Hostile Cyber Operations between States in International Law

Ius, Lex et Res Publica
Studies in Law, Philosophy and Political Cultures

Edited by Barbara Janusz-Pohl

Volume 43

Paul von Chamier Cieminski

Hostile Cyber Operations between States in International Law

PETER LANG
Berlin · Bruxelles · Chennai · Lausanne · New York · Oxford

Bibliographic Information published by the Deutsche Nationalbibliothek
The Deutsche Nationalbibliothek lists this publication in the Deutsche Nationalbibliografie; detailed bibliographic data is available online at http://dnb.d-nb.de.

Library of Congress Cataloging-in-Publication Data
Names: Cieminski, Paul Caesar von Chamier, 1990- author.
Title: Hostile Cyber Operations between States in International Law / Paul Caesar von Chamier Cieminski.
Description: New York : Peter Lang, 2026. | Series: Ius, lex et res publica studies in law, philosophy and political cultures, 2191-3250 ; 43 | "Doctoral thesis written under academic advisership of Professor Karol Karski." | Includes bibliographical references.
Identifiers: LCCN 2025029217 (print) | LCCN 2025029218 (ebook) | ISBN 9783631930458 (hardback) | ISBN 9783631930489 (pdf) | ISBN 9783631942093 (epub)
Subjects: LCSH: Information warfare (International law) | Cyberspace operations (International law) | Cyberterrorism–Law and legislation. | Cyberspace–Security measures. | Computer networks–Security measures.
Classification: LCC KZ6718 .C54 2026 (print) | LCC KZ6718 (ebook) | DDC 344.05/325–dc23/eng/20250621
LC record available at https://lccn.loc.gov/2025029217
LC ebook record available at https://lccn.loc.gov/2025029218

This publication was funded with a scientific grant from Johanna und Fritz Buch Gedächtnis-Stiftung.

JOHANNA UND FRITZ BUCH
GEDÄCHTNIS-STIFTUNG

ISSN 2191-3250
ISBN 978-3-631-93045-8 (Print)
ISBN 978-3-631-93048-9 (ePDF)
ISBN 978-3-631-94209-3 (ePUB)
DOI 10.3726/b23137

Published by Peter Lang GmbH, Berlin (Germany)

info@peterlang.com

This publication has been peer reviewed.

www.peterlang.com

I'm dedicating this book to my loving wife,
Chelsea Ilana von Chamier Garbell.

Principles of networked communication, if applied correctly to the realm of international affairs, could help solve age-old problems of violent conflict. Traditional ethnic and sectarian rivalries may be muted in the Internet age.

HENRY KISSINGER, WORLD ORDER, 2014

If someone used nuclear weapons 20 years ago against us, or we used them against someone else, the party affected would know where these weapons came from. One of my concerns here is that this kind of indirect [cyber] warfare becomes more pervasive and simultaneously more destructive and more anonymous in origin. And that, I think, is just a paralyzing, frightening prospect for humanity, and could undermine the stability of the international system.

ZBIGNIEW BRZEZIŃSKI, THE NEW RULES OF CYBER-WAR, 2013

Table of Contents

List of Figures

List of Tables

Foreword

As the supervisor in the doctoral proceedings of Paul von Chamier Cieminski, I would like to share my highest praise of the research that is the foundation of this book. The author focuses on the development of international law in the area of regulating hostile cyber-attacks between subjects of public international law, primarily between sovereign entities, that is, States. This dynamically developing phenomenon creates a series of questions about application of existing legal rules in cyberspace and a potential need for new ones. Effective regulation of cyberspace may become a source of stability for the public international law system in the new technological era. Nevertheless, ineffective structuring of rules in this space at the international level may have serious negative results.

The development path of public international law to date in the area covered by the book has had a *sui generis* character. Recognized norms of public international law regulating telecommunications technologies are not being applied, and State practice seems to develop in an original manner that defies regulatory patterns developed in other areas. Various aspects of this dynamic have already been analyzed in scholarly literature. However, an area that has not yet been adequately researched is the question of the status of this emerging set of norms and their application as a separate branch of public international law.

This question is the main focus of the book. For the sake of the analysis, the author relies on the formal legal model of *Specialized International Legal Regimes*, formulated by the UN International Law Commission. Dr. von Chamier Cieminski presents the hypothesis that the emerging system of norms and their application relating to hostile cyber operations between subjects of public international law has not yet achieved this status but that it is making progress in that direction. This research problem serves as the starting point for an in-depth and structured analysis of the legal criteria that must be met for the answer to turn positive down the road. The book also presents in a structured manner the developing practice of States and other subjects of international law that contribute to the movement in that direction. The analysis of the research problem in the book draws on the historical-legal and political-legal context as well as rich scholarly achievements in the subject of international legal regulation of cyberspace. The author reliably synthesizes existing research works and presents a new dimension of the issue while taking into account literature and current events. In sum, it is a great, panoramic source of insight into the subject of hostile cyber operations in public international law.

Prof. Dr. habil. Dr. h.c. mult. Karol Karski
Head of the Department of Public International Law
Faculty of Law and Administration
University of Warsaw, Poland

Preface

The book focuses on an emergent new branch of Public International Law that deals with the subject of hostile cyber operations between States (and other subjects of Public International Law). Dynamic technological development over the past decades led to the creation of cyberspace, a brand-new dimension in which States can interact, collaborate, and compete. This has given rise to an array of legal questions regarding the application of existing international rules and the need to create new ones. The analysis is structured around the core question: has this new area of Public International Law developed sufficiently to qualify as a new *special regime of Public International Law*?

Recognition of the emerging practices on hostile cyber operations between States as a *special regime of Public International Law* would create a robust framework for establishment of specialized interpretative rules and unique legal norms that apply exclusively in international cyberspace, thus accelerating development of the field. The thorough analysis of the current state of the field supports the hypothesis that the set of existing practices has not yet reached the necessary threshold for such recognition. However, the evolution of relevant State practice is moving in that direction, setting ground for achievement of the status of a special regime in the foreseeable future. The book lays out the full context of that process, highlights its outcomes, and anticipates its direction. It also structures the necessary legal criteria for achieving the status of a special regime and provides a comprehensive summary of relevant State practice, position statements by States, and relevant scientific literature that contribute to the final assessment.

Chapter 1 explores the key legal definitions relevant for the analysis, including those of cyberspace and hostile cyber operations between States. This analysis sets the ground for the rest of the book, providing alternative definitional models and explaining their legal consequences. Chapter 2 offers a structured insight into the historical legal and international political developments that shaped the current state of the field, delineating the main factors impacting the state of regulation of cyberspace in Public International Law. The chapter concludes with a review of potential future models of regulating cyberspace that might replace the existing one. Chapter 3 engages with the question of applying the existing framework of hostile acts between States to the cyber context, analyzing cyber equivalents of categories developed in the conventional context such as: Violation of Sovereignty, Prohibited Intervention, Act of Aggression, or Armed Attack. The chapter puts emphasis on points of divergence of the application of the existing norms in cyberspace as a potential early precursor for development of a special regime. Chapter 4 explores the notion of lawful cyber hostilities between States, akin to lawful Countermeasures or UN Security Council-approved interventions, which are allowed in the conventional realm. This aspect of the analyzed subject is currently hypothetical but could become highly relevant in the future as ever more State functions and interactions take place in the cyber realm. Chapter 5 deals with one of the most challenging aspects of the field which is attribution of cyber hostilities to a responsible State. Tools developed in the conventional realm appear insufficient in the cyber context, leading to various adaptations and practices on the part of States that are the focus of this chapter. Chapter 6 synthesizes the findings from the previous chapters and provides the final verification of the hypothesis. It also offers insight into the future development of the field and what it would take for it to achieve the status of a *special regime of Public International Law.*

Introduction

Rarely in the history of international law does one technological advancement create a ripple effect potent enough to profoundly change the very nature of interactions between States. The development of cyberspace is a historical breakthrough of that magnitude. The meteoric rise of the internet since its inception as ARPANET back in the 1960s has remodeled the way humans experience culture, economy, politics, and even their basic social connections. Cyberspace, which emerged on the basis of the internet platform, is a completely new dimension of human interactions, whose consequences we are still learning. As of 2023, the majority of mankind has access to it and the ratio continues to rise continuously. This level of connectivity is unprecedented in the history of our species, minimizing the relevance of physical distance and exposing communities to one another like never before. Meanwhile, the technology continues to display potency, offering ever more ways for a human to immerse oneself in the digital realm.

The system of Public International Law experienced a slow start in terms of regulating this phenomenon. The reasons for that were multifold. At first, the internet emerged as a niche academic and military project, missing international policymakers' attention. As its disruptive potential became obvious in the early 1990s, the vested interest of the United States of America to prevent international oversight that would limit its governance control over cyberspace became an important factor stymieing formation of new public international legal norms. A complex web of State interests and broader systemic developments in the international community, including a large increase of stakeholder States, have also contributed to the stalemate since then. The situation forced the system of Public International Law to play catch-up with rapidly progressing cyber technologies.

Creative ways to address this challenge have been deployed. The United Nations, alongside a few high-level multilateral initiatives such as the Global Commission on the Stability of Cyberspace, has put forward *soft law* proposals, in hope that they become binding customary law over time. Proactive States have expressed their *opinio juris* and demonstrated relevant practice that could catalyze development of rules if their approach were to be assumed by enough other States. Attempts are made intermittently to draft an overarching treaty that would consolidate the key international legal rules on cyberspace. However, this path proves especially challenging due to diverging interests of the main stakeholders and has failed so far.

As States grapple with the challenge of regulating cyberspace, it has become obvious that it is a source of both tremendous positive potential and serious risks. Cyberspace creates a dynamic of anonymity and plausible deniability. Hostile States and their affiliate non-State actors, such as hacker groups, can conduct operations against peaceful governments from a far-away distance with seeming impunity. The nature of attacks can be instantaneous and preparations for such hostilities are not visible using conventional means such as satellite monitoring. All this sets hostile cyber operations apart from their conventional equivalents, for which measures have been developed to identify and prevent them before they create damage. Moreover, a two-tier system has emerged with a small group of powerful high-cyber-capacity States on one side and everyone else on the other. The high-capacity States, which are mostly the leading global military powers, benefit from this imbalance. Other States struggle to mount a defensive response or even to effectively attribute cyber hostilities hurting them. Unlike for conventional operations, attribution in cyberspace requires advanced IT capacity and usually willing participation from third States through which territory hostile operations were routed, making it doubly difficult. The overall result is that of a rapidly growing volume of international cyber hostilities coupled with inadequate legal tools, essentially unfit for the novel digital context.

That is why it is essential to develop better understanding of the public international legal dynamics surrounding cyberspace. Specifically, understanding and addressing hostile cyber operations is the most urgent element of the slowly emerging cyberspace law and the main subject of this book.

There is urgency to reduce the level of uncertainty and identify paths forward that would enable the existing system of rules and norms to be effectively applied to the cyber context, with development of additional novel norms if necessary. It has now become clear that the scale, dynamism, and impact of cyberspace are so momentous that they substantiate formation of a new branch of Public International Law, much like it happened with earlier technological frontiers. Examples include the planet's airspace or exploration of outer space, both of which are now covered by special regimes. The broad purpose driving this book is to contribute to solving the public international legal challenge posed by cyberspace and reduce the level of related uncertainty. The specific objective is to verify the research hypothesis whether the emerging unique State practice and statements concerning cyberspace constitute a *special regime of Public International Law.*

The hypothesis was selected based on the current stage of development of cyberspace and the scholarly discourse on it. Decades after the internet's creation and with a demonstrated track record of large-scale impact of State-on-State cyber hostilities, there is still no clarity on cyberspace law's status in Public International Law. Drawing on past technological and political advancements, the framework of special legal regimes, sometimes also described as self-contained regimes, provides a specific and time-proven litmus test on the state of maturity and consolidation of a novel branch of international law. There are established international jurisprudence cases and UN General Assembly resolutions that set up the definitional terms and conditions for emergence of special regimes. There is also a rich selection of existing special regimes of varying strength to compare against emerging cyberspace law, enabling for contextualizing of the current legal trends and their likely trajectory in the future.

More broadly, the research work required to verify the hypothesis offers a cohesive and structured insight into the current state of international public law concerning cyberspace. It establishes definitions of key notions, analyzes the historical legal context, dissect positions of the main stakeholders, including the UN Security Council member States and key multilateral organizations, reviews feasibility and limitations of applying existing public legal norms in the cyber context, and identifies the emerging patterns of State practice and *opinio juris* that can lead to development of novel international rights and obligations pertaining solely to cyberspace. The research also delves into the philosophical and conceptual underpinnings of legal systems and specialized regimes and their application in the cyber context. This book rests on a wide range of diverse sources including multiple monographies, international and domestic sources of law, scientific articles in peer-reviewed academic journals, doctoral dissertations, as well as official statements by governments and international organizations. The author also conducted three library queries to complement and deepen the research at: the United Nations Library, the Library of the Faculty of Law of New York University, and the Library of the Faculty of Law of University of Warsaw.

The following methodologies are utilized in the book:

1. Comparative legal methodology: Legal norms contained within the system of Public International Law were analyzed and compared given their context and status as part of various special legal regimes in order to identify their most accurate application in the cyber context. The same method was applied when assessing State practice, *opinio juris*, and relevant international jurisprudence cases. Cyberspace law, due to being a relatively new phenomenon, largely rests on analogy and equivalence with the norms established in the conventional real, which puts much emphasis on utilizing the comparative legal methodology as the key tool in the analysis.

2. Methods of legal text interpretation: Established ways of interpretating sources of law in Public International Law provide guidance on accurate assessment of documents. These methods have been developed over centuries of State practice and treaty signing and are primarily based on the linguistic and systemic interpretation of the source text to ensure coherence within the overarching international legal system. They can be utilized to deduce and clarify the binding rules in the novel cyber context as well as provisions contained within legal documents. A special role in that regard is extended to the most qualified international scholars who provide guidance on the interpretative process, based on established law and landmark jurisprudence cases.

3. Statistical analysis: This book draws on insights provided by statistical analysis to shed light on dynamics such as: proportions of international hostile cyber acts over time, distribution of State positions on international legal debates, and accretion and prevalence of State practice that

might contributing to formation of customary legal norms concerning cyberspace. Given the early stage at which cyberspace law is at present, these statistical insights can offer guidance on the trends and possible future developments.

4. Historical analysis: Utilizing the historical analysis allows for identifying trends and patterns that have developed over decades, positioning development of international cyberspace regulations during various political eras: the Cold War, the period between the fall of the Soviet Union and the 9/11 terrorist attacks, and the time since. It also allows for identifying long-term impacts of international legal processes that took place in the nineteenth and the early twentieth century, such as the establishment of the International Telegraph Union and the sinking of Titanic, on the current legal dynamics surrounding cyberspace. Drawing a wide historical arc also allows for more contextualized predictions of the future of cyberspace law.

Chapter 1 titled *Cyberspace and cyber operations—definitional scope of the concepts and their contextualization in Public International Law* engages with several definitions of cyberspace that currently exist in parallel. Each of them represents a different focus and reflects the interests of States that promote it. Those considerations can have tangible impact on legal classification of hostile acts and hence all these dynamics are analyzed and structured into a cohesive overview. The chapter offers an analogous analysis of related terms such as a cyber *Unfriendly Act* or a hostile cyber operation. In this way, Chapter 1 lays the foundation for the research work conducted in the subsequent ones.

Chapter 2 titled *History of the international legal framework regulating cyberspace* introduces the historical legal context that determines current challenges surrounding international public regulation of cyberspace. It explains the origins of the internet and the related vested interests that prevent new norms from forming. Moreover, it discussed the broader framework of oversight over communication technologies that has been developed as part of Public International Law and that is currently defied by the United States of America in regard to cyberspace, creating a precedent. Chapter 2 also presents the recent international efforts to structure and regulate cyberspace, including the initiatives introduced by the United Nations and States, contextualizing the legal analysis.

Chapter 3 titled *Typology of hostile cyber operations between States which are Internationally Wrongful Acts* engages with the subject of application of the existing norms of the system of Public International Law in the cyber context. There exist a number of legal categories to draw on, some of them being especially relevant. These include *Violations of Sovereignty*, *Prohibited Interventions*, *Acts of Aggression*, and *Armed Attacks*. Each of these consecutive categories constitutes a progressively more severe form of an *Internationally Wrongful Act* than the previous one. However, nuanced adaptations of these terms are required to fit the unique context of cyberspace, such as the unique status of IT critical infrastructure and the instantaneous nature of cyber attacks. Chapter 3 dissects each of these terms, providing insights into what aspects of them are inapplicable or require special interpretation in cyberspace. Whenever such considerations are subject to a dispute within the international community, stances of key States are highlighted, including their demonstrated practice and statements.

Chapter 4 titled *Typology of hostile cyber operations between States which are not Internationally Wrongful Acts* deals with the question of lawful hostile cyber operations. Such a term might sound like a contradiction. However, it is a logical consequence of applying the existing framework of Public International Law in cyberspace. The framework allows for self-help measures and circumstances that preclude wrongfulness of hostile acts. There exists no general prohibition of such measures in cyberspace but adaptation of general rules in that regard remains a largely uncharted territory. A number of proposals have been put forward by States on specialized norms that would modify these rules in cyberspace, including for instance Estonia's idea of collective legal cyber *Countermeasures*, possibly executed as a joint digital NATO operation. One of the biggest fears of the international community is that the scale and instantaneous nature of cyber operations, coupled with limited ability to seek redress using legal measures might lead to a destructive spiral of escalation between States, including acts of *Use of Force* by cyber means. Chapter 4 analyzes all those considerations in depth, presenting the likely course of development in that regard in the future.

Chapter 5 titled *Jurisdiction and attribution of hostile cyber operations in Public International Law* engages with one of the most complex and difficult aspects of regulating cyberspace in Public International Law which are the considerations on attribution, jurisdiction, and limits of *State Sovereignty*. The chapter explains all the main constraints and States' positions on how those could be resolved. These constraints are mostly driven by the technical features of cyberspace such as a high level of anonymity, plausible deniability, and the need to collaborate across States in order to trace back a hostile cyber act to its source. However, some of them stem from the vested interests of main stakeholder States, which benefit from the current legal flux. Limits of State jurisdiction in cyberspace are highly problematic, as internet data traffic usually passes through a number of States without any control or insight from the States hosting the pass-through infrastructure. Should every State exert sovereign control over each and every bit of data flowing through its servers? If so, how could that even be enforced and what legal responsibility would it bestow on such a host State? There exists no clear-cut answer to this question, but Chapter 5 presents possible solutions, based on State practice and international scholars' analysis.

Finally, Chapter 6 titled *Cyberspace norms as a special regime of Public International Law* brings together all the analysis conducted in this book, taking stock of the research to verify the main hypothesis whether the emerging unique State practice and statements concerning cyberspace constitute a special regime of Public International Law. In doing so, it sums up all the main State practice and statements that might give an indication as to whether unique legal norms pertaining to cyberspace are currently developing. Moreover, the chapter presents the main philosophical, methodological, and legal underpinnings of the notion of special regimes of Public International Law and applies them in the context of cyberspace. In doing so, it anticipates the inherent trade-off within special regimes of better adapting the system to a specific field on one side and making that overall system less cohesive on the other.

Taken together, the six chapters offer a deep insight into the history, present, and potential future of regulations concerning cyberspace in Public International Law. The emerging patterns help understand which direction the system might move in and what could be the main obstacles in the process. The scale of the challenge of effectively regulating cyberspace is daunting. However, if done right, the system of Public International Law can become well prepared for the digital age, developing a framework that ensures fairness and stability.

CHAPTER 1

Cyberspace and cyber operations—definitional scope of the concepts and their contextualization in Public International Law

1.1 Introduction

The starting point for the book has to be the definition of cyberspace as it will demarcate the its scope. Putting it in a broader context, the notion of cyberspace is the pinnacle of a rapid development of the information society that we have witnessed over the course of the twentieth and twenty-first century. This phenomenon has affected every dimension of human life, eventually impacting the shape of Public International Law and relations between sovereign States too. This novel situation creates both opportunities and challenges for the subjects of international law. One of the questions that have arisen is how to position cyberspace within the existing international legal context. While certain legal concepts can be transposed into cyberspace, there remain aspects of the digital world that escape conventional frameworks or require modifications when applied.

At the same time, the international community, including States and other subjects of international law, does not speak in unison on the matter. Conflicting interests and approaches have resulted in a state of flux that stokes ongoing uncertainty. The legal definitions of cyberspace and hostile cyber operations sit at the center of that flux. In this chapter, I aim to clarify various positions in that regard, their origin, and their potential consequences in the field of Public International Law. By contextualizing these dynamics and providing scholarly commentary, I offer better understanding of the extent of the *Sui Generis* character of public international rules regulating cyberspace and of the direction in which this evolution is heading.

1.2 Cyberspace—range of definitions and their legal impact

1.2.1 Definitions of cyberspace proposed by States and leading international experts

A review of various positions taken by governments, leading legal scholars, and the European Commission on the question of what constitutes cyberspace reveals far-ranging differences in perception of the term with potential profound legal consequences. However, before we delve into them, it is worth taking a step back and considering the origin of the term and its evolution before the advent of the digital era. The word *cyber* derives from the ancient Greek word *kubernētēs* (κυβερνᾶν), meaning a ship steersman.[1] It evolved into the French word *cybernetique*, first denoting the art of navigating, and then more generally governing.[2] In the twentieth century, it inspired a U.S. mathematician Norbert Wiener to transpose the idea into the English language. In 1948, he defined the term *cybernetics* as a "theory or study of communication and control."[3] It became popular in the fields of IT and engineering where the notion of using scientific methods to navigate and control the physical world reflected well the technological aspirations.[4] The term was not only used by scientists though. It made its way into popular culture and became a widely used concept in the nascent Sci-Fi movement.[5] Cyber became a prefix added to existing words in order to lend them an aura of futuristic flair. This phenomenon laid ground for the emergence of the term *cyberspace*. It appeared for the first time in the 1982 Sci-Fi novel "Burning Chrome" by William Gibson. Two years later,

---

1 Oxford University Press. "Where Does the Word Cyber Come From?" OUP, July 10, 2015. Retrieved November 21, 2023. <https://blog.oup.com/2015/03/cyber-word-origins/>

2 Centre National de Ressources Textuelles et Lexicales. "TLFI." CYBERNÉTIQUE : Définition de CYBERNÉTIQUE. Retrieved November 21, 2023. <https://www.cnrtl.fr/definition/cybern%C3%A9tique>

3 Online Etymology Dictionary. "Cybernetics (n.)." Etymology. Accessed November 21, 2023. <https://www.etymonline.com/word/cybernetics?ref=etymonline_crossreference>

4 Oxford University Press. "Where Does the Word Cyber Come From?" OUP, July 10, 2015. Retrieved November 21, 2023. <https://blog.oup.com/2015/03/cyber-word-origins/>

5 Ibid.

in his most popular book "Neuromancer" he defined cyberspace, through a characters' dialogue, as: "Graphic representation of data abstracted from the banks of every computer in the human system. Unthinkable complexity. Lines of light ranged in the nonspace of the mind, clusters and constellations of data."[6]

While far-removed from the legal world, the novel gave rise to a heated debate about humanity's digital future and captured well with the term *cyberspace* the substance of internet-based data systems that by the 1980s were already taking shaping. Gibson's vision of a data network that feels like an immersive space, qualitatively different from physical reality, still resonates and its echo is present in legal definitions proposed by both States and legal scholars.

1982 was a fitting moment to bring the subject to the general public's attention as the ARPANET, the internet's forbear, was already being developed in California, extending its branches to various U.S.-based universities. As it turned out, cyberspace was much less abstract than it might have seemed at the time. The following years and decades brought a rapid development and scaling-up of the ARPANET into the global network that we are familiar with nowadays. Chapter 2 describes in detail the international legal impacts of internet's evolution but for the sake of discussing the notion of cyberspace itself, it is important to introduce the formal definition of internet, which unlike cyberspace is a technical and specific term—internet is a global network of interconnected computers using standardized communication protocols for information exchange, enabled by electromagnetic processes.[7] A very consistent set of definitions of the internet, encapsulated in the sentence earlier, can be found in domestic legal codes across States, for example, the U.S.-American one.[8]

The original novel-based and futuristic definition of cyberspace was disconnected from the actual legal, political, and technological context of

---

6 Gibson, William. Neuromancer, page 128. New York: Penguin Group, 1984.

7 Own elaboration, based on Oxford English Dictionary. Retrieved November 22, 2023. <https://www.oed.com/viewdictionaryentry/Entry/248411.>

8 Cornell University Legal Information Institute. "47 U.S. Code § 230 - Protection for Private Blocking and Screening of Offensive Material." Legal Information Institute. Retrieved November 21, 2023. <https://www.law.cornell.edu/uscode/text/47/230#f_1.>

the late 1980s and the early 1990s. The internet was still in its rudimentary, nascent form and its development toward becoming a space for more complex forms of communication and collaboration was gradual. However, as that became the case eventually, the need to define this new type of space, a *cyber* space, emerged. The government of the United States, the birthplace of the internet, was the first subject of international law to attempt developing a formal definition of cyberspace. In 2010, U.S. Department of Defense defined it as: "a global domain within the information environment consisting of the interdependent network of information technology infrastructures, including the Internet, telecommunications networks, computer systems, and embedded processors and controllers."[9]

This was followed by a slew of other States proposing their own definitions over the course of the 2010s. Some prominent examples include: Poland, United Kingdom, Canada, New Zealand, Italy, and Germany. Their proposed definitions are summarized in Table 1. As this process unfolded, crucial differences started emerging between States. The four key components of the definitional scope became the subject of a legal debate. These are:

- The physical infrastructure component (servers, cords, operating systems, etc.);
- The stored data component (databases, websites, private and public services provided online);
- Social interactive component (interactions between users of cyberspace, both amicable and adversarial ones);
- Non-networked devices component (e.g., separate parallel systems that have only a partial or intermittent connection to the internet or no direct connection at all, e.g., a large company's intranet or an electricity plant's internal computer network).

[9] Ning, Huansheng, Xiaozhen Ye, Mohammed Amine Bouras, Dawei Wei, and Mahmoud Daneshmand. "General Cyberspace: Cyberspace and Cyber-Enabled Spaces." IEEE Internet of Things Journal 5, no. 3 (2018): 1843–56. <https://doi.org/10.1109/jiot.2018.2815535.>

Table 1. Definitions of cyberspace proposed by key States and the European Commission

Source	Cyberspace Definition	Infrastructure Component	Data Component	Social Interactive Component	Non-networked Devices Included
Poland 2019 (Cybersecurity Strategy of the Republic of Poland for 2019–2024)	Cyberspace is the space for processing and exchanging information formed by ICT systems defined in Article 3(3) of the Act of 17 February 2005 on the computerization of activities of entities performing public tasks (Journal of Laws of the Republic of Poland of 2019, items 700, 730, 848 and 1590), including relations between them and relationships with the users—in accordance with Article 2(1b) of the Act of 29 August 2002 on the martial law and competences of the Supreme Commander of the Armed Forces and the rules of his subordination to the constitutional authorities of the Republic of Poland (Journal of Laws of the Republic of Poland of 2017, item 1932).[10]	✓	✓	✓	×
Poland 2015 (Cybersecurity Doctrine of the Republic of Poland)	Cyberspace is the space for processing and exchanging information formed by ICT systems (networks of integrated ICT devices and software that together enable processing, maintenance, as well as sending and receiving of data via ICT systems by utilizing a specialized end-node device designed to connect into the systems) including relations between them and relationships with users.[11]	✓	✓	✓	×

(*Continued*)

10 Ministry of Digital Affairs, Republic of Poland. Rep. Cybersecurity Strategy of The Republic of Poland For 2019 – 2024. Page 6. <https://www.gov.pl/web/cyfryzacja/strategia-cyberbezpieczenstwa-rzeczypospolitej-polskiej-na-lata-2019-2024>.

11 Bureau of National Security, Republic of Poland. Doctrine of Cybersecurity of the Republic of Poland, January 22, 2015. Page 7. <https://en.bbn.gov.pl/ftp/dok/01/DCB.pdf.>

Table 1. *(Continued)*

Source	Cyberspace Definition	Infrastructure Component	Data Component	Social Interactive Component	Non-networked Devices Included
United States 2021 (Congress Act 50 U.S.C. 1708—Actions to address economic or industrial espionage in cyberspace)	The term "cyberspace"— (A)means the interdependent network of information technology infrastructures; (B)includes the Internet, telecommunications networks, computer systems, and embedded processors and controllers.[12]	✓	✓	×	✓
United States 2010 (Department of Defense Dictionary of Military and Associated Terms)	Cyberspace—a global domain within the information environment consisting of the interdependent network of information technology infrastructures, including the Internet, telecommunications networks, computer systems, and embedded processors and controllers.[13]	✓	✓	×	✓
United States 2017 (Department of Defense Dictionary of Military and Associated Terms)	Cyberspace—a global domain within the information environment consisting of the interdependent network of information technology infrastructures and resident data, including the Internet, telecommunications networks, computer systems, and embedded processors and controllers.[14]	✓	✓	×	✓

12 United States Code, Supplement 3, Title 50, Section 1708 - WAR AND NATIONAL DEFENSE, December 3, 2021. <http://www.govinfo.gov/app/details/USCODE-2021-title50/USCODE-2021-title50-chap35-sec1708>.

13 Ning, Huansheng, Xiaozhen Ye, Mohammed Amine Bouras, Dawei Wei, and Mahmoud Daneshmand. "General Cyberspace: Cyberspace and Cyber-Enabled Spaces." IEEE Internet of Things Journal 5, no. 3 (2018): 1843–56. <https://doi.org/10.1109/jiot.2018.2815535>.

14 Ibid.

Source	Cyberspace Definition	Infrastructure Component	Data Component	Social Interactive Component	Non-networked Devices Included
United Kingdom 2011 (The U.K. Cyber Security Strategy)	Cyberspace is an interactive domain made up of digital networks that are used to store, modify and communicate information. It includes the internet, but also the other information systems that support our businesses, infrastructure and services.[15]	✓	✓	×	✓
Canada 2010 (Canada's Cyber Security Strategy)	Cyberspace is the electronic world created by interconnected networks of information technology and the information on those networks. It is a global commons where more than 1.7 billion people are linked to exchange ideas, services, and friendship.[16]	✓	✓	✓	×
New Zealand 2011 (New Zealand Cyberspace Strategy)	Cyberspace is the global network of interdependent information technology infrastructures, telecommunications networks, and computer processing systems in which online communication takes place.[17]	✓	✓	✓	×
Germany 2011 (Cyber Security Strategy for Germany)	Cyberspace is the virtual space of all IT systems linked at data level on a global scale. The basis for cyberspace is the Internet as a universal and publicly accessible connection and transport network which can be complemented and further expanded by any number of additional data networks. IT systems in an isolated virtual space are not part of cyberspace.[18]	✓	✓	×	×

(Continued)

15 Ibid.
16 Ibid.
17 Ibid.
18 Ibid.

Table 1. *(Continued)*

Source	Cyberspace Definition	Infrastructure Component	Data Component	Social Interactive Component	Non-networked Devices Included
Italy 2013 (Decree of the President of the Council of Ministers of Italy)	Cyberspace is the overall system of interconnected computer infrastructures, including hardware, software, data and users, as well as the logical relationships among them, regardless of how they are established.[19]	✓	✓	×	×
European Commission 2013 (Information Society Glossary)	Virtual space in which the electronic data of worldwide PCs circulate.[20]	✓	✓	×	×

Source: Own elaboration

There exists a consensus that the first two components: the infrastructure and the stored data are foundational parts of cyberspace. These components essentially overlap definitionally with the internet and therefore constitute cyberspace's core foundation. Inclusion of the two other components: the social interactive layer and non-networked systems is disputed and sparks controversy. Three main camps have emerged thus far. In the first group are the States that embrace the social aspect as an integral, defining part of cyberspace. This group includes, for example, Poland, New Zealand, and Canada. What logically follows is that they perceive non-networked IT systems as not part of cyberspace, presumably because their isolation means they are not part of that interactive layer. The second group are countries

19 Ibid.

20 Wasilewski, Janusz. "Zarys Definicyjny Cyberprzestrzeni." Przegląd Bezpieczeństwa Wewnętrznego 5, no. 9 (2013): 225–34. <http://cejsh.icm.edu.pl/cejsh/element/bwmeta1.element.desklight-fad9287e-d6f2-4713-ad9e-472717378ab4.>

that do see non-networked systems as part of cyberspace, with all relevant regulations also applicable to them. This group includes the United States of America and the United Kingdom. Consequently, for them, the social interactive layer is not critically important for a system to be considered part of cyberspace and is therefore not emphasized in their formal definitions. Finally, the third group of States is the most minimalist one. States and other international legal actors that embrace this approach include neither the social component nor the non-networked systems in the core definition of cyberspace. Germany and Italy can be counted in this group, alongside the European Commission.

1.2.2 Infrastructure, data, and social dimensions of cyberspace

The legal debate on inclusion of non-networked systems or social interactive aspects in the definition is not idle and can have a tangible impact in the sphere of international law as norms on cyberspace are slowly forming in Public International Law. Let us consider the Siberian gas pipeline explosion of 1982, which depending on the assumed definition, might or might not be considered the first recorded hostile operation between States in cyberspace. In June of that year, an American satellite detected a massive explosion in remote Siberia. As it turned out, it was a Soviet gas pipeline. KGB spies had stolen software that operated it sometime earlier from an engineering company in Canada. What they were not aware of was that the CIA had intercepted their communication and tampered with the software ahead of time. It was thus programmed to function correctly for a duration, after which time the valves would hike gas pressure in the pipe until it bursts. This and similar operations were approved by President Ronald Reagan himself.[21] The result was the most monumental non-nuclear explosion and fire ever seen from space, according to Thomas Reed, a former U.S. Air Force Secretary.[22] The system regulating oil and gas pipelines across the Soviet Union was not

---

21 Hoffman, David E. "Reagan Approved Plan to Sabotage Soviets." The Washington Post, February 27, 2004. <https://www.washingtonpost.com/archive/politics/2004/02/27/reagan-approved-plan-to-sabotage-soviets/a9184eff-47fd-402e-beb2-63970851e130/.>

22 "War in the Fifth Domain." The Economist, July 6, 2010. <https://www.economist.com/briefing/2010/07/01/war-in-the-fifth-domain.>

connected to the ARPANET and the malicious payload was shipped by means of stolen software that was physically smuggled out of Canada. The operation was thus a "cyber" operation only if such means of connectivity between physically separate systems are included in the definition.

Let us also consider another, more recent case where this definitional flux could have had a tangible impact on international legal qualification of an event and its implications. Possibly the most impressive, publicized case of a hostile cyber operation against a sovereign State so far has been the disruption caused to Iran's nuclear facilities in 2010 by the Stuxnet Virus. In June of that year, a Belarusian cybersecurity company VirusBlokAda warned the public of a sophisticated virus targeting computers using specific IT industrial systems procured by Siemens.[23] The virus would spread online and affect USB devices plugged into infected computers with seemingly no malicious impact at all. However, if the infected USB device was then used on a computer with the targeted Siemens Programmable Logic Control (PLC) software, the malware would modify instructions for industrial machinery responsible for switching on and off motors and controlling temperature in a way that would cause the machinery to break down beyond repair.[24] If no targeted software was detected on a computer, the virus would stay dormant forever. As it happened, Iran's nuclear facilities were using exactly that type of software.[25] Because its systems were not connected to the internet, they were assumed to be impermeable to online viruses. The sophisticated design of Stuxnet managed to cross this so-called air gap. While Iran was not the sole State affected by Stuxnet (some 200,000 computers were infected around the world with around 1,000 of them physically degrading due to the impact[26]), around 60% of all the impactful infections took place

---

23 Mills, Elinor. "Details of the First-Ever Control System Malware (FAQ)." CNET, July 21, 2010. <https://www.cnet.com/news/privacy/details-of-the-first-ever-control-system-malware-faq/.

24 Fildes, Jonathan B. "Stuxnet Worm 'Targeted High-Value Iranian Assets.'" BBC, September 23, 2010. <https://www.bbc.com/news/technology-11388018.>

25 Ibid.

26 Katz, Yaakov B. "Stuxnet may have destroyed 1,000 centrifuges at Natanz." The Jerusalem Post, December 24, 2010. <https://www.jpost.com/defense/stuxnet-may-have-destroyed-1000-centrifuges-at-natanz.>

in the country.[27] Stuxnet reportedly destroyed around 20% of its nuclear centrifuges, which tore themselves apart as the scientists were watching helplessly.[28] The key uranium enrichment facility in Natanz lost 30% of its capacity that year, setting back the timeline for the country acquiring nuclear bomb capacity significantly.[29]Attribution of the brazen cyber operation is still under debate. No State came forward claiming authorship, but some substantial clues have been identified. A 2011 presentation commemorating the service of recently retired Israeli Defense Forces Chief Gabi Ashkenazi featured a reference to Stuxnet as one of the achievements accomplished during his tenure.[30] Some IT specialists also claim to have found biblical references in the string of code making up Stuxnet that purportedly allude to the story behind the Jewish holiday of Purim, set in the capital city of ancient Persia.[31] 2011 WikiLeaks documents included files confirming that the United States was considering using cyber warfare to target Iranian nuclear facilities.[32] Finally, a 2012 article by New York Times purported that the operation was part of a covert collaboration between the United States and Israel called Olympic Games.[33] Stuxnet disruption showcased how a serious infringement of sovereignty could come to bear in cyberspace although whether it was "just" a *Prohibited Intervention* or rather an *Act of Aggression* is still being debated. Stuxnet provides a vivid example that is still being invoked on the forum of international bodies debating the subject

---

27 Fildes, Jonathan B. "Stuxnet Worm 'Targeted High-Value Iranian Assets.'" BBC, September 23, 2010. <https://www.bbc.com/news/technology-11388018.>

28 Kelley, Michael B. "The Stuxnet Attack On Iran's Nuclear Plant Was 'Far More Dangerous' Than Previously Thought." Business Insider, November 20, 2013. <https://www.businessinsider.com/stuxnet-was-far-more-dangerous-than-previous-thought-2013-11.>

29 Melman, Yossef. "Computer virus in Iran actually targeted larger nuclear facility." Haaretz, September 28, 2010. <https://www.haaretz.com/1.5118389.>

30 Williams, Christopher. "Israel video shows Stuxnet as one of its successes." The Telegraph, February 15, 2011. <https://www.telegraph.co.uk/news/worldnews/middleeast/israel/8326387/Israel-video-shows-Stuxnet-as-one-of-its-successes.html.>

31 Zetter, Kim. Countdown to zero day: Stuxnet and the launch of the world's first digital weapon. Crown, 2015. Page 67.

32 Sanger, David E. "Obama Order Sped Up Wave of Cyberattacks Against Iran." The New York Times, June 1, 2012. <https://www.nytimes.com/2012/06/01/world/middleeast/obama-ordered-wave-of-cyberattacks-against-iran.html.>

33 Ibid.

such as the UN Group of Governmental Experts (UN GGE) and the UN Open-Ended Working Group (UN OEWG), two United Nations bodies set up to analyze developments in the field of information and telecommunications in the context of international security.[34]

Prominent international legal scholars have weighed in on the debate on various defining dimensions of cyberspace. One of the most relevant expert opinions on the definitional scope of cyberspace was provided by the Tallinn Manual in 2013:

> Cyberspace is the environment formed by physical and non-physical components characterized by the use of computers and the electro-magnetic spectrum to store, modify and exchange data using computer networks.[35]

Tallinn Manual is a result of an effort conducted by NATO in the wake of the 2008 Bronze Soldier controversy in Estonia, in which the country's parliament, president's office, non-Russian political parties, three biggest news outlets in the country, and two biggest banks saw their website shut down by a wave of DDoS attacks coming from the Russian Federation. The attacks were seen as a response to the removal of the statue of a soldier commemorating Soviet victory in World War 2.[36] NATO's response was to conduct an assessment of their cyber security and critical infrastructure defenses. A few months later, in May 2008, it also established NATO Cooperative Cyber Defence Center of Excellence (CCDCOE) with headquarters in Tallinn. One of the Center's main initiatives is Tallinn Manual on the International Law Applicable to Cyber Warfare—an academic juristic effort, officially backed by the alliance, to clarify international legal rules and norms in the context of cyberspace and to propose new ones.[37] The definition in the Tallinn Manual

---

34 Geneva Internet Platform. "UN OEWG in 2023." Digital Watch Observatory, October 18, 2023. <https://dig.watch/processes/un-gge/.>

35 Schmitt, Michael N. Tallinn Manual on the international law applicable to cyber warfare. Cambridge: Cambridge University Press, 2013. Page 278.

36 Traynor, Ian. "Russia Accused of Unleashing Cyberwar to Disable Estonia." The Guardian, May 17, 2007. <https://www.theguardian.com/world/2007/may/17/topstories3.russia>; British Broadcasting Corporation. "Estonia Fines Man for 'Cyber War.'" BBC News, January 25, 2008. <http://news.bbc.co.uk/2/hi/technology/7208511.stm.>

37 NATO Cooperative Cyber Defence Center of Excellence. "The Tallinn manual Initiative." Accessed November 23, 2023. <https://ccdcoe.org/research/tallinn-manual/.>

is important because its authors enjoy international scholarly prominence and also because the publication enjoys official backing by NATO, a key factor in international law. The publication claims to lay out a "black-letter rule," meaning that the authors claim their definitions describe the state of legal affairs as they already are in State practice rather than being just a proposition.[38] Due its prominence and concise character, NATO CCDCOE's definition will be used as the basis for analysis in this book (given the interpretative choices laid out in the previous section).

Cyberspace's definition in the Manual is minimalist as it focuses on basic physical (infrastructure) and non-physical (data & software) components, leaving it open whether there's an additional required social interpretative interactive aspect to it. It also leaves it undecided whether parallel intranet systems are part of cyberspace, unlike sources that provide a clear yes (e.g., the definition espoused by the United States) or a clear no (the definition espoused by Germany). In trying to resolve this ambiguity, Tomasz Welanyk for example invokes linguistic interpretative logic to suggest that the phrasing points to cyberspace's definition scope being at the conjunction of physical and non-physical aspects listed in the definition. This would imply, according to him, that non-networked devices and systems, such as the one running nuclear centrifuges in Iran, are not included as part of NATO CCDOCOE's definition of cyberspace.[39] However, this appears to be a very restrictive reading. First, functional interpretation of the definition implies that the mere possibility of an isolated network getting occasionally connected to the internet by utilizing the listed physical and non-physical components is enough to qualify it as being part of a broader cyberspace, especially if it demonstrably does happen occasionally (e.g., a power plant which normally is isolated from the internet network getting temporarily connected to it). Second, NATO CCDOCOE's definition does not insist that all networks making up cyberspace must be connected to it at all times. The only listed requirements are that those networks retain ability to store, modify, and

38 Georgetown University Law School. "Guides: International and Foreign Cyberspace Law Research Guide: Tallinn Manual & Primary Law Applicable to Cyber Conflicts." Guides at Georgetown Law Library. Accessed November 23, 2023. <https://guides.ll.georgetown.edu/cyberspace/cyber-conflicts.>

39 Welanyk, Tomasz, "Istnienie i granice suwerenności w cyberprzestrzeni. Analiza prawna." Ph.D. dissertation, University of Warsaw, 2019. Page 19.

exchange data from elsewhere in the cyberspace environment. For instance, if the Iranian power plant facility possesses required physical components (interoperable device insertion sockets such as USB ports, CD ports, LAN cables) and non-physical components (inter-intelligible operating systems such Windows that can easily store, modify and process data brought over from the broader internet) that serve as connective tissue enabling it to interact with the broader system occasionally, it technically meets the Tallinn Manual's definition of being part of cyberspace, with all the international legal consequences that this entails.

Daniel Kuehl from the U.S. National Defense University defines cyberspace as "a domain characterized by the use of electronics and the electromagnetic spectrum to store, modify and exchange information via networked information systems and physical infrastructures."[40] He was instrumental in formulating one of the earliest formal definitions of cyberspace in a U.S. Armed Forces Joint Staff's internal publication back in 2006 titled National Military Strategy for Cyberspace. The definition is much like the one included in NATO's Tallinn Manual although the role of the non-physical component is downplayed in it, which was usually the case with the earliest definitions of cyberspace.[41] He also provides reasoning for an expansionary interpretation of cyberspace that is inclusive of critical infrastructure systems only partially or occasionally connected into the broader internet network. According to him, the events of September 11, 2001, and the following political sensitivity around the subjects of safety and security of military and government information networks led George W. Bush's presidential administration to issue the 2008 Cybersecurity Policy that went so far as to even include networked machines and processors inside private industrial plants as part of cyberspace, thus extending related international legal protections onto them.[42]

Other scholars also tend to propose an expanded definition of cyberspace, although for reasons other than national security. For instance, Klaus Krippendorff argued in 2010 that cyberspace "results from the human

---

[40] Kuehl, Daniel T. "From Cyberspace to Cyberpower:" Cyberpower and National Security, June 16, 2009, page 25. <https://doi.org/10.2307/j.ctt1djmhj1.7.>

[41] Ibid.

[42] Ibid.

collective ability to articulate possibilities in which technological artifacts are designed, used, and conceptualized,"[43] thus proposing to see cyberspace as an abstract space facilitating further technological progress of humanity rather than being a specific communication and data exchange system. In a similar vein, John P. Barlow suggested in his Declaration of the Independence of Cyberspace that "cyberspace consists of transactions, relationships, and thought itself, arrayed like a standing wave in the web of our communications. Ours is a world that is both everywhere and nowhere, but it is not where bodies live."[44] Such attempts are inspired by the original vision of William Gibson but they have not received much following. Ryszard Tadeusiewicz soundly points out that it is the word "space" in cyberspace that stimulates imagination. He stated: "cyberspace evokes semantic and emotional associations with the ideas of a wide reach and absolute freedom. Such a space compels one to move in multiple directions, to overcome barriers, and to initiate interactions with others that would not have been possible if the space did not exist."[45] Other scholars still try to make the definition more nuanced by focusing on strengthening of the social interactive component. For example, Nazli Choucri said: "cyberspace is created through the interconnection of millions of computers by a global network such as the Internet which is built as a layered construct, where physical elements enable a logical framework of interconnection that permits the processing, manipulation, exploitation, augmentation of information, and the interaction of people and information. Cyberspace is enabled by institutional intermediation and organization, and characterized by decentralization and interplay among

---

43 Krippendorff, Klaus. "The Growth of Cyberspace and the Rise of a Design Culture, workshop on Social Theory and Social Computing." University of Hawaii. May 22, 2010. <https://www.iosrjournals.org/iosr-jce/papers/Vol17-issue3/Version-6/C017361724.pdf.>

44 Barlow, John P. "A Declaration of the Independence of Cyberspace." Electronic Frontier Foundation, April 8, 2018. <https://www.eff.org/cyberspace-independence.>

45 Tadeusiewicz Ryszard. "Wychowywanie dla cyberprzestrzeni jednym z warunków zapobiegania cyberuzależnieniom," [in:] Mastalerz, Elżbieta, Krzysztof Pytel, and Henryk Noga. Cyberuzależnieni: Przeciwdziałanie uzależnieniom od Komputera I Internetu: Publikacja Pokonferencyjna. Kraków: Niezależne Zrzeszenie Studentów Akademii Pedagogicznej, 2007. Page 23.

these actors, constituencies and interests."[46] However, several scholars question whether the social interactive component should be considered a core part of cyberspace. For example, Marcin Rojszczak aptly points out that a large share of activity in cyberspace, including sophisticated operations, are automated software-to-software interactions, without direct involvement of any humans.[47] With the rise of Artificial Intelligence the scale and complexity of such non-human interactions is bound to grow. This weakens the case for the social interactive component being a foundational part of cyberspace but rather just its emanation, unless we classify AI-to-AI communication as equally meaningful as human-to-human communication.

A balanced approach can account for the social interactive dimension while remaining firmly rooted in the formal definitions formulated by key actors of Public International Law. That view is represented, among others, by Karol Dobrzeniecki who proposed perceiving cyberspace as consisting of two main components: the infrastructure, including both the physical and software aspects, and the social interactive part, consisting of the internet users and their interactions.[48]

In the current context, numerous definitions of cyberspace function in parallel both in the realm of statements released by sovereign States as well as among academic publications. No consistent practice or *opinio juris* on the matter means the state of legal flux might remain protracted. The observable trend however is to progressively embrace more expansive definitions that include non-networked systems and only occasionally networked systems. Those definitions also don't require any human-to-human interaction. Going forward, developments in the area of Artificial Intelligence might mean that actually most of cyberspace activity won't even involve any direct human input, being conducted instead by AI agents, strengthening this broad definitional approach.

---

46 Choucri, Nazli. "Co-Evolution of Cyberspace and International Relations: New Challenges for the Social Sciences." SSRN Electronic Journal, October 13, 2014, 3–23. <https://doi.org/10.2139/ssrn.2514532.>

47 Rojszczak, Marcin. Ochrona prywatności W cyberprzestrzeni Z uwzględnieniem Zagrożeń Wynikających Z nowych Technik Przetwarzania Informacji. Warszawa: Wolters Kluwer, 2019. Page 45.

48 Dobrzeniecki, Karol. Prawo a Etos cyberprzestrzeni. Toruń: Wydawnictwo Adam Marszałek, 2004. Page 21.

1.2.3 Cyberspace as the new domain of State interactions and warfare

Since antiquity, nations have recognized land and water as the two domains of warfare. We can identify several international rules that were developed for each of them respectively in the works of Thucydides who vividly described Peloponnesian Wars in the fifth century B.C.[49] Over the course of history, airspace was added to the list of domains. First reports of utilizing airborne means for conducting warfare can be found in ancient China, where manned kites were used in warfare by General Han Xin.[50] At the advent of modernity, the three domains of warfare: land, water, and air were already well recognized and established in Public International Law.[51] The framework of three domains has been traditionally deployed to talk about *Jus in bello* and *Jus ad bellum* (The rules on States engaged in armed conflict and the rules on conditions under which States might resort to using their armed forces respectively). More broadly however, the three domains are the types of physical space in which States can come into interaction in general. Peacetime international arrangements have developed that apply solely to each respective domain.[52] In that respect, domains are a useful tool to discuss interactions between States that take place both at the time of war and peace.

The twentieth century brought changes to the framework as rapid technological progress led to the development of additional international laws, such as in the area of underwater warfare, a semi-separate sub-domain within the

---

49 Kelly, Thomas. "Thucydides and Spartan Strategy in the Archidamian War." The American Historical Review 87, no. 1 (1982). Page 25. <https://doi.org/10.2307/1863307>; Thibault, Edward A. "Thucydides on the influence of sea power." Naval War College Review 25, no. 4 (1973). Pages 31–35. <http://www.jstor.org/stable/44639794.>

50 Manheim, Noa. "The Strange and Violent History of Kites." Haaretz, June 28, 2018. <https://www.haaretz.com/israel-news/2018-06-28/ty-article-magazine/.premium/the-strange-and-violent-history-of-kites/0000017f-db94-d856-a37f-ffd483610000.>

51 Seebeck, Lesley. "Why the Fifth Domain Is Different." Australian Strategic Policy Institute, September 4, 2019. <https://www.aspistrategist.org.au/why-the-fifth-domain-is-different/.>

52 For example: "United Nations Convention on the Law of the Sea of 1982." United Nations. Accessed November 23, 2023. <https://www.un.org/depts/los/convention_agreements/convention_overview_convention.htm;> "Convention on International Civil Aviation of 1944 - Overview." Accessed November 23, 2023. <https://www.icao.int/publications/pages/doc7300.aspx.>

water one. Then, with the launch of Sputnik by the Soviet Union in 1957, yet another new domain was opened for human exploration and competition—outer space. Outer space was soon proclaimed to be the 4th *domain*, and a slew of new international public norms, covering subjects ranging from launching communication satellites to deploying weapons on the Moon were developed by the international community.[53] Outer space has been effectively the 4th domain since the time of the Cold War although some international organizations, most importantly NATO, only formally confirmed their consent to that legal framing in 2019.[54]

The emergence of cyberspace set the ground for a heated debate as to whether it can be defined as the 5th *domain*. First such proposals have been recorded in the late 1990s, including by Darrel Menthe.[55] That debate is far from settled, creating a state of legal uncertainty at the international level. Let us first consider the key characteristics of cyberspace as compared to the other four domains:

- It is man-made and subject to shaping by technological, social, and political forces.
- It can be either fully de-localized or geographically specific depending on the nature of a cyber operation.
- It is not a separate physical space unlike the other domains.
- It permeates all the other domains (see Figure 1).

---

53 United Nations - Office for Outer Space Affairs. Space Law Treaties and Principles. Accessed November 23, 2023. <https://www.unoosa.org/oosa/en/ourwork/spacelaw/treaties.html#:~:text=These%20five%20treaties%20deal%20with,with%20space%20activities%20and%20the.>

54 North Atlantic Treaty Alliance. NATO's official policy on the outer space, October 7, 2022. <https://www.nato.int/cps/en/natohq/topics_175419.htm#:~:text=At%20the%20June%202019%20Defence,%2C%20land%2C%20maritime%20and%20cyberspace.>

55 Darrel C. Menthe. Jurisdiction in Cyberspace: A Theory of International Spaces. 4 Mich. Telecomm. & Tech. L. Rev. 69 (1998). Page 71. <https://repository.law.umich.edu/mttlr/vol4/iss1/3.>

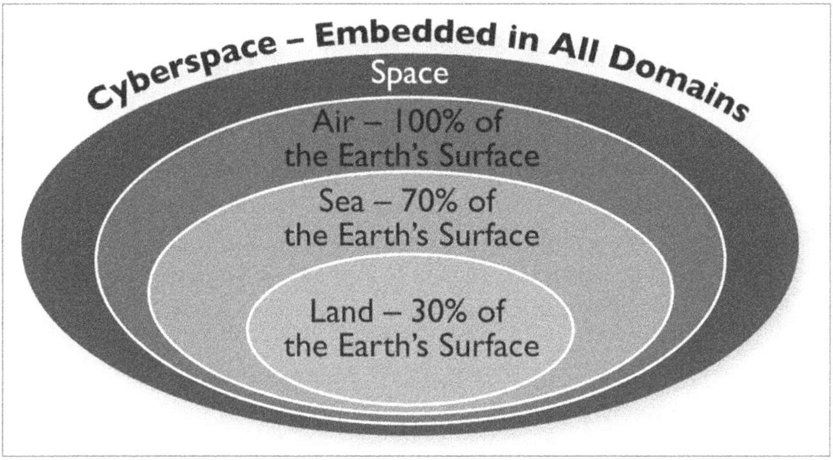

Figure 1. Five domains of warfare with cyberspace having a unique status
Source: Cyberspace—The Fifth Operational Domain, Gen. Larry D. Welch USAF (Ret.)

These features gave rise to much critique among scholars, some of them even suggesting that labeling cyberspace as a domain of warfare is a marketing maneuver that weakens international law. For example, Martin Libicki stated that "this concept is misleading, perhaps even pernicious. Faced with the question—if cyberspace is not a 'domain' what is it—one answer may be that 'it' does not exist in a sufficiently meaningful form to make conflict-related (legal) statements about it."[56] U.S. Armed Forces General Michael Hayden resonated with that statement, claiming that "cyberspace is the creation of man. Man can actually change this geography, and anything that happens there actually creates a change in someone's physical space. Are these differences important enough for us to rethink our doctrine?"[57] Michael Kreuzer stated that cyberspace is more of a metaphor than anything tangible enough to be treated as a domain: "The original three domains

56 Libicki, Martin C. "Cyberspace is Not a Warfighting Domain." I/S A Journal of Law and Policy for the Information Society 8, no. 2 (2012). Pages 325–340. <https://kb.osu.edu/server/api/core/bitstreams/0f5c21be-28f3-5951-926c-6bdcab243319/content>

57 Ibid.

of land, maritime, and air developed separate identities and independent services because unique characteristics dictated distinct requirements for humans to fight in those domains. (…) Cyberspace appeared a natural extension to this evolution, and in its early years it likely appeared the ability to control and exploit cyberspace was the next iteration for defense. The problem, however, is there is no cyberspace. There is instead a metaphor to help humans understand the near instantaneous sharing of information across widespread computer networks."[58] Daniel Ventre claimed that cyberspace is not a separate domain but rather a connective tissue that connects the four traditional ones.[59]

Other scholars still, such as Chris McGuffin and Paul Mitchell, take a balanced stance, acknowledging that cyberspace has not yet fully matured as a domain and is substantially different from the traditional four ones, but has potential to evolve to become an established one. Interestingly, they quoted Victorian Era similarly dismissive statements by British generals about air-to-air combat not being a genuine dimension of warfare. Comparing that past discussion to the current discourse on cyberspace, they implied that it might take a full-scale war whose large part takes place solely within the digital realm of cyberspace for the new domain to finally mature. This would constitute a rite of passage similar to what World War 1 was for aircraft combat.[60] The response of the critics, such as Thomas Rid, is that they doubt a truly digital war is ever going to take place.[61]

This critique, while salient, seems to underestimate important aspects of cyberspace. Scholars such as the International Group of Experts that

---

58 Kreuzer, Michael P. "Cyberspace Is an Analogy, Not a Domain: Rethinking Domains and Layers of Warfare for the Information Age." The Strategy Bridge, July 8, 2021. <https://thestrategybridge.org/the-bridge/2021/7/8/cyberspace-is-an-analogy-not-a-domain-rethinking-domains-and-layers-of-warfare-for-the-information-age.>

59 Ventre, Daniel. Cyberespace et acteurs du cyberconflit. Paris: Hermès Science publications, 2011. Pages 87–88.

60 McGuffin, Chris, and Paul Mitchell. "On Domains: Cyber and the Practice of Warfare." International Journal: Canada's Journal of Global Policy Analysis 69, no. 3 (2014): Page 411. <https://doi.org/10.1177/0020702014540618.>

61 Rid, Thomas. "Cyber War Will Not Take Place." Journal of Strategic Studies 35, no. 1 (2012): Pages 5–32. <https://doi.org/10.1080/01402390.2011.608939.>

authored the Tallinn Manual[62] believe that there can already occur adverse impacts that exist solely within cyberspace. Examples can include defacement or a blockade of a government website. For this reason, fully virtual actions done by States, even when there is no direct physical impact, can constitute *Internationally Wrongful Acts*, including those that are acts of *Use of Force* if their effects are severe enough. Cyber operations can also produce physical effects, such as was the case with the Stuxnet virus. If such legally consequential damaging impacts can be created in cyberspace, it should be considered as a domain of interactions between States, even if its nature is novel.

This brings us to the term *Internationally Wrongful Act*, which stems from *Draft Articles on Responsibility of States for Internationally Wrongful Acts*, issued by the International Law Commission (ILC) in 2001.[63] While not formally adopted as binding international law, the Draft Articles have been designed from the beginning to slowly become part of the customary international law through the process of forming of *opinio juris* and consistent practice within the international community. Twenty-two years after their publication, a hypothesis can be proposed that certain parts of the *Draft Articles*, especially the basic ones which enjoy the widest consensus, have in fact become part of agreed-upon customary international law.[64] This is because: one, the *Draft Articles* have been cited by the ICJ as a source for its legal rulings.[65] Two, at the time of their publication the *Draft Articles* were announced both as formalization of existing customary norms and laying out of proposed new norms that can become binding law following solidification of *opinio juris*, without a clear delineation between the two

62 Schmitt, Michael N. et al. Tallinn Manual 2.0 on the International Law Applicable to Cyber Operations. Cambridge, United Kingdom: Cambridge University Press, 2017. Pages 328–330.

63 United Nations International Law Commission. Draft articles on Responsibility of States for Internationally Wrongful Acts with commentaries. United Nations Office of Legal Affairs (2001). Retrieved February 15, 2022. <https://legal.un.org/ilc/texts/instruments/english/commentaries/9_6_2001.pdf.>

64 Czapliński, Władyslaw. "Un Codification of Law of State Responsibility." Archiv des Völkerrechts 41, no. 1 (2003): Pages 62–82. <https://doi.org/10.1628/0003892034410754.>

65 For instance: Case concerning the Gabcikovo-Nagymaros Project—Judgement, International Court of Justice Reports 1997, 92. Page 35.

categories.[66] Three, International Law Commission is a UN system body, which consists of 34 renowned experts recognized for their qualifications in the field of international law and who are elected by the UN General Assembly for a five-year term.[67] This means that the ILC is well positioned for its statements to be regarded as *teachings of the most highly qualified publicists of the various nations*, which qualify as a subsidiary source of international law according to Article 38 of the Statute of the International Court of Justice.[68] For these reason, depending on the context, the *Draft Articles*, especially the basic parts of it such as the definition of an *Internationally Wrongful Act*, can be seen as a general source of international law applicable to all treaty regimes[69] (unless an alternative exemptional framework is applied in a specific legal area such as it is the case for instance with the European Convention on Human Rights).[70] According to the *Draft Articles on State Responsibility*, an *Internationally Wrongful Act*:

1) is attributable to the State under international law; and
2) constitutes a breach of an international obligation of the State.[71]

A hostile cyber operation that constitutes an *Internationally Wrongful Act* can lead to consequences such as deploying *Countermeasures* by the injured State. The International Group of Experts proposed using the notion of

---

66 Georgetown University. Law Guides: International Investment Law Research Guide: Customary Law on State Responsibility. Retrieved February 15, 2022. <https://guides.ll.georgetown.edu/c.php?g=371540&p=2511830.>

67 United Nations General Assembly Resolution 174 (II). Establishment of an International Law Commission, A/RES/174(II) (1947, November 21). Retrieved February 15, 2022. <https://daccess-ods.un.org/access.nsf/Get?OpenAgent&DS=A/RES/174(II)&Lang=E.>

68 International Court of Justice. Statute of the Court (1945, June 26). Retrieved February 15, 2022. <https://www.icj-cij.org/en/statute. Article 38.>

69 Ibid.

70 Council of Europe. European Convention on Human Rights (1950, November 4). Retrieved February 15, 2022. <https://www.echr.coe.int/documents/convention_eng.pdf.>

71 United Nations International Law Commission. Draft articles on Responsibility of States for Internationally Wrongful Acts with commentaries. United Nations Office of Legal Affairs (2001). Retrieved February 15, 2022. <https://legal.un.org/ilc/texts/instruments/english/commentaries/9_6_2001.pdf.>

"consequential harm" stemming from a cyber operation as a method to gauge whether a cyber hostility reached the minimum threshold for being considered an *Internationally Wrongful Act* and if so, what legal classification to ascribe to it. The term consequential harm "encompasses any reasonably foreseeable consequential damage, destruction, injury or death."[72] The question then is whether purely digital impacts can reach that minimal level. The authors of the Manual suggest that they can.[73]

However, several experts still express their ambivalence about this expansionary interpretation. François Delerue claimed that while hostile cyber operations can amount to *Use of Force* solely based on impacts in the digital space,[74] cyberspace does not constitute the 5th domain. His argument is that the physical character of the traditional four domains means that humans and objects can travel between them, which means acts such as *Use of Force* can directly carry between those domains. For example, a missile launched from one domain can reach a target in the other. That same cannot be said of cyberspace.[75] Matthew Hoisington noted that assuming that purely digital operations, with no direct physical manifestation, can potentially reach the threshold of *Use of Force*, would cause the currently prevailing interpretation of Article 2(4) of the UN Charter to become untenable.[76] This is because acts of economic and political coercion listed in it, such as economic sanctions, have been traditionally excluded from that definition and instead classified as examples of an intervention, which is a less acute type of a disruption to a State's sovereignty than *Use of Force*. If virtual blockades or operations with no direct physical impact could potentially reach the level of an act of use of force, then why should not economic sanctions with no direct physical damage component be classified similarly? However, recognizing an economic sanction as *Use of*

---

72 Schmitt, Michael N. Tallinn Manual on the international law applicable to cyber warfare. Cambridge: Cambridge University Press, 2013. Page 107.

73 Ibid.

74 Delerue, François. Cyber Operations and international law. Cambridge: Cambridge University Press, 2020. Page 298.

75 Ibid. Page 11.

76 Hoisington, Matthew. "Cyberwarfare and the Use of Force Giving Rise to the Right of Self-Defense." SSRN Electronic Journal, 2009. Page 447. <https://doi.org/10.2139/ssrn.1542223.>

Force, would go against established practices and the logic of the system Public International Law. This creates a potential contradiction and an inconsistency within the legal system.

Much of the tension among scholars stems from their differential focus. The skeptics focus on the existing possibilities for hostile cyber operations in cyberspace, deeming them not substantial enough to justify establishment of a whole new domain. Those in favor of embracing the new domain, point to future possibilities that include new kinds of damage that are only possible inside cyberspace, serious enough to validate the status of cyberspace as a new domain. As technology progresses and human-computer interfaces allow for more of an immersive experience within cyberspace, new sophisticated forms of cyber operations and interactions are indeed likely to emerge that will have no direct bearing on the physical reality. Franklin Kramer captured this expanding nature of cyberspace with the following words: "Cyber has a number of characteristics that suggest its future may differ importantly from its present. Policymakers must, therefore, establish cyber strategy in a dynamic context—not knowing what the future will be, but nonetheless creating structures, processes, and people sufficiently flexible to adapt to change. Cyber is malleable because, although it exists in the physical world of electrons, transmission capabilities, and computers, it is a man-made creation subject to the power of human invention."[77] Joanna Worona claims that while it is near-impossible to predict what cyberspace will look like 50 years from now, its past dynamic evolution is a good indicator that we can expect a continuation of the rapid pace of development of new capabilities permeating ever more spheres of human life.[78] A recent example of an early development in that direction comes from the United Arab Emirates. The State has launched their Metaverse Strategy, a part of which is developing virtual reality presence for its government ministries that could be visited virtually via an avatar.[79] Those new virtual venues could

---

77 Kramer, Franklin D., Stuart H. Starr, and Larry K. Wentz. Cyberpower and national security. Washington, D.C.: Center for Technology and National Security Policy, 2009. Page 2.

78 Worona, Joanna, "Cyberprzestrzeń a Prawo Międzynarodowe - Status Quo i Perspektywy." Ph.D. dissertation, University of Bialystok, 2017. Page 26.

79 "WAM - Emirates News Agency." Hamdan bin Mohammed launches Dubai Metaverse Strategy -وكالة أنباء الإمارات, July 18, 2022. <https://wam.ae/en/details/1395303067141.>

be at risk of getting hacked or defaced as part of a hostile cyber operation by another State.

Some scholars proposed that cyberspace as the 5th domain should be modeled on outer space as it is the most similar to it from among the four physical domains. For instance, Joanna Worona wrote: "Cyberspace is the most similar to outer space in its characteristics. The latter is free, unpossessable by any State, open to free access and exploration, [its order] based on the principles of responsibility and international cooperation in terms of using its resources by all."[80]

Despite the controversies and ongoing debates, ever more States and international organizations have embraced cyberspace as a unique domain of State interactions, both the war and peacetime-related ones. In 2011, the U.S. Department of Defense officially recognized it in its Strategy for Operating in Cyberspace.[81] In 2016, NATO States jointly espoused that stance at the Summit in Warsaw.[82] The conduct of other key military powers, coupled with lack of dissent from their governments on the matter implies that the position is progressively gaining recognition within the international community.[83] It appears then that cyberspace is now defined as the 5th domain of warfare (and peacetime) interactions between States. To the extent that the evolution of the other four can serve as a forecast, this means that *Sui Generis* specialized international legal rules could develop that apply specifically and uniquely to actions taken in cyberspace.

---

80 Worona, Joanna, "Cyberprzestrzeń a Prawo Międzynarodowe - Status Quo i Perspektywy." Ph.D. dissertation, University of Bialystok, 2017. Page 547.

81 US Department of Defense. Strategy for Operating in Cyberspace, July 2011. <https://csrc.nist.gov/CSRC/media/Projects/ISPAB/documents/DOD-Strategy-for-Operating-in-Cyberspace.pdf.>

82 North Atlantic Treaty Organization. "NATO Recognises Cyberspace as a 'domain of Operations' at Warsaw Summit." NATO CCDCOE, July 9, 2016. <https://ccdcoe.org/incyder-articles/nato-recognises-cyberspace-as-a-domain-of-operations-at-warsaw-summit/.>

83 Seebeck, Lesley. "Why the Fifth Domain Is Different." Australian Strategic Policy Institute, September 4, 2019. <https://www.aspistrategist.org.au/why-the-fifth-domain-is-different/.>

1.3 Cyber operations—range of definitions and their legal impact

1.3.1 Hostile cyber operations between States as *Unfriendly Acts*

Defining "a cyber operation" or more specifically "a hostile cyber operation" is challenging. The opening key finding is that there is no general prohibition of cyber operations in Public International Law, not even of hostile ones. The existing framework of Public International Law provides guidelines on how to classify various non-consensual types of behavior that can take place between sovereign States and cyber operations, including their minimal threshold criteria. However, such operations would be prohibited not due to the fact of being "hostile cyber operations" but rather because they meet general well-established criteria set for prohibited acts such as, for example, *Prohibited Intervention* or *Prohibited Use of Force*. The question then arises—should those general rules be adjusted in any way to accommodate the unique context of cyber hostilities between States? Are there any precedents implying that we are moving in that direction?

At the highest level, all hostile cyber operations between States can be classified as *Unfriendly Acts*. It's one of the broadest categories in the system of Public International Law and also one that has never been formally defined despite being routinely used by States, the UN General Assembly, and the ICJ. For that reason, we can first lean on a non-legal source—the Max Planck Encyclopedia of Public International Law, which defines it the following way:

> An 'unfriendly act' is a conduct (act or omission) of a subject of international law which inflicts a disadvantage, disregard or discourtesy on another subject of international law. (...)[84]

François Delerue adds that an *Unfriendly Act* is perceived by its recipient as a breach of good relations and can complicate future relations.[85]

Because the term has not been formalized, uncertainties remain such as, for example, whether only States or all subjects of Public International Law

---

84 Oxford Public International Law. Unfriendly Act - definition. Retrieved February 17, 2022. <https://opil.ouplaw.com/view/10.1093/law:epil/9780199231690/law-9780199231690-e423.>

85 Delerue, François. Cyber Operations and international law. Cambridge: Cambridge University Press, 2020. Page 194.

can receive and conduct *Unfriendly Acts*. François Delerue for instance suggests that only States can conduct *Unfriendly Acts*.[86] This however seems to be a very narrow definition. The fact that the European Union was accused of perpetrating an *Unfriendly Act* by the Russian Federation[87] implies that at least certain other categories of subjects of Public International Law can commit *Unfriendly Acts*. An additional point of debate is whether all types of *Internationally Wrongful Acts* can also simultaneously be classified as *Unfriendly Acts*.[88] The linguistic interpretative logic implies that this should be the case. Acts such as a *Prohibited Intervention* or an *Armed Attack* are quite literally *Unfriendly Acts*. They also meet more restrictive requirements that classify them as more egregious acts, but this does not remove them from the broad category of *Unfriendly Acts*. It is then logically consistent to see the term *Unfriendly Act* as an umbrella notion that includes all the other progressively more severe categories. Therefore, one can claim that the term *Unfriendly Acts* includes all *Internationally Wrongful Acts* as well as some acts that are lawful but nevertheless perceived as unfriendly, inimical, or hostile by the subject of Public International Law who is the act's recipient. For example, the Russian Federation stated that the European Union's sanctions against it, following its invasion of Ukraine's region of Crimea, were an *Unfriendly Act*.[89] Importantly, the *Unfriendly Acts* that are lawful do not make the affected State eligible for any kind of *Countermeasures*. It is essentially a term that spans the gap between legal and diplomatic relations.

While an *Unfriendly Act* is not a strictly formal category, it draws on existing legal sources:

---

86 Ibid.

87 Polityuk, Pavel, and Aleksandar Vasovic. "Putin Likens Western Sanctions to War as Russian Assault Traps Ukrainian Civilians." Reuters, March 5, 2022. <https://www.reuters.com/markets/europe/top-wrap-1-europes-largest-nuclear-power-plant-fire-after-russian-attack-mayor-2022-03-04/.>

88 Moynihan, Harriet. The Application of International Law to State Cyberattacks. Chatham House (December 2019). Page 50. <https://www.chathamhouse.org/2019/12/application-international-law-state-cyberattacks.>

89 "Russia Says 'unfriendly' EU Sanctions Will Hinder Ties." Reuters, July 10, 2014. <https://www.reuters.com/article/us-ukraine-crisis-sanctions-russia/russia-says-unfriendly-eu-sanctions-will-hinder-ties-idUSKBN0FF1A820140710.>

- Article 2 paragraph 2 of the UN Charter;
- Article 33 paragraph 1 of the UN Charter;
- *Declaration on Principles of International Law concerning Friendly Relations and Cooperation among States in accordance with the Charter of the United Nations* adopted by the UN General Assembly in 1970;
- ICJ ruling on the case Nicaragua v. United States of America (Paramilitary Activities) issued in 1986.

Article 2 paragraph 2 of the UN Charter states:

> All Members shall settle their international disputes by peaceful means in such a manner that international peace and security, and justice, are not endangered.[90]

While there's no general prohibition of *Unfriendly Acts*, art. 2 paragraph 2 can be interpreted as an obligation of all subjects of international law to make a good faith effort toward avoiding them. Similar message can be deduced from Article 33 of the UN Charter, which states:

> The parties to any dispute, the continuance of which is likely to endanger the maintenance of international peace and security, shall, first of all, seek a solution by negotiation, enquiry, mediation, conciliation, arbitration, judicial settlement, resort to regional agencies or arrangements, or other peaceful means of their own choice.[91]

The same message is present in the *Declaration on Principles of International Law concerning Friendly Relations and Cooperation among States in accordance with the Charter of the United Nations*, unanimously adopted by the UN General Assembly in 1970.[92] The declaration undergirds the prevailing

---

90 United Nations. Charter of the United Nations, June 26, 1945. 1 UNTS XVI. Article 2, Point 2. <https://www.un.org/en/about-us/un-charter.>

91 Ibid. Article 33.

92 United Nations General Assembly Resolution 2625 (XXV). Declaration on Principles of International Law concerning Friendly Relations and Cooperation among States in Accordance with the Charter of the United Nations, A/RES/2625(XXV) (1970, October 24). Retrieved February 17, 2022. <https://legal.un.org/avl/ha/dpilfrcscun/dpilfrcscun.html.>

paradigm of respectful, friendly, international relations. In the Declaration, the UN GA asserted:

> Bearing in mind the importance of maintaining and strengthening international peace founded upon freedom, equality, justice and respect for fundamental human rights and of developing friendly relations among nations irrespective of their political, economic and social systems or the levels of their development.[93]

The ICJ has confirmed that stance in its Nicaragua ruling, where it confirmed that there is no general prohibition of *Unfriendly Acts* in Public International Law:

> Such a duty (to avoid committing Unfriendly Acts) might of course be expressly stipulated in a treaty or might even emerge as a necessary implication from the text; but as a matter of customary international law, it is not clear that the existence of such a far-reaching rule is evidenced in the practice of States. There must be a distinction, even in the case of a treaty of friendship.[94]

In this context, launching an *Unfriendly Act* against a State without resorting to peaceful means of resolving tension first impinges upon the spirit of the UN Charter and the Declaration on Principles of International Law concerning Friendly Relations but it is not prohibited *per se*. This leads us back to hostile cyber operations. A hostile cyber operation can be defined as:

> An Unfriendly Act of a subject of international law which inflicts damage, disadvantage, disregard, or discourtesy on another subject of international law conducted via cyberspace.[95]

This definition draws upon the already established definition of an *Unfriendly Act* and cyberspace. By being based on the notion of an *Unfriendly Act*, it recognizes that there is no general prohibition of hostile cyber operations in

---

93 Ibid.

94 Military and Paramilitary Activities in and against Nicaragua (Nicaragua v. United States of America)—Judgment, International Court of Justice Reports 1986, 273. Page 126.

95 Own elaboration, based on: "Unfriendly Act - Definition in the Public International Law." Oxford University Public International Law. Retrieved November 25, 2023. <https://opil.ouplaw.com/display/10.1093/law:epil/9780199231690/law-9780199231690-e423.>

Public International Law. Additionally, by utilizing the word *via*, it includes both the acts that took place fully within the domain of cyberspace as well as those that only utilized cyberspace as a means to create effects in one of the other four domains: on land, in air, in water, or in outer space.

1.3.2 Status of espionage in the context of hostile cyber operations

The volume of international hostile cyber operations has been growing exponentially over the past few years (Section I.4 presents details on the trends). Nevertheless, the overwhelming majority of those operations are activities that are well below the threshold of severity necessary for classification as an *Internationally Wrongful Act*. Most of that below-threshold activity can be broadly described as cyber espionage. This is no coincidence. Cyber espionage is a natural extension and evolution of conventional espionage, which has been taking place between States since time immemorial. Rather than being a completely new phenomenon, these espionage activities are deploying modern technologies to satisfy the universal and timeless demand of States for classified intelligence on foreign governments. Of course, some of those spying activities utilize methods so egregious and severe that they can be also qualified as breaches of international obligations, but this is due to the means chosen rather than espionage itself. This section engages with the question of definition and impact of below-threshold hostile cyber operations, with cyber espionage being the prime example.

Similarly to hostile cyber operations, there exists no general prohibition of espionage in Public International Law although the methods deployed to conduct it may deem it an *Internationally Wrongful Act*. Christian Schaller framed it the following way: "Although there are no specific international norms designed to contain or regulate espionage activities, it is inherent in the nature of such activities that they always run the risk of conflicting with certain principles under international law. First and foremost, a covert intrusion into a foreign State usually interferes with the sovereignty of that State and violates the prohibition of intervention."[96] Another parallel between espionage and hostile cyber operations is that there also exists no

[96] Schaller, Christian. Spies. In: Rüdiger Wolfrum (ed.), The Max Planck Encyclopedia of Public International Law (2008), online edition (<www.mpepil.com>), paras. 6–12.

formal definition of espionage in international law. This opens up space for non-binding academic sources to help frame the discussion. According to the *Oxford University Bibliographies*, espionage consists of:

> the access, on behalf of a state, to information that is held by another state and considered as confidential or strategic, in the military, security, or economic field.[97]

The key element of the definition is that espionage operations do not carry any disruptive payload, their only purpose being collection of information, preferably without causing any impact. Tallinn Manual 2.0., a non-binding, NATO-sponsored publication that pools together insights from an International Group of Renowned Experts, proposed a specific definition that focuses solely on cyber espionage. It proposes that cyber espionage is:

> an information-gathering cyber operation, encompassing any act undertaken clandestinely or under false pretenses by a State that uses cyber capabilities to gather, or attempt to gather, information [from another State].[98]

There are four main elements of this definition of cyber espionage:

- The act must be geared toward collecting valuable information;
- The act must be done in a covert or clandestine manner;
- The act must rely on cyber capabilities;
- The act must be attributable to a State and aimed at another State.

---

97 Dubuisson, François, and Agatha Verdebout. "Espionage in International Law." Oxford Bibliographies Online Datasets, 2018. <https://doi.org/10.1093/obo/9780199796953-0173.>

98 Schmitt, Michael N. et al. Tallinn Manual 2.0 on the International Law Applicable to Cyber Operations. Cambridge, United Kingdom: Cambridge University Press, 2017. Supra n.3, page 168; Buchan, Russell. Cyber espionage and international law (1st Edition). Oxford: Hart, 2019. Chapter 1; Lubin, Asaf M. "The Liberty to Spy." Articles by Maurer Faculty. Harvard International Law Journal, 61(185), 2020. Pages 1–61. <https://www.repository.law.indiana.edu/facpub/2905/>; Sander, Barrie. "The Sound of Silence: International Law and the Governance of Peacetime Cyber Operations." 2019 11th International Conference on Cyber Conflict (CyCon), 2019, Pages 1–21. <https://doi.org/10.23919/cycon.2019.8756882>.

Such activity is for the most part below-threshold and makes up the vast majority of non-consensual cyber interactions between States. For instance, U.S. Deputy Secretary of Defense William J. Lynn III stated in a Foreign Affairs article that *the theft of intellectual property may be the most significant cyber threat that the United States will face over the long term*, even if it is less noticeable than hostile cyber acts aimed at disrupting critical national infrastructure (which would surely qualify as *Internationally Wrongful Acts*).[99]

Governments readily employ cyber espionage tools and peacetime espionage is lawful in international law.[100] Essentially all countries outlaw foreign espionage domestically, within their jurisdiction. At the same time, customary international law provides that a foreign espionage incursion during peacetime does not per se violate State sovereignty.[101] It is also not considered a *casus belli*, meaning that it is not covered by international law related to armed conflict.[102] In fact, most States maintain a deliberate policy of strategic silence on the status of espionage in international law, a practice

---

99 Lynn, William J. III. "Defending a New Domain - The Pentagon's Cyberstrategy." Foreign Affairs, September 1, 2010. <https://www.foreignaffairs.com/articles/united-states/2010-09-01/defending-new-domain.>

100 Sander, Barrie. "The Sound of Silence: International Law and the Governance of Peacetime Cyber Operations," 2019. 11th International Conference on Cyber Conflict (CyCon), 2019, Pages 1–21. <https://doi.org/10.23919/cycon.2019.8756882>; Moynihan, Harriet. The Application of International Law to State Cyberattacks. Chatham House (December 2019). <https://www.chathamhouse.org/2019/12/application-international-law-state-cyberattacks>; Deeks, Ashley. "An International Legal Framework for Surveillance," 2014. Virginia Journal of International Law, 55(291), Pages 300–319. <https://www.ilsa.org/Jessup/Jessup16/Batch%202/DeeksLegalFramework.pdf>; Pun, Darien. "Rethinking Espionage in the Modern Era," 2017. Chicago Journal of International Law," 353, Pages 359–368. <https://chicagounbound.uchicago.edu/cjil/vol18/iss1/10/>; Lubin, Asaf M. "Cyber Law and Espionage Law as Communicating Vessels," 2018. SSRN Electronic Journal, Pages 203–225. <https://doi.org/10.2139/ssrn.3099769>; Egan, Brian. "US Department of State's Transparency Regarding International Law in Cyberspace," 2019. Just Security. <https://www.justsecurity.org/34465/transparency-international-law-cyberspace/>.

101 Ibid.

102 Lin, Herbert. "Responding to Sub-Threshold Cyber Intrusions: A Fertile Topic for Research and Discussion," 2011. Georgetown Journal of International Affairs, 2011, Pages 127–135.

that led to a customary assumption of its legality.[103] Its legality can be also inferred from the 1961 Vienna Convention on Diplomatic Relations, which, according to expert interpretations, *explicitly recognizes the well-established right of nations to engage in espionage during peacetime.*[104] There is also consensus on that subject in the academia[105] (albeit with some divergent interpretations[106]). Tallinn Manual 2.0 echoed that sentiment: *The International Group of Experts agreed that customary international law does not prohibit espionage per se. (…) On the contrary, a number of States have by domestic law authorised their security services to engage in espionage, including cyber espionage.*[107]

Lawfulness of international espionage is confirmed by State practice, that is, the objective component of *opinio juris.* There exist many publicly available government documents confirming that States order their intelligence services engage in cyber espionage abroad. Some of those States include: Austria, Germany, Netherlands, Sweden, Switzerland, United Kingdom, and the United States.[108] The fact that such prominent countries reveal their

---

103 Ziolkowski, Katharina. Peacetime regime for state activities in Cyberspace: International law, International Relations and Diplomacy. Tallinn, Estonia: NATO Cooperative Cyber Defence Centre of Excellence, 2013. Page 425, 437–443.

104 Wingfield, Thomas C. The law of information conflict: National security law in Cyberspace. Falls Church, VA: Aegis Research Corp., 2000. Supra note 110, page 350.

105 Lubin, Asaf M. "Cyber Law and Espionage Law as Communicating Vessels," 2018. SSRN Electronic Journal, pages 203–225. <https://doi.org/10.2139/ssrn.3099769>.

106 Navarrete Inaki Mr., and Buchan, Russell. "Out of the Legal Wilderness: Peacetime Espionage, International Law and the Existence of Customary Exceptions," 2019. Cornell International Law Journal, 51(4), 897–953. <https://scholarship.law.cornell.edu/cilj/vol51/iss4/4/>.

107 Schmitt, Michael N. et al. Tallinn Manual 2.0 on the International Law Applicable to Cyber Operations. Cambridge, United Kingdom: Cambridge University Press, 2017. Supra n.3, page 169.

108 The government of Austria. Bundesgesetz über Aufgaben und Befugnisse im Rahmen der militärischen Landesverteidigung, April 27, 1999. Section 20(a). Retrieved February 17, 2022. <https://www.ris.bka.gv.at/GeltendeFassung.wxe?Abfrage=Bundesnormen&Gesetzesnummer=20000864>; The government of Germany. Gesetz über den Bundesnachrichtendienst (BND-Gesetz - BNDG), December 20, 1990. Section 2(1)(40). Retrieved February 17, 2022. <https://www.gesetze-im-internet.de/bndg/BJNR029790990.html>; The government of Netherlands. Wet op de inlichtingen- en veiligheidsdiensten 2017,, February 7, 2017. Sections 1–2. Retrieved February 17, 2022. <https://wetten.overheid.nl/BWBR0039896/2022-01-01#:~:text=2%20De%20Algemene%20Inlichtingen%2D%20en,zijn%20verstrekt%20

intent to spy does not contradict the definition of cyber espionage since the actual acts of spying and their targets are not revealed.

Identifying the threshold that delineates between cyber espionage acts that are only *Unfriendly Acts* and those that constitute *Internationally Wrongful Acts* is challenging. Unlike conventional espionage, which typically takes place on the physical territory of a target State, cyber espionage is geographically unbound. It can take place remotely and instantaneously. It also allows for transfers of data that are much bigger than conventional espionage would ever allow for.[109] This means that cyber espionage can easily inflict much more negative impact on a target State than its conventional equivalent. This issue was discussed by the International Group of Experts behind the Tallinn Manual 2.0, who proposed:

> Cyber espionage may be conducted in a manner that violates international law due to the fact that certain of the methods employed to conduct cyber espionage are unlawful. (...) In other words, if an aspect of a cyber espionage operation is unlawful under international law, it renders the cyber espionage unlawful. By styling a cyber operation as a 'cyber espionage operation', a State cannot therefore claim that it is by definition lawful under international law;[110]

This framing appears to be consistent with State practice. For instance, United States of America and China, stated in its 2015 agreement on cyber security implicitly that certain instances of cyber espionage can

dat%20noodzakelijk%20maken>; The government of United Kingdom. Regulation of Investigatory Powers Act 2000, July 20, 2000. Section 8(4). Retrieved February 17, 2022. <https://www.legislation.gov.uk/ukpga/2000/23/contents>; The government of Switzerland. Bundesgesetz vom 3. Oktober 2008 über die Zuständigkeiten im Bereich des zivilen Nachrichtendienstes (ZNDG), October 3, 2008. Articla 1(a). Retrieved February 17, 2022. <https://www.fedlex.admin.ch/eli/cc/2009/809/de>.

109 Kilovaty, Ido. "World Wide Web of Exploitations – The Case of Peacetime Cyber Espionage Operations Under International Law: Towards a Contextual Approach," January 18, 2017. Columbia University Science and Technology Law Review 18(1), page 53. <https://doi.org/10.7916/stlr.v18i1.4012>.

110 Schmitt, Michael N. et al. Tallinn Manual 2.0 on the International Law Applicable to Cyber Operations. Cambridge, United Kingdom: Cambridge University Press, 2017. Supra n.3, page 170.

constitute a breach of international obligations.[111] Sometimes the difference between espionage acts that are only *Unfriendly Acts* and those that constitute *Internationally Wrongful Acts* boils down to nuances of jurisdiction (addressed in detail in Chapter 5). For instance, the act of cyber wiretapping of a military submarine would likely constitute a violation of sovereignty, and hence an *Internationally Wrongful Act*, if hacking into the submarine's systems took place at the time when it was located within a country's territorial waters. That same act would constitute just an *Unfriendly Act* if the same happened in international waters.[112]

This growing gap between treatment of conventional and cyber espionage gives rise to a debate on whether a specialized international legal regime is emerging that deals specifically with cyber espionage and applies differentials standards to it. The International Group of Experts appears to be implying just that by proposing Rule 32 that deals with cyber espionage in the section of the Tallinn Manual 2.0 titled "Cyber operations not *per se* regulated by international law" and Rule 33 on hostile cyber operations done by non-State actors attributable to their host States. This treatment is different from the one enjoyed by conventional international espionage, which traditionally has not been directly regulated at all.[113]

In the context of insufficient amount of State practice and international jurisprudence, various approaches have been proposed to classify hostile cyber operations between States in a way that would clearly distinguish between those that are likely only *Unfriendly Acts* and those that constitute *Internationally Wrongful Acts*. Those approaches do not have a binding character and are academic proposals. Potentially, they can inform future government conduct contributing to emergence of an internationally binding method. For now however, they are a form of intellectual exercise rather than anything else. For instance, Herbert Lin constructed the notion of the *nature of payload*, distinguishing between *cyber-exploitations*

---

111 The government of the United States of America. Fact Sheet: President Xi Jinping's State Visit to the United States. September 25, 2015. Retrieved February 17, 2022. <https://obamawhitehouse.archives.gov/the-press-office/2015/09/25/fact-sheet-president-xi-jinpings-state-visit-united-states>.

112 Ibid. Point 7.

113 Buchan, Russell. Cyber espionage and international law (1st Edition). Oxford: Hart, 2019. Chapter 1.

(his term for international hostile cyber operation) whose *payload* is destructive (which means it seeks to disrupt functioning of the targeted system, e.g., when a virus has the purpose of stalling a power on top of gathering intelligence) and those whose *payload* is non-destructive (e.g., their sole purpose is to get access to information).[114] The former are potentially *Internationally Wrongful Acts* while the latter are mostly below-threshold activities.

The fast-growing number of publicly decried international cyber incidents has drawn public attention and outcry in a number of countries. It propelled a debate as to whether peaceful cyber espionage should be regulated more restrictively than its conventional equivalent.[115] For example, Barrie Sander argues that since cyber espionage impacts non-State actors on an unprecedented scale (both as perpetrators as well as targets) compared to conventional spying, States might invoke mass violation of individuals' rights (such as human rights, including the right to privacy), and in that way drive the wedge between cyber and conventional espionage, leading to development of differential international legal rules that deal with each.[116]

Public pressure to address the growing problem of hostile international cyber operations is partially also driven by the fact that States are reluctant to invoke more serious categories of international law violation, meaning that most instances of such activity are officially presented as forms of espionage by the victim States. This is likely due to the challenges with legal attribution of more severe cyber breaches of international law, as described in Chapter 4. It is much harder to successfully attribute a cyber violation to a State than it is the case with traditional conventional hostilities. It might also have to do with the policy of ambivalence and secrecy, discussed in Chapter 2, according to which, victim States do not want to limit their own legal and

---

114 Lin, Herbert. "Responding to Sub-Threshold Cyber Intrusions: A Fertile Topic for Research and Discussion," 2011. Georgetown Journal of International Affairs, 2011, pages 129–130; Leonhard Kreuzer, "Disentangling the Cyber Security Debate," Völkerrechtsblog, 20 June 2018. <https://doi.org/10.17176/20180620-183041-1>.

115 Sander, Barrie. "The Sound of Silence: International Law and the Governance of Peacetime Cyber Operations." 2019 11th International Conference on Cyber Conflict (CyCon), 2019, page 11. <https://doi.org/10.23919/cycon.2019.8756882>.

116 Ibid.

operational latitude to perform cyber operations abroad in the future. Finally, States might be reluctant to claim that the hostile cyber operations they were affected by are *Internationally Wrongful Acts* due to their inability to project a symmetrical response. For example, a State that acknowledges being on the receiving end of *Prohibited Use of Force* by another State and does not seek recourse or *Countermeasures* (for instance because it is incapable of doing so) can be perceived as weak or publicly accepting of other States compromising its sovereignty.

1.3.3 *State Sovereignty* as the guiding principle in assessing hostile cyber operations in Public International Law

Two concepts have emerged so far in terms of what constitutes the threshold above which a hostile cyber operation constitutes an *Internationally Wrongful Act* and both of them operate using the notion of *State Sovereignty*. The first one posits that State-sponsored intrusions below a certain threshold do not constitute a violation of international law. The second, more absolutist, claims that all hostile cyber operations in another country that can be attributed to a State are by definition a *Violation of Sovereignty*.[117] This position, championed by France, implies that even lack of any kind of damage, material or otherwise, would not preclude a hostile cyber operation from being a *Violation of Sovereignty*.[118]

France's stance defies the established norms regarding conventional activities, specifically espionage. There is no general prohibition in Public International Law of either espionage or hostile cyber operations. Numerous States conduct intelligence-gathering activities in foreign countries at any given point in time and this is not seen as a *Violation of Sovereignty* as long as intensity and character of such activity does not reach the threshold of

117 Moynihan, Harriet. The Application of International Law to State Cyberattacks. Chatham House (December 2019). <https://www.chathamhouse.org/2019/12/application-international-law-state-cyberattacks>.

118 Ministry of Armed Forces of the Republic of France. "Droit International Applique Aux Operations Dans Le Cyberspace', 2019. <https://www.defense.gouv.fr/salle-de-presse/communiques/communiques-du-ministere-des-armees/communique_la-france-s-engage-a-promouvoir-un-cyberespace-stable-fonde-sur-la-confianceet-le-respect-du-droit-international>.

other transgressions such as *Prohibited Intervention* or *Prohibited Use of Force*.[119] A counter-argument can be to invoke a slowly changing State practice in that regard. For instance, the Federal Court of Canada refused to grant permission to the Canadian Security Intelligence Service in 2008 to conduct espionage operations abroad on the basis that it would contravene the *Principles of Sovereignty and Non-Intervention*.[120] President of the Russian Federation, Vladimir Putin, stated in 2014 that he perceives international cyber espionage of any kind to constitute a *Violation of Sovereignty*.[121] Tallinn Manual 2.0, which is an academic publication sponsored by the NATO and designed as a reflection of views of the leading experts in the field suggests that while hostile cyber operations do not have to violate sovereignty, they are very likely to do it.[122]

It was not always obvious that *Violation of Sovereignty* would be the guiding principle in assessing hostile cyber operations in Public International Law. The 2013–2015 period marked a crucial milestone for clarifying this uncertainty. The two reports by the UN Group of Government Experts (UN GGE) passed during that time (both subsequently approved by a UN General Assembly Resolution) laid down the groundwork for the future system of binding customary international norms. At the time of writing this book, the norms included in the reports have not yet reached that status and they are bound to undergo a process of modification and expansion before they eventually transition toward becoming customary law. Nevertheless, there exist strong signs that *opinio juris* on those norms' binding status has already started forming, as demonstrated by statements of international

---

119 Oppenheim, Lassa, Robert Y. Jennings, and Arthur Watts. Oppenheim's international law. Oxford: Oxford University Press, 2008. Page 391.

120 Buchan, Russell. Cyber espionage and international law (1st Edition). Oxford: Hart, 2019. Page 51; Watts, Sean, and Richard, Theodore. T. "Baseline Territorial Sovereignty and Cyberspace," 2018. Lewis & Clark Law Review, pages 866–867. <https://papers.ssrn.com/sol3/papers.cfm?abstract_id=3142272>.

121 Interfax. "Vladimir Putin: cyber espionage is direct violation of state's sovereignty," July 11, 2014. <https://interfax.com/newsroom/top-stories/41982/>.

122 NATO Cooperative Cyber Defence Center of Excellence. "The Tallinn manual Initiative." Accessed November 23, 2023. <https://ccdcoe.org/research/tallinn-manual/>.

organizations and States.[123] Both reports are also a product of a careful consensus within the international community, with all permanent member States on the UN Security Council formally endorsing them. This allows us to utilize the norms contained within the reports as the legal framework for analysis.

Prior to the 2013–2015 period, it was uncertain exactly which international obligations could be breached by a hostile cyber operation. Essentially, there were three main "candidates" for the main axis of the legal framework of State accountability discussed by international scholars: *Prohibition of Use of Force*, *Principle of Non-Intervention*, and *Principle of State Sovereignty*, with the first one being the most restrictive term and the last one being the broadest in terms of scope of potential violations (i.e., it sets the lowest, easiest-to-clear threshold for considering a cyber hostility an *Internationally Wrongful Act*).[124] This distinction has tangible consequences. In order to call out an *Internationally Wrongful Act* and attribute it to another State, a government has to specify a valid obligation stemming from an international legal norm or principle that was purportedly breached. A *Violation of Sovereignty*, being the broadest of the three potential options, also includes the other two categories, *Prohibited Use of Force* and *Prohibited Intervention*, on top of other acts of lesser severity. Choosing it as the main category implies a low bar for a hostile cyber operation to be considered an *Internationally Wrongful Act.* This is the legal approach that was chosen by the UN Group of Government Experts. Its historic 2015 report stated:

> In their use of ICTs, States must observe, among other principles of international law, State sovereignty, sovereign equality, the settlement of disputes by peaceful means and nonintervention in the internal affairs of other States. Existing

123 United Nations General Assembly Resolution 76/136. Official compendium of voluntary national contributions on the subject of how international law applies to the use of information and communications technologies by States submitted by participating governmental experts in the Group of Governmental Experts on Advancing Responsible State Behaviour in Cyberspace in the Context of International Security established pursuant to General Assembly resolution, A/76/136 (2021, July 13). Retrieved February 16, 2022. <https://front.un-arm.org/wp-content/uploads/2021/08/A-76-136-EN.pdf>.

124 Moynihan, Harriet. The Application of International Law to State Cyberattacks. Chatham House (December 2019). Page 9. <https://www.chathamhouse.org/2019/12/application-international-law-state-cyberattacks>.

> obligations under international law are applicable to State use of ICTs. States must comply with their obligations under international law to respect and protect human rights and fundamental freedoms.[125]

It was a legal milestone, comparable in scale to the recognition of applicability of the existing international legal framework in general to cyberspace, which was the main conclusion of the 2013 UN GGE report. Between 2013 and 2015, a number of organizations, NATO in particular, were pushing to recognize *Principle of Sovereignty* as an operational obligation in cyberspace (rather than a general guideline), framing it as the very first rule of the Tallin Manual, its flagship publication released in the aftermath of the cyber assault on Estonia.[126] Rule 4 of the Manual rule contains prohibition of utilizing of cyber operations to infringe upon sovereignty and Rule 5 expands the definition of *Violation of Sovereignty* to *any interference by a State with cyber infrastructure aboard a platform, wherever located, that enjoys sovereign immunity by a State with cyber infrastructure aboard a platform*.[127] This strong stance represented a signal from NATO regarding its view on hostile cyber operations.[128] The 2015 UN GGE report largely embraced a similar sentiment and chose a sovereignty-center approach, making it the leading way in which hostile cyber operations are being legally framed. The 2015 Report was approved by the UN General Assembly, just like the 2013 one, and its identification of the *Principle of Sovereignty* as the fundamental concept in understanding cyber hostilities has been espoused since by a number of States and multilateral organizations. Some of those include: OSCE (2016),[129] Shanghai Cooperation

---

125 United Nations General Assembly Resolution A/70. Group of Governmental Experts on Developments in the Field of Information and Telecommunications in the Context of International Security - Note by the Secretary-General, A/70/174 (2015, July 22). Retrieved February 15, 2022. <https://documents-dds-ny.un.org/doc/UNDOC/GEN/N15/228/35/PDF/N1522835.pdf?OpenElement>.

126 Schmitt, Michael N. Tallinn Manual on the international law applicable to cyber warfare. Cambridge: Cambridge University Press, 2013. Page 25.

127 Schmitt, Michael N. et al. Tallinn Manual 2.0 on the International Law Applicable to Cyber Operations. Cambridge, United Kingdom: Cambridge University Press, 2017. Supra n.3, page 17.

128 Ibid.

129 Organization for Security and Co-operation in Europe - Permanent Council. Decision no. 1202 OSCE confidence-building measures to reduce the risks of Conflict

Organization,[130] Uzbekistan (2016),[131] Council of the EU (2017),[132] People's Republic of China (2017),[133] The Commonwealth (2018),[134] Islamic Republic of Iran (2019),[135] Netherlands (2019),[136] and France (2019).[137]

Several prominent international scholars such as, for example, Michael Schmitt, Gary Corn, and Robert Taylor, expressed a similar sentiment.[138]

Stemming from the Use of Information and Communication Technologies, March 10, 2016. <https://www.osce.org/files/f/documents/d/a/227281.pdf.>

130 Shanghai Cooperation Organization. The Tashkent Declaration of the Fifteenth Anniversary of the Shanghai Cooperation Organization, July 18, 2018. <https://uzbekistan.lv/en/the-tashkent-declaration-of-the-fifteenth-anniversary-of-the-shanghai-cooperation-organization/.>

131 Ibid.

132 Council of the European Union. Council Conclusions on the Joint Communication to the European Parliament and the Council: Resilience, Deterrence and Defence: Building strong cybersecurity for the EU, November 20, 2017. <https://www.consilium.europa.eu/media/31666/st14435en17.pdf.>

133 The Government of the People's Republic of China. China's International Strategy of Cooperation on Cyberspace, March 1, 2017. Xinhua Press Agency. <http://www.xinhuanet.com//english/china/2017-03/01/c_136094371_5.htm>.

134 Commonwealth Heads of Government Meeting. Commonwealth Cyber Declaration, April 20, 2018. <https://production-new-commonwealth-files.s3.eu-west-2.amazonaws.com/migrated/inline/Commonwealth-Cyber-Declaration.pdf>.

135 The government of the Islamic Republic of Iran. Submission by the Islamic Republic of Iran to the Open Ended Working Group on Developments in the Field of Information and Telecommunications in the context of International Security, September 2019. United Nations Office of Disarmament Affairs. Paragraph 10. <https://ceipfiles.s3.amazonaws.com/pdf/CyberNorms/UNGGE/Submission+by+the+Islamic+Republic+of+Iran+to+the+Open-Ended+Working+Group+on+Developments+in+the+Field+of+Information+and+Telecommunications+in+the+Context+of+International+Security.pdf.>

136 The government of Netherlands. Letter to the parliament on the international legal order in cyberspace, September 26, 2019. <https://www.government.nl/documents/parliamentary-documents/2019/09/26/letter-to-the-parliament-on-the-international-legal-order-in-cyberspace.>

137 The government of France. Communiqué -La France s'engage à promouvoir un cyberespace stable, fondé sur la confiance et le respect du droit international, October 4, 2019. French Ministry of Defense. <https://www.defense.gouv.fr/fre/salle-de-presse/communiques/communique_la-france-s-engage-a-promouvoir-un-cyberespace-stable-fonde-sur-la-confiance-et-le-respect-du-droit-international.>

138 Corn, Gary P., and Taylor, Robert. "Sovereignty in the Age of Cyber." AJIL Unbound, 111, August 22, 2017. Page 210. <https://doi.org/10.1017/aju.2017.57.>

Applying the *Principle of Sovereignty* to cyber operations represents an expansionary interpretation of international law. Despite progressing solidification of the *opinio juris* on this legal choice, there are governments which have publicly withheld their endorsement of that stance. Most notably United Kingdom and United States of America, two permanent member States on the UN Security Council, have expressed their hesitance. While United Kingdom refrained from expressing a clear position on the matter, on the few occasions that its government representatives spoke about it, they only stated their position that the *Principles of Non-Intervention* and the *Prohibition of Use of Force* apply in cyberspace. They stopped short of confirming that the same is the case for a much broader *Principle of Sovereignty*.[139] A similar position has been assumed by the United States.[140] However in the case of United States of America, there appears to exist an ongoing internal discussion between various parts of the government, with some of them endorsing application of sovereignty in cyberspace as the basic operational framework for holding States accountable.[141] This reluctance to follow the framework laid out by the United

---

139 The government of the United Kingdom. Cyber and International Law in the 21st Century—position of the United Kingdom on applying international law to cyberspace, May 23, 2018. Retrieved February 16, 2022. <https://www.gov.uk/government/speeches/cyber-and-international-law-in-the-21st-century.>

140 Buchan, Russell. Cyber espionage and international law (1st Edition). Oxford: Hart, 2019. Page 51;

Watts, Sean, and Richard, Theodore. T. "Baseline Territorial Sovereignty and Cyberspace," 2018. Lewis & Clark Law Review, page 827. <https://papers.ssrn.com/sol3/papers.cfm?abstract_id=3142272>; Corn, Gary. "Tallinn Manual 2.0 – Advancing the Conversation." Just Security, October 8, 2021. <https://www.justsecurity.org/37812/tallinn-manual-2-0-advancing-conversation/#more-37812>.

141 The government of the United States - Department of Defense. An Assessment Of International Legal Issues In Information Operations, May, 1999. <https://irp.fas.org/eprint/io-legal.pdf>; Watts, Sean, and Richard, Theodore. T. "Baseline Territorial Sovereignty and Cyberspace," 2018. Lewis & Clark Law Review, page 853. <https://papers.ssrn.com/sol3/papers.cfm?abstract_id=3142272>; Corn, Gary. "Tallinn Manual 2.0 – Advancing the Conversation." Just Security, October 8, 2021. <https://www.justsecurity.org/37812/tallinn-manual-2-0-advancing-conversation/#more-37812>; The government of the United States - Department of State. International Law in Cyberspace, Response #9, September 18, 2012. <https://2009-2017.state.gov/s/l/releases/remarks/197924.htm.>

Nations might stem from the fact that sovereignty is a wide-ranging, composite concept. Its application could potentially constrain operational possibilities in cyberspace of high-capability States such as United State of America s and United Kingdom. Unlawfulness of *Prohibited Use of Force* and the *Principle of Non-Intervention* are two principles that are already covered by *State Sovereignty*. Narrowing the scope of potential *internationally wrongful acts* in cyberspace to just them would limit State accountability to a certain class of the most serious sovereignty breaches in cyberspace, leaving much space for maneuver. In other words, limiting application of international law only to events reaching this level of severity would effectively establish a high threshold, enabling cyber activity below it to be treated as legally acceptable, much like it is currently the case with international espionage.[142]

There is no reason, in principle, to distinguish between cyber and conventional *Violations of Sovereignty*, especially if tangible and verifiable harm has been done.[143] Just like other existing legal categories, sovereignty is subject to development and expansion, as societies and technology progress. In fact, the definition of sovereignty has been expanded in relatively recent past when the issue of national ownership and accountability for communications satellites in outer space was considered.[144]

Having said that, application of the *Principle of Sovereignty* in cyberspace requires adaptation of the way in which it is applied to conventional State

---

142 Moynihan, Harriet. The Application of International Law to State Cyberattacks. Chatham House (December 2019). Page 11. <https://www.chathamhouse.org/2019/12/application-international-law-state-cyberattacks>.

143 Watts, Sean, and Richard, Theodore. T. “Baseline Territorial Sovereignty and Cyberspace,” 2018. Lewis & Clark Law Review, page 866. <https://papers.ssrn.com/sol3/papers.cfm?abstract_id=3142272>; Schmitt, Michael N. et al. Tallinn Manual 2.0 on the International Law Applicable to Cyber Operations. Cambridge, United Kingdom: Cambridge University Press, 2017. Rule 4, paragraph 16; Oppenheim, Lassa, Robert Y. Jennings, and Arthur Watts. Oppenheim’s international law Vol. 1. Peace (9th ed.). Oxford: Oxford University Press, 2008. Page 385.

144 United Nations Office for Outer Space Affairs. The Outer Space Treaty, December 19, 1966. <https://www.unoosa.org/oosa/en/ourwork/spacelaw/treaties/introouterspacetreaty.html>.

activity. L. F. L. Oppenheim described sovereignty's core elements in the following way:

> (...) as it excludes subjection to any other authority, and in particular the authority of another state, sovereignty is independence. It is external independence with regard to the liberty of action outside its borders. It is internal independence with regard to the liberty of action of a state inside its borders. As comprising the power of a state to exercise supreme authority over all persons and things within its territory, sovereignty involves territorial authority.[145]

Three key elements emerge from this description that jointly denote the substance of sovereignty:

- External sovereignty (sovereign equality of States);
- Internal sovereignty (independence of internal State powers); and
- Territorial sovereignty (inviolability of borders and a State's jurisdiction space).

Jerzy Kranz emphasized in his scholarship the importance of defining sovereignty as equally and uniformly applicable to all States, regardless of the amount of power they hold within the international community.[146] Indeed, *Principle of Sovereignty*, formulated in this way, is very strongly embedded in the framework of international law, including the UN Charter[147] and is seen as a fundamental attribute of self-determination.[148] Based on this framework, infringement upon any of the three dimensions of sovereignty of one country at the behest of another is a breach of an international obligation

---

145 Oppenheim, Lassa, Robert Y. Jennings, and Arthur Watts. Oppenheim's international law Vol. 1. Peace (9th ed.). Oxford: Oxford University Press, 2008. Page 385; Watts, Sean, and Richard, Theodore. T. "Baseline Territorial Sovereignty and Cyberspace," 2018. Lewis & Clark Law Review, pages 866–867.

146 Kranz, Jerzy, and Barcz, Jan. Pojęcie Suwerenności we Współczesnym Prawie Międzynarodowym. Warszawa: Dom Wydawniczy Elipsa, 2015. Page 12.

147 United Nations. Charter of the United Nations, June 26, 1945. 1 UNTS XVI. Article 2, Point 1. <https://www.un.org/en/about-us/un-charter>.

148 United Nations General Assembly Resolution 375 (IV). Draft Declaration on Rights and Duties of States with commentaries - United Nations International Law Commission, December 6, 1949. <https://legal.un.org/ilc/texts/instruments/english/commentaries/2_1_1949.pdf>.

and hence an *Internationally Wrongful Act* (unless there is some consensual arrangement that limits their application, either through a shared treaty, a customary legal norm, or a case-specific agreement). Let us analyze each of these three dimensions.

Historically, the principle of sovereign equality was acknowledged by the Western international community already in the year 1648 in the Treaty of Westphalia. The Treaty ended the Thirty Years' War and granted international legal status to a mosaic of small German States making up the Holy Roman Empire. The Treaty formally established the principle of sovereign equality as the defining feature, by which every State, regardless how large or small, has an equal legal status in international law.[149] This formula ushered in a new model of international relations, which remains the foundation of the system of international law. In the realm of cyber operations, this aspect of sovereignty is most likely to surface in cases involving attempts to coerce or scare a State into changing the course of its action in the international sphere.

Independence in conducting its internal affairs is the core of internal sovereignty. To that end, the ILC Draft Declaration on the Rights and Duties of States proclaims in Article 1 that

> Every State has the right to independence and hence to exercise freely, without dictation by any other State, all its legal powers, including the choice of its own form of government.[150]

This stance is also embedded into the UN Charter in its Article 2(7):

> Nothing contained in the present Charter shall authorize the United Nations to intervene in matters which are essentially within the domestic jurisdiction of any state or shall require the Members to submit such matters to settlement under the present Charter; but this principle shall not prejudice the application of enforcement measures under Chapter 7.[151]

---

149 Simpson, Gerry J. Great powers and outlaw states: Unequal sovereigns in the International Legal Order. Cambridge: Cambridge University Press, 2004. Page 35.

150 United Nations General Assembly Resolution 375 (IV). Draft Declaration on Rights and Duties of States with commentaries - United Nations International Law Commission, December 6, 1949. <https://legal.un.org/ilc/texts/instruments/english/commentaries/2_1_1949.pdf.>

151 United Nations. Charter of the United Nations, June 26, 1945. 1 UNTS XVI. Article 2, Point 7. <https://www.un.org/en/about-us/un-charter.>

The Permanent Court of Arbitration has expressed a similar stance on this aspect of sovereignty in its verdict on the *Island of Palmas* case back in 1928:

> Sovereignty in the relations between States signifies independence. Independence in regard to a portion of the globe is the right to exercise therein, to the exclusion of any other State, the functions of a State.[152]

The ICJ has confirmed this line of reasoning in the ruling on the Case Concerning the Military and Paramilitary Activities in and Against Nicaragua in 1986.[153] In the context of State interactions in cyberspace, this aspect of sovereignty is most likely to surface with regard to operations aimed at disrupting or altering the course of internal politics and the functioning of a State. The alleged interference by hackers sponsored by the Russian Federation during the Brexit referendum and the U.S. presidential election in 2016 can serve as potential examples.[154] The principle of internal sovereignty is tightly linked to the concept of Domaine Réservé—areas of State activity that are

---

152 Island of Palmas Case (or Miangas), United States v Netherlands, Award, (1928). April 4, 1928, Permanent Court of Arbitration, II RIAA 829, ICGJ 392. Pages 117, 118, 829, 838. <https://pca-cpa.org/en/cases/94/>.

153 Case Concerning the Application of the Convention on the Prevention and Punishment of the Crime of Genocide (Bosnia and Herzegovina v Serbia)—Judgment. International Court of Justice Reports 43, February 26, 2007. Paragraphs 205–209. <https://www.icj-cij.org/en/case/91/judgments>. The judgment referred to "matters in which each State is permitted, by the principle of State sovereignty, to decide freely. One of these is the choice of a political, economic, social and cultural system, and the formulation of foreign policy:" (para 205). Although this was stated in the context of the *Principle of Non-Intervention*, it is relevant to the *Principle of Sovereignty* inasmuch the former is derived from the latter.

154 Howard, Philip N., and Bence Kollanyi. "Bots, #strongerin, and #Brexit: Computational Propaganda during the UK-EU Referendum." SSRN Journal, June 21, 2016, pages 1–6. <https://doi.org/10.2139/ssrn.2798311>; Gorodnichenko, Yuriy, Tho Pham, and Oleksandr Talavera. Social media, sentiment and public opinions: Evidence from #Brexit and #uselection, May 2018, pages 1–40. <https://doi.org/10.3386/w24631>; Reuters. "Russian Twitter Accounts Promoted Brexit Ahead of Eu Referendum - Times Newspaper," November 15, 2017. <https://www.reuters.com/article/us-britain-eu-russia/russian-twitter-accounts-promoted-brexit-ahead-of-eu-referendum-times-newspaper-idUSKBN1DF0ZR>; Smialek, Jeanna. "Twitter Bots Helped Trump and Brexit Win, Economic Study Says." Bloomberg, May 21, 2018. <https://www.bloomberg.com/politics/articles/2018-05-21/twitter-bots-helped-trump-and-brexit-win-economic-study-says>.

regarded as exclusively domestic affairs and hence are excluded from any external interference, legal or otherwise.[155] This latter concept however has not been as well anchored by international treaties and customary norms as sovereignty and therefore can only serve as an auxiliary means to further specify understanding of the substance of internal sovereignty.

Territorial sovereignty takes on an additional measure of relevance in the context of international cyber operations. The principle is applicable to a State's land territory, territorial sea, territorial skies, aerial space, the maritime zones as well as all spaces where a State's jurisdiction applies.[156] When conceptualizing the applicability of international law in cyberspace, the UN GGE focused on ICT infrastructure located within a State's jurisdiction due to an important reason—this physical element constitutes a proxy between conventional, physical theaters of State interactions and the new one that is located within cyberspace. ICT infrastructure, its location and usage, play a fundamental role in understanding whether territorial sovereignty of a State has been breached during a cyber operation or not.

An important aspect of the application of the territorial sovereignty principle to cyberspace is whether data transmission through a third State and usage of its infrastructure, such as cables, servers, or satellites, while targeting another State, constitutes a breach on its own. Importantly, breaching territorial sovereignty does not have to involve direct use of force, as ruled by the ICJ in the case *Nicaragua in the Border Area* (adjudicated in 1949) and later confirmed in 2015.[157] These rulings support the claim that routing a cyber operation through the territory of a third-State, which almost always

---

155 Oxford Public International Law. Domaine Réservé - definition. Retrieved February 17, 2022. <https://opil.ouplaw.com/view/10.1093/law:epil/9780199231690/law-9780199231690-e1398>; Ossoff, William. "Hacking the Domaine Reserve: The Rule of Non-Intervention and Political Interference in Cyberspace," April 18, 2021. Harvard International Law Journal, 62(1), pages 1–40. <https://harvardilj.org/wp-content/uploads/sites/15/HLI115_crop.pdf>.

156 Moynihan, Harriet. The Application of International Law to State Cyberattacks. Chatham House (December 2019). Page 11. <https://www.chathamhouse.org/2019/12/application-international-law-state-cyberattacks>.

157 Certain Activities Carried Out by Nicaragua in the Border Area (Costa Rica v. Nicaragua)—Judgment. International Court of Justice Reports 150, December 16, 2015. Paragraph 93. <https://www.icj-cij.org/en/case/150>; Case concerning Corfu Channel (United Kingdom of Great Britain and Northern Ireland v.

happens while targeting another State, is an internationally wrongful act in its own right. This subject will be explored in-depth in Section 5.5 on jurisdiction in cyberspace.

Sovereignty over ICT infrastructure is an exclusive right of a State within its jurisdiction space, which includes, most importantly, their territory. The right is adjusted for limitations and contextualization resulting from a State's international legal obligations, most importantly the UN Charter, its self-imposed treaty commitments, and human rights norms.[158] Certain States have also developed a set of internal law that are aimed at regulating the issue of data traffic over domestic ITC infrastructure.[159] This has led to conceptualization of the term of *cyber sovereignty*, which develops a new dimension of sovereignty rather than seeking to expand application of the existing ones in cyberspace. Russia and China are two States that promote this approach especially actively.[160] Despite their effort, the notion has not been embraced by the international State community more widely.

Albania)—Judgment (Merits). International Court of Justice Reports 4 and 9, April 9, 1949. Paragraphs 69–70. <https://www.icj-cij.org/case/1>.

158 For example, the UN Human Rights Council has held that human rights such as freedom of expression, freedom of assembly and privacy apply online as much as offline in its Resolution A/HRC/20/L.13 on the Promotion and Protection and Enjoyment of Human Rights on the Internet; United Nations General Assembly Resolution. Group of Governmental Experts on Developments in the Field of Information and Telecommunications in the Context of International Security - Note by the Secretary-General, July 22, 2015. Paragraph 13(e). <https://documents-dds-ny.un.org/doc/UNDOC/GEN/N15/228/35/PDF/N1522835.pdf?OpenElement>; Tsagourias, Nicholas. "The Slow Process of Normativizing Cyberspace." AJIL Unbound 113 (2019): pages 71–75. <https://doi.org/10.1017/aju.2019.9>; Schmitt, Michael N., and Vihul, Liis. "Respect for Sovereignty in Cyberspace." Texas Law Review, 95(7), 2017, pages 1639–1670. <https://texaslawreview.org/respect-sovereignty-cyberspace/>; Tyranowski, Jerzy. Integralność Terytorialna, nienaruszalność granic i Samostanowienie w Prawie Międzynarodowym. Warszawa: Państwowe Wydawnictwo Naukowe, Warszawa 1990. Page 243.

159 Centre for European Policy Studies. The impact of the German NetzdG law, November 30, 2018. Retrieved February 17, 2022. <https://www.ceps.eu/ceps-projects/the-impact-of-the-german-netzdg-law/>; Government of France. Against information manipulation, November 20, 2018. Retrieved February 17, 2022. <https://www.gouvernement.fr/en/against-information-manipulation>.

160 Wang, Yaqiu. "In China, the 'Great Firewall' Is Changing a Generation," September 1, 2020. Politico. <https://www.politico.com/news/magazine/2020/09/01/

The Permanent Court of International Justice has established in its landmark 1927 *Lotus* case ruling the general process of identifying a violation of sovereignty:

> First and foremost restriction imposed by international law upon a State is that – failing the existence of a permissive rule to the contrary – it may not exercise its power in any form in the territory of another State.[161]

This is a strong definition that implies the actions of a State in another State's territory are generally unlawful unless there is an explicit permission from the host State. In the 1949 *Corfu Channel* case, the ICJ ruled that the United Kingdom sending warships through territorial waters of Albania was enough to constitute a breach of territorial integrity, and as a result, a *Violation of Sovereignty*.[162] Importantly, it did not have to involve an intervention or use of force in order to do so. In the 2015 case *Certain Activities carried out by Nicaragua in the Border Area (Costa Rica v. Nicaragua)*, the ICJ doubled down on territorial sovereignty being an operational norm of international law, whose breach is an *Internationally Wrongful Act*.[163] In that case, Nicaragua dredged a boat traffic channel on Costa Rican soil (as well as deployed army troops to protect the construction site), an action that can be seen as a precursor for utilizing another State's territory for transferring data. There also exist legal precedents on violating territorial sovereignty "remotely." The 1935 Trail Smelter arbitration case between the governments of the United States of America and Canada pertained to an ironworks facility (located on territory of Canada) whose toxic fumes polluted the environment and

---

china-great-firewall-generation-405385>; British Broadcasting Corporation. "Russia internet: Law introducing new controls comes into force," November 1, 2019. <https://www.bbc.com/news/world-europe-50259597>.

161 The Case of the S.S. Lotus (France v. Turkey). Permanent Court of International Justice, Award. September 7, 1927. Permanent Court of International Justice (series A). Page 18. Retrieved February 17, 2022. <https://www.icj-cij.org/public/files/permanent-court-of-international-justice/serie_A/A_10/30_Lotus_Arret.pdf>.

162 Case concerning Corfu Channel (United Kingdom of Great Britain and Northern Ireland v. Albania)—Judgment (Merits). International Court of Justice Reports, April 9, 1949. Gen L No. 1. Paragraphs 69–70. <https://www.icj-cij.org/en/case/1>.

163 Case Concerning Certain Activities Carried Out by Nicaragua in the Border Area (Costa Rica v. Nicaragua). International Court of Justice Reports, December 16, 2015. Paragraph 95. <https://www.icj-cij.org/en/case/150>.

poisoned communities on the soil of the United States.[164] In their conclusions, arbiters wrote:

> No State has the right to use or permit the use of its territory in such a manner as to cause injury by fumes in or to the territory of another or the properties of persons therein, when the case is of serious consequence and the injury established by clear and convincing evidence.

State practice has not yet developed enough to establish whether there exists a minimal threshold for cyber operations to surpass in order to be considered a *Violation of Sovereignty*. Certain types of breaches of sovereignty can be so grave that they meet the threshold necessary to trigger the *Principle of Non-Intervention* or the *Prohibition of Use of Force* (the distinction between various types of breaches of international rules in cyberspace is the focus of Chapter 3) At the same time, there is no established *opinio juris* or sufficient State practice to discern what kinds of hostile cyber operations that are less severe than those two categories also qualify as *Violations of Sovereignty*. There are two main approaches in that regard. The first approach is that any infringement of a State's sovereignty, regardless of how severe it is, by another State constitutes a *Violation of Sovereignty*.[165] What is challenging about this approach is that at present, despite widespread conventional spying activity taking place across States, for the most part it is not considered as a violation of international norms. Why would then an equivalent type of activity in cyberspace be considered differently? State practice over centuries has developed in a way that includes a certain level of tolerance toward infringements of sovereignty.[166] The second approach acknowledges existence of a minimal threshold. It recognizes that for practical reasons, not all unpermitted cyber

---

164 Trail smelter Case (United States v. Canada). Permanent Court of Arbitration, March 11, 1941. <https://legal.un.org/riaa/cases/vol_III/1905-1982.pdf>.

165 Tsagourias, Nicholas. "Law, Borders and the Territorialisation of Cyberspace." SSRN Electronic Journal, 2018, page 19. <https://doi.org/10.2139/ssrn.3213511>; Watts, Sean, and Richard, Theodore. T. "Baseline Territorial Sovereignty and Cyberspace," 2018. Lewis & Clark Law Review, pages 866–867. <https://papers.ssrn.com/sol3/papers.cfm?abstract_id=3142272>.

166 Buchan, Russell. Cyber espionage and international law (1st Edition). Oxford: Hart, 2019. Page 51; Watts, Sean, and Richard, Theodore. T. "Baseline Territorial Sovereignty and Cyberspace," 2018. Lewis & Clark Law Review, pages 866–867. <https://papers.ssrn.com/sol3/papers.cfm?abstract_id=3142272>.

operations infringe upon *State Sovereignty*. Oppenheim in his scholarly works suggested that *independence is a question of degree*, implying existence of a spectrum of sovereignty violation, with certain types of unfriendly acts being too mild to qualify.[167] Incorporating the degree of intensity into the definition of *Violation of Sovereignty* and denoting its bottom threshold makes sense in practical terms. Otherwise, even a hostile public statement could be construed as a *Violation of Sovereignty*. Certain comments by States, such as Netherlands,[168] suggest there might be an *opinio juris* forming that would validate the existence of a minimal threshold. Unfortunately, the dearth of legal cases involving cyber operations limits our ability to define this potential threshold. In this context, each case has to be considered separately. A hypothesis can be stated though that in the future, accumulating State practice and jurisprudence will lead to definition of such a minimal threshold.

In the absence of binding guidelines on where the threshold for *Violation of Sovereignty* in cyberspace is, one can analyze some of the main proposals in existence that can potentially become the basis of the legal standard on that matter in the future. The two main ones are:

- The approach assumed by the EU Council;
- The approach proposed in the NATO-sponsored Tallinn Manual 2.0 publication.

The EU Council has laid out its approach to gauging severity of cyber breaches of sovereignty in its document titled *Restrictive measures against cyber-attacks threatening the Union or its Member States*. The legal document is based on a term *significant effect*, meaning one that would substantiate EU sanctions and other restrictive measures.[169] As a non-State organization, the EU Council

---

167 Oppenheim, Lassa, Robert Y. Jennings, and Arthur Watts. Oppenheim's international law Vol. 1. Peace (9th ed.). Oxford: Oxford University Press, 2008. Page 391.

168 Government of Netherlands. "Letter to the parliament on the international legal order in cyberspace - Parliamentary Document," September 26, 2019. <https://www.government.nl/documents/parliamentary-documents/2019/09/26/letter-to-the-parliament-on-the-international-legal-order-in-cyberspace>.

169 Council of the European Union. "Council Decision concerning restrictive measures against cyber-attacks threatening the Union or its Member States," May 14, 2019. <https://data.consilium.europa.eu/doc/document/ST-7299-2019-INIT/en/pdf>.

did not use the term *Sovereignty* in the document even though the spirit of the *significant effect* doctrine overlaps well with *Violation of Sovereignty* in practical terms. To assess whether a *significant effect* has taken place, the EU Council resolved to assess the following seven aspects:

A. The scope, scale, impact or severity of disruption caused, including to economic and societal activities, essential services, critical State functions, public order or safety;
B. The number of natural or legal persons, entities or bodies affected;
C. The number of Member States affected;
D. The amount of economic loss caused, such as through large-scale theft of funds, economic resources or intellectual property;
E. The economic benefit gained by the perpetrator, for himself or for others;
F. The amount or nature of data stolen or the scale of the data breaches; or
G. The nature of commercially sensitive data accessed.[170]

The international group of experts convened by NATO to deliberate on the matter proposed the following assessment framework in the Tallinn Manual 2.0:

- Physical harm (real-world impact—such as, for example, shutting down of the electricity grid in Ukraine in 2015);
- Loss of functionality of ICT infrastructure (paralyzing IT operations, governmental or otherwise, in a State—such as, for example, the Sony hack in 2014);
- Cyber intrusions below loss of functionality (e.g., stealing of intelligence information).[171]

---

170 Ibid. Art 3.

171 Schmitt, Michael N. et al. Tallinn Manual 2.0 on the International Law Applicable to Cyber Operations. Cambridge, United Kingdom: Cambridge University Press, 2017. Rule 4, Paragraph 13.

These scenarios represent three levels of harm, from the most to the least damaging respectively. Scholars framed this approach to gauging the extent of *Violation of Sovereignty* as the *effects doctrine*.[172] The international group of experts could not come to an agreement on what would define the threshold of *loss of functionality*, due to insufficient volume of State practice. This loops back to the problem of lack of clarity regarding the minimal severity threshold for *Violation of Sovereignty* to take place. Since *loss of functionality* is construed as the mildest form of *Violation of Sovereignty*, it is the one that is the most important to delineate since it divides between events that are *Internationally Wrongful Acts* on one side and those that are mere *Unfriendly Acts* on the other. Another challenge to this framework is that the hierarchy of events is not as straightforward in real life as proposed in it. For instance, certain cases of stealing intelligence documentation by cyber spies might be perceived as causing more damage to a government than loss of ICT functionality (which would be classified as a more severe impact according to the framework).

The challenge of identifying the minimal severity threshold for a *Violation of Sovereignty* in cyberspace is one of the main limitations of the UN-proposed legal framework. While alternative principles of international law such as *Non-Intervention* and *Prohibition of Use of Force* would come with a volume of legal cases and State practice that could be transposed onto cyberspace, *State Sovereignty* provides a much vaguer basis that still has to be solidified. This lack of clarity was recognized by the U.S. Department of State, which acknowledged that the system of international law is *faced with a relative vacuum of public State practice* on the matter.[173] The future of Sovereignty-based model

---

172 Moynihan, Harriet. The Application of International Law to State Cyberattacks. Chatham House, December 2019. Paragraph 66. <https://www.chathamhouse.org/2019/12/application-international-law-state-cyberattacks>; Schmitt, Michael N. et al. Tallinn Manual 2.0 on the International Law Applicable to Cyber Operations. Cambridge, United Kingdom: Cambridge University Press, 2017. Rule 69, Commentary.

173 Egan, Brian. J. “International Law and Stability in Cyberspace,” November 10, 2016. Berkeley Journal of International Law, 35(1), pages 1–26. <https://www.law.berkeley.edu/wp-content/uploads/2016/12/BJIL-article-International-Law-and-Stability-in-Cyberspace.pdf>; Jensen, Eric T. “The Tallinn Manual 2.0: highlights and insights,”

of legal attribution of hostile cyber operations is therefore still uncertain and depending on the direction of State practice and prevailing *opinio juris* that will emerge over coming years.[174]

1.4 Current global trends in the area of cyberspace and hostile cyber operations

The intensity of the debate on the subject of cyberspace and hostile cyber operations becomes clear when put in the context of dynamically unfolding global trends. The internet infrastructure now enmeshes the entire planet and ever more vital State functions are primarily serviced in cyberspace, creating a vulnerability. For example, it takes 18 minutes 49 seconds for Russian State-sponsored hackers to penetrate a computer network after they launch an initial breach. This world record of sorts is followed by North Korean hackers, who need 2 hours on average to take over a network and the Chinese, who need 4 hours to do it. A number of other countries have developed similar capabilities.[175] This measure, called breakout time, *shows how much time defenders have on average to detect an initial intrusion, investigate it and eject the attacker from the network, before sensitive data is stolen or destroyed.*[176] As presented in this section, a number of governments do not hesitate to deploy hostile cyber operations, or threat thereof, in international relations. Current dynamic development of cyberspace and the possibilities it offers bears an ever-growing impact on interactions between States. For those reasons, the phenomenon of hostile cyber operations launched by

March 15, 2017. Georgetown Journal of International Law, 48(735), pages 735–778. <https://papers.ssrn.com/sol3/papers.cfm?abstract_id=2932110>.

174 Ibid. Page 743.; Ansley, Rachel. "Tallinn Manual 2.0: Defending Cyberspace," February 15, 2017. Atlantic Council. Retrieved February 17, 2022. <https://www.atlanticcouncil.org/blogs/new-atlanticist/tallinn-manual-2-0-defending-cyberspace/>.

175 Crowdstrike. "2019 Global Threat Report: Adversary Tradecraft and the Importance of Speed," February 2019. Page 14. Retrieved February 13, 2022. <https://www.crowdstrike.com/blog/2019-global-threat-report-shows-it-takes-innovation-and-speed-to-win-against-adversaries/>.

176 Crowdstrike. "2018 Global Threat Report: Blurring The Lines Between Statecraft And Tradecraft," February 2018. Page 2. Retrieved February 13, 2022. <https://go.crowdstrike.com/2018ThreatReport.html>.

one State against another has become a threat to both global stability and domestic order across the globe.[177]

At the same time, the international community appears ill-equipped to cope with this growing challenge. The combined impacts of weakness of low defensive IT capabilities of many States and the rudimentary and fragmented international framework regulating cyber operations are generating a state of legal flux.

Hostile cyber operations between States are not an isolated phenomenon. At the broadest level, they are part of surging malicious cyber activity in general. Every year, around 820,000 breaches and breach attempts by sophisticated hacker groups are identified, with targets ranging from private, through corporate, to public. That translates to 2,244 attacks every single day.[178] The estimated economic loss of cybercrime now runs at approximately $6 trillion annually.[179] The scale and intensity of these operations are growing rapidly. The bulk of those operations are criminal acts aimed at theft of money or private property and handled by domestic courts rather than international bodies (see Figure 2 for details). Only a small fraction of hostile cyber operations possibly meet the following three criteria:

- they are attributable to a State;
- they create an impact in another States, (i.e., a different one than the one from which the operation originated); and
- they reach a level of severity that would potentially qualify them as hostile cyber operations.

For example, in 2022 there were approximately 149 such cases worldwide (0.015% of the estimated average annual number of cyber breaches in general)

---

177 Council on Foreign Relations. "Cyber Operations Tracker." Retrieved February 13, 2023. <https://www.cfr.org/cyber-operations/>.

178 Sobers, Robert. "Cybersecurity Statistics and Trends for 2021," March 13, 2021. Varonis. Retrieved February 13, 2022. <https://www.varonis.com/blog/cybersecurity-statistics>.

179 Morgan, Steven. "Cybercrime To Cost The World $10.5 Trillion Annually By 2025," April 27, 2021. Cybercrime Magazine. Retrieved February 13, 2022. <https://cybersecurityventures.com/hackerpocalypse-original-cybercrime-report-2016/>; AT&T. "2022 AT&T Cybersecurity Insights Report," February 2022. Page 6. <https://www.business.att.com/categories/cybersecurity-insights-report.html>.

according to the CFR Cyber Operations Tracker (see Figure 2).[180] While low, this number represents a sharp uptick from 14 in 2012, just one decade ago.[181]

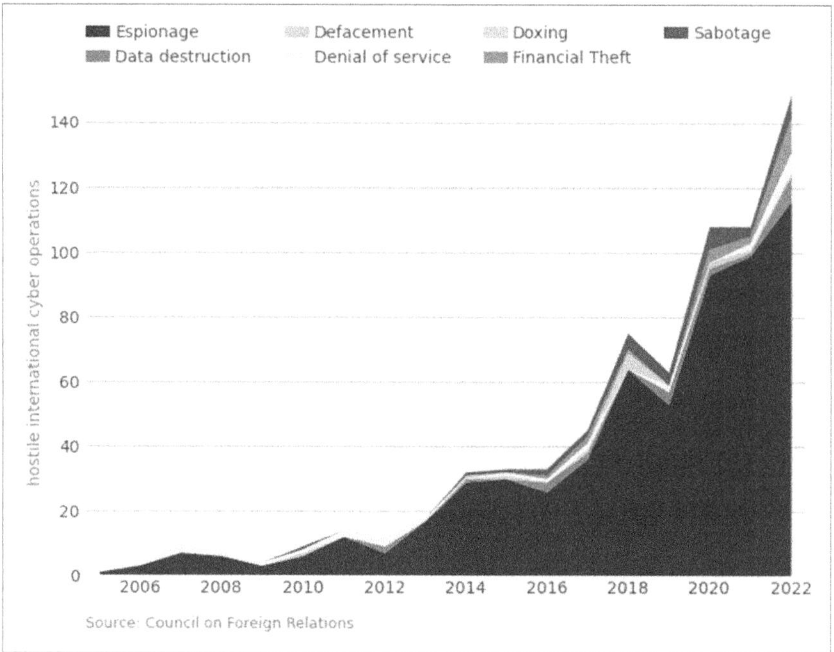

Figure 2. Number and types of international cyber incidents involving States 2005–2022
Source: own elaboration, based on CFR Cyber Operations Tracker

The international legal system is still adapting to this new reality. Cyberspace is a relatively new dimension, different from land, sea, air, or space, in which nations can typically come into conflict. Capable governments can exploit and weaponize tools in this new dimension and judging by the extent of cyber investment across nations, some of them waste no time to develop that early

180 Council on Foreign Relations. "Cyber Operations Tracker." Retrieved February 13, 2023. <https://www.cfr.org/cyber-operations/>.

181 Ibid.

mover advantage.[182] This novel reality cannot be easily compared to any past technological advances, such as invention of planes or launching of space programs. Cyber interactions are often de-territorialized, which cannot be said of any of these previous technological expansions. At the same time, the division between tangible physical reality and the virtual one is starting to blur as various aspects such as hardware, software, and the transnational infrastructure all blend together to create cyberspace. As a result a situation of legal ambiguity and flux emerges.

An important feature of cyberspace is also the distributed and private character of the underlying internet network. While governments retain oversight over their national digital domains, the reality is that many of the targets such as cable infrastructure, laptops, servers, phones, and databases are for the most part private property belonging to civilians.[183] These assets are placed on the front line of modern cyber warfare. This situation engenders complex questions on issues such as division of responsibility for overseeing cyberspace, attribution of digital malicious acts, the role of the private sector, and application of the existing international legal framework on sovereignty, non-intervention, and the right to self-defense. Even the definition of what exactly an international cyber delict might be is an intensely contested topic.

Figure 2 summarizes 18 years of tracking of international cyber incidents and reveals some emerging trends. The actual numbers probably differ from the ones established by scholars since there have likely been a number of instances of State-sponsored cyber operations over that period that ended up not being revealed to the public. Nevertheless, enough cases have been revealed to give us a general sense of unfolding trends. The data suggest that there were hardly any big-ticket cases of State-sponsored cyber intrusion prior to 2005. Between 2005 and 2010 the incidents were very scarce, mostly staying in the one-digit territory. The dynamic shifted in the beginning of

182 International Institute for Strategic Studies. "Cyber Capabilities and National Power: A Net Assessment," June 28, 2021. Retrieved February 13, 2022. <https://www.iiss.org/blogs/research-paper/2021/06/cyber-capabilities-national-power>.

183 Smith, Brad. "The need for a Digital Geneva Convention," May 15, 2018. Microsoft. Retrieved February 13, 2022. <https://blogs.microsoft.com/on-the-issues/2017/02/14/need-digital-geneva-convention/>.

the 2010s. The number of recorded cases started growing rapidly and the variety of the types of attacks became more diverse. Espionage in its various forms remains the dominant class of cyber intrusions by far throughout the analyzed period. Distributed Denial of Service (DDoS), one of the simplest ways of paralyzing a network by means of a concerted wave of data requests from many computers at once, was a popular mode of cyber intrusion during the 2000s, but lost its position to more sophisticated methods afterward, as technical possibilities expanded, and governments learned to repel such crude attacks. Then, Doxing, Sabotage, and Data Destruction have been gaining some momentum since the mid-2010s. All three classes of malicious cyber behavior involve inserting malware into the target system in order to expose confidential and sensitive information, disrupt processes and critical services, and to destroy data or hardware respectively. Defacement, a category that encompasses instances of breaking into IT systems for the sole purpose of changing the appearance of websites and social media profiles, was a minor, occasional presence during the analyzed period.

Some clear trends emerge when all of them are taken together. In terms of the operations' target, the majority were aimed at a government institution (426 operations). The second biggest class of targets were private sector entities. There were 363 attacks against private companies that with a high measure of probability can be attributed to a foreign government or a government-aligned hacker group. Civil society sector was the least exposed class of targets. There were around 214 attacks that attempted to disrupt or otherwise hurt actors in that space. Many of the aforementioned cases overlapped across sectors as oftentimes multiple targets are attacked at once (see Figure 3 for details). For instance, that was the case in Estonia in 2007 during the Bronze Soldier escalation.[184]

[184] Traynor, Ian. "Russia Accused of Unleashing Cyberwar to Disable Estonia." The Guardian, May 17, 2007. https://www.theguardian.com/world/2007/may/17/topstories3.russia; British Broadcasting Corporation. "Estonia Fines Man for 'Cyber War.'" BBC News, January 25, 2008. http://news.bbc.co.uk/2/hi/technology/7208511.stm.

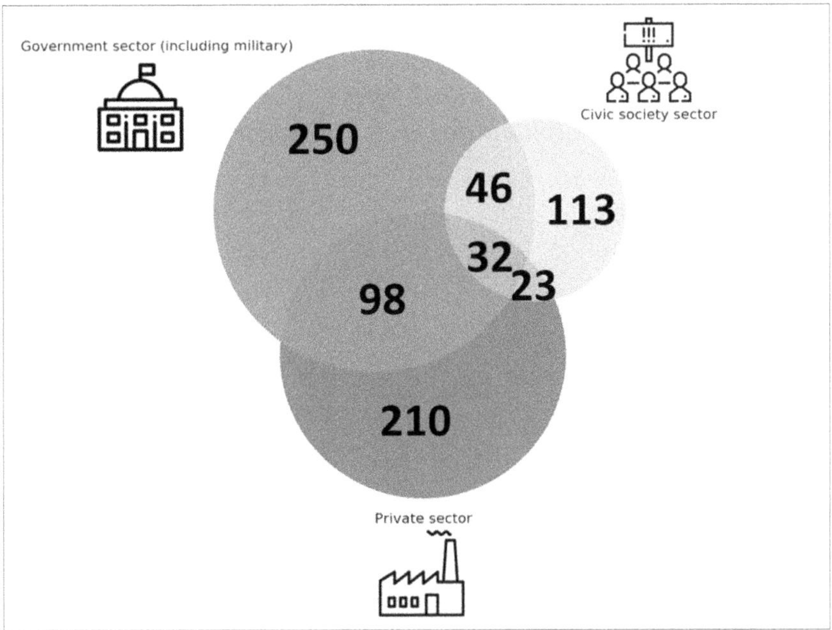

Figure 3. Three main classes of hostile cyber acts based on the type of the target 2005–2023
Source: own elaboration, based on CFR Cyber Operations Tracker

Certain States keep reappearing as potential sponsors of hostile cyber operations. China, Russia, Iran, North Korea, the United States, and Israel have been most frequently accused of sponsoring malicious cyber activity aimed at foreign countries, although a large number of other States also have a track record of international cyber activism (see Figure 4 for details). Some of these States use rhetoric that projects their cyber muscle. China talks of *winning informationized wars by the mid-twenty-first century.*[185]

[185] The Economist. "War in the fifth domain," July 6, 2010. <https://www.economist.com/briefing/2010/07/01/war-in-the-fifth-domain.>

Iran publicly boasts of having the world's second-largest cyber army.[186] David Rothkopf, a Columbia University professor, wrote in Foreign Policy in 1997: *For the United States, a central objective of an Information Age foreign policy must be to win the battle of the world's information flows, dominating the*

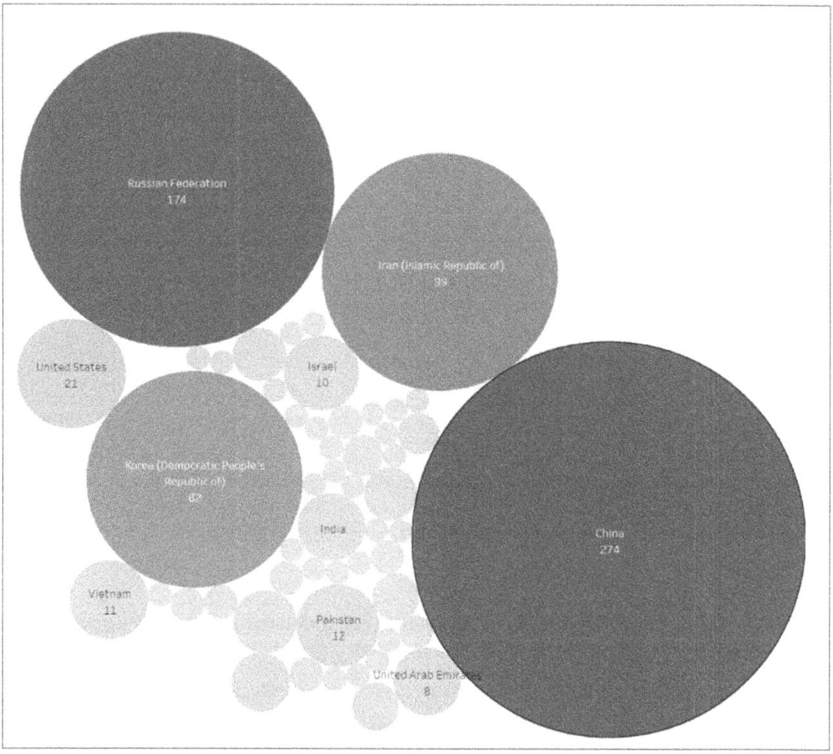

Figure 4. Fifty-two countries have been publicly accused of conducting hostile cyber operations during the 2005–2023 period; the ten most frequent States are labeled[187]
Source: own elaboration, based on CFR Cyber Operations Tracker

---

[186] Ibid.

[187] Some hostile cyber acts can be attributed to a group of States while other are perpetrated by just one. Hence, the number of attributions in Figure 4 does not directly translate to the number of hostile acts in Figure 5.

airwaves as Great Britain once ruled the seas.[188] This sentiment is well reflected in the United States' stance on international legal oversight over the internet, as described in Chapter 2, which describes the State's efforts to maintain a *Sui Generis* character of internet and cyberspace vis-à-vis other communication technologies when it comes to international oversight.

Taking stock of data on hostile cyber operations attributed to sovereign States, we can identify a few governments that are leaders in terms of the number and scale of their cyber activity. The data reveals a lopsided landscape. Three groups of countries can be delineated based on this analysis: five champions that dominate the field, catchers-up—a group of approximately 20 countries with some measure of cyber capacity, and all the remaining countries in the world, around 175, that lack external cyber power projection capacity and remain vulnerable to attacks.

The majority of these State-on-State cyber interferences consist of low-intensity acts that do not produce any discernible physical effects and can be placed below the threshold needed to invoke a breach of *State Sovereignty*, even less so to meet the criteria of a *Prohibited Intervention*. For example, in December 2018, the *Five Eyes* intelligence-sharing alliance, consisting of the United States, Canada, Australia, New Zealand, and the United Kingdom attributed a Chinese cyber espionage group, aligned with the Chinese government, with conducting a 12-year campaign of tracking the IP addressed and stealing trade secrets of companies in 12 countries.[189] This kind of sensitive data gathering, similar in nature and purpose to traditional espionage, to date still makes up the majority of State-on-State cyber transgressions.

Most States maintain a policy of *ambiguity and silence* in terms of their stance on how international law applies in cyberspace. Oftentimes they will lay out their general approach but will refuse to commit to details or delineate definitional scopes that would allow for identifying cyber operations as specific violations of international law. Some of the key actors, such as the

---

188 Rothkopf, David. "In Praise of Cultural Imperialism?," July 1997. Foreign Policy, No. 107, pages 38–53. <https://doi.org/10.2307/1149331>.

189 Center for Strategic & International Studies. "Significant International Cyber Incidents - a list." Retrieved February 13, 2022. <https://www.csis.org/programs/strategic-technologies-program/significant-cyber-incidents>

United States, United Kingdom, China, and Russia to name four, prefer to retain a degree of flexibility that such a situation creates as they are frequently both on the receiving and dispensing end of cyberattacks. This ambiguity applies to the scope of definitions of key terms such as *Prohibited Intervention* or *Prohibited Use of Force* in the cyber context as well as the threshold of intensity of a cyberattack needed to determine whether a violation of the *Principle of Sovereignty* took place. Those considerations are the subject of Chapter 3.

1.5 Conclusion

The framing of hostile cyber operations as *Unfriendly Acts* is now well established in Public International Law. While some hostile cyber activity conducted by States may meet the definitional criteria of more severe acts, such as *Prohibited Interventions* or *Prohibited Use of Force,* most of them are structurally close to espionage, placing them in a sort of liminal space—not formally unlawful but likely to constitute a *Violation of Sovereignty* based on the methods they employ. The line delineating *Unfriendly Acts* in cyberspace that are lawful and those that reach the level of intensity classifying them also as *Internationally Wrongful Acts* is a violation of another State's sovereignty. After more than a decade of debate, the international community is leaning toward that framing, which was confirmed by the UN General Assembly Resolution, based on the UN GGE's report in 2015. This is an expression of an expansionary interpretation of what constitutes internationally wrongful activity in cyberspace. An alternative approach, which eventually was not embraced was to set *Prohibited Intervention* as the minimal threshold for internationally wrongful cyber activity, which would narrowed down the scope of what is considered internationally wrongful activity by States in cyberspace.

The hybrid character of cyberspace, combining both physical and non-physical aspects, makes application of existing rules difficult. Hostile cyber operations can pass through a number of third States without causing harm on their way toward a target in a fraction of a second, blurring conventional separations of territorial jurisdictions. This compelled several States to propose a more flexible and expansionary definition of *State Sovereignty,* that includes non-material online expressions of sovereignty. This however remains a postulate rather than a customary legal norm.

Cyberspace as the environment in which hostile cyber operations take place, is not precisely defined and the contours of the notion are still subject to a heated international debate, both among States and scholars. One of the main differences is whether to include non-networked systems (i.e., those behind an "air gap") as part of cyberspace as long as they interact with the broader network occasionally. Doing so would mean that incidents such as the Stuxnet virus, which damaged Iranian nuclear facilities, could be classified as hostile cyber operations. The emerging consensus is to accept this expansionary definition. Another point of disagreement is whether cyberspace is the fifth domain of warfare, like land, air, water, and outer space. This would imply that specialized international legal norms could develop to deal with warfare-related situations specific to cyberspace. Opinions among scholars are split but most States, including those which are NATO members, have formally embraced that approach.

Statistical data on hostile cyber operations involving States reveals a rapidly growing scale of such activity. The number of such operations rose 10-fold over the ten years between 2012 and 2022 with the bulk of them being a form of cyber espionage below the threshold required to be classified as *Internationally Wrongful Acts*. Some legal scholars, including the NATO-backed International Group of Experts who authored the Tallinn Manual, are now proposing to handle conventional and cyber espionage differently in Public International Law due to the pervasive nature and larger impact of cyber acts. Some State practice, for example, in Canada, appears to be leaning in that direction too. At the same time, cyber capabilities to conduct such operations are distributed in a highly unequal way around the world. Five most powerful States (out of almost two hundred) are responsible for the majority of publicized hostile cyber operations against other States. This lopsided dynamic contributes to the prevailing approach of ambiguity and silence. Target States have no capacity to retaliate and seeking redress via Public International Law is perceived as futile. Therefore, most victim States are reluctant to publicize the fact that they were attacked. Meanwhile, the cyber-capable States often find themselves being both a target and perpetrator of numerous cyber operations. They possess the means to retaliate and do not need to seek redress via international law. For that reason, they have no incentive to advocate for stronger norms within the system of Public International Law.

All these dynamics suggest a slowly developing *Sui Generis* framework covering cyberspace that encompasses a range of ways in which States adapted existing rules of international law to the novel field. Classification as the fifth domain of warfare, proposed special treatment of cyber espionage, and more flexible expansionary norms regarding violations of the territorial dimension of State sovereignty when they take place in cyberspace all contribute to this emergent trend.

CHAPTER 2

History of the international legal framework regulating cyberspace

2.1 Introduction

Cyberspace, while being a relatively new phenomenon, is another iteration of a continuous chain of technological advancements in the area of human communication that has been taking place for millennia. At this point, all the previous technological iterations of methods of information exchange have been essentially accounted for and regulated by the system of international law. This indicates that the same fate awaits cyberspace. Its emergence has not taken place in an international legal vacuum but is situated in a broader existing context, including well-established rules and a body of precedents.

The analysis of international legal sources covering historical technological developments preceding the emergence of the internet reveals a complex train of events that all set the ground for the current heated debate among States on how to regulate and oversee cyberspace. These events include the international arrangements on telegraph, the legal impact of the sinking of Titanic, and Cold War era U.S. military preparations, among many other factors. As cyberspace became a global success, more actors started weighing in on the subject, contributing to the development of a complex web of stakeholders, all trying to influence the evolution of the new domain. An unprecedented number of non-State actors are involved in this effort, potentially challenging the traditional path for setting norms in Public International Law.

This unique process reinforces the notion that cyberspace is being treated differently than other communication technologies by the system of Public International Law. It remains to be seen whether the future brings more convergence in that respect or rather continued divergence. As this chapter demonstrates, the analysis of historical dynamics is pointing toward the latter outcome.

2.2 The international legal framework regulating telecommunication before the internet

2.2.1 Agreements regulating telegraph as the foundation of the international legal system on telecommunication

In legal terms, modern cyberspace is developing against the backdrop of an international framework designed back in the nineteenth century to regulate the transatlantic telegraph cables network. Both technical and legal arrangements set up to organize international telegraphs continue to define the contours of the system regulating oversight over communication technologies in Public International Law. As demonstrated in this chapter, it is the gap between that legal framework and the actual way in which the internet operates that is a source of much unresolved international tension.

Let us restate the definition of the internet invoked in Chapter 1: Internet is a global network of interconnected computers using standardized communication protocols for information exchange, enabled by electromagnetic processes.[190] This technical definition places the internet firmly as a follow-up technology to the electric telegraph. First conceived of in 1753 in Scotland,[191] the idea of harnessing electromagnetic induction for instantaneous long-distance information dispatches was explored by a string of European inventors for another eight decades.[192] It finally found its first real-world application in

[190] Own elaboration, based on Oxford English Dictionary. Retrieved November 22, 2023. <https://www.oed.com/viewdictionaryentry/Entry/248411>.

[191] Marland, E. A. Early Electrical Communication. London: Abelard-Schuman, 1964. Pages 17–19.

[192] Michaelis, Anthony R. From semaphore to satellite. UN International Telecommunication Union. 1965. Section: Electrochemical Telegraph, pages 1808–1810; Menon, R. V. G. Technology and Society. Pearson India. 2012. Section: Telegraph; Henry, Joseph. “Inventor of the Telegraph?.” 2007. Accessed November 26, 2023. <https://siarchives.si.edu/oldsite/siarchives-old/history/jhp/joseph20.htm>.

England's Great Western Railway system in 1838.[193] The system did not convey text messages but rather simple signals for rope-hauling of locomotives over a distance of 13 miles (21 km).[194] The astonishing commercial success of the technology led to a rapid expansion across the United Kingdom and in North America, precipitating the advent of the Second Industrial Revolution.[195] The first long-distance text telegraph was sent on May 24th 1844 by an American inventor Samuel Morse from the Capitol in Washington D.C. to Mount Clare railway station in Baltimore, 44 miles (71 km) away.[196] The text consisted of just four words: WHAT HATH GOD WROUGHT—a passage from the Bible's Book of Numbers.[197] Just 14 years later, on August 16, 1858, the first transatlantic communication occurred. It was a courteous letter from Queen Victoria to the President of the United States James Buchanan by means of the newly created Atlantic Telegraph Company.[198] The new system reduced the time needed to pass on information between the two continents from ten days (the duration of a ship cruise) to around one minute.[199]

A swift expansion of the globe-covering telegraph web created an urgent need for international legal coordination. Between 1849 and 1865, Western European governments signed a series of bilateral and regional agreements. In 1865, representatives of 20 States gathered in Paris, upon invitation of

---

193 BT Group Connected Earth Online Museum. "The telegraphic age dawns," 2010. BT Group Connected Earth Online Museum. Page 129; Huurdeman, Anton A. The worldwide history of Telecommunications. Hoboken, NJ: J. Wiley, 2003. Page 103.

194 Ibid.

195 Ibid.

196 History.com Editors. "Morse Code & the Telegraph," November 9, 2009. History. Com. Retrieved February 14, 2022. <http://www.history.com/topics/inventions/telegraph>. The Telegraph. "A significant demonstration of Morse Code," May 4, 2017. The Telegraph. <https://www.telegraph.co.uk/technology/connecting-britain/significant-demonstration-morse-code>.

197 "English Standard Version Online - Literal Word." English Standard Version Bible. Retrieved November 26, 2023. <https://esv.literalword.com/. Section Numbers 23:23>.

198 Fisher, Smith Norman Alfred. History of technology. London: Mansell Publishing, 1985. | Section: de Cogan, D. Dr. E. O. W. Whitehouse and the 1858 trans-Atlantic cable. History of Technology, 10, 1–15. Section History of the Atlantic Cable & Undersea Communications; Guarnieri, Massimo. "The Conquest of the Atlantic [Historical]." IEEE Industrial Electronics Magazine 8, no. 1 2014, pages 53–67. <https://doi.org/10.1109/mie.2014.2299492>.

199 Ibid.

Emperor Napoléon III, to create a global framework, which would standardize telegraph equipment, lay out consistent operating procedures, and define common international tariff rules that would apply worldwide.[200] Thus, the first globe-covering international organization was born—ITU (International Telegraph Union). The original treaty bears official seals of States that are since long gone such as Kingdom of Württemberg, United Kingdoms of Sweden and Norway, and the Ottoman Empire.[201] All existing States were welcome to join the ITU. The consensual and multilateral character of the accord set a strong precedent for international co-governance of communication technologies. More broadly, it also ascertained the philosophy of a global multilateral consent that underpins the modern international legal order embodied by the United Nations.[202] When radio broadcasting was regulated in the International Wireless Telegraph Convention in 1906, it was modeled on the inclusive co-governance framework developed for ITU.[203]

2.2.2 The impact of the Titanic's sinking on the forward-expanding mandate of the UN ITU

The sinking of *Titanic* in 1912 was an event that forever changed the trajectory of the ITU. It did so by giving an impulse for the ITU to assert a legal supposition of its automatically expanding regulatory domain in a process that led to the creation of anew customary legal norm. In April that year, as the ship started to sink and its crew were frantically broadcasting S-O-S signals through radio, another large vessel, the *Californian*, was located only around 5 miles (8 km) away. Unfortunately, the *Californian* did not receive the signals. Hundreds of people, of the 1,500 that ended up perishing that

---

200 UN International Telecommunication Union. "Plenipotentiary Conferences." ITU. Retrieved November 26, 2023. <https://www.itu.int/en/history/Pages/PlenipotentiaryConferences.aspx?conf=4.1>.

201 UN International Telecommunication Union. "International Telegraph Convention, May 17, 1865." ITU. Retrieved November 26, 2023. <https://search.itu.int/history/HistoryDigitalCollectionDocLibrary/4.1.43.fr.201.pdf>.

202 UN International Telecommunication Union. "The 1865 International Telegraph Conference." ITU. Retrieved November 26, 2023. <https://www.itu.int/en/history/Pages/ITUBorn1865.aspx>.

203 UN International Telecommunication Union. "International Telegraph Convention, May 17, 1865." ITU. Retrieved November 26, 2023. <https://search.itu.int/history/HistoryDigitalCollectionDocLibrary/4.1.43.fr.201.pdf>.

night, could have been saved, had the signal been captured. When this fact was realized by the public in the aftermath of the tragedy, it added to the outcry on both sides of the Atlantic. Ships were oftentimes turning off their radio at nights, which could have been the cause of the missed opportunity to save more lives.[204] However, there exist accounts of a grimmer potential cause of the *Californian* missing the S-O-S signal. Historian Keith Dawson presents it as follows:

> In 1912, the radiomen were not ships crew, but employees of the radio company they hired and subscribed to. There were two major companies that provided the equipment and operators: The Marconi Company in New York City and Telefunken in Germany. The Titanic was subscribed to Marconi. Shortly before the Titanic set to sea, there was a big flap about exchanging weather and iceberg information between ships, that is, between these two different companies. So Marconi Company issued an edict that any operator who "talked" to a Telefunken ship would be immediately relieved of duty upon his return. Telefunken, in turn, issued the same order to their operators. Therefore, at the time of the Titanic, Marconi operators did not talk to Telefunken operators and vice versa for fear of losing their jobs. This is why the Titanic SOS's went unanswered by the Californian, a Telefunken ship, which we know now was adrift for the night only miles away. The Carpathia was a Marconi ship, and at midnight when the operator checked his gear following some repairs, heard the SOS and was able to respond, even though they were some distance away.[205]

The *Carpathia* ship he mentions was located 58 miles (93 km) from Titanic at the moment of receiving the S-O-S signal. The ship's captain took the decision to rush to the crash scene at the top speed in the middle of the night, navigating ice fields. His actions earned him a Congressional Medal of Honor, but his crew could only save 711 people by the time they had

---

204 Spaulding Ryan, P. "The ITU and the Internet's Titanic Momen," 2012. Stanford Technology Law Review, 2012(8), pages 8–36. <https://papers.ssrn.com/sol3/papers.cfm?abstract_id=2110509#>; Congressional Records – GovInfo. "48 Congressional Records S7282 - Statement of Sen. Smith," May 28, 1912. <https://www.govinfo.gov/app/collection/crecb/_crecb/Volume%20048%20(1912)>.

205 Dawson, Keith. "Browser wars of the wireless telegraphy age," March 1, 1999. Technology Front. Retrieved February 14, 2022. <https://tbtf.com/resource/telegraph-browser-wars.html>.

arrived.[206] This catastrophe could have been avoided, had there been an established uniform international radio protocol. The finding prompted the International Radiotelegraph Union (IRU) that same year to introduce its first International Table of Frequency Allocations, despite no explicit mandate for those competences in the International Wireless Telegraph Convention.[207]

Importantly, IRU was effectively a radio-related extension of the ITU, responsible for executing the convention, with little or no separation between the two bodies, which meant that by doing so the ITU assumed a new competence.[208] The international community consented to this act through their State practice (i.e., behaving in accordance with the act and consistently following the new rules) and so a precedent in Public International Law was born. In 1932 IRU was formally merged into the ITU, whose name was also adjusted to International Telecommunication Union, which it bears until today. From then on, it assumed international oversight over all future communication technologies that had not been invented yet at the time, assuming that their continuous emergence and replacing of the old ones is inevitable, thus anchoring its *forward-expanding mandate* as a customary rule.[209]

---

206 Wade, Wyn Craig. The Titanic: End of a dream. New York, USA. Penguin Books, 1992.

207 Spaulding Ryan, P. "The ITU and the Internet's Titanic Moment," 2012. Stanford Technology Law Review, 2012(8), pages 8–36. <https://papers.ssrn.com/sol3/papers.cfm?abstract_id=2110509#>; UN International Telecommunication Union. "Radio Regulations Board (RRB): It's place, role and functioning in the ITU (by Wladyslaw Moron, Member RRB)," 2010, March 22, 2010. Retrieved February 14, 2022. <https://www.itu.int/net/ITU-R/information/promotion/e-flash/4/article7.html>

208 Spaulding Ryan, P. "The ITU and the Internet's Titanic Moment," 2012. Stanford Technology Law Review, 2012(8), pages 8–36. <https://papers.ssrn.com/sol3/papers.cfm?abstract_id=2110509#>; Codding, George. A. Jr. "The International Telecommunications Union: 130 Years of Telecommunications Regulation," January 1995. Denver Journal of International Law and Policy, 23, pages 501–513; Allison, A. L. "Meeting the Challenges of Change: The Reform of the International Telecommunication Union," 1993. Federal Communications Law Journal, 45, pages 491–498.

209 UN International Telecommunication Union. "International Telegraph Conference (Madrid, 1932)," October 7, 2007. Retrieved February 14, 2022. <https://www.itu.int/en/history/Pages/PlenipotentiaryConferences.aspx?conf=4.5>; Orji, Uchenna Jerome. International Telecommunications Law and policy. Newcastle upon Tyne, UK: Cambridge Scholars Publishing, 2018. Page 175; Spaulding Ryan, P. "The ITU

2.2.3 The central role of the UN ITU as the international body regulating telecommunication

ITU still exists today and became a part of the UN system after 1945 as a so-called specialized agency.[210] The organization defines its three main work areas as:

- setting worldwide technical standards for telecommunications technologies;
- coordinating rational use of radio frequency spectrum and assigning satellite orbit bands;
- running programs aimed at closing the digital divide between countries.[211]

One hundred and 55 years after its foundation, regulating the telegraph network is no longer the core activity of the organization. Its flexible model, built around technical governance and multilateralism, worked well as mankind's technological frontier organically progressed from electric telegraph, through radio, phone, GSM technology, to orbit satellites, all without ever changing its underlying treaty. The organization serves as an arbiter between States in areas such as orbit slot allotment or frequency bandwidth rights negotiations.

The internet, however, is not overseen or regulated by the ITU. Despite being covered by ITU's mandate, the most relevant of all modern communication technologies broke the historic pattern of joint international oversight, defying the customary legal rule that had been in place before. The part of the UN ITU envisioned to hold the technical oversight over the internet is called ITU-T, standing for *Telecommunication Standardization Sector*. While the organization has some say over the medium, including data compression standards, it is removed from deciding over key areas such as IP addresses and domain assignment, which can be utilized to identify the source of a hostile

---

and the Internet's Titanic Momen," 2012. Stanford Technology Law Review, 2012(8), pages 8–36.

210 Malamud, Carl. Exploring the internet: A technical travelogue. Englewood Cliffs, N.J: Prentice Hall, 1993. Page 384.

211 UN International Telecommunication. "What does ITU do?." Retrieved February 14, 2022. <https://www.itu.int/en/about/Pages/whatwedo.aspx>.

cyber operation.[212] As the next section demonstrates, these competencies are mostly concentrated in a small number of NGOs operating as domestic organizations in the United States of America. Therefore, the peculiar shape of the internet's technical governance model has a tangible impact on the development of Public International Law applicable to cyberspace.

This situation is a source of much international tension and has a direct impact on the development of the legal arrangements governing cyberspace. The following sections of this chapter explain how this state of affairs came to be and how it impacts development of Public International Law.

2.3 Genesis of the internet

2.3.1 Evolution of ARPANET

The internet, which provides the platform sustaining cyberspace, has become a basic staple on which people around the planet depend in all key areas of life such as work, education, culture, and government services. As of 2022, 68% of humanity around the world, that is 5.4 billion persons, were internet users.[213] Around 21% of the planet's GDP growth every year is generated thanks to the internet.[214] Our perception of the internet is also evolving. A momentum grows for elevating the internet to the status of a utility,[215]

---

212 Ibid.

213 Internet World Stats. "World Internet Users Statistics and 2021 World Population Stats," March 31, 2021. Retrieved February 14, 2022. <https://www.internetworldstats.com/stats.htm>.

214 McKinsey Global Institute. "Internet Matters: The Net's Sweeping Impact on Growth, Jobs, and Prosperity, May, 2011. Page 3. <https://www.mckinsey.com/industries/technology-media-and-telecommunications/our-insights/internet-matters.>

215 Kang, Cecilia. "Court Backs Rules Treating Internet as Utility, Not Luxury," June 14, 2016. The New York Times. <https://www.nytimes.com/2016/06/15/technology/net-neutrality-fcc-appeals-court-ruling.html>; Gilbert, Ben. "Bernie Sanders has a $150 billion plan to turn the internet into a public utility with low prices and fast speeds — here's how his plan works," January 22, 2020. Business Insider Nederland. <https://www.businessinsider.nl/bernie-sanders-internet-as-utility-plan-explainer-2019-12?international=true&r=US>; Livni, Ephrat. "The pandemic proves internet should be a public utility," March 26, 2020. Quartz. <https://qz.com/1826043/the-coronavirus-crisis-proves-internet-should-be-a-public-utility/>; Andriole, Steve. "It's Time For An Internet-For-All Public Utility (Before Corona Crashes It)," March 31, 2020. Forbes. <https://www.forbes.com/sites/steveandriole/2020/03/30/

which would strengthen people's case for permanent uninterrupted access, and even framing it as a human right.[216]

It is virtually impossible to imagine the modern world, as well as its future, without the internet's central role in it. Technology's meteoric career is even more stunning when one realizes that only 25 years ago it was still a niche project. The rapid emergence of the internet partially explains why this telecommunication technology evaded the established ITU-based model of international coordination although there were other complex political and legal processes at play. As this section shows, the internet is a special case in which the lion's share of the technical and political control is in the hands of just one government, that of the United States of America.

The internet started as a U.S. military project spearheaded by the country's Armed Forces unit called Advanced Research Projects Agency (ARPA). The Agency started developing the project in 1969, calling it ARPANET at the time, at the height of the Cold War, as a way of building a communication network without a center but rather a mesh of links and computer nodes that would continue operating through any assault, including a nuclear attack by Soviet Russia.[217] The idea of such a communication mesh was conceptualized some years earlier as Packet Switching method, and published in the form of an academic paper in 1964. The idea was for the system to route communication between computer nodes through the

---

its-time-for-an-internet-for-all-public-utility-before-corona-crashes-it/#2638b-7f2af95>.

216 Howell, Catherine, and West, Darrell. M. "The internet as a human right. Brookings Institution," 2016, November 4, 2016. Retrieved February 14, 2022. <https://www.brookings.edu/blog/techtank/2016/11/07/the-internet-as-a-human-right/>; Feldstein, Steven. "Why Internet Access Is a Human Right. Carnegie Endowment for International Peace," June 1, 2017. Retrieved February 14, 2022. <https://carnegieendowment.org/2017/06/01/why-internet-access-is-human-right-pub-70151>; Bode, Karl. "The Case for Internet Access as a Human Right," November 13, 2019. Vice. Retrieved February 14, 2022. <https://www.vice.com/en/article/3kxmm5/the-case-for-internet-access-as-a-human-right;>

217 Timberg, Craig. "Your Internet is working. Thank these Cold War-era pioneers who designed it to handle almost anything," April 6, 2020. The Washington Post. <https://www.washingtonpost.com/technology/2020/04/06/your-internet-is-working-thank-these-cold-war-era-pioneers-who-designed-it-handle-almost-anything/.>

fastest node-and-links path and automatically reroute that path whenever some of the computer nodes stop working.[218] By the end of the year 1970, the ARPANET was connecting 20 academic sites across the United States (see Figure 5 for details). The proto-internet was born.[219] In Parallel, ARPA had been developing another project—Nuclear Monitoring Research Office, which coordinated an electronic network of seismic activity measurement stations including two abroad—in Norway and the United Kingdom.[220] In 1973, The Agency, now renamed as American Defense Advanced Research Projects Agency (DARPA) combined the two systems, enabling leading American and British universities to engage in instantaneous international data exchange.[221]

In those early days of the internet, its development and usage were limited to a small community of academics at a handful of American and British universities. This is reflected in how informal the process of regulating the internet was at the time. For instance, when a person accesses the internet, they do it by using the TCP/IP protocol. It was pitched by Vint Cerf and Bob Kahn back in 1973 among their fellow professors from participating universities, which was enough for the protocol to become a global standard until today.[222] The system's architecture finally took the modern shape we are familiar with later, in the year 1990, when DARPA, in collaboration with the European Organization for Nuclear Research (CERN), deployed the World Wide Web (WWW) address linkage system, allowing users to access websites using text addresses rather than strings of numbers and dots.[223] The system was rapidly expanding and as more universities from an array of

---

218 Kirstein, Peter T. "Early Experiences with the ARPANET and INTERNET in the UK," City University of London. Retrieved February 14, 2022. <http://www0.cs.ucl.ac.uk/research/darpa/internet-history.html.>

219 Ibid.; Klein, Robert E. Oral history interview with Robert E. Kahn. April 24, 1990. Charles Babbage Institute. Page 213.

220 Kirstein, Peter T. "Early Experiences with the ARPANET and INTERNET in the UK," City University of London. Retrieved February 14, 2022. <http://www0.cs.ucl.ac.uk/research/darpa/internet-history.html.>

221 Ibid.

222 Klein, Robert E. Oral history interview with Robert E. Kahn. April 24, 1990. Charles Babbage Institute. Page 214.

223 UN International Telecommunication Union. "Overview of ITU's History." Retrieved February 14, 2022. <https://itu.int/en/history/documents/itu-history-overview.pdf.>

countries started lining up to join the network, the project was transformed into a shared initiative of the United States Armed Forces and the American National Science Foundation (NSF), becoming a part of America's soft power toolkit. In fact, the American government started actively encouraging ally countries to plug their universities and civilian telecommunication grids into the network.

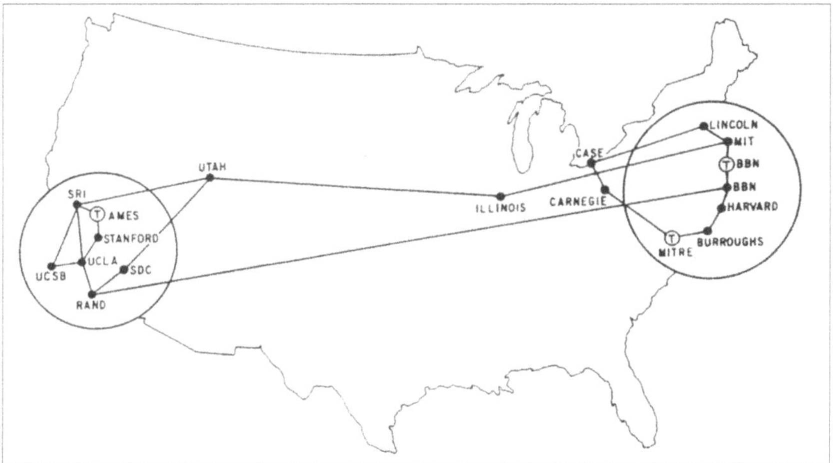

Figure 5. ARPANET in 1971
Source: International Telecommunication Union

In the year 1988, the first malicious cyber operation of sorts took place (although not one that would infringe upon any State's sovereignty). That year, the so-called Morris worm, written by a Cornell University student Robert Morris, ended up infecting 10% of all 60,000 computers connected to the internet, slowing them down to a point of being unusable.[224] The laurel of the first virus might be also contested by the Creeper, which would self-replicate across ARPANET-connected computers as early as 1971. It was not malicious though, the only impact being a message on the screen

224 Legal case United States v. Morris—the judgment. Case Brief for Law School | LexisNexis. Retrieved February 14, 2022. <https://www.lexisnexis.com/community/casebrief/p/casebrief-united-states-v-morris>; Seeley, Donn. "A tour of the worm," February 1989. University of Utah Computer Science Technical Report, 89(009). Pages 1–16. <https://collections.lib.utah.edu/details?id=702918>.

reading *I'm the creeper: catch me if you can.*[225] Another cyber incident that could claim the mantle of the first one ever was the Soviet gas pipeline explosion of 1982 discussed in Chapter 1. These three incidents show that malicious cyber incidents emerged as an issue almost as soon as cyberspace itself. Nevertheless, expansion of the internet continued unimpeded. As a result of a growing number of users and the threat posed by viruses, U.S. armed forces decided to split the military network from the progressively more popular ARPANET. In 1983, MILNET was set up as a separate tool for information exchange, freeing ARPANET to become a global information exchange platform for civilian purposes.

2.3.2 Establishment of the unique international system regulating the internet

In 1994, commercial activity began moving onto the Internet. The first company ever to offer online purchases was Pizza Hut, which set up its online delivery website that year.[226] In parallel, by the mid-1990s, the internet's idiosyncratic governance system gained formal international recognition. Unlike other telecommunication technologies, it remained outside of the scope of the UN ITU, breaking with the paradigm of the organization's *forward-expanding mandate*. Instead, initial informal initiatives by the American academics to coordinate growth of the project on behalf of DARPA and American National Science Foundation acquired a legal status, usually as nonprofit public benefit corporations under various U.S. states' civil regulations. It would not have been possible without the backing of the government of the United States, which had a clear interest in the internet retaining its unique legal oversight model, despite having an international reach. For instance, the Internet Engineering Task Force (IETF), a California-based nonprofit, was founded in 1986 at the behest of Internet Architecture Board (IAB), which in turn was formed

---

225 Meltzer, Tom, and Phillips, Sarah. "From the first email to the first YouTube video: a definitive internet history," October 23, 2009. The Guardian. <shttps://www.theguardian.com/technology/2009/oct/23/internet-history>.

226 Schrage, Michael. "On-Line Pizza Idea Is Clever but Only Half-Baked," 2019, March 6, 2019. Los Angeles Times. <https://www.latimes.com/archives/la-xpm-1994-08-25-fi-31168-story.html>.

a few years earlier, in 1979, as a committee within DARPA.[227] IETF is a volunteer-based organization (consisting mostly of professors of the universities originally involved in ARPANET), whose role is to develop and oversee operational protocols for the global digital architecture, such as TCP/IP.[228] IETF's sister organization—Internet Research Task Force (IRTF), set up in 1989, works on the long-term vision for internet's development.[229] Vint Cerf, TCP/IP's creator, was seminal in setting up IAB and continued to convene the community of IETF/IRTF-involved engineers and professors known as The Internet Society throughout the 1990s.[230] Another American nonprofit, which became a formal expression of earlier informal workings of the community of engineers involved in DARPA is the World Wide Web Consortium (W3P). It was incorporated as a nonprofit organization under Massachusetts state law in 1994 at Massachusetts Institute of Technology (MIT) Laboratory for Computer Science (MIT/LCS) and is in charge of assuring compatibility of coding standards for the internet platform, such the HTML language, among the key companies in the industry.[231] The Consortium has since expanded its network of offices to 18 countries,[232] three of which: in France, Japan, and China co-administer the organization together with the American headquarters.[233] All this goes to say that cyberspace has a radically different oversight model than, for instance, global GSM or satellite communication technologies, which are overseen by a UN body (ITU), that has a balanced State representation. The internet international legal oversight

227 Cerf, Vint. "The Internet Activities Board Memo. Internet Engineering Task Force, May 1, 1990. Retrieved February 14, 2022. <https://www.ietf.org/rfc/rfc1160.txt>.

228 Cerf, Vint. "IETF and the Internet Society. Internet Society," September 28, 2021. Retrieved February 14, 2022. <https://www.internetsociety.org/internet/history-of-the-internet/ietf-internet-society/>.

229 Internet Research Task Force. "Internet Research Task Force," January 11, 2022. Retrieved February 14, 2022. <https://irtf.org/>.

230 Cerf, Vint. "IETF and the Internet Society. Internet Society," September 28, 2021. Retrieved February 14, 2022. <https://www.internetsociety.org/internet/history-of-the-internet/ietf-internet-society/>.

231 World Wide Web Consortium. "Facts About W3C." Retrieved February 14, 2022. <https://www.w3.org/Consortium/facts>

232 Ibid.

233 Ibid.

system is fragmented and “organic” in that it emerged from practice of academics involved in its creation.

Internet Assigned Numbers Authority (IANA), a nonprofit organization that assigns IP numbers to decipherable, alphabet-based website addresses perhaps best represents the specific evolution of the internet’s governance model. In the early days of ARPANET, Professor Jonathan Postel of University of Southern California (USC) was involved in assigning the so-called socket-numbers (proto-website addresses) to each host in the new system. In May 1972, Postel circulated a memo, in which he asked potential hosts to leave him a note or call him in case they wanted to request a socket. He also called himself in it *the czar of socket numbers.*[234] As the internet started to grow in importance, the U.S. federal government moved to regulate this function by asserting oversight and signing a contract with USC in 1988, therefore formally establishing IANA.[235] In practice though, it meant that Jonathan Postel continued to have uninterrupted control over the domain assignment system from his faculty office in Los Angeles’ Marina Del Rey. When the U.S. Congress was reviewing the internet’s architecture in 1997, it summoned Jonathan Postel to testify on how the vital function of domain assignment is handled under the agreement. He stated that coordinating the system was a *side task* to his research work at the university.[236] In 1998 the government resolved to further institutionalize IANA functions and that same year The Internet Corporation for Assigned Names and Numbers (ICANN) was established as a nonprofit

234 Postel, Jon. “RFC 349 - Proposed Standard Socket Numbers. Internet Engineering Task Force,”May 30, 1972. Retrieved February 14, 2022. <https://datatracker.ietf.org/doc/html/rfc349.>

235 Internet Society. “The History of IANA An Extended Timeline with Citations and Commentary,” November, 2016. Retrieved February 14, 2022. <https://www.yumpu.com/en/document/view/56851186/the-history-of-iana-an-extended-timeline-with-citations-and-commentary>.

236 U.S. House of Representatives, Committee on Science. “Public Hearing on Internet Domain Names, Part I,” September 25, 1997. U.S. House of Representatives Committee Hearings. Retrieved February 14, 2022. <http://commdocs.house.gov/committees/science/hsy268140.000/hsy268140_0.HTM>.

public benefit corporation, located in Los Angeles.[237] The U.S. Department of Commerce signed a *joint program agreement* with ICANN that outlined its mandate and priorities as well as designated it as the body responsible for managing IANA.[238] This direct oversight of U.S. government over the internet domain system continued until 2016 when ICANN transitioned to a multi-stakeholder governance model due to international pressure (more on in Subsection 2.4).

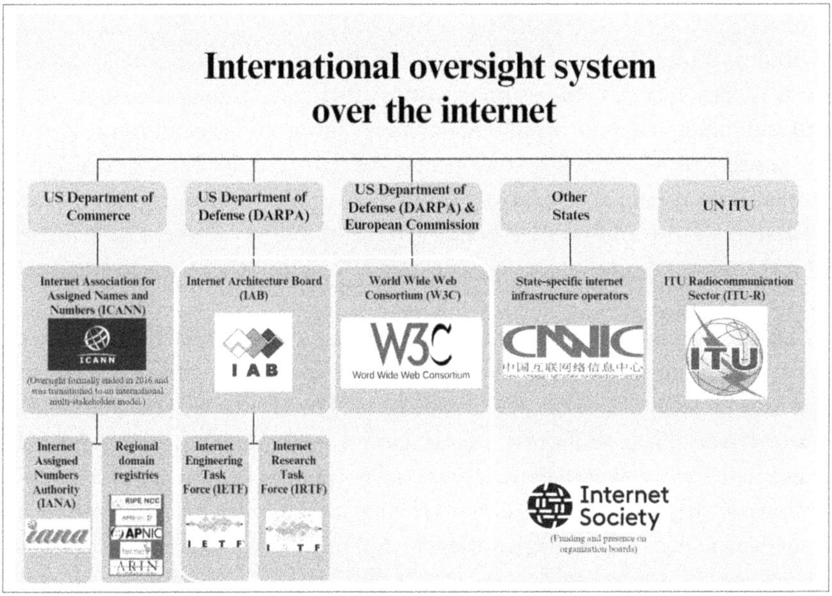

Figure 6. The international technical governance model of internet
Source: own elaboration

[237] State of California - Business Portal. California Secretary of State - California Business Search. Retrieved February 14, 2022. https://web.archive.org/web/20070321194344/;<http://kepler.ss.ca.gov/corpdata/ShowAllList?QueryCorpNumber=C2121683>.

[238] Internet Corporation for Assigned Names and Numbers. "ICANN's Major Agreements and Related Reports." Retrieved February 14, 2022. <https://www.icann.org/resources/pages/agreements-en.>

2.4 Development of the public international norms on cyberspace

2.4.1 Efforts to establish international legal oversight over the internet

By the turn of millennia, the internet became a global sensation. Companies such as Google, Amazon, and Alibaba started operating and hundreds of millions of new people were getting connected every year. It became a subject of controversy that such a powerful tool was defying the established international legal order and remained in the firm grasp of just one government, through several domestic nonprofit subsidiaries. Some of the first signs of other States' resentment toward this arrangement came in 1995. In December that year, President Jacques Chirac of France announced to the leaders of 47 French-speaking nations gathered in Benin: "if English States to dominate the information highway, our future generations will be economically and culturally marginalized. Ninety percent of information transmitted on the internet is in English, and it threatens to steamroll French language and culture."[239]

The position of the United States regarding international governance of the internet, defined initially in the late 1990s, became entrenched during the first 12 years of the twenty-first century. The United States had obvious reasons to be defensive about it. The amount of economic, cultural, and intelligence-gathering power that cyberspace started generating was unprecedented. Following the events of September 11, 2001, the country became even more assertive in terms of holding onto its clout. The internet acquired an essential role in the country's newly waged *war on terror*.[240] For the same reasons, other countries ramped up political pressure to merge the internet into the fold of the established multi-stakeholder system with the ITU at its center. The first high-profile initiative by the international community was launched in 1998, when UN ITU's Plenipotentiary Conference in Minneapolis, acting on Tunisia's proposal, passed Resolution 73 to convene a World Summit

239 Negroponte, Nicholas. "Pluralistic, Not Imperialistic," March 1, 1996. Wired. <https://www.wired.com/1996/03/negroponte-51/.>

240 Perl, Raphael. F. "National Strategy for Combating Terrorism: Background and Issues for Congress," November, 2007. Congressional Research Service. <https://sgp.fas.org/crs/terror/RL34230.pdf.>

on the Information as a United Nations-sponsored event.[241] Passing of the resolution and engaging the United Nations was an attempt to compel the United States to allow the ITU to expand its mandate onto international governance of the internet. Due to the efforts of the American side, this process stalled for another three years. In June 2001, the ITU announced its intent to hold the Summit in two stages, the first one in Switzerland in December 2003, and the second one in Tunisia in November 2005.[242] The disruption caused by the 9/11 terrorist attack, which occurred some three months later, lent the initiative unexpected momentum. ITU's decision was endorsed in December 2001 by the UN General Assembly Resolution, which designated the organization as the convener of interested organizations and summit participants.[243] One seventy five States sent delegations to the Geneva Summit, a sign of widespread interests of governments around the world in the issue of international legal oversight over the internet. The summit led to signing of an historic document—*Declaration of Principles on Building the Information Society.*[244] It laid out a global vision of achieving *an information society accessible to all and based on shared knowledge* by realizing the potential of the internet and formulated the Plan of Action with its main goal of bringing 50% of the world's population online by 2015.[245] The most contentious point of the agenda—discussion on international governance over the internet—ended in an impasse. The subject was left unresolved. Nevertheless, Working Group on Internet Governance (WGIG) was formed following the summit to prepare

---

241 UN International Telecommunication Union. "Resolution 73 of the ITU Plenipotentiary Conference," 1998. <https://www.itu.int/net/wsis/docs/background/resolutions/73.html.>

242 Ibid.; UN International Telecommunication Union. ("Agenda of the 2001 Session of Council," June 19, 2001. <https://www.itu.int/itudoc/gs/council/c01/pdagn/001rev1.html.>

243 United Nations General Assembly Resolution 56/183. "World Summit on the Information Society," A/RES/56/183. January 31, 2002. <https://undocs.org/en/A/RES/56/183.>

244 UN International Telecommunication Union. "WSIS: Declaration of Principles - Building the Information Society: a global challenge in the new Millennium," December 3, 2003. Retrieved February 15, 2022. <https://www.itu.int/net/wsis/docs/geneva/official/dop.html>.

245 Ibid.

an array of potential solutions ahead of the Tunis Summit.[246] Come July 2005, it released a statement delineating four potential models that would overhaul the existing system based on a fragmented network of United States-based NGOs.[247] They could be summarized in the following way:

- **Option One:** Establishing a new UN organ called the Global Internet Council that would consist of government representatives and other stakeholders. It would take over the oversight role of ICANN from the United States of America;
- **Option Two:** Leaving in place the ecosystem of American nonprofit organizations in charge of regulating the internet with a small adjustment of strengthening ICANN's Governmental Advisory Committee to become a multilateral forum for high-profile debate;
- **Option Three:** Relegating ICANN to a narrow technical role, transitioning it to a multilateral oversight and setting up a new body called International Internet Council for political and legal decisions on cyberspace's development;
- **Option Four:** Creating three new organizations, one would replace ICANN and take over its functions, one would become a debating chamber for UN member states, businesses and the public, and one would be meant to develop solutions on cyber space-related international public policy issues.[248]

At the time of the publication of WGIG's report, the United States promptly announced its opposition to all four options and intent to retain its role as an overseer of ICANN, setting the stage for a confrontation at the summit.

The course of events that followed in Tunis, during the conclusive ITU summit, was fairly chaotic. The run-up to the 2005 summit was marred by media accusations against the Tunisian government, suggesting it was harassing journalists and human rights activists trying to draw the World's

246 Ibid.

247 United Nations Working Group on Internet Governance. (2005, June). United Nations Working Group on Internet Governance 2005 Report. Retrieved February 15, 2022. <http://www.wgig.org/WGIG-Report.html>.

248 BBC News - Technology. (2005, July 18). UN at odds over internet's future. BBC News - Technology. <http://news.bbc.co.uk/2/hi/technology/4692743.stm>.

attention to the state of civic liberties in their country.[249] Domestic human rights protesters were arrested shortly before the summit. French journalist Robert Ménard, the president of Reporters Without Borders, was denied entry into Tunisia at the Tunis airport. A French journalist representing the newspaper Libération was stabbed and beat up by unidentified perpetrators on the streets of Tunisia's capital city. Police forces confiscated footage on human rights protests recorded by a Belgian TV crew. Tunisia also refused admission to the representatives of an organization called *Human Rights in China* following a request from the Chinese government.[250] Inside the plenary hall of the summit, the dispute over transforming the governance model for the internet brought the conference to the brink of a collapse without any conclusion. A last-minute compromise saved the event—the United States got to retain the *status quo* at the expense of one concession: creation of an organization called Internet Governance Forum—a purely consultative body of countries and industry representatives under United Nations' control.[251] The wording of the new organization's 5-year mandate was vague. It was instructed to, among other consultative tasks, *identify emerging issues, bring them to the attention of the relevant bodies and the general public, and, where appropriate, make recommendations, help contribute to capacity building,* and *facilitate the exchange of information and best practices.*[252]

The assumption behind this decision on the part of the governments aiming to reduce the level of control exerted by the United States was that the renewal of the mandate might provide a chance to expand the IGF's role. However, 15 years on and two renewals later, the mandate has not been

---

249 MacKinnon, R. (2013). Consent of the Networked - The Worldwide Struggle For Internet Freedom. Basic Books. Page 187.

250 Ibid.

251 United Nations International Telecommunication Union. (2005, November 18). World Summit on Information Society: Tunis Agenda for the Information Society. Retrieved February 15, 2022, from <https://www.itu.int/net/wsis/docs2/tunis/off/6rev1.html>

252 United Nations Internet Governance Forum (n.d.). Organization Mandate. United Nations Internet Governance Forum. Retrieved February 15, 2022, from <http://www.intgovforum.org/en/about>.

broadened.[253] In spite of the failure to force-bring the internet into the fold of telecommunication areas overseen by the United Nations, the organization has had a positive impact in terms facilitating knowledge sharing that allowed many developing States to enhance their internet infrastructure.[254] Following the contentious summit in Tunis, the United States also ratified (which it had signed earlier but whose implementation process it would not finalize until then) the Convention on Cybercrime. The Budapest Convention, as it is popularly known, is a treaty spearheaded by the Council of Europe and while it lacks any sanctions for cyber hostilities against States and does not set explicitly and international norms, it harmonizes national laws on cybercrime and prosecuting individuals involved in illicit activity online as well as establishes voluntary coordination mechanisms.[255] Ratifying it was seen as a way of the United States signaling goodwill on the subject in the wake of a contentions summit.

Continued international pressure resulted in 2009 in the issuance of Affirmation of Commitments between the United States government and ICANN. The Affirmation was not a legally binding document but rather a declaration of intent to expand the internet legal governance framework toward a multi-stakeholder model in the future.[256] It followed an international outcry in 2008, when the United States Department of Commerce reiterated its resolve to retain control over internet governance and refused

---

253 Ibid. United Nation Internet Governance Forum. (2014, April). The Global Multistakeholder Forum for Dialogue on Internet Governance Issues. <http://intgovforum.org/cms/2014/IGFBrochure.pdf>.

254 United Nations. (2015, December 16). Communique from the UN Under-Secretary-General For Economic and Social Affairs. United Nations Internet Governance Forum. Retrieved February 15, 2022, from <http://www.intgovforum.org/cms/Message%20from%20Mr%20Wu_adoption%20outcome%20doc%20WSIS_16%20Dec%202015.pdf>.

255 Council of Europe. (2001, November 23). Convention on Cybercrime - Council of Europe. Council of Europe Treaty Office (ETS No. 185). Retrieved February 15, 2022, from <https://www.coe.int/en/web/conventions/full-list?module=treaty-detail&treatynum=185>

256 United States government. (2009, September 30). ICANN - Affirmation of Commitments Information. Internet Corporation for Assigned Names and Numbers. Retrieved February 15, 2022, from <https://www.icann.org/resources/pages/governance/aoc-en>.

to transfer the so-called root-zone file to ICANN.[257] The 2009 Affirmation of Commitment was a soft shift in policy formulated by the new presidential administration of Barack Obama. While it marked a change of tone compared with the previous president, the U.S. nevertheless remains steadfast in maintaining its internet policy established in the 1990s. The consecutive U.S. government had a good reason to stay the course. The root-zone file is in essence the focal point of internet traffic. It contains the IP linkages to the authoritative DNS root servers, which are in charge of running top-level domains (TLDs) such as.com,.edu,.gov,.org,.net,.pl, or.de. Whenever we type in an internet address such as google.com, our computer first has to connect with the authoritative DNS server in charge of the.com TLD, which in turn connects us with the server of the Google company using the root-zone file. There are 13 authoritative DNS root server service providers (also called logical root name servers), 10 of which are located in the United States (the other three are in Tokyo, Amsterdam, and Oslo).[258] The State that controls root-zone processes can effectively track and police most of the worldwide cyber space activity. Concentration of that role in the hands of the United States government is essentially inconsistent with a multilateral legal governance model and has direct impact on development of the international customary order in terms of attributing and sanctioning hostile cyber operations (DNS root-zone tracking data allows the United States to identify the source of a cyber operation with a much higher precision than any other State).

The United States could very easily spy on almost all internet users by collecting data as it flows through the DNS root servers located in the United States. Controlling the root-zone file also gave the Americans an effective veto power over domain names. Both of these advantages appear all the more obvious when one takes a look at who are the operators of the ten DNS root server service providers located in the United States. Three of them are governmental bodies: U.S. Army Research Lab, U.S. Defense Communications Agency, and NASA Ames Research Center; two are universities: University of Maryland and University of Southern California; two are American private companies:

---

257 McCarthy, K. (2005, July 1). Bush administration annexes internet. The Register. <https://www.theregister.com/2005/07/01/bush_net_policy/>.

258 Root Server Technical Operations Association. (n.d.). Root Server Technical Operations Association. Retrieved February 15, 2022, from <https://root-servers.org/>.

Verisign (two service centers), and Cogent Communications; and two are non-profits in California: ICANN, and Internet Systems Consortium.[259]

The following four years between 2009 and 2012 passed without much overt tension. International initiatives attempting to wrestle internet legal governance away from the U.S. were being presented but none gained any significant momentum. One of the most prominent ones was the so-called 2011 IBSA proposal named after the three States behind the initiative (India, Brazil, South Africa). Their draft UN General Assembly resolution proposed that a new specialized body of the United States—UN Committee on Internet-Related Policy (UN-CIRP)— be established to directly oversee ICANN.[260] However, following U.S. pressure, India backed away from the bid, leading to its withdrawal and preservation of the status quo.[261]

The 2012 ITU World Conference on International Telecommunications (WCIT-12) in Dubai led to a stand-off between a United States-led coalition of Western States on one side and a number of developing States, led by Russia and China, on the other. The official premise of the conference was to update the International Telecommunication Regulations (ITR)—a legacy treaty from 1988 in custody of the UN ITU that sets out actual binding international norms rather than recommendations.[262] The most important update was meant to expand the ITR's mandate to include the internet, effectively putting the UN ITU in charge of its oversight. The ITR is rooted in the early days of the UN ITU in the nineteenth century when its universal mandate was first established and it was periodically updated to bring new telecommunication technologies under the legal governance arm of the UN ITU. Up until 2012, the latest update to the ITR had taken place in 1988. At

---

259 Ibid.

260 Governments of India, Brazil, and South Africa. (2011, September 2). IBSA Multistakeholder Meeting on Global Internet Governance. IBSA Multistakeholder Meeting on Global Internet Governance. Retrieved February 15, 2022, from https://web.archive.org/web/20111005063245/;<http://www.culturalivre.org.br/artigos/IBSA_recommendations_Internet_Governance.pdf>.

261 Kaul, M. (2012, October 29). India changes its internet governance position — backs away from UN proposal. Uncut. https://web.archive.org/web/20121103094900/;<http://uncut.indexoncensorship.org/2012/10/india-internet-governance/.>

262 United Nations International Telecommunication Union. (1989). Final Acts of World Administrative Telegraph and Telephone Conference. Retrieved February 15, 2022, from <https://www.itu.int/dms_pub/itu-t/oth/3F/01/T3F010000010001PDFE.pdf>.

the time, the international community agreed in a treaty to expand the UN ITU's agency over GSM technologies. By 2012, the era of smartphones was in full swing, meaning that the GSM systems were increasingly blended together with the internet. This provided a rationale to consider expanding the UN ITU's mandate to cover the latter. Additionally, ever since 1963, the UN ITU had been managing telecommunication satellite orbit slot allocation, which by the late 2000s became part of mobile internet infrastructure.

The ITU and a coalition of States supporting it hoped to use these two points of entry to try and expand the organization's role in internet governance. To that end, the ITU scheduled a conference for December 2012 in Dubai, United Arab Emirates, invoking a periodical review clause embedded in the 1988 treaty. States such as Russia, China, Brazil, and South Africa revealed themselves to be among the most vocal proponents of an ITU-sponsored reform. On the other side, besides the United States with a clear national interest, a coalition of Western nations has emerged, including such States as Germany, United Kingdom, and Canada, who expressed concern that a multilateral governance model would effectively devolve management of the internet to national governments. According to them, this would entail creating an archipelago of subsystems with parallel rules in place of the existing United States-dominated platform, rather than creation of a multilateral legal framework. In such a case, illiberal regimes would find it much easier to use the internet as a tool of invigilation and censorship.[263]

Proposals under consideration, tendered by the ITU, included establishing regulatory oversight over IANA and ICANN functions by the United Nations (implying effective control by the ITU). The move was denounced by many American media outlets,[264] Google,[265] as well as the European

---

263 Thimm, J., & Schaller, C. (2014, October 22). Internet Governance and the ITU: Maintaining the Multistakeholder Approach - The German Perspective. Council on Foreign Relations. Retrieved February 15, 2022, from <https://www.cfr.org/report/internet-governance-and-itu-maintaining-multistakeholder-approach>.

264 McDowell, R. M. (2012, February 21). Robert McDowell: The U.N. Threat to Internet Freedom. The Wall Street Jorunal. <https://www.wsj.com/articles/SB10001424052970204792404577229074023195322>; Crovitz, G. L. (2012, June 18). Crovitz: The U.N.'s Internet Power Grab. The Wall Street Journal. <https://www.wsj.com/articles/SB10001424052702303822204577470532859210296>.

265 BBC News. (2012, November 21). Google attacks UN's internet treaty conference. BBC News. <https://www.bbc.co.uk/news/technology-20429625>.

Parliament[266] and the U.S. Congress.[267] The European Parliament claimed in its resolution that if successful, WCIT-12 would *negatively impact the internet, its architecture, operations, content and security, business relations, internet governance and the free flow of information online*. It capped the document by saying that *the ITU […] is not the appropriate body to assert regulatory authority over the internet*.[268] The U.S. House of Representatives decided by a rare 398-0 unanimous vote to denounce the ITU's bid. In its resolution it stated: *Proposals have been put forward for consideration at the WCIT-12 that would fundamentally alter the governance and operation of the Internet … [and] would attempt to justify increased government control over the Internet …*[269] It then invoked the 2009 Affirmation of Commitments as a proof that the United States is already moving toward a multi-stakeholder model on its own terms.

WCIT-12 ended in an impasse. At first, 600 gathered delegates were moving toward a compromise. According to the draft, the new ITR treaty would not mention the internet explicitly, but a separate non-binding resolution titled *To foster an enabling environment for the greater growth of the Internet* would express the international community's intent to create a multilateral oversight system sometime in the future. 89 of the 152 present State representatives signed up to this formula but a group of influential States, including the

266 European Parliament. (2012, November 19). Motion for a Resolution on the forthcoming World Conference on International Telecommunications (WCIT-12) of the International Telecommunication Union, and the possible expansion of the scope of international telecommunication regulations. European Union, 2012 - Source: European Parliament. Retrieved February 15, 2022, from <https://www.europarl.europa.eu/doceo/document/B-7-2012-0499_EN.html?redirect>.

267 Kasperowicz, P. (2016, February 3). House approves resolution to keep Internet control out of UN hands. TheHill. <https://thehill.com/blogs/floor-action/house/271153-house-approves-resolution-to-keep-internet-control-out-of-un-hands>.

268 European Parliament. (2012, November 19). Motion for a Resolution on the forthcoming World Conference on International Telecommunications (WCIT-12) of the International Telecommunication Union, and the possible expansion of the scope of international telecommunication regulations. European Union, 2012 - Source: European Parliament. Retrieved February 15, 2022, from <https://www.europarl.europa.eu/doceo/document/B-7-2012-0499_EN.html?redirect>.

269 Kasperowicz, P. (2016, February 3). House approves resolution to keep Internet control out of UN hands. TheHill. <https://thehill.com/blogs/floor-action/house/271153-house-approves-resolution-to-keep-internet-control-out-of-un-hands>.

United States, Canada, France, Germany, India, Japan, New Zealand, and the United Kingdom eventually refused to do so. The U.S. delegation head Terry Kramer said: "We cannot support a treaty that is not supportive of the multi-stakeholder model of Internet governance." The main point of tension was the last-minute revision in the draft update to the ITR's that referenced the ITU's role in addressing unsolicited bulk communications and network security on the internet.[270] Despite the apparent disunity and a strong block of States, rejecting the new treaty, the ITU published a press release stating: *New global telecoms treaty agreed in Dubai*.[271] Due to the discord between States and especially due to the final act's rejection by the United States, the international status of the WCIT-12 treaty remains unclear until today.

Soon after the WCIT-12 conference, a high-profile event contributed to the tension between States on the subject of international legal framework regulating cyberspace. In 2013, Edward Snowden, a former employee of the U.S. National Security Agency (NSA), revealed an array of classified government documents confirming that the United States is continuously using its control over the internet to conduct cyber espionage operations. The scale of the Snowden's revelation was monumental. He revealed 160,000 emails and 7,900 documents he intercepted from the NSA, as well as 900,000 top secret files of the U.S. Department of Defense.[272] Among those many files, a system of surveillance was described, which was used by the United

---

270 Pfanner, E. (2012, December 14). Citing Internet Standoff, U.S. Rejects International Telecommunications Treaty. The New York Times. <https://www.nytimes.com/2012/12/14/technology/14iht-treaty14.html>; Japan, West snub rules for Net curbs | The Japan Times Online. (2012, December 16). Japan Times. <https://web.archive.org/web/20121221143609/>;<http://www.japantimes.co.jp/text/nn20121216a7.html>; World Conference on International Telecommunications. (2012, December 14). WCIT-12 Final Acts Signatories. United Nations International Telecommunication Union. Retrieved February 15, 2022, from <https://www.itu.int/osg/wcit-12/highlights/signatories.html>.

271 United Nations International Telecommunication Union. (2012, December 14). New global telecoms treaty agreed in Dubai. Retrieved February 15, 2022, from <https://www.itu.int/net/pressoffice/press_releases/2012/92.aspx>

272 Leopold, J. (2015, June 4). Exclusive: Inside Washington's Quest to Bring Down Edward Snowden. Vice. <https://news.vice.com/en/article/qv54gd/exclusive-inside-washingtons-quest-to-bring-down-edward-snowden>; Gellman, B., Tate, J., & Soltani, A. (2014, July 6). In NSA-intercepted data, those not targeted far outnumber the foreigners who are. The Washington Post. <https://www.washingtonpost.com/world/

States to spy on all internet traffic, utilizing the fact that the internet root infrastructure is almost entirely located within its sovereign borders. The system's name is XKeyscore.[273] The shock caused by this information gave a new lease of life to the international movement aimed at transitioning legal control over the internet away from the United States. On October 7, 2013, the leading internet governance organizations (mapped out in Figure 6) agreed to sign the Montevideo Convention, which called for an accelerated transition toward a multi-stakeholder, effectively defying the United States policy to retain the status quo.[274]

Following the Montevideo Convention, ICANN's CEO Fadi Chehade and Brazil's President Dilma Rousseff released a joint statement, expressing their wish to organize a global conference on the future of international governance over the internet. At the time Dilma Rousseff was publicly decrying NSA's tapping of all her electronic communication through XKeyscore, as revealed by Edward Snowden. To counter this momentum, the United States resolved to actually join the new partnership, influencing it from within. Thus, the NET Mundial Initiative (NMI) was formed. It was co-sponsored by Brazil, the United States, and ICANN. The NMI organized a conference in 2014 to discuss a transition toward a multi-stakeholder internet governance model. The international community reacted with much skepticism that then turned into an open denouncement when the draft of the resolution prepared ahead of the conference was published. It would grant the United States, Brazil, ICANN, the Internet Society, and the Internet Architecture Board permanent seats on an otherwise rotational 25-member international governance council. This formula drew comparisons with the UN Security Council, with its embedded privilege for the permanent member States, and was immediately rejected by States such as China and Russia. The initiative

---

national-security/in-nsa-intercepted-data-those-not-targeted-far-outnumber-the-foreigners-who-are/2014/07/05/8139adf8-045a-11e4-8572-4b1b969b6322_story.html>.

273 Greenwald, G., & Ackerman, S. (2017, July 15). How the NSA is still harvesting your online data. The Guardian. <https://www.theguardian.com/world/2013/jun/27/nsa-online-metadata-collection>.

274 Internet Corporation for Assigned Names and Numbers. (2013, October 7). Montevideo Statement on the Future of Internet Cooperation. Retrieved February 15, 2022, from <https://www.icann.org/en/announcements/details/montevideo-statement-on-the-future-of-internet-cooperation-7-10-2013-en>.

was also diminished by then-ongoing impeachment proceedings in Brazil and the following imprisonment of Dilma Rousseff.[275] NMI's mandate expired in July 2016 without any conclusion or legal impact.

In March 2016, in an effort to defuse a growing tension in the international community, the United States unexpectedly announced that it would revoke its direct oversight over ICANN later that year.[276] The announcement took place in the context of Barack Obama's presidential term nearing its end. In October 2016, the Joint Program Agreement between the U.S. government and ICANN lapsed without extension, technically leaving the U.S.-based nonprofit organization to oversee vital functions of the internet globally. Oversight over ICANN itself was transitioned from the U.S. government to a board of 21 members, representing all world regions and key industrial stakeholders such as companies Google or Cisco, as laid out in the NGO's bylaws. This was perceived as a legacy-building decision on behalf of President Barack Obama's administration.[277] In actuality, the United States has retained plenty of technical control over the internet as well as political clout over ICANN. The root infrastructure is still located on U.S. soil and XKeyscore is up and running. Moreover, since ICANN formally remains a nonprofit organization in California, The United States retains an array of hard and soft means of influencing its conduct.

The current struggle over international oversight over the internet fits the theory of international regimes developed by Stephen Krasner. At the height of the Cold War, long before cyberspace a point of contention for the international community, he theorized a hegemonic power, whose clout is declining or about to decline, is bound to experience growing dissent and incongruence from smaller countries. The dissent mostly concentrates around the systems developed by the hegemonic power. At the height of their power,

275 Marcello, M. A., & Boadle, A. (2016, September 1). Brazil's Rousseff ousted by Senate, Temer sworn in. REuters. <https://www.reuters.com/article/us-brazil-impeachment/brazils-rousseff-ousted-by-senate-temer-sworn-in-idUSKCN114071>.

276 Farrell, M. (2017, February 21). Quietly, symbolically, US control of the internet was just ended. The Guardian. <https://www.theguardian.com/technology/2016/mar/14/icann-internet-control-domain-names-iana>.

277 Westby, J. (2016, September 24). 7 Days Before Obama Gives Away Internet & National Security. Forbes. <https://www.forbes.com/sites/jodywestby/2016/09/24/7-days-before-obama-gives-away-internet-national-security/>.

hegemonic States tend to establish systems that benefit them. As they then lose clout, other participants of those systems start calling for a more equal distribution of power within the developed structures. This theory was first articulated by Stephen Krasner to describe dynamics at the United Nations but it since has been interpreted more universally to describe the historical trajectory of many international systems.[278]

2.4.2 Efforts to establish norms regulating conduct of States in cyberspace

In parallel to the discussion on the internet oversight model, an equally tense process has been taking place among international actors when it comes to legal rules governing State conduct in cyberspace. Due to the internet's meteoric rise, the true scale of its potential international impact was only realized around the turn of the millennia, some 30 years after ARPANET's deployment. The international legal framework governing the technical oversight of cyberspace, while fragmented and disconnected from the established UN-based system, at least has been developing organically alongside the internet's expansion. The same cannot be said about the international rules governing application of the existing international law on State responsibility for breaches of their legal obligations in cyberspace. As a result, the process of integrating cyberspace into the international legal order only started relatively recently and has been progressing rapidly to catch-up with the digital reality.

The watershed moment came in 2003 when the World Summit on the Information Society was held at the behest of the UN ITU. The summit was mentioned before in Section 1.4 in the context of the struggle over the international legal framework on technical oversight of the internet. That same event also tackled the issue of broader application of international law in cyberspace. The Geneva Convention, passed at the summit, provided political momentum for launching a new initiative at the UN General Assembly. In December that year, UN GA established *The United Nations Group of Governmental Experts on Developments in the field of information and telecommunications in the context of*

278 Krasner, Stephen D. "Transforming International Regimes: What the Third World Wants and Why." International Studies Quarterly 25, no. 1 (1981): pages 119–28. <https://doi.org/10.2307/2600213>.

international security or UN GGE for short.[279] It was framed as an expansion of annual reports on the subject that the UN Secretary-General had been presenting to the UN General Assembly since 1998.[280] The mandate for the group was designed in a particularly narrow fashion, in order to avoid a veto from the United States. UN GGE exists until today and is overseen by the UN First Committee, whose scope of competence is Disarmament & International Security.[281] Thus, any resolutions and discussions on the subject of political oversight over the internet have to stay within that specific context of international security. This has an impact on the shape of development of international norms in cyberspace. Subjects such as espionage, technical governance, or digital privacy are not only shunned by the Group's members but also essentially forbidden from being discussed. At the same time, the UN GGE focuses on topics such as cybercrime, digital terrorism, or cyberwarfare. Six GGEs have been established since 2003, each with a biannual mandate.[282] The latest UN GGE was established in 2019.

During the initial 2004–2005 Mandate, the GGE consisted of 10 UN member states. This number has grown to 25 during the most recent 2019–2021 mandate. Five permanent members of the UN Security Council are customarily always included, while the rest of the slots are filled on the basis of equitable

279 United Nations General Assembly Resolution 58/32. (2003, December 18). 58/32 - Developments in the field of information and telecommunications in the context of international security. Retrieved February 15, 2022, from <https://undocs.org/A/RES/58/32>.

280 United Nations Office for Disarmament Affairs. (n.d.). Developments in the field of information and telecommunications in the context of international security—UNODA. Retrieved February 15, 2022, from <https://www.un.org/disarmament/ict-security/>.

281 Permanent Mission of Switzerland to the United Nations. (2017). The GA Handbook A practical guide to the United Nations General Assembly. Retrieved February 15, 2022, from <https://www.eda.admin.ch/dam/mission-new-york/en/documents/UN_GA__Final.pdf>.

282 Six GGEs have been convened so far—in 2004/2005 (A/RES/58/32), 2009/2010 (A/RES/60/45), 2012/2013 (A/RES/66/24), 2014/2015 (A/RES/68/243), 2016/2017 (A/RES/70/237), and 2019/2021 (A/RES/73/266); Elżbieta Karska, & Karol Karski (2014), Introduction: The Use of Private Military and Security Companies by the United Nations, International Community Law Review 16(4), pages 399–404, <https://doi.org/10.1163/18719732-12341286>, <https://www.researchgate.net/publication/286258554>.

geographic distribution among members of the five UN Regional Groups.[283] States interested in participating in UN GGE send an official request for a seat upon a biannual call for expression of interest, issued by the Office of the High Representative for Disarmament Affairs. The High Representative is tasked with proposing a composition to the UN Secretary-General who in turn makes the final decision on the matter. While doing so, UNSC takes into account not only the geographic balance, but also the political, cultural, and economic one as well as other factors such as demonstrated interest in the topic, personnel capacity, representation in other UN bodies, and even general conduct.[284] Over the past years, countries began launching extensive lobbying campaigns with the aim of facilitating their request with the UN Secretary-General. Initial UN GGE saw many member countries nominate technical experts to represent them in the group. However, over time they became replaced by professional diplomats and international lawyers, who are better versed with sometimes intense diplomatic negotiations. A practice has developed in which each member State is represented by a diplomatic expert, who is accompanied by a technical adviser. UN GGE usually organizes two formal sessions a year with a number of informal meetings in between. Every decision has to be reached by consensus and proceedings are not open to the public. As long as the discussion abides by the thematic mandate of the UN First Committee, the Group enjoys much latitude in shaping the agenda and the work plan. A Chairperson, chosen through an internal vote from among the members, coordinates the work. The choice of the Chairperson can strongly influence the selected topics and group's goals. The Russian Federation chaired the UN GGE in the period 2004–2005 and then again in the period 2009–2010. Australia led the GGE during the period 2012–2013, Brazil did so during 2014–2015, and Germany did so during 2016–2017. The current UN GGE is again led by Brazil (see Figure 7 for details).[285]

---

283 United Nations - Department for General Assembly and Conference Management. (n.d.). United Nations Regional Groups. Retrieved February 15, 2022, from <https://www.un.org/dgacm/>.

284 Geneva Internet Platform. (2022, January 28). UN GGE and OEWG. Digital Watch Observatory. Retrieved February 15, 2022, from <https://dig.watch/processes/un-gge>.

285 United Nations Office for Disarmament Affairs. (n.d.-b). Fact Sheet Developments In The Field Of Information And Telecommunications In The Context Of International

The UN Group of Government Experts became the main platform for shaping the process of delineating application of international law in cyberspace. The bulk of its work is research on existing and potential cyber threats to international security and potential remedies.

The UN GGE's 2009–2010 cohort established a three-pillar system for international coordination on those challenges and it has been espoused by all subsequent UN GGEs.[286]

The three-pillar system is also referred to as a *Framework for Responsible State Behaviour in Cyberspace.* It consists of:

Resolutions on application of international law, as well as defining voluntary non-binding norms, rules and principles of responsible behavior of States	**Capacity building**	**Confidence-building measures**

This framework and the language of the three-prong approach was espoused by G-20 and the OSCE, confirming its role as the basis for broader international collaboration.[287] Between 2009 and now, the African Union, European Union, The Organization of American States, and The ASEAN Regional Forum have all joined the GGE consultation process coordinated by the United Nations Office for Disarmament Affairs, elevating its role as the focal point on the matter.[288]

Security. Retrieved February 15, 2022, from <https://unoda-web.s3.amazonaws.com/wp-content/uploads/2019/07/Information-Security-Fact-Sheet-July-2019.pdf>.

286 United Nations Secretary-General. (2010, July 30). Group of Governmental Experts on Developments in the Field of Information and Telecommunications in the Context of International Security - Note by the Secretary-General. Retrieved February 15, 2022, from <https://undocs.org/A/65/201>.

287 Geneva Internet Platform. (2022, January 28). UN GGE and OEWG. Digital Watch Observatory. Retrieved February 15, 2022, from <https://dig.watch/processes/un-gge>.

288 Ibid.

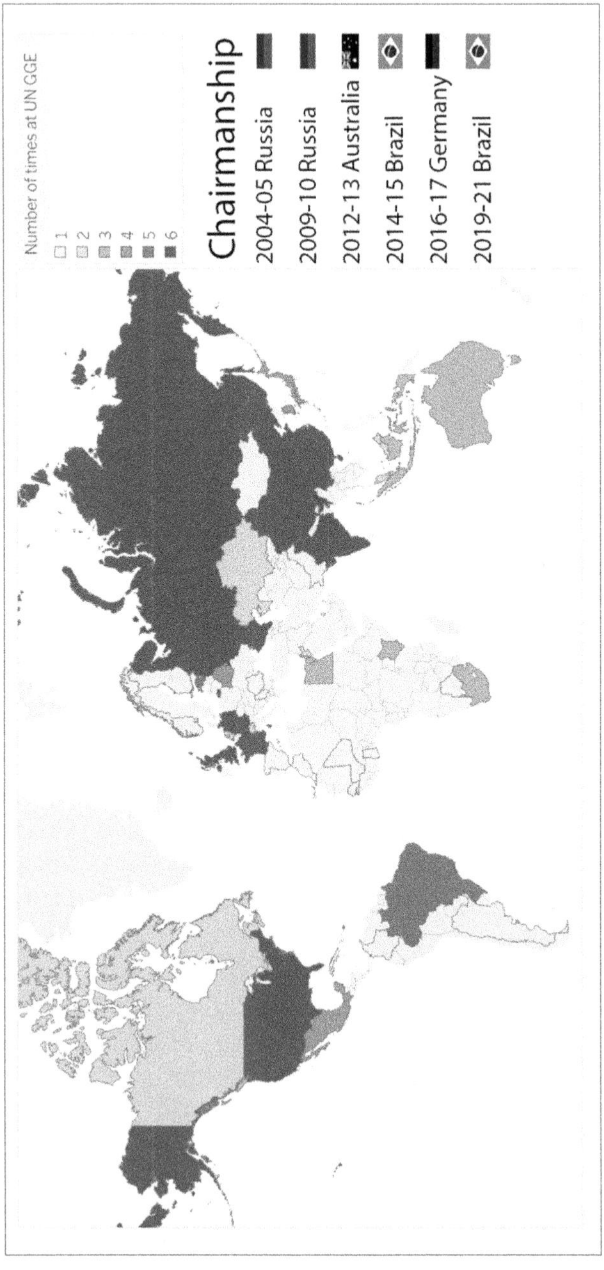

Figure 7. States, which have sent representatives to the UN GGE
Source: Own elaboration using Tableau

In 2013, the UN GGE emerged with a historic consensus, reporting to the UN General Assembly its conclusion that the existing international law applies to cyberspace. This conclusion, approved by the UN General Assembly in a resolution, clarified application of the existing legal norms in cyberspace:

> The report reflects the Group's conclusion that international law and in particular the United Nations Charter, is applicable and is essential to maintaining peace and stability and promoting an open, secure, peaceful and accessible ICT environment. The Group also concluded that State sovereignty and the international norms and principles that flow from it apply to States' conduct of ICT-related activities and to their jurisdiction over ICT infrastructure with their territory; States must meet their international obligations regarding internationally wrongful acts attributable to them.[289]

The key conclusion coming from this report is that international legal norms and principles do apply to States' ICT-related activities. ICT here stands for information communications technologies and includes operations in cyberspace. This implies that all the existing notions such as the *Principle of Non-Intervention*, *Prohibited Use of Force*, or *Armed Attack* can potentially be breached by cyber means. While this conclusion might sound obvious to modern ears, that was not the case back in 2013 when acts committed in cyberspace were still often considered less real or impactful than those committed through conventional, physical actions, despite mounting evidence to the contrary. The fact that the report was co-authored by all five UN Security Council permanent member States and approved by UN General Assembly in a resolution gives it a very strong claim to be a manifestation of *opinio juris* (emergence of a binding international customary rule). *International custom, as evidence of a general practice accepted as law* is one of the four potential sources of international law, as laid out by the Statute of the International Court of Justice.[290] For the emergence of a customary rule to take place, there must exist consensus within the international community on the matter as

---

289 United Nations Secretary-General. (2013, June 24). Group of Governmental Experts on Developments in the Field of Information and Telecommunications in the Context of International Security - Note by the Secretary-General. Retrieved February 15, 2022, from <https://undocs.org/A/68/98>.

290 International Court of Justice. (1945, June 26). Statute of the Court. Article 38. Retrieved February 15, 2022, from <https://www.icj-cij.org/en/statute>.

to a certain practice being a legal obligation, and the State conduct must be consistent with that consensus.[291] Both of those criteria have arguably been met for a customary rule that applies existing international legal obligations of States in cyberspace to emerge (see Figure 8 for the key developments in the area of cyberspace in the international community over the past years).[292]

The subsequent UN GGE seized on that momentum in its 2015 report and *offered for consideration by States* the so-called 11 voluntary, non-bindings norms, rules, and principles (bolding added):

> (a) Consistent with the purposes of the United Nations, including to maintain international peace and security, **States should cooperate in developing and applying measures to increase stability and security in the use of ICTs and to prevent ICT practices that are acknowledged to be harmful** or that may pose threats to international peace and security.
>
> (b) **In case of ICT incidents, States should consider all relevant information, including the event's larger context**, the challenges of attribution in the ICT environment and the nature and extent of the consequences.
>
> (c) **States should not knowingly allow their territory to be used for internationally wrongful acts using ICTs.**
>
> (d) **States should consider how best to cooperate** to exchange information, assist each other, prosecute terrorist and criminal use of ICTs and implement other cooperative measures to address such threats. States may need to consider whether new measures need to be developed in this respect.
>
> (e) **States, in ensuring the secure use of ICTs, should respect Human Rights Council resolutions** 20/8 and 26/13 on the promotion, protection and enjoyment of human rights on the Internet, as well as General Assembly resolutions 68/167 and 69/166 on the right to privacy in the digital age, to guarantee full respect for human rights, including the right to freedom of expression.
>
> (f) **A State should not conduct or knowingly support ICT activity contrary to its obligations under international law that intentionally damages critical**

---

291 Oxford University References. (n.d.). Opinio Juris. Retrieved February 15, 2022, from <https://www.oxfordreference.com/view/10.1093/oi/authority.20110803100251755>.

292 For more insights on how international customary norms emerge see: Harris, D., & Sivakumaran, S. (2020). Cases and Materials on International Law (9th edition). Sweet & Maxwell.

infrastructure or otherwise impairs the use and operation of critical infrastructure to provide services to the public.

(g) **States should take appropriate measures to protect their critical infrastructure from ICT threats**, taking into account General Assembly resolution 58/199 on the creation of a global culture of cybersecurity and the protection of critical information infrastructures, and other relevant resolutions.

(h) **States should respond to appropriate requests for assistance by another State whose critical infrastructure is subject to malicious ICT acts.** States should also respond to appropriate requests to mitigate malicious ICT activity aimed at the critical infrastructure of another State emanating from their territory, taking into account due regard for sovereignty.

(i) **States should take reasonable steps to ensure the integrity of the supply chain so that end users can have confidence in the security of ICT products.** States should seek to prevent the proliferation of malicious ICT tools and techniques and the use of harmful hidden functions.

(j) **States should encourage responsible reporting of ICT vulnerabilities and share associated information on available remedies** to such vulnerabilities to limit and possibly eliminate potential threats to ICTs and ICT dependent infrastructure.

(k) **States should not conduct or knowingly support activity to harm the information systems of the authorized emergency response teams** (sometimes known as computer emergency response teams or cybersecurity incident response teams) of another State. A State should not use authorized emergency response teams to engage in malicious international activity.[293]

In laying out the list, the UN GGE aimed to contribute to the first of the three pillars laid out in the 2013 report, namely the one titled *Resolutions on application of international law, as well as defining voluntary non-binding norms, rules and principles of responsible behavior of States*. Some of the points of focus of the 11 norms are: framing cyberwarfare as an *internationally wrongful act*, applicability of the international human rights framework to the digital interactions, and forbidding states from willingly hosting malicious international cyber activities. Some interpretations of the norms might even imply States' responsibility for unwilling hosting of such

293 United Nations General Assembly Resolution 228/35. (2015, July 22). Group of Governmental Experts on Developments in the Field of Information and Telecommunications in the Context of International Security - Note by the Secretary-General. Retrieved February 15, 2022, from <https://documents-dds-ny.un.org/doc/UNDOC/GEN/N15/228/35/PDF/N1522835.pdf?OpenElement>.

operations as they are compelled to *take reasonable steps to ensure the integrity of the supply chain* as per the document. This norm establishing states' responsibility is also sometimes called *Due Diligence* (this subject is analyzed in-depth in Chapter 2).[294] The 11 non-binding norms put forward by the UN GGE are not customary rules of international law since, by their very definition, they lack an international agreement on their binding character. In time, however, some, if not all, of the proposed norms are likely to be recognized by several States as binding. This organic process can result in the norms becoming binding international law.[295]

The second pillar maned in the 2013 UN GGE report, capacity building, provides guidelines for countries on how to strengthen their ICT infrastructure and oversight, as well to on how to establish a network of national CERTs—Computer Emergency Response Teams. This task was formally assumed and endorsed by six regional organizations: the African Union, the ASEAN Regional Forum, the European Union, the League of Arab States, the Organization of American States, the OSCE, and the Shanghai Cooperation Organization (with the door remaining open for other regional organizations willing to join).[296] The case for coordinated capacity building and State responsibility in that area, made by UN GGE, was strengthened by the UN General Assembly Resolution 64/211 titled *Creation of a global culture of cybersecurity and taking stock of national efforts to protect critical information infrastructures*.[297] Despite its seemingly neutral character, the capacity-building pillar stirred much controversy in the United States, where it is frequently perceived as a backdoor way of expanding the UN ITU's mandate over the internet. There are signs suggesting that this might be the case. For instance, the

---

294 Moynihan, Harriet. (2019, December). The Application of International Law to State Cyberattacks. Chatham House. Page 2—Summary. <https://www.chathamhouse.org/2019/12/application-international-law-state-cyberattacks>.

295 More on the subject can be read here: Schmitt, Michael. N. (2021, October 8). The Sixth United Nations GGE and International Law in Cyberspace. Just Security. <https://www.justsecurity.org/76864/the-sixth-united-nations-gge-and-international-law-in-cyberspace/>.

296 United Nations General Assembly Resolution 228/35. (2013, June 24). Group of Governmental Experts on Developments in the Field of Information and Telecommunications in the Context of International Security - Note by the Secretary-General. Retrieved February 15, 2022, from <https://undocs.org/A/68/98>.

297 United Nations General Assembly Resolution. (2010, March 17). 64/211. Creation of a global culture of cybersecurity and taking stock of national efforts to protect critical information infrastructures. Retrieved February 15, 2022, from <https://undocs.org/pdf?symbol=en/A/RES/64/211>.

UN General Assembly Resolution 64/211 calls for the UN ITU's greater involvement in coordinating the capacity building work.[298]

The third pillar listed in the 2013 UN GGE report, confidence-building measures, became a platform for a number of multi- and bilateral initiatives around the world. These range from a movement by certain States to publicly assert the 11 voluntary norms as binding international law, through intellectual property protection and anti-spying arrangements, to an array of statements on good relations. This is especially crucial in the context of the developing international legal customary environment, which is shaping up whenever country practice and collective understanding of binding legal commitments solidifies. International law regulating cyberspace is still a new phenomenon and emerging legal trends become clear with each of these initiatives. To that end, a visual summary of 98 key initiatives and statements between 2006 and 2018 can be found as follows:

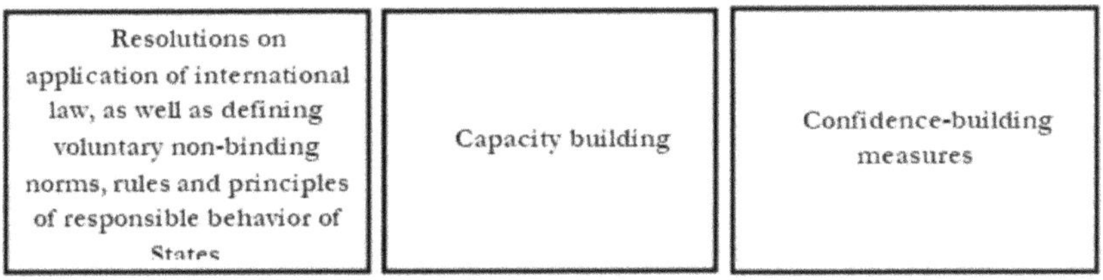

Figure 8. Chronology of the key events pertaining to regulation of cyber activities
Source: Own elaboration

Cyberspace law is at an early stage of development as a branch of the international legal system. For this reason, it is still very malleable and susceptible to impact by the outcomes of relevant international events and treaties. In this context, the above-assembled list is serving the purpose of identifying the emerging trends. When consistent State practice, coupled by collective perception by States that a certain norm constitutes an obligation (*opinio juris*), a customary international law might emerge.[299] At the center of many of the events on the list are the 11 voluntary, non-binding norms put forward by the UN GGE in 2015. A number of States and regional organizations embraced

298 Ibid.

299 Cornell University - Legal Information Institute. (n.d.). Opinio Juris (international law). Retrieved February 15, 2022, from <https://www.law.cornell.edu/wex/opinio_juris_(international_law)>.

them and asserted them to be binding parts of international law, potentially launching the process of their transition toward becoming customary laws. In general, six key events between the years 2006–2022 deserve particular attention due to their potential international legal impact on development of the field:

- 2015 bid for the UN to recognize the Internet Code of Conduct for Information Security;
- 2017 adoption by the European Council of *The Cyber Diplomacy Toolbox;*
- 2018 subscription in principle to the 11 voluntary, non-binding norms by ASEAN;
- 2018 publication of the *Singapore Package* by the Global Commission on the Stability of Cyberspace;
- 2021 UN GGE Report;
- 2021 UN OEWG Report.

In 2015, member states of the Shanghai Cooperation Organization (Russian Federation, China, Kazakhstan, Kyrgyzstan, Tajikistan, and Uzbekistan) submitted to the UN Secretary-General a revised draft of the Internet Code of Conduct for Information Security (originally proposed in 2011). It was subsequently acknowledged in the UN GGE's 2015 report.[300] The draft sparked backlash from Western States, as its wording implied extended government control over civic society activity on the internet. The draft revived tensions from WCIT-12 in Dubai, with many Global South States supporting Shanghai Cooperation Organization's call for more sovereign power over the internet (defying the existing United States-centric) as a form of democratizing it.

[300] United Nations General Assembly Resolution. (2015, January 13). Letter dated 9 January 2015 from the Permanent Representatives of China, Kazakhstan, Kyrgyzstan, the Russian Federation, Tajikistan and Uzbekistan to the United Nations addressed to the Secretary-General. Retrieved February 15, 2022, from <https://documents-dds-ny.un.org/doc/UNDOC/GEN/N15/014/02/PDF/N1501402.pdf?OpenElement>; Rõigas, H. (n.d.). An Updated Draft of the Code of Conduct Distributed in the United Nations—What's New? NATO Cooperative Cyber Defence Center of Excellence. Retrieved February 15, 2022, from <https://ccdcoe.org/incyder-articles/an-updated-draft-of-the-code-of-conduct-distributed-in-the-united-nations-whats-new/<; <https://www.cfr.org/blog/will-china-and-russias-updated-code-conduct-get-more-traction-post-snowden-era>;

The draft was rejected by the United Nations but it managed to signal disunity and lack of consensus on legal matters surrounding international oversight of the internet among States.
The issue of the current international legal setup, concentrating power in the hands of the United States government and defying the established UN ITU-based mode, continues to be a source of tension.

In 2017, The Council of European Union adopted *The Cyber Diplomacy Toolbox*,[301] in which it formulated a joint European Policy on malicious cyber-activity. First, it stated that malicious cyber activities can constitute wrongful acts under international law, embracing the key legal postulate of the UN GGE 2013 Report. Based on that assertion, it assumed its ability to impose sanctions toward both State and non-State actors that engage in such malicious activity. Third, it defined the rules of EU diplomatic response to such activity, writing, among other provisions, that it must be *proportionate to the scope, scale, duration, intensity, complexity, sophistication and impact of the cyber activity*.[302] To date, only the United States has ever imposed sanctions pertaining to malicious cyber activity (following the purported Sony Corporation hack by North Korea described in Section 1.2). The Cyber Diplomacy Toolbox asserts the EU's ability to do so too. Besides minimally impactful measures, such as statements and recalling ambassadors, the possible means also include reduced access to the EU single market and freezing of assets held at EU-based financial institutions.[303]

In 2018, ASEAN Ministerial Conference on Cybersecurity formally espoused in principle the 11 voluntary, non-binding norms recommended in the 2015 Report of the United Nations Group of Governmental Experts, embracing them as binding international law among the organization's member States.[304] The ten member States of the multilateral platform sent a strong

---

301 Council of the European Union. (2017, June 19). Cyber attacks: EU ready to respond with a range of measures, including sanctions. Retrieved February 15, 2022, from <https://www.consilium.europa.eu/en/press/press-releases/2017/06/19/cyber-diplomacy-toolbox/>.

302 Ibid.

303 Ibid.

304 Cyber Security Agency of Singapore. (2018, September 20). Singapore International Cyber Week 2018 - Highlights and Testimonials. Retrieved February 15, 2022, from <https://www.csa.gov.sg/news/press-releases/sicw-2018-highlights-and-testimonials>

signal this way that they commit to observe the norms. This type of act can be seen as an important step on the way to establishing *opinio juris* within the international community regarding the 11 voluntary norms' transition toward becoming binding customary international law. That same year, Global Commission on the Stability of Cyberspace (GCSC), has published the *Singapore Package*—a document embracing the 11 voluntary non-binding norms and proposing six additional legal norms regulating State and non-State actor behavior in cyberspace.[305] The norms build on and expand the UN GGE's, using a much stronger language to define States' responsibilities and rights. The six additional legal norms are:

- Norm to Avoid Tampering;
- Norm Against Commandeering of ICT Devices into Botnets;
- Norm for States to Create a Vulnerability Equities Process;
- Norm to Reduce and Mitigate Significant Vulnerabilities;
- Norm on Basic Cyber Hygiene as Foundational Defense;
- Norm Against Offensive Cyber Operations by Non-State Actors.[306]

The GCSC initiative is sponsored by the Netherlands, France, Estonia, Japan, Singapore, and Switzerland, with active engagement from other developed States and key civic society and private sector actors, such as the Internet Society, Microsoft, or Google.[307] The proposed additional norms would create a set of responsibilities related to maintenance of the internet system and monitoring of access to it by potential malicious actors within States' own borders.

One of the most recent key developments in the area of international cyber law is the UN GGE Report of 2021. It is an effect of a multi-State consensus, including all five UN Security Council permanent members. The report was in the making for two years and was supported by six regional consultations with AU, EU, OAS, OSCE, ARF, and ASEAN. It was also approved by a UN

---

305 Global Commission on the stability of Cyberspace. (2018, November). Norm Package Singapore. Retrieved February 15, 2022, from <https://cyberstability.org/wp-content/uploads/2018/11/GCSC-Singapore-Norm-Package-3MB.pdf>.

306 Ibid.

307 Ibid.

General Assembly Resolution.[308] The fact that the UN GGE managed to find a consensus is a success in its own right after the 2016–2017 term of the Group failed to find an agreed-upon conclusion.

The main achievement within the Report was the acknowledgment that the International Humanitarian law does apply in cyberspace.[309] While this statement is technically included in the 2013 UN GGE Report's assertion that international law applies in cyberspace in general, there remained an opened question regarding the parts of international that do not directly link to the *Principle of Sovereignty* (since it was presented as the main backbone if the international law's applicability in cyberspace). The Report did not explicitly assert that countermeasures are applicable in cyberspace. Neither did it propose for the so-called *Due Diligence* requirement to be applicable. Nevertheless, the UN GGE left both subjects open to deliberation in the future.[310] Both those aspects are some of the most hotly debated subjects in the context of international law in cyberspace. Those subjects are discussed in Chapter 4 (*Countermeasures*) and Chapter 5 (*Due Diligence*) respectively.

Not all developments in the area of cyber international law take the form of a document. As legal arrangements on cyber-activity emerge as the new branch of international law, international political coalitions emerge too. One of them has already been mentioned in the paragraph earlier. It is the Russian–Chinese alliance, with active support of an array of other, mostly non-Western States. Another active alliance is called *Five Eyes* (FVEY). The intelligence-sharing arrangement was established in 1941 between five Anglophone States: United States, United Kingdom, Canada, Australia, and New Zealand, with the immediate purpose of helping defeat Nazi Germany. The alliance then became instrumental in combating Soviet spying activities during the Cold War. Following the collapse of the Soviet Union, FVEY

---

308 United Nations General Assembly Resolution 228/35. (2021, July 14). Group of Governmental Experts on Developments in the Field of Information and Telecommunications in the Context of International Security - Note by the Secretary-General. Retrieved February 15, 2022, from <https://front.un-arm.org/wp-content/uploads/2021/08/A_76_135-2104030E-1.pdf>.

309 Schmitt, Michael. N (2021, October 8). The Sixth United Nations GGE and International Law in Cyberspace. Just Security. <https://www.justsecurity.org/76864/the-sixth-united-nations-gge-and-international-law-in-cyberspace/>.

310 Ibid.

lost some of its relevance until the emergence of malicious cyber-activity became a threat to Western-style democracies. At present, it is a strategic intelligence cooperation program, which frequently attributes hostile cyber operations to State and non-State actors based on its digital and conventional capacities. This for instance gave the United States the rationale to impose sanctions on North Korea in 2015. However, Five Eyes is not only a defensive program. On at least a few occasions, publications have emerged that called out FVEY's offensive actions. For example, in 2013 Russia Today announced that the United States' National Security Agency hacked Aeroflot, Russian Federation's national air carrier. This was then attributed to Five Eyes' hacking cooperation.[311]

Somewhat in parallel to the UN GGE, which is run by UN ODA, another crucial process is taking place under auspices of the United Nations. The Open-Ended Working group of the UN General Assembly launched its work in 2019. It is open to any interested UN member States. Ambassador Jürg Lauber of Switzerland was voted in as the OEWG's chairman. The resolution, which led to its creation, was sponsored by the Russian Federation.[312] The OEWG has been tasked with an analysis of the existing international legal norms formulated in past UN GGE reports. The resolution reserves the possibility of *introducing changes to the rules, norms and principles of responsible behaviour of States* agreed in the 2013 and 2015 UN GGE reports.[313] This means, some rules might be actually weakened. This would constitute undoing of the consistent progress observed over the past few years. The OEWG defined *six substantive issues* for discussion:

- Existing and potential threats;
- International law;

311 Russia Today International. (2013, September 1). NSA hacked Al-Jazeera and Russia's Aeroflot—report. Russia Today International. <https://www.rt.com/news/nsa-jazeera-aeroflot-spy-272/>.

312 United Nations General Assembly Resolution 73/27. (2018, December 11). 73/27. Developments in the field of information and telecommunications in the context of international security. Retrieved February 15, 2022, from <https://undocs.org/en/A/RES/73/27>.

313 United Nations Office for Disarmament Affairs. (n.d.-c). Open-ended Working Group—UNODA. Retrieved February 15, 2022, from <https://www.un.org/disarmament/open-ended-working-group/>.

- Rules, norms and principles;
- Regular institutional dialogue;
- Confidence-building measures;
- Capacity building.

More aspects of the UN GA OEWG might become potential points of contention. The UN GGE's mandate explicitly excludes the subject of internet governance by means of limiting its scope to the thematic domain of the United Nations Office for Disarmament Affairs. The resolution forming the UN OEWG does not contain such a limitation. The Russian Federation might be compelled to utilize the latter group as a platform for promoting its draft Internet Code of Conduct for Information Security, refuted earlier by many Western States.

What complicates the negotiations is that differences in interpretation of the UN OEWG's mandate have emerged between States. While the United States see its role mostly as space for promoting existing confidence-building measures and to getting other States involved in the GGE-led process, The Russian Federation expressed hopes for the UN OEWG to develop new kinds of measures and potentially establish a new permanent entity under UN auspices to discuss cyber issues in the future.[314] In 2021 both the UN GGE and UN OEWG released their reports broadly confirming earlier findings.[315] The UN General Assembly then took the decision to not set up UN GGE for another term, leaving UN OEWG as the only remaining platform within the UN system directly dealing with the subject of application of Public International Law in cyberspace. It is due to deliver its final report in 2025 for UN GA's consideration.

2.4.3 The role of non-State entities in developing the international legal framework regulating cyberspace

The rules-creation process in Public International Law is primarily the domain of States, with other subjects of international law having only a derivative

---

314 Digital Watch Observatory - Geneva Internet Platform. (2022, January 28). UN GGE and UN OEWG. Retrieved February 13, 2022, from <https://dig.watch/processes/un-gge/>.

315 "UN OEWG in 2023 - DW Observatory." Digital Watch Observatory. Retrieved November 27, 2023, from <https://dig.watch/processes/un-gge>.

legal standing.[316] This foundational understanding can be traced back to at least the Peace of Westphalia of 1648.[317] However, over the course of the twentieth and twenty-first century, an evolution of that framework could be observed whereas ever more international organizations and sometimes even domestic law entities, such as NGOs and private companies, started exerting more influence on the shape of international relations, eventually influencing the reality of how international law is being applied. This situation weakens the distinction of law-makers and law-takers in international law, potentially undermining its stability. Nevertheless, many scholars, such as Noortman and Ryngaert, claim that this has always been the case and recent scaling up of such activity is just a matter of proportions. Additionally, every State by definition is a law-maker and law-taker in international law, which prepares ground for a more lateral model than the one utilized in internal affairs.[318]

Certainly, the impact of non-State entities is indirect and formally only influencing States, which then make a decision to establish a new rule or acknowledge their existence via emergence of consistent customary practice coupled with an intent—*opinio juris*. However, it can help the process when traditional paths of law-making fail. François Delerue stated that "the recent failure of the UN GGE, and thus the current blockage of the inter-State multilateral discussions, may leave more space for non-State actors and, thus, reinforce their participation, or at least influence, in these matters."[319]

Taking stock of the civil society organizations' and the private companies' contributions to the field reveals a wealth of diverse initiatives. I listed them extensively in Figure 8. A few of them however are especially worth mentioning due to their scale and impact. These are:

---

316 Advisory Opinion on Legality of the Threat or Use of Nuclear Weapons. International Court of Justice. (1996, July 8). ICJ Reports 66, 74–75, paragraphs 18,19. Retrieved February 18, 2022, from <https://www.icj-cij.org/en/case/95>.

317 <https://www.jstor.org/stable/40109077>

318 Math Noortman and Cedric Ryngaert "International Law-Making by Non-State Actors: Changing the Model or Putting the Phenomenon into Perspective?" in "Non-State Actor Dynamics in International Law: From Law-Takers to Law-Makers" (Ashgate 2010)

319 Delerue, François. Cyber Operations and international law. Cambridge: Cambridge University Press, 2020. Page 24.

- 2014 Global Commission on Internet Governance initiative;
- 2015 Microsoft initiative to establish a *Digital Geneva Convention*;
- 2018 Charter of Trust on Cybersecurity;
- 2018 Geneva Dialogue on Responsible Behaviour in Cyberspace;
- 2019 Cybersecurity Tech Accord initiative;
- 2019 Digital Peace Now initiative.

The Global Commission on Internet Governance (the Bildt Commission) is an initiative launched at the 2014 World Economic Forum with the goal of articulating and advancing a strategic vision for the future of internet governance, including international legal norms. The initiative was housed at the famous Chatham House, and in 2016 produced a report summarizing its work.[320]

The company Microsoft has been also leading an initiative titled *Digital Geneva Convention*. Its new framing of the situation focuses on civilians and private sector actors, who might be caught in the crossfire of cyber conflicts between States in a similar fashion to how it is happening during conventional conflicts. The risk they envision is all the more palpable that the digital infrastructure, which is a frequent target of malicious cyber activity, is almost entirely owned by private companies and persons. For that reason, Microsoft is calling for a *Digital Geneva Convention*, that much like the Fourth Geneva Convention, would aim to reduce the harm to civilians.[321]

Charter of Trust on Cybersecurity was signed during the 2018 Munich Security Conference by Siemens and eight high-profile industry partners. The charter called for binding international legal rules to develop more trust and clarity on the subject of international relations in cyberspace. By 2020, the Charter signatories' group has grown to 16 members, including

320 Moynihan, Harriet. (2019, December). The Application of International Law to State Cyberattacks. Chatham House. <https://www.chathamhouse.org/2019/12/application-international-law-state-cyberattacks>; World Economic Forum. (2014, January 20). Global Commission on Internet Governance (2014–2016). Centre for International Governance Innovation. Retrieved February 15, 2022, from <https://www.cigionline.org/activities/global-commission-internet-governance-2014-2016/>.

321 Smith, Brad. (2018, May 15). The need for a Digital Geneva Convention. Microsoft. Retrieved February 13, 2022, from <https://blogs.microsoft.com/on-the-issues/2017/02/14/need-digital-geneva-convention/>.

companies such as Allianz, Airbus, Atos, Cisco, Daimler, Dell, Deutsche Telekom (T-Mobile parent firm), and IBM.[322]

Geneva Dialogue on Responsible Behaviour in Cyberspace, initiated in 2018, focuses on clarifying the roles and responsibilities of main actors in contributing to greater security and stability in cyberspace.[323] The main process for achieving this result is by combining the expertise of the private sector with the capacity of States to shape or clarify international legal norms. The initiative is spearheaded by a public-private partnership of Switzerland and more than 20 partner entities, including Microsoft, Cisco, Huawei, Siemens, and UBS.

The 2019 Cybersecurity Tech Accord has been signed by 39 companies, which are leaders in the field of cybersecurity. They include such industry giants as Microsoft, Dell, SAP, Oracle, and Facebook.[324] The accord promotes collaboration across tech companies on stability and resilience in cyberspace. It is regularly engaged with by the OECD, the United Nations, and other multilateral organizations as a valuable partner providing technical insights facilitating discussion on international legal norms.

Digital Peace Now is a global movement of over 130,000 persons from over 170 countries. By crowdsourcing information on digital harm caused by malicious cyber activity and showcasing the findings, it aims to enable attribution of hostile cyber operations and compel States to accelerate the process of developing a viable international framework for addressing the challenge.[325]

Another development is the emergence of private cyber-security companies, which provide services to both governments and private companies. Two of such companies, Crowdstrike and iSight, were mentioned earlier in this chapter. Another company, Tiversa, became known after its 2009 allegations that they discovered a security breach that had exposed President Barack Obama's helicopter operating protocols, Marine One, to

---

322 Charter of Trust. (2020). Charter of Trust. Retrieved February 15, 2022, from <https://www.charteroftrust.com/>.

323 Geneva Dialogue. Retrieved November 27, 2023. <https://genevadialogue.ch/>.

324 Cybersecurity Tech Accord. (2019, October 12). Cybersecurity Tech Accord. Retrieved February 15, 2022, from <https://cybertechaccord.org/about/>.

325 Demand Digital Peace Now. (2020, June 24). Demand Digital Peace Now. Retrieved February 15, 2022, from <https://digitalpeacenow.org/>.

the Iranian government.[326] This was however refuted by a whistleblower, who provided clues suggesting the company itself fabricated the leak in order to compel the government to hire it.[327] Similar controversies followed the company in its later activities.[328] Area1Security is a company offering email protection services to those concerned by international cyber security.[329] It provided analysis of American President Joe Biden's son Hunter's involvement with the Ukrainian company Burisma.[330] The aforementioned companies are just examples of a multi-billion-dollar industry that has been growing rapidly as the international legal framework on cyber activity is slowly forming.

2.4.4 The role of *soft law* in developing the international legal framework regulating cyberspace

In light of the hesitation of States to declare or recognize the existence of new binding norms covering cyberspace, and the growing role of non-State entities stepping in to fill the void, a unique dynamic has emerged. Cyberspace is exceptional in terms of scale non-State-led efforts to regulate its international legal status. The reason for this appears to be that States realize that the stakes are high, given how defining cyber technologies might be for every sphere of human existence in the future. Therefore, they are only willing to engage in discussion on two levels and even that in a very careful and limited manner:

---

326 Khatchadourian, R. (2019, October 28). A Cybersecurity Firm's Sharp Rise and Stunning Collapse. The New Yorker. <https://www.newyorker.com/magazine/2019/11/04/a-cybersecurity-firms-sharp-rise-and-stunning-collapse>.

327 Ibid.

328 Pagliery, J. (2015, May 7). Whistleblower accuses cybersecurity company of extorting clients. CNNMoney. <https://money.cnn.com/2015/05/07/technology/tiversa-labmd-ftc/index.html>; Schectman, J. (2016, March 18). Exclusive: DOJ probes allegations that Tiversa lied to FTC about data breaches. Reuters. <https://www.reuters.com/article/us-tiversa-doj-probe-exclusive-idUSKCN0WK027>.

329 Area 1 Security, Inc. (n.d.). Area 1 Security, Inc. Retrieved February 15, 2022, from <https://www.area1security.com/>.

330 Haaretz. (2020, January 14). Russians hacked key Ukrainian company in Trump impeachment inquiry, researchers say. Haaretz. <https://www.haaretz.com/world-news/europe/russians-hacked-key-ukrainian-company-in-trump-impeachment-inquiry-researchers-say-1.8399586>.

- Interpretation and clarification of application in cyberspace of existing norms;
- Proposing new non-binding voluntary norms that express responsible behavior of States in cyberspace.

As Peter Muchlinski put it, these two kinds of developments can be described as *soft law*, meant to create conditions for slow emergence of obligations by States that can then turn into a binding norm, rather than forcing them into it.[331] Meanwhile, new *hard law*, which means binding rules, is still controversial to the point of not being a feasible subject. While this might change with the new UN Programme of Action, due to launch after the last UN OEWG runs its course in 2025 (the Programme includes a provision on a possible international conference that could propose new binding norms[332]), the current vacuum is being filled in by non-State-led initiatives. This conduct by State is consistent with the policy of *ambiguity and silence*, mentioned in Chapter 1, meaning that States have no incentive to push for more regulation if they possess significant cyber capabilities or to reveal their cases of being a target of a hostile cyber operation (which could advance the process of regulating cyberspace) if they possess low cyber capabilities. This dynamic was especially reinforced by the failure of the UN GGE in 2017, when State representatives were not able to find consensus, preventing creation of a report that could be approved by the UN GA.[333] However, in any case, UN GGE was only generating *soft law* already. The only qualitative difference between activity by the United Nations and State-private partnerships in the area is

---

331 Peter Muchlinski "Multinational Enterprises as Actors in International Law: Creating "Soft Law" Obligations and "Hard Law" rights, page 1 4. <https://www.researchgate.net/publication/287448877_Multinational_enterprises_as_actors_in_international_law_Creating_'soft_law'_obligations_and_'hard_law'_rights>

332 United Nations General Assembly Resolution 77/L.73. "Programme of action to advance responsible State behaviour in the use of information and communications technologies in the context of international security." A/C.1/77/L.73. <https://digitallibrary.un.org/record/3991743?ln=en>.

333 "Back to Square One? The Fifth UN GGE Fails to Submit a Conclusive Report at the United Nations General Assembly." CCDCOE. Retrieved November 27, 2023. <https://ccdcoe.org/incyder-articles/back-to-square-one-the-fifth-un-gge-fails-to-submit-a-conclusive-report-at-the-un-general-assembly/.>

that the former enjoys the additional measure of validity and proof of *opinio juris* that comes with an approval by the UN General Assembly.

More broadly, this phenomenon fits into a trend observable in Public International Law, where multilateral treaties appear to be in decline, being replaced by non-committal declarations and proposals for voluntary rules of conduct. Timothy Meyer claims that this proves a structural shift in Public International Law that is an effect of multilateralism as opposed to old-style deal making by strongest powers: "The traditional treaty, conceived of as a contract between states, is in decline. [e.g.] Recent climate change negotiations have produced nonbinding instruments such as the Copenhagen and Cancun Accords; the financial crisis prompted governments to negotiate Basel III, a nonbinding framework for global banking regulation. (…) the contractual treaty's decline is symptomatic of a more fundamental shift in international governance: a turn towards collective decision-making at the expense of a state's individual authority over its obligations. (…) We are in the midst of a change in the processes through which international rules are negotiated. (…) The collective institutions work as a costly commitment device, limiting states' ability to choose which other states to negotiate with on an issue-by-issue basis and thereby ensuring states that they will have the right to participate in future negotiations. But because they can be more confident of a seat at the table tomorrow, states are willing to make greater concessions today."[334]

Władysław Czapliński and Anna Wyrozumska summarized this broad phenomenon, noting that the *soft law* ends up frequently being the basis for an international treaty of a binding character. This way, *soft law* is a precursor, helping States set up the direction for development of Public International in an environment of an increasingly large numbers of States (the UN currently recognizes 206 States as compared to 51 founding member States in 1945[335]) where traditional methods of codifying a new legal space became near impossible. They wrote: "Without any doubt, subjects of international law utilize to an ever-larger extent the instruments of non-binding character,

334 Meyer, Timothy. "Collective Decision-Making in International Governance." AJIL Unbound 108 (2014): 30–36. <https://doi.org/10.1017/s239877230000180x>.

335 United Nations. "List of the member states." Retrieved November 28, 2023. <https://www.un.org/en/about-us/member-states>.

such as various principles, norms, standards or rules of engagement. Despite their non-binding character, the creators of such instruments expect that they will actually be followed in practice. This political and moral obligation is necessarily limited to those subjects which participated in the creation of the non-binding rules. (…) "Soft" rules can become the basis for emergence of legal norms, offer support in their application, and can be treated as the element of *State practice* when the later binding norms are being interpreted."[336]

A number of scholarly voices criticize the rising status of *soft law*, as an imperfect way to cope with inertia and indecisiveness of multilateral bodies. Joel Trachtman stated that as the international community resembles ever more an interconnected society, it should embrace in more cases the majority-voting model that is present in most countries. He said: "The requirement of consent or unanimity-based decision-making cannot be defended by a reference to democracy. It can only be defended by such a reference to the extent that the national desire is negative or defensive—to the extent that the goal is to defeat legislation that may be adverse, in contrast with a goal to pass legislation that is beneficial. This can easily be seen where a single small state has the capacity to block decisions that are desired by the overwhelming majority of states. This cannot be explained in terms of democracy. François Delerue went one step further and called the embrace of *soft law* in the context of cyberspace a challenge to the system of international law. He stated: "the situation may lead States to neglect existing norms of international law and thus weaken the scope of application of these norms in the future."[337] This critique consists of two points: that *soft law* might impair development of a robust effective framework of new binding rules and that it would also weaken the existing binding rules. While the first point is substantiated, the second one is not reflected in current State practice or statements. There is no evidence so far of States trying to relativize and weaken the binding character of the existing norms of Public International Law by means of discussion on their application in cyberspace.

---

[336] Czapliński, Władysław, and Anna Wyrozumska. Prawo Międzynarodowe publiczne: Zagadnienia Systemowe. Warszawa: Beck, 2014. Pages 15–16.

[337] Delerue, François. Cyber Operations and international law. Cambridge: Cambridge University Press, 2020. Page 26.

Soft law can be a double-edged sword. Guzman and Meyer captured that duality the following way: "*soft law* may serve well where the only goal is coordination—where states do not gain from defection. Where, on the other hand, a state may gain by violation, as in cases of externalities or public goods, cooperation as opposed to coordination is needed. *Soft law* can support cooperation, provided that the incentives for compliance are sufficient. There will, however, be circumstances in which *hard law* will provide a stronger basis for cooperation, while soft law will fall short. Thus, *soft law* would not be a satisfactory method of cooperation in all cases." Indeed, cyberspace, with its ability to conceal identity and the source of a hostile cyber operation is a case where at least some measure of *hard law* might be necessary to ensure responsible State conduct. It remains to be seen whether the prevailing *soft law* initiatives will be able to pave a way toward binding rules.

2.5 Future evolution of the international legal framework regulating cyberspace

The UN GGE-based formula for advancement of development of Public International Law norms in cyberspace appears to have run its course. After the last report in 2021, the United Nations General Assembly decided not to extend the Group's mandate for a new term. The last big milestone coming from the effort was in 2015, when the UN GGE report, approved by a UN GA resolution, confirmed application of principles of State Sovereignty and Non-Intervention, as well as the commitments stemming broadly from the specialized regime of Humanitarian Law, in cyberspace.[338] The UN OEWG process, which has been running in parallel to the UN GGE one since 2018, is now the main vehicle by which United Nations is playing the leading role in orchestrating common understanding of application of Public International Law in cyberspace. The OEWG started its second mandate in 2021 and will

338 United Nations General Assembly Resolution A/70. Group of Governmental Experts on Developments in the Field of Information and Telecommunications in the Context of International Security - Note by the Secretary-General, A/70/174 (2015, July 22). <https://documents-dds-ny.un.org/doc/UNDOC/GEN/N15/228/35/PDF/N1522835.pdf?OpenElement>.

conduct its sessions through 2025, at which point it is scheduled to present a report to the UN General Assembly.[339]

Given historic reluctance by either UN GGE or UN OEWG to propose new binding norms, the biggest impact of these reports might be in the area of confidence and capacity-building measures, which is to say closing the gap between States, which have a high level of cyber capabilities and those that do not. In fact, closing that gap and its impact on application of Public International Law in cyberspace has already become one of the main theme of UN OEWG sessions. Unlike UN GGE, UN OEWG is marked by high participation from African States. Kenya has distinguished itself for appealing that operationalization of the 2015 UN GGE report must be consistent and should not discriminate along the digital divide.[340] One example of a risk of inconsistency is in the area of *Due Diligence* responsibility for actions done by non-State actors from the territory of a State. Governments with lower cyber capabilities might find themselves more vulnerable to accusations for such conduct. This sentiment has been picked up and amplified by Russian Federation.[341] Ghana has argued for UN OEWG becoming a nexus for cooperation on capacity-building measures, including a global repository and a tracker.[342]

A new development in the area took place in October 2020, when France and Egypt, supported by more than 40 States, put forward a proposal to set up a permanent UN forum, named Programme of Action (PoA) that would replace the UN OEWG/GGE format. Every five years, the forum would

---

339 United Nations General Assembly Resolution 73/27. Developments in the field of information and telecommunications in the context of international security, A/RES/73/27 (December 11, 2018). Operative Clause 5, <https://documents-dds-ny.un.org/doc/UNDOC/GEN/N18/418/04/PDF/N1841804.pdf?OpenElement>.

340 "Africa in OEWG and Ad Hoc Cybercrime Committee - Diplo Resource." Diplo, January 25, 2023. <https://www.diplomacy.edu/resource/report-stronger-digital-voices-from-africa/africa-participation-international-processes-cybersecurity-cybercrime/#Cybersecurity_UN_GGE_and_OEWG>.

341 Geneva Internet Platform. "UN OEWG in 2023." Digital Watch Observatory, October 18, 2023. <https://dig.watch/processes/un-gge/>.

342 "Africa in OEWG and Ad Hoc Cybercrime Committee - Diplo Resource." Diplo, January 25, 2023. <https://www.diplomacy.edu/resource/report-stronger-digital-voices-from-africa/africa-participation-international-processes-cybersecurity-cybercrime/#Cybersecurity_UN_GGE_and_OEWG>.

organize a global international conference, at which new binding and voluntary legal norms could be put forward for consideration.[343] The proposal was approved by the UN General Assembly, paving the way for the forum's launch in two years.[344] The fact that Programme of Action explicitly includes a competence to propose new norms is already a qualitative improvement from the current format. Its permanent character adds to a sense of continuity as compared to the existing ad-hoc approach. In that respect, the international debate on application of Public International Law in cyberspace will get more institutionalized and elevated in importance compared to an wide array of subjects that United Nations deals with.

The civil society and private sector organizations will remain key actors in the multilateral dialogue, to the extent unseen in other spheres of Public International Law. The private sector remains the engine of development of cyber technologies and source of expertise on attribution. In recognition of that, the Swiss government came up with the initiative called Geneva Dialogue on Responsible Behavior in Cyberspace, which convenes States alongside some of the biggest brands in the tech world.[345] Together, they aim to come up with "Geneva Manual" that would "clarify the roles and responsibilities of all stakeholders stemming from accepted norms on responsible behaviour in cyberspace, promoting a free, open, and secure internet."[346] This and other similar initiatives are now at the forefront of defining *soft law*, that while not binding, will set the framework and expectations for binding international norms for cyberspace that will eventually develop, including some of the notoriously sticking points: *Due Diligence*

---

343 "France and Partners Propose a Programme of Action for Advancing Responsible State Behaviour in Cyberspace." Digital Watch Observatory, February 26, 2022. <https://dig.watch/updates/france-and-partners-propose-programme-action-advancing-responsible-state-behaviour>.

344 "Resolution on the Programme of Action (POA) on Cybersecurity Adopted." Digital Watch Observatory, November 9, 2022. <https://dig.watch/updates/resolution-on-the-programme-of-action-poa-on-cybersecurity-adopted>; United Nations General Assembly Resolution 77/L.73. "Programme of action to advance responsible State behaviour in the use of information and communications technologies in the context of international security." A/C.1/77/L.73. <https://digitallibrary.un.org/record/3991743?ln=en>.

345 Geneva Dialogue. Retrieved November 27, 2023. <https://genevadialogue.ch/>.

346 Ibid.

responsibility of States, attribution, jurisdiction, and allowed response to hostile cyber operations.

2.6 Conclusion

There is an ongoing disagreement among States on how to reconcile the established UN ITU-based international legal framework for international oversight of telecommunication technologies with the separate oversight system governing cyberspace that emerged in defiance of pre-existing norms. At present, the special status of the internet persists, which benefits the United States of America and engenders tangible political tensions with other States. As a result of the disagreement, no consistent *opinio juris* has developed as to what the future state of norms governing the internet should be. This disagreement is continuously inflamed by the enormous privilege enjoyed by the birthplace of the internet—the United States of America. Maintaining the separate track for international technical oversight means that the United States retains edge in matters such as capacity to attribute hostile cyber operations or to block a country from the network, as demonstrated with regard to North Korea in 2014.

The existing international framework for overseeing communication technologies stems from the original arrangements set up for telegraph. This system, embodied by the UN ITU, received a powerful reinforcement following the sinking of the Titanic, which led to establishment of a customary international legal norm of a forward-expanding mandate of the organization. This means that every new telecommunications technology was assumed to be included in the remit of the UN ITU. The internet was the first large technological development in the area of informational exchange that defied this model, creating an ongoing international legal and political stand-off.

Instead of the UN ITU, the international oversight model for cyberspace rests on a mosaic of domestic American non-governmental organizations, most of them based in two regions of the United States: California and Massachusetts. The reason for it is that the internet, the underlying platform that sustains cyberspace, started as a joint project of the U.S. Armed Forces and several American universities. The current organizations overseeing the internet represent institutionalization of semi-formal ways in which a small academic community involved in creating the internet was self-regulating. Rapid scaling up of the internet in the 1990s granted staying power to this model, which has no precedent in Public International Law.

In terms of the development of legal norms regulating conduct of States in cyberspace, there is also an impasse that effectively prevents new binding rules from being established. Most States embrace the approach of *ambiguity and silence* in cyberspace, which limits development of consistent *opinio juris*. Those States that have strong offensive cyber capabilities, which also tend to be the most powerful States in general, are reluctant to advocate for more regulation that could curtail their space for maneuver. Those States that become a target of hostile cyber operations have no incentive to popularize their vulnerability given no effective redress can be provided via the system of Public International Law.

To circumvent this impasse, the United Nations has resorted to *soft law*. It proposed 11 voluntary non-binding norms of responsible behavior by States via its Group of Government Experts. A few governments, supported by a large ecosystem of involved NGOs and companies specializing in the subject, have started parallel efforts geared toward proposing other potential future norms, around which State practice and *opinio juris* could develop over time. However, it remains debatable whether this route would bear fruit.

The unique evolution path of the international legal framework regulating cyberspace sets it aside from other areas of Public International Law. The continuation of the existing impasse might further contribute to this dynamic but also stunt development of international legal norms that are progressively more needed as the scale of hostile cyber operations between States increases exponentially.

Typology of hostile cyber operations between States which are *Internationally Wrongful Acts*

3.1 Introduction

When attributing an international hostile cyber operation to a specific sovereign State, it is essential to determine the specific norm of Public International Law that is purportedly breached by the act. This is relatively easier in the realm of conventional *Unfriendly Acts*. Layers of jurisprudence and State practice provide a foundation for assessing any given transgression. However, the process of transposing the existing legal framework into the cyber context generates uncertainties and open-ended questions driven by the unique characteristics of cyberspace. Examples include the near-instantaneous nature of cyber operations and ease with which multiple below-threshold cyber acts can be launched that would not amount to an *Internationally Wrongful Act* individually. Conversely, certain aspects of physical reality do not apply in cyberspace, rendering various existing norms obsolete. Examples include the notion of border clashes, which is less relevant in largely de-territorialized cyberspace where barriers between different States' jurisdiction spheres are fluid.

This chapter engages with these challenges and presents the most up-to-date evidence on State practice and scholarly analysis that aim to address them. It also proposes a stage-based classification of hostile cyber operations based on their severity that reflects the main categories of *Internationally Wrongful Acts* applicable in cyberspace. The analysis offers insight on the extent to which Public International Law has started developing unique applications of existing norms and sometimes even brand-new norms to regulate hostile cyber operations.

3.2 Overview of the legal typology of international hostile cyber operations

The existing framework of international law provides guidelines on how to classify various non-consensual cyber operations that can take place between sovereign States. However, only a specific set of international legal categories is applicable in that novel context. At the highest level, all hostile cyber operations between States can be classified as *Unfriendly Acts*, as delineated in Chapter 1. Launching a hostile cyber operation against another State impinges upon the spirit of the UN Charter and constitutes an *Unfriendly Act*, even if the act does not meet the threshold of severity that would qualify it as an *Internationally Wrongful Act*. There exists an ongoing debate as to whether *Unfriendly Acts* include only activities below the threshold for *Internationally Wrongful Acts* or are a broader term that encompasses the full spectrum of "unfriendly" conduct in international law, including more severe events such as *Acts of Aggression*.[347] Both the linguistic and systemic interpretative logic point to the latter formulation. An *Act of Aggression* is an act that is unfriendly. Systemically, it also contributes to the sense of cohesiveness to perceive consecutively harsher forms of hostile conduct between States as qualified forms of *Unfriendly Acts*.

Based on this interpretation, within the broad pool of *Unfriendly Acts* in cyberspace, some also qualify as more serious transgressions. Additional sets of requirements can be applied, each making an *Unfriendly Act* in cyberspace that meets them graver than the previous one. Figure 9 presents these categories of hostile cyber operations between States. Within the broad category of *Unfriendly Acts*, only some meet the threshold of an *Internationally Wrongful Act*. This chapter demonstrates how such *Internationally Wrongful Acts* can be then further delineated into: *Violations of Sovereignty*, *Prohibited Interventions*, *Acts of Aggression*, and *Armed Attacks*, each consecutive category meeting the

[347] Moynihan, Harriet. (2019, December). The Application of International Law to State Cyberattacks. Chatham House. Page 50. <https://www.chathamhouse.org/2019/12/application-international-law-state-cyberattacks>.

criteria for the previous category and also some additional ones. The final three categories: *Prohibited Interventions involving Use of Force, Acts of Aggression*, and *Armed Attacks*, qualify not only as *Internationally Wrongful Acts* but also as cases of *Prohibited Use of Force.*

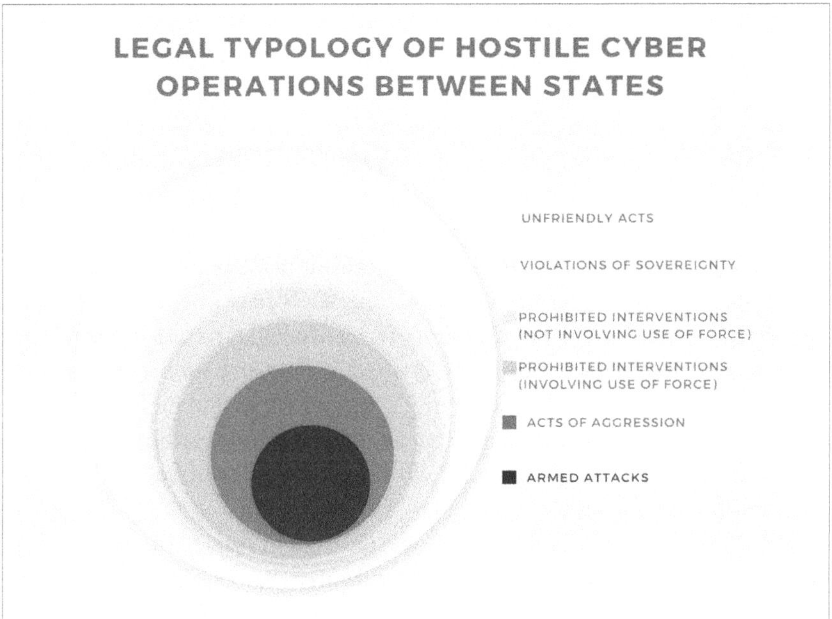

Figure 9. Legal typology of hostile cyber operations between States
Source: Own elaboration

As of 2022, more than 80% of publicly identified international cyber incidents can be defined as *Unfriendly Acts* only (see Figure 2 for reference). This group is composed mostly of cases of international cyber espionage. In addition, several cases of a *Violation of Sovereignty* and a *Prohibited Intervention* have been recorded. Depending on interpretation of criteria, some isolated *Acts of Aggression* took place too. Arguably, no cases of cyber *Armed Attacks* have taken place yet. The rest of Chapter 3 is dedicated to each of the delineated categories of hostile cyber operations between States and also, as a separate section, the role of international humanitarian and criminal law in that context.

3.3 Hostile cyber operations below the threshold denoting *Internationally Wrongful Acts*

3.3.1 Cyber espionage as the main type of *Unfriendly Acts* in cyberspace

As shown in Figure 2, the volume of international hostile cyber operations has been growing exponentially over the past decade. Nevertheless, the overwhelming majority of those operations are activities that are well below the threshold of *Internationally Wrongful Acts*. Specifically, those below-threshold activities can be broadly described as either cyber espionage or public *Unfriendly Acts* (such as disrupting a website by sending multiple server requests, i.e., doxing). By and large, cyber espionage acts constitute most of the below-threshold activity. They are a natural extension and evolution of conventional espionage, which has been taking place between States since time immemorial. Rather than being a completely new phenomenon, these espionage activities are deploying modern technologies to satisfy a universal and timeless demand of States for classified intelligence on foreign governments. Of course, some of those spying activities are so egregious and severe that they can also be qualified as breaches of international obligations. This section deals with the question of definition and impact of below-threshold hostile cyber operations.

There exists no formal definition of espionage in international law. This opens up space for non-binding academic sources to help frame the discussion. According to the *Oxford University Bibliographies*, espionage consists of:

> the access, on behalf of a state, to information that is held by another state and considered as confidential or strategic, in the military, security, or economic field.[348]

The key element of the definition is that espionage operations do not carry any disruptive payload, their only purpose being collection of information, preferably without causing any impact. Tallinn Manual 2.0., a non-binding, NATO-sponsored publication that pools together insights from an

[348] Dubuisson, François, and Agatha Verdebout. "Espionage in International Law." Oxford Bibliographies Online Datasets, 2018.

international group of renowned experts, proposed a specific definition that focuses solely on cyber espionage. It proposes that:

> an information-gathering cyber operation, encompassing any act undertaken clandestinely or under false pretenses by a State that uses cyber capabilities to gather, or attempt to gather, information [from another State].[349]

There are four main elements of this definition:

- The act must be geared toward collecting valuable information;
- The act must be done in a covert or clandestine manner;
- The act must rely on cyber capabilities;
- The act must be attributable to a State and aimed at another State.

Such activity is for the most part below the threshold of an *Internationally Wrongful Act* and makes up the vast majority of non-consensual cyber interactions between States. For instance, U.S. Deputy Secretary of Defense William J. Lynn III stated in a Foreign Affairs article that *the theft of intellectual property may be the most significant cyber threat that the United States will face over the long term*, even if it is less noticeable than hostile cyber acts aimed at disrupting critical national infrastructure (which would surely qualify as *internationally wrongful acts*).[350]

Governments readily employ cyber espionage tools due to one fundamental reason—peacetime espionage is lawful in international law.[351]

---

349 Schmitt, Michael. N. & NATO Cooperative Cyber Defence Centre of Excellence. (2017). Tallinn Manual 2.0 on the International Law Applicable to Cyber Operations. Cambridge University Press. Supra n.3, page 168; Buchan, R. (2018). Cyber Espionage and International Law (1st ed.). Hart Publishing. Chapter 1. <https://doi.org/10.1017/S0922156519000359>; Lubin, Asaf. M (2020). The Liberty to Spy. Harvard International Law Journal, 61(185), Pages 1–61. <https://www.repository.law.indiana.edu/facpub/2905/>; Sander, Barrie. (2019). The Sound of Silence: International Law and the Governance of Peacetime Cyber Operations. Pages 1–21.

350 Lynn III, W. J. (2020, October 16). Defending a New Domain: The Pentagon's Cyberstrategy. Foreign Affairs. <https://www.foreignaffairs.com/articles/united-states/2010-09-01/defending-new-domain>.

351 Sander, Barrie. (2019). The Sound of Silence: International Law and the Governance of Peacetime Cyber Operations. Pages 1–21; Moynihan, Harriet. (2019, December). The Application of International Law to State Cyberattacks. Chatham House.

Essentially all countries outlaw foreign espionage domestically, within their jurisdiction. At the same time, customary international law provides that a foreign espionage incursion during peacetime does not per se violate *State Sovereignty.*[352] It is also not considered a *casus belli*, meaning that it is not covered by international law related to armed conflict.[353] In fact, most States maintain a deliberate policy of strategic silence on the status of espionage in international law, a practice that led to a customary assumption of its lawfulness.[354] Its lawfulness can be also inferred from the 1961 Vienna Convention on Diplomatic Relations, which, according to expert interpretations, *explicitly recognizes the well-established right of nations to engage in espionage during peacetime.*[355] There is also consensus on that subject in the academia[356] (albeit with some divergent interpretations[357]). Tallinn Manual 2.0 echoed that sentiment: *The International Group of Experts agreed that customary international law does not prohibit espionage per se. (…) On the*

Section Sovereignty and Non-intervention. <https://www.chathamhouse.org/2019/12/application-international-law-state-cyberattacks>; Deeks, Ashley (2015). An International Legal Framework for Surveillance. Virginia Journal of International Law, 55(291), 300–319. <https://www.ilsa.org/Jessup/Jessup16/Batch%202/DeeksLegalFramework.pdf>; Pun, D. (2017). Rethinking Espionage in the Modern Era. Chicago Journal of International Law, pages 353, 359–368. <https://chicagounbound.uchicago.edu/cjil/vol18/iss1/10/>; Lubin, Asaf. M. (2018). Cyber Law and Espionage Law as Communicating Vessels. SSRN Electronic Journal, pages 203–225. <https://doi.org/10.2139/ssrn.3099769>; Brian Egan, US State Department Legal Adviser - Schmitt, M. (2019a, March 21). US Transparency Regarding International Law in Cyberspace. Just Security. <https://www.justsecurity.org/34465/transparency-international-law-cyberspace/>.

352 Ibid.

353 Lin, Herbert. (2011). Responding to Sub-Threshold Cyber Intrusions: A Fertile Topic for Research and Discussion. Georgetown University Press, 2011, pages 127–135.

354 Ziolkowski, K. & NATO Cooperative Cyber Defence Centre of Excellence. (2013). Peacetime regime for state activities in cyberspace: international law, international relations and diplomacy. NATO CCD COE Publications, pages 425, 437–443.

355 Wingfield, Thomas. C. (2000). The Law of Information Conflict: National Security Law in Cyberspace (1st ed.). Aegis Research Corp. Supra note 110, page 350.

356 Lubin, Asaf. M. (2018). Cyber Law and Espionage Law as Communicating Vessels. SSRN Electronic Journal, 203–225. <https://doi.org/10.2139/ssrn.3099769>.

357 Navarrete Inaki Mr., and Buchan, Russell. "Out of the Legal Wilderness: Peacetime Espionage, International Law and the Existence of Customary Exceptions," 2019. Cornell International Law Journal, 51(4), 897–953. <https://scholarship.law.cornell.edu/cilj/vol51/iss4/4/>.

contrary, a number of States have by domestic law authorised their security services to engage in espionage, including cyber espionage.[358]

The lawfulness of international espionage is confirmed by State practice, that is, the objective component of *opinio juris.* There exist many publicly available government documents confirming that States order their intelligence services engage in cyber espionage abroad. Some of those States include: Austria, Germany, Netherlands, Sweden, Switzerland, the United Kingdom, and the United States.[359] The fact that such prominent countries reveal their intent to spy does not contradict the definition of cyber espionage since the actual acts of spying and their targets are not revealed.

3.3.2 Determining the threshold beyond which cyber espionage becomes an *Internationally Wrongful Act*

Identifying the threshold that delineates between cyber espionage acts that are only *Unfriendly Acts* and those that constitute *Internationally Wrongful Acts* is challenging. Unlike conventional espionage, which typically takes place mostly on the physical territory of a target State, cyber espionage is less geographically bound. It can take place remotely and instantaneously.

---

358 Schmitt, M. N. & NATO Cooperative Cyber Defence Centre of Excellence. (2017). Tallinn Manual 2.0 on the International Law Applicable to Cyber Operations. Cambridge University Press. Page 169.

359 The government of Austria. (1999, April 27). Bundesgesetz über Aufgaben und Befugnisse im Rahmen der militärischen Landesverteidigung. Section 20(a). Retrieved February 17, 2022, from <https://www.ris.bka.gv.at/GeltendeFassung.wxe?Abfrage=Bundesnormen&Gesetzesnummer=20000864>; The government of Germany. (1990, December 20). Gesetz über den Bundesnachrichtendienst (BND-Gesetz - BNDG). Section 2(1)(40). Retrieved February 17, 2022, from <https://www.gesetze-im-internet.de/bndg/BJNR029790990.html>; The government of Netherlands. (2017, February 7). Wet op de inlichtingen- en veiligheidsdiensten 2017. Sections 1–2. Retrieved February 17, 2022, from <https://wetten.overheid.nl/BWBR0039896/2022-01-01#:~:text=2%20De%20Algemene%20Inlichtingen%2D%20en,zijn%20verstrekt%20dat%20noodzakelijk%20maken>.; The government of United Kingdom. (2000). Regulation of Investigatory Powers Act 2000. Section 8(4). Retrieved February 17, 2022, from <https://www.legislation.gov.uk/ukpga/2000/23/contents>; The government of Switzerland. (2008, October 3). Bundesgesetz vom 3. Oktober 2008 über die Zuständigkeiten im Bereich des zivilen Nachrichtendienstes (ZNDG). Articla 1(a). Retrieved February 17, 2022, from <https://www.fedlex.admin.ch/eli/cc/2009/809/de>.

It also allows for transfers of data that are much bigger than conventional espionage would ever allow for.[360] This means that cyber espionage can easily inflict much more negative impact on a target State than conventional one. This issue was discussed by the International Group of Experts behind the Tallinn Manual 2.0, who proposed:

> Cyber espionage may be conducted in a manner that violates international law due to the fact that certain of the methods employed to conduct cyber espionage are unlawful. (...) In other words, if an aspect of a cyber espionage operation is unlawful under international law, it renders the cyber espionage unlawful. By styling a cyber operation as a 'cyber espionage operation', a State cannot therefore claim that it is by definition lawful under international law;[361]

This framing appears to be consistent with State practice. For instance the United States and China, in its 2015 agreement on cyber security stated implicitly that certain instances of cyber espionage can constitute a breach of international obligations.[362] Sometimes the difference between espionage acts that are only *Unfriendly Acts* and those that constitute *internationally wrongful acts* boils down to nuances of jurisdiction. For instance, the act of cyber wiretapping of a military submarine would likely constitute a violation of sovereignty, and hence an *Internationally Wrongful Act*, if hacking into the submarine's systems took place at the time when it was located within a country's territorial waters. That same act would constitute just an *Unfriendly Act* if the same happened in international waters.[363]

In the context of insufficient amount of State practice and international jurisprudence, various approaches have been proposed to classify hostile

---

360 Kilovaty, Ido. (2017). World Wide Web of Exploitations—The Case of Peacetime Cyber Espionage Operations Under International Law: Towards a Contextual Approach. Columbia University Science and Technology Law Review, 18(1), 42–78. Page 53. <https://doi.org/10.7916/stlr.v18i1.4012>.

361 Schmitt, Michael. N. & NATO Cooperative Cyber Defence Centre of Excellence. (2017). Tallinn Manual 2.0 on the International Law Applicable to Cyber Operations. Cambridge University Press. Page 170.

362 The government of the United States of America. (2015, September 25). Fact Sheet: President Xi Jinping's State Visit to the United States. Retrieved February 17, 2022, from <https://obamawhitehouse.archives.gov/the-press-office/2015/09/25/fact-sheet-president-xi-jinpings-state-visit-united-states>.

363 Ibid. Point 7.

cyber operations between States in a way that would clearly distinguish between those that are likely only *Unfriendly Acts* and those that have constitute *Internationally Wrongful Acts*. Those approaches do not have a binding character and are academic proposals. Potentially, they can inform future government conduct contributing to emergence of an internationally binding method. For now however they are a form of intellectual exercise rather than anything else. For instance, Herbert Lin constructed the notion of *nature of payload*, distinguishing between *cyber-exploitations* (his term for international hostile cyber operation) whose *payload* is destructive (which means it seeks to disrupt functioning of the targeted system, for example, when a virus has the purpose of stalling a power plant) and those whose *payload* is non-destructive.[364] The former are potentially *Internationally Wrongful Acts* while the latter are mostly below-threshold activities.

The fast-growing number of publicly decried international cyber incidents has drawn public attention in a number of countries. It propelled a debate as to whether peaceful cyber espionage should be regulated more restrictively than its conventional equivalent.[365] For example, Barrie Sander argues that since cyber espionage implicates non-State actors on an unprecedented scale (both as perpetrators as well as targets) compared to conventional spying, States might invoke rights reserved for dealing individuals (such as human rights, including the right to privacy), and in that way drive the wedge between how cyber and conventional espionage is dealt with.[366]

Public pressure to address the growing problem of hostile international cyber operations is partially also driven by the fact that States are reluctant to invoke more serious categories of international law, meaning that most instances of such activity are officially presented as forms of espionage by the victim States. This is likely due to the challenges with legal attribution of more severe breaches of international law, as described in Chapter 2 It might also

---

364 Lin, Herbert. (2011). Responding to Sub-Threshold Cyber Intrusions: A Fertile Topic for Research and Discussion. Georgetown University Press, 2011, 127–135. Pages 129–130; Kreuzer, Leonhard. (2020, December 9). Disentangling the cyber security debate. Völkerrechtsblog. Retrieved February 17, 2022, from <https://voelkerrechtsblog.org/disentangling-the-cyber-security-debate/>.

365 Sander, Barrie. (2019). The Sound of Silence: International Law and the Governance of Peacetime Cyber Operations. 1–21. Page 11.

366 Ibid.

have to do with the policy of ambivalence and secrecy, discussed in Chapter 1, according to which, victim States do not want to limit their own legal and operational latitude to perform cyber operations abroad in the future.

Finally, States might be reluctant to claim that the hostile cyber operations they were affected by are internationally wrongful acts due to their inability to project a symmetrical response. For example, a State that acknowledges being on the receiving end of *Prohibited Use of Force* by another Stata and does not seek a recourse or countermeasures can be perceived as weak or accepting of others compromising its sovereignty.

3.4 Hostile cyber operations that constitute a *Violation of Sovereignty*

3.4.1 Evolution of the term *Violation of Sovereignty* in Public International Law

3.4.1.1 *Violation of Sovereignty* as an operational norm in Public International Law

The roots of the notion of State sovereignty, as described in Chapter 1, go all the way back to the ancient law of nations. The term *Violation of Sovereignty* is a more modern legal term with a central role in the framework regulating hostile cyber operations between States. As laid out in Chapter 2, its centrality was confirmed in the UN GGE's decision from 2013[367] (further expanded in 2015[368]) to structure State accountability in cyberspace around the notion of *State Sovereignty* over ICT infrastructure within its jurisdiction. This framing implies that *State Sovereignty* is an operational norm that can be breached rather than a general guideline.

---

367 United Nations General Assembly Resolution. (2013, June 24). Group of Governmental Experts on Developments in the Field of Information and Telecommunications in the Context of International Security - Note by the Secretary-General. Retrieved February 15, 2022, from <https://undocs.org/A/68/98>.

368 United Nations General Assembly Resolution. (2015, July 22). Group of Governmental Experts on Developments in the Field of Information and Telecommunications in the Context of International Security - Note by the Secretary-General. Retrieved February 15, 2022, from <https://documents-dds-ny.un.org/doc/UNDOC/GEN/N15/228/35/PDF/N1522835.pdf?OpenElement>.

It also means that prohibition of *Violation of State Sovereignty is* an *erga omnes* obligation on part of States, and whose violation constitutes an *Internationally Wrongful Act.*[369] *State Sovereignty* is also a composite norm,[370] meaning that encompasses a number of prerogatives. It is also the foundation of more specific, narrow international legal categories, such as *Prohibition of Prohibited Intervention*, or *Prohibition of Prohibited Use of Force*, all of them drawing on the notion of State Sovereignty.[371] For instance, ICJ Judge Alejandro Alvarez in the 1949 *Corfu Channel* case, in his separate opinion, wrote that when we speak about *State Sovereignty, we understand the whole body of rights and attributes which a State possesses in its territory, to the exclusion of all other states, and also in its relations with other States.*[372]

The 1970 UN Friendly Relations Declaration, invoked in Chapter 1, describes *rights inherent in full sovereignty*, reinforcing the notion that State Sovereignty covers an array of rights.[373] The 1975 Helsinki Accords also supported that approach committing all of its signatory States to:

> Article I
> respect each other's sovereign equality and individuality as well as all the rights inherent in and encompassed by its sovereignty, including in particular the right of every State to juridical equality, to territorial integrity and to freedom and

369 Schmitt, Michael N. & NATO Cooperative Cyber Defence Centre of Excellence. (2017). Tallinn Manual 2.0 on the International Law Applicable to Cyber Operations. Cambridge University Press. Page 741.

370 Moynihan, Harriet. (2019, December). The Application of International Law to State Cyberattacks. Chatham House. Paragraph 29. <https://www.chathamhouse.org/2019/12/application-international-law-state-cyberattacks>.

371 Schmitt, Michael N. & NATO Cooperative Cyber Defence Centre of Excellence. (2017). Tallinn Manual 2.0 on the International Law Applicable to Cyber Operations. Cambridge University Press. Page 741.

372 Case concerning Corfu Channel (United Kingdom of Great Britain and Northern Ireland v. Albania). I.C.J. Reports 1949, 244, Gen L No. 1. (1949). <Https://Www.Icj-Cij.Org/En/Case/1. Retrieved February 15, 2022, from https://www.icj-cij.org/en/case/1>.

373 United Nations General Assembly Resolution. (1970, October 24). 2625 (XXV) Declaration on Principles of International Law concerning Friendly Relations and Cooperation among States in Accordance with the Charter of the United Nations - Main Page. Retrieved February 17, 2022, from <https://legal.un.org/avl/ha/dpilfrcscun/dpilfrcscun.html>.

> political independence. They will also respect each other's right freely to choose and develop its political, social, economic and cultural systems as well as its right to determine its laws and regulations.[374]

This formulation means that, for example, a *Prohibited Intervention* by a State in another country would, by definition, also constitute a *Violation of Sovereignty* of the victim State. However, this approach is not the only one receiving recognition within the international community. An alternative view is that sovereignty is a broad concept that guides international relations and constitutes a component of operational notions (such as *Prohibited Intervention*, *Act of Aggression*, or *Armed Attack*) but does not enjoy the same practical status. United Kingdom has shared such a divergent stance a number of times, most recently in 2021.[375] Another State, which appears to not fully support this interpretation is the United States. For example, Colonel Gary Corn, the U.S. Cyber Command Senior Legal Advisor, stated: *An opposing view holds that sovereignty is a baseline principle of the Westphalian international order undergirding binding norms such as the prohibition against the Use of Force in Article 2(4) of the UN Charter, or the customary international law rule of non-intervention, which States have assented to as an exercise of their sovereign equality.*[376] At the same time, U.S. Department of State representatives went on record stating that they support the UN GGE approach.[377]

Nevertheless, the supposition that violating sovereignty (without meeting a threshold for any more specific *Internationally Wrongful Act*) is a legally non-material concern, akin to an *Unfriendly Act*, is inconsistent with the prevalent State practice and the judiciary line of the ICJ. In the *Corfu Channel* case judgment mentioned earlier, the ICJ ruled that *all* unauthorized exercises

---

374 Organization for Security and Co-operation in Europe. (1975, August 1). Helsinki Final Act. Article I. Retrieved February 17, 2022, from <https://www.osce.org/helsinki-final-act>.

375 Schmitt, Michael N. (2021, October 8). The Sixth United Nations GGE and International Law in Cyberspace. Just Security. <https://www.justsecurity.org/76864/the-sixth-united-nations-gge-and-international-law-in-cyberspace/>.

376 Corn, Gary C. (2021, October 8). Tallinn Manual 2.0 – Advancing the Conversation. Just Security. <https://www.justsecurity.org/37812/tallinn-manual-2-0-advancing-conversation/#more-37812>.

377 Koh, Harold H. (2012, September 18). International Law in Cyberspace. U.S. Department of State. Retrieved February 15, 2022, from <https://2009-2017.state.gov/s/l/releases/remarks/197924.htm>.

of State authority can be subject to legal scrutiny based on the *Principle of Sovereignty*, rendering the latter very operational.[378] State practice appears to mostly toe that line. An example of a State that interprets prohibition of *Violation of Sovereignty* very strictly is France. In September 2019, it laid out its position on the matter. In this official document, titled *Droit International Applique Aux Operations Dans Le Cyberspace*, the government stated that *unauthorized State cyber intrusions into French systems, or any negative effects on French territory created by cyber methods, might constitute a Violation of Sovereignty.*[379]

3.4.1.2 Ambiguity about the scope of the term *Violation of Sovereignty*

While the UN GGE approach remains the prevalent one, residual ambiguity about the status of *State Sovereignty* in cyberspace will likely remain a discussion subject over the coming years. More examples of hostile cyber operations and States' reactions to them might need to take place before consistent practice is established. In that vein, U.S. Department of State Legal Advisor Brian Egan stated even that the international community *is faced with a relative vacuum of public State practice* [on State sovereignty in cyberspace].[380] During the launch event for Tallinn Manual 2.0, Michael Schmitt (Director of the Tallinn Manual process, Chairman of the Stockton Center for the Study of International Naval War College, and Professor of public international law and Exeter Law School) acknowledged as much. When answering a question about which part of the Manual was most likely to change over the following

---

378 I.C.J. Reports 1949, 244, Gen L No. 1. (1949). Case concerning Corfu Channel (United Kingdom of Great Britain and Northern Ireland v. Albania). Retrieved February 15, 2022, from <https://www.icj-cij.org/en/case/1>.

379 The government of France. (2019, October 4). Communiqué -La France s'engage à promouvoir un cyberespace stable, fondé sur la confiance et le respect du droit international. French Ministry of Defense. Retrieved February 16, 2022, from <https://www.defense.gouv.fr/fre/salle-de-presse/communiques/communique_la-france-s-engage-a-promouvoir-un-cyberespace-stable-fonde-sur-la-confiance-et-le-respect-du-droit-international>.

380 Egan, Brian J. (2017). International Law and Stability in Cyberspace. Berkeley Journal of International Law, 35(1), 1–26. <https://www.law.berkeley.edu/wp-content/uploads/2016/12/BJIL-article-International-Law-and-Stability-in-Cyberspace.pdf>.

five years, he stated it would likely be clarification of States' legal positions on the question of *State Sovereignty.*[381]

For a *Violation of Sovereignty* to occur, the following three conditions must be met:

- a State has to exercise its authority in another's State's jurisdiction;
- without an explicit consent of that another State;
- over an aspect which that another State has the *exclusive right to exercise State powers independently.*

This definition and the requirements stem from the jurisprudence of the Permanent Court of International Justice (the predecessor of the ICJ, which was provided for in the Covenant of the League of Nations) in the 1927 S.S. *Lotus* case and evolved to become part of customary international law.[382] They was further reinforced by the *Corfu Channel* case,[383] the *Case Concerning Military and Paramilitary Activities in and against Nicaragua (Nicaragua v. the United States),*[384] and the *Case Concerning Certain Activities carried out by Nicaragua in the Border Area (Costa Rica v. Nicaragua).*[385] State here can encompass categories of entities such as State's organs, State agents, and non-State actors such as organizations and proxy groups, whose actions are attributable to it. These rules are explained in detail in Chapter 5.

---

381 Ansley, Rachel. (2017, February 15). Tallinn Manual 2.0: Defending Cyberspace. Atlantic Council. Retrieved February 17, 2022, from <https://www.atlanticcouncil.org/blogs/new-atlanticist/tallinn-manual-2-0-defending-cyberspace/>.

382 The Case of the S.S. Lotus (France v. Turkey). Permanent Court of International Justice (series A) No. 1. (1927, September 7). Page 18. Retrieved February 17, 2022, from <https://www.icj-cij.org/public/files/permanent-court-of-international-justice/serie_A/A_10/30_Lotus_Arret.pdf>.

383 Case concerning Corfu Channel (United Kingdom of Great Britain and Northern Ireland v. Albania). I.C.J. Reports 1949, 244, Gen L No. 1. (1949). Paragraphs 69–70. <https://Www.Icj-Cij.Org/En/Case/1. Retrieved February 15, 2022, from https://www.icj-cij.org/en/case/1>.

384 Case Concerning the Military and Paramilitary Activities in and Against Nicaragua (Nicaragua v. United States of America). ICJ Reports 1986. Retrieved February 17, 2022, from <https://www.icj-cij.org/case/70>

385 Certain Activities Carried Out by Nicaragua in the Border Area (Costa Rica v. Nicaragua). International Court of Justice. ICJ Reports 2015. (2015, December 16). Paragraphs 221–223. Retrieved February 17, 2022, from <https://www.icj-cij.org/en/case/150>.

Areas over which States have the exclusive rights to exercise independent powers are those where States retain *inherently governmental functions*.[386] Jurisprudence and State practice point to functions such as delivery of social services, conduct of elections, utilities provision, collection of taxes, effective conduct of diplomacy, and national defense activities.[387] Areas covered by the concept *Domain Réservé* discussed in Chapter 2 provide further examples of *inherently governmental functions*.

3.4.1.3 Aiding and abetting by a State as a *Violation of Sovereignty*

If a State aids and assists another State in a way that enables another it to conduct an *Internationally Wrongful Act*, it can also be liable for unlawful conduct from the standpoint of Public International Law.[388] It is important to note that aiding and assisting according to this formula is a separate, additional *Internationally Wrongful Act*, different from the *Internationally Wrongful Act* of the original perpetrator State. In the comments to the *Draft Articles on State responsibility*, the UN ILC experts claimed the threshold for qualifying the aid as unlawful is that it "contributed significantly" to the *Internationally Wrongful Act* by the original perpetrator State.[389] It also has to make it "materially easier" for the State receiving aid to conduct the *Internationally Wrongful Act*.[390] Finally, the experts also asserted that in certain contexts the aid and assistance can be so integral to an act, that the aiding State will bear legal responsibility for it on par with the perpetrating State.[391]

---

386 Oppenheim, Lassa, Robert Y. Jennings, and Arthur Watts. Oppenheim's international law. Oxford: Oxford University Press, 2008. Page 385; The Case of the S.S. Lotus (France v. Turkey). Permanent Court of International Justice. Permanent Court of International Justice (series A) No. 1. (1927, September 7). Page 18. Retrieved February 17, 2022, from <https://www.icj-cij.org/public/files/permanent-court-of-international-justice/serie_A/A_10/30_Lotus_Arret.pdf>.

387 Schmitt, Michael N. & NATO Cooperative Cyber Defence Centre of Excellence. (2017). Tallinn Manual 2.0 on the International Law Applicable to Cyber Operations. Cambridge University Press. Rule 4, Commentary paragraph 16.

388 United Nations International Law Commission. Draft articles on Responsibility of States for Internationally Wrongful Acts with commentaries. United Nations Office of Legal Affairs (2001). Article 16. Retrieved February 15, 2022. <https://legal.un.org/ilc/texts/instruments/english/commentaries/9_6_2001.pdf>.

389 Ibid. Article 16, Commentary paragraph 5.

390 Ibid. Article 16, Commentary paragraph 1.

391 Ibid. Article 16, Commentary paragraph 10.

Because aiding and assisting is a norm included in the *Draft Articles* that is not rooted in ICJ jurisprudence, it can be perceived as a proposal of a new norm rather than an expression of an already existing customary rule. Even though it is popular among many international scholars, including the group of international experts behind the Tallin Manual 2.0,[392] and it reflects the logic of domestic criminal codes in many States, the norm is still in the process of forming of *opinio juris*. Tallinn Manual 2.0, one of the key academic publications on the matter of application of Public International Law in cyberspace, embraced the notion of State accountability for aid and abetting. Rule 18 of the Tallinn Manual 2.0 covers the subject of aiding and assisting other States in their cyber assaults, identifying it as an *Internationally Wrongful Act*. This provision, however, is only a scholarly proposal. While Tallinn Manual 2.0 enjoys a special status as a NATO-sponsored document and a summary of contributions by some of the best legal experts in the field worldwide, it can be seen as a subsidiary means for the determination of existing rules of law at best, per Article 38 of the Statute of the International Court of Justice.[393] For these reasons, it can be determined that aid and abetting has not been regulated in the framework of Public International Law, effectively creating a gap that can be exploited by bad-actor States in cyberspace.

3.4.2 Application of the term *Violation of Sovereignty* in cyberspace

3.4.2.1 Criteria for qualifying a hostile cyber operation as a *Violation of Sovereignty*

A case of a *Violation of Sovereignty* in cyberspace must meet the general conventional criteria for that category laid out in the Lotus case by the Permanent Court of International Justice.[394] However, beyond that, the established body

---

392 Schmitt, Michael N. & NATO Cooperative Cyber Defence Centre of Excellence. (2017). Tallinn Manual 2.0 on the International Law Applicable to Cyber Operations. Cambridge University Press. Rule 18.

393 International Court of Justice. (1945, June 26). Article 38. Statute of the Court. Retrieved February 15, 2022, from <https://www.icj-cij.org/en/statute>.

394 The Case of the S.S. Lotus (France v. Turkey). Permanent Court of International Justice, Award. September 7, 1927. Permanent Court of International Justice (series A). Page 18. Retrieved February 17, 2022. <https://www.icj-cij.org/public/files/permanent-court-of-international-justice/serie_A/A_10/30_Lotus_Arret.pdf>.

of international legal practice does not provide guidelines on how to handle hostile cyber operations and their impact in the area of *State Sovereignty*, which is a novel application of the term. The reason for it is that the legal cases and State conduct that shaped them are of conventional nature whereas cyberspace represents a new type of interaction domain. Specifically, there are two key challenges that uniquely define cyberspace:

- Ease with which States can launch hostile cyber operations, which raises questions about the threshold at which they should be considered a *Violation of Sovereignty;*
- The fact that cyberspace allows for de-territorialized instantaneous interactions between States, including operations executed remotely and operations that only have impact inside cyberspace.

These two factors are driving a wedge between the conventional *Violations of Sovereignty* and the cyber ones, potentially leading to establishment of separate legal regimes (which remains a future possibility). While there is no general prohibition of hostile cyber operations, because of the two unique challenges, the mood in the international community might have started shifting on that matter. To that end, many States see the notion of *Violation of Sovereignty* as a tool for limiting the space for lawful hostile cyber operations. There is still not enough State practice on the subject to ascertain how this process will end. In the absence of hard evidence, academic scholars, public-private organizations, and think-tanks have stepped in to propose interpretations and formulas that would help conceptualize the emerging unique features of cyberspace and gauge their potential impact on the shape of Public International Law.

Whatever little State practice there is on *Violation of Sovereignty* in cyberspace can be put on the spectrum between the formal positions taken by France and the United Kingdom. The former went on record stating that sovereignty applies in cyberspace as an operational concept and that any unauthorized penetration of "French systems" constitutes a *Violation of Sovereignty* and therefore is an *Internationally Wrongful Act.*[395] On the other end of the

395 The government of the Republic of France. International law applied to operations in cyberspace – UN ODA, 2021. Page 2. <https://documents.unoda.org/wp-content/uploads/2021/12/French-position-on-international-law-applied-to-cyberspace.pdf>.

spectrum is the United Kingdom, which stated explicitly that it does not recognize sovereignty as an operational concept but rather a guideline and therefore a *Violation of Sovereignty* is not a form of an *Internationally Wrongful Act*, especially in cyberspace.[396] These stances represent two extreme interpretations of the UN GGE's Report ascertaining that sovereignty applies in cyberspace—one makes it into a sharp defensive tool while the other acknowledges but completely defangs it. Przemysław Roguski calls these two interpretations: "Sovereignty-as-a-rule" and "Sovereignty-as-a-principle."[397]

Most States as well as internationally recognized scholars opt for a balanced approach that is in between these two stances, where a *Violation of Sovereignty* can take place but only if conditions are met. The question of the threshold needed for a hostile cyber operation to be considered a *Violation of Sovereignty* also puts in new light cyber espionage, especially since it makes up more than 80% of all the cases of hostile cyber operations (as noted in Chapter 1). It is worth restating here that there is no general prohibition of espionage in international law. However, that might not be entirely the case as far as cyber espionage is concerned, depending on interpretation of recent State practice.[398] Recent State practice and scholarly interpretation essentially groups Cyber espionage together with other forms of hostile cyber operations. Therefore, its international lawfulness is gauged based on methods employed and the effects it caused.[399] This is a split compared with conventional espionage, which is criminalized in domestic legal orders but remains lawful in Public International Law. Meanwhile, there is now a clear trend of States and international organizations speaking up publicly and strongly condemning acts of cyber espionage as something unacceptable from the standpoint of

---

396 The government of the United Kingdom. "Cyber and International Law in the 21st Century." GOV.UK, May 23, 2018. <https://www.gov.uk/government/speeches/cyber-and-international-law-in-the-21st-century>.

397 Roguski, Przemysław. "Application of International Law to Cyber Operations: A Comparative Analysis of States' Views." The Hague Program for Cyber Norms, 2020. Page 7. <https://ruj.uj.edu.pl/xmlui/bitstream/handle/item/153989/roguski_application_of_international_law_to_cyber_operations_2020.pdf?sequence=1>.

398 See section I.3.2 - "Status of espionage in the context of hostile cyber operations" for the analysis of the status of cyber espionage in Public International Law.

399 Delerue, François. Cyber Operations and international law. Cambridge: Cambridge University Press, 2020. Pages 203–232.

international law. For example, the European Commission and the European Parliament released a statement in 2013 after a case of cyber spying by the United States of America was revealed, denouncing it as "unacceptable."[400] That same year, Angela Merkel criticized in similarly harsh words American spying agencies tapping her phone.[401] In 2018, after a hack of the German Parliament by the Russian Federation was uncovered, another statement was released by Germany in a similar tone.[402] Germany itself was denounced for using cyber espionage methods to collect confidential information on the Afghan government.[403] Statements by the Parliament of Canada and President of the Russian Federation describing international cyber espionage as a *Violation of Sovereignty* were invoked in Chapter 1.[404]

The point at which cyber espionage as well as other more severe forms of hostile cyber operations start constituting a *Violation of Sovereignty* in Public International Law is still unclear. Michael Schmitt stated that international law on that subject is not fully formed.[405] Navarrete and Buchan claim that remote cyber penetration of State IT systems by another State is likely a breach of territorial integrity and therefore a *Violation of Sovereignty*, although they refrain from rendering that finding conclusive due to insufficient State

---

400 Deighton, Ben, and Annika Breidthardt. "EU Confronts U.S. over Reports It Spies on European Allies." Reuters, July 1, 2013. <https://www.reuters.com/article/usa-eu-spying-reports/eu-confronts-u-s-over-reports-it-spies-on-european-allies-idINDEE95T06G20130701/>.

401 Baker, Luke, and Andreas Rinke. "Merkel Says U.S. Spying an Unacceptable Breach of Trust." Reuters, October 24, 2013. <https://www.reuters.com/article/uk-eu-summit-idUKBRE99N0ED20131024/>.

402 "Germany Detects New Cyber Attack by Russian Hacker Group - Spiegel." Reuters, November 30, 2018. <https://www.reuters.com/article/germany-cyber-russia/germany-detects-new-cyber-attack-by-russian-hacker-group-spiegel-idUSL8N1Y47J5/>.

403 Deutsche Welle. "New BND Spy Scandal – German Intelligence Admits to Spying in Afghanistan." dw.com, December 7, 2008. <https://www.dw.com/en/german-intelligence-admits-to-spying-on-charities-in-afghanistan/a-3855839>; Delerue, François. Cyber Operations and international law. Cambridge: Cambridge University Press, 2020. Page 217.

404 See section I.3.2 - "Status of espionage in the context of hostile cyber operations" for the analysis of the status of cyber espionage in Public International Law.

405 Schmitt, Michael N. & NATO Cooperative Cyber Defence Centre of Excellence. (2017). Tallinn Manual 2.0 on the International Law Applicable to Cyber Operations. Cambridge University Press. Page 25.

practice.[406] Jared Beim comes to a comparable conclusion and attempts to reconcile it with the general lack of prohibition of espionage in Public International Law by claiming that most cyber espionage necessarily constitutes a *Prohibited Intervention* due to the intrusive penetration methods it employs.[407] Russell Buchan leaned toward the French approach, framing any exercise of State authority within jurisdiction of another State using cyber means as a *Violation of Sovereignty*.[408] Others still, such as Gary Corn, Robert Taylor, and Benedict Pirker, lean against the idea of cyber espionage having an ambiguous status, emphasizing instead the general lack of prohibition of espionage.[409]

Other scholars attempted to develop a framework that answers whether hostile cyber operations are a *Violation of Sovereignty* based on the cause of an operation.[410] Asaf Lubin proposed seven categories of the purpose of a cyber operation, three of them "just" and four of them "unjust." The just ones include: international stability, cooperation, and preserving national security. The unjust ones are: spying for the sake of corporate interests, spying for the sake of exploitation of former colonies, spying to pursue personal interests, and spying with the intent of committing *Internationally*

---

406 Navarrete Inaki Mr., & Buchan, Russell. (2019). Out of the Legal Wilderness: Peacetime Espionage, International Law and the Existence of Customary Exceptions. Cornell International Law Journal, 51(4), pages 897–953. <https://scholarship.law.cornell.edu/cilj/vol51/iss4/4/>.

407 Beim, Jared (2018) "Enforcing a Prohibition on International Espionage," Chicago Journal of International Law: Vol. 18: No. 2, Article 6.

408 French, D. (2019). Russell Buchan, Cyber Espionage and International Law, Hart Publishing, 2018, 248pp. Leiden Journal of International Law, 32(4), pages 883–885. <https://doi.org/10.1017/S0922156519000359>.

409 Corn, Gary, and Taylor, Robert. (2017). Sovereignty in the Age of Cyber. AJIL Unbound, 111, pages 207–212. <https://doi:10.1017/aju.2017.57>; Buchan, Russell.J. The International Legal Regulation of Cyber Espionage - The International Legal Regulation of State-Sponsored Cyber Espionage. In: Osula, A.-M. and Rõigas, H., (eds.) International Cyber Norms: Legal, Policy & Industry Perspectives. NATO CCD COE Publications, pages 65–86.

410 For example, Jupillat, Nicolas, "From the Cuckoo's Egg to Global Surveillance: Cyber Espionage that Becomes Prohibited Intervention" (June 19, 2017). North Carolina Journal of International Law and Commercial Regulation, Vol. 42, No. 4, 2017. <https://ssrn.com/abstract=3050619>

Wrongful Acts.[411] This approach focuses on the purpose and context of a cyber espionage act. On the other hand, the approach proposed by Tallinn Manual concentrates on damage, also known as the Doctrine of Effects, as the main way to gauge whether a hostile cyber operation violated sovereignty. The Manual distinguishes three main degrees of damage: physical damage, loss of functionality of cyber infrastructure, and damage below the loss of functionality of cyber infrastructure.[412] According to the approach, the first category would definitely constitute a *Violation of Sovereignty*, for the second one it would depend on the circumstances, while the last one would typically only qualify as an *Unfriendly Act.* The ongoing debate reflects lack of certainty on how to classify cyber hostilities between States. While scholars focus on identifying the threshold for a State-sponsored hack to constitute a *Violation of Sovereignty*, most States, which fall victim to such hostile cyber activity, prefer to hide that fact, effectively rendering threshold conversations moot.

3.4.2.2 *Violations of Sovereignty* that penetrate ICT infrastructure and those that do not

The damage and purpose-based approaches offer an interesting way of handling the two challenges listed in the beginning of the section: the ease with which States can launch hostile cyber operations against other States and their partially or wholly de-territorialized character. However, both of them suffer from a problem of inconsistency with the contents of the principle of sovereignty in Public International Law. Just the mere fact of a State penetrating the jurisdiction of another Space without permission is enough for a *Violation of Sovereignty* to occur. That notion was established in the landmark Corfu case, where the United Kingdom conducted searches in Albanian territorial waters without permission.[413] This is because such conduct is interpreted as a

---

411 Corn, Gary, and Taylor, Robert. (2017). Sovereignty in the Age of Cyber. AJIL Unbound, 111, pages 207–212. <https://doi:10.1017/aju.2017.57. Pages 231–242>.

412 Schmitt, Michael N. & NATO Cooperative Cyber Defence Centre of Excellence. (2017). Tallinn Manual 2.0 on the International Law Applicable to Cyber Operations. Cambridge University Press. Rule 16.

413 Case concerning Corfu Channel (United Kingdom of Great Britain and Northern Ireland v. Albania)—Judgment (Merits). International Court of Justice Reports, April 9, 1949. Gen L No. 1. 35, Reports 3, 43, paragraph 93. <https://www.icj-cij.org/en/case/1>.

State exercising its authority within a jurisdiction of another State.[414] There is no requirement for minimum damages in that regard in Public International Law. For instance, after the Soviet satellite Cosmos 954 crashed in Canada in 1978, the fact that the airspace and territory of the State were trespassed on, was enough for *Violation of Sovereignty* to take place. Both States accepted this legal interpretation in the international settlement.[415] If damage was the sole criterion dictating whether an *Internationally Wrongful Act* occurred, then all kinds of cyber penetration operations, including the overt ones, could be taking place between States without any legal consequences, as long as they did not incur physical damage. Since there is no clear border in cyberspace a clear distinction between transit and penetration has to be delineated, the latter meaning that computers and servers physically within the jurisdiction of a victim State are being targeted. François Delerue phrased it the following way:

> "Territorial sovereignty extends to ICT infrastructure located in the territory of the State. (...) Data are constantly traveling from server to server, which involves crossing physical borders of States. (...) The unlawful penetration only violates the territorial sovereignty of the State where computers or servers are located."[416]

Therefore, in analyzing hostile cyber operations (including cyber espionage), a two-step process should be utilized. In the first step, a question should be asked about whether ICT infrastructure of the target State has been penetrated or an attempt at doing so has happened. If the answer is positive, then a *Violation of Sovereignty* took place. Even if an attempt at breaking into the systems completely failed, the hostile action is still classified as a *Violation of Sovereignty*. Examples can include installing malware on State agency computers or establishing a connection with a government server, through which confidential data is moved out. If no penetration of ICT systems took place, the doctrine of physical effects or the doctrine of purpose could be deployed (the former enjoys more prominence among scholars) to distinguish between

---

414 Ibid.

415 "Canada: Claim Against The Union Of Soviet Socialist Republics For Damage Caused By Soviet Cosmos 954." International Legal Materials 18, no. 4 (1979): 899–930. Paragraph 21.

416 Delerue, François. Cyber Operations and international law. Cambridge: Cambridge University Press, 2020. Page 222.

hostile cyber operations that reach the threshold of a *Violation of Sovereignty* and those that do not. An example can be a doxing attack, during which a website is connected to by so many devices at once, it stops responding for lack of server capacity. It does not involve a system penetration (visiting a website does not constitute a penetration of its server) and the damage caused by can vary, ranging from none at all to critical (as was the case during a Russian hostile cyber operation in Ukraine in 2015[417]). Lassa Oppenheim stated that *independence is a question of degree.*[418] and this could serve as an important guideline when delineating non-penetrative hostile cyber operations that are *Violations of Sovereignty* from those that are not.

A good example of a potential *Violation of Sovereignty* is the 2018 attempt at hacking into the Organization for the Prevention of Chemical Weapons (OPCW), an international body based in Hague, Netherlands. In April 2018, Netherlands Defense Intelligence found out that Russian intelligence officers were present in Hague and attempting to conduct a cyber operation geared toward breaking into the system of the targeted organization. The Dutch counterintelligence service proceeded to arrests and expel the operatives from the country.[419] In this situation, it appears that Russian Federation attempted to exercise its authority within a jurisdiction of another State (in form of its GRU agents executing tasks unauthorized by Netherlands), without any consent from that State, and while impinging on an area where Netherlands had an exclusive authority to exercise State powers (national security and policing). At the same time, there was no coercive behavior or demands on the part of Russia, meaning that a more specific category of a *Prohibited Intervention* was not applicable. At the same time a penetration of Dutch territorial sovereignty took place when Russian agents engaged in

417 "Connect the Dots on State-Sponsored Cyber Incidents - Compromise of a Power Grid in Eastern Ukraine." Council on Foreign Relations, December 2015. <https://www.cfr.org/cyber-operations/compromise-power-grid-eastern-ukraine>;
"Cyber-Attack against Ukrainian Critical Infrastructure: CISA." Cybersecurity and Infrastructure Security Agency CISA, March 4, 2021. <https://www.cisa.gov/news-events/ics-alerts/ir-alert-h-16-056-01>.

418 Oppenheim, Lassa. F. (1996). International Law A Treatise Vol. 1. Peace (9th ed.). Longman. Page 391.

419 British Broadcasting Corporation. (2018, October 4). How the Dutch foiled Russian "cyber-attack" on OPCW. BBC News. <https://www.bbc.com/news/world-europe-45747472>.

their illicit conduct, while in Hague. This puts this incident in the *Violation of Sovereignty* category.

While certain *Unfriendly Acts* are not severe enough to meet the threshold of *Violations of Sovereignty*, some *Unfriendly Acts* are so severe that not only do they constitute *Violations of Sovereignty* but also meet the criteria of a more severe type of breach of international obligations—a prohibited intervention. This subject will be explored in depth in the next section. The key difference between the two categories is that *coercive behavior* is required on behalf of the intervening State for an event of *Violation of Sovereignty* to breach also the *Principle of Non-Intervention*. In practice however, the distinction can prove very difficult with uncertainty as to which of the two labels fits better.

3.5 Hostile cyber operations that constitute a *Prohibited Intervention*

3.5.1 Evolution of the term *Prohibited Intervention* in Public International Law

3.5.1.1 International treaties regulating the issue of *Prohibited Intervention*

The roots of the *Principle of Non-Intervention* come from the *Principle of Sovereign Equality*, which was formally established as part of the post-Westphalian international legal order. However, it took more than a hundred years after the signing of the Treaty of Westphalia in 1648 for the *Principle of Non-Intervention* to be first put forward in writing in a formula that was a precursor to our modern understanding of it. The Swiss thinker, Emer de Vattel is widely credited with doing that. In 1758 he wrote in his treatise titled *The Law of Nations or Principles of the Law of Nature Applied to the Conduct and Affairs of Nations and Sovereigns*:

> §36. We may conclude from what has been said (§31), that if any disputes arise in a state respecting the fundamental laws, the public administration, or the rights of the different powers of which it is composed, it belongs to the nation alone to judge and determine them conformably to its political constitution.
>
> §37. In short, all these affairs, being solely a national concern, no foreign power has a right to interfere in them, nor ought to intermeddle with them otherwise than by its good offices, unless requested to do it, or induced by particular reasons.

> If any intrude into the domestic concerns of another nation and attempt to put a constraint on its deliberations, they do it an injury.[420]

Anchoring the principle within the concept of *Sovereign Equality* and inviolability of domestic affairs strengthens the notion that a prohibited intervention is a specific type of event within a broader category of violations of sovereignty. Its status as a binding legal norm gained further recognition during the nineteenth century as burgeoning Western empires were making an effort to maintain a fragile balance of power. The young United States even made steps to expand the notion of non-intervention onto the whole Western Hemisphere of the planet, when in 1823, U.S. President James Monroe stated that European military and political interventions in either of Americas or the Caribbean would be read in Washington D.C. *as the manifestation of an unfriendly disposition toward the United States.*[421] By the interbellum period, the principle started acquiring the status of a customary rule of international law. 1933 Montevideo Convention on the Rights and Duties of States' Article 8 stated:

> No State has the right to intervene in the internal or external affairs of another.[422]

The Additional Protocol Relative to Nonintervention to the Montevideo Convention, signed in 1936, doubled down on and expanded the original Article 8:

> The High Contracting Parties declare inadmissible the intervention of any one of them, directly or indirectly, and for whatever reason, in the internal or external affairs of any other of the Parties.[423]

---

420 Vattel, Emer D., Chitty, Joseph, and Ingraham, Edward D. (1758). The Law of Nations: Or, Principles of the Law of Nature, Applied to the Conduct and Affairs of Nations and Sovereigns. Page 11.

421 Yale University Law School. (n.d.). Avalon Project - Monroe Doctrine; December 2 1823. Retrieved February 17, 2022, from <https://avalon.law.yale.edu/19th_century/monroe.asp>.

422 Organization of American States. (1933, December 26). Montevideo Convention on the Rights and Duties of States. Article 8. Retrieved February 17, 2022, from <https://www.jus.uio.no/english/services/library/treaties/01/1-02/rights-duties-states.xml>.

423 Organization of American States. (1936, December 23). Montevideo Convention on the Rights and Duties of States - Additional Protocol Relative to Non-intervention. Article

The Montevideo Convention was seen at first as binding only its signatories—a number of North and South American States. However, over time, its main provisions, including the Principle of Non-intervention, evolved to be seen as *erga omnes*-binding customary international law. This means that they are applicable not just among the signatories but across the whole system of international law. This is reflected for example in the fact that the Arbitration Commission of the Peace Conference on Yugoslavia (The Badinter Commission) invoked the Convention as a source of law in its First Opinion on the conflict in West Balkans.[424] The government of Switzerland was also citing the Convention as a source of customary international law.[425]

The UN Charter took a specific angle at the subject of non-intervention. While no provision in it directly forbids States from engaging in interventions in other States, article 2(7) applies such a standard to the United Nations itself:

> Nothing contained in the present Charter shall authorize the United Nations to intervene in matters which are essentially within the domestic jurisdiction of any state.[426]

The predecessor of UN Charter Article 2(7) was Article 15(8) of the League of Nations Covenant, which stated that:

> If the dispute between the parties is claimed by one of them, and is found by the Council, to arise out of a matter which by international law is solely within the domestic jurisdiction of that party, the Council shall so report, and shall make no recommendation as to its settlement.[427]

---

1. Retrieved February 17, 2022, from <https://history.state.gov/historicaldocuments/frus1947v08/d566>.

424 Arbitration Commission of the Peace Conference on Yugoslavia (The Badinter Commission). (1991, November 29). The Opinions of the Badinter Arbitration Committee A Second Breath for the Self-Determination of Peoples. Retrieved February 17, 2022, from <http://www.ejil.org/pdfs/3/1/1175.pdf>.

425 The government of Switzerland. (n.d.). The recognition of states and governments. Retrieved February 17, 2022, from <https://www.eda.admin.ch/eda/en/fdfa/foreign-policy/international-law/respect-promotion/the-recognition-of-states-and-governments.html>.

426 United Nations. (1945, June 26). Charter of the United Nations. Article 2(7). Retrieved February 17, 2022, from <https://www.un.org/en/about-us/un-charter>.

427 League of Nations. (1924, December). Article 15(8). The Covenant of the League of Nations. Retrieved February 17, 2022, from <https://avalon.law.yale.edu/20th_century/leagcov.asp>.

While it contained no prohibition for the organization itself, it acknowledged that there exist matters which by *international law should remain solely within the domestic jurisdiction*, without weighing in by the League of Nations' organs. This provision then evolved in the UN Charter into a more forceful prohibition of intervention by the United Nations. It shows that following the failures of the League of Nations, the international community wanted to reinforce the notion that joining the new organization (the UN) would not expose States to any interference. Some legal experts also argue that the scope of domestic jurisdiction was expanded in Article 2(7), since the term *essentially within the domestic jurisdiction* can be read more widely than *by international law solely within the domestic jurisdiction*.[428]

Even though Article 2(7) does not cover the interactions between individual states, a case can be made that it nevertheless strengthened prohibition of intervention at the State-on-State level and that such a principle is a part of the UN legal system. Three UN Regional Agencies: Organization of American States (OAS), the African Union (AU), and The Association of Southeast Asian Nations (ASEAN) included either the *Principle of Non-Intervention* or its broader variant, the *Principle of Non-Interference*, in their founding charters. The components point to a consistent *opinio juris* across States and their widespread practice on the matter, two components necessary for emergence and maintenance of customary international law.[429] The OAS Chapter, signed in 1948, states the following:

> Article 15
> No State or group of States has the right to intervene, directly or indirectly, for any reason whatever, in the internal or external affairs of any other State. The foregoing principle prohibits not only armed force but also any other form of interference

---

[428] Simma, Bruno et al. (2013). The Charter of The United Nations 3E, Vol 1. Oxford Commentaries on International Law, 1. Page 293. <https://doi.org/10.1093/law/9780199639762.001.0001>.

[429] Max Planck Encyclopedia of Public International Law. (n.d.). State Practice. Oxford Public International Law. Retrieved February 17, 2022, from <https://opil.ouplaw.com/view/10.1093/law:epil/9780199231690/law-9780199231690-e1107?prd=MPIL#:%7E:text=State%20practice%20is%20creative%2C%20or,law%2C%20or%20opinio%20iuris)>.

or attempted threat against the personality of the State or against its political, economic and cultural elements.

Article 16
No State may use or encourage the use of coercive measures of an economic or political character in order to force the sovereign will of another State and obtain from it advantages of any kind.[430]

The 2000 Constitutive Act of the African Union included a non-interference as its key principle:

Article 4 Principles
The Union shall function in accordance with the following principles:

(a) sovereign equality and interdependence among Member States of the Union;

(…)

(f) prohibition of the Use of Force or threat to use force among Member States of the Union;

(g) non-interference by any Member State in the internal affairs of another;[431]

Finally, the ASEAN included similar provisions in its 2007 Charter:

2. ASEAN and its Member States shall act in accordance with the following Principles:

(a) respect for the independence, sovereignty, equality, territorial integrity and national identity of all ASEAN Member States;

(b) shared commitment and collective responsibility in enhancing regional peace, security and prosperity;

(c) renunciation of aggression and of the threat or Use of Force or other actions in any manner inconsistent with international law;

---

430 Organization Of American States. (1948). Charter Of The Organization Of American States. Articles 15–16. Retrieved February 17, 2022, from <https://www.oas.org/en/sla/dil/inter_american_treaties_A-41_charter_OAS.asp>.

431 African Union. (2000, July 11). Constitutive Act Of The African Union. Retrieved February 17, 2022, from <https://au.int/sites/default/files/pages/34873-file-constitutiveact_en.pdf>.

(d) reliance on peaceful settlement of disputes;

(e) non-interference in the internal affairs of ASEAN Member States;

(f) respect for the right of every Member State to lead its national existence free from external interference, subversion and coercion;[432]

3.5.1.2 Difference between an *Intervention* and *Interference*

Regarding the difference between the *Principle of Non-Intervention* or its broader variant, the *Principle of Non-Interference*, those terms are regularly used interchangeably, despite the latter's notionally broader scope. As proposed by Niki Aloupi, definitionally, while a *Prohibited Intervention* always involves violating jurisdiction of a State, it is not the case with *Prohibited Interference*.[433] The coercive element is also not always required for *Prohibited Interference*, while it remains a mandatory feature of a *Prohibited Intervention*. Nevertheless, two permanent UN Security Council member States appear to claim equivalence between these terms: Russia and China. Russia's official Russian-language versions of UN documents and international treaties consistently use the term невмешательство (*Nye-Vmeshatelstvo*) for both non-intervention and non-interference. For instance, that is the case for the Russian-language version of the Helsinki Accords.[434] It directly translates as *Non-Mixing-In*, and is closer in substance to non-interference, potentially being even broader in meaning than it. In a similar vein, China understands non-intervention broadly, in a way that includes non-interference. For example, its high-profile statement titled *Five Principles of Peaceful Co-Existence* claims that non-interference is covered by *State Sovereignty*:

---

432 Association of Southeast Asian Nations. (2008, January). The ASEAN Charter. Retrieved February 17, 2022, from <https://asean.org/wp-content/uploads/images/archive/publications/ASEAN-Charter.pdf>.

433 Aloupi, Niki. "The Right to Non-Intervention and Non-Interference." Cambridge Journal of International and Comparative Law 4, no. 3 (2015): pages 566–587. <https://doi.org/10.7574/cjicl.04.03.566>.

434 Organization for Security and Co-operation in Europe. (1975b, August 1). СОВЕЩАНИЕ ПО БЕЗОПАСНОСТИ И СОТРУДНИЧЕСТВУ В ЕВРОПЕ - ЗАКЛЮЧИТЕЛЬНЫЙ АКТ. Retrieved February 17, 2022, from <https://www.osce.org/files/f/documents/0/c/39505_1.pdf>.

> Mutual respect for sovereignty and territorial integrity and 'non-interference in each other's internal affairs[435]

This approach reveals the two States' tendency to see a broader scope of activities as protected from other international subjects' interference. Western countries on the other hand, including the United States and the United Kingdom, drive a wedge between the two. In this interpretation, intervention is the narrower of the two terms and is covered by the body of jurisprudence dealing with *Prohibition of Prohibited Intervention.* Interference on the other hand is perceived as a broader category that includes activities, which cannot be repelled using tools designed to deal with *Prohibited Interventions.*[436] One exception here is Germany. The core meaning of the German term *Nichteinmischung* means *Non-Mixing-In*, similarly to the Russian framing. The State joins Russian Federation and China in claiming that both interference and intervention are prohibited categories covered by the rules developed to deal with *Prohibited Interventions.*[437]

3.5.1.3 *Principle of Non-Intervention* as an *erga omnes* rule of Public International Law

In addition to international charters and treaties espousing the *Principle of Non-Intervention*, ICJ jurisprudence (more on that in the following paragraph), and three UN GA Resolutions also assert its status as an international legal norm of *erga omnes* character. The three UN GA Resolutions in question are:

- 1965 Declaration on the Inadmissibility of Intervention in the Domestic Affairs of States and the Protection of Their Independence and Sovereignty;

---

435 The government of China. (2014, June 28). Carry Forward the Five Principles of Peaceful Coexistence To Build a Better World Through Win-Win Cooperation. Retrieved February 17, 2022, from <https://www.fmprc.gov.cn/mfa_eng/wjdt_665385/zyjh_665391/201407/t20140701_678184.html>.

436 Moynihan, Harriet. (2019, December). The Application of International Law to State Cyberattacks. Chatham House. Paragraph 83. <https://www.chathamhouse.org/2019/12/application-international-law-state-cyberattacks>.

437 The government of Germany. (n.d.). Die Souveränität Deutschland. Retrieved February 17, 2022, from <https://www.bundestag.de/resource/blob/579364/034b11190e6f59a-da9686600ee020f37/WD-3-119-09-pdf-data.pdfmenschenrechte-data.pdf>.

- 1970 Declaration on Principles of International Law concerning Friendly Relations and Cooperation among States in accordance with the Charter of the United Nations;
- 1981 Declaration on the Inadmissibility of Intervention and Interference in the Internal Affairs of States.

The 1965 Declaration, (drafted as part of the de-colonization political momentum prevalent at that time) stated:

> 1. No State has the right to intervene, directly or indirectly, for any reason whatever, in the internal or external affairs of any State. Consequently, armed intervention and all other forms of interference or attempted threats against the personality of the State or against its political, economic and cultural elements, are condemned.
>
> 2. No State may use or encourage the use of economic, political or any other type of measures to coerce another State in order to obtain from it the subordination of the exercise of its sovereign rights or to secure from it advantages of any kind. Also, no State shall organize, assist, foment, finance, incite or tolerate subversive, terrorist, or armed activities directed towards the violent overthrow of the regime of another State, or interfere in civil strife in another State.
>
> 3. The Use of Force to deprive peoples of their national identity constitutes a violation of their inalienable rights and of the principle of non-intervention. [...]
>
> 4. Every State has an inalienable right to choose its political, economic, social and cultural systems, without interference in any form by another State.
>
> 6. All States shall respect the right of self-determination and independence of peoples and nations, to be freely expressed without any foreign pressure [...][438]

Due to its unanimous support at the UN (with just one abstention—from the United Kingdom), the Declaration is seen as a strong expression of *opinio juris*. The 1970 Declaration largely repeated the same messaging and additionally had a broader scope, covering a diverse range of subjects pertaining to friendly

438 United Nations General Assembly Resolution. (1965, December 21). 2131 (XX) Declaration on the Inadmissibility of Intervention in the Domestic Affairs of States and the Protection of Their Independence and Sovereignty General Assembly resolution. Retrieved February 17, 2022, from <https://legal.un.org/avl/ha/ga_2131-xx/ga_2131-xx.html>.

relations between States. Its full unanimous support at the UN GA makes it one of the most prominent resolutions to date.[439] Non-intervention is mentioned as many as eight times throughout the document, which underscores the principle's importance and laying out a number of areas of domestic jurisdiction protected by it:

> Considering that the progressive development and codification of the following principles:
>
> (a) The principle that States shall refrain in their international relations from the threat or Use of Force against the territorial integrity or political independence of any State, or in any other manner inconsistent with the purposes of the United Nations, (...)
>
> (c) The duty not to intervene in matters within the domestic jurisdiction of any State, in accordance with the Charter, (...)
>
> No State or group of States has the right to intervene, directly or indirectly, for any reason whatever, in the internal or external affairs of any other State. Consequently, armed intervention and all other forms of interference or attempted threats against the personality of the State or against its political, economic and cultural elements, are in violation of international law.
>
> No State may use or encourage the use of economic political or any other type of measures to coerce another State in order to obtain from it the subordination of the exercise of its sovereign rights and to secure from it advantages of any kind. Also, no State shall organize, assist, foment, finance, incite or tolerate subversive, terrorist or armed activities directed towards the violent overthrow of the regime of another State, or interfere in civil strife in another State.
>
> The Use of Force to deprive peoples of their national identity constitutes a violation of their inalienable rights and of the principle of non-intervention.
>
> Every State has an inalienable right to choose its political, economic, social and cultural systems, without interference in any form by another State.[440]

---

[439] Ibid.

[440] United Nations General Assembly Resolution. (1970, October 24). 2625 (XXV) Declaration on Principles of International Law concerning Friendly Relations and Cooperation among States in Accordance with the Charter of the United Nations - Main Page. Retrieved February 17, 2022, from <https://legal.un.org/avl/ha/dpilfrcs-cun/dpilfrcscun.html>.

1981 was a tumultuous time in international affairs. The risk of an armed intervention by the Soviet Union in Poland was discussed in wake of pro-democratic protests in the latter. Iran-Iraq war started a few months prior and was now in full swing. It was also the year Israel's Air Force bombarded the Iraqi nuclear reactor in Osirak and residential buildings in Beirut. This volatile context is reflected in the preamble of the UN GA Declaration on the Inadmissibility of Intervention and Interference in the Internal Affairs of States, passed that year. The document reasserts the *Principle of Non-Intervention* as stated in the 1965 and 1970 resolutions adding additional aspects that aimed to expand the scope of domestic jurisdiction, thus setting a lower bar for a *Prohibited Intervention*:

> 1. No State or group of States has the right to intervene or interfere in any form or for any reason whatsoever in the internal and external affairs of other States.
>
> 2. The principle of non-intervention and non-interference in the internal and external affairs of States comprehends the following rights and duties:
>
> (a) Sovereignty, political independence, territorial integrity, national unity and security of all States, as well as national identity and cultural heritage of their peoples;
>
> (b) The sovereign and inalienable right of a State freely to determine its own political, economic, cultural and social system, to develop its international relations and to exercise permanent sovereignty over its natural resources, in accordance with the will of its people, without outside intervention, interference, subversion, coercion or threat in any form whatsoever; [...]
>
> (a) The duty of States to refrain in their international relations from the threat or Use of Force in any form whatsoever to violate the existing internationally recognized boundaries of another State, to disrupt the political, social or economic order of other States, to overthrow or change the political system of another State or its Government, to cause tension between or among States or to deprive peoples of their national identity and cultural heritage;
>
> (b) The duty of a State to ensure that its territory is not used in any manner which would violate the sovereignty, political independence, territorial integrity and national unity or disrupt the political, economic and social stability of another State; this obligation applies also to States entrusted with responsibility for territories yet to attain self-determination and national independence;

> (c) The duty of a State to refrain from armed intervention, subversion, military occupation or any other form of intervention and interference, overt or covert, directed at another State or group of States, or any act of military, political or economic interference in the internal affairs of another State, including acts of reprisal involving the Use of Force;
>
> (d) The duty of a State to refrain from any forcible action which deprives peoples under colonial domination or foreign occupation of their right to self-determination, freedom and independence;
>
> (e) The duty of a State to refrain from any action or attempt in whatever form or under whatever pretext to destabilize or to undermine the stability of another State or of any of its institutions;
>
> (f) The duty of a State to refrain from the promotion, encouragement or support, direct or indirect, of rebellious or secessionist activities within other States, under any pretext whatsoever, or any action which seeks to disrupt the unity or to undermine or subvert the political order of other States;[…][441]

Despite its ambitious language and wide scope, the 1981 Declaration is seen as a less valuable legal document than the other two declarations. While it managed to pass at the UN GA, as many as 22 States, including prominent Western countries, voted against it. This weakens the Resolution's status as a source of consistent *opinio juris*. The Friendly Declaration of 1970 is seen as the most impactful one since it was passed with full unanimity, no abstentions, and because it included a statement that it *reflects basic principles of international law*.[442] The Helsinki Accords of 1975, mentioned earlier in the context of the *Principle of Sovereignty*, also provided additional reinforcement of the *Principle of Non-intervention*, nested within the broader concept of sovereignty. They stated:

---

441 United Nations General Assembly Resolution. (1981, December 9). 36/103. Declaration on the Inadmissibility of Intervention and Interference in the Internal Affairs of States. Retrieved February 17, 2022, from <https://digitallibrary.un.org/record/27066?ln=en>.

442 Case Concerning Military and Paramilitary Activities in and Against Nicaragua, Nicaragua v. United States -Judgment. I.C.J Reports 14, ICGJ 112 (ICJ 1986). (1986). Paragraphs 106–107, 202–203. <https://Www.Icj-Cij.Org/En/Case/70/Judgments>. Retrieved February 15, 2022, from <https://www.icj-cij.org/en/case/70/judgments>.

> VI. Non-intervention in internal affairs
>
> The participating States will refrain from any intervention, direct or indirect, individual or collective, in the internal or external affairs falling within the domestic jurisdiction of another participating State, regardless of their mutual relations. They will accordingly refrain from any form of armed intervention or threat of such intervention against another participating State. They will likewise in all circumstances refrain from any other act of military, or of political, economic or other coercion designed to subordinate to their own interest the exercise by another participating State of the rights inherent in its sovereignty and thus to secure advantages of any kind. Accordingly, they will, inter alia, refrain from direct or indirect assistance to terrorist activities, or to subversive or other activities directed towards the violent overthrow of the regime of another participating State.[443]

Importantly, consistently with the typology proposed in Figure 8, Helsinki Accords put the *Principle of Non-intervention* in the broader context of *State Sovereignty* on one end and provide a more specific prohibition of *armed interventions* and *acts of military* as a qualified case of a prohibited intervention on the other.

The legal documents laid out earlier undergird the claim that the *Principle of Non-Intervention* is a norm of international law that is binding *erga omnes* and enjoys both a statutory as well as customary character. However, it is jurisprudence of the ICJ that made the principle truly operational by applying it in a specific legal case between two States. That case is the 1986 judgment on *Military and Paramilitary Activities in and against Nicaragua (Nicaragua v. United States of America)*. In its ruling, the ICJ established three main aspects of the *Principle of Non-Intervention*:

- it nested it within the broader *Principle of State Sovereignty*;
- it laid out criteria and evidentiary tests necessary to determine whether the principle has been breached and applied them to a specific case.
- it confirmed explicitly its universally binding, customary character;

---

443 Organization for Security and Co-operation in Europe. (1975a, August 1). Helsinki Final Act. Article VI. Retrieved February 17, 2022, from <https://www.osce.org/helsinki-final-act>.

Regarding the first two points, the ICJ, drawing on the language of the *Friendly Relations Declaration,* stated that:

> In view of the generally accepted formulations, the principle forbids all States or groups of States to intervene directly or indirectly in internal or external affairs of other States. A prohibited intervention must accordingly be one bearing on matters in which each State is permitted, by the principle of State sovereignty, to decide freely. One of these is the choice of a political, economic, social and cultural system, and the formulation of foreign policy. Intervention is wrongful when it uses methods of coercion in regard to such choices, which must remain free ones. The element of coercion, which defines, and indeed forms the very essence of, prohibited intervention, is particularly obvious in the case of an intervention which uses force, either in the direct form of military action, or in the indirect form of support for subversive or terrorist armed activities within another State. As noted above (paragraph 191), General Assembly resolution 2625 (XXV) equates assistance of this kind with the Use of Force by the assisting State when the acts committed in another State "involve a threat or Use of Force." These forms of action are therefore wrongful in the light of both the principle of non-Use of Force, and that of non-intervention.[444]

Finally, the ICJ also recognized the universal, customary status of the norm:

> They therefore accept a treaty-law obligation to refrain in their international relations from the threat or Use of Force against the territorial integrity or political independence of any State, or in any other manner inconsistent with the purposes of the United Nations. The Court has however to be satisfied that there exists in customary international law an opinio juris as to the binding character of such abstention.
>
> Expressions of an opinio juris regarding the existence of the principle of non-intervention in customary international law are numerous and not difficult to find. (…) The existence in the opinio juris of States of the principle of non-intervention is backed by established and substantial practice. It has moreover been presented as a corollary of the principle of the sovereign equality of States. A particular instance of this is General Assembly resolution 2625 (XXV), the Declaration on the Principles of International Law concerning Friendly Relations and Co-operation among States.[445]

---

444 Case Concerning Military and Paramilitary Activities in and Against Nicaragua, Nicaragua v. United States. I.C.J Reports 14, ICGJ 112 (ICJ 1986). (1986). <https://Www.Icj-Cij.Org/En/Case/70/Judgments>. Retrieved February 15, 2022, from <https://www.icj-cij.org/en/case/70/judgments>.

445 Ibid.

3.5.1.4 Criteria for qualifying an act of a State as a *Prohibited Intervention*

In the 1949 Corfu Channel case, the ICJ rebuked the claim by a State that it can intervene in another State in order to furnish evidence necessary for making a legal claim in front of an international judiciary body:

> The alleged right of intervention as the manifestation of a policy of force, such as has, in the past, given rise to most serious abuses and such as cannot, whatever be the present defects in international organization, find a place in international law. Intervention is perhaps still less admissible in the particular form it would take here; for, from the nature of things, it would be reserved for the most powerful States, and might easily lead to perverting the administration of international justice itself.[446]

The two main conditions for a State's activity to be considered a *Prohibited Intervention*, based on the 1986 Nicaragua judgment by the ICJ, it has to meet two conditions:

- coercion by one State of another State;
- in relation to matters *in which each State is permitted, by the principle of State Sovereignty, to decide freely*.[447]

The ICJ addressed the issue of a gap between prevalent State declarations on non-intervention and the mixed track record of State practice, rife with violations of the principle (the judgment was rendered at the height of the Cold War with a number of proxy wars between the United States and the Soviet Union taking place around the world). The ICJ stated:

> It is not to be expected that in the practice of States the application of the rules in question should have been perfect, in the sense that States should have refrained, with complete consistency, from the Use of Force or from intervention in each other's internal affairs.[448]

---

446 Case concerning Corfu Channel (United Kingdom of Great Britain and Northern Ireland v. Albania). I.C.J. Reports 1949, 244, Gen L No. 1. (1949). Page 35. Retrieved February 15, 2022, from <https://www.icj-cij.org/en/case/1>.

447 Case Concerning Military and Paramilitary Activities in and Against Nicaragua, Nicaragua v United States. I.C.J Reports 14, ICGJ 112 (ICJ 1986). (1986). Paragraph 235. Retrieved February 15, 2022, from <https://www.icj-cij.org/en/case/70/judgments>.

448 Ibid. Paragraph 205.

This approach, which allows for the *Principle of Non-Intervention* to bind despite an imperfect State conduct was confirmed in another judgment, *Armed Activities on the Territory of the Congo*, 19 years later.[449]

The key element that distinguishes a prohibited *intervention* from a more generic *violation of sovereignty* is coercion by one State of another State. The ICJ went so far as to say that it *defines, and indeed forms the very essence of, prohibited intervention*. Some legal experts wrote that the condition of coercion *is a crucial limit in the principle of non-intervention. Without it, any act which had an effect on another state could fall within the prohibition*.[450] As noted earlier, an intervention can either proceed with or without *Use of Force*, the latter making it a prohibited *Use of Force* (more on that in Section 3.5). This implies that coercion does not have to include engagement of armed forces or physical imposition. There is however lack of a specific definition of the term *coercion* in the ICJ ruling, which led to debates as to what conduct qualifies as such (e.g., does it have to involve forcing a State to make a decision or is deprivation of control over certain area of State matters sufficient). Nevertheless, the ICJ included a number of clues in its ruling that help narrow down the scope of the definition of both coercion and the relevant matters covered by the principle.

Coercion requires a measure of pressure from the intervening State. As Oppenheim stated, independence is a question of degree,[451] which can be applied in this context to claim that there exists a certain threshold of external pressure on matters of *State Sovereignty* beyond which coercion takes place. Where the threshold lies should be determined by State practice, ICJ jurisprudence, and individual circumstances of each case (e.g., which specific State matters have been affected by an intervention). At one end of the spectrum, there is dictatorial behavior—*do this or otherwise I will do that*. Dictatorial action implies by definition that the victim State is aware

---

449 Armed Activities on the Territory of the Congo (Democratic Republic of the Congo v. Uganda). International Court of Justice. ICJ Reports 2005. (2005, December 19). Retrieved February 17, 2022, from <https://www.icj-cij.org/en/case/116>.

450 Jamnejad, Maziar., & Wood, Michael. (June 1, 2009). The Principle of Non-intervention. Leiden Journal of International Law, 22(2), 345–381. Page 381. <https://doi.org/10.1017/s0922156509005858>.

451 Oppenheim, Lassa. F. (1996). International Law A Treatise Vol. 1. Peace (9th ed.). Longman. Page 391.

of coercion. Such a stance was presented by some scholars, including Robert Nozick.[452]

On the other end of the spectrum of possible coercion are actions that infringe upon matters of *State Sovereignty* in a more nuanced way. This broader understanding of the notion coercion is fitting for the evolving nature of interactions between States, especially when technological progress, such as development of cyberspace is considered. It is also the prevalent approach among international legal scholars. For instance, Lori Fisler Damrosch wrote that:

> The traditional formulation of intervention as "dictatorial interference" resulting in the "subordination of the will" of one sovereign to that of another is also unsatisfactory, because some subtle techniques of political influence may be as effective as cruder forms of domination and because the metaphoric abstraction of the "sovereign will" of the target state tends to confuse rather than assist analysis.[453]

Oppenheim appears to concur with such an expansive statement, suggesting that coercion can take form other than dictatorial, as long as it results in deprivation of control over *Sovereign Matters* on the part of the victim State:

> To constitute intervention the interference must be forcible or dictatorial, or otherwise coercive, in effect depriving the state intervened against of control over the matter in question.[454]

Importantly, the ICJ did not focus on the motive or purpose of the intervening State. As long as coercive conduct of one State takes place in relation to another State's matters which, by the principle of *State Sovereignty*, are a domain in which a State can *decide freely*, a *Prohibited Intervention* occurs. Such conduct, by definition, is designed to achieve a goal or contribute to achievement of some goal in the future. However, the nature of intentions

---

452 Nagel, Ernest et al. (1969). Philosophy, Science, and Method: Essays in Honor of Ernest Nagel. St. Martin's Press. Pages 440–472.

453 Damrosch, Lori. F. (1989). Politics Across Borders: Nonintervention and Nonforcible Influence Over Domestic Affairs. American Journal of International Law, 83(1), pages 1–50. <https://doi.org/10.2307/2202789>.

454 Ibid. Page 432.

does not bear any direct legal consequences. This is in fact consistent with the general approach toward State responsibility. Article 2(10) of the *Draft articles on Responsibility of States for Internationally Wrongful Acts*, which formulates existing customary law, reads:

> A related question is whether fault constitutes a necessary element of the internationally wrongful act of a State. This is certainly not the case if by "fault" one understands the existence, for example, of an intention to harm. In the absence of any specific requirement of a mental element in terms of the primary obligation, it is only the act of a State that matters, independently of any intention.

By the same token, identifying the benefit that the intervening State is seeking to achieve is immaterial for the legal classification of its actions. While existence of some kind of a purpose is assumed, its range can be extremely wide. The most typical intervention is geared toward effecting a specific behavior by the victim State. However, any action that deprives the victim State of its free will with regard to *matters in which each State is permitted, by the principle of State Sovereignty, to decide freely*, can be seen as coercive in a broad sense. This interpretation makes the ICJ's ruling consistent with the Friendly Relations Declaration, which states that:

> No State may use or encourage the use of economic, political or any other type of measures to coerce another State in order to obtain from it the subordination of the exercise of its sovereign rights and to secure from it advantages of any kind.[455]

This understanding is reinforced by the ICJ ruling, which stated that the coercive behavior can be either direct or indirect and an actual intervention or just a threat of it.[456] Indirect intervention, which in the case at hand consisted of financing and arming anti-Sandinista guerrillas in Nicaragua

455 United Nations General Assembly Resolution. (1970, October 24). 2625 (XXV) Declaration on Principles of International Law concerning Friendly Relations and Cooperation among States in Accordance with the Charter of the United Nations - Main Page. Retrieved February 17, 2022, from <https://legal.un.org/avl/ha/dpilfrcscun/dpilfrcscun.html>.

456 Case Concerning Military and Paramilitary Activities in and Against Nicaragua, Nicaragua v United States. I.C.J Reports 14, ICGJ 112 (ICJ 1986). (1986). Paragraph 205. Retrieved February 15, 2022, from <https://www.icj-cij.org/en/case/70/judgments>.

by the United States, might not include a direct threat or demand raised against a State. Yet, as long as it affects matters covered by *State Sovereignty* in a way that can induce an outcome in terms of the victim State's conduct, it qualifies as a prohibited *intervention.*[457] Such broad interpretation has been since officially endorsed by governments. For instance, the government of Australia defined a *Prohibited Intervention* as:

> one that interferes by coercive means (in the sense that they effectively deprive another state of the ability to control, decide upon or govern matters of an inherently sovereign nature), either directly or indirectly, in matters that a state is permitted by the principle of state sovereignty to decide freely. Such matters include a state's economic, political and social systems, and foreign policy[458]

While whether a coercive behavior was effective does not directly influence the legal classification of State conduct, some legal scholars argue that weighing of the effect might have some measure of indirect influence in marginal cases, where presence of the effects itself determines if any inherently sovereign matters were affected.[459] Harmful effects can also provide more readily available evidence to make the case in front of an international court by a suing State.

The second definitional requirement of a *Prohibited Intervention*, that the hostile act is aimed at *matters in which each State is permitted, by the principle of State Sovereignty, to decide freely*, is as vague as the first one. The ICJ gave a number of examples in its judgment that can be perceived as the core of such matters. However, it didn't define the outer limits of that scope. At the highest level, the matters covered by the *Principle of Non-Intervention*, since it is a reflection of the *Principle of Sovereignty*, should fit into the scope covered by the latter. As stated in Section 3.3, these are aspects which a State has *the exclusive right to exercise State powers over independently*. Also, as quoted

457 Ibid.

458 The government of Australia. (2019). 2019 International Law Supplement to Australia's International Cyber Engagement Strategy. Page 2. <https://www.internationalcybertech.gov.au/sites/default/files/2020-11/2019%20Legal%20Supplment_0.PDF>.

459 Watts, Sean. (2015). Low-Intensity Cyber Operations and the Principle of Non-Intervention. Baltic Yearbook of International Law Online, 14(1), pages 137–161. <https://doi.org/10.1163/22115897-90000111>.

earlier, the ICJ specified some *Sovereign Matters* covered by the principle: *One of these is the choice of a political, economic, social and cultural system, and the formulation of foreign policy.*[460]

3.5.1.5 Application of the term *Domaine Réservé* in the context of *Prohibited Interventions*

To further specify the scope, many scholars link the notion of *Sovereign Matters* in the context of the *Principle of Non-Intervention* with the term *Domaine Réservé*, discussed already in Chapter 1. *Domaine Réservé* is not a formal term in international law but rather a concept of a bundle of areas of State activity that are regarded as exclusively domestic affairs and hence are excluded from any external interference, lawful or otherwise.[461] The term originates from the Permanent Court of International Justice's Advisory Opinion, issued in 1923 for the dispute known as *Nationality Decrees Issued in Tunis and Morocco*.[462] The dispute took place between France and the United Kingdom, with the latter claiming that France's decrees in Tunis and Morocco (its colonial territories) do not apply to British citizens. The Court determined that *Domestic Jurisdiction* matters, such as the question of nationality eligibility, are unregulated by international law, defining them as *Reserved Domain* in the English-language version of the Opinion or *Domaine Réservé* in the French-language one. The Court also claimed that:

> The question whether a certain matter is or is not solely within the jurisdiction of a State is an essentially relative question; it depends upon the development of international relations.[463]

---

[460] Case Concerning Military and Paramilitary Activities in and Against Nicaragua, Nicaragua v. United States. International Court of Justice. I.C.J Reports 14, ICGJ 112 (ICJ 1986). Retrieved February 15, 2022, from <https://www.icj-cij.org/en/case/70/judgments>.

[461] Ziegler, Katja. S. (n.d.). Domaine Réservé. Max Planck Encyclopedias of International Law. Retrieved February 18, 2022, from <https://opil.ouplaw.com/view/10.1093/law:epil/9780199231690/law-9780199231690-e1398>;

Ossoff, William. (2021). Hacking the Domaine Reserve: The Rule of Non-Intervention and Political Interference in Cyberspace. Harvard International Law Journal, 62(1), pages 1–40. <https://journals.law.harvard.edu/ilj/2021/04/hacking-the-domaine-reserve-the-rule-of-non-intervention-and-political-interference-in-cyberspace/>.

[462] Nationality Decrees Issued in Tunis and Morocco, Advisory Opinion. International Court of Justice. Permanent Court Of International Justice. (1923, February 7). Paragraph 4. Retrieved February 18, 2022, from <https://www.icj-cij.org/en/pcij-series-b>.

[463] Ibid. Paragraph 40.

A question arises as to how helpful it is to apply the notion of *Domaine Réservé* to the *Principle of Non-Intervention*. For instance, Jens D. Ohlin claimed that it has no added value:

> Despite the patina of precision in its French rendering, the concept has little internally generated content. It has to be spelled out with reference to theories and concepts that are external to the notion of sovereignty.[464]

More problematic still, as pointed out by Harriet Moynihan, is the potential inconsistency between *Domaine Réservé* and the aspects of *State Sovereignty* such as formulation of external policy, which thanks to the ICJ judgment we know for a fact should be included.[465] In this context, the scope of *Sovereign matters* covered by the *Principle of Non-Intervention* can be better defined by utilizing two other sources mentioned earlier, which preceded the ICJ *Nicaragua v. United States* judgment: the OAS Charter and the Friendly Relations Declaration. The former states:

> Article 19. No State or group of States has the right to intervene, directly or indirectly, for any reason whatever, in the internal or external affairs of any other State. The foregoing principle prohibits not only armed force but also any other form of interference or attempted threat against the personality of the State or against its political, economic, and cultural elements.[466]

The latter source, the Friendly Relations Declaration, echoed the key elements included in the OAS charter: *Every State has an inalienable right to choose its political, economic, social and cultural systems.*[467] Between these two sources and the ICJ judgment, the list of *Sovereign Matters* includes broadly defined:

---

464 Ohlin, Jens D. (2018). Did Russian Cyber-Interference In The 2016 Election Violate International Law? Cornell University Law School - Cornell Law School Research Paper, 17(15), pages 1–24. <https://archive.law.upenn.edu/live/files/6477-ohlin-jens-david-did-russina-cyber-interference-in>.

465 Moynihan, Harriet. (2019, December). The Application of International Law to State Cyberattacks. Chatham House. Page 34. <https://www.chathamhouse.org/2019/12/application-international-law-state-cyberattacks>.

466 Organization Of American States. (1948). Charter Of The Organization Of American States. Retrieved February 17, 2022, from <https://www.oas.org/en/sla/dil/inter_american_treaties_A-41_charter_OAS.asp>.

467 United Nations General Assembly Resolution. (1970, October 24). 2625 (XXV) Declaration on Principles of International Law concerning Friendly Relations and Cooperation among States in Accordance with the Charter of the United

- political system;
- social policies;
- economic policies;
- cultural policies;
- foreign policies;
- legal personality of a State.

Table 2 compiled by William Ossoff, summarizes some States' official interpretation of the definitional requirements necessary to identify a *Prohibited Intervention:*

Table 2. States' stances regarding definitional requirements for a prohibited *intervention*[468]

State	Definition of "Protected Domain of State Actions"	Definition of "Coercion" over State Actions
Netherlands	*Exclusive authority*	*Compel state to take action it would not otherwise take*
United Kingdom	*Matters at the heart of sovereignty*	*Coercive intervention*
United States	*Core functions*	*Actions without a state's consent in contravention of its rights*
Australia	*Matters of sovereignty*	*Depriving a state of "control" over governance*
France	*Political, cultural, economic, social systems*	*To harm*
Iran	*Political, cultural, economic, social organs*	*Impediment, denying, and … restricting sovereign rights*
China	*Stability*	*To undermine*

Source: Hacking the Domaine Réservé: The Rule of Non-Intervention and Political Interference in Cyberspace, William Ossoff 2021

Nations - Main Page. Retrieved February 17, 2022, from <https://legal.un.org/avl/ha/dpilfrcscun/dpilfrcscun.html>.

468 Ossoff, William. (2021). Hacking the Domaine Reserve: The Rule of Non-Intervention and Political Interference in Cyberspace. Harvard International Law Journal, 62(1), pages 1–40. <https://journals.law.harvard.edu/ilj/2021/04/hacking-the-domaine-reserve-the-rule-of-non-intervention-and-political-interference-in-cyberspace/>.

3.5.2 Application of the term *Prohibited Intervention* in cyberspace

3.5.2.1 Contextualizing the definition of *Prohibited Intervention* in cyberspace

Application of the *Principle of Non-Intervention* in cyberspace is now a widely accepted premise. The notion has been effectively included in the UN GA resolution endorsing general application of international law in cyberspace.[469] It has also been specifically supported by a number of governments. Most States now agree that hostile cyber operations can infringe upon *Sovereign Matters* of a State, creating a prohibited coercive effect. Some examples of prominent States expressing such a stance include: Poland[470], the United Kingdom,[471] Australia,[472] Netherlands,[473] the United States,[474] and France.[475]

---

469 United Nations General Assembly Resolution. (2013, June 24). Group of Governmental Experts on Developments in the Field of Information and Telecommunications in the Context of International Security - Note by the Secretary-General. Retrieved February 15, 2022, from <https://undocs.org/A/68/98>.

470 The government of the Republic of Poland. "The Republic of Poland's Position on the Application of International Law in Cyberspace - Ministry of Foreign Affairs Republic of Poland - Gov.Pl Website." Ministry of Foreign Affairs Republic of Poland, December 29, 2022. <https://www.gov.pl/web/diplomacy/the-republic-of-polands-position-on-the-application-of-international-law-in-cyberspace>.

471 The government of the United Kingdom. "Cyber and International Law in the 21st Century." (2018). Speech by Attorney General Jeremy Wright QC MP on 23 May 2018 <https://www.gov.uk/government/speeches/cyber-and-international-law-in-the-21st-century>.

472 The government of Australia. (2017). "Annex A: Australia's position on how international law applies to State conduct in cyberspace," in: Australia's International Cyber Engagement Strategy. Commonwealth of Australia, Department of Foreign Affairs and Trade. <https://www.dfat.gov.au/sites/default/files/DFAT%20AICES_AccPDF.pdf>.

473 The government of Netherlands. Letter of 5 July 2019 from the Minister of Foreign Affairs to the President of the House of Representatives on the international legal order in cyberspace (2019). <https://www.government.nl/ministries/ministry-of-foreign-affairs/documents/parliamentary-documents/2019/09/26/letter-to-the-parliament-on-the-international-legal-order-in-cyberspace>

474 Egan, Brian. J. "International Law and Stability in Cyberspace," November 10, 2016. Berkeley Journal of International Law, 35(1), pages 1–26. <https://www.law.berkeley.edu/wp-content/uploads/2016/12/BJIL-article-International-Law-and-Stability-in-Cyberspace.pdf>.

475 The government of the Republic of France. "International Law Applied to Operations in Cyberspace," (2019). French Ministry of the Armies. <https://www.defense.

In the absence of resistance from any other subject of Public International Law, this matter is all but settled. In fact, some States such as the United Kingdom, argue that the *Principle of Non-Intervention*, rather than *Principle of Sovereignty*, is the main benchmark for gauging whether a hostile cyber operation constitutes an *Internationally Wrongful Act*.[476]

There remain, however, nuanced differences between how various States perceive applicability of the *Principle of Non-Intervention* in cyberspace. For instance, in its official position paper on the subject, Poland implied that if a cyber disinformation campaign by another State forces the target State to make choices or take actions falling within *Sovereign Matters*, then such a hostile cyber campaign takes away the target State's freedom and coerces it into action, thus qualifying as a *Prohibited Intervention*.[477] Germany on the other hand claims that "spreading disinformation [at the behest of a State] via the internet may deliberately incite violent political upheaval, riots and/or civil strife in another State, thereby significantly impeding the orderly conduct of an election and the casting of ballots and thus may be comparable in scale and effects to the support of insurgents and may hence be akin to coercion."[478] This framing proposed the scale and effects doctrine as the main test, focusing on analyzing the direct impact of the intervention itself whereas Poland proposes to verify whether there was a direct impact and the Target State was actually forced into taking action as a result of said impact.

The distinction between a *Prohibited Intervention* and *Prohibited Interference*, oftentimes a problematic matter in the realm of conventional operations, is also a subject of an ongoing debate in the context of cyberspace. While a *Prohibited Intervention* definitionally always involves violating jurisdiction

---

gouv.fr/content/download/567648/9770527/file/international+law+applied+to+operations+in+cyberspace.pdf>.

476 The government of the United Kingdom. "Cyber and International Law in the 21st Century." (2018). Speech by Attorney General Jeremy Wright QC MP on 23 May 2018 <https://www.gov.uk/government/speeches/cyber-and-international-law-in-the-21st-century>.

477 Roguski, Przemysław. "Poland's Position on International Law and Cyber Operations: Sovereignty and Third-Party Countermeasures." Just Security, January 18, 2023. <https://www.justsecurity.org/84799/polands-position-on-international-law-and-cyber-operations-sovereignty-and-third-party-countermeasures/>.

478 Ibid.

of a State, it is not the case with *Prohibited Interference.*[479] Tomasz Welanyk stated that "nearly every hostile cyber operation takes place within the jurisdiction of a State other than the one initiating it."[480] This approach would render the term *Prohibited Interference* largely obsolete in the cyber context. Michael Schmitt and other authors of the Tallinn Manual proposed a different way of capturing this difference. According to them, the coercive element of a *Prohibited Intervention* (which is not required in the case of *Prohibited Interference*) is the key distinction between the two notions, especially in cyberspace. This notion would relegate *Prohibited Interference* to the realm of *Unfriendly Acts* and *Violations of Sovereignty* at most while more transgressive hostile cyber operations would be all classified as *Prohibited Interventions.* Since *Prohibition of Prohibited Intervention* is a much more established term in terms of ICJ judgments and State practice, this debate remains mostly academic.

There are a few other open-ended aspects of application of the *Principle of Non-Intervention* in cyberspace that reflect unique features of the domain that are still subject to debate by States and international scholars. These are:

- Evolution of the scope of *Sovereign Matters* in the cyber context;
- Whether the notion of *Use of Force applies* in cyberspace and whether a hostile cyber operation can qualify as a *Prohibited Intervention* with the element of *Prohibited Use of Force;*
- Whether a victim State has to be aware of a hostile cyber operation taking place for it to qualify as a *Prohibited Intervention.*

3.5.2.2 Evolution of the scope of Sovereign Matters in the cyber context

Most experts agree that the scope of *Sovereign Matters* can evolve over time. For instance, as aptly pointed out by Jerzy Kranz, the scope of *Domaine Réservé* is subject to change as States agree on treaties and customs that cut

479 Ossoff, William. (2021). Hacking the Domaine Reserve: The Rule of Non-Intervention and Political Interference in Cyberspace. Harvard International Law Journal, 62(1), pages 1–40. <https://journals.law.harvard.edu/ilj/2021/04/hacking-the-domaine-reserve-the-rule-of-non-intervention-and-political-interference-in-cyberspace>

480 Welanyk, Tomasz, "Istnienie i granice suwerenności w cyberprzestrzeni. Analiza prawna." Ph.D. dissertation, University of Warsaw, 2019. Page 86.

into previously purely domestic affairs. There exists no sphere of domestic affairs that could not potentially be subject to an international agreement. Therefore, the general tendency is for *Domaine Réservé* to shrink over time as the scope of international regulation grows.[481] For example, perpetrating grave crimes against humanity such as a genocide by a State is now prohibited by Public International Law, following the events of Word War 2.[482] Importantly, expanding international regulation onto a new area does not mean that it is now completely excluded from *Sovereign Matters* but rather creates an overlap that puts in place legal guardrails.[483] For instance, the Permanent Court of International Justice stated in its decision on the case of S. S. Wimbledon in 1923:

> Furthermore, the abandonment of the rights in question cannot be regarded as inadmissible for reasons connected with Germany's sovereignty; for the Court declines to see in the conclusion of any treaty by which a State undertakes to perform or refrain from performing a particular act, an abandonment of its sovereignty; on the contrary, the right of entering into international engagements is an attribute of State sovereignty.[484]

The language of this judgment implies that even if international law has influence over or limits certain aspects of what used to be solely *Sovereign Matters*, a State still retains authority over them. That is especially the case for those matters that are not regulated by *erga omnes* international legal rules but rather lower-grade multilateral treaty commitments. This sets the ground for considering the legal status of critical ICT infrastructure systems

---

481 Kranz, Jerzy. Pojęcie suwerenności we współczesnym prawie międzynarodowym, Warszawa PWN 2015. Page 137.

482 The Case of the S.S. Lotus (France v. Turkey). Permanent Court of International Justice. Permanent Court of International Justice (series A) No. 1. (1927, September 7). Paragraph 18. Retrieved February 17, 2022, from <https://www.icj-cij.org/public/files/permanent-court-of-international-justice/serie_A/A_10/30_Lotus_Arret.pdf>; Besson, Samantha. (n.d.). Sovereignty. Max Planck Encyclopedias of International Law. Retrieved February 18, 2022, from <https://opil.ouplaw.com/view/10.1093/law:epil/9780199231690/law-9780199231690-e1472?prd=MPIL>.

483 Crawford, James. (2012). Sovereignty as a legal value. The Cambridge Companion to International Law. Page 122. <https://doi.org/10.1017/cco9781139035651.009>.

484 The Case of S.S. "Wimbledon" Judgment (Series A, No. 1). Permanent Court of International Justice. (1923, August 17). Paragraph 25. Retrieved February 18, 2022, from <https://legal.un.org/PCIJsummaries/documents/english/5_e.pdf>.

in the cyber context. Damage to critical ICT infrastructure done through hostile cyber operations can now easily match that done by conventional international interventions. The cases of computers running Iranian nuclear facilities being destroyed in 2010 and of Ukraine's electricity grid being disrupted in 2015 are just two examples. While these systems are not mentioned in the ICJ Nicaragua ruling or the UN GA Friendly Relations Declaration although most States that expressed their position implicitly accepted their inclusion on the list of *Sovereign Matters/Domain Réservé.*[485] This is important because the principle can only be invoked if an intervention had bearing on areas where a State has an exclusive right to exercise its sovereign functions and in a way that either affects the outcomes or limits the State's control in such an area. This notion was supported by the EU Council's *Decision Concerning Restrictive Measures Against Cyber-Attacks Threatening The Union Or Its Member States*. It states:

> Cyber-attacks constituting a threat to Member States include those affecting information systems relating to, i.e.:
>
> (a) **critical infrastructure**, including submarine cables and objects launched into outer space, which is essential for the maintenance of vital functions of society, or the health, safety, security, and economic or social well-being of people;
>
> (b) **services necessary for the maintenance of essential social and/or economic activities**, in particular in the sectors of: energy (electricity, oil and gas); transport (air, rail, water and road); banking; financial market infrastructures; health (healthcare providers, hospitals and private clinics); drinking water supply and distribution; digital infrastructure; and any other sector which is essential to the Member State concerned;
>
> (c) **critical State functions**, in particular in the areas of defence, governance and the functioning of institutions, including for public elections or the voting process, the functioning of economic and civil infrastructure, internal security, and external relations, including through diplomatic missions;[486]

---

485 Ossoff, William. (2021). Hacking the Domaine Reserve: The Rule of Non-Intervention and Political Interference in Cyberspace. Harvard International Law Journal, 62(1), pages 1–40. <https://journals.law.harvard.edu/ilj/2021/04/hacking-the-domaine-reserve-the-rule-of-non-intervention-and-political-interference-in-cyberspace>

486 Council of the European Union. (2019, May 14). COUNCIL DECISION concerning restrictive measures against cyber-attacks threatening the Union or its Member States. Retrieved February 17, 2022, from <https://data.consilium.europa.eu/doc/document/ST-7299-2019-INIT/en/pdf>.

3.5.2.3 *Prohibited Interventions* with the element of *Use of Force* in cyberspace

Prohibition of Prohibited Use of Force is laid down in Article 2(4) of the UN Charter and strengthened by customary international law.[487] It enjoys the status of an *erga omnes* rule, which gives it the highest priority in the system of Public International Law.

Prohibited Interventions can be split into those that include the element of *Use of Force* and those that do not. Moreover, according to *the Advisory Opinion of the ICJ on the Legality of the Threat or Use of Nuclear Weapons*, *Use of Force* can take on any form as long as effects of the taken action are tantamount to *Use of Force.* A number of States, such as Poland, Germany, France, and Australia, have now endorsed the notion that *Use of Force* is possible in cyberspace should be gauged using the scale and effects test developed by the ICJ in the Nicaragua judgment (more on that in Section 3.6).[488]

Przemysław Roguski has proposed key factors to assess the impact scale and effects caused by hostile cyber operations with the element of *Use of Force* based on State practice and position papers. These are:

---

487 United Nations. Charter of the United Nations, June 26, 1945. 1 UNTS XVI. Article 2(4). <https://www.un.org/en/about-us/un-charter>.

488 The government of Australia. "Australia's International Cyber Engagement Strategy," November 2020. <https://www.internationalcybertech.gov.au/sites/default/files/2020-11/The%20Strategy.pdf>. Page 90; Auswärtiges Amt. "'cyber Security as a Dimension of Security Policy'. Speech by Ambassador Norbert Riedel, Commissioner for International Cyber Policy, Federal Foreign Office, Berlin, at Chatham House, London." German Federal Foreign Office, May 18, 2015. <https://www.auswaertiges-amt.de/en/newsroom/news/150518-ca-b-chatham-house/271832>; The government of the Republic of France. "International Law Applied to Operations in Cyberspace," (2019). French Ministry of the Armies. Page 8. <https://www.defense.gouv.fr/content/download/567648/9770527/file/international+law+applied+to+operations+in+cyberspace.pdf>; The government of Netherlands. Letter of 5 July 2019 from the Minister of Foreign Affairs to the President of the House of Representatives on the international legal order in cyberspace (2019). Pages 3–4. <https://www.government.nl/ministries/ministry-of-foreign-affairs/documents/parliamentary-documents/2019/09/26/letter-to-the-parliament-on-the-international-legal-order-in-cyberspace>; Koh, Harold H. (2012, September 18). International Law in Cyberspace. U.S. Department of State. Page 4. Retrieved February 15, 2022, from <https://2009-2017.state.gov/s/l/releases/remarks/197924.htm>.

- the origin of the operation;
- the military/civilian status of the perpetrator;
- the military/civilian status of the target;
- the scope of the operation;
- the actual and/or intended effects;
- the immediacy of the effects;
- the depth of penetration of the cyber infrastructure.[489]

While *opinio juris* appears to be slowly forming in favor of recognizing that it is possible to project State force inside cyberspace, it is not settled yet and will take more time and State practice to fully form.

3.5.2.4 Does the victim State have to be aware it is being targeted with a *Prohibited Intervention?*

Another challenge that is characteristic especially of cyber hostilities is that the affected State might not be aware of an operation taking place against it, even when the perpetrator State is deploying means that are designed to constrain victim State's freedom of choice such as manipulating election results or voting patterns. NATO-related experts behind the Tallinn Manual 2.0 suggested that in fact victim States do not have to be aware of a breach of international obligations by another State for it to take place.[490] Several scholars approve of this approach. For instance, Sean Watts stated that: "actions merely restricting a state's choice with respect to a course of action or compelling a course of action may be sufficient to amount to violations of the principle of non-intervention."[491] These are however not binding opinions and there are others in the academic world that claim to the contrary. More State and judiciary practice will be necessary to clarify these aspects.

---

[489] Roguski, Przemysław. "Application of International Law to Cyber Operations: A Comparative Analysis of States' Views." The Hague Program for Cyber Norms, 2020. Page 10. <https://ruj.uj.edu.pl/xmlui/bitstream/handle/item/153989/roguski_application_of_international_law_to_cyber_operations_2020.pdf?sequence=1>.

[490] Schmitt, Michael. N. & NATO Cooperative Cyber Defence Centre of Excellence. (2017). Tallinn Manual 2.0 on the International Law Applicable to Cyber Operations. Cambridge University Press. Rule 66, paragraph 25.

[491] Watts, Sean. (2015). Low-Intensity Cyber Operations and the Principle of Non-Intervention. Baltic Yearbook of International Law Online, 14(1), 137–161. <https://doi.org/10.1163/22115897-90000111>.

An important aspect of the cyber interactions between States is that they oftentimes take place with use of private companies and networks.

The interpretative logic based on analogy would support the notion that awareness is not a requirement for a *Prohibited Intervention* to take place. It would also reinforce a sense of systemic consistency in Public International Law. Since an intervention does not need to be successful in order to be classified as prohibited, it also follows that it does not have to be fully revealed to the public. This is because the coercive element, as defined by the ICJ, appears to be more tied to the perpetrator State's intent as well as the scale and effects of the intervention act itself rather than its actual impact or visibility. For example, in the Nicaragua case, the Sandinista government managed to survive the intervention stage by the United Stated and subsequently filed a complaint with the ICJ. Additionally, nesting the *Principle of Non-Intervention* within the broader *Principle of Sovereignty* implies that damage is done regardless of the actual outcome as even an unsuccessful challenge to a State's sovereignty creates a form of damage. This approach was espoused, among others, by the International Group of Experts behind the NATO-sponsored Tallinn Manual 2.0, who wrote that:

> The International Group of Experts agreed that the fact that a coercive cyber operation fails to produce the desired outcome has no bearing on whether this Rule has been breached. As an example, a State may impose a ban on exports to another State. The latter launches highly disruptive cyber operations against the former's Ministry of Commerce in an effort to force that State to rescind the ban. Irrespective of whether rescission results, the cyber operations constitute prohibited intervention.[492]

Finally, Table 3 summarized some States' official positions on the most widespread types of non-consensual cyber operations, listing whether they would qualify as *Prohibited Interventions*:

---

492 Schmitt, Michael. N. & NATO Cooperative Cyber Defence Centre of Excellence. (2017). Tallinn Manual 2.0 on the International Law Applicable to Cyber Operations. Cambridge University Press. Rule 66, paragraph 29.

Table 3. State stances on specific non-consensual cyber operations. Would they be considered *Prohibited Interventions*?[493]

Hostile Cyber Operation	Nether lands	U.K.	U.S.A.	Australia	France	Iran	China
Altering election results and systems	Yes	Yes	Yes	Yes	Yes	Yes	Yes
Causing harm to a State's political, economic, social, or cultural systems	Yes	Yes	Yes	Yes	Yes	Yes	Yes
Destabilizing a State's financial system	Yes	Yes	Yes	Yes	Yes	Yes	Yes
Damage or destruction of physical objects	Yes	Yes	Yes	Yes	Yes	Yes	Yes
Penetrating critical infrastructure systems, including ICT, hospitals, the energy grid, and military sites	Yes	Yes	Yes	Yes	Yes	Yes	Yes
Disrupting government and parliament operations	Maybe	Yes	Yes	Yes	Yes	Yes	Yes
Politically motivated Doxing	Maybe	Maybe	Maybe	Yes	Yes	Yes	Yes
Covert disinformation campaigns	No	No	Maybe	Maybe	Yes	Yes	Yes
Open propaganda campaigns	No	No	No	No	Maybe	Maybe	Maybe

Source: Own elaboration, based on Hacking the Domaine Réservé: The Rule of Non-Intervention and Political Interference in Cyberspace, William Ossoff 2021 and Application of International Law to Cyber Operations: A Comparative Analysis of States' Views, Przemysław Roguski 2020

493 Ossoff, William. (2021). Hacking the Domaine Reserve: The Rule of Non-Intervention and Political Interference in Cyberspace. Harvard International Law Journal, 62(1), pages 1–40. <https://journals.law.harvard.edu/ilj/2021/04/hacking-the-domaine-reserve-the-rule-of-non-intervention-and-political-interference-in-cyberspace/>.

3.6 Hostile cyber operations that constitute an *Act of Aggression*

3.6.1 Evolution of the terms *Act of Aggression* and Armed Attack in Public International Law

3.6.1.1 Sources of law on *Acts of Aggression* and *Armed Attacks* in Public International Law

Certain severe instances of *Prohibited Interventions*, which include the element of *Prohibited Use of Force* and also meet other conditions, qualify as *Acts of Aggression*. It is challenging to lay out a clear definitional distinction between *Acts of Aggression* on one side and *Armed Attacks* on the other. The reasons for that are twofold.

- The first one is that the key sources of international law consciously avoid setting up binding definitions of legal notions, typically preferring to only provide their core components and examples. That is also the case when it comes to *Acts of Aggression*.
- The second reason, which can also offer an explanation for avoidance of clear formal definitions by legal sources, is the dynamic development and evolution of interactions between States that creates an element of uncertainty. There is no better example of that than cyberspace, which presents a completely new way for States to collaborate and compete using methods unknown to humanity as recently as 20 years ago.

There are a number of sources of international law that explicitly address the notion of *Prohibited Use of Force*, and its nesting within the broader framework of *Prohibited Interventions*. These are:

- London Conventions For The Definition Of Aggression, 1933
- UN Charter Art. 2(4), 1945
- Declaration on the Inadmissibility of Intervention in the Domestic Affairs of States and the Protection of Their Independence and Sovereignty UN GA resolution 2131, 1965
- Declaration on Principles of International Law concerning Friendly Relations and Cooperation among States in accordance with the Charter of the United Nations. 1970

- Definition of Aggression UN GA resolution 3314, 1974
- ICJ Judgment on the case of Military and Paramilitary Activities in and against Nicaragua (Nicaragua v. United States of America), 1986
- Declaration on the Enhancement of the Effectiveness of the Principle of Refraining from the Threat or Use of Force in International Relations UN GA resolution 42/22, 1987
- Amendment to the Rome Statute of the International Criminal Court Art. 8 bis, 2010
- UN GA resolution approving the Report of the Group of Governmental Experts on Developments in the Field of Information and Telecommunications in the Context of International Security, 2015

To the extent that publications of renowned legal experts can serve as subsidiary means for the determination of rules of international law,[494] the NATO-sponsored Tallinn Manual 2.0, published in 2015, can also serve as a point of reference on *acts of aggression* in cyberspace.

The *London Conventions For The Definition Of Aggression*, three parallel international agreements signed in 1933, are among the earliest modern international legal sources that deal with *Acts of Aggression*. Signed at the Soviet embassy in London, between the Soviet Union and eight of its neighbors (Afghanistan, Estonia, Finland, Latvia, Persia, Poland, Romania, and Turkey) with three different compositions of signatory States due to ongoing diplomatic tensions within the group, they identify five actions, taking of which would apply the label of an *aggressor* to a State. It also invoked the Kellogg-Briand Pact of 1928, which condemned and renounced recourse to war by States. The Convention stated:

> Article 2
> Accordingly, the aggressor in an international conflict shall, subject to the agreements in force between the parties to the dispute, be considered to be State which is the first to commit any of the following actions:

---

494 International Court of Justice. (1945, June 26). Statute of the Court. Article 38(1), point d. Retrieved February 15, 2022, from <https://www.icj-cij.org/en/statute>.

(1) Declaration of war upon another State;

(2) Invasion by its armed forces, with or without a declaration of war, of the territory of another State;

(3) Attack by its land, naval or air forces, with or without a declaration of war, on the territory, vessels or aircraft of another State;

(4) Naval blockade of the coasts or ports of another State;

(5) Provision of support to armed bands formed in its territory which have invaded the territory of another State, or refusal, notwithstanding the request of the invaded State, to take, in its own territory, all the measures in its power to deprive those bands of all assistance or protection.

Article 3
No political, military, economic or other considerations may serve as an excuse to justification for the aggression referred to in Article 2.[495]

The Convection was soon breached by one of its initiators, the Soviet Union, which attacked and annexed land of Estonia, Latvia, Lithuania, and Poland in 1939. It also had limited geographic scope as the nine signatory nations only represented a regional grouping. Nevertheless, it provides a valuable framework of potential *Acts of Aggression* that is a point of reference for later sources of international law. Importantly, the Convention provides examples of *Armed Attacks* (such an invasion by armed forces or an attack by air forces) as well as more nuanced situations constituting *Acts of Aggression* without being *Armed Attacks* such as a naval blockade or supporting non-State actors on own territory that invade another State. Linguistic and systemic interpretative logic of the conventions implies that *Armed Attacks* are a qualified form of *Acts of Aggression*. This approach is supported by other international legal sources:

495 Convention for the Definition of Aggression. Parties: Roumania, Estonian Republic, Latvian Republic, Polish Republic, Turkish Republic, Persia, USSR, Afghanistan, Finland. (1933, July 3). Institute for International Law and Justice. Retrieved February 18, 2022, from <https://www.iilj.org/wp-content/uploads/2016/08/Convention-for-the-Definition-of-Aggression-1933.pdf>.

UN Charter, the foundational document for the modern system of international law,[496] states:

> Art. 2 The Organization and its Members, in pursuit of the Purposes stated in Article 1, shall act in accordance with the following Principles.
>
> (...)
>
> 4. All Members shall refrain in their international relations from the threat or Use of Force against the territorial integrity or political independence of any state, or in any other manner inconsistent with the Purposes of the United Nations.[497]

Art. 2(4) states that UN Member States shall refrain from resorting to *Use of Force* or threat thereof that is in any manner inconsistent with the Purposes of the United Nations. This raises questions about the definition of the term *Force* and where to draw the line between those events that qualify as *Use of Force* and those that do not. Since an *Act of Aggression* is a qualified form of a *Prohibited Intervention*, by definition it has to meet the requirement set for it, that is the coercive element and impact on *Sovereign Matters*. The UN Charter provides two examples or areas especially exposed to *Acts of Aggression*: territorial integrity and political independence. *Use of Force* against these two *Sovereign Matters* is especially egregious. *The UN GA Declaration on the Inadmissibility of Intervention in the Domestic Affairs of States and the Protection of Their Independence and Sovereignty* provides some further insights on the matter. It was already invoked in the previous section when discussing *Prohibited Interventions.* Two parts of it are particularly relevant when discussing *Acts of Aggression*:

> 1. No State has the right to intervene, directly or indirectly, for any reason whatever, in the internal or external affairs of any State. Consequently, armed intervention and all other forms of interference or attempted threats against the personality of the State or against its political, economic and cultural elements, are condemned. [...]

---

496 Henkin, Louis. (1971). "The Reports of the Death of Article 2(4) Are Greaty Exaggerated." American Journal of International Law, 65(3), pages 544–548. <https://doi.org/10.2307/2198975>.

497 United Nations. (1945, June 26). Charter of the United Nations. Article 2(4). Retrieved February 17, 2022, from <https://www.un.org/en/about-us/un-charter>.

> 3. The Use of Force to deprive peoples of their national identity constitutes a violation of their inalienable rights and of the principle of non-intervention.[498]

The Declaration distinguishes between *Prohibited Interventions* in general and *Armed Interventions*, implying that the latter is a more severe variant of a broader category of interventions. Moreover, it states that *Use of Force* aimed at depriving peoples of their national identity constitutes a *Prohibited Intervention*:

> Considering that the progressive development and codification of the following principles:
>
> (a) The principle that States shall refrain in their international relations from the threat or Use of Force against the territorial integrity or political independence of any State, or in any other manner inconsistent with the purposes of the United Nations, (…)
>
> (c) The duty not to intervene in matters within the domestic jurisdiction of any State (…)
>
> No State or group of States has the right to intervene, directly or indirectly, for any reason whatever, in the internal or external affairs of any other State. Consequently, armed intervention and all other forms of interference or attempted threats against the personality of the State or against its political, economic and cultural elements, are in violation of international law. (…)
>
> The Use of Force to deprive peoples of their national identity constitutes a violation of their inalienable rights and of the principle of non-intervention.[499]

This UN GA resolution confirmed the language from the 1965 one and expanded the scope of situations and areas covered prohibition of *prohibited*

[498] United Nations General Assembly Resolution. (1965, December 21). 2131 (XX) Declaration on the Inadmissibility of Intervention in the Domestic Affairs of States and the Protection of Their Independence and Sovereignty General Assembly resolution. Retrieved February 17, 2022, from <https://legal.un.org/avl/ha/ga_2131-xx/ga_2131-xx.html>.

[499] United Nations General Assembly Resolution. (1970, October 24). 2625 (XXV) Declaration on Principles of International Law concerning Friendly Relations and Cooperation among States in Accordance with the Charter of the United Nations - Main Page. Retrieved February 17, 2022, from <https://legal.un.org/avl/ha/dpilfrcscun/dpilfrcscun.html>.

intervention to include depriving people of their national identity. The UN GA resolution titled *Definition of Aggression*, passed in 1974 was a key development on the matter. It states:

> 3. Calls upon all States to refrain from all acts of aggression and other uses of force contrary to the Charter of the United Nations and the Declaration on Principles of International Law concerning Friendly Relations and Cooperation among States in accordance with the Charter of the United Nations; (…)
>
> Article 1
> Aggression is the use of armed force by a State against the sovereignty, territorial integrity or political independence of another State, or in any other manner inconsistent with the Charter of the United Nations, as set out in this Definition. (…)
>
> Article 3
> Any of the following acts, regardless of a declaration of war, shall, subject to and in accordance with the provisions of article 2, qualify as an act of aggression:
>
> (a) The invasion or attack by the armed forces of a State of the territory of another State, or any military occupation, however temporary, resulting from such invasion or attack, or any annexation by the Use of Force of the territory of another State or part thereof,
>
> (b) Bombardment by the armed forces of a State against the territory of another State or the use of any weapons by a State against the territory of another State;
>
> (c) The blockade of the ports or coasts of a State by the armed forces of another State;
>
> (d) An attack by the armed forces of a State on the land, sea or air forces, or marine and air fleets of another State;
>
> (e) The use of armed forces of one State which are within the territory of another State with the agreement of the receiving State, in contravention of the conditions provided for in the agreement or any extension of their presence in such territory beyond the termination of the agreement;
>
> (f) The action of a State in allowing its territory, which it has placed at the disposal of another State, to be used by that other State for perpetrating an act of aggression against a third State;
>
> (g) The sending by or on behalf of a State of armed bands, groups, irregulars or mercenaries, which carry out acts of armed force against another State of

such gravity as to amount to the acts listed above, or its substantial involvement therein.[500]

Linguistic analysis of Point 3 of the resolution implies that an *Act of Aggression* necessarily involves *Use of Force* but also that there exist other instances of *Use of Force* that are something else than *Acts of Aggression*. This fits the interpretation that there exist *Prohibited Interventions* that involve *Use of Force* without constituting *Acts of Aggression*. It then proceeds to list examples of *Acts of Aggression*, all of which involved use of armed forces by a perpetrator State. The systemic interpretative logic, drawing on the context of other sources of international law listing examples rather than giving a complete definition, such as the ICJ's Nicaragua judgment, implies that this list is not exhaustive but rather presents the most obvious core cases of State-on-State aggression. This approach is consistent with the interpretation that all *Acts of Aggression* take the form of an *Armed Attack*.

3.6.1.2 Definition of an *Act of Aggression* in Public International Law

The ICJ ruling on the case of Military and Paramilitary Activities in and against Nicaragua from 1986 (discussed earlier in the context of the *Principle of Non-Intervention*) contributed three key elements to the definition of an *Act of Aggression*:

- First, it stated that United States' support for anti-government insurgents in Nicaragua amounted to *Prohibited Use of Force*, providing a tangible example on that matter.
- Second, it confirmed that *Prohibition of Use of Force* has become a customary legal norm that enjoyed an *erga omnes* character.[501]
- Third, it reinforced the difference in the scopes of the *Principle of Non-Intervention* and the *Principle of Non-Use of Force*. It is visible in the

500 United Nations General Assembly Resolution. (1974, December 14). 3314 (XXIX) Definition of Aggression General Assembly resolution. Retrieved February 18, 2022, from <https://legal.un.org/avl/ha/da/da.html>.

501 Case Concerning Military and Paramilitary Activities in and Against Nicaragua, Nicaragua v. United States. International Court of Justice. I.C.J Reports 14, ICGJ 112 (ICJ 1986). (1986). Paragraph 227. Retrieved February 15, 2022, from <https://www.icj-cij.org/en/case/70/judgments>.

distinction between *Prohibited Interventions* in general and *Prohibited Interventions* which utilize force in particular, which the ICJ laid out in the following passage of the judgment: *The element of coercion, which defines, and indeed forms the very essence of, prohibited intervention, is particularly obvious in the case of an intervention which uses force, either in the direct form of military action, or in the indirect form of support for subversive or terrorist armed activities within another State. As noted above (paragraph 191), General Assembly resolution 2625 (XXV) equates assistance of this kind with the Use of Force by the assisting State when the acts committed in another State "involve a threat or Use of Force." These forms of action are therefore wrongful in the light of both the principle of non-Use of Force, and that of non-intervention.*[502] This passage conveys a few important statements, stating that *Armed Attacks* are a form of a *Prohibited Intervention* and also that prohibited interventions can be divided into those that involve *Prohibited Use of Force* and those that do not, reinforcing the step-wise framework presented in Section 3.2.

There is now a strong consensus that norm enjoys an even stronger status than *erga omnes*, namely *jus cogens* (i.e., it is universally accepted and applicable to all States without a possibility of a derogation).[503] In addressing the subject of *Use of Force* and *Armed Attacks*, the 1987 *UN GA Declaration on the Enhancement of the Effectiveness of the Principle of Refraining from the Threat or Use of Force in International Relations* repeated verbatim the language of the *Definition of Aggression* resolution from 1974. Three important additions that can be found there are the following:

> 2. In accordance with the purposes and principles of the United Nations, States have the duty to refrain from propaganda for wars of aggression.
>
> 3. Neither acquisition of territory resulting from the threat or Use of Force nor any occupation of territory resulting from the threat or Use of Force in contravention of international law will be recognized as le gal acquisition or occupation.

---

502 Ibid.

503 Simma, Bruno. (1999). NATO, the UN and the use of force: legal aspects. European Journal of International Law, 10(1), 1–22. Page 3. <https://doi.org/10.1093/ejil/10.1.1>.

4. A treaty is void if its conclusion has been procured by the threat or Use of Force in violation of the principles of international Jaw embodied in the Charter.[504]

The norm obliging States to refrain from propaganda is a relic of the late Cold War context, in which the resolution was developed. This provision is gaining currency in the context of internet-based fake news and cyber info wars that have an increasingly large impact. The provisions asserting no legal consequences of treaties concluded *Use of Force* or threat thereof is consistent with the provisions of the *Vienna Convention on the Law of Treaties* from 1969. Its Art. 52 states:

Article 52 Coercion of a State by the threat or Use of Force
A treaty is void if its conclusion has been procured by the threat or Use of Force in violation of the principles of international law embodied in the Charter of the United Nations.[505]

The Rome Statute of the International Criminal Court, which entered into force in 2002, also addressed the subject of *Acts of Aggression.* Specifically, Art. 8 bis, added to the Statute in 2010 (it went into force in 2018) delineated the definition of *Acts of Aggression* and provided key examples*:*

Article 8 bis - Crime of aggression (...)

2. For the purpose of paragraph 1, "act of aggression" means the use of armed force by a State against the sovereignty, territorial integrity or political independence of another State, or in any other manner inconsistent with the Charter of the United Nations. Any of the following acts, regardless of a declaration of war, shall, in accordance with United Nations General Assembly resolution 3314 (XXIX) of 14 December 1974, qualify as an act of aggression:

(a) The invasion or attack by the armed forces of a State of the territory of another State, or any military occupation, however temporary, resulting from such invasion

---

504 United Nations General Assembly Resolution. (1987, November 18). 42/22. Declaration on the Enhancement of the Effectiveness of the Principle of Refraining from the Threat or Use of Force in International Relations, General Assembly resolution. Retrieved February 18, 2022, from <https://legal.un.org/avl/ha/ga_42-22/ga_42-22.html>.

505 Vienna Convention on the Law of Treaties. United Nations. (1969, May 23). Retrieved February 18, 2022, from <https://legal.un.org/ilc/texts/instruments/english/conventions/1_1_1969.pdf>.

or attack, or any annexation by the Use of Force of the territory of another State or part thereof;

(b) Bombardment by the armed forces of a State against the territory of another State or the use of any weapons by a State against the territory of another State;

(c) The blockade of the ports or coasts of a State by the armed forces of another State;

(d) An attack by the armed forces of a State on the land, sea or air forces, or marine and air fleets of another State;

(e) The use of armed forces of one State which are within the territory of another State with the agreement of the receiving State, in contravention of the conditions provided for in the agreement or any extension of their presence in such territory beyond the termination of the agreement;

(f) The action of a State in allowing its territory, which it has placed at the disposal of another State, to be used by that other State for perpetrating an act of aggression against a third State;

(g) The sending by or on behalf of a State of armed bands, groups, irregulars or mercenaries, which carry out acts of armed force against another State of such gravity as to amount to the acts listed above, or its substantial involvement therein.[506]

Art. 8 bis directly invokes the UN GA Resolution from 1974, in an attempt to anchor itself in a broader context of State practice and their expressed *opinio juris*.[507] However, there is one important, albeit nuanced difference between both sources in terms of identifying the aggressor State. While the UN General Assembly Resolution uniformly embraced the rule of anteriority, putting the onus on the first State to reach the threshold of international aggression in its conduct, the Rome Statute of the International Criminal Court proposed a slightly modified approach, which also takes into consideration whether

---

506 Rome Statute of the International Criminal Court. International Criminal Court. (2010). Retrieved February 18, 2022, from <https://www.icc-cpi.int/resource-library/documents/rs-eng.pdf>.

507 Karska, Elżbieta. (2010). „Dorobek Konferencji Rewizyjnej Statutu MTK ze szczególnym uwzględnieniem poprawki definiującej zbrodnię agresji. Kwartalnik Prawa Publicznego," 2010(3), pages 9–39. <https://bazhum.muzhp.pl/media/files/Kwartalnik_Prawa_Publicznego/Kwartalnik_Prawa_Publicznego-r2010-t10-n3/Kwartalnik_Prawa_Publicznego-r2010-t10-n3-s9-39/Kwartalnik_Prawa_Publicznego-r2010-t10-n3-s9-39.pdf>.

any side of a conflict pushed toward *Prohibited Use of Force* by consciously provoking the other one to use force.[508] Importantly, Art. 8 bis defines an *Act of Aggression* as use of armed forces by a State against sovereignty, territorial integrity, or political independence of a State. Compared to a the broader category of *Prohibited Interventions* that involve *Use of Force, Acts of Aggression* require two specific circumstances:

- Use of armed forces by the perpetrator State;
- The narrower potential set of targets within the broader set of *Sovereign Matters.* Specifically, the target against which force is used has to be *sovereignty, territorial integrity or political independence* of the injured State.

Security Council remains the sole authoritative source that can determine the existence of an *Act of Aggression* in a legally binding way. The UN Charter states:

> Art. 39 The Security Council shall determine the existence of any threat to the peace, breach of the peace, or act of aggression and shall make recommendations, or decide what measures shall be taken in accordance with Articles 41 and 42, to maintain or restore international peace and security.[509]

The UN GA *Definition of Aggression* Resolution from 1974, reinforced that point and underscored that the *examples of Acts of Aggression enumerated in are not exhaustive and the Security Council may determine that other acts constitute aggression under the provisions of the Charter.*[510] The 2010 amendment

---

508 The latter approach, which recognizes the responsibility of a State pushing for a conflict even if it is not the first one to reach the threshold of *Act of Aggression* (such a State is sometimes being called *Amicus Aggressionis*) draws on a few cases of State practice. One of the most prominent ones is the Ems Dispatch that provoked the Second French Empire to launch the Franco-Prussian War of 1870. The subject is described in-depth in: Verdebout, Agatha. (2021). Rewriting Histories of the Use of Force: The Narrative of "Indifference." Cambridge University Press. <https://doi.org/10.1017/9781108937375>.

509 United Nations. (1945, June 26). Charter of the United Nations. Article 39. Retrieved February 17, 2022, from <https://www.un.org/en/about-us/un-charter>.

510 United Nations General Assembly Resolution. (1974, December 14). 3314 (XXIX) Definition of Aggression General Assembly resolution. Retrieved February 18, 2022, from <https://legal.un.org/avl/ha/da/da.html>.

to the Rome Statute of the International Criminal Court aims to modify this process by extending the ability to identify and prosecute Crimes of Aggression (in a limited form—only for the sake of personal accountability) to the International Criminal Court (ICC) too. While the amendment has not entered into force yet, it laid out potential future rules for ICC's engagement in that aspect. Article 13 introduced by the 2010 Amendment builds a bridge between the foundational competence of the UN Security Council to identify Acts of Aggression and the ICC's competence to prosecute individuals responsible for them (which might also involve ICC's competence to identify an Act of Aggression for the sake of individual accountability). It states:

> Article 13 Exercise of jurisdiction
> The Court may exercise its jurisdiction with respect to a crime referred to in article 5 in accordance with the provisions of this Statute if:
>
> (a) A situation in which one or more of such crimes appears to have been committed is referred to the Prosecutor by a State Party in accordance with article 14;
>
> (b) A situation in which one or more of such crimes appears to have been committed is referred to the Prosecutor by the Security Council acting under Chapter 7 of the Charter of the United Nations; or
>
> (c) The Prosecutor has initiated an investigation in respect of such a crime in accordance with article 15.[511]

Either a State Party, the UN Security Council, or an ICC prosecutor can all initiate an investigation, a part of which would be the establishment of facts as to the purported *Act of Aggression*. However, even if a State Party or an ICC Prosecutor manage to launch an investigation on that matter, the UN Security Council can stay or pause it indefinitely, in 12-month increments. This situation, laid out in Art.16 of the Statute, confirms the primary role of the UN Security Council in determining occurrence of *Acts of Aggression*:

> Article 16 Deferral of investigation or prosecution
> No investigation or prosecution may be commenced or proceeded with under this Statute for a period of 12 months after the Security Council, in a resolution

511 Rome Statute of the International Criminal Court. International Criminal Court. (2010). Retrieved February 18, 2022, from <https://www.icc-cpi.int/resource-library/documents/rs-eng.pdf>.

> adopted under Chapter 7 of the Charter of the United Nations, has requested the Court to that effect; that request may be renewed by the Council under the same conditions.[512]

A qualified version of an *Act of Aggression* is an *Armed Attack.* It is arguably the gravest type of a *Violation of Sovereignty* of a State by another State. As a *casus belli*, it also creates a situation of *jus ad bellum,* that is, it provides *iusta causa* grounds justifying the transition from international legal norms of peaceful time to those regulating an armed conflict.[513] More broadly, all *Acts of Aggression* technically constitute a *casus belli* but an *Armed Attack* is the most canonical instance.[514] Art. 51 of the UN Charter states:

> Nothing in the present Charter shall impair the inherent right of individual or collective self-defense if an armed attack occurs against a Member of the United Nations.[515]

This article has arguably a narrower scope than article 2(4) mentioned earlier, which outlawed *Prohibited Use of Force* in general rather than *Armed Attacks* specifically. Importantly, between the two provisions, only article 51 invokes *the inherent right of individual or collective self-defense.* The logical consequence of article 51 is that not every type of *Prohibited Use of Force* qualifies as an *Armed Attack.*[516] How big the gap is between *Acts of Aggression* in general and *Armed Attacks* in particular is the subject of a debate. Yoram Dinstein for example wrote that the overlap is very tight and only *Use of Force* that does not result in deaths or property destruction would qualify as an *Act of Aggression* or a *Prohibited Intervention* rather than an *Armed Attack.*[517] The ICJ

---

512 Ibid.

513 Kowalski, Michał. (2005). Ius ad bellum a systemowy charakter prawa międzynarodowego. Wydawnictwo UMCS. Page 190.

514 Stahn, Carthen. (2006). "Jus ad bellum," "jus in bello" … "jus post bellum"? -Rethinking the Conception of the Law of Armed Force. European Journal of International Law, 17(5), 921–943. <https://doi.org/10.1093/ejil/chl037>.

515 United Nations. (1945, June 26). Charter of the United Nations. Article 51. Retrieved February 17, 2022, from <https://www.un.org/en/about-us/un-charter>.

516 Case Concerning Military and Paramilitary Activities in and Against Nicaragua, Nicaragua v United States. I.C.J Reports 14, ICGJ 112 (ICJ 1986). (1986). Paragraph 191. Retrieved February 15, 2022, from <https://www.icj-cij.org/en/case/70/judgments>.

517 Dinstein, Yoram. (2013). Cyber War and International Law: Concluding Remarks at the 2012 Naval War College International Law Conference. International Law

in its jurisprudence emphasized the difference between the two notions[518] but also assumed a broad interpretation of what could constitute an *Armed Attack*. For instance, in the *Oils Platform Case*, it stated that *the possibility that the mining of a single military vessel might be sufficient to bring into play the inherent right of self-defense*, implying this way that even a relatively minor act could potentially qualify as an *Armed Attack*.[519] The linkage between the *right to self-defense* and the *Armed Attack* shows that the distinction between *Acts of Aggression* and armed Attacks plays an important role. *Prohibited Use of Force* below the threshold for an *Armed Attack* is not a delict of sufficient gravity to self-defense, which is effectively an in-kind response. Access to self-defense is being guarded by both the UN Charter and the ICJ because the UN Charter framework leans away from that, preferring instead seeking a peaceful resolution of disputes.

3.6.1.3 Definition of an *Armed Attack* in Public International Law

Similarly to other forms of *Violation of Sovereignty*, there is no formal definition of an *Armed Attack* in official sources of international law.[520] The UN GA resolution *Definition of Aggression* and related later sources (such as the 2010 Amendment to the Rome Statute of the ICC) laid out useful examples, including: *attack by the armed forces of a State of the territory of another State, bombardment of State territory by armed forces of another State, attack by the armed forces of a State on the land, sea or air forces, or marine and air fleets of another State, or sending armed bands, groups, irregulars or mercenaries, which carry out acts of armed force against another State of such gravity as to amount to such acts*. The ICJ provided a measure of insight on that matter in its 1986 *Nicaragua* Judgment in which it listed a few examples of an *Armed*

Studies of the U.S. Naval War College, 89, 275–287. Page 280. <https://digital-commons.usnwc.edu/ils/vol89/iss1/2/>.

518 Case Concerning Military and Paramilitary Activities in and Against Nicaragua, Nicaragua v. United States. International Court of Justice. Paragraph 191. I.C.J Reports 14, ICGJ 112 (ICJ 1986). (1986). Retrieved February 15, 2022, from <https://www.icj-cij.org/en/case/70/judgments>.

519 Case Concerning Oil Platforms, (2003), (Iran v. United States). ICJ Reports 2003. (2003, November 6). Paragraph 72. Retrieved February 18, 2022, from <https://www.icj-cij.org/en/case/90>.

520 Lin, Herbert. (2011). Responding to Sub-Threshold Cyber Intrusions: A Fertile Topic for Research and Discussion. Georgetown University Press, 2011, 127–135. Page 128.

Attack. Importantly, it limited its definition scope by rejecting inclusion in the definition of acts such as provision of weapons to rebels or logistical support for them:

> The sending by or on behalf of a State of armed bands, groups, irregulars or mercenaries, which carry out acts of armed force against another State of such gravity as to amount to an actual armed attack, or its substantial involvement. (…)

Court does not believe that the concept of "armed attack" includes not only acts by armed bands where such acts occur on a significant scale but also assistance to rebels in the form of the provision of weapons or logistical or other support.[521]

The notion of *Armed Attack* also plays a big role in the system of intergovernmental military alliance NATO. The NATO Charter, which is the foundational document for the alliance of 30 North Atlantic States, states in its Article 5:

> The Parties agree that an armed attack against one or more of them in Europe or North America shall be considered an attack against them all and consequently they agree that, if such an armed attack occurs, each of them, in exercise of the right of individual or collective self-defence recognised by Article 51 of the Charter of the United Nations, will assist the Party or Parties so attacked by taking forthwith, individually and in concert with the other Parties, such action as it deems necessary, including the use of armed force, to restore and maintain the security of the North Atlantic area.[522]

François Delerue framed the relationship between *Use of Force*, *Act of Aggression*, and *Armed Attack* the following way: "It is broadly accepted that a cascading relationship exists between [the terms]. The term *Armed Attack* being the narrowest and constituting a sub-category of *Aggression*, and *Aggression* itself being a sub-category of *Force*. However, none of these terms are defined by

---

521 Case Concerning Military and Paramilitary Activities in and Against Nicaragua, Nicaragua v United States. International Court of Justice. I.C.J Reports 14, ICGJ 112 (ICJ 1986). (1986). Paragraph 195. Retrieved February 15, 2022, from <https://www.icj-cij.org/en/case/70/judgments>.

522 North Atlantic Treaty Organization (NATO). (1949, April 4). The North Atlantic Treaty. Retrieved February 18, 2022, from <https://www.nato.int/cps/en/natolive/official_texts_17120.htm>.

the UN Charter. Moreover, a certain ambiguity results from the use of different terms based on the different language versions of the UN Charter."[523]

Similarly to Article 51 of the UN Charter, self-defense measures invoked in Article 5 of the NATO Charter are only unlocked by an *Armed Attack* rather than an *Act of Aggression* or *Prohibited Use of Force* in general. So far, Article 5 was only invoked once in more than 70 years of the history of NATO. It took place in 2001, following the 9/11 attack on the World Trade Center.[524] The attack was perpetrated by Al-Qaida, an organization that can be classified as *armed bands, groups, irregulars or mercenaries* for the sake of classifying the event. The fact that they did not represent any State, and were only enabled by their hosts, the Taliban government of Afghanistan, potentially expanded understanding of how the link between a State and the *armed bands has to be* for the sake of attribution.

3.6.2 Application of the term *Act of Aggression* in cyberspace

3.6.2.1 Meaning of the term *Use of Force* in cyberspace

Use of Force is a requirement for qualifying State behavior as an *Act of Aggression. Prohibited Interventions*, discussed in the previous section, can include the element of *Force*, but it is not a precondition. That is why defining the notion of *Force* and *Use of Force* in the cyber context is essential when discussing *Acts of Aggression.*

Following the historic 2013 UN GGE Report, approved by the UN GA, which explicitly stated that the rules of international law apply in cyberspace, the 2015 follow-up report by the same body offered more specific guidelines on application of international law in the area of ICT usage. In terms of application of the terms *State Sovereignty, Non-Intervention,* and *Use of Force*, UN GGE stated that *Prohibition of Use of Force* in cyberspace is a commitment of all States that stems from the UN Charter and is of central importance:

> In considering the application of international law to State use of ICTs, the Group identified as of central importance the commitments of States to the following

---

523 Delerue, François. Cyber Operations and international law. Cambridge: Cambridge University Press, 2020. Page 328.

524 North Atlantic Treaty Organization (NATO). (2001, October 2). Invocation of Article 5 confirmed. Retrieved February 18, 2022, from <https://www.nato.int/docu/update/2001/1001/e1002a.htm>.

> principles of the Charter and other international law: sovereign equality; the settlement of international disputes by peaceful means in such a manner that international peace and security and justice are not endangered; refraining in their international relations from the threat or Use of Force against the territorial integrity or political independence of any State, or in any other manner inconsistent with the purposes of the United Nations; respect for human rights and fundamental freedoms; and non-intervention in the internal affairs of other States.[525]

The Report repeats the language of the UN GA Definition of Aggression Resolution from 1974, when it talks about *refraining in international relations from the threat or Use of Force against the territorial integrity or political independence of any State, or in any other manner inconsistent with the purposes of the United Nations.*

Application of the notions of *Acts of Aggression* and *Prohibited Use of Force* in cyberspace requires clarification on what the scope of the term *Force* is in international law and how it relates to cyber interactions between States. Since there is no source of international law that would directly define it, we should begin the attempt at reconstructing it by analyzing recognized academic works. Henry Campbell Black's Law Dictionary states that force means *power, violence, or pressure against a person or thing.*[526] This is a broad definition that could easily encompass cyber operations. The ICJ's 1996 *Advisory Opinion on the Legality of the Use of Nuclear Weapons* appears to support that broad and flexible approach to defining *Force.* In it, the ICJ stated that Articles 2(4), 51 and 41 of the UN Charter: *do not refer to specific weapons. They apply to any Use of Force, regardless of the weapons*[527] This wide understanding of the term *Force* in Public International Law can be derived from the language of the UN Chapter too. Yoram Dinstein noted that Article 2(4) of the Charter, which is the foundation of the *Principle of Prohibition of Use of Force* talks

525 United Nations General Assembly Resolution. (2015, July 22). Group of Governmental Experts on Developments in the Field of Information and Telecommunications in the Context of International Security - Note by the Secretary-General. Retrieved February 15, 2022, from <https://documents-dds-ny.un.org/doc/UNDOC/GEN/N15/228/35/PDF/N1522835.pdf?OpenElement>.

526 Black, Henry., & Garner, Bryan. (2009). Black's Law Dictionary. St. Paul, MN: West. Page 717.

527 Advisory Opinion on Legality of the Threat or Use of Nuclear Weapons. International Court of Justice. (1996, July 8). Retrieved February 18, 2022, from <https://www.icj-cij.org/en/case/95>.

about *Force* while the expression *Armed Force* can be found in other parts of the document, specifically Article 41 and 46.[528] The linguistic interpretative logic dictates that the fact that the two phrases are different, one being a more specific version of the other, means the interpretation of them should reflect that difference. This means that Article 2(4) talks about various types of *Force*, only one of them being *Armed Force*. The systemic interpretative logic, drawing on the context of the system, supports this understanding, as the system of international law aims to prevent escalations between States, pushing instead for consensual resolution of tensions. Interpreting the term *Force* too narrowly could lead to a risk of hostile States deploying some form of *Force* while maintaining plausible deniability about it not being *Armed Force* and hence not subject to the prohibition contained in Article 2(4) of the Charter. At the same time, not all types of force qualify as *Force* for the sake of Article 2(4) of the UN Charter and therefore the overall *Prohibition of Use of Force* between States. UN Charter Preparatory works (Travaux Préparatoires), which are the official record of the drafting process of the international legal document including authors' comments, reveal that economic, political, and indirect types of force are not encompassed by Article 2(4) and instead fall under the less severe category of *Coercion*, that is, the main ingredient of a *Prohibited Intervention*.[529] *Coercion* is a broad term that includes both acts that have the component of force as well as those that do not, making it a much softer category (see Figure 10 for details).

Prohibited Use of Force by a State against another by definition infringes upon *Sovereign Matters* as it violates *State Sovereignty* and potentially breaches other areas of *Domaine Réservé*. It also automatically includes the *coercive element* as it forces the injured State to respond and constrains its freedom of action. For these reasons, identifying *Prohibited Use of Force*, in absence of an ongoing armed conflict, simultaneously proves existence of a *Prohibited Intervention*.

---

528 Dinstein, Yoram. (2013). Cyber War and International Law: Concluding Remarks at the 2012 Naval War College International Law Conference. International Law Studies of the U.S. Naval War College. Page 88.

529 Delerue, François. Cyber Operations and international law. Cambridge: Cambridge University Press, 2020. Page 286.

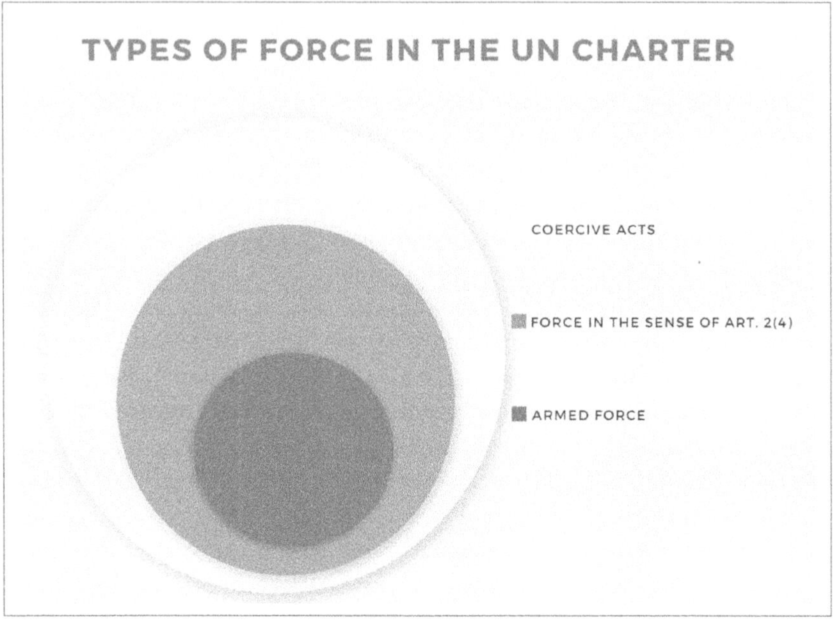

Figure 10. Types of *Force* in the UN Charter
Source: Own elaboration

Besides the fact that *Force* can take on various forms, the most egregious one of them being *Armed Force*, and the fact that some weaker forms of force do not actually qualify as such for the sake of the *Principle of Prohibition of Use of Force*, implying existence of a threshold, nothing else can be gleaned from the canonical sources of International Law. This opens space for developments in the field of technology and warfare that can fit into the ever-expanding notion of *Force*. However, it also creates uncertainty as to what new forms of force should be relegated to only constituting a *Coercion*.

The current reality is that there is neither established State practice nor documents from international courts or organizations that would point to an exact threshold of *Force* or a formula that would help determine it. This is even more so the case in cyberspace where additionally to that challenge, transposition of the few existing definitional cues is not fully clear either. This state of flux was summarized well by U.S. Armed Forces Vice Admiral Michael Rogers who stated in his formal deposition in front of the U.S. Senate: "As a matter of law, the Department of Defense believes that what constitutes a *Use of Force* in cyberspace is the same for all nations. Our activities in cyberspace would be governed by Article 2(4) of the UN Charter the same way other nations' would be. With that said, there is no international consensus on the precise definition of a *Use of Force*, in or [even] out of cyberspace."[530]

This situation is only reinforced by the fact that no State has claimed deployment of the Stuxnet virus, which remains the most tangible example of a hostile cyber operation creating serious physical effects on record, to be a case of *Prohibited Use of Force.* An additional challenge is that the Article 41 of the UN Charter explicitly states that *complete or partial interruption of (...) postal, telegraphic, radio, and other means of communication* is a measure not involving *Use of Force.*[531] Hostile cyber operations are in a certain way a form of interruption of means of communication. However, in the current reality their damaging impact can be much greater than envisioned back in 1945 and, as demonstrated by Stuxnet, very physical. François Delerue claims that Article 41 is written in a flexible enough manner to allow for a reinterpretation that would prevent hostile cyber operations from enjoying impunity in that regard.[532] Daniel Silver proposed that Article 41 is a reflection of the state of technology toward the end of World War 2 rather than a formal blockade for treating any hostile cyber operations as *Use of Force.*[533] Nevertheless, in the context of the current lack of consensus, it adds to the flux.

Faced with this challenge, various scholars weighed in to propose potential solutions. Ian Brownlie suggested that weapons and methods employed for the destruction of life and property should qualify as means of *Force* in the sense of Article 2(4) of the UN Charter, while those that create other types of damage are only means of coercion.[534] This model classifies some extreme forms of hostile cyber operations as *Prohibited Use of Force*. The example of the Stuxnet virus, which damaged Iranian nuclear facilities showcases damage

---

530 Ibid. Page 290

531 United Nations. (1945, June 26). Charter of the United Nations. Article 41. Retrieved February 17, 2022, from <https://www.un.org/en/about-us/un-charter>.

532 Delerue, François. Cyber Operations and international law. Cambridge: Cambridge University Press, 2020. Page 277.

533 Ibid.

534 Ibid. Page 287; Crawford, James, and Ian Brownlie. Brownlie's principles of Public International Law. Oxford: Oxford University Press, 2019. Page 362.

to property caused by cyber means. Albrecht Randelzhofer and Oliver Dörr, in a similar vein, proposed a narrow rule of equivalence where only those cyber methods and tools that can create effects similar to that caused by a conventional armed attack can be qualified as *Prohibited Use of Force.*[535] The Fact-Finding Commission on the Conflict in Georgia, formed by the EU Council in the wake of the Russian invasion in 2008, stated *Force* has to be physical in its manifestation, thus proposing a clear threshold that can be applied, among other acts, to hostile cyber operations.[536]

Certain legal cases that have taken place in front of international courts also provide guidance on what actions are not intense enough to constitute *Use of Force.* In the *Corfu Channel* case from 1948 British ships' incursion into Albanian territorial waters was classified as a *Violation of Sovereignty* but not as *Prohibited Use of Force* by the ICJ.[537] In the three *Fisheries Juridictions* judgments, rendered between 1974 and 1998, the ICJ also refused to classify minor displays of hostility and physical force between naval vessels of different States as *Use of Force.*[538]

At the current stage of development of law on the matter, cases of *Use of Force* in cyberspace must be analyzed on a case-by-case basis, taking into consideration the unique context alongside the totality of available norms and applicable precedents. Additionally, the Public International Law includes two general tools that can help guide this process:

- The Martens Clause;
- Article 31 of the Vienna Convention on the Law of Treaties.

The so-called "Martens Clause" was included in the 1899 Hague Convention II on the Laws and Customs of War on Land. It derives its name from the

[535] Dörr, Oliver, and Randelzhofer Albrecht. "Ch.I Purposes and Principles, Article 2 (4)." [in:] Simma, Bruno, and Nikolai Wessendorf. The charter of the United Nations: A commentary. Oxford: Oxford University Press, 2012. Page 210.

[536] Delerue, François. Cyber Operations and international law. Cambridge: Cambridge University Press, 2020. Page 292.

[537] Case concerning Corfu Channel (United Kingdom of Great Britain and Northern Ireland v. Albania). I.C.J. Reports 1949, 244, Gen L No. 1. (1949). Paragraph 35. Retrieved February 15, 2022, from <https://www.icj-cij.org/en/case/1>.

[538] Delerue, François. Cyber Operations and international law. Cambridge: Cambridge University Press, 2020. Page 293.

surname of its initiator, the Russian delegate Fyodor Fyodorovich Martens. Its contents are included in Article 1 §2 of the I Additional Protocol:

> Until a more complete code of the laws of war is issued, the High Contracting Parties think it right to declare that in cases not included in the Regulations adopted by them, populations and belligerents remain under the protection and empire of the principles of international law, as they result from the usages established between civilized nations, from the laws of humanity and the requirements of the public conscience.[539]

§4 of the Preamble to the II Additional Protocol, agreed upon in 1977, additionally included an abridged and modified version of the Martens Clause:

> In cases not covered by the law in force, the human person remains under the protection of the principles of humanity and the dictates of the public conscience.[540]

The clause was also invoked by the ICJ, which in its 1996 Advisory Opinion on the Legality of the Threat or Use of Nuclear Weapons stated:

> *The Martens Clause has proved to be an effective means of addressing the rapid evolution of military technology.*[541]

The clause's interpretation is that any State-on-State aggression and *Use of Force*-related situations not covered by the Hague (and Geneva) Protocols, are subject to the customary international public rules *of humanity and the requirements of the public conscience*. The clause remains generic in nature and while its inclusion in the body of Public International Law, including its customary law status, is now well established, it is not obvious how its application to concrete cases should proceed. Methods of hostile cyber operations can be well described as *military technology*, which makes the invocation by

---

539 Hague Convention II on the Laws and Customs of War on Land (1899). Article 1 §2 the I Additional Protocol. Retrieved February 15, 2022, from <https://ihl-databases.icrc.org/en/ihl-treaties/hague-conv-ii-1899>.

540 Ibid. §4 of the Preamble to the II Additional Protocol.

541 Advisory Opinion on Legality of the Threat or Use of Nuclear Weapons. International Court of Justice. (1996, July 8). ICJ Reports 66, 74–75, paragraph 78. Retrieved February 18, 2022, from <https://www.icj-cij.org/en/case/95>.

the ICJ helpful in terms of applicability of the Martens Clause in cyberspace. However, that invocation by Judge Simma did not include examples or further details. The debate at the UN General Assembly in 1995 on application of the Clause proved inconclusive and yielded inconsistent propositions by States.[542]

The one point of clarity came from the International Committee of the Red Cross, which stated in its official commentary on The First Geneva Convention that the sole undisputed function of the Martens Clause in modern International Public Law is to be *lex specialis* that prevents automatic permissibility of any acts or methods of an armed conflict that are not covered by existing law (i.e., this *lex specialis* does not extend to areas of Public International Law other than the one regulating armed conflict).[543] This interpretation enables the system of Public International Law to penalize the most severe cases of hostile cyber operations, albeit most likely only those that cause damage equivalent to that caused by conventional means and would qualify as *Use of Force*. Tomasz Welanyk stated that this means that the Martens Clause is a legal path for applying the doctrine of kinetic equivalence to hostile cyber operations above the threshold of *Use of Force*: "There is no doubt, that the Clause refers to acts surpassing the threshold of *Use of Force* according to the doctrine of kinetic equivalence. An Attack on civilian infrastructure, e.g. an airport network, that results in casualties, would by the power of the Clause be prohibited, regardless of the IT technology that was utilized to conduct it. (...) Continuous development of cyberspace leads to creation of an ever-broader range of IT technologies that can be used to conduct actions with results that are equivalent to those done with conventional kinetic means or even actions with direct real-world

---

542 Welanyk, Tomasz, "Istnienie i granice suwerenności w cyberprzestrzeni. Analiza prawna." Ph.D. dissertation, University of Warsaw, 2019. Page 134; United Nations General Assembly Resolution. (January 9, 1995). General and complete disarmament - A Prohibition of the dumping of radioactive wastes. Retrieved February 15, 2022, from <https://digitallibrary.un.org/record/193267?ln=en>.

543 Ticehurst, Rupert. "The Martens Clause and the Laws of Armed Conflict." ICRC, April 30, 1997. Paragraphs 3–5. <https://www.icrc.org/en/doc/resources/documents/article/other/57jnhy.htm>; "The Updated Commentary on the First Geneva Convention – a New Tool for Generating Respect for International Humanitarian Law." International Review of the Red Cross, November 1, 2016. Pages 1209–1226. <https://international-review.icrc.org/articles/updated-commentary-first-geneva-convention-new-tool-generating-respect-international>.

kinetic results. The terms *public conscience* or *humanity* that are used in the Clause allow for prohibition of cyberattacks based on their effects. Therefore, they are one of few ways allowing for effective regulation of cyberspace by utilizing traditional international law."[544]

Article 31 of the Vienna Convention on the Law of Treaties of 1969 states:

> A treaty shall be interpreted in good faith in accordance with the ordinary meaning to be given to the terms of the treaty in their context and in the light of its object and purpose.[545]

The article provides a *General Rule of Interpretation* of treaties. From the systemic perspective however, it also offers a basic rule for interpretation of legal commitments of States in general. The threat posed by hostile cyber operations can be easily tied to existing treaty commitments by States, the most important of which stem from the UN Charter. The commitment to international peace and *Prohibition of Use of Force* is now both a treaty and customary norm that is well anchored in the Charter, most importantly Article 2(4) but also many others. From that perspective, Article 31 provides a powerful path for holding States accountable for conducting hostile cyber operations and resorting to *Prohibited Use of Force* by cyber means. Two main requirements are provided by the article. First, it requires that legal norms be interpreted in good faith. This means that attempts at circumventing *Prohibition of Use of Force* by, say, conducting a series of small-intensity operations instead of a big one, could still be deemed prohibited. Second, it requires that legal terms be interpreted according to their ordinary meaning, in their context, and in the light of their object and purpose. This allows for some latitude in transposition of existing commitments into cyberspace where their object and purpose might require a specific application, as long as the ordinary meaning of the terms used can be maintained. Examples might include blockading of the functioning of State organs in cyberspace, which can be seen as equivalent to forcefully shutting down a physical site where a State organ is located.

---

544 Welanyk, Tomasz, "Istnienie i granice suwerenności w cyberprzestrzeni. Analiza prawna." Ph.D. dissertation, University of Warsaw, 2019. Page 136.

545 Vienna Convention on the Law of Treaties (May 23, 1969). UN Doc A/Conf39/27. Article 31(1) Retrieved February 15, 2022, from <https://legal.un.org/ilc/texts/instruments/english/conventions/1_1_1969.pdf>.

3.6.2.2 Measuring *Use of Force* in cyberspace

Measuring intensity of a hostile cyber operation is essential in determining the threshold beyond which they qualify as instances of *Use of Force.* While there are a few clues coming from State practice and statements, as well as case-specific ICJ judgments, as to how defining the intensity and the threshold should proceed, there is still much uncertainty as to what the general rules should be. It is especially difficult in cyberspace, where the additional complication of gauging equivalence with kinetic acts is present. Therefore, a number of scholars have weighed in, attempting to reconcile various legal cases and State practices into a one cohesive narrative. At the fundamental level, three main doctrines can be utilized to determine whether a hostile cyber operation meets the threshold of *Use of Force:*[546]

- Weapon-based Doctrine;
- Target-based Doctrine;
- Effects-based Doctrine.

The weapon-based doctrine (also known as the instrument-based approach) focuses on the instruments chosen to conduct a hostile act. In the cyber context, the examples might include broadcasting manipulative information using social media, launching a DDoS attack aimed at shutting down a government website providing a service to citizens, or devising a virus that can damage the electricity grid of a target State. The classification of a hostile cyber operation according to this doctrine stems from the selection of the instrument or weapon and matching it with reasonably expected results. Manipulative information in cyberspace aimed at influencing public opinion in the target State is a "weapon" that could potentially cause a *Violation of Sovereignty* but it is not an instrument typically designed for conducting a *Prohibited Intervention* or an *Act of Aggression.* Reese Nguyen argues that applying the Weapon-based Doctrine in cyberspace requires using analogy

---

546 University of Oslo Faculty of Law. (2016, April). "When do cyber operations amount to use of force and armed attack, and what response will they justify?." Page 24. <https://www.duo.uio.no/bitstream/handle/10852/50840/723.pdf?sequence=1>.

from the conventional world.[547] For instance, Internet propaganda could be an equivalent of paying for coverage in traditional media. Damaging a power grid using a computer virus could be an equivalent of conducting an incursion into sovereign territory with the aim of damaging electricity infrastructure, which can be classified as a *Prohibited Intervention* involving *Use of Force.* The weapon-based doctrine is an imperfect fit in the cyber context. Marco Roscini pointed out that it is difficult to identify specific IT methods as a weapon as many of them are of a dual, triple, or even multi-use nature.[548] François Delerue also criticized this approach saying "This approach is based on the similarity between cyber operations and traditional weapons; this resemblance is very difficult to ascertain and has the potential to lead to far-fetched analyses."[549]

The target-based doctrine is built on the premise that only cyber operations that aim to disrupt or destroy targets of certain importance can qualify as *Prohibited Use of Force.* This doctrine focuses less on the weapons or instruments involved. Nikolaos Tsagourias and Russell Buchan proposed that targets of significant enough importance in the cyber context are essentially all elements of critical infrastructure, such as the electricity grid or internet infrastructure cables.[550] This interpretation appears however to be too narrow. Critical infrastructure is the natural core type of target for *Prohibited Use of Force* in cyberspace because it can be affected remotely by electronic means. However, government-owned buildings or even sites of strategic importance such as top universities could be considered targets important enough to validate invoking *Prohibited Use of Force* by the injured State. The target-based doctrine might appear simplistic as it is grouping together very diverse types of action. Indeed, scholars such Yaroslaw Radziwill stated that the approach is too inclusive to be applied in cyberspace as it ignores

547 Nguyen, Reese. (2013). "Navigating Jus ad Bellum in the Age of Cyber Warfare." California Law Review, 101(4), 1079–1130. Page 1117. <https://www.jstor.org/stable/23784325>.

548 Roscini, Marco. Cyber Operations and the use of force in international law. New York: Oxford University Press, 2016. Page 54.

549 Delerue, François. Cyber Operations and international law. Cambridge: Cambridge University Press, 2020. Page 289.

550 Tsagourias, Nicholas, and Buchan, Russell. (2021). Research Handbook on International Law and Cyberspace (Research Handbooks in International Law series) (2nd ed.). Edward Elgar Publishing.

intensity or characteristics of a hostile cyber operation.[551] François Delerue provides an interpretation for this situation, explaining that the framework was mostly developed in the context of self-defense measures and was driven by the postulate that the *scale and effects* doctrine is not providing sufficient protection to key State facilities.[552] In the context of cyberspace, where most hostile cyber operations are a form of cyber espionage and there has been not a single instance of a cyber *Armed Attack* or an invocation of *Self-defense*, this doctrine is the least applicable.

Both these the aforementioned doctrines have the advantage of allowing for a clear categorization of hostile cyber operations. However, their weakness is that too many cyber acts would potentially qualify as *Internationally Wrongful Acts*, some of them without any tangible impact at all. In essence, they are based on hypothetical results rather than actual ones. That is the reason why most of the States and other subjects of Public International Law gravitate toward the effects-based doctrine. It has been dominant since at least the ICJ's Nicaragua judgment in 1986, when *scale and effects* were used as the main basis for gauging whether a *Prohibited Intervention* took place.

The effects-based approach looks at the character and scale of impact, equating cyber operations with more conventional ones in that it focuses on consequences rather than the technology chosen to cause them. Especially in cyberspace, the effects-based approach appears fitting. Oftentimes, the conduct of a hostile cyber operation is clandestine and can remain so for a much longer period than for an equivalently profound conventional operation, creating a delay that obscures the link between action and effect. For example, the =Stuxnet virus, which attacked Iran's nuclear facilities sometime before 2010 was designed to not cause much disruption or cause immediate damage and penetrated the Natanz facility for years before being uncovered.[553]

---

551 Radziwill, Yaroslav. Cyber-attacks and the exploitable imperfections of International Law. BRILL, 2015. Page 138.

552 Delerue, François. Cyber Operations and international law. Cambridge: Cambridge University Press, 2020. Page 288.

553 Finkle, Jim. (2013, February 26). Researchers say Stuxnet was deployed against Iran in 2007. Reuters. <https://www.reuters.com/article/us-cyberwar-stuxnet-idUSBRE91P0PP20130226>.

This approach rests upon the *Scale and Effects Doctrine*. It means that as long as the scale of and effects of the negative impact of an operation are commensurate to those created by conventional means of conveying force, *Prohibited Use of Force* can be invoked by an injured State.[554] This expansionary approach was in place well before hostile cyber operations were considered. Threat of use of biological and chemical means was recognized as potential *Use of Force* decades before.[555] The 1986 Nicaragua judgment by the ICJ also pushed the definition of force in the direction of broad and flexible understanding. In the judgment, training and arming of anti-government guerillas was rendered to constitute *Use of Force*.[556]

The term *scale and effects* stems from the Nicaragua Judgment, where the ICJ utilized it to distinguish between *prohibited Use of Force* and *mere frontier incidents*.[557] This approach is also officially assumed by key big States, such as the United States which presented its doctrine in a 2012 statement from Martin R. Flug, then Legal Adviser at the U.S. Department of State:

> Cyber activities may in certain circumstances constitute uses of force within the meaning of Article 2(4) of the UN Charter and customary international law. In analyzing whether a cyber operation would constitute a Use of Force, most commentators focus on whether the direct physical injury and property damage resulting from the cyber event looks like that which would be considered a Use of Force if produced by kinetic weapons. Cyber activities that proximately result in death, injury, or significant destruction would likely be viewed as a Use of Force. In assessing whether an event constituted a Use of Force in or through cyberspace, we must evaluate factors: including the context of the event, the actor perpetrating

---

554 Roscini, Marco. (2010). World Wide Warfare - "Jus Ad Bellum" and the Use of Cyber Force. Max Planck Yearbook of United Nations Law, 14, 85–130. Page 106. <https://papers.ssrn.com/sol3/papers.cfm?abstract_id=1683370>.

555 "Countering Chemical, Biological, Radiological and Nuclear Terrorism." United Nations : Office on Drugs and Crime. Retrieved on November 28, 2023. <https://www.unodc.org/unodc/en/terrorism/expertise/countering-chemical-biological-radiological-and-nuclear-terrorism.html>.

556 Case Concerning Military and Paramilitary Activities in and Against Nicaragua, Nicaragua v. United States. International Court of Justice. I.C.J Reports 14, ICGJ 112 (ICJ 1986). Paragraph 228. Retrieved February 15, 2022, from <https://www.icj-cij.org/en/case/70/judgments>.

557 Ibid. Paragraph 195.

the action (recognizing challenging issues of attribution in cyberspace), the target and location, effects and intent, among other possible issues.

Commonly cited examples of cyber activity that would constitute a Use of Force include, e.g.:

(1) operations that trigger a nuclear plant meltdown;

(2) operations that open a dam above a populated area causing destruction; or

(3) operations that disable air traffic control resulting in airplane crashes.

Only a moment's reflection makes you realize that this is common sense: if the physical consequences of a cyber attack work the kind of physical damage that dropping a bomb or firing a missile would, that cyber attack should equally be considered a Use of Force.[558]

In July 2021, The United Nations published *Official compendium of voluntary national contributions on the subject of how international law applies to the use of information and communications technologies by States submitted by participating governmental experts in the Group of Governmental Experts on Advancing Responsible State Behaviour in Cyberspace in the Context of International Security established pursuant to General Assembly resolution 73/266*, which includes positions of 15 States: Australia, Brazil, Estonia, Germany, Japan, Kazakhstan, Kenya, Netherlands, Norway, Romania, Russian Federation, Singapore,

---

558 Koh, Harold. H. (2012). International Law in Cyberspace. Harvard International Law Journal, 54, 1–12. <https://harvardilj.org/wp-content/uploads/sites/15/2012/12/Koh-Speech-to-Publish1.pdf>; U.S. Department of Defense. (2020, March 2). Department of Defense General Counsel Remarks at U.S. Cyber Command Legal Conference. The Government of the United States. Retrieved February 18, 2022, from <https://www.defense.gov/News/Speeches/Speech/Article/2099378/dod-general-counsel-remarks-at-us-cyber-command-legal-conference/>;

United Nations General Assembly Resolution. (2021, July 13). 73/266. Official compendium of voluntary national contributions on the subject of how international law applies to the use of information and communications technologies by States submitted by participating governmental experts in the Group of Governmental Experts on Advancing Responsible State Behaviour in Cyberspace in the Context of International Security established pursuant to General Assembly resolution. Retrieved February 16, 2022, from <https://front.un-arm.org/wp-content/uploads/2021/08/A-76-136-EN.pdf>.

Switzerland, United Kingdom, and the United States on the question of *Use of Force* in the cyberspace.[559] All of these States concurred that it is potentially possible for cyber operations to reach the threshold of *Use of Force*. All of those governments agreed that cyber operations between States can amount to *Use of Force*, including *Prohibited Use of Force*. All of them also listed the effects-based approach as the most important basis for determining whether a cyber operation constituted *Prohibited Use of Force*. Two States, the United States and Estonia also included a target-based component in their approach.[560] Here is the summary of the stances presented in the UN Compendium as well as two other large States (France and Poland) regarding determining whether *Prohibited Use of Force* took place:

- **Australia** went on record stating that both direct and indirect consequences of cyber activity, could cause serious or extensive ("scale") damage or destruction ("effects") to life, or injury or death, or result in damage to the victim State's objects, critical infrastructure, and/ or functioning, which at a certain level of intensity can amount to *Prohibited Use of Force*.
- **Brazil** also claimed that cyber operations can be classified as *Prohibited Use of Force* in international law as long as their impact is commensurate with conventional kinetic attacks that would reach that threshold.
- **Estonia** stated that cyber operations that target civilian infrastructure and result in serious damage, injury, or death (or are a threat of such acts) would constitute *Prohibited Use of Force*.
- **Germany** invoked Tallinn Manual 2.0 in its stance, which draws on the ICJ's Nicaragua Judgment focusing on scale and effects of an act to determine whether it constitutes *Prohibited Use of Force*. According to Germany's position, as long as these two metrics are comparable to conventional operations deemed to carry such a designation, they also qualify as such.

---

559 Ibid.

560 NATO Cooperative Cyber Defence Centre of Excellence. (2021, November 16). Use of Force in International Law - Statement of the Government of Estonia. Retrieved February 18, 2022, from <https://cyberlaw.ccdcoe.org/wiki/Use_of_force#Estonia_(2021)>.

- **Japan** issued a detailed statement saying that cyber operations can in general be classified as *Prohibited Use of Force* without specifying the method of evaluating an act in that regard.
- **Kazakhstan** issued a communique stating that cyber operations can constitute a breach of international law in general, without specifying details in regard to *Prohibition of Use of Force.*
- **Kenya**, similarly to Kazakhstan, expressed its agreement with general applicability of existing international law in the cyberspace and a possibility of a cyber operation constituting a breach of international obligations but refrained from engaging with the subject of *Prohibition of Use of Force.*
- **Netherlands** focused on the doctrine of effects, confirming that cyber operations can in general be classified as *Prohibited Use of Force.*
- **Norway** laid out a detailed position espousing key findings of the UN GGE, confirming that cyber operations can reach the threshold of *Prohibited Use of Force,* and embracing the scale and effects doctrine in assessing that.
- **Romania** expressed a view that cyber operations have to be analyzed in a case-by-case manner due to their diversity when considering whether they constitute *Prohibited Use of Force.* The analysis should consider the circumstances of the operation, its nature, scale and effects. Romania stated that in doing so the relevant jurisprudence of the ICJ should be utilized.
- **Russian Federation** issued a short open-ended statement that confirmed the international legal system's applicability and indirectly agreed that cyber operations can reach the threshold of *Prohibited Use of Force* (by stating that cyber *Countermeasures* are not allowed to reach the level of *Use of Force*). Otherwise, it called on the international community to continue the discussion on the matter.
- **Singapore** issued a short but succinct statement, confirming that cyber operations can not only reach the threshold of *Prohibited Use of Force* but also amount to an *Armed Attack.*
- **Switzerland** echoed the position that the notions of *Use of Force* and *Armed Attack* are applicable in cyberspace. Interestingly, it also added in its statement that the international norms regulating its neutral status are also relevant in cyberspace, sending a signal that it perceives

its national cyberspace as a safe zone of sorts, much like it is the case with its physical territory.

- **United Kingdom** shared a short statement that confirmed the cyber operations can amount to *Prohibited Use of Force* and embraced the doctrine of effects and scale.
- **United States** mentioned the scope of *Prohibited Use of Force* that draws on both Article 2(4) of the UN Charter and customary international law, implying a broader range. In that context, it focused on the doctrine of effect, mentioning direct physical injury and property damage as aspects most focused on by legal commentators. However, it also mentioned the circumstances of a cyber operation as relevant for determination of its legal status.[561]

Separately from the UN Compendium on the subject, below are legal stances of two additional large States:

- **France** expressed its support for the doctrine of effects in its statement on the subject. It wrote that as long as effects are similar to those resulting from conventional operations, a cyber operation can be considered in the same international legal categories. However, France reserved the possibility that cyber operations without physical impact can also be classified as *Prohibited Use of Force.*[562]

---

561 United Nations General Assembly Resolution. (2021, July 13). 73/266. Official compendium of voluntary national contributions on the subject of how international law applies to the use of information and communications technologies by States submitted by participating governmental experts in the Group of Governmental Experts on Advancing Responsible State Behaviour in Cyberspace in the Context of International Security established pursuant to General Assembly resolution. Retrieved February 16, 2022, from <https://front.un-arm.org/wp-content/uploads/2021/08/A-76-136-EN.pdf>.

562 The government of France. (2019, October 4). Communiqué -La France s'engage à promouvoir un cyberespace stable, fondé sur la confiance et le respect du droit international. French Ministry of Defense. Pages 12–18. Retrieved February 16, 2022, from <https://www.defense.gouv.fr/fre/salle-de-presse/communiques/communique_la-france-s-engage-a-promouvoir-un-cyberespace-stable-fonde-sur-la-confiance-et-le-respect-du-droit-international>.

- **Poland's** Internal Security Agency (Agencja Bezpieczeństwa Wewnętrznego—ABW), a part of the government apparatus, published an analysis claiming that international cyber operations can reach the level of *Use of Force* if its effects are comparable with such conventional operations that would also be classified as *Use of Force*.[563]

The earlier statements show the doctrine of scale and effects is now an established framework for assessing *Prohibited use of Force* as well general seriousness of a hostile cyber operation. Nevertheless, there exist no consistent international norms that would provide an explanation on how exactly to apply this standard in cyberspace. In the context of this vacuum, several international scholars proposed their non-binding interpretations of this process. Marco Roscini suggested sorting effects of cyber operations into three main categories to gauge whether an operation qualifies as *Use of Force*:

- Primary: direct impact on affected systems such as deletion or corruption of data, or disruption of software functioning;
- Secondary: the impact on the underlying infrastructure in the victim State;
- Tertiary: effects on persons, communities, and property (e.g., damage done to hospital operations due to shutting down of an electricity plant by foreign hackers).[564]

The doctrine of scale and effects, espoused by most of the States that went on record in the UN Compendium, was summarized well in Tallinn Manual 2.0 (this summary was later invoked by Germany in its official position for the UN Compendium mentioned earlier). Rule 69 of the Manual states that *a cyber operation constitutes a Use of Force when its scale and effects are comparable*

[563] Aleksandrowicz, Tomasz. R. (2016). Bezpieczeństwo w cyberprzestrzeni ze stanowiska prawa międzynarodowego. Agencja Bezpieczenstwa Wewnetrznego. <https://www.abw.gov.pl/download/1/2170/TomaszRAleksandrowicz.pdf>.

[564] Roscini, Marco. (2014). Cyber Operations and the Use of Force in International Law. British Yearbook of International Law, 84(1), 385–389. <https://doi.org/10.1093/bybil/bru014.>

to non-cyber operations rising to the level of a Use of Force.[565] The authors of the Manual invoked the ICJ Nicaragua Judgment, which utilized the *scale and effects* doctrine to determine whether an *Armed Attack* or rather a *Prohibited Intervention* took place at the behest of the United States.[566] Based on these considerations, Tallinn Manual 2.0 proposed a specialized approach in cyberspace, listing eight dimensions of a cyber operation's impact that should be gauged:

- Severity;
- Immediacy;
- Directness;
- Invasiveness;
- Measurability of effects;
- Military character;
- State involvement;
- Presumptive lawfulness.[567]

The Manual also listed auxiliary circumstances, which might additionally influence the assessment of the impact of a cyber act: *prevailing political environment, the identity of the hacker, any records of cyber operations by the hacker, and the nature of the target.*[568] The Manual did not specify the proportion in which different criteria should be weighed, suggesting instead that the assessment should be done in concert and on a case-by-case basis. This leads to a conclusion that as long as a cyber operation causes effects similar to those caused by a kinetic weapon that would be classified as *Use of Force,* it can be classified as such and also by extension as a *Prohibited Intervention.* Meeting the additional requirements of utilizing armed forces and targeting

565 Schmitt, Michael N. & NATO Cooperative Cyber Defence Centre of Excellence. (2017). Tallinn Manual 2.0 on the International Law Applicable to Cyber Operations. Cambridge University Press. Rule 69.

566 Case Concerning Military and Paramilitary Activities in and Against Nicaragua, Nicaragua v United States. International Court of Justice. I.C.J Reports 14, ICGJ 112 (ICJ 1986). (1986). Paragraph 195. Retrieved February 15, 2022, <from https://www.icj-cij.org/en/case/70/judgments>.

567 Schmitt, Michael N. & NATO Cooperative Cyber Defence Centre of Excellence. (2017). Tallinn Manual 2.0 on the International Law Applicable to Cyber Operations. Cambridge University Press. Page 51.

568 Ibid.

the sovereignty, territorial integrity or political independence of the affected State would classify it as an *Act of Aggression.*[569] Harold Hongju Koh, a Legal Adviser at U.S. Department of State at the time, described it the following way in Harvard International Law Journal in 2012:

> Only a moment's reflection makes you realize that this is common sense: if the physical consequences of a cyber attack work the kind of physical damage that dropping a bomb or firing a missile would, that cyber attack should equally be considered a Use of Force.[570]

Applying the *scale and effects* doctrine creates certain legal and interpretative challenges in cyberspace. This is due to the fact that the understanding of the doctrine developed based on "traditional" kinetic conflicts that only have partial equivalence in the digital realm. One such challenge is related to *jus ad bellum*—the conditions under which States may resort to war, self-defense, or the use of armed force in general. The system of Public International Law prefers low-intensity responses and avoidance of escalation. That is why the general principles of proportionality and peaceful resolution of tensions take central roles in *jus ad bellum*, the precursor to *jus in bello*, which regulates the conduct of parties that escalated the tension to the point of turning it into an armed conflict.[571] In that spirit, per ICJ jurisprudence, situations such as border clashes are not perceived as *Prohibited Use of Force*, as that could give rise to a spiral of escalation. In cyberspace, where physical borders between States are not clearly delimited, gauging such hostilities is unregulated. As of now, the system of Public International Law has not developed a framework for handling them. Another challenge are hostile cyber operations that mostly create non-physical, non-kinetic effects. Such acts have no obvious equivalent in the "traditional" jurisprudence, creating a problematic legal

---

569 Nguyen, Reese. (2013). Navigating Jus ad Bellum in the Age of Cyber Warfare. California Law Review, 101(4), 1079–1130. Page 1123. <https://lawcat.berkeley.edu/record/1125693/>.

570 Koh, Harold. H. (2012). International Law in Cyberspace. Harvard International Law Journal, 54, 1–12. Page 4. <https://harvardilj.org/wp-content/uploads/sites/15/2012/12/Koh-Speech-to-Publish1.pdf>

571 International Committee of the Red Cross. "What Are Jus Ad Bellum and Jus in Bello?" International Committee of the Red Cross, November 12, 2015. <https://www.icrc.org/en/document/what-are-jus-ad-bellum-and-jus-bello-0>.

vacuum. There exist however guidelines that allow for proposing a potential solution to this challenge. These are discussed in the following subsection.

3.6.2.3 Can hostile cyber operation with no physical effects qualify as *Use of Force?*

Hostile cyber operations can create both physical and non-physical effects. The exact balance between both shares can vary. At their core, hostile cyber operations always create a non-physical effect as they affect or penetrate IT systems of a State. The physical manifestations, such as the explosion of the 1982 Soviet Siberian pipeline mentioned in Chapter 1, damaging of the Iranian nuclear facilities in 2010, or shutting down of the Ukrainian electricity grid in 2015 are only featured in some hostile cyber operations that display the highest level of technical sophistication and severity. Around 90% of all hostile cyber operations between States currently are acts of cyber espionage or close to it in nature and have no direct physical effect.[572] At the same time, the *scales and effects* doctrine focuses on equivalence with the "traditional" kinetic impacts that is based on the physical effects. This creates a blind spot: cyber operations that have only non-physical effects.

Technically, even low-intensity damage to a computer network or an individual device caused by a hostile cyber operation is damage to property that can qualify as at least *coercive behavior.* If the damage is large enough, it can qualify as *Prohibited Use of Force*, although no State has ever invoked it in the context of hostile cyber operations, not even when Stuxnet hit nuclear facilities in Iran.[573] Any measure of physical damage, however small, could open space for claiming *Prohibited Use of Force* by the injured State if the non-physical impact is large enough. However, many hostile cyber operations leave no physical trace at all. This debate is hypothetical and future-oriented as no State has ever produced a non-physical effect large enough to even be considered *Use of Force.* However, with rapid expansion of IT technologies, such as generative AI and virtual reality, this uncharted area might come into sharp focus of the international community. First however, a sufficient

---

[572] See section I.2.2—"Infrastructure, data, and social dimensions of cyberspace" for further details.

[573] Zetter, Kim. Countdown to Zero Day: Stuxnet and the launch of the world's first Digital Weapon. New York: Broadway Books, 2015.

amount of human life and governmental processes would have to move entirely into cyberspace for that possibility to become a tangible threat.

The opinions among scholars are split on the matter with some supporting it[574] while others are adamantly against.[575] François Delerue has offered a two-step test that can help position and answer this question in the context of the existing framework of Public International Law.[576] The test is the following:

- Are the physical effects and their scale always by definition more severe than non-physical ones?
- Is the production of physical effects a necessary requirement for determining *Prohibited Use of Force* in itself?

François Delerue offers a negative answer to both questions, stating that purely digital effects of a hostile cyber operation can potentially be an instance of *Prohibited Use of Force* between States. Cyber operations can demonstrably produce large-scale digital effects. For example, the Slammer worm has infected thousands of servers worldwide in a matter of minutes in 2003.[577] It disrupted internet connectivity in several countries and had knock-on effects of shutting down Bank of America ATMs and leading to cancellation of a few Continental Airlines flights. NotPetya, a virus created by a State-sponsored Russian hacker group, spread globally in 2017, damaging operations of an international corporation.[578] While less visible physically, the hostile cyber

574 Silver, Daniel B. "Computer Network Attack as a Use of Force under Article 2(4) of the United Nations Charter." Page 85. <https://core.ac.uk/download/pdf/236321477.pdf>; Schmitt, Michael N. "Computer Network Attack and the Use of Force in International Law: Thoughts on a Normative Framework." The Use of Force in International Law, 2017, pages 379–431. <https://doi.org/10.4324/9781315084992-17>.

575 Hoisington, Matthew. "Cyberwarfare and the Use of Force Giving Rise to the Right of Self-Defense." SSRN Electronic Journal, 2009. Page 447. <https://doi.org/10.2139/ssrn.1542223>.

576 Delerue, François. Cyber Operations and international law. Cambridge: Cambridge University Press, 2020. Page 298.

577 "What Is the Slammer Worm/SQL Worm/Sapphire Worm?" North Carolina State University. Accessed November 29, 2023. <https://ethics.csc.ncsu.edu/abuse/wvt/Slammer/study.php>.

578 Villasenor, John, and Nicol Turner Lee Norman Eisen. "How the Notpetya Attack Is Reshaping Cyber Insurance." Brookings, December 1, 2021. <https://www.brookings.edu/articles/how-the-notpetya-attack-is-reshaping-cyber-insurance/>.

operations can be coercive and indeed forceful, especially in societies where large enough amount of human activity, including government processes, switched online. For these reasons, Tallinn Manual 2.0 offers an adjusted formula to the *effects and scale* doctrine when applied in cyberspace. Its Rule 71 states: "all reasonably foreseeable consequences of the cyber operations qualify," explaining in the commentary that this means non-physical effects should be taken into consideration when gauging whether the threshold of *Use of Force* has been met.[579] This proposal, if it takes root, would mean that despite lack of equivalence, non-physical effects would stop being discounted when deciding if a hostile cyber operation is an *Act of Aggression,* including its qualified form—*Armed Attack.*

3.6.2.4 The role of critical infrastructure in determining occurrence of *Prohibited Use of Force*

Critical infrastructure has been invoked several times in this book. There are two main reasons for that:

- Hostile cyber operations require some sort of critical infrastructure to be conducted. At minimum it is the electricity grid. Usually also the internet network and other systems such as GPS are involved. They spread through critical infrastructure and create physical and non-physical effects as they move along the nodes of systems.
- Foreign assaults on critical infrastructure are the most evocative, easiest to visualize, and clearly prohibited in the system Public International Law as they demonstrably breach spheres of jurisdiction of a State with the purpose of creating a negative impact.

An argument can be made that the role of critical infrastructure in the emerging Public International Legal Framework goes beyond these two arguments. This would mean that the currently developing rules on cyberspace would have unique features that set it aside from other areas of international law. One

---

579 Schmitt, Michael N. & NATO Cooperative Cyber Defence Centre of Excellence. (2017). Tallinn Manual 2.0 on the International Law Applicable to Cyber Operations. Cambridge University Press. Rule 71; Commentary to Rule 71, Paragraph 13, page 343.

such unique feature could be the notion of *Due Diligence*, which is analyzed in depth in Chapter 5. The other one is determining the threshold for *Use of Force*. Analyzing the issue of the role of critical infrastructure in cyberspace in the context of *Prohibited Use of Force* allows for a focused approach with a tangible threshold that organizes the discussion.

There are a few available definitions of critical infrastructure. Most States and some international organizations adopt their own ones. For example, François Delerue offers the following framing: "critical infrastructure refers to assets or systems that a State considers to be essential for the maintenance of vital societal functions or pose potential serious risk to the population if they are damaged, destroyed or disrupted."[580] The Australian government has defined critical infrastructure as: *physical facilities, supply chains, information technologies and communication networks which, if destroyed, degraded or rendered unavailable for an extended period, would significantly impact on the social or economic well-being of the nation or affect Australia's ability to conduct national defence and ensure national security.*[581] The United States defined critical infrastructure as: "systems and assets, whether physical or virtual, so vital to the United States that the incapacity or destruction of such systems and assets would have a debilitating impact on security, national economic security, national public health or safety or any combination of those matters."[582] The EU strategy distinguishes two tiers of critical infrastructure: National Critical Infrastructure and European Critical Infrastructure, the latter affecting at least two EU countries, creating a significant impact.[583] It general defines cyber infrastructure as: *an asset, system or part thereof located in Member States which is essential for the maintenance of vital societal functions, health, safety, security, economic or social well-being of people, and the disruption or destruction of which would have a*

580 Delerue, François. Cyber Operations and international law. Cambridge: Cambridge University Press, 2020. Page 299.

581 The government of Australia. Critical Infrastructure Resilience Strategy: Policy statement. Retrieved on November 29, 2023. <https://www.tisn.gov.au/Site%20 Documents/CriticalInfrastructureResilienceStrategyPolicyStatement.PDF>.

582 "42 U.S. Code § 5195C(e) - Critical Infrastructures Protection." Legal Information Institute. Accessed November 29, 2023. <https://www.law.cornell.edu/uscode/text/42/5195c>.

583 Delerue, François. Cyber Operations and international law. Cambridge: Cambridge University Press, 2020. Page 300.

significant impact in a Member State as a result of the failure to maintain those functions.[584] Other international organizations and States have come up with similar frameworks, all creating a general impression of a consensus on the areas covered by the term.

Most available definitions focus on systems pertaining to provision of: public services, security, food, water, transportation, communication services, energy, health, trade, and banking.[585] This list essentially overlaps with the areas highlighted by the UN General Assembly in its 2003 resolution titled "Creation of a global culture of cybersecurity and the protection of critical information infrastructures." Back in 2006, the European Union adopted its European Programme for Critical Infrastructure Protection (EPCIP). Importantly, what connects all the critical infrastructure systems is deep reliance on computers and computer networks, which makes them an obvious target for hostile cyber operations. The OECD proposed in 2008 that this connective tissue of IT networks inside and in between various critical infrastructure systems as Critical Information Infrastructure.[586]

The dominant approach of gauging whether an act against a State has met the threshold of *Use of Force*, which is the doctrine of *effects and scale*, might not be fully adequate in the context of hostile cyber operations. As Francois Delerue has stated: "The fact that the target is critical infrastructure constitutes an aggravating factor that may tip the balance in favor of the qualification as a *Use of Force*."[587] This would essentially mean blending of the *effects and scale* doctrine with the *target* doctrine, creating a modified approach that applies specifically in cyberspace. The 2007 Bronze Soldier

---

584 EU Council Directive 2008/114/EC of 8 December 2008 on the identification and designation of European critical infrastructures and the assessment of the need to improve their protection [2008] OJ L 345/75 art 2. <https://eur-lex.europa.eu/legal-content/en/TXT/?uri=CELEX:32008L0114>

585 United Nations General Assembly Resolution. (December 23, 2003 Creation of a global culture of cybersecurity and the protection of critical information infrastructures. Retrieved February 15, 2022, from <https://digitallibrary.un.org/record/509571?ln=en>

586 Critical Information Infrastructures Protection (CIIP) - OECD. 2008. Retrieved November 29, 2023. <https://www.oecd.org/sti/ieconomy/ciip.htm>; Delerue, François. Cyber Operations and international law. Cambridge: Cambridge University Press, 2020. Page 302.

587 Ibid. Page 298.

scandal, when the targeting of Estonia's Critical Information Infrastructure led to shutting down of an array of government websites and services shows the compounded impact that targeting critical infrastructure specifically can have.[588] In fact, international legal scholars such as Marco Roscini called for such a crucial adaptation in the context of cyberspace.[589] This shift would impact a variety of potential situations. Hostile cyber operations that failed to produce any physical effects but targeted sensitive systems such as the operating room of a dam would be seen differently than attempting and failing to disrupt operations of a company providing non-essential products. The same would be the case for a hostile cyber operation that produced only minor physical impact but attempted to damage a dam's operating room rather than a non-essential company. In both those cases, the qualification of the hostile operation could be more severe, more easily reaching the threshold of *Prohibited Use of Force* and therefore constituting an *Act of Aggression.* On the other hand, the dual-character of the internet infrastructure makes it a legitimate target in the context of wartime activities, reducing the risk of an attack on it being an *Internationally Wrongful Act.*[590] As Samuli Haataja pointed out, this introduces an element of uncertainty that makes application of Public International Law unclear when it comes to internet infrastructure. David Fidler suggested that governments lack confidence that existing norms of Public International Law on the matter are sufficient or effective, switching their focus instead to prevention and defensive measures.[591] This situation creates a sense of urgency for States to clarify the legal ramifications of targeting such facilities.

---

588 Juurvee, Ivo, and Anna-Mariita Mattiisen. "The Bronze Soldier Crisis of 2007: Revisiting an Early Case of Hybrid Conflict." International Centre for Defence and Security, February 14, 2022. <https://icds.ee/en/the-bronze-soldier-crisis-of-2007/>.

589 Roscini, Marco. (2014). Cyber Operations and the Use of Force in International Law. British Yearbook of International Law, 84(1), pages 385–389. <https://doi.org/10.1093/bybil/bru014>.

590 Haataja, Samuli. "Cyber Operations against Critical Infrastructure under Norms of Responsible State Behaviour and International Law." International Journal of Law and Information Technology 30, no. 4 (2022): pages 423–443. Page 442. <https://doi.org/10.1093/ijlit/eaad006>.

591 Fidler, D. P. (2015). Whither the Web?: International Law, Cybersecurity, and Critical Infrastructure Protection. Georgetown Journal of International Affairs - Articles by Maurer Faculty, 2452, 8–20. Page 18.

3.6.2.5 Accumulation of hostile cyber operations that collectively amount to *Use of Force*

Ease with which States can launch harassing hostile cyber operations creates the challenge of under-threshold acts that are designed to avoid meeting the definition of *Use of Force* while doing the most damage possible. Instantaneous and decentralized character of cyber acts makes that problem radically bigger than is the case with, for example, border clashes or missile tests. The notion of "accumulation of events" is not novel although emergence of hostile cyber operations puts it in a new light. German scholars have traditionally called it "Nadelstichtaktik" (needle prick tactic).[592]

In the landmark Nicaragua judgment of 1986, the ICJ stated:

> that a series of attacks, none of which individually could amount to an armed attack, might together constitute an armed attack,[593] thus embracing the idea. In the Law and Maritime Borders of Cameroon and Nigeria judgment of 2002, the ICJ did not reject Cameroon's claim that by launching a series of border clashes by Nigeria would amount to an Act of Aggression but it dismissed the case based on insufficient proof to justify attribution of the hostile acts to Nigeria.[594] In the Oil Platforms judgment of 2003, the ICJ claimed: "even taken cumulatively (…) these incidents do not seem to the Court to constitute an armed attack on the United States,"[595] thus again allowing for a possibility of accumulation of events to together constitute an instance of Use of Force (although judge Simma expressed

---

592 Yehuda Z. Blum, "State Response to Acts of Terrorism," 19 German Yearbook Of International Law 223 (1976).

593 Case Concerning Military and Paramilitary Activities in and Against Nicaragua, Nicaragua v United States. International Court of Justice. Supra note 23. I.C.J Reports 14, ICGJ 112 (ICJ 1986). (1986). Retrieved February 15, 2022, from <https://www.icj-cij.org/en/case/70/judgments>.

594 Land and Maritime Boundary between Cameroon and Nigeria (Cameroon v. Nigeria: Equatorial Guinea intervening)—Judgment. International Court of Justice. (ICJ 2002). Paragraphs 303, 323. Retrieved February 15, 2022, from <https://www.icj-cij.org/case/94>.

595 Oil Platforms (Islamic Republic of Iran v. United States of America)—Judgment. International Court of Justice. (ICJ 2003). Supra note 63, paragraph 64. Retrieved February 15, 2022, from <https://www.icj-cij.org/case/90>.

> his opposition to the idea in a dissenting opinion[596]). Finally, in the 2005 Armed Activities on the Territory of the Congo judgment the ICJ wrote: "even if this series of deplorable attacks could be regarded as cumulative in character [they could not be attributed to the Democratic Republic of Congo]."[597] While embracing the idea in principle, in each of those three cases, the ICJ did not find the accumulation of events at hand to constitute a joint instance of Use of Force. Instead, the court expressed its preference for a case-by-case approach, relegating the idea of accumulation to the realm of hypotheticals.

The notion of "accumulation of events" did not get endorsement of the UN Security Council when it was discussed there.[598] At the same time, several States such as the United States, the United Kingdom, and Israel, have utilized the terms, both in front of the ICJ[599] and outside of it.[600] Additionally, the UN International Law Commission proposed in its Draft Articles on State

---

596 Oil Platforms (Islamic Republic of Iran v. United States of America)—The separate opinion by Judge Bruno Simma. International Court of Justice. (ICJ 2003). Paragraph 14. Retrieved February 15, 2022, from <https://www.icj-cij.org/case/90>.Simma separate opinion para 14

597 Armed Activities on the Territory of the Congo (Democratic Republic of the Congo v. Uganda)—Judgment. (ICJ 2005). ICJ Rep 53, paragraph 147. Retrieved February 15, 2022, from <https://www.icj-cij.org/case/116>.

598 Kretzmer, David. "The Inherent Right to Self-Defence and Proportionality in Jus Ad Bellum." European Journal of International Law 24, no. 1 (April 1, 2013): pages 235–282. Page 244. <https://doi.org/10.1093/ejil/chs087>.

599 In the Oil Platforms case the US argued that the "pattern of Iranian conduct added to the gravity of the specific attacks, reinforced the necessity of action in self-defense, and helped to shape the appropriate response": Oil Platforms (Islamic Republic of Iran v. United States of America) -, Counter-Memorandum and Counter-Claim submitted by the United States of America. International Court of Justice. (ICJ 2003). Paragraph 4.10. Retrieved February 15, 2022, from <https://www.icj-cij.org/case/90>.

600 U.S. Naval War College. "Anticipatory Self-Defense in the Cyber Context." Digital Commons: U.S. Naval War College Research. Retrieved November 29, 2023. <https://digital-commons.usnwc.edu/>; Ronen, Yaël. "Israel, Hizbollah, and the Second Lebanon War." Yearbook of International Humanitarian Law 2006, 2007, pages 362–393. Page 372. <https://doi.org/10.1007/978-90-6704-755-5_10>.; Lubell, Noam. Extraterritorial use of force against non-state actors. Oxford: Oxford University Press, 2011. Supra note 19, page 51.

Responsibility introduction of a composite *Internationally Wrongful Act* as a formal category. The article 15(1) of the Draft Articles states:

> The breach of an international obligation by a State through a series of actions or omissions defined in aggregate as wrongful occurs when the action or omission occurs which, taken with the other actions or omissions, is sufficient to constitute the wrongful act.[601]

The Draft Articles are a combination of formalization of existing customary rules and proposed rules that the UN ILC hopes might become binding in the future. Article 15 belongs to the latter category. However, the support by such a respected body as the ILC might solidify State practice in that direction. Some emergent State practice already suggests that. For example, France has formally espoused the Public International Norm of accumulation of events in the context of hostile cyber operations.[602] There is now also renewed interest in giving the notion full recognition as a norm of Public International Law. Theresa Reinold claims that the international developments after the 9/11 terrorist attack call for embrace of the notion.[603] Christian Tams wrote: "States seem to have shown a new willingness to accept the *accumulation of events* doctrine which previously had received little support."[604] The consensus among legal scholars studying cyber operations is that the accumulation of events theory is fitting for cyberspace, in fact even more so than in the conventional one, and should be an operational norm.[605] Most

601 <https://legal.un.org/ilc/texts/instruments/english/commentaries/9_6_2001.pdf>

602 Grey, Christine. (2018) International Law and the Use of Force Oxford University Press, page 164.

603 Reinold, Theresa: "State Weakness, Irregular Warfare, and the Right to Self-Defense Post 9/11," 105 AJIL (2011) 244; Elżbieta Karska, & Karol Karski (2016), Introduction: The Phenomenon of Foreign Fighters and Foreign Terrorist Fighters: An International Law and H uman Rights Perspective, International Community Law Review 18(5), pages 377–387, <http://doi.org/10.1163/18719732-12341337>, <https://www.researchgate.net/publication/312064941>.

604 Tams, Christian: "The Use of Force against Terrorists," 20 EJIL (2009), supra note 49, page 388.

605 Roscini, Marco. (2014). Cyber Operations and the Use of Force in International Law. British Yearbook of International Law, 84(1), page 110. <https://doi.org/10.1093/bybil/bru014>; Delerue, François. Cyber Operations and international law. Cambridge: Cambridge University Press, 2020. Page 335.

of that discussion however takes place in the context of whether a State has a right to use *Force* as part of *Self-defense.* This pertains only to the qualified form of aggression which is the *Armed Attack.* It is uncertain whether the same degree of scholarly consensus would be reached when it comes to softer forms of *Force,* specifically those that constitute an *Act of Aggression* but do not reach the threshold of an *Armed Attack.*

A separate version of accumulation of events is when preparations for a hostile cyber operation are revealed, creating an effect of intimidation or a threat, that is then followed by execution which on its own would not amount to *Use of Force.* The preparation itself might also include a coercive component and be a *Violation of Sovereignty* of the target State, that can contribute to the overall cumulative classification as *Prohibited Use of Force.* This notion was highlighted in the Gabčíkovo-Nagymaros judgment, where the ICJ determined that Czechoslovakia's preparations to begin diverting the course of the Danube River to the detriment of Hungary were not part of a cumulative *Internationally Wrongful Act.*[606] Since preparations are a "weak" element of an accumulation of events, the ICJ has established a rule for accounting for them while determining whether an *Internationally Wrongful Act* took place. The rule is that the preparations that do not predetermine the final decision to be taken are not a cumulative part of an *Internationally Wrongful Act.* Those that do lock in the final decision can be counted toward a cumulative act.[607] In the case at hand, there existed several variants of diverting the river, one of which—Variant C—was the one most protested by Hungary. While Czechoslovakia started preparatory works toward implementing Variant C, they did not reach the point of no return, at which executing other variants would have become impossible or extremely complicated.

The notion of accumulation of events is especially applicable in cyberspace, where execution of many hostile operations against numerous targets is a

---

606 Case Concerning Gabčíkovo-Nagymaros Project (Hungary/Slovakia)—Judgment. International Court of Justice. Reports 7, 54, para 79. I.C.J Reports 14, ICGJ 112 (ICJ 1986). Retrieved February 15, 2022, from <https://www.icj-cij.org/case/92>.

607 United Nations International Law Commission. Draft articles on Responsibility of States for Internationally Wrongful Acts with commentaries. United Nations Office of Legal Affairs (2001). Commentary to the articles 61 and 62, paragraph 13. Retrieved February 15, 2022. <https://legal.un.org/ilc/texts/instruments/english/commentaries/9_6_2001.pdf>.

possible scenario. Additionally, many cyber operations are deployed in combination with conventional acts. For example, on February 24, 2022, a number of government servers and websites in Ukraine were assaulted by Russian State-sponsored hackers just as the country was also being physically invaded by the Russian armed forces.[608] The notion of accumulation of events allows to count these simultaneous acts toward a unified *Internationally Wrongful Act* that captures the full scale of Russian aggression.

3.6.2.6 Difference between *Acts of Aggression and Armed Attacks* in cyberspace

There is a nuanced difference between *Acts of Aggression* that constitute an *Armed Attack* and those that do not. For instance, based on ICJ judgments, a blockade of ports or blocking internet communication with the rest of the world by a foreign State would most likely be classified as an *Act of Aggression* but not necessarily as an *Armed Attack.* While there exists an international consensus that *Acts of Aggression* can take place in cyberspace, the situation is less certain when it comes to *Armed Attacks.* The division is crucial because as noted in the previous section, only an *Armed Attack* allows the injured State to use *Force* as part of *Self-Defense.* Therefore, acknowledging the possibility of *Armed Attacks* in cyberspace would open the door to potentially more States retaliating by using aggressive methods.

Since the definition of an *Armed Attack* is not clearly spelled out in any source of international law, identifying a cyber *Armed Attack* is an even harder feat. Art. 2(4) of the UN Charter prohibits *Prohibited Use of Force.* Art. 39 talks about the UN Security Council determining whether an *Act of Aggression* took place and art. 51 specifies that only an *Armed Attack* allows a State to use *Force* lawfully, as a way of *Self-Defense.* None of them are defined however, neither by the UN Charter nor by any other treaty, as confirmed by the ICJ in the Nicaragua judgment.[609] This multitude of terms creates

---

608 "Ukraine Computers Hit by Data-Wiping Software as Russia Launched Invasion." Reuters, February 24, 2022. <https://www.reuters.com/world/europe/ukrainian-government-foreign-ministry-parliament-websites-down-2022-02-23/>.

609 Case Concerning Military and Paramilitary Activities in and Against Nicaragua, Nicaragua v United States. International Court of Justice. I.C.J Reports 14, ICGJ 112 (ICJ 1986). (1986). Merits 94 paragraph 176. Retrieved February 15, 2022, from <https://www.icj-cij.org/en/case/70/judgments>.

a semantic challenge that is only compounded in cyberspace. As noted in Subsection 3.6.2.1, the broad consensus is that *Armed Attack* is a sub-category of *Aggression,* which in turn is a sub-category of *Force.* Since, it is now well established that a hostile cyber operation can generate *Force* in the sense of *Prohibited Use of Force,* theoretically, this should also cover more specific acute types of *Force,* such as an Armed Attack. Another way of confirming that *Armed Attacks* can indeed take place in cyberspace would be for the UN Security Council to issue a statement saying so. According to article 39 of the UN Charter they can determine if a situation constitutes an *Act of Aggression*, which includes *Armed Attacks.*[610] Finally, the lists of "model" cases of *Armed Attacks* included in the UN GA resolutions such as the one adopted in 1974, were designed to not be exhaustive, opening space for an ever-expanding repository of examples.[611] France and Germany came forward endorsing the notion, each with caveats. France stated that an *Armed Attack* in cyberspace takes place "if it caused substantial loss of life or considerable physical or economic damage."[612] Germany stated that the determination depends on "the seriousness of the attack, the immediacy of its effects, depth of penetration of the cyber infrastructure and its military character."[613] Netherlands came forward partially supporting the notion although it excluded hostile cyber operations with purely digital impacts from the scope: *at present there is no international consensus on qualifying a cyber attack as an Armed Attack if it does*

---

610 United Nations. (1945, June 26). Charter of the United Nations. Articles 39, 51. Retrieved February 17, 2022, from <https://www.un.org/en/about-us/un-charter>.

611 United Nations General Assembly Resolution. (1974, December 14). 3314 (XXIX) Definition of Aggression General Assembly resolution. Article 4. Retrieved February 18, 2022, from <https://legal.un.org/avl/ha/da/da.html>.

612 The government of France. Communiqué -La France s'engage à promouvoir un cyberespace stable, fondé sur la confiance et le respect du droit international, October 4, 2019. French Ministry of Defense. Page 8. <https://www.defense.gouv.fr/fre/salle-de-presse/communiques/communique_la-france-s-engage-a-promouvoir-un-cyberespace-stable-fonde-sur-la-confiance-et-le-respect-du-droit-international>.

613 Auswärtiges Amt. "Cyber Security as a Dimension of Security Policy." Speech by Ambassador Norbert Riedel, Commissioner for International Cyber Policy, Federal Foreign Office, Berlin, at Chatham House, London." German Federal Foreign Office, May 18, 2015. <https://www.auswaertiges-amt.de/en/newsroom/news/150518-ca-b-chatham-house/271832>;

not cause fatalities, physical damage or destruction yet nevertheless has very serious non-material consequences.[614]

International scholars appear largely to support the idea of *Armed Attacks* being possible in cyberspace in principle, albeit with several caveats attached. Albrecht Randelzhofer, in his UN Charter Commentary, wrote that a hostile cyber operation can amount to an *Armed Attacks.*[615] He hedged that statement somewhat by stating that in order to reach that threshold, a cyber attack would have to produce substantial and immediate effects, comparable to the effects produced by a conventional attack. The effects disrupt the elementary living conditions in a country or reduce a State's ability to act and should do so in an *inhibitive way* (i.e., not be easily fixable).[616] Since these conditions will differ from State to State, depending on its country context, including the level of dependence on cyber infrastructure, every situation should be evaluated in a case-by-case manner. Other scholars appear to propose similar solutions. For example, Arva Constantinou proposed that an *Armed Attack* is: *an act or the beginning of a series of acts of armed force of considerable magnitude and intensity (i.e., scale) which have as their consequences (i.e., effects) the infliction of substantial destruction upon important elements of the target State namely, upon its people, economic and security infrastructure, destruction of aspects of its governmental authority, i.e., its political independence, as well as damage to, or deprivation of its physical element namely, its territory.*[617] Henry Campbell Black's Law Dictionary states that the *Armed* component of an *Armed Attack* means *equipped with a weapon* or *involving the use of a weapon,*[618] where a

---

614 The government of Netherlands. Letter to the parliament on the international legal order in cyberspace, September 26, 2019. <https://www.government.nl/documents/parliamentary-documents/2019/09/26/letter-to-the-parliament-on-the-international-legal-order-in-cyberspace>.

615 Simmam Bruno et al. (2013). The Charter of The United Nations 3E, Vol 1. Oxford Commentaries on International Law, 1. Pages 1419–1420. <https://doi.org/10.1093/law/9780199639762.001.0001>.

616 Ibid.

617 Tsagourias, Nicholas. (2012). Cyber attacks, self-defence and the problem of attribution. Journal of Conflict and Security Law, 17(2), 229–244. Page 231. <https://doi.org/10.1093/jcsl/krs019>.

618 Black, Henry., & Garner, Bryan. (2009). Black's Law Dictionary. St. Paul, MN: West. Page 717.

weapon is *an instrument used or designed to be used to injure or kill someone*.[619] This definition combines the scale and effects-based doctrine with elements of the instruments-based doctrine. Karl Zemanek combined the doctrine of scale and effects with the notion of intent, which is similar in substance to the doctrine of target: *It is neither the designation of a device, nor its normal use, which make it a weapon, but the intent which it is used and the effect. The use of any device or number of devices, which results in a considerable loss of life and/or extensive destruction of property must therefore de deemed to fulfill the conditions of an 'armed attack'.*[620]

Yoram Dinstein listed number of situations of assault on critical ICT infrastructure, which he believes would constitute an *Armed Attack* against a State: "Fatalities causes by the loss of computer-controlled life-support systems; an extensive power grid outage (electricity blackout) creating considerable deleterious repercussions; a shutdown of computers controlling waterworks and dams, generating thereby floods of inhabited areas; deadly crashes deliberately engineered (e.g., through misinformation fed into aircraft computers) and "the wanton instigation of a core-meltdown of a reactor in a nuclear power plant, leading to the release of radioactive materials that can result in countless casualties if the neighboring areas are densely populated."[621]

The terrorist attack that took place on September 11, 2001 provided a case study on NATO's interpretation of the term *Armed Attack*. At the time, two civilian planes, hijacked by Al-Qaida operatives, were interpreted to have been used as a weapon with which an *Armed Attack* was perpetrated.[622]

---

619 Ibid. Page 123.

620 Zemanek, Karl. (2013, October). Definition of an Armed Attack in International Law. Max Planck Encyclopedias of International Law - Oxford Public International Law. Paragraph 21. Retrieved February 18, 2022, from <https://opil.ouplaw.com/view/10.1093/law:epil/9780199231690/law-9780199231690-e241>.

621 Dinstein, Yoram. (2002). Computer Network Attacks and Self-Defense. International Law Studies, 76, 99–114. Page 105. <https://digital-commons.usnwc.edu/cgi/viewcontent.cgi?article=1397&context=ils>.

622 United Nations Security Council. (2001a, September 12). Resolution 1368 (2001) of the United Nations Security Council. Retrieved February 18, 2022, from <https://home.treasury.gov/system/files/126/1368.pdf>; United Nations Security Council. (2001, September 28). Resolution 1373 (2001) of the United Nations Security Council. Retrieved February 18, 2022, from <https://www.un.org/press/en/2001/sc7158.doc.htm>

This provides a precedent for a broad definition of a weapon utilized in an *Armed Attack*. Other non-obvious objects, such as civilian cyber infrastructure, or private computers hijacked by hackers could be labeled as *weapons* for the sake of determining that an Armed Attack took place. It also intensified the debate on applying the term *Armed Attack* to actions taken by non-State-actors, such as Al-Qaeda. There is however no consensus on the matter as States have expressed opposite views. For instance Germany accepts the notion that hostile cyber operations can constitute an *Armed Attack* and validate *Self-Defense* measures in Public International Law.[623] France on the other hand rejected it although with two comments: that acts by quasi-State entities such as ISIS could qualify as *Armed Attacks* and also that the general practice might shift in the future close to the position held by Germany although it has not yet.[624] As a result, no consistent *opinio juris* has emerged yet on the subject although such convergence is not precluded in the future.

Some States also raised the notion of preemptive *Self-Defense* in cyberspace. Because hostile cyber operations can have instantaneous damaging effects, sometimes the only way to avoid them is a preemptive action. Australia and France have expressed their espousal of such a norm in the cyber context.[625] However, it remains to be seen whether other States will follow and whether this will become a norm of Public International Law.

3.7 Conclusion

The existing framework of *Internationally Wrongful Acts* in Public International Law is the foundation for how hostile cyber operations between States should be regulated. Following the approval by UN GA of the UN GGE Reports

---

623 The German Parliament. Antwort - Deutscher Bundestag, December 10, 2015. Page 11. <https://dserver.bundestag.de/btd/18/069/1806989.pdf>.

624 The government of France. Communiqué -La France s'engage à promouvoir un cyberespace stable, fondé sur la confiance et le respect du droit international, October 4, 2019. French Ministry of Defense. Page 9. <https://www.defense.gouv.fr/fre/salle-de-presse/communiques/communique_la-france-s-engage-a-promouvoir-un-cyberespace-stable-fonde-sur-la-confiance-et-le-respect-du-droit-international>.

625 Ibid.; The government of Australia. "Australia's International Cyber Engagement Strategy," November 2020. <https://www.internationalcybertech.gov.au/sites/default/files/2020-11/The%20Strategy.pdf>.

of 2013 and 2015, a consensus has emerged on applicability of the main categories such as *Violation of Sovereignty*, *Prohibited Intervention*, and *Act of Aggression* in the cyber context. However, there remain several open-ended questions regarding this transposition that are due to the unique characteristics of cyberspace.

Cyber espionage is the most widespread form of hostile cyber operations between States, constituting more than 80% of the total volume. While there is no general prohibition of espionage, State practice and statements start shaping in the direction of seeing cyber espionage as different from conventional one and perceiving it as internationally wrongful in principle. This is mostly due to the penetrative character of such espionage coupled with the ease with which large cyber espionage operations can be conducted.

Violations of Sovereignty are the lowest category of hostile cyber operations that cross the threshold of an *Internationally Wrongful Act.* After an initial debate that took a few years, there is now strong *opinio juris* among States pointing to an operational character of the norm, rather than being just a general guideline. State practice that has been emerging is to treat differently hostile cyber operations that penetrate IT systems of another State and those that do not. The former type of operation would be always treated as a Violation of Sovereignty due to its penetrative character, breaching into the sphere of jurisdiction of another State. Those that do not have the penetrative component are assessed based on the type of effects and their scale that they produce to gauge whether a *Violation of Sovereignty* took place anyway. This practice is different from conventional interactions between States, where the penetrative component is important but not as central to the analysis of an act.

States uniformly embrace the notion of application and relevance of the *Principle of Non-Intervention* in cyberspace and support the idea that Sovereign Matters, the area that is adversely impacted by a coercive action during a *Prohibited Intervention*, has expanded over time to include IT infrastructure-related functions such as provision of public services via the internet. There are still nuanced differences in *opinio juris* among States, such as whether a cyber hostile act actually or just potentially has to coerce a government into action. Those might get resolved as more State practice takes place to validate one of the options.

Some *Prohibited Intervention*-related concepts might become irrelevant in the cyber context. There are a number of scholarly opinions that due to the penetrative character of cyber operations all potential instances of interference actually turn into *Prohibited Interventions* in the cyber context. This is because interference does not breach territorial sovereignty of a State whereas executing a hostile cyber operation almost inevitably leads to delivering a payload, be it a virus or just information, into the servers and computers located within the targeted State's jurisdiction. The largely de-territorialized and clandestine character are typical features of hostile cyber operations rather than an exception as is the case with conventional *Prohibited Interventions.* For that reason, *opinio juris* is now forming in the international community that a targeted State does not have to be aware of a hostile cyber operation taking place against it for the act to constitute a *Prohibited Intervention.* In this regard, International Public Law is developing a somewhat different standard for cyber operations than it is the case for conventional acts, where while not required, awareness is expected and might affect legal determination.

There is no consistent *opinio juris* in terms of determining the threshold for an *Act of Aggression* in cyberspace with various States issuing their statements on the matter. Some definitions include the requirement for existence of physical damage, while others allow for purely digital *Acts of Aggression.* There is consensus however that hostile cyber operations can generate *Prohibited Use of Force,* which is the key ingredient of an *Act of Aggression.* There exists some resistance from several States to recognize either purely digital *Acts of Aggression* or cyber *Armed Attacks*, which are a qualified form of *Acts of Aggression*, although they recognize the possibility of emergence of such norms in the future. For that reason, several scholars proposed that over upcoming years, State practice might start forming that will allow for non-physical impact of a hostile cyber act to be enough to constitute an *Act of Aggression* and even an *Armed Attack.* For a sufficient scale of damage to take place this way however, more spheres of human life, including government processes, would likely have to move online than currently.

The main doctrine for assessing whether the threshold of severity of *Prohibited Use of Force* has been met in State-on-State hostilities is called *Effects and Scale*, although State practice started emerging that treats cyberspace differently in that regard. Instead, a modified doctrine of *Effects and Target* that adds the element of type of facility or object that is targeted by a hostile cyber operation is slowly emerging.

Critical infrastructure plays an outsized role in the context of International Public Law regulating cyberspace. Whether a hostile cyber operation targeted critical infrastructure can influence the legal classification of an act. This constitutes a modification compared to general rules of International Public Law, where damaging critical infrastructure can contribute to classification of an *Internationally Wrongful Act* but only to the extent that it aggravates the effects and scale of the created damage rather than being a factor in its own right.

Classifying an accumulation of events as one joint *Internationally Wrongful Act*, a legal theory that has been on the cusp of becoming a norm of Public International Law for decades but has never achieved that status, is getting a new lease of life in the cyber context. States such as France are now officially espousing the notion specifically in the cyber context, where it is more applicable than in the conventional one. Whether the rule is a binding norm is not clear yet and additional State practice coupled by *opinio juris* is required. If the rule emerges as part of customary law, it would create a unique feature of the international legal framework covering cyberspace. In the wake of terrorist attacks in the 2010s, several States also expressed their opinion that a cyber *Act of Aggression* can be launched by a non-State actor, including quasi-States, such as the now-defeated ISIS.

Finally, in the areas where there is no consistent *opinio juris* on transposition of existing rules into the novel cyber context, International Public Law provides two tools to guide lawfulness of State conduct. The first one is the Martens Clause, and the second one is Article 31 of the Vienna Convention on The Law of Treaties. The former talks about the obligation of acting in a humanitarian way in the context of *jus ad bellum*. The latter talks about interpreting States' legal commitments from treaties in good faith. Together, they provide guidelines that can curb excesses in cyberspace, keeping States accountable for their behavior in a situation of a protracted legal vacuum.

Typology of hostile cyber operations between States which are not *Internationally Wrongful Acts*

4.1 Introduction

All States are obliged to seek out a peaceful settlement to any dispute with another State. This fundamental principle of Public International Law enjoys a customary, *erga omnes* character[626] and is confirmed by Article 2(3) and 33(1) of the UN Charter. It is also reinforced by several other sources of international law, including the UN General Assembly *Friendly Relations* Declaration,[627] international treaties,[628]

---

626 Case Concerning Military and Paramilitary Activities in and Against Nicaragua, Nicaragua v. United States. International Court of Justice. I.C.J Reports 14, ICGJ 112 (ICJ 1986). (1986). Paragraphs 145, 290. Retrieved February 15, 2022, from <https://www.icj-cij.org/en/case/70/judgments>; United Nations General Assembly Resolution. (2015, July 22). Group of Governmental Experts on Developments in the Field of Information and Telecommunications in the Context of International Security - Note by the Secretary-General. Paragraphs 26, 28(b). Retrieved February 15, 2022, from <https://documents-dds-ny.un.org/doc/UNDOC/GEN/N15/228/35/PDF/N1522835.pdf?OpenElement>.

627 United Nations General Assembly Resolution. (1970, October 24). 2625 (XXV) Declaration on Principles of International Law concerning Friendly Relations and Cooperation among States in Accordance with the Charter of the United Nations - Main Page. Retrieved February 17, 2022, from <https://legal.un.org/avl/ha/dpilfrcs-cun/dpilfrcscun.html>.

628 For example, European Convention for the Peaceful Settlement of Disputes: Council of Europe. (1957, April 29). European Convention for the Peaceful Settlement of Disputes. Retrieved February 18, 2022, from <https://rm.coe.int/1680064586>.

and jurisprudence of the ICJ.[629] This rule also applies to all interactions between States, which includes cyberspace. The UN Charter confirms that state of affairs:

All Members shall settle their international disputes by peaceful means in such a manner that international peace and security, and justice, are not endangered.

States are obliged to make a good faith attempt at a peaceful settlement of any dispute among one another. However, that attempt does not have to be successful, nor do they have to exhaust every single possible peaceful means in order to be in compliance with the rule.[630] Most importantly, attempts at peaceful settlement of a dispute does not preclude State, which is a target of an *Armed Attack* to resort to *Use of Force* in *Self-defense* and to *Countermeasures* if it is a target of a *Prohibited Intervention* or other *Violation of Sovereignty* (unless the UN Security Council rules specifically on the issue).[631] Some of such *Self-defense acts* and *Countermeasures* can take on the form of a hostile cyber operation aimed back at the perpetrator. They would then constitute an example of a lawful hostile international operation between two States.

In fact, there exist several circumstances that would preclude *wrongfulness* of a non-consensual cyber act between States that would otherwise be warranted. Preclusion of *wrongfulness* means that a State would not be held accountable for an otherwise prohibited conduct. Naturally, there are a number of limitations to these exemptions. These preclusions can be organized into two groups: independent acts whose wrongfulness is precluded based on special conditions and forms of response to hostile conduct by other States (also known as self-help measures). The first group includes: *consent,*

---

629 For example, Fisheries Jurisdiction (Spain v. Canada). International Court of Justice. (1998, December 4). Paragraph 56. Retrieved February 18, 2022, from <https://www.icj-cij.org/en/case/96/judgments>.

630 Case Concerning Military and Paramilitary Activities in and Against Nicaragua, Nicaragua v United States. International Court of Justice. I.C.J Reports 14, ICGJ 112 (ICJ 1986). (1986). Paragraph 310. Retrieved February 15, 2022, from <https://www.icj-cij.org/en/case/70/judgments>.

631 Case Concerning Military and Paramilitary Activities in and Against Nicaragua, Nicaragua v United States. International Court of Justice. I.C.J Reports 14, ICGJ 112 (ICJ 1986). (1986). Paragraph 307. Retrieved February 15, 2022, from <https://www.icj-cij.org/en/case/70/judgments>.

force majeure, *distress*, and *necessity*.[632] The second group includes: *Retorsions*, *Countermeasures*, and *Self-defense*. International consensus regarding existence of circumstances precluding wrongfulness of acts that would otherwise be classified as prohibited dates back to at least the 1930 Hague Conference.[633] Difference variants of such circumstances have since been confirmed by the jurisprudence of the ICJ[634] and various multilateral treaties, including the 1969 Vienna Convention.[635] This organic process taking place over decades led to development of the list precluding circumstances presented in this chapter. All of the listed circumstances technically apply in cyberspace, albeit in a contextualized way. At the high level, each of the listed circumstances creates a unique legal context that defines the scope of latitude for States when transposed into the cyber context. The exact contours of application, however, are not fully clear as States still clash on details of how established legal norms of Public International Law should be interpreted in this realm. These points of contention are highlighted and analyzed in this chapter.

Nevertheless, the broad consensus on the general possibility of lawful hostile cyber operations between States is undeniable. For instance, the United Nations has directly engaged on the subject of self-defense in cyberspace, which is conceivably the most severe possible form of a lawful international

---

632 United Nations International Law Commission. (2001). Draft articles on Responsibility of States for Internationally Wrongful Acts with commentaries. United Nations Office of Legal Affairs. Page 71. Retrieved February 15, 2022, from <https://legal.un.org/ilc/texts/instruments/english/commentaries/9_6_2001.pdf>.

633 United Nations International Law Commission. (1958, March 6). Yearbook Of The International Law Commission 1958. Pages 219–225. Retrieved February 18, 2022, from <https://legal.un.org/ilc/publications/yearbooks/english/ilc_1958_v2.pdf>.

634 Case concerning the Gabcikovo-Nagymaros Project. I.C.J. Reports 88, ICJ GL No. 92. (1997). Page 39, paragraph 48. Retrieved February 15, 2022, from <https://www.icj-cij.org/en/case/92/judgments>; Case concerning the difference between New Zealand and France concerning the interpretation or application of two agreements, concluded on 9 July 1986 between the two States and which related to the problems arising from the Rainbow Warrior Affair. International Court of Justice. ICJ Reports 1990. (1990, April 30). Paragraph 79. Retrieved February 18, 2022, from <https://legal.un.org/riaa/cases/vol_XX/215-284.pdf>.

635 United Nations. (1969, May 23). Vienna Convention on the Law of Treaties. Article 61. Retrieved February 18, 2022, from <https://legal.un.org/ilc/texts/instruments/english/conventions/1_1_1969.pdf>.

cyber operation, as recently as in 2021, publishing a list of legal positions of ten States.[636]

Beyond the established list of seven precluding circumstances, any hostile cyber operations ordered by the UN Security Council would be lawful by definition. They do not enjoy preclusion from wrongfulness since they are lawful unconditionally. There also exist proposals of additional forms of lawful hostile cyber operations that are being debated. Those include: *Humanitarian Interventions*, *Responsibility to Protect*, and collective *Countermeasures*.

Finally, there is the question of how far lawful international cyber operations can go in their severity and damage that they cause. At present, there is no clear consensus among States on the matter. For example, in 2015 the United States released its cyber strategy, which emphasized offensive capabilities and the readiness to strike back as a deterrent. This substantiates some pundits' fears of potential *hacking back* exchanges between States.[637] There is also a growing concern over preemptive international cyber operations that would be framed as preventive *Countermeasures* or *Self-defense* measures, leading to a global spiral of cyber escalation. The UN Charter frames lawful *Use of Force* as a next hostile cyber tool of last resort, after all less invasive methods become unavailable. The nature of cyberspace, fast-paced, clandestine, and with potential of paralyzing a whole country in one swift hostile operation, might test the limits of this notion.

This chapter analyzes each of the aforementioned aspects explaining their historical legal context and likely application in cyberspace.

---

636 United Nations General Assembly Resolution. (2021, July 13). 73/266. Official compendium of voluntary national contributions on the subject of how international law applies to the use of information and communications technologies by States submitted by participating governmental experts in the Group of Governmental Experts on Advancing Responsible State Behaviour in Cyberspace in the Context of International Security established pursuant to General Assembly resolution. Retrieved February 16, 2022, from <https://front.un-arm.org/wp-content/uploads/2021/08/A-76-136-EN.pdf>.

637 Timberg, Craig, Nakashima, Ellen, & Douglas-Gabriel, Danielle. (2014, October 9). "Cyberattacks trigger talk of hacking back." The Washington Post. <https://www.washingtonpost.com/business/technology/cyberattacks-trigger-talk-of-hacking-back/2014/10/09/6f0b7a24-4f02-11e4-8c24-487e92bc997b_story.html>.

4.2 Conditions precluding wrongfulness of a hostile cyber operation between States

4.2.1 Necessity

4.2.1.1 *Necessity* in Public International Law

Necessity is one of the circumstances precluding wrongfulness of a State's act in Public International Law. This rule is a relatively new addition to the body of international law. For example, the ICJ considered the notion in its deliberations on the Rainbow Warrior case in 1986 and refused to recognize it as a binding norm.[638] In 1995 however, the ICJ judgment in the Gabcíkovo-Nagymaros Project accepted the norm's existence "in principle."[639] It then re-confirmed the norm's existence without any hedging in the 1998 Fisheries Jurisdiction case.[640]

The key difference between *Force Majeure* and *Distress* on one side and *Necessity* on the other is that the latter pertains to an impending situation rather than one that has already actualized. Necessity means that the only way of averting a grave and imminent peril would be to temporarily behave in a way that would otherwise constitute an *Internationally Wrongful Act*. The UN International Law Commission attempted to lay out the details of the norm in Article 25 of *Draft Articles on State Responsibility*. The Commission proposed four criteria for gauging whether act by a State can qualify as *Necessity*:

- The action concerns an essential interest of the State.
- There exists a threat of grave and imminent peril to said essential interest.

---

638 Case concerning the difference between New Zealand and France concerning the interpretation or application of two agreements, concluded on 9 July 1986 between the two States and which related to the problems arising from the Rainbow Warrior Affair. International Court of Justice. ICJ Reports 1990. (1990, April 30). Page 254. Retrieved February 18, 2022, from <https://legal.un.org/riaa/cases/vol_XX/215-284.pdf>.

639 Case concerning the Gabcikovo-Nagymaros Project. I.C.J. Reports 88, ICJ GL No. 92. (1997). Pages 40– 41, paragraphs 51–52. Retrieved February 15, 2022, from <https://www.icj-cij.org/en/case/92/judgments>.

640 Fisheries Jurisdiction (Spain v. Canada). International Court of Justice. (1998, December 4). Page 432. Retrieved February 18, 2022, from <https://www.icj-cij.org/en/case/96/judgments>.

- The State's act is the only way to safeguard the essential interest.
- The essential interest is of greater value than whatever is being violated by the State's act.[641]

Article 25 of *Draft Articles* is not a source of law but rather a proposition of how the existing norm of *Necessity* could be understood and applied. At the same time, the status of UN ILC, coupled with the fact that States have overall embraced their formulation suggests that the four criteria are at least in the process of becoming customary law, if not already have concluded that process. UN ILC offered three additional clarifications, based on a study of States' practice and statements. First, *Necessity* cannot be invoked if a State contributed in any way to creation of the situation. Second, "grave and imminent peril" can arise even when there was no conduct, rightful or wrongful, by another State. For example, sometimes it might be non-State-actors' actions or even acts of nature (e.g., a tsunami). Henning Lahmann found that the scope of invocable situations is fairly wide, including for instance financial emergencies or terrorist threats.[642] Third, *Necessity* cannot infringe upon norms of international law enjoying the status of *jus cogens.* Despite the speculative nature of necessity (no actual damage of any sort is needed for *Necessity* to be invokable), the ICJ and arbitration bodies have since confirmed its operational character in Public International Law, for example in the 2004 *Advisory Opinion on Legal Consequences of the Construction of a Wall in the Occupied Palestinian Territory.*[643]

Similarly to *Force Majeure* and *Distress*, the mainstream opinion is that *Necessity* never allows for measures rising to the level of *Use of Force* (although

---

641 United Nations International Law Commission. (2001). Draft articles on Responsibility of States for Internationally Wrongful Acts with commentaries. United Nations Office of Legal Affairs. Article 25. Retrieved February 15, 2022, from <https://legal.un.org/ilc/texts/instruments/english/commentaries/9_6_2001.pdf>.

642 Lahmann, Henning. (2020) Unilateral Remedies to Cyber Operations: Self-Defence, Countermeasures, Necessity, and the Question of Attribution. 1st ed. Cambridge: Cambridge University Press on p. 208.

643 Advisory Opinion - Legal Consequences of the Construction of a Wall in the Occupied Palestinian Territory. International Court of Justice. ICJ Report 2004. (2004, July 9). Paragraph 140. Retrieved February 18, 2022, from <https://www.icj-cij.org/en/case/131>; Argentina-US Bilateral Investment Treaties Arbitration Body. (2007, July 25). LG&E Energy Corp., LG&E Capital Corp., LG&E International Inc.

there are scholars who argue otherwise).[644] This is consistent with the approach that lawful *Use of Force* is only allowed as an act of *Self-defense* in face of an *Armed Attack.*[645] However, there exists a minority opinion among academic scholars claiming that it is possible if imminent peril is especially grave and would match the impact of an *Armed Attack.*[646] This proposal however has not found yet resonance in State practice or government statements.

There remain a few gaps in understanding of the definitional scope of *Necessity*. The notion of "an essential interest" has not been clearly delineated in international law, especially in the context of invoking *Necessity*, although there exist sources of law that offer several definitional guidelines. The ICJ judgment in the Gabčíkovo-Nagymaros Project case stated that "an essential interest should be fundamental, and of great importance to the State concerned and the threat to it should be imminent."[647] Importantly, the ICJ established in that case that the imminence does not necessarily have to be short-lived or recent. It might take place over a long period as long as it does

---

v. The Argentine Republic. Paragraph 201–266. Retrieved February 19, 2022, from <https://www.biicl.org/files/3908_2007_lg&e_v_argentina.pdf>;

Case between CMS Gas Transmission Company and The Argentine Republic. The World Bank. International Centre For Settlement Of Investment Disputes. (2005, May 12). Paragraphs 304–394. Retrieved February 19, 2022, from <http://icsidfiles.worldbank.org/icsid/ICSIDBLOBS/OnlineAwards/C4/DC504_En.pdf>;

Argentina-US Bilateral Investment Treaties Arbitration Body. (2007a, May 22). Enron Corporation and Ponderosa Assets, L.P. v The Argentine Republic. Paragraphs 288–345. Retrieved February 19, 2022, from <https://www.biicl.org/files/3909_2007_enron_v_argentina.pdf>; Argentina-US Bilateral Investment Treaties Arbitration Body. (2007c, September 28). Sempra Energy International v. Argentine Republic. Paragraphs 325–397. Retrieved February 19, 2022, from <https://www.biicl.org/files/3906_2007_sempra_energy_v_argentina.pdf>.

644 Schmitt, Michael N. & NATO Cooperative Cyber Defence Centre of Excellence. (2017). Tallinn Manual 2.0 on the International Law Applicable to Cyber Operations. Cambridge University Press. Page 140, commentary on Rule 26, paragraph 18.

645 Advisory Opinion on Legality of the Threat or Use of Nuclear Weapons. International Court of Justice. ICJ Reports. (1996, July 8). Paragraph 96. Retrieved February 18, 2022, from <https://www.icj-cij.org/en/case/95>.

646 Schmitt, Michael N. & NATO Cooperative Cyber Defence Centre of Excellence. (2017). Tallinn Manual 2.0 on the International Law Applicable to Cyber Operations. Cambridge University Press. Page 141.

647 Case concerning the Gabcikovo-Nagymaros Project. International Court of Justice. I.C.J. Reports 88, ICJ GL No. 92. (1997). Paragraph 54. Retrieved February 15, 2022, from <https://www.icj-cij.org/en/case/92/judgments>.

not render the risk of damage less likely.[648] What is decisive is that *the window of opportunity* to take action and prevent an imminent grave peril is shrinking fast. Besides targeting an essential interest and being imminent, the definition of *Necessity* states that the peril should also be grave. This last part implies that only the most severe perils would qualify although where the threshold of severity of the graveness lies remains unclear for now. However, Henning Lahmann's analysis found however that the most challenging requirement for invocation of *Necessity* is not the gravity of action taken or imminence of the threat but proving that the chosen response is "is the only way to safeguard the essential interest."[649] *Necessity* can be subjected to a treaty modification that supplants, adjusts or even removes that legal pathway through consent of contracting States.[650]

4.2.1.2 Application of *Necessity* in cyberspace

Application of *Necessity* in8 8the cyber context requires an adaptation to its specific features. Two of them are especially relevant:

- The near-instantaneous nature of hostile cyber operations that makes the window of opportunity to prevent them shorter;
- Classification of preservation of functioning ITC infrastructure as an essential interest.

International scholars who authored the Tallinn Manual put much emphasis on *Necessity*, dedicating a separate rule to it (Rule 26), as well as a mention within another one (Rule 19) that deals with circumstances precluding wrongfulness.[651] They proposed that in the cyber context the peril is always imminent if "the window of opportunity to take action to prevent it is about to close" focusing on the time during which it is possible to prevent the peril

648 Ibid.

649 Lahmann, Henning. (2020) Unilateral Remedies to Cyber Operations: Self-Defence, Countermeasures, Necessity, and the Question of Attribution. 1st ed. Cambridge: Cambridge University Press on p. 209

650 Ibid. page 225

651 Schmitt, Michael N. & NATO Cooperative Cyber Defence Centre of Excellence. (2017). Tallinn Manual 2.0 on the International Law Applicable to Cyber Operations. Cambridge University Press. Pages 135, 137.Manual pages 135, 137

rather than the time until the peril actualizes into a disaster.[652] This seemingly slight change of focus fits the cyber context. Hostile cyber operations can take place at any time without any warning and in a much less predictable fashion than in the conventional context. This however would constitute a split from the way the norm is interpreted outside of cyberspace, implying formation of a separate set of rules for cyberspace in Public International Law. In fact, scholars such as Christian Schaller have called out the Tallinn Manual for advocating for that direction, describing *Necessity* as described in the Manual as a proposal of a specialized norm rather than a description of application of an existing general norm.[653]

Regarding the second feature of cyberspace, its critical dependence on the ICT infrastructure, some existing international legal cases provide evidence that its continued operation is included in the definition of *essential interest.* For example, an arbitration award from 2007 between Argentina and LG&E extended that notion of essential interest to the electric grid.[654] This potentially provides a precedent for potentially extending *Necessity* to internet infrastructure. Some scholars advocate for an elevated status of critical infrastructure in the context of *Necessity.* For example, Henning Lahmann suggested that contextual nature is not relevant when critical infrastructure is even partially disrupted. According to him, such a situation would automatically be eligible for invoking *Necessity.*[655] However, validating this interpretation in the international legal system would require more State practice that would validate such a broad definitional scope. The following two examples present how application of *Necessity* to cyberspace could proceed in practice.

Let us consider the following case: a State discovers through intelligence operations that preparations are taking place in another State to release a

---

652 Ibid. Page 140, Commentary on Rule 26, paragraph 18.

653 Schaller, Chrisitan. "Beyond Self-Defense and Countermeasures: A Critical Assessment of the Tallinn Manual's Conception of Necessity" 2016, 95 Texas Law Review. Page 1619.

654 Argentina-US Bilateral Investment Treaties Arbitration Body. (2007, July 25). LG&E Energy Corp., LG&E Capital Corp., LG&E International Inc. v. The Argentine Republic. Paragraph 251. Retrieved February 19, 2022, from <https://www.biicl.org/files/3908_2007_lg&e_v_argentina.pdf>.

655 Lahmann, Henning. (2020) Unilateral Remedies to Cyber Operations: Self-Defence, Countermeasures, Necessity, and the Question of Attribution. 1st ed. Cambridge: Cambridge University Press on p. 209

new Stuxnet-like virus with the aim of infecting IT systems of a domestic nuclear power plant and causing its meltdown. The peril is so grave and imminent that the State decides to order its military IT unit to strike first, locating the server in the other State on which the virus is being developed and breaking into it to read the virus's code and insulate the domestic systems against it. The preemptive strike would normally constitute at least a *Violation of Sovereignty* and possibly also a *Prohibited Intervention*. However, because the State operated in the context of *Necessity*, the cyber operation would not be wrongful.

Let us consider a hypothetical scenario based on an actual existing dangerous situation. A vast stranded oil tanker, F. S. O. Safer, is moored outside of the Yemeni port city of Hodeidah (at the time of writing this book). Its tanks currently store around one million barrels of oil, four times as much as was spilled by Exxon Valdez during the infamous 1989 Alaska spill.[656] The ship is likely to explode at any moment due to its decrepit state and lack of maintenance caused by the ongoing civil war in Yemen. If and when that happens, the Suez Canal shipping route might be closed for months. The port of Hodeidah, the main passage point for food and medications, of critical importance to the nation ravaged by a terrible humanitarian crisis,[657] would be cut off. UNICEF claimed that should the port close, some three hundred thousand children would be at risk of dying from starvation and disease.[658] The fire would pollute air breathed by some eight million Yemenis, forcing many of them to relocate. Impact on marine life and the local fishing industry would be as disastrous. The United Nations tried, unsuccessfully, to broker a deal with the Houthi rebels to remove oil from the tanker. If Eritrea, whose population, economy, and environment would be severely affected by the explosion, tried to use a cyber operation to breach into the ship's systems as part of an operation to siphon off the oil, it could invoke *Necessity*, even

---

656 Caesar, Ed. (October 4, 2021). The Ship That Became a Bomb. The New Yorker. <https://www.newyorker.com/magazine/2021/10/11/the-ship-that-became-a-bomb>.

657 Ferguson, Jane. (2018, July 11). Is Yemen's Man-Made Famine the Future of War? The New Yorker. <https://www.newyorker.com/news/news-desk/is-yemen-intentional-starvation-the-future-of-war>.

658 United Nations. (2018, June 15). Assault on key Yemeni port would endanger 300,000 children and choke. Retrieved February 19, 2022, from <https://news.un.org/en/story/2018/06/1012032>.

though the situation has been going on incessantly since at least 2014. This would constitute a hybrid operation with both the cyber and the conventional component being precluded from constituting *Internationally Wrongful Acts.*

4.2.2 Force Majeure

4.2.2.1 *Force Majeure* in Public International Law

Force Majeure, sometimes translated from French as "Higher Power," denotes: *the occurrence of an irresistible force or of an unforeseen event, beyond the control of the State, making it materially impossible in the circumstances to perform the obligation.*[659] It is a customary rule of international law that is also reflected in international treaties, PCIJ rulings[660] and ICJ judgments.[661]

Sandra Szurek proposed that the definition of *Force Majeure* encompasses three requirements:

- Irresistibility
- Unpredictability
- Externality.[662]

---

659 United Nations International Law Commission. (2001). Draft articles on Responsibility of States for Internationally Wrongful Acts with commentaries. United Nations Office of Legal Affairs. Article 23. Retrieved February 15, 2022, from <https://legal.un.org/ilc/texts/instruments/english/commentaries/9_6_2001.pdf>.

660 Case Concerning the Payment of Various Serbian Loans Issued in France (France v. Kingdom of the Serbs, Croats and Slovenes). Permanent Court Of International Justice Series A No. 20. (1929, July 12).. Pages 39–40. Retrieved February 19, 2022, from <https://www.icj-cij.org/public/files/permanent-court-of-international-justice/serie_A/A_20/62_Emprunts_Serbes_Arret.pdf>; Case Concerning The Payment In Gold Of Brazilian Federal Loans Contracted In France (France v. Brazil). Permanent Court Of International Justice Series A No. 21. (1929, July 12). Page 120. Retrieved February 19, 2022, from <https://www.icj-cij.org/public/files/permanent-court-of-international-justice/serie_A/A_20/64_Emprunts_Bresiliens_Arret.pdf>.

661 Case concerning the Gabcikovo-Nagymaros Project. I.C.J. Reports 88, ICJ GL No. 92. (1997). Page 63, paragraph 102. Retrieved February 15, 2022, from <https://www.icj-cij.org/en/case/92/judgments>.

662 Szurek, Sandra. "Circumstances precluding Wrongfulness in the ILC Articles on State Responsibility: Force Majeure." [in:] James Crawford, Alain Pellet, and Simon Olleson "The Law of International Responsibility," page 477.

The norm concerns non-performance of obligations under international law. Active actions do not fall under *Force Majeure* since they include the element of choice on the part of a State. The rule means that lack of certain action on part of a State, which would normally be internationally wrongful, is not if a State finds itself in a situation where it is impossible to deliver on its commitments. The UN International Law Commission clarified that force is irresistible when it becomes *a constraint that the State was unable to avoid or oppose by its own means.*[663] Some additional clarification came from the 1983 Gould Marketing, Inc. v. Ministry of Defence of Iran arbitration case, which provided that *the irresistible force or event must be the cause of the material impossibility of performing the obligation.*[664] The Anaconda-Iran, Inc. v. Iran et al., Interlocutory Award from 1986 also included a passage about *Force Majeure*, stating that *social and economic forces beyond the power of the state to control through the exercise of due powers* can be classified as irresistible force.[665]

Force Majeure has to render an international obligation completely impossible, not merely more difficult to deliver on.[666] It would also not apply if the impossibility is a direct result of the State's negligent behavior.[667] By

---

663 United Nations International Law Commission. (2001). Draft articles on Responsibility of States for Internationally Wrongful Acts with commentaries. United Nations Office of Legal Affairs. Article 23, paragraph 2 of Commentary. Retrieved February 15, 2022, from <https://legal.un.org/ilc/texts/instruments/english/commentaries/9_6_2001.pdf>.

664 Gould Marketing, Inc. v. Ministry of National Defence, 3 IRAN-U.S. C.T.R., at 147 et seq. Trans-Lex.Org. Iran-U.S. Claims Tribunal. (1983, July 27). Paragraph 153. Retrieved February 19, 2022, from <http://translex.uni-koeln.de/230700/_/iran-us-claims-tribunal-gould-marketing-inc-v-ministry-of-national-defence-3-iran-us-ctr-at-147-et-seq/>.

665 Anaconda Iran Ltd. v. Iran, 13 IRAN-U.S. C.T.R. 1986, at 199 et seq. Trans-Lex.Org. Iran-US Claims Tribunal. (1986, December 10). Paragraph 213. Retrieved February 19, 2022, from <http://translex.uni-koeln.de/231800/_/iran-us-claims-tribunal-anaconda-iran-ltd-v-iran-13-iran-us-ctr-1986-at-199-et-seq/>.

666 Case concerning the difference between New Zealand and France concerning the interpretation or application of two agreements, concluded on 9 July 1986 between the two States and which related to the problems arising from the Rainbow Warrior Affair. International Court of Justice. ICJ Report 1990. (1990, April 30). Page 253. Retrieved February 18, 2022, from <https://legal.un.org/riaa/cases/vol_XX/215-284.pdf>.

667 Libyan Arab Foreign Investment Company (Lafico) v. the Republic of Burundi. International Law Review. World Trade Organization Arbitration. (1994). Pages 279,

the same token, a State that directly contributed to a *Force Majeure* event in another State, will not be able to invoke wrongfulness of the resulting lack of ability to comply with related international obligations by the affected State. However, there is no norm preventing States from precluding *Force Majeure* from having any impact on treaty obligations within a treaty, thus in a way precluding a preclusion.

Force Majeure is similar in substance to supervening impossibility of performance of an international obligation, laid out in Article 61 of the Vienna Convention on the Law of Treaties. The article states that permanent disappearance or destruction of an object indispensable for the execution of a treaty provision precludes the wrongfulness of a violation of that treaty.[668] It is important to stress however that disappearance or destruction does not include malfunction or more difficult maintenance. This means that Force Majeure is broader in its scope than Article 61 of the Vienna Convention on the Law of Treaties.

4.2.2.2 Application of *Force Majeure* in cyberspace

The scope of application of *Force Majeure* in cyberspace is limited because almost all *Internationally Wrongful Acts* or more broadly *Unfriendly Acts* in cyberspace result from States' action rather than lack thereof. Application of *Force Majeure* in cyberspace can then pertain to:

- *Due Diligence* commitments, which would be based on the as-of-now non-binding notion that States can commit an *Internationally Wrongful Act* by failing to prevent a hostile cyber operation from taking advantage of the ICT infrastructure located within their jurisdiction;

---

318. Retrieved February 19, 2022, from <https://www.cambridge.org/core/journals/international-law-reports/article/abs/libyan-arab-foreign-investment-company-lafico-and-the-republic-of-burundi/62B205440734B90983D02B51A712780D>; United Nations International Law Commission. (2001). Draft articles on Responsibility of States for Internationally Wrongful Acts with commentaries. United Nations Office of Legal Affairs. Article 23(2)(a). Retrieved February 15, 2022, from <https://legal.un.org/ilc/texts/instruments/english/commentaries/9_6_2001.pdf>.

668 United Nations. (1969, May 23). Vienna Convention on the Law of Treaties. Article 61. Retrieved February 18, 2022, from <https://legal.un.org/ilc/texts/instruments/english/conventions/1_1_1969.pdf>.

- Future situations that have not been conceptualized yet, at a stage of technological development where enough human activity has moved to cyberspace that it creates new types of risk, including cyber *Force Majeure*.

Due Diligence in the cyber context is one of the voluntary non-binding norms proposed by the UN GGE and will be discussed in-depth in Chapter 5, together with other aspects of attribution in cyberspace. Its conjunction with *Force Majeure* would occur if lack of *Due Diligence* in cyberspace was caused by *Force Majeure*, inadvertently resulting in harm done to another State. Let us consider a potential future case: in the wake of chaos caused by an unpredictable massive flood, a State was not able to prevent private hackers from exploiting ICT infrastructure on its territory to perpetrate a hostile cyber operation against another State. The injured State could then invoke lack of proper *Due Diligence* on the part of the State, whose territory was used to perpetrate the hostile cyber act (provided *Due Diligence* is already a binding norm of Public International Law in this scenario). However, the latter state could invoke *Force Majeure* as the reason for it not being able to oversee its cyberspace properly.

Regarding future situations where something akin to cyber *Force Majeure* could take place, certain legal scholars, for example, Johann-Christoph Woltag, proposed a vision of a world in which spread of an internet virus could cause damage similar to that done by a tsunami, or a tornado.[669] The WannaCry virus, which spread virally around the globe and disrupted functioning of hospitals in the United Kingdom in 2017 can be seen as an early example of that possible phenomenon.[670] In such a situation, a State affected by this force-of-nature-like disaster could attempt to invoke cyber *Force Majeure*, in case it is unable to meet some of its international obligations due to profound disruption of State functioning caused by the virus. This, however,

---

669 Woltag, Johann-Christoph, Computer Network Operations Below the Level of Armed Force (May 26, 2011). ESIL 2011 4th Research Forum. Page 155. Retrieved on November 29, 2023. <https://ssrn.com/abstract=1967593>.

670 British Broadcasting Corporation. "NHS Cyber-Attack: GPS and Hospitals Hit by Ransomware." BBC News, May 12, 2017. <https://www.bbc.com/news/health-39899646>.

is subject to all standard caveats, such as the one that a State cannot invoke *Force Majeure* if its conduct has contributed to the problem's emergence.

4.2.3 Distress

4.2.3.1 *Distress* in Public International Law

Distress is another circumstance that can preclude wrongfulness of a cyber operation. It is defined as a situation where an individual or individuals have no other reasonable way of saving their life or lives of other persons entrusted to their care than to commit an act that would normally qualify as internationally wrongful. Such individuals' also need to be attributable to a State.[671] There are subtle but significant differences between *Distress* and other types of norms precluding wrongfulness:

- An important difference between *Distress* and *Force Majeure* is that the latter applies to lack of conduct due to a situation beyond a State's control while the former pertains to State's conduct (or lack thereof) that was the only way of saving life at a moment. Hence, *Distress* describes situations that involve a measure of decision-making and free will.
- The difference between *Distress* and *Necessity* is that the former pertains only to saving lives at a particular moment and is committed by an individual or individuals while the latter pertains to essential interests of a State.

The historical context of development of that norm are maritime catastrophes and accidents.[672] The phrasing *Distress* derives from the *Distress Call* that a ship or an airplane can send. Applicability of *Distress* in Public International Law was acknowledged in various contexts, besides calls from vessels, by the ICJ

---

671 United Nations International Law Commission. (2001). Draft articles on Responsibility of States for Internationally Wrongful Acts with commentaries. United Nations Office of Legal Affairs. Article 24. Retrieved February 15, 2022, from <https://legal.un.org/ilc/texts/instruments/english/commentaries/9_6_2001.pdf>.

672 United Nations. (1958, April 29). Convention on the Territorial Sea and the Contiguous Zone. United Nations Treaty Collection. Article 14, paragraph 3. Retrieved February 19, 2022, from <https://treaties.un.org/pages/ViewDetails.aspx?src=TREATY&mtdsg_no=XXI-1&chapter=21>.

in the 1990 *Rainbow Warrior* ruling.[673] The logic of *Distress* was also expanded onto airspace, such as when a military aircraft needs to violate borders of a foreign State in order to conduct an emergency landing.[674]

Distress only applies to situations that include a threat to human life and are attributable to a State. One caveat is that if an act caused by *Distress* can be reasonably expected to cause more harm than if no action is taken (for instance by shifting the burden onto another State), then it would still be internationally wrongful. This stems from the principle of proportionality, applicable to the norm. Additionally, even *Distress* cannot preclude violation of a preemptory rules of international law (per Vienna Convention on the Law of Treaties).[675] Finally, if the circumstance creating a *Distress* subside, compliance with international legal obligations must resume or else an *Internationally Wrongful Act* is committed.

4.2.3.2 Application of *Distress* in cyberspace

The application of Distress to cyberspace is very limited, if not non-existent at present. Some international scholars, such as François Delerue, doubt that the norm of *Distress* would offer the most effective way of saving lives in case of any cyber incident.[676]

However, certain potential cases can be proposed. Take a situation, in which due to a natural disaster, an electricity plant in a certain region bordering another State gets destroyed, resulting in a dramatic humanitarian

---

673 Case concerning the difference between New Zealand and France concerning the interpretation or application of two agreements, concluded on 9 July 1986 between the two States and which related to the problems arising from the Rainbow Warrior Affair. International Court of Justice. ICJ Report 1990. (1990, April 30). Pages 254–255, paragraph 78. Retrieved February 18, 2022, from <https://legal.un.org/riaa/cases/vol_XX/215-284.pdf>.

674 United Nations International Law Commission. (2001). Draft articles on Responsibility of States for Internationally Wrongful Acts with commentaries. United Nations Office of Legal Affairs. Commentary on Article 24, paragraph 2. Retrieved February 15, 2022, from <https://legal.un.org/ilc/texts/instruments/english/commentaries/9_6_2001.pdf>.

675 United Nations. (1969, May 23). Vienna Convention on the Law of Treaties. Article 53. Retrieved February 18, 2022, from <https://legal.un.org/ilc/texts/instruments/english/conventions/1_1_1969.pdf>.

676 Delerue, François. Cyber Operations and international law. Cambridge: Cambridge University Press, 2020. Page 348.

crisis and a rising death count. If the affected State uses a non-consensual cyber operation to reroute electricity from another State through inter-border connectors toward the affected region, allowing hospitals to operate, it could invoke *Distress* to precludes international wrongfulness. However, if the natural disaster is a direct result of its own negligence (e.g., lack of proper maintenance of a dam) or if it could reroute electricity from other parts of its own country rather than a foreign State, the acting State would still be committing an *Internationally Wrongful Act*.

4.2.4 *Consent*

4.2.4.1 *Consent* in Public International Law

Article 20 of the Draft Articles on State Responsibility addresses the subject of *Consent* for all types of international interactions. It states:

> Valid consent by a State to the commission of a given act by another State precludes the wrongfulness of that act in relation to the former State to the extent that the act remains within the limits of that consent.[677]

This statement is a manifestation of a customary rule of Public International Law. The customary rule of *Consent* is reflected in a number of written sources of international law. For example, it can be deducted from the 1969 Vienna Convention on the Law of Treaties, whose Article 54 (b) states that State parties can agree to terminate or suspend a treaty, rendering its obligations null.[678]

Consent is also only valid if extended by an authorized State organ, designated to have agency over the specific aspect of *State Sovereignty* that is the subject of the agreement. Moreover, the agreed-upon act shall not exceed the scope of a State's consent. This begs the question of what happens if such a consent from an unauthorized organ or representative, acting outside of their remit, takes place. *Consent* will then be valid if two conditions are met: the authorized organs of the target State confirm the consent and the acting

---

677 United Nations International Law Commission. (2001). Draft articles on Responsibility of States for Internationally Wrongful Acts with commentaries. United Nations Office of Legal Affairs. Article 20. Retrieved February 15, 2022, from <https://legal.un.org/ilc/texts/instruments/english/commentaries/9_6_2001.pdf>.

678 United Nations. (1969, May 23). Vienna Convention on the Law of Treaties. Retrieved February 18, 2022, from <https://legal.un.org/ilc/texts/instruments/english/conventions/1_1_1969.pdf>.

State assumed initial consent in good faith.[679] Otherwise, an abuse of *Consent* constitutes an *Internationally Wrongful Act.*

Consent does not have to be explicit. There have been international legal arbitrage cases where implicit consent was found to be sufficient.[680] The ICJ jurisprudence has however established that there should be clear understanding regarding the scope of consent, and it should be interpreted in good faith.[681] Timing of *Consent* is also crucial. *Consent* can be given only before or during execution of the act in question. A retroactive agreement has a different legal status—that of a waiver or acquiescence by the targeted State following occurrence of an *Internationally Wrongful Act.*[682] *Consent* also cannot breach the preemptory rules of international law (*jus cogens*). However, the ICJ appears to have allowed for some borderline cases in this respect. For example, in the 2005 judgment on *Armed Activities on Territory of Congo*, it allowed for an invitation by a State to another one to intervene militarily on its territory to help subdue anti-government insurgents, which raised questions regarding the scale of human rights violation.[683]

---

679 United Nations International Law Commission. (2001). Draft articles on Responsibility of States for Internationally Wrongful Acts with commentaries. United Nations Office of Legal Affairs. Article 20, paragraph 4 of the Commentary. Retrieved February 15, 2022, from <https://legal.un.org/ilc/texts/instruments/english/commentaries/9_6_2001.pdf>.

680 Permanent Court of Arbitration. (1911, February 24). Arrest and Return of Savarkar, France v Great Britain, Award, (1911) XI RIAA 243, ICGJ 401 (PCA 1911). Oxford University Public International Law. Page 446. Retrieved February 18, 2022, from <https://opil.ouplaw.com/view/10.1093/law:icgj/401pca11.case.1/law-icgj-401pca11>.

681 Armed Activities on the Territory of the Congo (Democratic Republic of the Congo v. Uganda). International Court of Justice. ICJ Reports 168. (2005, December 19). Paragraph 99. Retrieved February 17, 2022, from <https://www.icj-cij.org/en/case/116>;
United Nations International Law Commission. (2001). Draft articles on Responsibility of States for Internationally Wrongful Acts with commentaries. United Nations Office of Legal Affairs. Article 20, paragraph 6 of the Commentary. Retrieved February 15, 2022, from <https://legal.un.org/ilc/texts/instruments/english/commentaries/9_6_2001.pdf>.

682 Ibid. Article 45.

683 Armed Activities on the Territory of the Congo (Democratic Republic of the Congo v. Uganda). International Court of Justice. ICJ Reports 168. (2005, December 19). Paragraphs 105, 106, 113, 149. Retrieved February 17, 2022, from <https://www.icj-cij.org/en/case/116>.

This leads to an important aspect of *Consent*, which is the unforeseen negative consequences. As long as such consequences are the result of the consented act, they do not constitute an *Internationally Wrongful Act.* However, in case such negative consequences are anticipated and explicitly forbidden as part of *Consent*, they do constitute an *Internationally Wrongful Act.*

Important aspects of consent are that it is freely given and that the following act stays within the limits of that consent. For instance, during the Soviet invasion in 1939, the Estonian parliament voted to express its consent to the Soviet Union's request to establish military bases in the country. However, this decision was coerced by the Soviet Army and cannot qualify as genuine *Consent* that was freely given.[684] For this reason, the international community never recognized Estonia's occupation by the Soviet Union, laying groundwork for the country's reemergence as an independent State in the 1990s.

4.2.4.2 Application of *Consent* in cyberspace

Application of *Consent* in cyberspace is a straightforward transposition. There exist however nuances that play out differently in cyberspace as compared to the conventional realm:

- The exact contours of a hostile act are not obvious, due to their non-physical character, creating a great risk of abuse of *Consent.*
- A high number of non-State actors conducting hostile cyber operations makes the remit of *Consent* less obvious.

The established rules on *Consent* regulate the question of the limit of remit of *Consent* and the risk of its abuse. For instance, if a head of a diplomatic mission can, in their capacity, agree to an entry onto the premises of the mission, including the access to ICT infrastructure, to another State's operative, it would only be limited to those premises. This means no other diplomatic mission or location within the sphere of jurisdiction of the mission's home

684 Lane, Thomas, Pabriks, Artis, Purs, Aldis, & Smith, David J. (2002). The Baltic States: Estonia, Latvia and Lithuania (Postcommunist States and Nations) (1st ed.). Routledge. Page 24.

State would be covered by the remit.[685] The limits of reach covered by *Consent* are less obvious in cyberspace where websites and other digital resources are part of the complex mesh of the global internet network. Accessing them could inevitably lead to disrupting other States' jurisdiction. Public International Law still does not have a way of handling such a challenge.

The second point pertains to non-State actors. Let us consider the following case: if a State asks to gain access to another State's ICT infrastructure to go after hackers residing within the target State, knowing that they might resist or retaliate, creating damage, without explaining fully those risks to the receiving State, the *Consent* might be void and the potential resulting damage can be attributed to the acting State. To address this challenge in the cyber realm, Michael Schmitt and other co-authors of the Tallinn Manual proposed a new norm that voids *fraudulently solicited Consent* in cyberspace.[686] They offered the following example for it:

> Consider the case of cyber operations being conducted by one State in another's territory with the latter's consent. The former knows of a flaw in the malware it is using that will have negative effects on systems that are not the target of the operation. It intentionally fails to inform the latter. The consent would not preclude any wrongfulness of the conduct in question because the former knew that the operation would have deleterious consequences for the latter and the latter was unaware of those consequences at the time it agreed to the operation.[687]

Whether *Fraudulently Solicited Consent* in cyberspace will take on remains an open subject. There have been however real cases of cyber *Consent.* For example, in 2008, during the Russian invasion of Georgia, the State's institutions were hit by hacker attacks. Georgia accepted international support and cooperation on the matter, letting IT teams representing foreign States

685 United Nations. (1961, April 18). Vienna Convention on Diplomatic Relations. Article 22(1). Retrieved February 17, 2022, from <https://legal.un.org/ilc/texts/instruments/english/conventions/9_1_1961.pdf>.

686 Schmitt, Michael N. & NATO Cooperative Cyber Defence Centre of Excellence. (2017). Tallinn Manual 2.0 on the International Law Applicable to Cyber Operations. Cambridge University Press. Article 19, Commentary.

687 Ibid. Pages 106–107.

help them handle the attacks.[688] Similar cooperation took place in Ukraine following the 2022 full-scale invasion by the Russian Federation.[689]

4.3 Acts of response to hostile cyber operations

4.3.1 Countermeasures

4.3.1.1 *Countermeasures* in Public International Law

Countermeasures are a well-established international legal customary norm. The *Draft Articles on State Responsibility* presented by the UN ILC suggested the following formula for this customary norm: *Measures that would otherwise be contrary to the international obligations of an injured State vis-à-vis the responsible State, if they were not taken by the former in response to an Internationally Wrongful Act by the latter in order procure cessation and reparation*[690]

Countermeasures can only be deployed by a targeted State to compel the perpetrator State to resume conduct that is compliant with its international obligations. They do not have to be of the exact same nature as the initial hostile act, allowing for flexibility in picking response by the injured State, as long as requirements of necessity and proportionality are met.[691]

Countermeasures as a norm of Public International Law were slowly emerging in the second half of the twentieth century as a way of offsetting a hostile act by a State without leading to an escalation. They were invoked for the first time as a binding rule in the Air Services Agreement

---

688 Delerue, François. Cyber Operations and international law. Cambridge: Cambridge University Press, 2020. Page 346; See also: Markoff, John. "Georgia Takes a Beating in the Cyberwar with Russia." The New York Times, August 11, 2008. <https://archive.nytimes.com/bits.blogs.nytimes.com/2008/08/11/georgia-takes-a-beating-in-the-cyberwar-with-russia/>.

689 Mueller, Grace B., Benjamin Jensen, Brandon Valeriano, Ryan C. Maness, and Jose M. Macias. "Cyber Operations during the Russo-Ukrainian War." CSIS, July 13, 2023. <https://www.csis.org/analysis/cyber-operations-during-russo-ukrainian-war>.

690 United Nations International Law Commission. (2001). Draft articles on Responsibility of States for Internationally Wrongful Acts with commentaries. United Nations Office of Legal Affairs. Page 128. Retrieved February 15, 2022, from <https://legal.un.org/ilc/texts/instruments/english/commentaries/9_6_2001.pdf>.

691 Ibid. Chapeau to Chapter II of Part 3, paragraph 5.

case of 1978.[692] Countermeasures were also featured in the ICJ's 1980 Teheran Hostages judgment.[693] By far the most comprehensive and thorough analysis of *Countermeasures* was provided by the ICJ in its 1997 judgment on the case of Gabčikovo-Nagymaros Project, in which the Court invoked several other ICJ rulings, arbitration awards, and customary norms. In the judgment, the ICJ listed the definitional requirements of *Countermeasures*, describing them as measures that:

- must be taken in response to an *Internationally Wrongful Act* of another State;
- shall be preceded by notifications of the State targeted by the *Countermeasure*: demanding cessation of the offensive act and another one that a *Countermeasure* is about to be taken;
- shall be temporary in nature;
- shall be reversible as far as possible;
- shall be proportionate to the violation they address;
- cannot reach the threshold of *Use of Force;*
- cannot breach preemptory (*jus cogens*) norms of international law.[694]

These requirements define *Countermeasures* in a way that they are not allowed to ever be so severe as to reach the level of *Use of Force*. This choice is shaped by the historical context. The predecessor of *Countermeasures* were *Reprisals*,

692 Air Service Agreement of 27 March 1946 between the United States of America and France. United Nations -Reports of International Arbitral Awards. Permanent Court of Arbitration. (1978, December 9). Paragraph 83. Retrieved February 18, 2022, from <https://legal.un.org/riaa/cases/vol_XVIII/417-493.pdf>.

693 United States Diplomatic and Consular Staff in Tehran (United States of America v. Iran). International Court of Justice. ICJ Reports 1980. (1980, May 24). Pages 27–28, paragraph 53. Retrieved February 17, 2022, from <https://www.icj-cij.org/en/case/64.3>

694 Case concerning the Gabcikovo-Nagymaros Project. I.C.J. Reports 88, ICJ GL No. 92. (1997). Page 55, paragraph 83. Retrieved February 15, 2022, from <https://www.icj-cij.org/en/case/92/judgments>; Additional sources engaging with the subject of definitional requirements for *Countermeasures*:

Air Service Agreement of 27 March 1946 between the United States of America and France. United Nations -Reports of International Arbitral Awards. Permanent Court of Arbitration. (1978, December 9). Paragraph 83. Retrieved February 18, 2022, from <https://legal.un.org/riaa/cases/vol_XVIII/417-493.pdf>.

a term in broad use until the mid-twentieth century, which is also discussed in the next subsection of this chapter.[695] *Reprisals* have a wide scope and are more symmetrical in nature to the act that gave rise to them. This creates a risk of a cycle of escalation between States.

One of the major developments following World War II was to reduce the role of *Reprisals*, which can contain the *Use of Force* component, and replace them with *Countermeasures* as the main way of self-help in wake of a hostile act by another State. At the same time, legitimate responses utilizing force were described as *Self-defense* measures, available only when a State is hit by an *Armed Attack*.[696] This framing serves better the purpose of restoration of peaceful relations. The *Air Service Agreement* arbitration ruling provides:

> Counter-measures (...) should be a wager on the wisdom, not on the weakness of the other Party. They should be used with a spirit of great moderation and be accompanied by a genuine effort at resolving the dispute.[697]

Reprisals still exist in Public International Law, but they are limited to only the realm of armed conflicts—*jus in bello*. Per Geneva Conventions, they are actions that can be taken by a State that would be otherwise prohibited if not for prior prohibited conduct by another State.[698] They are prohibited during

---

695 Grafton Wilson, G. (1925). "A Treatise on International Law." By William Edward Hall, M.A. 8th Edition. Edited by A. Pearce Higgins Professor. New York: Oxford University Press, 1924. pp. xlvii, 952. American Journal of International Law, 19(3), 656–657 <https://doi.org/10.2307/2188905>;
Lawrence, Thomas. J. (1910). The Principles of International Law. Forgotten Books. Pages 311–315.

696 Schmitt, Michael N. & NATO Cooperative Cyber Defence Centre of Excellence. (2017). Tallinn Manual 2.0 on the International Law Applicable to Cyber Operations. Cambridge University Press. Rule 71.

697 Air Service Agreement of 27 March 1946 between the United States of America and France. United Nations -Reports of International Arbitral Awards. Permanent Court of Arbitration. (1978, December 9). Paragraph 91. Retrieved February 18, 2022, from <https://legal.un.org/riaa/cases/vol_XVIII/417-493.pdf>.

698 International Committee of the Red Cross. (n.d.-b). Customary International Humanitarian Law - Rule 148. Reprisals in Non-International Armed Conflicts. Retrieved February 18, 2022, from <https://ihl-databases.icrc.org/customary-ihl/eng/docs/v1_rul_rule148>; International Committee of the Red Cross. (2016). Treaties, States parties, and Commentaries - Geneva Convention (I) on Wounded and Sick in Armed Forces in the Field,1949 - 3 - Article 3: Conflicts not of an international

peacetime. *Countermeasures* on the other hand are a tool designed for times of peace. *Countermeasures* are also different from *Retorsions*. *Retorsions* are measures taken in response to another State's conduct that is lawful, even if visibly unfriendly (i.e., they are *Unfriendly Acts* below the severity threshold for *Internationally Wrongful Acts*). *Countermeasures* in turn are measures that would constitute *Internationally Wrongful Acts* if not for their being a response to another State's *internationally wrongful act.*[699]

Self-defense measures, discussed in a separate subsection of this chapter, are a qualified form of *Countermeasures*, reserved only in the face of an *Armed Attack*. A key difference between *Self-defense* measures and *Countermeasures* is that the latter must not rise to the threshold of *Use of Force*.[700] Therefore, *Countermeasures* can be a proportionate response to *Violations of Sovereignty* and *Prohibited Interventions* but not to *Armed Attacks*.

There exists a legal gray area in regard to deploying *Countermeasures* against *Acts of Aggression*, that is, instances of *Prohibited Use of Force* that are grave enough to establish a *casus belli* but not quite grave enough to qualify as an *Armed Attack*. The international scholars who authored the Tallinn Manual were split on the matter and could not come to a shared interpretation.[701] Article 50 of the Draft Articles on State Responsibility proposes strongly

---

character - Commentary of 2016. Paragraphs 904–905. Retrieved February 18, 2022, from <https://ihl-databases.icrc.org/ihl/full/GCI-commentaryArt3>.

699 International Committee of the Red Cross. (n.d.-b). Customary International Humanitarian Law. Rule 147 - Reprisals against Protected Objects. International Committee of the Red Cross - Customary International Humanitarian Law. Retrieved February 18, 2022, from <https://ihl-databases.icrc.org/customary-ihl/eng/docs/v1_rul_rule147>; United Nations International Law Commission. (2001). Draft articles on Responsibility of States for Internationally Wrongful Acts with commentaries. United Nations Office of Legal Affairs. Chapeau to Chapter II of Part 3, paragraph 3 of Commentary. Retrieved February 15, 2022, from https://legal.un.org/ilc/texts/instruments/english/commentaries/9_6_2001.pdf>.

700 Schmitt, Michael N. (2014). "Below the threshold" cyber operations: the countermeasures response option and international law. Virginia Journal of International Law, 54(3), 697–732. Pages 718–719. <https://centaur.reading.ac.uk/89821/1/SSRN-id2353898.pdf>.

701 Schmitt, Michael N. & NATO Cooperative Cyber Defence Centre of Excellence. (2017). Tallinn Manual 2.0 on the International Law Applicable to Cyber Operations. Cambridge University Press. Pages 125–126, Commentary on Rule 22, paragraphs 11–12.

that *Countermeasures* cannot amount to a *Use of Force*.[702] In that it spells out a well-established customary legal norm that was first formalized in the UN General Assembly 1970 Resolution titled *Declaration on Principles of International Law concerning Friendly Relations and Cooperation among States in accordance with the Charter of the United Nations*. In this unanimously passed expression of collective *opinio juris*, the international community wrote that *States have a duty to refrain from acts of reprisal involving the use of force*[703] (reprisals being the precursor of *Countermeasures*). However, despite that, some experts are of the opinion that Countermeasures might, in exceptional cases, reach the level of *Use of Force*, in order to create an adequate and symmetrical deterrent.[704] The separate opinion of Judge Simma in the Oil Platforms case, substantiates that position:

> But we may encounter also a lower level of hostile military action, not reaching the threshold of an 'armed attack' within the meaning of Article 51 of the United Nations Charter. Against such hostile acts, a State may of course defend itself, but only within the more limited range and quality of responses (the main difference being that the possibility of collective self-defence does not arise, cf. Nicaragua) and bound to necessity, proportionality and immediacy in time in a particular strict way.[705]

Additionally, nothing prevents a State from conducting an asymmetrically soft response, in which it responds with an act of lesser severity, for example, a *Countermeasure*, to a forceful *Act of Aggression*.

---

702 United Nations International Law Commission. (2001). Draft articles on Responsibility of States for Internationally Wrongful Acts with commentaries. United Nations Office of Legal Affairs. Article 50. Retrieved February 15, 2022, from <https://legal.un.org/ilc/texts/instruments/english/commentaries/9_6_2001.pdf>.

703 United Nations General Assembly Resolution. (1970, October 24). 2625 (XXV) Declaration on Principles of International Law concerning Friendly Relations and Cooperation among States in Accordance with the Charter of the United Nations - Main Page. Retrieved February 17, 2022, from <https://legal.un.org/avl/ha/dpilfrcscun/dpilfrcscun.html>.

704 Schmitt, Michael N. & NATO Cooperative Cyber Defence Centre of Excellence. (2017). Tallinn Manual 2.0 on the International Law Applicable to Cyber Operations. Cambridge University Press. Page 126.

705 Case Concerning Oil Platforms, (2003), (Iran v. United States). International Court of Justice. (2003, November 6). Separate opinion of Judge Simma, paragraph 13. Retrieved February 18, 2022, from <https://www.icj-cij.org/en/case/90>.

Countermeasures should also not be conflated with measures imposed by the UN Security Council. Measures agreed on by the UN Security Council are lawful *ab initio*, by their definition. Such measures, if taken, would not be subject to the requirements that constrain *Countermeasures*. Therefore, based on Chapter 7 of the UN Charter, cyber measures mandated by the UN Security Council would be lawful. For instance, Article 41 of the UN Charter states:

> The Security Council may decide what measures not involving the use of armed force are to be employed to give effect to its decisions, and it may call upon the Members of the United Nations to apply such measures. These may include complete or partial interruption of economic relations and of rail, sea, air, postal, telegraphic, radio, and other means of communication, and the severance of diplomatic relations.[706]

Unlike with *Self-defense* measures, there is no ambiguity in terms of States and non-State actors. *Countermeasures* can only be conducted against a State or an organization whose actions are attributable to a State. This provision was spelled out in relation to reprisals, the predecessor term for modern *Countermeasures*, by the Hamburg Prize Court in the *Cysne* case[707] and confirmed by the Arbitral Tribunal in the Air Service Agreement case.[708] However, there exist scholarly voices in favor of expanding States' ability to deploy *Countermeasures* against non-State actors.[709] If that development took

---

[706] United Nations. (1945, June 26). Charter of the United Nations. Article 41. Retrieved February 17, 2022, from <https://www.un.org/en/about-us/un-charter>.

[707] Portugal v. Germany. (The Cysne). Hamburg Prize Court. (1915). Cambridge University - Annual Digest of Public International Law Cases. Pages 1056–1057. Retrieved February 18, 2022, from <https://www.cambridge.org/core/journals/annual-digest-of-public-international-law-cases/article/abs/portugal-v-germany-the-cysne/AC04379DA13F524F709EF6789D825D4A>; German-Portugese Arbitral Award (The Naulilaa Case). Arbitral Commission. (1930, June 30). United Nations - Report of International Arbitral Awards. Page 1011. Retrieved February 18, 2022, from <https://legal.un.org/riaa/cases/vol_III/1371-1386.pdf>;

[708] Air Service Agreement of 27 March 1946 between the United States of America and France. Permanent Court of Arbitration. (1978, December 9). United Nations -Reports of International Arbitral Awards. Retrieved February 18, 2022, from <https://legal.un.org/riaa/cases/vol_XVIII/417-493.pdf>.

[709] Schmitt, Michael N. & NATO Cooperative Cyber Defence Centre of Excellence. (2017). Tallinn Manual 2.0 on the International Law Applicable to Cyber Operations. Cambridge University Press. Rules 15, and 17.

place, it would allow a small number of States with extensive cyber capacity to gain the ability to pursue targets beyond their borders. While it might be compelling to States often targeted by foreign cyber activity, such as the United States, it would create a risk of abuse.

Countermeasures are mutable via international agreements. For example, States can agree in a regional treaty to render a certain type of a *Countermeasure* prohibited in disputes. In such a situation, that particular type of a circumstance would be prohibited even if all the standard requirements would be met. This is demonstrated by State practice such as the EU treaties, which include alternative methods of resolution and rules enforcement[710] as well as the provisions of the WTO Appellate Body, which is operating based on its Dispute Settlement Understanding document that includes ways of providing redress.[711]

While there is an ongoing discussion as to whether preemptive *Self-defense* measures should be allowed, the situation is clearer when it comes to *Countermeasures*—they can only follow an actual *Internationally Wrongful Act*. The ICJ stated that explicitly in the Gabčíkovo-Nagymaros Project Case: [*Countermeasures*] *must be taken in response to a previous internationally wrongful act of another State.*[712] This limitation on *Countermeasures* appears to fit well the cyber context, where the risk of escalation is potentially higher than in the conventional space due to relative logistical ease with which hacker groups can launch hostile cyber operations.

Temporariness and reversibility of *Countermeasures* are directly linked to their main purpose—restoring compliance with international law (rather than causing lasting damage). The UN International Law Commission stated that *Countermeasures must be as far as possible reversible in their effects in terms*

710 European Parliament. (n.d.). Fact Sheet - The internal market: General principles. Retrieved February 18, 2022, from <https://www.europarl.europa.eu/factsheets/en/sheet/33/the-internal-market-general-principles>.

711 World Trade Organization. (1994, April 15). Marrakesh Agreement Establishing the World Trade Organization. Annex 2, article. 3, paragraphs 7,22. Retrieved February 18, 2022, from <https://www.wto.org/english/docs_e/legal_e/04-wto_e.htm>.

712 Case concerning the Gabcikovo-Nagymaros Project. I.C.J. Reports 88, ICJ GL No. 92. (1997). Retrieved February 15, 2022, from <https://www.icj-cij.org/en/case/92/judgments>.

of future legal relations between the two States.[713] This stance stems from the ICJ jurisprudence[714] and is consistent with the purpose of *Countermeasures*, which is restitution of compliance with international law, rather than causing lasting damage. For that reason, *Countermeasures* also must be proportionate. Those actions that do not meet the requirement of proportionality don't enjoy the benefit of precluded wrongfulness.[715] This is especially relevant in cyber space because the actual source of the operation can be concealed for much longer than the conventional ones and the risk of escalation of mutual hostile operations is high.

Countermeasures should be suspended and new ones cannot be undertaken by a State, if a dispute is pending in front of an Arbitration Tribunal or an international court.[716] This is however subject to debate as a number of legal experts claim there is no such obligation and it is a mere guideline that demonstrates good faith during legal proceedings.[717]

---

713 United Nations International Law Commission. (2001). Draft articles on Responsibility of States for Internationally Wrongful Acts with commentaries. United Nations Office of Legal Affairs. Chapeau to Chapter II of Part 3, paragraph 6. Retrieved February 15, 2022, from <https://legal.un.org/ilc/texts/instruments/english/commentaries/9_6_2001.pdf>.

714 Case concerning the Gabcikovo-Nagymaros Project. I.C.J. Reports 88, ICJ GL No. 92. (1997). Paragraph 87. Retrieved February 15, 2022, from <https://www.icj-cij.org/en/case/92/judgments>; United Nations International Law Commission. (2001). Draft articles on Responsibility of States for Internationally Wrongful Acts with commentaries. United Nations Office of Legal Affairs. Article 49(3). Retrieved February 15, 2022, from <https://legal.un.org/ilc/texts/instruments/english/commentaries/9_6_2001.pdf>.

715 German-Portugese Arbitral Award (The Naulilaa Case). Arbitral Commission. (1930, June 30). United Nations - Report of International Arbitral Awards. Page 1028. Retrieved February 18, 2022, from <https://legal.un.org/riaa/cases/vol_III/1371-1386.pdf>; Air Service Agreement of 27 March 1946 between the United States of America and France. Permanent Court of Arbitration. (1978, December 9). United Nations -Reports of International Arbitral Awards. Paragraph 83. Retrieved February 18, 2022, from <https://legal.un.org/riaa/cases/vol_XVIII/417-493.pdf>.

716 United Nations International Law Commission. (2001). Draft articles on Responsibility of States for Internationally Wrongful Acts with commentaries. United Nations Office of Legal Affairs. Article 52(3). Retrieved February 15, 2022, from <https://legal.un.org/ilc/texts/instruments/english/commentaries/9_6_2001.pdf>.

717 Schmitt, Michael N. & NATO Cooperative Cyber Defence Centre of Excellence. (2017). Tallinn Manual 2.0 on the International Law Applicable to Cyber Operations. Cambridge University Press. Page 122.

Countermeasures should also not breach any preemptory norms of international law. One of the most important ones is the *Prohibition of Use of Force*, a customary rule nested within the UN Charter.[718] The same goes for fundamental human rights. The Arbitration Tribunal in the Naulilaa case stated that *Countermeasures* must be *limited by the requirements of humanity and the rules of good faith applicable in relations between States*.[719] Which human rights qualify as fundamental is the subject of a debate. The International Law Commission provided some core examples informed by customary law: prohibition of genocide, slavery, racial discrimination, crimes against humanity, and torture.[720] This list overlaps to a large extent with the provisions laid out in the first 16 articles of the International Covenant on Civil and Political Rights from 1966.[721]

Diplomatic and consular missions as well as staff enjoy legal immunity from *Countermeasures*. This provision is inscribed in the Vienna Convention on Consular Relations,[722] Draft Articles on State Responsibility,[723] and was confirmed by the ICJ in its Tehran Hostages judgment.[724] This means that no

---

718 United Nations. (1945, June 26). Charter of the United Nations. Article 2(4). Retrieved February 17, 2022, from <https://www.un.org/en/about-us/un-charter>.

719 German-Portugese Arbitral Award (The Naulilaa Case). Arbitral Commission. (1930, June 30). United Nations - Report of International Arbitral Awards. Page 1028. Retrieved February 18, 2022, from <https://legal.un.org/riaa/cases/vol_III/1371-1386.pdf>.

720 United Nations International Law Commission. (2001). Draft articles on Responsibility of States for Internationally Wrongful Acts with commentaries. United Nations Office of Legal Affairs. Article. 26, paragraph 5 of Commentary, Article 40, paragraphs 4–5 of Commentary. Retrieved February 15, 2022, from <https://legal.un.org/ilc/texts/instruments/english/commentaries/9_6_2001.pdf>.

721 United Nations. (1966, December 16). International Covenant on Civil and Political Rights. Retrieved February 19, 2022, from <https://www.ohchr.org/en/professionalinterest/pages/ccpr.aspx>.

722 United Nations. (1963, April 24). Vienna Convention on Consular Relations. Articles 33, 35. Retrieved February 17, 2022, from <https://legal.un.org/ilc/texts/instruments/english/conventions/9_2_1963.pdf>.

723 United Nations International Law Commission. (2001). Draft articles on Responsibility of States for Internationally Wrongful Acts with commentaries. United Nations Office of Legal Affairs. Article 50(2)(b). Retrieved February 15, 2022, from <https://legal.un.org/ilc/texts/instruments/english/commentaries/9_6_2001.pdf>.

724 United States Diplomatic and Consular Staff in Tehran (United States of America v. Iran). ICJ Reports 1980. (1980, May 24). International Court of Justice. Paragraphs 83, 86. Retrieved February 17, 2022, from <https://www.icj-cij.org/en/case/64>.

matter what *Countermeasures* are devised by a State, they are never allowed to target diplomatic missions and staff.

Enzo Cannizzaro proposed four main purposes of *Countermeasures*. These are:

- Normative function
- Retributive function
- Coercive function
- Executive function[725]

The normative function implies an attempt to re-establish a normative balance in Public International Law that was disrupted by a hostile act. The retribute function pertains to putting a cost on committing an *Internationally Wrongful Act*. The coercive function means that a *Countermeasure* is geared toward compelling the offending State to cease and desist such conduct. Finally, the executive function pertains to those effects of a *Countermeasure* that neutralize the negative physical effects or of an *Internationally Wrongful Act*. A fifth purpose of *Countermeasures* could also be proposed—the punitive function. It would pertain to satisfy the injured State's desire to avenge being targeted by a hostile act. However, this function was rejected by experts, such as François Delerue,[726] as going against the grain of the core understanding of what *Countermeasures* are, namely a tool that was designed to avoid escalation. He wrote: "It is undisputed that *Countermeasures* must be conciliatory."[727]

4.3.1.2 Application of *Countermeasures* in cyberspace

Countermeasures are potentially the key tool at States' disposal to address hostile cyber operations launched against them by foreign governments. However, the layered and interconnected character of cyberspace makes it especially difficult to gauge what a proportionate response should be to a hostile act. This situation requires that States err on the side of caution and

725 Enzo Cannizzaro. "The Role of Proportionality in the Law of International Countermeasures," 2001. European Journal of International Law 889, pages 899–900

726 Delerue, François. Cyber Operations and international law. Cambridge: Cambridge University Press, 2020. Pages 436, 442.

727 Ibid.

precede deployment of *Countermeasures* with analysis of their consequences. States can decide less impactful measures might be enough to compel the hostile State to resume compliance with its international obligations. As pointed out by Nicholas Tsagourias: "Whether states will claim that a violation of international law occurred and take countermeasures depends on many factors, primarily political ones. There is no automaticity as far as the application and enforcement of international law is concerned because states are at the same time law creators, interpreters, and enforcers."[728] At the end of the day, whether to deploy *Countermeasures* is a discretionary decision of States that is made on a case-by-case basis. Additionally, a non-cyber violation can be countered with a cyber *Countermeasure* and a cyber delict can be countered with a conventional *Countermeasure.* The measures also do not have to target the activity of a hostile State that specifically led to the *Internationally Wrongful Act.* In sum, States have much latitude in terms of what *Countermeasures* to deploy.

There are four aspects of the legal notion of *Countermeasures* in cyberspace that deviate from standard application in the conventional realm:

- Targeting non-State actors as part of *Countermeasures;*
- The notification requirements;
- Automatic *Countermeasures* targeting recurring hostile cyber operations;
- Affecting third States while executing cyber *Countermeasures.*

The outsize role of non-State actors is a challenge that is more acute in cyberspace compared to the conventional space. *Countermeasures* can be only deployed against States, which potentially creates a risk of impunity for hostile cyber operations. Proving a linkage between non-State entities and a State can prove challenging when there is no visual proof. However, no States have raised a claim to expand applicability of *Countermeasures* in this context. For that reason, relevance of *Countermeasures* in cyberspace in the future will likely depend on progress in the area of attribution (discussed

728 Tsagourias, Nicholas. (2019). The Slow Process of Normativizing Cyberspace. AJIL Unbound, 113, 71–75. Supra note 4, page 74. <https://doi.org/10.1017/aju.2019.9>; See also, Sander, Barrie. (2019). The Sound of Silence: International Law and the Governance of Peacetime Cyber Operations. Pages 1–21. Supra note 1.

in Chapter 5). Scholars who authored the Tallinn Manual provided the following theoretical example to present how this limitation might play out in practice:

> Consider a situation in which a hacktivist group located in one State exploits a buffer overflow vulnerability in a SCADA system located in another. Whether the latter may launch a remote take-down operation against the hacktivist group's server as a Countermeasure depends, inter alia, on whether the group's activities are attributable to the former.[729]

Oscar Schachter proposed an expansionary version of the norm, suggesting that while non-State actors cannot be the target of *Countermeasures,* they can be their victim.[730] This interpretation would provide a measure of flexibility that could enable States to utilize *Countermeasures* more frequently. However, such an approach would be fraught with risk of abuse, as States could create much collateral negative impact via such *Countermeasures.* Much of cyber infrastructure is of dual nature and serves both civilian and governmental purposes. Creating negative impact that directly affects the civilian sphere in a foreign State would go against the foundational understanding that *Countermeasures* are meant to prevent escalation. No solution has been found yet to address this challenge.

Another aspect of *Countermeasures,* whose application in cyberspace is not straightforward is the obligation of notification of the offending State that a measure will be taken. This is because the element of surprise is very important in cyberspace, more so than it is the case with conventional operations. Oftentimes, the success of a cyber operation rests entirely on the element of surprise. Hostile cyber operations can cut deeper and in radically quicker fashion than conventional acts but they can also be prevented more much more easily if information about the preparations is available. Notifying the target State could easily neutralize the whole

---

729 Schmitt, Michael. N. & NATO Cooperative Cyber Defence Centre of Excellence. (2017). Tallinn Manual 2.0 on the International Law Applicable to Cyber Operations. Cambridge University Press. Page 113.

730 Schachter, Oscar. "Dispute Settlement and Countermeasures in the International Law Commission." American Journal of International Law 88, no. 3 (1994): 471–77. <https://doi.org/10.2307/2203714>.

operation. There are two notification requirements listed in the ICJ jurisprudence: the first one demanding cessation of the offending conduct and the second one signaling the *Countermeasure* that is about to be taken. Of the two, for the listed reasons, the second one specifically is the most problematic.

The existing framework of Public International Law allows for an exception that could accommodate this specific nature of cyber operation—*Urgent Countermeasures*. This is not a fully formed norm of international law—State practice and their *opinio juris* are too scarce and not consistent enough yet. However, there exist legal precedents that point to a potential process of forming of the norm. For example, Protocol Additional to the Geneva Conventions from August 12, 1949, when relating to the Protection of Victims of International Armed Conflicts states that:

> In the case of bombardment by long-distance projectiles or bombs dropped from aircraft, giving warning may be inconvenient when the element of surprise in the attack is a condition of its success. For this reason the rule allows for derogation: "unless circumstances do not permit."[731]

The passage comes from the International Committee of the Red Cross and applies to *jus in bello*, that is, it pertains to Stat es in the midst of an armed conflict. This is an obstacle to a direct transposition of the logic into the context of cyber *Countermeasures*, which pertain to the peacetime context. Emergence of urgent cyber *Countermeasures* that do not require prior notification would mean taking a partially formed exception rule from another realm of Public International Law and applying it in the cyber context. However, such expansionary transposition in the context of cyber *Countermeasures* would help adapt the existing legal framework to the new context. In fact, some scholars, including Michael Schmitt, have called for

---

731 International Committee of the Red Cross. (1977b, June 8). Commentary to Protocol Additional to the Geneva Conventions of 12 August 1949, and relating to the Protection of Victims of International Armed Conflicts (Protocol I). Retrieved February 18, 2022, from <https://ihl-databases.icrc.org/applic/ihl/ihl.nsf/1a13044f3bbb5b8ec12563fb0066f226/d80d14d84bf36b92c12563cd00434fbd>.

this solution.[732] Others, including François Delerue[733] and Mary O'Connell[734] have critiqued the idea. Since no State has come forward supporting such an expansion as of yet, the notion of urgent cyber *Countermeasures* remains only a proposition.

The third specific characteristic of a hostile cyber operation is that it can reach multiple disparate targets at once or at various moments. The ease with which a State can launch instantaneous hostile cyber acts is unmatched by any conventional operations. As a result, hostile cyber operations oftentimes occur in batches. For instance, the WannaCry virus attacked numerous public and private-sector servers, many of them in the United Kingdom and the United States, over a few days in May 2017. By December 2017, both States attributed the cyber operation to North Korea.[735] Had they decided to deploy *Countermeasures* against North Korea in May 2017, they could have also set a recurring schedule of *Countermeasures* set to be triggered with every recurring assault, rather than a one-off response. While this approach does not constitute a separate legal norm, it presents an application of *Countermeasures* that is specifically tailored to the cyber context.

The wrongfulness of a *Countermeasure* is only precluded to the extent to which it affects the offending State. This was laid out in the Cysne Case ruling[736] as well as the ICJ's Gabčíkovo-Nagymaros Project judgment.[737] This

---

732 Schmitt, Michael N. & NATO Cooperative Cyber Defence Centre of Excellence. (2017). Tallinn Manual 2.0 on the International Law Applicable to Cyber Operations. Cambridge University Press. Supra note 14, paragraph 120.

733 Delerue, François. Cyber Operations and international law. Cambridge: Cambridge University Press, 2020. Pages 445.

734 Mary E. O'Connell, Attribution and Other Conditions of Lawful Countermeasures to Cyber Misconduct, 10 Notre Dame J. Int'l Comp. L. 1 (2020). Page 251. Retrieved on November 29, 2023. <https://scholarship.law.nd.edu/law_faculty_scholarship/1437>.

735 British Broadcasting Corporation. "Cyber-Attack: US and UK Blame North Korea for WannaCry." BBC News, December 19, 2017. <https://www.bbc.com/news/world-us-canada-42407488>.

736 German-Portuguese Arbitral Award of June 30th, 1930 (Germany v. Portugal—The Cysne Case). Arbitral Commission. (1933, February 16). United Nations - Report of International Arbitral Awards. Pages 1056–1057. Retrieved February 18, 2022, from <https://legal.un.org/riaa/cases/vol_III/1371-1386.pdf>.

737 Case concerning the Gabcikovo-Nagymaros Project. I.C.J. Reports 88, ICJ GL No. 92. (1997). Para 83. Retrieved February 15, 2022, from <https://www.icj-cij.org/en/case/92/judgments>;

creates a tension when it comes to utilizing cyber tools for *Countermeasures.* The data packets can easily travel through the ICT infrastructure of other States and sometimes might even negatively affect them. For instance an operation aimed at overwhelming servers of the offending State with multiple requests can also slow down data traffic speed on the servers of a State, through which such an operation would be routed. In any case, routing a hostile cyber operation through a third State might be seen as a *Violation of Sovereignty* even if there is no material impact. Michael Schmitt proposed that in cases where there is no material impact on third States or the impact is minimal, such cyber *Countermeasures* would still enjoy preclusion of wrongfulness due to necessity, which would constitute a combination of norms of *Necessity* and *Countermeasures* for the sake of accommodating the unique nature of cyberspace.[738] This however remains a proposition that still has to be considered by States before becoming a binding rule.

Such considerations are not entirely hypothetical. For instance, in 2012 it was revealed that the Japanese government had contracted in 2008 a private-sector entity, the Fujitsu company, to develop software that would counter hostile cyber operations against the State and work to identify the perpetrator by tracing the hostile operation back to its source, including by penetrating the intermediate servers in third States.[739] This case touches upon two of the presented challenges: automatic *Countermeasures* that are triggered whenever a hostile cyber operation takes place, without a pre-notification and the problematic situation of affecting third States while deploying a *Countermeasure.*

Since *Countermeasures* are positioned to be the main tool at States' disposal to address hostile cyber operations, how the four main considerations get resolved will have a lasting impact on the international dynamics in cyberspace. More consistent *opinio juris* and additional enduring State practice

---

738 Schmitt, Michael N., and Christopher M. Pitts. "Cyber Countermeasures and Effects on Third Parties: The International Legal Regime." International Law from a Baltic Perspective, 2020, 258–80. <https://doi.org/10.1163/9789004433151_011>.

739 Shimbun, Yomiuri. "Japanese Govt Working on Defensive Cyberweapon." Communications of the ACM, January 4, 2012. <https://cacm.acm.org/news/144941-japanese-govt-working-on-defensive-cyberweapon/fulltext?mobile=false>.

will be necessary to discern the future shape of Public International Law on each of them.

4.3.2 Retorsions

4.3.2.1 *Retorsions* in Public International Law

Responses to other States' *Unfriendly Acts*, which would not meet the threshold of wrongfulness, even if deployed independently, are called *Retorsion*. The UN International Law Commission proposed the following definition of a *Retorsion* in the *Draft Articles on Responsibility of States for Internationally Wrongful Acts*:

> [Retorsion is] an 'unfriendly' conduct which is not inconsistent with any international obligation of the State engaging in it even though it may be a response to an internationally wrongful act.[740]

UN ILC's *Draft Articles* are not a source of international law but rather a combination of articulations of existing customary norms alongside proposals of new ones that are at various stages of formation. The part presenting *Retorsions* is widely perceived to belong to the first group, which allows us to draw on the definition in the analysis. There is a broad consensus on what *Retorsions* are as confirmed by very similar definitions offered by international scholars such as Lassa Oppenheim,[741] Alphonse Rivier,[742] Jean Salmon,[743] and François Delerue.[744] All of them contain the same two core elements:

---

740 United Nations International Law Commission. (2001). Draft articles on Responsibility of States for Internationally Wrongful Acts with commentaries. United Nations Office of Legal Affairs. Supra note 19, page 128. Retrieved February 15, 2022, from <https://legal.un.org/ilc/texts/instruments/english/commentaries/9_6_2001.pdf>.

741 Oppenheim, Lassa. International Law: a Treatise, vol II, "War and Neutrality." Longmans, 1903. Page 31. Quote: "Retorsion is a technical term for the retaliation of discourteous or unkind or unfair and inequitable acts by acts of the same or a similar kind."

742 Rivier, Alphonse. Principes du droit des gens, vol II. A Rousseau, 1896. Page 189.

743 Salmon, Jean (ed.). Dictionnaire de droit international public. Bruxelles, Bruyant/AUF, 2001. Page 1007.

744 Delerue, François. Cyber Operations and international law. Cambridge: Cambridge University Press, 2020. Pages 424.

- It is an act below the threshold of severity necessary for constituting an *Internationally Wrongful Act*;
- It takes place in response to another State's unfriendly conduct, which might or might not be wrongful.

Retorsions are not *Countermeasures.* The latter are acts that would be wrongful if not for preclusion that they possess due to being a response to a an *Internationally Wrongful Act. Retorsion* can take on a diverse range of forms as long as they remain lawful. Additionally, they are not limited by the notions of proportionality or necessity.[745] States also have latitude in terms of what conduct to deploy *Retorsions* in response to. A State might decide to react asymmetrically and only utilize *Retorsions,* even though it is being targeted with an *Internationally Wrongful Act*, such as a *Violation of Sovereignty*, a *Prohibited Intervention*, or even an *Armed Attack*. It cannot however deploy *Countermeasures,* if the hostile conduct aimed at it by another State only amounts to an *Unfriendly Act*. In that case, *Retorsions* are the only available lawful response. Because *Retorsions* are a soft measure, the UN ILC did not delve into the details of the notion in the *Draft Articles on Responsibility of States for Internationally Wrongful Acts*, as it is outside of the scope of acts indicated by the title.[746]

Some of the most frequent forms of *Retorsions* include downgrading or severing diplomatic relations, expelling diplomats, restricting visa access, reducing economic ties, introducing trade blockades, and publicly calling out a State for conducting hostile acts.[747] However, none of these actions are allowed to amount to a breach of an international obligation as that would meet the definition of an *Internationally Wrongful Act*. For instance, introducing certain trade barriers is prohibited under the rules of the World

---

745 Bannelier, Karine and Christakis, Theodore, Cyber-Attacks—Prevention-Reactions: The Role of States and Private Actors (February 25, 2017). Les Cahiers de la Revue Défense Nationale, Paris, 2017. Page 34. <https://ssrn.com/abstract=2941988>.

746 2 Yearbook of the International Law Commission. Part II 31, 2001. Commentary to Part II, Chapter II, para 3 of the Draft Articles on Responsibility of States for Internationally Wrongful Acts.

747 Crawford, James, and Kate Parlett. The law of international responsibility. Oxford: Oxford University Press, 2013. Pages 1057–1058, paragraph 573.

Trade Organization, which limits space for maneuver for States that are party to this organization.

4.3.2.2 Application of *Retorsions* in cyberspace

Retorsion could play a secondary role in the cyber context if not for the fact that no State has ever described its response to a hostile cyber operation, no matter how harsh, as a *Countermeasure* or *Self-defense*.[748] This means that all the available evidence of actual State practice is formally contained within the category of *Retorsions*. In fact, even that interpretation is somewhat limited as only three States (Australia,[749] Netherlands,[750] and the United States[751]) have so far publicly recognized that responses to hostile cyber operations by other States can amount to *Retorsions*. States so far have not refrained from claiming that their responses to hostile cyber operations are acts that would be wrongful if not for a preclusion. Instead, they mostly do not publicly elaborate on this aspect at all. Despite this limitation, labeling responses to hostile cyber acts by a State that are below the threshold of wrongfulness as *Retorsions* appears to be accepted by the doctrine. For instance, Przemysław Roguski stated: "While only [a few States] specifically refer to retorsions as response options to cyber assaults, it is safe to assume that the recourse to actions which do not violate international obligations is largely unproblematic."[752]

---

748 Delerue, François. Cyber Operations and international law. Cambridge: Cambridge University Press, 2020. Pages 431.

749 The government of Australia. "Australia's International Cyber Engagement Strategy," November 2020. <https://www.internationalcybertech.gov.au/sites/default/files/2020-11/The%20Strategy.pdf>.

750 The government of Netherlands. Letter to the parliament on the international legal order in cyberspace, September 26, 2019. Page 7. <https://www.government.nl/documents/parliamentary-documents/2019/09/26/letter-to-the-parliament-on-the-international-legal-order-in-cyberspace>.

751 Egan, Brian. J. "International Law and Stability in Cyberspace," November 10, 2016. Berkeley Journal of International Law, 35(1), pages 1–26. <https://www.law.berkeley.edu/wp-content/uploads/2016/12/BJIL-article-International-Law-and-Stability-in-Cyberspace.pdf>.

752 Roguski, Przemysław. "Application of International Law to Cyber Operations: A Comparative Analysis of States' Views." The Hague Program for Cyber Norms, 2020. Page 18. <https://ruj.uj.edu.pl/xmlui/bitstream/handle/item/153989/roguski_application_of_international_law_to_cyber_operations_2020.pdf?sequence=1>.

For example, following the 2014 Sony hack that the United States attributed to North Korea, the U.S. government limited itself to diplomatic denouncements and a series of criminal cases opened against specific hackers. At the same time however, the internet connectivity in all North Korea ground to a halt for a day. This event was publicly attributed to the United States by the North Korean government, although the former never confirmed nor denied it.[753] Following the 2016 hack of the Democratic National Committee in the United States by Russian State-sponsored hackers, and a subsequent attribution to Russia by the U.S. government, the victim State also limited itself, at least publicly, to diplomatic (expelling 35 diplomats) and domestic criminal reaction.[754] However, President Barack Obama vowed publicly to respond to Russia using both overt and covert methods.[755] When Iran's nuclear facilities were paralyzed and damaged by the Stuxnet virus, it reacted with a diplomatic denouncement. At the same time, a number of American banks were hit with a virus as part of what became known as Operation Ababil.[756] While the operation was never formally attributed to Iran, a number of signs implied that the operation was State sponsored.[757]

The pattern that emerges is that States by hostile cyber operations orchestrated by other States limit themselves to *Retorsions* in the public sphere while pursuing more damaging and aggressive forms of response in private. This dynamic might imply that the formula of *Countermeasures* does not offer a compelling path for injured States to respond to hostile cyber operations. *Retorsions* have so far been the sole response of States to hostile cyber operations not because States find them the most fitting or because they want to avoid escalation. The evidence suggests that they might seek more damaging

---

753 Kim, Jack. "North Korea Blames U.S. for Internet Outages, Calls Obama 'Monkey.'" Reuters, December 27, 2014. <https://www.reuters.com/article/us-northkorea-cybersecurity/north-korea-blames-u-s-for-internet-outages-calls-obama-monkey-idUSKBN0K502920141228>.

754 Delerue, François. Cyber Operations and international law. Cambridge: Cambridge University Press, 2020. Pages 431.

755 Detrow, Scott (December 15, 2016). "Obama On Russian Hacking: 'We Need To Take Action. And We Will'". National Public Radio.

756 Delerue, François. Cyber Operations and international law. Cambridge: Cambridge University Press, 2020. Pages 429.

757 Ibid.

responses while enjoying the plausible deniability granted by the anonymous character of cyberspace.

4.3.3 Self-defense

4.3.3.1 *Self-defense* in Public International Law

Self-defense is a lawful *Use of Force* by a State in response to another State's *Armed Attack* by another State that is precluded from qualifying as an *Internationally Wrongful Act.* At the core of *Self-defense* is the notion that a State can respond to an *Armed Attack* with lawful *Use of Force*. The right to *Self-defense* begins when an *Armed Attack* starts taking place and ends with the cessation of it. This high-level definition is a reconstruction based on the UN Charter and international jurisprudence. In fact, no one source of international law contains a full definition of *Self-defense.*

The norm however enjoys a long-standing customary status. In its current form it is conventionally dated back to the Caroline Case.[758] The case pertains to a confrontation in 1837 between a band of British subjects and the crew of the ship Caroline, anchored at an American port on Niagara River. The British subjects destroyed the ship in retaliation for it having been used to raid Canadian territory (which at the time was an overseas part of the United Kingdom). In a retributive move, a band of American civilians burned down a British ship. In the aftermath of those incidents, the U.S. Secretary of State launched a negotiation process with the British, which led to signing of the Webster-Ashburton Treaty in 1842, in which both sides acknowledged their wrongdoing. Importantly, the Treaty laid out the so-called *Caroline Test.* The test states that a necessity of *Self-Defense must be instant, overwhelming, leaving no choice of means, and no moment for deliberation.*[759] Many scholars believe that thus a customary international rule began forming that remains in force until this day.[760]

---

758 Kretzmer, David. (2013). "The Inherent Right to Self-Defence and Proportionality in Jus Ad Bellum." European Journal of International Law, 24(1), pages 235–282. <https://doi.org/10.1093/ejil/chs087>.

759 Wiltse, Charles M. (1973). Daniel Webster and the British Experience. Proceedings of the Massachusetts Historical Society, 85, pages 58–77. <https://www.jstor.org/stable/25080745>.

760 Nichols, Tom M. (2008). Eve of Destruction: The Coming Age of Preventive War. University of Pennsylvania Press. Page 2.

The right to *Self-defense* is also acknowledged in the UN Charter, which states in Article 51:

> Nothing in the present Charter shall impair the inherent right of individual or collective self-defense if an armed attack occurs against a Member of the United Nations.

Two main points emerge from this framing. First, *Self-defense* can happen in response to an *Armed Attack*, which sets a high bar for invoking the norm. Second, *Self-defense* can be exercised on an individual or collective basis by States. Collective *Self-defense* is the foundational component of NATO Charter Article 5:

> The Parties agree that an armed attack against one or more of them in Europe or North America shall be considered an attack against them all and consequently they agree that, if such an armed attack occurs, each of them, in exercise of the right of individual or collective self-defence recognised by Article 51 of the Charter of the United Nations, will assist the Party or Parties so attacked by taking forthwith, individually and in concert with the other Parties, such action as it deems necessary, including the use of armed force, to restore and maintain the security of the North Atlantic area.[761]

The rule is also indirectly invoked in the UN GA Declaration on *The Principles of International Law Concerning Friendly Relations and Co-operations among States in accordance with the Charter* by way of its invocation of cases of lawful *Use of Force*. The Declaration states:

> Nothing in the foregoing paragraphs shall be constructed as enlarging or diminishing in any way the scope of these provisions of the Charter concerning cases in which the use of force is lawful.[762]

---

761 North Atlantic Treaty Organization (NATO). (1949, April 4). The North Atlantic Treaty. Article 5. Retrieved February 18, 2022, from <https://www.nato.int/cps/en/natolive/official_texts_17120.htm>.

762 United Nations General Assembly Resolution. (1970, October 24). 2625 (XXV) Declaration on Principles of International Law concerning Friendly Relations and Cooperation among States in Accordance with the Charter of the United Nations - Main Page. Retrieved February 17, 2022, from <https://legal.un.org/avl/ha/dpilfrcscun/dpilfrcscun.html>.

An important milestone for application of *Self-defense* was the 1986 Nicaragua Judgment, in which the Court confirmed the customary, *erga omnes* character of the rule and its four fundamental requirements (later confirmed by the 1996 ICJ Advisory Opinion on the Legality of the Threat or Use of Nuclear Weapons):

- proportionality;
- necessity;
- immediacy;
- Immediate notification of the UN Security Council.[763]

The ICJ underscored a number of times across its various Judgments and Advisory Opinions that *Self-defense* can only be invoked to execute measures, which are *proportional to the armed attack and necessary to respond to it, a rule well established in international customary law.*[764] The principle of

---

763 Case Concerning Military and Paramilitary Activities in and Against Nicaragua, Nicaragua v United States. International Court of Justice. I.C.J Reports 14, ICGJ 112 (ICJ 1986). Paragraph 176. Retrieved February 15, 2022, from <https://www.icj-cij.org/en/case/70/judgments>;

Melzer, Nils. (2009). Targeted Killing in International Law (Oxford Monographs in International Law) (1st ed.). Oxford University Press. Page 16. <https://doi.org/10.1093/law/9780199577903.001.0001>; United Nations General Assembly Resolution. (2011, July 15). 66/152. Developments in the field of information and telecommunications in the context of international security - Report of the Secretary-General. Page 19. Retrieved February 18, 2022, from <https://www.un.org/ga/search/viewm_doc.asp?symbol=A/66/152>.

764 Case Concerning Military and Paramilitary Activities in and Against Nicaragua, Nicaragua v United States. International Court of Justice. I.C.J Reports 14, ICGJ 112 (ICJ 1986). Paragraphs 176, 194. Retrieved February 15, 2022, from <https://www.icj-cij.org/en/case/70/judgments>; Advisory Opinion on Legality of the Threat or Use of Nuclear Weapons. International Court of Justice. (1996, July 8). Paragraphs 38, 41, 96. Retrieved February 18, 2022, from <https://www.icj-cij.org/en/case/95>;

Case Concerning Oil Platforms, (2003), (Iran v. United States). International Court of Justice. (2003, November 6). Paragraph 74. Retrieved February 18, 2022, from <https://www.icj-cij.org/en/case/90,=>; ICJ Reports 2005. (2005, December 19); Armed Activities on the Territory of the Congo (Democratic Republic of the Congo v. Uganda). International Court of Justice. Paragraph 147. Retrieved February 17, 2022, from <https://www.icj-cij.org/en/case/116>.

proportionality requires that the act chosen by a State as a way of *Self-defense* is commensurate in terms of its intended purpose of either halting and repelling an *Armed Attack* or preventing it.[765] This setting implies that the scope of possible options of *Self-defense* available to the injured State will depend on the type of an *Armed Attack* mounted by the hostile State.

Necessity is the second requirement that has to be met when launching *Self-defense.* For it to be met, the injured State must demonstrate that *non-forcible remedies must either prove futile in limine or have in fact been exhausted in an unsatisfactory manner.*[766] In short, it means that the State can prove that there was no other way to defend itself from an *Armed Attack* than to engage in *use of force*. To be able to do that, a State must attribute the *Armed Attack* to a specific State actor, identify the motive behind the attack, and determine that *Use of Force* is necessary to successfully repel it.[767] Such *Use of Force* measures can be accompanied by less forcible measures too, such as economic sanctions or diplomatic efforts.

The requirement of necessity in the context of self-defense measures was introduced by the ICJ in its Nicaragua Judgment.[768] It was also confirmed in the Nuclear Weapons advisory opinion[769] and the Oil Platforms Judgment.[770]

---

765 Dinniss, Heather H. (2012). Cyber Warfare and the Laws of War (Cambridge Studies in International and Comparative Law). Cambridge University Press. Page 104. <https://doi.org/10.1017/CBO9780511894527>.

766 Dinstein, Yoram. (2013). Cyber War and International Law: Concluding Remarks at the 2012 Naval War College International Law Conference. International Law Studies of the U.S. Naval War College, 89, 275–287. Page 209. <https://digital-commons.usnwc.edu/ils/vol89/iss1/2/>.

767 Jensen, Eric T. (2002). Computer Attacks on Critical National Infrastructure: A Use of Force Invoking the Right of Self-Defense. Stanford Journal of International Law, 38(207), 207–240. Page 231. <https://digitalcommons.law.byu.edu/faculty_scholarship/212/>.

768 Case Concerning Military and Paramilitary Activities in and Against Nicaragua, Nicaragua v United States. I.C.J Reports 14, ICGJ 112 (ICJ 1986). International Court of Justice. Paragraphs 176, 194. Retrieved February 15, 2022, from <https://www.icj-cij.org/en/case/70/judgments>.

769 Advisory Opinion on Legality of the Threat or Use of Nuclear Weapons. International Court of Justice. (1996, July 8). Paragraph 41. Retrieved February 18, 2022, from <https://www.icj-cij.org/en/case/95>.

770 Case Concerning Oil Platforms, (2003), (Iran v. United States). International Court of Justice. (2003, November 6). Paragraph 43, 73, 74, 76. Retrieved February 18, 2022, from <https://www.icj-cij.org/en/case/90>.

The rule requires that self-defense measures only go to the point, in terms of severity, to which they are necessary to reinstate compliance with international law on part of the aggressor. This formulation implies the application of proportionality as a guiding principle when gauging what type of measures is necessary.

The final requirement for *Self-defense* is immediacy. It pertains to sequencing of events and accounts for passage of time as an aspect that might render otherwise lawful measures *Internationally Wrongful Acts.* Nevertheless, an *Armed Attack* is a *casus belli*, meaning that it potentially might switch gears from peaceful to wartime relations between States (*jus ad bellum*), with all the consequences. Therefore, an injured State should be given enough time, from a legal standpoint, to calibrate its response. Hence, immediate does not mean instantaneous.

This notion of *Self-Defense* was expounded on in the 1996 ICJ Advisory Opinion on the Legality of the Threat or Use of Nuclear Weapons. The Court tied the notion of *Self-defense* to a State's survival, potentially narrowing down the scope of application of the norm. The Court wrote:

> The Court cannot lose sight of the fundamental right to every State to survival, and thus its right to resort to self-defense, in accordance with Article 51 of the Charter, when its survival is at stake.[771]

While the Court linked the right to *Self-defense* with the fundamental issue of survival of a State, most scholars point out that it does not require such dramatic circumstances.[772] The difference is explained by the fact that in the case at hand, the Court formulated its opinion in the hypothetical context of a State using nuclear bombs as a form of *Self-Defense*, which is possibly the most dangerous weapon ever created by humanity.[773] In this context, the

---

771 Advisory Opinion on Legality of the Threat or Use of Nuclear Weapons. International Court of Justice. (1996, July 8). Paragraph 96. Retrieved February 18, 2022, from <https://www.icj-cij.org/en/case/95>.

772 Dinstein, Yoram. (2013). Cyber War and International Law: Concluding Remarks at the 2012 Naval War College International Law Conference. International Law Studies of the U.S. Naval War College, 89, 275–287. Page 286. <https://digital-commons.usnwc.edu/ils/vol89/iss1/2/>.

773 Advisory Opinion on Legality of the Threat or Use of Nuclear Weapons. International Court of Justice. (1996, July 8). Paragraph 97. Retrieved February 18, 2022, from <https://www.icj-cij.org/en/case/95>.

Court might have just considered when using nuclear weapons would be a proportionate reaction rather than narrowing down the scope of the whole notion of *Self-defense.*

There is an ongoing dispute regarding the possibility to deploy *Self-defense* measures, including the cyber ones, directly against non-State actors. According to the Caroline Case, invoked in the beginning of this section, States can exercise *Use of Force* against non-State actors.[774] This is perceived as part of customary international law by several States, including the United States and Israel.[775] However, the International Court of Justice, as well as a large number of States, have assumed an alternative approach, in which *Self-defense* is available only against an armed attack by *one State against another State*. This framing was present in the ICJ's 1986 Nicaragua judgment[776] and was reinforced in its 2004 Advisory Opinion on *Legal Consequences of the Construction of a Wall in the Occupied Palestinian Territory*[777] as well as its 2005 judgment on Armed Activities on the Territory of Congo.[778] Only those non-State-actor acts, which are attributable to a State, would allow for deployment of *Self-defense* measures according to this understanding. The debate has been unresolved until now, with the context of surging international terrorism only adding complexity to it. The issues of anticipatory *Self-defense* and preemptory strikes are equally controversial.

---

774 Tsagourias, Nicholas. (2012). "Cyber attacks, self-defence and the problem of attribution." Journal of Conflict and Security Law, 17(2), pages 229–244. <https://doi.org/10.1093/jcsl/krs019>.

775 D'Aspremont, Jean. (2012). Participants in the International Legal System: Multiple Perspectives on Non-State Actors in International Law (Routledge Research in International Law) (1st ed.). Routledge. Pages 326ff.

776 Case Concerning Military and Paramilitary Activities in and Against Nicaragua, Nicaragua v. United States. International Court of Justice. I.C.J Reports 14, ICGJ 112 (ICJ 1986). (1986). Paragraph 195. Retrieved February 15, 2022, from <https://www.icj-cij.org/en/case/70/judgments>; Legal Consequences of the Construction of a Wall in the Occupied Palestinian Territory. International Court of Justice. ICJ Report 136, 2004. (2004, July 9). Paragraph 139. Retrieved February 18, 2022, from <https://www.icj-cij.org/en/case/131>.

777 Ibid. Paragraph 136.

778 Armed Activities on the Territory of the Congo (Democratic Republic of the Congo v. Uganda). International Court of Justice. ICJ Reports 2005. (2005, December 19). Paragraph 146. Retrieved February 17, 2022, from <https://www.icj-cij.org/en/case/116>.

In 1968, the so-called 13 powers (Colombia, the Democratic Republic of Congo, Cyprus, Ecuador, Ghana, Guyana, Indonesia, Iran, Mexico, Spain, Uganda, Uruguay, and Yugoslavia) presented a draft UN GA resolution, which stated their position on the matte—according to them, anticipatory self-defense, self-defense against non-State actors in another State, disproportionate force in self-defense were all unlawful.[779] While the draft never got voted on, it is a source on *opinio juris* of the signatory States and represents evidence of disagreement on the subject. Numerous other States have since criticized the notion of preemptory or anticipatory *Self-defense*.[780] In the absence of consistent *opinio juris*, it must be concluded that *Self-defense* cannot precede an *Armed Attack* according to Public International Law. This does not however apply to interceptive *Self-defense*, which describes a response to an *Armed Attack* that has already started but has not created damage or hit its target yet. This form of *Self-defense* is generally perceived to be included in the scope of the norm.[781]

In response to uncertainty on the matter of non-State entities, a number of States, led by the United States, developed a standard of *toleration and unwillingness* in terms of *Use of Force* against non-State actors. This controversial State practice assumes that acts of non-State actors are attributable to a State, which hosts the said actors, if the act of hosting amounts to enabling preparation and execution of an *Armed Attack*. This standard was deployed in the aftermath of the 9/11 terrorist attacks.[782] In that case, the United States accused Afghanistan of tolerating Al-Qaeda, the organization responsible for the attack. A number of UN Security Council resolutions calling on the Taliban government to arrest Al-Qaeda operatives and prevent Afghanistan's territory from being used as a sanctuary for terrorist activities, dating from

779 United Nations General Assembly Resolution. (1968, November). Report of the Special Committee on the Problem of Defining Aggression. Retrieved February 18, 2022, from <https://digitallibrary.un.org/record/774843/files/A_7185_Rev-1-EN.pdf#page=11>.

780 Corten, Olivier. Le droit contre la guerre: L'interdiction du recours à la force en droit international contemporain. Paris: Éditions Pédone, 2020. Pages 694–698.

781 Gazzini, Tarcisio. The changing rules on the use of force in international law. Huntington, NY: Juris Publ., 2005. Page 151.

782 Simma, Bruno et al. (2013). The Charter of The United Nations 3E, Vol 1. Oxford Commentaries on International Law, 1. Page 802. <https://doi.org/10.1093/law/9780199639762.001.0001>.

before the attack, were presented as evidence that the threshold of *toleration and unwillingness* was met.[783] The UN Security Council Resolution 1373, issued a few weeks after the 9/11 attack, strongly asserts the ability of States to use *Force* against terrorists residing in other States.[784]

By 2006, the International Court of Justice acknowledged the existence of the *toleration and unwillingness* standard. Its Congo v. Uganda Case Judgment ruled that toleration by a State of non-State actors, who perpetrate attacks against another State can bestow the right of *Self-defense* on the injured State. However, for that specific case, the Court did not conclude whether passivity on the part of Democratic Republic of Congo toward armed groups on its territory qualified as toleration or allowed attribution of the acts to the host State, leaving that term lacking a firm reference point.[785] Still, separate individual opinion of Judge Kooijmans, attached to Congo v. Uganda Case Judgment openly endorsed the notion of *Self-defense* against non-State actors:

> if armed attacks are carried out by irregular bands from such territory against a neighbouring State, they are still armed attacks even if they cannot be attributed to the territorial State. It would be unreasonable to deny the attacked State the

---

783 United Nations Security Council. (1999, October 15). Resolution 1267 (1999) Adopted by the Security Council at its 4051st meeting on 15 October 1999. Paragraph 1. Retrieved February 17, 2022, from <https://www.undocs.org/S/RES/1267%20(1999)>; United Nations Security Council. (2001a, September 12). Resolution 1368 (2001) of the United Nations Security Council. Retrieved February 18, 2022, from <https://home.treasury.gov/system/files/126/1368.pdf>; The government of the United States of America. (2001a, October 7). Letter dated 2001/10/07 from the Permanent Representative of the United States of America to the United Nations addressed to the President of the Security Council. United Nations Digital Library System. Retrieved February 18, 2022, from <https://digitallibrary.un.org/record/449476?l-n=en>; The government of United Kingdom. (2001, October 7). Letter from the Charge d'affaires ai of the Permanent Mission of the United Kingdom of Great Britain and Northern Ireland to the United Nations addressed to the President of the Security Council. United Nations Digital Library. Retrieved February 18, 2022, from <https://digitallibrary.un.org/>.

784 United Nations Security Council. (2001b, September 28). Resolution 1373 (2001) of the United Nations Security Council. Retrieved February 18, 2022, from <https://www.un.org/press/en/2001/sc7158.doc.htm>.

785 Armed Activities on the Territory of the Congo (Democratic Republic of the Congo v. Uganda). International Court of Justice. ICJ Reports 2005. (2005, December 19). Retrieved February 17, 2022, from <https://www.icj-cij.org/en/case/116>.

> right to self-defence merely because there is no attacker State, and the Charter does not so require.[786]

Similar sentiment was expressed by Judge Higgins in his separate opinion to the 1986 Nicaragua Judgment.[787] The consensus appears to be thus slowly shifting toward the ability of mounting *Self-defense* measures against non-State actors in a specific set of circumstances, which might include cyber operations. The view has been tentatively embraced by scholars such as Michael Schmitt,[788] Sean Murphy[789] and François Delerue.[790] There is however still no certainty as to whether there exists enough *opinio juris* among States for such a customary rule of Public International Law to emerge.

4.3.3.2 Application of *Self-defense* in cyberspace

The subject of applying the notion of *Self-defense* in cyberspace is a source of controversy. There still exist scholars that claim that impacts created by cyber activities have no capacity of reaching the threshold necessary for meeting the definition of an *Armed Attack*.[791] These voices however are in a minority. At this stage, most States and scholars that voiced their stance embraced the understanding that hostile cyber operations can reach such a level in principle. Some scholars, such as Marco Roscini argue even that due to the interconnectedness that characterizes cyberspace, hostile cyber operations can potentially reach an even bigger scale than conventional acts.[792] Overall,

---

786 Ibid. Separate Opinion of Judge Kooijmans, paragraph 30.

787 Case Concerning Military and Paramilitary Activities in and Against Nicaragua, Nicaragua v United States. International Court of Justice. I.C.J Reports 14, ICGJ 112 (ICJ 1986). Separate Opinion of Judge Higgins. Retrieved February 15, 2022, from <https://www.icj-cij.org/public/files/case-related/90/090-20031106-JUD-01-03-EN.pdf.>

788 Schmitt, Michael N., and Vihul, Liis. "Respect for Sovereignty in Cyberspace." Texas Law Review, 95(7), 2017, pages 1639–1670. <https://texaslawreview.org/respect-sovereignty-cyberspace/>;

789 Murphy, Sean. "Terrorism and the Concept of Armed Attack in Article 51 of the U.N. Charter." 43 Harvard International Law Journal. 41 (2002). Page 50

790 Delerue, François. Cyber Operations and international law. Cambridge: Cambridge University Press, 2020. Pages 464.

791 Welanyk, Tomasz, "Istnienie i granice suwerenności w cyberprzestrzeni. Analiza prawna." Ph.D. dissertation, University of Warsaw, 2019. Page 260.

792 Roscini, Marco. Cyber Operations and the use of force in international law. New York: Oxford University Press, 2016. Page 68.

the application of *Self-defense* in cyberspace was confirmed by the 2010 UN GGE Report, endorsed by a UN GA resolution, which stated:

> The use of force in self-defence must be limited to what is necessary to address an imminent or actual armed attack and must be proportionate to the threat that is faced.[793]

There also exists a camp of scholars who insist hostile cyber acts need to create physical damage equivalent to those caused by conventional means in order for it to qualify as an *Armed Attack*. This however is an overly restrictive approach. While at present purely cyber impacts are not capable of causing *Armed Attack*-grade damage, such a scenario could be potentially possible in the future.

There are four aspects of application of *Self-defense* in cyberspace that deserve special attention:

- Civilian damage caused by *Self-defense* in cyberspace;
- The impact of damaging critical ICT infrastructure;
- Adjusting the requirement of immediacy for *Self-defense* in cyberspace;
- Preemptive and interceptive *Self-Defense* in cyberspace.

The problem of civilian damage done as part of deployment of *Self-defense* measures is especially relevant in cyberspace. This is caused by the fact that most of the internet infrastructure is private property and serves civilian purposes. Meanwhile, *Self-defense* is meant to target military or dual-use targets. Choosing purely civilian targets for causing damage as part of *Self-defense* is prohibited.[794] According to the Geneva Conventions and their Additional Protocols, regarding jus in bellum (the law of armed conflicts),

793 United Nations General Assembly Resolution. (2010, July 30). Group of Governmental Experts on Developments in the Field of Information and Telecommunications in the Context of International Security— Note by the Secretary-General. Retrieved February 15, 2022, from <https://documents-dds-ny.un.org/doc/UNDOC/GEN/N10/469/57/PDF/N1046957.pdf?OpenElement>

794 "Rule 54—Attacks against Objects Indispensable to the Survival of the Civilian Population." International Committee of the Red Cross—International Humanitarian Law. Retrieved November 29, 2023. <https://ihl-databases.icrc.org/en/customary-ihl/v1/rule54>.

even if civilian objects, such as critical infrastructure are targeted with an operation (e.g., a *Self-defense* cyber counter-operation), the acting State must differentiate between combatants and civilians.[795] This is near-impossible in the context of ICT infrastructure, routinely used for dual, civilian and military, purposes. The rules on *non*-perfidy, a principle stating that military forces shall not purposefully hide behind civilian objects (e.g., by locating headquarters in the basement of a hospital) would not apply here since over-layering of civilian and military functions of the ICT network is its structural feature.[796] A measure of collateral damage on the civilian side is actually permissible, but should be proportionate to the *anticipated military advantage* gained from operation.[797] If, for example, a State decides to hit another State's ICT infrastructure, purporting that the act would be covered by one of the eight circumstances listed in Section 4.1, it would have to be able to demonstrate that it had an assessment showing no disproportionate civilian damage would take place.

This raises the question of what proportion of damage can be of civilian nature for *Self-defense* measures to remain legitimate. There exist no clear answer to that question in sources of Public International Law, which forces us to seek legal analogy in areas where more State practice and international jurisprudence has occurred. ICJ expressed its view on environmental damage in the context of deploying *Self-defense* measures in its *Advisory Opinion on Legality of the Threat or Use of Nuclear Weapons*:

> The Court does not consider that the treaties in question could have intended to deprive a State of the exercise of its right of self-defence under international law because of its obligations to protect the environment. Nonetheless, States must take environmental considerations into account when assessing what is necessary and proportionate in the pursuit of legitimate military objectives. Respect for the

795 International Committee of the Red Cross. (1977, June 8). Additional Protocol I to the Geneva Conventions. Article 48. Retrieved February 18, 2022, from <https://www.icrc.org/en/doc/assets/files/other/icrc_002_0321.pdf>.

796 International Committee of the Red Cross. (n.d.). Customary International Humanitarian Law—Rule 65. Perfidy. Retrieved February 18, 2022, from <https://ihl-databases.icrc.org/customary-ihl/eng/docindex/v1_rul_rule65>.

797 International Committee of the Red Cross. (1977, June 8). Additional Protocol I to the Geneva Conventions. Articles 51(5)(b), 51(3). Retrieved February 18, 2022, from <https://www.icrc.org/en/doc/assets/files/other/icrc_002_0321.pdf>.

> environment is one of the elements that go to assessing whether an action is in conformity with the principles of necessity and proportionality.[798]

In a rather elegant way, the ICJ framed the challenge of damaging by-effects of *Self-defense* as a matter of assessing necessity and proportionality of utilized measures. This way, the by-effects do not close off the ability of a State to exercise its right to *Self-defense* but rather they limit the scope of measures that can be deployed as part of it. Similar sentiment, expressing the need to balance the commitment to limit environmental damage with the right to exercise *Self-defense* measures was expressed by the UN General Assembly Resolution titled *Protection of the Environment in Times of Armed Conflict*[799] and the Rio Declaration on Environment and Development,[800] both from 1992. This logic can be applied in cyberspace by analogy. The dual nature of internet infrastructure, serving both civilian and military purposes, creates a situation where negative by-effects of cyber *Self-defense* are almost inevitable. Oftentimes cyber hostilities between States spill over into the civilian part of cyberspace, either by accident or by design. For example, internet-based hospital communication systems were disrupted by the WannaCry Virus in the United Kingdom in 2015.[801] When assessing validity of a cyber measure, the principles of proportionality and necessity allow for factoring in civilian damage.

A related issue is the amplifying effect that utilizing critical ICT infrastructure can have on the scale of damage caused by cyber acts. This phenomenon and its impact on assessing severity of hostile cyber operations was discussed

798 Advisory Opinion on Legality of the Threat or Use of Nuclear Weapons. International Court of Justice. (1996, July 8). Paragraph 41. Retrieved February 18, 2022, from <https://www.icj-cij.org/en/case/95>.

799 United Nations General Assembly Resolution. (1993, February 9). 47/37. Protection of the environment in times of armed conflict. United Nations Digital Library System. Retrieved February 18, 2022, from <https://digitallibrary.un.org/record/158808?ln=en>.

800 United Nations Conference on Environment and Development. (1992, June 14). Rio Declaration on Environment and Development. Article 24. Retrieved February 18, 2022, from <https://www.jus.uio.no/lm/environmental.development.rio.declaration.1992/24.html>.

801 Ghafur Saira et al., (2019). "A retrospective impact analysis of the WannaCry cyber-attack on the NHS." Nature, 2019, 1–6. <https://doi.org/10.1038/s41746-019-0161-6>.

in the previous chapter in the context of wrongful cyber operations.[802] It can also have an impact on assessing cyber *Self-defense* measures. This amplifying effect of targeting critical ICT infrastructure must be accounted for when measuring necessity and proportionality of cyber *Self-defense.* It might be proposed that choosing this type of target over others as part of cyber *Self-defense* limits the scope of proportionate measures. A cyber measure that shuts down a State's vital ITC systems can create dramatic civilian damage if it disables the decision-making nerve center of a country. Attacking national critical infrastructure via a hostile cyber operation is an easy way to create instantaneous country-wide negative impact in the target State. Even if such systems are of dual-use nature, *Self-defense* measures of this kind could be wrongful. This was acknowledged by the United States, which defined critical infrastructure in its 2001 Patriot Act as:

> systems and assets, whether physical or virtual, so vital to the United States that the incapacity or destruction of such systems and assets would have a debilitating impact on security, national economical security, national public health or safety, or any combination of those matters[803]

The UN GGE Report from 2015, endorsed by a UN GA, includes a voluntary non-binding norm whose purpose is to discourage assaults on critical infrastructure:

> (f) A State should not conduct or knowingly support ICT activity contrary to its obligations under international law that intentionally damages critical infrastructure or otherwise impairs the use and operation of critical infrastructure to provide services to the public;[804]

---

802 See Section III.6.2.4—"The role of critical infrastructure in determining occurrence of Prohibited Use of Force" for details.

803 The government of the United States of America. (2001, October 26). USA PATRIOT Act. Retrieved February 18, 2022, from <https://www.fincen.gov/resources/statutes-regulations/usa-patriot-act>.

804 United Nations Secretary-General. (2015, July 22). Group of Governmental Experts on Developments in the Field of Information and Telecommunications in the Context of International Security—Note by the Secretary-General. Page 8. Retrieved February 15, 2022, from <https://documents-dds-ny.un.org/doc/UNDOC/GEN/N15/228/35/PDF/N1522835.pdf?OpenElement>.

Following a wave of cyber assaults on electronic election infrastructure, a number of States formally designated it as critical infrastructure, in line with the framing proposed by the UN GGE. One of them was the United States in the wake of the U.S. Democratic National Convention hack of 2016.[805]

National critical infrastructure plays a special role in the context of repelling cyber *Internationally Wrongful Acts.* Assault on critical infrastructure is among the most likely cyber *Internationally Wrongful Acts* as suggested by experience so far.[806] Due to the fundamental role of continuous functioning of critical infrastructure for States, they employ both multilateral and domestic legal means to deter potential assaults on ICT infrastructure. In terms of the former pathway, the most advanced framework is the Council of Europe's Convention on Cybercrime (COE Convention), which harmonizes national regulations and sets up enforcement cooperation in terms of trans-border cyber crime (ratified by 46 States),[807] The African Union's Convention on Cyber Security and Personal Data Protection contains similar goals (signed in 2014 and awaiting ratification by a required number of AU States).[808] Governments can also use Interpol extradition agreements and mutual legal assistance treaties to hold accountable perpetrators who target critical infrastructure.

There exists a general prohibition of attacks on civilian critical infrastructure. During an armed conflict however, those rules could not apply if said infrastructure is of dual nature (i.e., civilian and military at the same time). This is especially problematic when applied to cyberspace since the vast majority of the ICT infrastructure across countries is of primarily civilian

805 The government of the United States of America. (2019, September 18). The Designation of Election Systems as Critical Infrastructure. Retrieved February 18, 2022, from <https://sgp.fas.org/crs/misc/IF10677.pdf>.

806 Kozłowski, Andrzej. (2014). Comparative Analysis of Cyberattacks on Estonia, Georgia and Kyrgyzstan. European Scientific Journal ESJ, 10(7). <http://dx.doi.org/10.19044/esj.2014.v10n7p%25p>.

807 Council of Europe. (2001, November 23). Convention on Cybercrime—Council of Europe. Council of Europe Treaty Office (ETS No. 185). Retrieved February 15, 2022, from <https://www.coe.int/en/web/conventions/full-list?module=treaty-detail&treatynum=185>.

808 African Union. (2014, June 27). African Union Convention on Cyber Security and Personal Data Protection. Retrieved February 18, 2022, from <https://au.int/en/treaties/african-union-convention-cyber-security-and-personal-data-protection>.

character but is being extensively used by military forces for its internal purposes. An assault on such dual-use ICT infrastructure (a term which can apply to almost all ICT infrastructure) would still violate the prohibition of attacking civilian targets if it was done using indiscriminate means and caused disproportionate civilian damage.[809] Some scholars, such as Eric Jensen, went as far as to suggest that any cyber operation against national critical infrastructure is an *Armed Attack* and enables the injured State to engage in *Self-defense* measures.[810] This stance however appears to be an outlier. Nevertheless, a consensus is emerging to treat critical infrastructure differently in the cyber context, in recognition of its inevitable dual nature. If that consensus satisfies both the objective element (State practice) and the subjective one (*opinio juris* on part of States that expresses their collective conviction that a new norm of international law has emerged and is binding), it will likely point toward treating cyber assaults on critical infrastructure as broadly speaking *Violations of Sovereignty*, with potential for a more severe classification in case the additional established requirements are met.

The International Civil Aviation Organization (ICAO)[811] and the International Atomic Energy Agency (IAEA)[812] spearhead development of the notion of a special status of critical infrastructure in international law, including its heighted protection from cyber threats. The Council of the European Union *Directive on the Identification and Designation of European Critical Infrastructure and the Assessment of the Need to Improve Their Protection*

---

809 Schmitt, Michael N. & NATO Cooperative Cyber Defence Centre of Excellence. (2017). Tallinn Manual 2.0 on the International Law Applicable to Cyber Operations. Cambridge University Press. Supra note 3, page 54.

810 Jensen, Eric T. (2002). Computer Attacks on Critical National Infrastructure: A Use of Force Invoking the Right of Self-Defense. Stanford Journal of International Law, 38(207), 207–240. Pages 221–26. <https://digitalcommons.law.byu.edu/faculty_scholarship/212/>.

811 International Civil Aviation Organization. (2012, November 30). Working Paper on Cyber Security for Civil Aviation, Twelfth Air Navigation Conference. Retrieved February 18, 2022, from <https://www.icao.int/meetings/anconf12/workingpapers/anconfwp122.1.1.enonly.pdf>.

812 Fidler, David P. (2015). Whither the Web?: International Law, Cybersecurity, and Critical Infrastructure Protection. Georgetown Journal of International Affairs - Articles by Maurer Faculty, 2452, 8–20. Page 19. <https://www.repository.law.indiana.edu/cgi/viewcontent.cgi?article=3452&context=facpub>.

obligates EU States to designate *European Critical Infrastructure*, with special emphasis on ICT infrastructure and systems.[813] Meanwhile, the Shanghai Cooperation Organization agreed on a treaty to elevate the status of critical ICT infrastructure and set up security measures in cyberspace.[814]

Unilateral individual-level response is also possible as an alternative to responding to a hostile international cyber operation with a counter-operation. For example, in 2015, the U.S. President Barack Obama issued an executive order titled *Blocking the Property of Persons Engaging in Significant Malicious Cyber-Enabled Activities*. It envisioned sanctions on individuals outside of the United States, who perpetuate hostile cyber activities deemed a threat to *U.S. national security, foreign policy, economic health, or financial stability*.[815] Additionally, the International Convention for the Suppression of Terrorist Bombings from 1997, ratified by 168 countries, presumably covers cyber attacks, including disruption to critical infrastructure. It obliges signatory States to criminalize acts perpetrated with an *explosive or other lethal device*, whose definition arguably includes cyber means.[816]

Several legal experts weighed in, arguing for a high threshold of necessity in the cyber context, in order to prevent escalation that might be easier due to the nature of cyberspace. Marco Roscini stated that even those cyber *Armed Attacks* that severely disrupt the critical infrastructure do not automatically

---

813 Council of the European Union. (2008, December 8). Council of the European Union Directive 2008/114/EC on the identification and designation of European critical infrastructures and the assessment of the need to improve their protection. Official Journal of the European Union. Retrieved February 18, 2022, from <https://eur-lex.europa.eu/LexUriServ/LexUriServ.do?uri=OJ:L:2008:345:0075:0082:EN:PDF>.

814 Shanghai Cooperation Organization. (2009, June 16). Agreement of the Member States of the Shanghai Cooperation Organization on Cooperation in the Field of International Information Security. Article 3. Retrieved February 18, 2022, from <https://ccdcoe.org/uploads/2018/10/SCO-090616-IISAgreement.pdf>.

815 The government of the United States. (2015, April 1). Presidential Executive Order—Blocking the Property of Persons Engaging in Significant Malicious Cyber-Enabled Activities. Retrieved February 18, 2022, from <https://www.federalregister.gov/documents/2015/04/02/2015-07788/blocking-the-property-of-certain-persons-engaging-in-significant-malicious-cyber-enabled-activities>.

816 United Nations General Assembly Resolution. (1997, December 15). International Convention for the Suppression of Terrorist Bombings. United Nations Treaty Collection. Retrieved February 18, 2022, from <https://treaties.un.org/pages/ViewDetails.aspx?src=IND&mtdsg_no=XVIII-9&chapter=18&clang=_en>.

ensure that the necessity requirement for *Self-defense* is met.[817] Especially if a response below the threshold of *Use of Force* could be sufficient, responding in-kind to an attack might actually be wrongful.[818] Yoram Dinstein expressed a similar viewpoint—he stated that only extreme circumstances (*outré circumstances*), such as a nuclear power plant emergency caused by a cyber attack, could warrant invoking *Self-defense* measures amounting to *Use of Force*.[819]

Another challenge related to the application of *Self-defense* in cyberspace is of temporal nature. Concealing the perpetrator's identity and the scale of an *Armed Attack* is much easier in cyberspace. As a result, injured States might require additional time to effectively attribute it to the right State or uncover the full scale of an operation and its effects. In this context, some scholars, such as Marco Roscini, suggested that States should be given more time to gather evidence that would allow it to attribute an *Armed Attack* and deploy *Self-defense* measures.[820] One way of handling this situation would be to lower international legal evidence standards in cyberspace as compared to other spheres of States' interactions. Another way would be to allow for targeting non-State actors with *Self-defense* measures, a solution that is espoused by a number of States. It is, however, fraught with danger. François Delerue offered tentative support for the latter idea: "In the cyber context it may be difficult to establish the relationship between the perpetrating non-State actor and an alleged sponsoring State. Thus, the extension of the right of self-defense to threats arising from non-state actors could be seductive in the cyber context; however, this constitutes a very slippery slope and should be exercised with extreme caution."[821]

---

817 Roscini, Marco. (2014). Cyber Operations and the Use of Force in International Law. British Yearbook of International Law, 84(1), pages 385–389. <https://doi.org/10.1093/bybil/bru014>.

818 Ibid.

819 Dinstein, Yoram. (2002). Computer Network Attacks and Self-Defense. International Law Studies, 76, 99–114. Page 110. <https://digital-commons.usnwc.edu/cgi/viewcontent.cgi?article=1397&context=ils>.

820 Roscini, Marco. (2014). Cyber Operations and the Use of Force in International Law. British Yearbook of International Law, 84(1), pages 385–389. <https://doi.org/10.1093/bybil/bru014>.

821 Delerue, François. Cyber Operations and international law. Cambridge: Cambridge University Press, 2020. Pages 465.

Most hostile cyber operations are of instantaneous nature, which limits the scope of application of interceptive *Self-defense*. However, it is theoretically possible to conceive of cyber operations that have a delayed impact, such as a form of a cyber bomb that can be planted within an IT system with a countdown clock. As long as the countdown mechanism has been activated and the harm would reach the severity amounting to an *Armed Attack*, the victim State could invoke *Self-defense* in response to such a hostile cyber act.[822] This example is not far-fetched. The Stuxnet virus was present in the system of Iranian nuclear facilities before it started causing harm. Had the harm amounted to an *Armed Attack* (for instance by way of making the nuclear centrifuges explode rather than just malfunction) and Iran had uncovered it ahead of time, *Self-defense* could be theoretically warranted.

The international scholars who authored the Tallinn Manual, led by Michael Schmitt, have argued for the existence of preemptive *Self-defense* in cyberspace specifically, arguing that such a measure might be particularly suiting the domain.[823] To identify an imminent hostile cyber operation that will amount to an *Armed Attack*, Michael Schmitt introduced the notion of "last feasible window of opportunity."[824] The argument for preemptive *Self-defense* in cyberspace rests upon the notion that cyber acts can be near-instantaneous, which creates limited ability to respond to after damage has been done. Some tentative support for the notion was also extended by Marco Roscini[825] and Heather Dinnis.[826] Examples offered in the Tallinn Manual 2.0 include hostile cyber operations that harbinger launching of other, much more severe cyber or conventional acts or logical bombs that are set on a

822 Schmitt, Michael N. & NATO Cooperative Cyber Defence Centre of Excellence. (2017). Tallinn Manual 2.0 on the International Law Applicable to Cyber Operations. Cambridge University Press. Commentary to Rule 15, paragraph 6.

823 Ibid. Rule 73.

824 Ibid.

825 Roscini, Marco. (2014). Cyber Operations and the Use of Force in International Law. British Yearbook of International Law, 84(1), pages 385–389. <https://doi.org/10.1093/bybil/bru014>.

826 Dinniss, Heather H. (2012). Cyber Warfare and the Laws of War (Cambridge Studies in International and Comparative Law). Cambridge University Press. Page 88. <https://doi.org/10.1017/CBO9780511894527>.

countdown timer.[827] This approach however does not pass closer scrutiny. Resorting to *Use of Force* in response to soft hostile cyber operations that might precede more severe ones would be speculative and disproportionate. From the systemic point of view, it would also go against the grain of Public International Law, which tends to favor normative frameworks that gravitate toward de-escalation and avoidance of *Use of Force* as a matter of principle. Cyber preemptive *Self-defense* might then be a proposal, whose balance of benefits and risks is sub-optimal and implies it is not worth pursuing it as a binding norm of Public International Law.

4.4 Proposals of future forms of response to hostile cyber operations conducted by States

4.4.1 Humanitarian Interventions

Humanitarian Intervention in Public International Law is a controversial subject. It has not been defined or even confirmed in any binding source of international law, leaving us dependent on States' pronouncements and scholarly analysis. J. L. Holzgrefe of Oxford University described it the following way in his 2003 publication on the subject: "The threat or use of force across state borders by a state (or a group of states) aimed at preventing or ending widespread and grave violations of the fundamental human rights of individuals other than its own citizens, without the permission of the state within whose territory force is applied."[828] This definition draws on the norm of *Prohibited Intervention*. Just as a *Prohibited Intervention* can amount to *Prohibited Use of Force*, a *Humanitarian Intervention* constitutes a form of *Lawful Use of Force* toward another State, predicated on the fact that it aims to stop violations of fundamental human rights that reach a certain level of severity. It would still be a violation of *State Sovereignty* but it would enjoy preclusion from wrongfulness in the system of Public International Law. It is important to clarify what would not constitute as a *Humanitarian Intervention:*

---

827 Ibid.; Schmitt, Michael N. & NATO Cooperative Cyber Defence Centre of Excellence. (2017). Tallinn Manual 2.0 on the International Law Applicable to Cyber Operations. Cambridge University Press. Commentary to Rule 73, paragraph 7.

828 Holzgrefe, Jeff L. (2009). Humanitarian Intervention: Ethical, Legal and Political Dilemmas. Cambridge University Press. Page 18. <https://doi.org/10.1017/CBO9780511494000>.

- Consensual humanitarian assistance or presence based on an official invitation;
- *Use of Force* by a State to extricate its own citizens;
- UN Peacekeeping Operations.

Humanitarian Intervention is a non-consensual act, taking place against the will of a target State. The ICJ noted in the Nicaragua judgment:

> There can be no doubt that the provision of strictly humanitarian aid to persons or forces in another country, whatever their political affiliations or objectives, cannot be regarded as unlawful intervention, or as in any other way contrary to international law.[829]

On the second point, extracting citizens from within other States, practice and doctrine have established that such actions would not be covered by the term *Humanitarian Intervention*. The two key cases in that regard were: the rescue of Israeli civilians from Uganda in 1976 and American entrance into Grenada in 1984.[830] UN Peacekeeping missions are established by the UN Security Council and are an instrument of maintaining international peace and security. As such, they are lawful by definition and do not need to enjoy any preclusion.

There have been five large-scale examples that could potentially qualify as *Humanitarian Interventions*, which took place since the Cold War's end. These are operations that took place in: Iraq (1991), Somalia (1992), Kosovo (1999), Sierra Leone (2000), Darfur and Sudan (2004). The first three were undertaken by the United States (including the Kosovo one which was formally designated as a NATO operation). The United States described its 1991 intervention in Iraq as a response to mass-murder of Kurds in the north of the country.[831]

---

829 Case Concerning Military and Paramilitary Activities in and Against Nicaragua, Nicaragua v United States. International Court of Justice. I.C.J Reports 14, ICGJ 112 (ICJ 1986). (1986). Paragraph 242. Retrieved February 15, 2022, from <https://www.icj-cij.org/en/case/70/judgments>.

830 Britannica. "Entebbe raid." Encyclopedia Britannica. Retrieved 10 Nov. 2023, <https://www.britannica.com/event/Entebbe-raid>; Swift, John. "U.S. invasion of Grenada." Encyclopedia Britannica. Retrieved 21 Nov. 2023, <https://www.britannica.com/event/U-S-invasion-of-Grenada>.

831 Karlin, Mara E., Suzanne Maloney, Tea Ivanovic Sasha Toperich, Maya Nir Marsin Alshamary, Ranj Alaaldin, Kevin Huggard Jeffrey Feltman, Adrianna Pita Patricia M.

The Somalian intervention was explained as a reaction to a humanitarian crisis and inability of the UN to safely deliver food provisions to civilians.[832] The Kosovo intervention was a response to ethnic cleansing of Muslims in former Yugoslavia by Serbs.[833] The Sierra Leone intervention was conducted by the United Kingdom in response to gross violations of human rights committed by rebel groups in the country.[834] Finally, the Darfur intervention was formally conducted by the African Union and geared toward stopping the violence perpetrated toward the indigenous populace there by the central government.[835]

The notion of *Humanitarian Intervention* is tightly bound to the international human rights regime. At the core of this framework is the generally accepted claim that humanitarian law enjoys universal applicability across the world.[836] However, this approach creates a tension between two values integral to the system of international law: respecting *State Sovereignty* on one side and protecting fundamental human rights on the other. The Rwandan genocide of 1994 presents an example of what happens when the international community stays passive when confronted with this dilemma. The resulting humanitarian crisis and deaths could have been prevented. However, it would have involved an intervention that would violate *State Sovereignty.* For those reasons, Jerzy Kranz, alongside many other scholars and practitioners, claim

---

Kim, and Yingyi Ma. "Imperfect Allies and Non-State Actors: Lessons from the 1991 No-Fly Zone in Iraq." Brookings, March 9, 2022. <https://www.brookings.edu/articles/imperfect-allies-and-non-state-actors-lessons-from-the-1991-no-fly-zone-in-iraq/>.

832 U.S. Army Center of Military History—After Action Report. Retrieved November 30, 2023. <https://history.army.mil/html/documents/somalia/SomaliaAAR.pdf>.

833 NATO. "Kosovo Air Campaign (March-June 1999)." NATO, May 17, 2022. <https://www.nato.int/cps/en/natohq/topics_49602.htm>.

834 Roberson, Walter G, and Army Command And General Staff Coll Fort Leavenworth Ks. "British Military Intervention into Sierra Leone: A Case Study." DTIC, December 14, 2007. <https://apps.dtic.mil/sti/citations/ADA475595>.

835 Lefkow, Leslie. "Darfur Destroyed - Ethnic Cleansing by Government and Militia Forces in Western Sudan." Human Rights Watch, March 28, 2023. <https://www.hrw.org/report/2004/05/06/darfur-destroyed/ethnic-cleansing-government-and-militia-forces-western-sudan>.

836 Karska, Elżbieta, & Karski, Karol. (2015). Introduction: Extraterritorial Scope of Human Rights. International Community Law Review, 17(4–5), 395–401. <https://doi.org/10.1163/18719732-12341311>.

that *State Sovereignty* can be circumscribed in light of egregious acts that defy basic human rights.[837]

Humanitarian Intervention could potentially take place within cyberspace. Let us consider a case where a State intervenes to delete a database of individuals who the target State is wishing to exterminate. Another example could be a theoretical situation, in which a State conducts a cyber operation to temporarily paralyze armed forces in another State, rather than let them assault a region inhabited by a religious minority. While this seems far off now, the same was the case with the idea of cyber operations targeting nuclear power plants or shutting down the electricity grid, both of which scenarios have taken place over the past few years.

The 2021 UN GGE Report stated that international humanitarian law is applicable to cyber operations during the time of an armed conflict.[838] While this does not resolve the question on whether *Humanitarian Interventions* are permitted, it makes the need for finding it all the more urgent. The International Committee of the Red Cross did not take a stance on the matter although it expressed its opinion that international humanitarian law should limit the scope of hostile cyber operations:

> there is no question that IHL applies to, and therefore limits, cyber operations during armed conflict – just as it regulates the use of any other weapon, means and methods of warfare in an armed conflict, whether new or old. This holds true whether cyberspace is considered as a new domain of warfare similar to air, land, sea and outer space; a different type of domain because it is man-made while the former are natural; or not a domain as such.[839]

---

837 Kranz, Jerzy. (2005). "Suwerenność państwa. Rekonstrukcja i znaczenie idei w prawie międzynarodowym," Roman Kwiecień, Kraków 2004 : [recenzja]. Kwartalnik Prawa Publicznego, 5(1/2), pages 329–334. <https://bazhum.muzhp.pl/media/files/Kwartalnik_Prawa_Publicznego/Kwartalnik_Prawa_Publicznego-r2005-t5-n1_2/Kwartalnik_Prawa_Publicznego-r2005-t5-n1_2-s329-334/Kwartalnik_Prawa_Publicznego-r2005-t5-n1_2-s329-334.pdf>.

838 United Nations General Assembly Resolution. (2021, July 14). Group of Governmental Experts on Developments in the Field of Information and Telecommunications in the Context of International Security - Note by the Secretary-General. Retrieved February 15, 2022, from <https://front.un-arm.org/wp-content/uploads/2021/08/A_76_135-2104030E-1.pdf>.

839 International Committee on the Red Cross. (2019, November). ICRC Position Paper - International Humanitarian Law and Cyber Operations during Armed Conflicts.

4.4.2 Responsibility to Protect

A concept similar in substance to *Humanitarian Intervention* is *Responsibility to Protect*. The debate on *Responsibility to Protect* was reflected in the work of the UN International Law Committee, which was finalizing its work on *Draft articles on Responsibility of States for Internationally Wrongful Acts* in the period 2000–2001. The 2000 draft version, which was ultimately dropped, contained article 54 paragraph 2, which stated:

> In the cases referred to in article 41 [serious breach by a State of an obligation owed to the international community as a whole and essential for the protection of its fundamental interests], any State may take countermeasures, in accordance with the present chapter in the interest of the beneficiaries of the obligation breached.[840]

Members of the UN ILC suggested that article 54 paragraph 2 would cover cases of violations such as slavery, genocide, or apartheid.[841] This sentiment was supported by the then UN Secretary-General Kofi Annan.[842] However, a number of States expressed strong opposition to this notion,[843] which resulted in its removal from the final version of *Draft Articles.*

In 2001, this idea re-emerged in wake of the Report of the International Commission on Intervention and State Sovereignty (ICISS) crafted as a response to the UN Secretary-General Kofi Annan:[844]

Retrieved February 19, 2022, from <https://unoda-web.s3.amazonaws.com/wp-content/uploads/2020/01/icrc_ihl-and-cyber-operations-during-armed-conflicts.pdf>.

840 United Nations International Law Commission. (2000). Draft articles on State Responsibility Provisionally Adopted by the Drafting Committee on Second Reading. United Nations Office of Legal Affairs—Document A/55/10: Report of the International Law Commission on the Work of Its Fifty-Second Session. Article 54, paragraph 2.

841 Ibid. Commentary to the Draft Article 54.

842 "United Nations Office on Genocide Prevention and the Responsibility to Protect." United Nations. Retrieved November 29, 2023. <https://www.un.org/en/genocide-prevention/about-responsibility-to-protect.shtml>.

843 Crowford, James. "State Responsibility: Fourth Report on State Responsibility." United Nations International Law Commission, April 3, 2001. <https://legal.un.org/ilc/documentation/english/a_cn4_517.pdf>.

844 "United Nations Office on Genocide Prevention and the Responsibility to Protect." United Nations. Retrieved November 29, 2023. <https://www.un.org/en/genocide-prevention/about-responsibility-to-protect.shtml>.

> Sovereign States have a responsibility to protect their own citizens from avoidable catastrophe – from mass murder and rape, from starvation – but when they are unwilling or unable to do so, that responsibility must be borne by the broader community of states.[845]

The ICISS was a multilateral initiative led by the Canadian government to promote *Responsibility to Protect* as a new legal norm in international law. There are a number of significant differences between a *Humanitarian Intervention* and an intervention conducted based on *Responsibility to Protect:*

- It is framed as a duty rather than an option;
- It is borne by the whole international community rather than any particular State;
- It combines three types of commitment: to prevent, to react, to rebuild.

The UN Secretary-General continued spearheading the idea after the report's publication, seeing it as a narrower-scope response to resistance that emerged against the notion of humanitarian intervention. His two annual reports, both endorses by a UN GA resolution, included a reference to every State's obligation to protect its population from genocide and other grave atrocities by utilizing proportionate response that justify the cause, adding that in case of inability to do so, the burden of the obligation shifts onto the international community as a whole.[846] Then at the 2005 high-level UN World Summit, the majority of States agreed to such a formulation in the Summit Outcome Document.[847] This was followed

845 The Responsibility to Protect—Report of The International Commission on Intervention and State Sovereignty. (2001, December). International Commission on Intervention and State Sovereignty. Page VIII. <https://walterdorn.net/pdf/Responsibility-to-Protect_ICISS-Report_Dec2001.pdf>;

846 United Nations General Assembly Resolution. (2003, December 2). Follow-up to the outcome of the Millennium Summit—Note by the Secretary-General. Retrieved February 15, 2022, from <https://documents-dds-ny.un.org/doc/UNDOC/GEN/N04/602/31/PDF/N0460231.pdf>.

847 United Nations General Assembly Resolution. (2005, October 24). 2005 World Summit Outcome. Paragraphs 138 and 139. Retrieved February 15, 2022, from <https://documents-dds-ny.un.org/doc/UNDOC/GEN/N05/487/60/PDF/N0548760.pdf>.

by an appointment of a Special Adviser on the Responsibility to Protect by the Secretary-General in 2008.[848]

As part of the academic debate on the subject, Carsten Stahn suggested that the proposed norm heralds a shift away from the focus on *State Sovereignty* in Public International Law:

> R2P forms an example of a 'broader systemic shift in international law, namely, a growing tendency to recognize that the principle of state sovereignty finds its limits in the protection of "human security"'[849]

Jerzy Kranz has noted that all the Reports and Summit Documents put forward by the UN emphasize a preference for multilateral action rather than an individual action by a State. This additional measure of safety is meant to prevent abuse of *Responsibility to Protect* as a pretext to invade a country. He found that this puts the primary duty of coordinating such action on regional organizations, including, for example, the Organization of American States or the European Union.[850]

Bertrand Ramcharan pointed to Bank Ki-Moon's continuation of an effort to promote the norm of *Responsibility to Protect.* The late UN Secretary-General called on the United Nations to be more ambitious and bolder in mobilizing States to prevent genocide and other great atrocities.[851] This aspiration, while commendable, did not bear out. As of 2023, no tangible example of a measure taken under *Responsibility to Protect* exists. Given a lack of State practice and no consistent *opinio juris,* it must be concluded that the norm has not taken root. It is also difficult to conceive of hostile cyber acts amounting to grave violations that would justify action under *Responsibility to Protect.* However, if such a norm emerges in the future, its application in cyberspace would mean that the international community

848 "United Nations Office on Genocide Prevention and the Responsibility to Protect." United Nations. Accessed November 29, 2023. <https://www.un.org/en/genocideprevention/about-responsibility-to-protect.shtml>.

849 Stahn, Carsten. (2006). "Jus ad bellum," "jus in bello" … "jus post bellum"?—Rethinking the Conception of the Law of Armed Force. European Journal of International Law, 17(5), 921–943. <https://doi.org/10.1093/ejil/chl037>.

850 Kranz, Jerzt. Pojęcie suwerenności we współczesnym prawie międzynarodowym, Warszawa 2015, page 189.

851 Ramcharan, Bertrand. A new international Law of Security and Protection UN Chronicle 2015 No. 4, page 42.

could instantaneously deploy cyber operations against specific sovereign States with few to none geographic and logistical limitations.

4.4.3 Collective Countermeasures

In 2019, during the opening remarks at the *International Conference on Cyber Conflict*, president of Estonia Kersti Kaljulaid put forward a bold proposal of collective *Countermeasures* in cyberspace: "Estonia is furthering the position that States which are not directly injured may apply *Countermeasures* to support the State directly affected by the malicious cyber operation. The *Countermeasures* applied should follow the principle of proportionality and other principles established within the international customary law. It is therefore important that States may respond collectively to unlawful cyber operations where diplomatic action is insufficient, but no lawful recourse to use of force exists. Allies matter also in cyberspace."[852] Estonia has been the target of hostile cyber operations for years. The most publicized case, the Bronze Soldier incident of 2007, led to a denouncement by NATO and creation of the NATO Cyber Defence Centre of Excellence in Tallinn.[853] This context explains the State's support for collective *Countermeasures.*

The idea is analogous to the *Self-defense* provision included in Article 5 of the North Atlantic Treaty that obligates NATO member States to support any of them experiencing an *Armed Attack*. Developing a similar mechanism for hostile acts below the threshold of *Armed Attack* would provide an additional measure of deterrent against potential hostile actors, like those behind the 2007 cyber assault on websites of various public bodies in Estonia. However, considering that cyber hostilities are relatively frequent between States, this new rule would constitute a serious commitment. Soon after the Estonian President's statements, the French Ministry of Foreign Affairs repudiated

---

[852] The government of Estonia. (2019, May 29). Remarks from President of the Republic of Estonia at the opening of CyCon 2019. Retrieved February 19, 2022, from <https://ceipfiles.s3.amazonaws.com/pdf/CyberNorms/LawStatements/Remarks+by+the+President+of+the+Republic+of+Estonia+at+the+Opening+of+CyCon+2019.pdf>

[853] Juurvee, Ivo, and Anna-Mariita Mattiisen. "The Bronze Soldier Crisis of 2007: Revisiting an Early Case of Hybrid Conflict." International Centre for Defence and Security, February 14, 2022. <https://icds.ee/en/the-bronze-soldier-crisis-of-2007/>.

the idea.[854] While collective James Crawford proposed in 1997, as the ILC Special Rapporteur, collective *Countermeasures*, framing them as a response to a violation of collective obligations a concept similar in substance to obligations *erga omnes*) even if they were not directly affected by the violation.[855] However, this notion was rejected by UN member States, which cited their potentially destabilizing impact.[856] One of the current requirements for deploying *Countermeasures* is that only injured States are entitled to do it.[857] Collective *Countermeasures* would mean a modification to that binding customary rule. Moving in that direction could pitch the whole international community directly against any potential offending States, regardless of who the target State is. It remains to be seen if this idea takes root.

The proposed norm of collective *Countermeasures* overlaps with the notion of third-party *Countermeasures.* Certain States, such as Estonia and Poland expressed their direct support for States' right to deploy *Countermeasures* in response to hostile cyber operations conducted in another State. In its official policy document Poland stated:

> The Republic of Poland expresses the view that the evolution of customary international law over the last two decades provides grounds for recognising that a state may take countermeasures in pursuit of general interest as well. In particular, the possibility of taking such measures materialise itself in response to states' violations of preemptory norms, such as the prohibition of aggression."[858]

---

854 The government of France. (2019a). International Law Applied to Operations in Cyberspace. Retrieved February 19, 2022, from <https://www.defense.gouv.fr/content/download/567648/9770527/file/international+law+applied+to+operations+in+-cyberspace.pdf>.

855 Crwaford, James. (2000, August 15). Third report on State responsibility. United Nations Digital Library System. Paragraph 386. Retrieved February 19, 2022, from <https://digitallibrary.un.org/record/420754?ln=en>.

856 Schmitt, Michael N., & Watts, Sean. (2021). Collective Cyber Countermeasures? Harvard National Security Journal, 12, 373–411. <https://harvardnsj.org/wp-content/uploads/sites/13/2021/07/HNSJ-Vol-12-Schmitt-and-Watts-Collective-Cyber-Countermeasures.pdf>.

857 Ibid.

858 The government of the Republic of Poland. "The Republic of Poland's Position on the Application of International Law in Cyberspace - Ministry of Foreign Affairs Republic of Poland - Gov.Pl Website." Ministry of Foreign Affairs Republic of Poland, December 29, 2022. <https://www.gov.pl/web/diplomacy/the-republic-of-polands-position-on-the-application-of-international-law-in-cyberspace>.

The ICJ has established that third States *Countermeasures* or collective *Countermeasures* are prohibited in the Nicaragua case.[859] James Crawford argued that the ICJ would have reached a different conclusion if the injured State had asked for support.[860] This is however a hypothetical argument. In this context, the proponents of the new norm would have to prove that the state of international customary law has sufficiently evolved over the past 35 years to allow for them. The evidence points to collective or third-party *Countermeasures* remain only a proposal rather than a binding norm. Thus, the only forms of a lawful collective response are the actions ordained by the UN Security Council or conducted as part of a military alliance such as NATO.

The 2022 full-scale invasion of Ukraine by the Russian Federation has brought the attention of the international and scholarly community. Roman Kwiecień, for example, aptly pointed out *collective Countermeasures* could be a form of the international community's responsibility to breaches of *jus cogens*, the preemptory norms of Public International Law.[861] The pending case against Russian president Vladimir Putin in front of the International Criminal Court might shed light on the possible extent of breaches in that regard.[862] Whether this then creates additional impetus toward recognizing *collective Countermeasures* as a legal norm remains to be seen.

4.5 Conclusion

The concept of hostile cyber operations being a legitimate, lawful tool for handling inter-State relations logically stems from the fact that general principles of international law have been applied to cyberspace in their entirety

859 Case Concerning Military and Paramilitary Activities in and Against Nicaragua (Nicaragua v United States)—Merits. I.C.J Reports 14, (ICJ 1986). Paragraph 249.

860 Crawford, James. State responsibility the general part. Cambridge: Cambridge University Press, 2013. Page 704.

861 Kwiecień, Roman (2022), "Aggression and Responsibility Under International Law—A Case of the Aggression of the Russian Federation Against Ukraine." Page 201. Retrieved on November 28, 2023. <https://www.nomos-elibrary.de/10.5771/0030-6444-2022-2-201.pdf>.

862 "Situation in Ukraine: ICC Judges Issue Arrest Warrants against Vladimir Vladimirovich Putin and Maria Alekseyevna Lvova-Belova." International Criminal Court, March 17, 2023. <https://www.icc-cpi.int/news/situation-ukraine-icc-judges-issue-arrest-warrants-against-vladimir-vladimirovich-putin-and>.

following the historic UN General Assembly Resolution approving the UN GGE 2013 Report. However, the exact adaptation of existing legal rules in that regard is still uncertain, especially since there are very few cases of State practice to draw on. As cyber capabilities proliferate and more governments enter the ranks of sovereign nations with the ability to project cyber power externally, hostile cyber operations are likely to become more widespread and impactful. In such a case, the ability to distinguish the wrongful and lawful ones might become essential.

The existing framework for preclusions of wrongfulness of acts that would otherwise be prohibited applies in cyberspace. However, State practice and other sources of law, such as UN GA resolutions, point to nuanced but relevant adaptations that are developing to accommodate its unique nature. Collateral damage is much more likely in cyberspace, which relies mostly on dual-use private civilian infrastructure. Additionally, the fungible nature of data flows in cyberspace means that inadvertently affecting non-military targets is much more likely compared to the realm of conventional operations. Instead of outright prohibiting lawful cyber hostile acts, the State practice appears to be evolving toward applying harsher standards of necessity and proportionality in that regard. The standards are well established requirements for lawfulness of *Countermeasures* and *Self-defense.* Applying a higher standard in that regard to cyber acts limits the scope of what operations can be pursued by States without becoming wrongful. When assessing the severity of hostile cyber operations, special attention is bestowed on critical infrastructure. It is the most likely target of both prohibited hostile cyber acts as well as potential retributive ones due its digital connectedness that raises exposure and vulnerability coupled with the scale of negative impact that targeting it might cause.

The instantons and clandestine nature of hostile cyber acts led some States and scholars to advocate for modifying some of the requirements for *Countermeasures,* specifically the mandatory notification preceding a cyber response and prohibition of targeting of non-State actors. The notification aspect is related to the fact that time is of essence in cyber operations and knowing ahead of time of their coming might completely neutralize them. That is why some States argue that *Urgent Countermeasures,* which do not require a prior notification, are more befitting of the cyber context. This norm was developed in the conventional realm to capture exceptional cases, but it could be expanded in the future to become the default type of *Countermeasures* in cyberspace.

Another point of divergence between the broader conventional realm and cyberspace is the treatment of non-State actors. The nature of cyberspace creates a situation of plausible deniability for States. They can order non-State groups of hackers to conduct hostile cyber acts without assuming responsibility. Some States and scholars argue for a looser standard of proving attribution that would allow for easier deployment of lawful responses. Whether that will become a binding standard is still unclear but, in the meantime, many States, when being targeted by a hostile cyber operation, decide to limit their official response to *Retorsion* acts while possibly pursuing ways of hacking back behind the scenes.

Proposed new ways of responding to being targeted by hostile cyber acts are a source of controversy. A cyber *Humanitarian Intervention*, is a concept that never took enough root to be considered a legal norm. The same is the case with *Responsibility to Protect* and collective *Countermeasures.* While they have not yet become binding norms of Public International Law (nor is it certain that they ever will), they reflect *opinio juris* of a large segment of States, which strive to develop new types of tools that would effectively respond to cyber era challenges. Overall, the existing framework of *Public International Law* is slowly expanding and adjusting its ways to accommodate the specific characteristics of cyberspace, albeit at a pace that is slower than technological progress of cyberspace itself.

CHAPTER 5

Jurisdiction and attribution of hostile cyber operations in Public International Law

5.1 Introduction

A growing volume of international hostile cyber incidents over the past few years indicates that development of clear legal rules on State accountability in that area is urgently needed. However, attempts at transposition of the model for delineating State jurisdiction and attributing *Internationally Wrongful Acts*, developed in the conventional realm, create a series of challenges that make it dysfunctional in this novel realm. In fact, at present, most States avoid pursuing formal international legal paths for restoring their rights wronged by hostile cyber operations. This is a strong indication that the public international legal attributive system in cyberspace is still at an early stage of development with a long way to go before it becomes fit for purpose.

One of the reasons for the inadequacy of existing legal tools for identifying jurisdiction over and attribution of hostile cyber operations of States lies in the structural characteristics of the internet infrastructure. The ease with which actions can be concealed and routed through the internet infrastructure of third States creates a scope for plausible deniability on the part of offending States. The international community has adapted to this reality by developing an approach of different types of attribution, with varying legal impacts, that help them navigate this context. That State practice and its consequences for the system of Public International Law are discussed in Section 5.2.

One of the notoriously difficult elements of the legal proceedings before an international judiciary body is amassing a sufficient amount of evidence on the part of the injured State. This challenge is dramatically compounded in cyberspace, where much of the activity leaves no physical trace and recovering and analyzing most evidence requires a high degree of sophisticated IT expertise. The fact that hostile cyber acts can be routed via a string of States only adds to the difficulty as evidence gathering requires a high level of international cooperation. All these facts have an impact on the emerging consensus as to how the rules regulating the burden of proof and evidence should be applied in cyberspace. This aspect is the focus of Section 5.3.

Another dimension of the debate on attribution in Public International Law is the question of non-State actors acting either as organs of a State or under their effective control. The system of Public International Law has developed rules and practices geared toward ensuring accountability of States for their proxies, many of them being heritage of the Cold War era conflicts. However, those rules never reached a satisfying level of effectiveness and are currently put to a test in the cyber context. The unique nature of hacker groups, which are usually behind State-sponsored hostile cyber acts, has led to a reconceptualization of those rules. The current shape of that evolution is presented in Section 5.4.

The questions of attribution and jurisdiction in Public International Law are in a complex relationship. Wielding the ultimate jurisdiction is one of the pillars of State sovereignty, as conceptualized in the Peace of Westphalia Treaty of 1648, which in many aspects is foundational to the existing system of international law. Cyberspace escapes the traditional framing of jurisdiction, accelerating the process of de-territorialization of jurisdiction and presenting a slew of challenges when it comes to classifying global data flows happening at all times via physical ICT infrastructure located within sovereign territory. There exist proposals on how to capture the nature of cyberspace by analogy with existing models, such as that of vessels in territorial models or exterritoriality of certain areas. Some scholars call for an absolutist approach of extending States' jurisdiction onto every single data flow utilizing physical infrastructure within their territory. However, none of these approaches fully solves all the legal challenges posed by the nature of cyberspace, forcing the international community to shift its focus toward a hybrid legal model of State jurisdiction for cyberspace. This process is analyzed in Section 5.5.

The UN GGE Report of 2015 introduced the notion of a voluntary non-binding norm of *Due Diligence* in cyberspace. The norm would imply a duty of a State hosting physical ICT infrastructure that is part of the global internet system (which describes essentially every single State on the planet) to monitor its network and prevent the most abusive excesses against public international legal rights of third States utilizing said network that could take place. The norm is present within other branches of Public International Law, such as humanitarian law, where it enjoys the binding status. Introducing such a norm in cyberspace would put pressure on underdeveloped States that have fewer cyber capabilities to monitor for and prevent international hostile cyber operations. Nevertheless, the efforts to transform the norm into a binding one in the cyber context proceed. This complex subject is at the center of Section 5.6.

Finally, Section 5.7 focuses on the existing proposals to establish an international body that would facilitate legal and technical attribution in cyberspace. Such an organization would serve to level the playing field between States possessing varying degrees of sophisticated ICT capacity. It would also foster international cooperation on the subject and act as a discouragement to any potential offending States. There are various legal models that have been proposed although none of them has entered the path toward actually being established. Nevertheless, the potential magnitude of creation of such a body justifies analysis of the possible legal consequences.

5.2 State practice on legal attribution of hostile cyber operations perpetrated by other States

5.2.1 Reasons for differential practice on attribution in cyberspace

5.2.1.1 Technical challenges to attributing hostile cyber operations to a State

The dynamics of attributing a hostile cyber operation present a significant departure from the equivalent process for conventional operations in the international legal system. There is neither a clear legal procedure nor an established body of State practice that would provide consistent guidelines for governments on how to respond to a hostile cyber operation conducted by another State. Disparate and often secretive ways of handling cyber threats across States lends itself to an impression of a legal area at an early stage of its development where various approaches are still being tested.

The state of flux is to a large extent caused by the unique features of cyberspace that set it apart from the conventional realm in which the framework of Public International Law has developed. These unique circumstances that make attributing international cyber operations much more difficult than it is the case with conventional ones, are summarized in Table 4.

Table 4. Key differences between cyber operations and conventional ones making attribution of the former more difficult

Feature	Cyber operations	Conventional operations
National boundaries	De-territorialized, unclear, and overlapping	Physically manifest
Geographic distance	Irrelevant	Relevant
Non-State actors	High degree of operational capacity	Low to medium degree of operational capacity
Overlap between civilian and military realms	Operational theaters inseparable from civilian spaces and infrastructure	Operational theaters are separable from civilian spaces and infrastructure to a large degree
Visibility of operations	Operations can be conducted in a more clandestine way and with delayed impact	States maintain ability to physically observe the operations to a large extent
Clarity regarding the threshold of wrongfulness	Lack of clarity about the character and extent of an ongoing operation	The character and extent difficult to discern but less so than in the cyber context
Balance of power across States	Offensive and defensive capabilities asymmetrical across States	Offensive and defensive capabilities mostly balanced between main adversaries

Source: Own elaboration

All the factors that make attribution of cyber operations difficult lend themselves to an amplified challenge of *plausible deniability* in cyberspace. Compared with conventional operations, it is easier for an aggressor State to perpetrate an internationally wrongful act in cyberspace without getting caught while it is much harder for a victim State to muster technical and legal evidence that would unequivocally prove who has done it.[863] It is also much easier to perpetrate a hostile cyber operation than it is to prepare all the IT systems in a country for a potential assault.

5.2.1.2 Anonymity in cyberspace

Among many differences between conventional and cyber operations done by one State against another, one stands out as an especially challenging aspect. It is the fact that it is relatively easy to route hostile operations through infrastructure of third States and private servers, a maneuver that can last as shortly as a fraction of a second, which greatly amplifies the difficulty of technical and legal attribution to the original perpetrator.[864] Ambiguity shrouding the attribution issue has led some international legal scholars to suggest that the standards for evidence substantiating the attribution should be lowered in the cyber area as a systemic exception.[865] For the time being however, no exception norm has developed in that area, meaning that cyber operations need to meet the same high standards of proof as conventional operations, which, as this chapter demonstrates, proves to be challenging. Joel Brenner described it the following way: *The internet is one big masquerade ball. You can hide behind aliases, you can hide behind proxy servers, and you can surreptitiously enslave other computers to do your dirty work.*[866]

Anonymity granted by cyberspace is neither absolute nor objective. Most hostile cyber operations perpetrated by States are technically traceable. It is the question of effort and capabilities whether a victim State is able to actually prove this link. The ability to muster required capabilities in turn varies between States with some of the most developed economies being in

---

863 Koh, Harold H. (2012, September 18). International Law in Cyberspace. U.S. Department of State. Retrieved February 15, 2022, from <https://2009-2017.state.gov/s/l/releases/remarks/197924.htm>.

864 Finnemore, Martha, and Hollis, Duncan B. (2020). Beyond Naming and Shaming: Accusations and International Law in Cybersecurity. European Journal of International Law, 31(3), Pages 969–1003. <https://doi.org/10.1093/ejil/chaa056>.

865 Lin, Herbert. (2011). Responding to Sub-Threshold Cyber Intrusions: A Fertile Topic for Research and Discussion. Georgetown University Press, 2011, Pages 127–135.

866 Brenner, Joel. (2011). America the Vulnerable: Inside the New Threat Matrix of Digital Espionage, Crime, and Warfare. Penguin Press. Page 32;

Ohlin, Jens David, Kevin Govern, and Claire Oakes Finkelstein. Cyberwar: Law and ethics for virtual conflicts. Oxford: Oxford University Press, 2015. Page 215.

a much better position than States with modest means at their disposal.[867] Therefore anonymity of perpetrators of hostile cyber operations against States in cyberspace can be understood in a twofold manner:

- Objective anonymity, achieved when an operation is truly untraceable;
- Effective anonymity, when establishing the source is impossible given available capabilities.

The challenge of attribution and proving a causal link is a recurring theme in Public International as showcased by ICJ rulings such as the 2005 Congo v. Uganda Case Judgment[868] or the famous 1986 Armed Activities in Nicaragua Judgment.[869] The problem is exponentially compounded in cyberspace. Problematically, none of the diverse rights of an injured State can be invoked against the perpetrating State if the attribute link has not been proved. Hostile States are aware of that, setting up an elaborate network on non-State actors and third-State rerouting of cyber operations to exploit this weakness.

The degree of anonymity in cyberspace is raised by the way the system has been established and operated. The United States as the birthplace of the internet has arguably the highest capability of attributing hostile cyber actions to perpetrator States. After all, most root servers, as well as the ICANN organization, are located in the United States[870] and the Edward Snowden affair revealed that the scope of insight into global data flows by the U.S. government might be actually near-total.[871] The State however has no incentive to democratize this access or publicize its full scale, leaving other States vulnerable to unattributed hostile cyber operations.

---

867 Loshin, Peter. Practical anonymity hiding in plain sight online. Syngress, 2013. Page 10.

868 Armed Activities on the Territory of the Congo (Democratic Republic of the Congo v. Uganda)— Judgment. International Court of Justice. ICJ Reports 2005. (2005, December 19). Retrieved February 17, 2022, from <https://www.icj-cij.org/en/case/116>.

869 Case Concerning Military and Paramilitary Activities in and Against Nicaragua, Nicaragua v United States. International Court of Justice. I.C.J Reports 14, ICGJ 112 (ICJ 1986). (1986). Retrieved February 15, 2022, from <https://www.icj-cij.org/en/case/70/judgments>.

870 See Section II.3.2—"Establishment of the unique international system regulating the internet" for an in-depth analysis of the subject.

871 Ibid.

Lastly, the dearth of public cases of legal attribution to States of hostile cyber operations is stunting development of cyber rules as a separate branch of Public International Law or development of relevant State practice on the matter in general. The challenge of anonymity then creates a series of challenges that require addressing, possibly via a new treaty on cyberspace.[872]

5.2.1.3 Legal and political challenges to attributing hostile cyber operations to a State

Beyond technical constraints, there are several reasons why States find themselves unable or unwilling to publicly and legally attribute a hostile cyber operation to the perpetrator State. These include:

- States' reluctance to reveal their domestic systems' vulnerabilities;
- Avoidance of escalation;
- Inability to achieve redress or to retaliate;
- Lack of confidence in Public International Law as an effective too to address the problem;
- Conflicting internal interests.

Reluctance to reveal their domestic systems' vulnerabilities

Prevalence of the first motive, reluctance to reveal systems' vulnerabilities, will never be fully disclosed by affected States. This is because many victim governments are strongly incentivized to keep the occurrence of a hostile cyber operation against them confidential. Existence of weak spots in their national critical infrastructure or public IT systems might attract other assailants and also reflect negatively on a government's reputation both externally and internally. Oftentimes governments take time, months or even years, after an assault, to make sure that the exploited vulnerabilities are first fixed. That was the case with the 2018 FASTCash breach in Chile, which was perpetrated by a hacker group called Apt38, physically located at

[872] See Section II.5—"Future evolution of the international legal framework regulating cyberspace" for an analysis of this aspect.

government facilities in Pyongyang, North Korea.[873] While the assault has been geared solely toward material benefits, due to its cross-border character and the perpetrators' association with a foreign government, it qualified as an international cyber operation. During the breach, the hackers tried to steal large amounts of money from a Chilean bank. Despite identifying and foiling the attack, the Chilean government chose to spend the next few months strengthening the country's security systems before acknowledging publicly that an assault had happened.

Avoidance of escalation

Avoidance of escalation is another factor considered by governments. The geopolitical context might not permit a smaller State to call out a larger one that is perpetrating hostile cyber operations. It might also choose to reveal some attacks while concealing others. For instance, in 2018 a virus called *Olympic Destroyer* permeated Winter Olympic Games facilities in South Korea. The malware was designed to shut down the Wi-Fi systems at sports venues, the ticketing portal and communication systems servicing Olympic events. It was scheduled to go off exactly at the start of the opening ceremony in Seoul. The crisis was narrowly averted due an almost accidental discovery of a Wi-Fi malfunction shortly before that time. The United States government and a private cybersecurity company Crowdstrike soon identified a Russian GRU-affiliated group Sandworm as the source of the attack.[874] However, the government of the Republic of Korea chose to remain quiet on the subject, possibly due to a complex geopolitical context and its role as the host of Olympic Games that were still taking place.[875]

---

873 Caesar, Ed. (2021, April 19). The Incredible Rise of North Korea's Hacking Army. The New Yorker. <https://www.newyorker.com/magazine/2021/04/26/the-incredible-rise-of-north-koreas-hacking-army>.

874 Nakashima, Ellen. (2018, February 25). Russian spies hacked the Olympics and tried to make it look like North Korea did it, U.S. officials say. Washington Post. <https://www.washingtonpost.com/world/national-security/russian-spies-hacked-the-olympics-and-tried-to-make-it-look-like-north-korea-did-it-us-officials-say/2018/02/24/44b5468e-18f2-11e8-92c9-376b4fe57ff7_story.html>.

875 Greenberg, Andrew. (2019b, October 17). Inside Olympic Destroyer, the Most Deceptive Hack in History. Wired. <https://www.wired.com/story/untold-story-2018-olympics-destroyer-cyberattack/>.

Inability to achieve redress or to retaliate

Technical inability to retaliate or even identify the source of attack can disincentivize governments from attributing a hostile cyber operation. As presented in Figure 4. Only a handful of countries, between five and eight, have managed to develop profound cyber capabilities. Most of the world's nations lack the ability to effectively attribute a cyber assault even if they wanted to. In such a situation, revealing an intrusion would only create an impression of powerlessness. J. Goldsmith and S. Russell explained in the following way: *Unless a nation is able to effectively redress a cyber intrusion, it can be harmful or self-defeating to publicize it, since public knowledge of loss and the failure to respond effectively invite more attacks.*[876] Summarizing one of the UN GGE rounds in 2017, Michael Schmitt and Liis Vihul confirmed that impression, noting that *some States, such as Cuba, lack the technical wherewithal of more advanced States to reliably attribute hostile cyber operations and therefore will be less able to establish the necessary basis for resorting to self-defense or taking countermeasures.*[877]

Lack of confidence in Public International Law as an effective too to address the problem

Weakness of the international legal framework in cyberspace is another consideration. D. Efrony and Y. Shany note that the current body of international norms and customs concerning cyber operations is too weak and underdeveloped to lend any enforceability to victim States.[878] There are no cyber operations-related ICJ rulings that would link cyber delicts with specific laws. Neither is there a strong international consensus on the Voluntary Non-Binding Norms issued by the UN. Only recently did a slow process of forming *opinio juris* around their status as binding international norms

876 Hoover Institution. (2018). Strengths Become Vulnerabilities—How a Digital World Disadvantages the United States in Its International Relations (Aegis Series Paper No. 1806). <https://www.hoover.org/sites/default/files/research/docs/381100534-strengths-become-vulnerabilities.pdf>.

877 Schmitt, Michael, and Vihul, Liis. (2017, June 30). International Cyber Law Politicized: The UN GGE's Failure to Advance Cyber Norms. Just Security. <https://www.justsecurity.org/42768/international-cyber-law-politicized-gges-failure-advance-cyber-norms/>.

878 Efrony, Dan, and Shany, Yuval. (2018). A Rule Book on the Shelf? Tallinn Manual 2.0 on Cyberoperations and Subsequent State Practice. American Journal of International Law, 112(4), pages 583–657. <https://doi.org/10.1017/ajil.2018.86>.

started. In principle, State behavior, which is not explicitly forbidden by international laws and norms is legal. At present, this general principle places most hostile cyber operations closer to espionage (lawful) than a conventional physical attack against another State (prohibited).[879] This uncertainty makes international law a tool that might not be fit for the purpose of achieving a redress to an internationally wrongful act in cyberspace.

Conflicting internal interests

Finally, governments with high cyber capabilities might prefer to keep attacks they experience secret. States with the best cyber capabilities retain both defensive and offensive tools and oftentimes prefer to maintain the current state of international legal uncertainty that allows them to conduct their own external cyber operations.[880] Kubo Mačák described this situation as a *Glass house dilemma*[881] that makes some of the most powerful countries, such as the United States and United Kingdom, torn between different legal and political stances on the subject, sometimes leading to inconsistent behavior.[882] The United States' muted response to the 2014 Sony hack can be construed in these terms.

Should States become more comfortable with calling out international hostile cyber operations by other States, it could accelerate a drive toward a more regulated and effective legal framework on cyberspace. First, it would provide a volume of legal case studies that could help clarify application of legal terms in cyberspace. Second, it could create a stronger sense of urgency for the international community to address the growing phenomenon. For the time being however, such a change of dynamic has not happened yet.

---

879 Navarrete Inaki Mr., & Buchan, Russell. (2019). Out of the Legal Wilderness: Peacetime Espionage, International Law and the Existence of Customary Exceptions. Cornell International Law Journal, 51(4), pages 897–953. <https://scholarship.law.cornell.edu/cilj/vol51/iss4/4/.>; Sander, Barrie. (2019). The Sound of Silence: International Law and the Governance of Peacetime Cyber Operations. Pages 1–21.

880 Ibid.

881 Mačák, Kubo. (2019). On the Shelf, But Close at Hand: The Contribution of Non-State Initiatives to International Cyber Law. AJIL Unbound, 113, 81–86. <https://doi.org/10.1017/aju.2019.8>.

882 Sander, Barrie. (2019). The Sound of Silence: International Law and the Governance of Peacetime Cyber Operations. Pages 1–21.

5.2.2 Results of differential practice on attribution in cyberspace

5.2.2.1 Policy of ambiguity and plausible deniability

State practice so far suggests that most governments prefer to maintain the policy of ambiguity and plausible deniability, even if they are on the receiving end of cyber assaults. Whether a State publicly attributes a cyber assault to a specific actor, especially another State, is a result of a combination of technical and political factors. The main four levels of State response to an international cyber assault that have developed can be summarized as follows:

- Remain silent and neither call out the potential perpetrator nor even reveal the fact that an international cyber assault has occurred;
- Reveal the fact that an operation has occurred but remain silent or vague as to who might have conducted it or whether any countermeasures were taken;
- Reveal the cyber operation and attribute it to the potential perpetrator but remain silent or vague as to whether any specific international legal regulation was breached;
- Formal attribution: reveal the hostile cyber operation and publicly attribute it to another State invoking obligations and norms of the international law that have been violated.

The four kinds of response listed are ordered from the one requiring the least evidence on the part of the victim State to the one necessitating profound and exhaustive evidence.

While there is no exact data on the first type of response (since by definition all the details are kept secret in such a case), there exist clues that it is a very common policy among States.[883] Among the publicized cases of international hostile cyber operations, the next type of response, acknowledging an assault but stopping short of doing or saying anything else, is the most widespread. The least utilized type of response is one that combines acknowledging

883 Sander, Barrie. (2019). The Sound of Silence: International Law and the Governance of Peacetime Cyber Operations. Pages 1–21.

occurrence of an operation, an official attribution, and evidence facilitating the claim, which could be considered a proper attribution.

5.2.2.2 Types of attribution of hostile cyber operations utilized by States

Of the four main types of possible State responses to a hostile cyber operation, a formal attribution is the legally most consequential one and at the same time the one least frequently invoked by States. It is important to emphasize that a technical and legal attribution take place concurrently in principle. This is because invoking specific norms of international law allegedly breached by another State requires presenting at least an outline of evidence facilitating such an accusation. Political, technical, and legal attribution are oftentimes conflated in the public discourse on hostile cyber operations. It is important that only the legal attribution has formal consequences in Public International Law, with the political one being in the gray zone, its status uncertain from the legal perspective.

Nevertheless, for a variety of reasons described in this section, this type of response is usually shunned by governments. The few cases when they did include an attribution made in 2018 by the United Kingdom, when London accused the Russian Federation of *reckless campaign of cyber assaults* by GRU, leading to *flagrant violation of international law.*[884] The announcement was made in coordination with Canada and Ukraine, two countries also targeted by Russian hostile cyber operations, which purportedly aimed to disrupt work done by the World Anti-Doping Agency in Montreal, and the transport oversight systems in Kyiv respectively. Attribution was facilitated by technical analysis delivered by the U.K. National Cyber Security Centre. This however remains an exception from the norm. Usually, States stop short of formally attributing a hostile cyber operation, option instead for a softer response. The types of attribution made by States can be categorized into: political, technical, and legal one as summarized by Table 5.

---

[884] The government of United Kingdom. (n.d.). Reckless campaign of cyber attacks by Russian military intelligence service exposed. United Kingdom National Cyber Security Center. Retrieved February 15, 2022, from <https://www.ncsc.gov.uk/news/reckless-campaign-cyber-attacks-russian-military-intelligence-service-exposed>.

Table 5. Categories of responses to a cyber assault and their attributive elements

Elements Response	Official acknowledgment of a cyber assault	Political attribution	Technical attribution	Legal attribution
Complete silence	×	×	×	×
Acknowledgment of the assault only	✓	×	×	×
Attribution purporting the responsible State	✓	✓	×	×
Full attribution carrying both political and legal impact	✓	✓	✓	✓

Source: Own elaboration

5.2.2.3 Case Study—Shamoon operation against Saudi Arabia and Qatar between 2012 and 2018

A good example of States remaining quiet in reaction to a cyber operation is the response to the Shamoon virus in 2012. The malware was deployed between 2012 and 2018 against a slew of public and private targets in Saudi Arabia and Qatar. The malware was uniquely designed to disrupt the State-owned oil conglomerates Saudi Aramco Qatar's RasGas.[885] However, despite widespread suspicion that the Islamic Republic of Iran was the actor responsible for the assault, the international nature of the attack was never even publicly acknowledged by the targeted States.[886] All the insights regarding the operations are a result of leaks and activity of private companies engaged in the field of cyber security.

885 British Broadcasting Corporation. (2012a, August 17). Shamoon virus targets energy sector infrastructure. BBC News. "Shamoon Virus Targets Energy Sector Infrastructure." BBC News, August 17, 2012. <https://www.bbc.com/news/technology-19293797>.

886 Sander, Barrie. (2019). The Sound of Silence: International Law and the Governance of Peacetime Cyber Operations. Pages 1–21.

5.2.2.4 Case Study—Cyber assault on the U.S. civil service in 2014

The 2014 cyber assault on the U.S. Office of Personnel Management fits well into the second category of responses—operations that were acknowledged by the targeted State without a formal attribution being made. At the time, an international cyber assault from Chinese IP addresses led to 22.1 million confidential government records being copied by hackers. The assault disrupted functioning of the office and put a large number of individuals at risk of their sensitive personal information being abused. The operation was dubbed the biggest data breach in history.[887] Several sources pointed to a clear connection between the perpetrators and the Chinese government.[888] Despite this, no formal attribution was ever made, although a number of U.S. officials privately expressed their being very impressed by the Chinese cyber operation.[889]

5.2.2.5 Case Study—Wannacry ransomware and disruption of public health services in 2017

Response to the 2017 WannaCry ransomware assault fits the third category—attacks that get acknowledged and publicly attributed to a potential perpetrator country, but for which the affected countries raise no specific international legal regulation or norms that were purportedly breached. At the time, around 300,000 computers in more than 150 countries had their files encrypted overnight by a malicious virus that required a Bitcoin-based payment to release them back.[890] The total damages due to function disruption

887 Hackett, Robert. (2015, June 13). A product demo may have revealed what could be the biggest ever government data breach. Fortune. <https://www.govinfo.gov/content/pkg/CHRG-114hhrg99659/html/CHRG-114hhrg99659.htm>.

888 Fruhlinger, Josh. (2020, February 12). The OPM hack explained: Bad security practices meet China's Captain America. CSO Online. Retrieved February 15, 2022, from <https://www.csoonline.com/article/3318238/the-opm-hack-explained-bad-security-practices-meet-chinas-captain-america.html>; Graff, Garrett. M. (2020, February 11). China's Hacking Spree Will Have a Decades-Long Fallout. Wired. <https://www.wired.com/story/china-equifax-anthem-marriott-opm-hacks-data/>.

889 Pepitone, Julianne (2015, June 25). China Is "Leading Suspect" in OPM Hacks, Says Intelligence Chief James Clapper. NBC News. <https://www.nbcnews.com/tech/security/clapper-china-leading-suspect-opm-hack-n381881>.

890 British Broadcasting Corporation. (2017, December 19). Cyber-attack: US and UK blame North Korea for WannaCry. BBC News. <https://www.bbc.com/news/world-us-canada-42407488>.

and ransom payments are estimated to be billions of U.S. dollars.[891] The virus attacked indiscriminately, infecting personal computers, companies, as well as public sector providers.

That latter group of victims created a social pressure on affected governments to treat the crisis as an international issue, seeking to identify the responsible state. The country with public services most disrupted by WannaCry was the United Kingdom. On May 12, 2017 (the initial day of the attack), National Health Service (NHS) was forced to turn away non-critical emergencies and a number of ambulances had to be diverted.[892]

In October 2017, the United Kingdom government issued a statement accusing North Korea of perpetrating the hostile cyber operations against it.[893] Public attribution of the hostile operations to North Korea followed a thorough technical analysis. Two months later, it was followed by similar assertions by the United States, Australia, Canada, New Zealand, and Japan.[894] Private technological companies targeted by the ransomware, Google and Microsoft, lent their technical credence to amplify this conclusion with their own communiques.[895]

---

891 Whittaker, Zack. (2019, May 12). TechCrunch is part of the Yahoo family of brands. TechCrunch. <https://techcrunch.com/2019/05/12/wannacry-two-years-on/>.

892 British Broadcasting Corporation. (2017a, May 13). NHS cyber-attack: GPs and hospitals hit by ransomware. BBC News. <https://www.bbc.com/news/health-39899646>; Wong, Julia C., and Solon, Olivia. (2017, November 28). Massive ransomware cyber-attack hits nearly 100 countries around the world. The Guardian. <https://www.theguardian.com/technology/2017/may/12/global-cyber-attack-ransomware-nsa-uk-nhs>.

893 Withnall, Adam. (2017, October 27). British security minister says North Korea was behind WannaCry hack on NHS. The Independent. <https://www.independent.co.uk/news/uk/home-news/wannacry-malware-hack-nhs-report-cybercrime-north-korea-uk-ben-wallace-a8022491.html>.

894 Korea, M. U. S. (2017, December 21). Press Briefing on the Attribution of the WannaCry Malware Attack to North Korea. U.S. Embassy & Consulate in the Republic of Korea. Retrieved February 15, 2022, from <https://kr.usembassy.gov/121917-press-briefing-attribution-wannacry-malware-attack-north-korea/>.

895 Hills, Joel. (2017, October 13). North Korean government behind NHS cyber attack, says Microsoft boss. iTV. <https://www.itv.com/news/2017-10-13/hacking-threat-is-as-serious-as-terrorism-says-microsoft-boss>; Smith, Brad. (2017, May 14). The need for urgent collective action to keep people safe online: Lessons from last week's cyberattack. Microsoft. Retrieved February 15, 2022, from <https://blogs.microsoft.com/on-the-issues/2017/05/14/need-urgent-collective-action-keep-people-safe-online-lessons-last-weeks-cyberattack/#Idi5LfUGG87joatu.99>.

However, none of these actors invoked any specific rules or norms that would have been purportedly breached by WannaCry. The United Kingdom only went as far as to conclude its statement saying that *international law applies online as it does offline*. The United States did mention international law at all in its release. Following the events, cybersecurity companies Kaspersky Lab and Symantec were quick to identify the hackers behind the attack—the so-called Lazarus Group, which is hosted by the North Korean Reconnaissance General Bureau in Pyongyang.[896] This diplomatic reaction that shied away from engaging with the international legal framework was actually consistent with the response to an earlier attack attributed to the same hacking group—the Sony attack 2014, mentioned earlier. At the time, President Barack Obama referred to North Korean activities as *an act of cyber vandalism*, a statement with no direct international legal implications.[897]

5.2.2.6 Case Study—Pager explosion attack in Lebanon in 2024

Israel and Lebanon have been at the formal state of war since the former State's founding in 1948. The following decades have been punctuated by a series of conflicts, additionally complicated by a civil war in Lebanon and the rise of an Iran-sponsored State-like military organization named Hezbollah. The organization's base is the Shia-Muslim sector of the Lebanese society, and its stated goal is destruction of Israel. It practically controls the southern part of Lebanon, serving as the *de facto* State structure, and regularly clashes with the Israeli Army. Following the commencement of the Hamas–Israel war on October 7, 2023, Hezbollah launched a series of deadly rockets toward Israel, averaging more than 700 a month. The attacks resulted in killing of 52 Israeli citizens (25 soldiers and 27 civilians), including 12 children during the July 27, 2024 Majdal Shams attack. 60,000 Israeli civilians were forcibly relocated away from the border due to safety concerns. This was followed by intensification of missile assaults. In August 2024 alone, around 1,300

---

[896] Solon, Olivia. (2017, September 5). WannaCry ransomware has links to North Korea, cybersecurity experts say. The Guardian. <https://www.theguardian.com/technology/2017/may/15/wannacry-ransomware-north-korea-lazarus-group>.

[897] Holland, Steve., & Chiacu, Doina. (2014, December 22). Obama says Sony hack not an act of war. Reuters. <https://www.reuters.com/article/us-sony-cybersecurity-usa/obama-says-sony-hack-not-an-act-of-war-idUSKBN0JX1MH20141222>.

rockets were launched by Hezbollah. Israel responded with counterattacks, killing 564 people in Lebanon, including 133 civilians.[898]

As part of the escalation, on September 17 and 18, 2024, Israel executed a targeted cyber operation aimed at Hezbollah operatives, which they dubbed "Grim Beeper." On September 17, around 5,000 pagers procured by the organization for its members exploded simultaneously (the same happened with their walkie-talkies a day later). According to Hezbollah, 1,500 of their fighters lost their combat ability due to injuries, while sources close to Israel put the number at nearly 3,000. The Lebanese government reported that 42 people perished in the attack, including 12 civilians. One of the killed was the ambassador of Iran to Lebanon. Most of the injuries involved loss of eyes and fingers, as the explosion was triggered by the operatives opening a message, set by the Israeli Army to trigger the explosion. This was followed by Israeli assassination of Hezbollah's leader Hassan Nasrallah on September 27 and a ceasefire between the two belligerents signed on November 27, 2024.[899]

This impressive operation was made possible by Israel setting up a shell company in Hungary selling Taiwanese pagers via a complex scheme geared toward obscuring the Israeli connection. The Israeli Army was able to modify the devices, introducing combustible materials that were not easily noticeable, turning the pagers (and separately walkie-talkies) into remotely detonated bombs. The company, named BAC, was able to secure a bid to procure the pagers to Hezbollah at market rates. In fact, Israel even made profit by selling them to the Lebanese organization.[900]

---

898 "Lebanon: Flash Update #25—Escalation of hostilities in South Lebanon, as of 23 August 2024 – Lebanon." United Nations Office for the Coordination of Humanitarian Affairs. 27 August 2024. Archived from the original on 23 September 2024. Retrieved 27 August 2024. <https://web.archive.org/web/20240923020751/https://reliefweb.int/report/lebanon/lebanon-flash-update-25-escalation-hostilities-south-lebanon-23-august-2024>

899 Seddon, Max; Kynge, James; Rathbone, John Paul (28 December 2024). "How Israel's 'Operation Grim Beeper' rattled global spy chiefs." Financial Times. Retrieved 28 December 2024. <https://www.ft.com/content/f578b6c0-d534-4a04-ae25-3b97d11b6e71>

900 "What was Hungarian company's role in manufacturing pagers that exploded in Lebanon?". Euronews. 18 September 2024. Archived from the original on 19 September 2024. Retrieved 23 September 2024. <https://www.euronews.com/2024/09/18/dozens-of-hezbollah-members-wounded-in-lebanon-by-exploding-pagers>.

A number of legal scholars raised their concern about potential unlawfulness of the operation. Most notably, a group of UN experts, gathered by the UN Office of the High Commissioner on Human Rights (UN OHCHR) released a joint statement in that vein.[901] This sentiment was echoed by Amnesty International,[902] Research Society of International Law,[903] and the European Journal of International Law.[904] However, there has been at least an equal number of experts weighing in in favor of the operation being lawful in international law.[905] Below is a structured list of the main problematic aspects of the operation and their assessment from the perspective of public international law:

Israel's use of force inside of Lebanon

The debate over the attribution of actions of non-State actors to their host States has been one of the focal points of the debate among international law scholars even since the 9/11 2001 terrorist attacks. So far it has proven inconclusive.[906] However, in the case of Hezbollah, its actions can be attributed to the government of Lebanon since it is a part of it and Lebanon has had a track record of claiming Hezbolalh's actions as attributable to it.[907] Since the two States are formally at war and Hezbollah had been attacking Israel with missile barrages and artillery shellings for almost a year in the build-up to the cyber operation, it appears to fulfill the criteria for being an act of self-defense.[908]

---

[901] <https://www.ohchr.org/en/press-releases/2024/09/exploding-pagers-and-radios-terrifying-violation-international-law-say-un#:~:text=A%20booby%2Dtrap%20is%20a,and%20justice%2C%E2%80%9D%20they%20said>.

[902] <https://www.amnesty.org.uk/press-releases/lebanon-pager-attacks-bear-hallmarks-sinister-dystopian-nightmare-witness>

[903] <https://rsilpak.org/2024/battery-anxiety-cyber-attacks-with-kinetic-effect-and-international-humanitarian-law/>

[904] <https://www.ejiltalk.org/were-the-israeli-pager-and-walkie-talkie-attacks-on-hezbollah-indiscriminate/>

[905] <https://www.justsecurity.org/108719/israel-pager-operation-hezbollah/>

[906] <https://opiniojuris.org/2015/02/17/unable-unwilling-test-unstoppable-scholarly-imagination/>

[907] <https://crsreports.congress.gov/product/pdf/IF/IF10703>; <https://www.chathamhouse.org/2021/06/how-hezbollah-holds-sway-over-lebanese-state/05-influence-over-military-and-security>

[908] <https://lieber.westpoint.edu/well-it-depends-explosive-pagers-attack-revisited/>

Distinction

When using force in another country, even in the context of a war, every actor of international law must distinguish in its actions between active militants ("direct participants in hostilities"), who are legitimate targets and civilians, who must not be targeted. Article 52(2) of the First Additional Protocol to the Geneva Conventions, itself reflecting a customary norm, states that attacks can only be directed at miliary targets: "those objects which by their nature, location, purpose or use make an effective contribution to military action and whose total or partial destruction, capture or neutralization, in the circumstances ruling at the time, offers a definite military advantage."[909] From that perspective, Israel made a clear distinction between Hezbollah operatives and anyone else. Pagers were bought by Hezbollah for military purposes and only distributed to its operatives. Small amount of the explosive material ensured that the risk of indiscriminate damage on the part of civilians was minimal. In fact, there exists ample CCTV footage showing that while operatives were impacts doing groceries, people in the same shop were not impacted at all.

Proportionality & precautions

Any use of force is subject to the test of proportionality. At its core, it is a probabilistic assessment of whether the expected harm to civilians and civilian objects from an attack would be excessive in relation to the gained direct military advantage. What matters is also whether the attacking party took precautions to minimize whatever collateral damage among civilians might take place. The very high militant-to-civilian injury ratio, the very high maiming-to-killing ratio, and a minimal overall death toll imply this was an incisive, proportionate operation. In fact, hardly any modern military operation even comes close in terms of the strategic impact coupled with minimal collateral civilian damage. 12 killed civilians compared to 1,500–3,000 Hezbollah operatives taken out of action imply a ratio of 188 militants to one civilian.

---

909 Article 52(2) of the First Additional Protocol to the Geneva Conventions

Prohibition of "booby traps"

The Amended Protocol II of the Convention on Certain Conventional Weapons[910] (to which both Israel and Lebanon are parties) describes a booby trap in Article 7(2) as a device or material which is designed, constructed, or adapted to kill or injure, and which functions unexpectedly when a person disturbs or approaches an apparently harmless object or performs an apparently safe act.

Additionally, Article 7(3) of the same Protocol prohibits use of *weapons to which this Article applies [booby-traps] in any city, town, village or other area containing a similar concentration of civilians in which combat between ground forces is not taking place or does not appear to be imminent, unless either:*

(a) *they are placed on or in the close vicinity of a military objective; or*
(b) *measures are taken to protect civilians from their effects, for example, the posting of warning sentries, the issuing of warnings or the provision of fences.*

The definition of a booby trap from the Amended Protocol II of the Convention on Certain Conventional Weapons does not appear to apply to the pagers in question. Receiving a message on a pager does not meet the definition of the phrase "approaches or disturbs." According to CCTV, some of the pagers did not even need a confirmations of the message received from their owner, simply exploding whenever it was delivered.

The debate on the status of the operation continues. In any eventuality, it has proven that, as Herb Lin put it:

> the [pager and walkie-talkie] attacks raise the uncomfortable fear that every device connected to the internet could be turned into a physical—kinetic—weapon. Expressing fears that their smartphones were being used by Israeli intelligence to gather information, Hezbollah apparently decided to use pagers and handheld radios based on the theory that low-tech devices are more resistant (or even immune) to cyberattack because they lack computerized components that can be easily hacked.[911]

---

910 <https://treaties.un.org/doc/Treaties/1996/05/19960503%2001-38%20AM/Ch_XXVI_02_bp.pdf>

911 <https://www.lawfaremedia.org/article/reflections-on-the-lebanon-pager-attack>

5.3 Evidence requirements for legal attribution

5.3.1 The general framework on evidence in Public International Law

5.3.1.1 The burden of proof in Public International Law

The existing framework on evidence requirements is the result of hundreds of years of development of international legal relations between States.[912] However, following the formation of the United Nations and the International Court of Justice in 1945, the institutions became the standard-bearers for defining the application of evidentiary rules in Public International Law. The ICJ's jurisprudence, binding resolutions of the UN Security Council, and resolution of the UN General Assembly expressing the prevailing stances among States remain the main sources for analysis of the state of Public International Law.

It is in this context that one should consider ICJ regulations and the Court's practice on the subject of evidence. According to the Statute and Rules of the Court as well as the Rules of Court that aim to further clarify the procedures, each party to a case in front of the ICJ bears the burden of proof of their claims.[913] In the 1953 *Minqueirs and Ecrehos* judgment, the Court confirmed it by writing:

> Each Party has to prove its alleged title and the facts upon which it relies.[914]

Similarly, in the 2003 *Oil Platforms* judgment, the ICJ stated that a State invoking *Self-defense* must prove necessity and proportionality of the measures

---

912 Aufricht, Hans (1950), "Extrinsic Evidence in International Law." Cornell Law Review, vol. 35. Page 338. <https://scholarship.law.cornell.edu/cgi/viewcontent.cgi?article=1574&context=clr>

913 International Court of Justice. Statute of the Court (1945, June 26). Retrieved February 15, 2022. <https://www.icj-cij.org/en/statute>. Articles 48–52. Rules of the Court, 14 April 1978 (entered into force 1 July 1978), Handbook of the International Court of Justice;

See also Kolb, Robert. La Court Internationale de Justice (a pedone 2014). Pages 956–958.

914 Minqueirs and Ecrehos (France v. United Kingdom) 1953, ICJ reports 47. Retrieved November 29, 2023. <https://www.icj-cij.org/case/17>

it applied.[915] This common-sense approach mirrors the general notion of burden of proof in most domestic legal systems across the world. There are however a number of differences between such internal systems and the one developed as part of Public International Law, especially when it comes to assessing evidence. For one, the ICJ is not bound by the evidence and even facts provided by parties to a case. It may also arbitrarily decide to collect evidence independently, without regard for the parties' opinion.[916]

What evidence is aiming to attribute is also not "illegal conduct of a State." Legality, as understood in domestic law, is a notion that exists in the system of Public International Law. At least not in the same form. Instead, the focus is on proving a breach of a public international obligation by a State that stems either from contractual commitments, treaties, or customary international norms, including the *erga omnes* and *jus cogens* ones. Importantly, various States might be subject to different sets of international obligations, forcing the ICJ and other judiciary and arbitration bodies to analyze each case brought before them individually and oftentimes with varying results, despite considering the same legal norms. The framing of breaches of obligation is customarily to describe them as *Internationally Wrongful Acts*, which were already analyzed in Chapter 1. In using the key term *Internationally Wrongful Act*, the ICJ leans on the *Draft Articles on Responsibility of States for International Wrongful Acts*, issued by the UN International Law Commission (ILC) in 2001.[917] According to the *Draft Articles on State Responsibility*, a State bears legal responsibility when an act:

(a) is attributable to the State under international law; and
(b) constitutes a breach of an international obligation of the State.[918]

---

915 Oil Platforms (Islamic Republic of Iran v. United States of America)— Judgment. International Court of Justice. (ICJ 2003). Supra note 63, page 2. Retrieved February 15, 2022, from <https://www.icj-cij.org/case/90>.

916 Kolb, Robert. La Court Internationale de Justice (a pedone 2014). Page 956.

917 United Nations International Law Commission. (2001). Draft articles on Responsibility of States for Internationally Wrongful Acts with commentaries. United Nations Office of Legal Affairs. Retrieved February 15, 2022, from <https://legal.un.org/ilc/texts/instruments/english/commentaries/9_6_2001.pdf>.

918 Ibid. Article 2.

According to the framing, evidence brought before the ICJ or another judiciary or arbitration body must prove both points—that an act was attributable to a State and that it constituted a breach of its international obligation, in that order. The practice shows that attribution of an act is oftentimes the biggest obstacle in seeking justice in front of the ICJ. This challenge seems compounded in the cyber context. Successfully attributing an act to a State is notoriously more difficult than it is the case with deeds committed by individuals in domestic criminal orders. However without an attribution, even the most egregious act against a State bears no public international legal consequences.

While not formally adopted as binding international law, the *Draft Articles* are part reflection of existing customary norms and part proposition for future ones, with no clear distinction between the two groups. The *Draft Articles* have been designed from the beginning to slowly become part of customary international law as a whole through the process of forming of *opinio juris* within the international community.[919] Twenty years following their publication and endorsement by the UN General Assembly,[920] a hypothesis can be proposed that certain parts of the *Draft Articles*, especially the basic ones which enjoy the widest consensus, such as the definition of an *Internationally Wrongful Act*, have in fact become part of agreed-upon customary international law.[921] The reasons are threefold:

- One, the *Draft Articles* have been cited by the ICJ as a source for its judgments.[922]
- Two, the International Law Commission is a UN body, which consists of 34 renowned experts recognized for their qualifications in the field

---

919 Georgetown University. (n.d.). Law Guides: International Investment Law Research Guide: Customary Law on State Responsibility. Retrieved February 15, 2022, from <https://guides.ll.georgetown.edu/c.php?g=371540&p=2511830>.

920 United Nations General Assembly Resolution. (2002, January 28). 56/83. Responsibility of States for internationally wrongful act. Retrieved February 15, 2022, from <https://documents-dds-ny.un.org/doc/UNDOC/GEN/N01/477/97/PDF/N0147797.pdf?OpenElement>.

921 Czapliński, Władyslaw. (2003). UN Codification of Law of State Responsibility. Archiv Des Völkerrechts, 41(1), 62–82. <https://doi.org/10.1628/0003892034410754>.

922 For instance: Case concerning the Gabcikovo-Nagymaros Project. I.C.J. Reports 88, ICJ GL No. 92. (1997). Page 35. Retrieved February 15, 2022, from <https://www.icj-cij.org/en/case/92/judgments>.

of international law and who are elected by the UN General Assembly for a five-year term.[923] This means that the ILC is well positioned for its statements to be regarded as *teachings of the most highly qualified publicists of the various nations*, which qualify as a subsidiary source of international law according to Article 38 of the Statute of the International Court of Justice.[924]

- Three, as found by international scholars such as Przemysław Roguski, most States explicitly or implicitly endorsed the bases for attribution as found in the UN International Law Commission *Draft Articles*.[925]

For these reasons, the definition of an *International Wrongful Acts* can be seen as a general source of international law applicable to considerations of evidence[926] (unless an alternative exceptional framework is applied in a specific legal area such as it is the case for instance with the European Convention on Human Rights).[927]

5.3.1.2 Standards for assessing the level of required evidence

Unfortunately, Public International Law does not offer a unified source of clear standards for assessing and weighing evidence for the sake of legal attribution.[928] Instead, one can make an attempt at a legal reconstructing

---

923 United Nations General Assembly Resolution. (1947, November 21). 174 (III). Establishment of an International Law Commission. Retrieved February 15, 2022, from <https://www.un.org/ga/search/view_doc.asp?symbol=A/RES/174(II)>

924 International Court of Justice. (1945, June 26). Statute of the Court. Retrieved February 15, 2022, from <https://www.icj-cij.org/en/statute>. Article 38.

925 Roguski, Przemysław. "Application of International Law to Cyber Operations: A Comparative Analysis of States' Views." The Hague Program for Cyber Norms, 2020. Page 14. <https://ruj.uj.edu.pl/xmlui/bitstream/handle/item/153989/roguski_application_of_international_law_to_cyber_operations_2020.pdf?sequence=1>.

926 Ibid.

927 Council of Europe. (1950, November 4). European Convention on Human Rights. Retrieved February 15, 2022, from <https://www.echr.coe.int/documents/convention_eng.pdf>.

928 Buchan, Russell. (2014). Cyber Operations and the Use of Force in International Law. By MARCO ROSCINI. British Yearbook of International Law, 84(1), 385–389. <https://doi.org/10.1093/bybil/bru014>; University of Oslo. (2016, April). When do cyber operations amount to use of force and armed attack, and what response will they justify? <https://www.duo.uio.no/bitstream/handle/10852/50840/723.pdf?sequence=1>

of them based on the ICJ jurisprudence, State practice, and interpretative conclusions of recognized international scholars. A general guideline for assessing evidence in international law can be found in the ICJ's landmark judgment on the *Nicaragua* case:

> Within the limits of its Statute and Rules... [The Court] has freedom in estimating the value of the various elements of evidence.[929]

This approach extends much latitude to the Court and essentially amounts to full freedom in the process. Despite this open-ended guideline, the analysis of judgments rendered by the ICJ over decades reveals more specific patterns on the subject of assessing evidence. One of the key findings in thar regard is that the graver the alleged breach of an international obligation, the higher the evidentiary threshold for the invoking State.[930] This means that the most severe types of wrongful acts in the system of Public International Law, which are breaches of *jus cogens* obligations such as an *Armed Attack*, would require much more evidence than, for instance, a minor violation of territorial continuity. This interpretation can be deduced from the 2005 ICJ judgment on the Congo v. Uganda case, in which the Court stated:

> Claims against a State involving charges of exceptional gravity must be proved by evidence that is fully conclusive. The same standard applies to the proof of attribution for such acts.[931]

This approach was further strengthened by remarks in a separate opinion in the ICJ ruling on Bosnia Genocide Case from 2007.[932] However, even that qualified level of evidence is at the *beyond a reasonable doubt* threshold, which is perceived

---

929 Case Concerning Military and Paramilitary Activities in and Against Nicaragua (Nicaragua v United States), Merits, Paragraph 60, (1986) I.C.J Reports 14, ICGJ 112 (ICJ 1986). Retrieved February 26, 2022. <https://www.icj-cij.org/case/70>.

930 Riddell, Anna, and Plant, Brendan. (2009). Evidence before the International Court of Justice. British Institute of International and Comparative Law. Page 18.

931 Case Concerning Armed Activities on the Territory of the Congo (Democratic Republic of Congo v Uganda) (2005) ICJ Rep 168. Paragraphs 91 and 172. Retrieved February 26, 2022. <https://www.icj-cij.org/en/case/116>.

932 Case Concerning the Application of the Convention on the Prevention and Punishment of the Crime of Genocide (Bosnia and Herzegovina v Serbia) (2007) ICJ Rep 43 para 209 (Bosnia Genocide Case); Separate Opinion of Judge Higgins (n 23) Paragraph 33.

as softer than the *beyond any doubt* threshold that is predominant when it comes to the most severe criminal cases in domestic legal regimes.[933] The *balance of probabilities* threshold was utilized in some cases pertaining to violations in former Yugoslavia and is perceived as less demanding than the *beyond a reasonable doubt* one.[934] For example, in both the Bosnia Genocide Case and the Corfu Channel Case, the ICJ did not demand the production of classified documents by the Parties (a fact criticized in one of the separate opinions in the Bosnia Genocide Case).[935] This did not prevent the Court in either of them from rendering a binding ruling attributing a breach of international legal obligations.

This relation between the severity of claimed wrongfulness and the necessary evidence can be described as the rule of proportionality. It means that the more serious a breach of obligation is, the more conclusive evidence it will require in front of an international judiciary body.[936] Based on an array of judgments rendered by the ICJ, one can even preliminarily map this relationship on a chart (see Figure 11). While visual proportions are only illustrative, the general notion of evidentiary proportionality follows the presented pattern. The spectrum of standards for required evidence ranges from "balance of probabilities" in low-stakes issues, through "fully conclusive," and "beyond a reasonable doubt," to "beyond any doubt" in case of the most serious accusations, such as breaches of *jus cogens* obligations.[937]

---

933 Tsagourias, Nicholas. (2012). Cyber attacks, self-defence and the problem of attribution. Journal of Conflict and Security Law, 17(2), 229–244. <https://doi.org/10.1093/jcsl/krs019>.

934 Bosnia Genocide Case (n 24) para 208; Memorial of the Government of the Republic of Bosnia and Herzegovina (1994) 5.3.2.5–5.3.3.10. ME O'Connell, "Rules of Evidence for the Use of Force in International Law's New Era' (2006) 100 ASIL Proceedings 44.; Tsagourias, Nicholas. (2012). Cyber attacks, self-defence and the problem of attribution. Journal of Conflict and Security Law, 17(2), 229–244. <https://doi.org/10.1093/jcsl/krs019>.

935 Case Concerning Corfu Channel I.C.J. Reports 1949, 24, Page 32. Retrieved February 2022. <https://www.icj-cij.org/case/1>; Case Concerning the Application of the Convention on the Prevention and Punishment of the Crime of Genocide (Bosnia and Herzegovina v Serbia) (2007) ICJ Rep 43 para 209 (Bosnia Genocide Case); Merits, Paragraph 207.

936 Barela, Steven. J. (2016). Jens David Ohlin, Kevin Govern and Claire Finkelstein (eds),Cyber War: Law and Ethics for Virtual Conflicts. Journal of International Criminal Justice, 14(1), 225–226. <https://doi.org/10.1093/jicj/mqw003>.

937 Quintana, Juan Jose. (2015). Litigation at the International Court of Justice, Brill Nijhoff: pages 382–480;

While *Armed Attacks*, *Use of Force*, *Prohibited Interventions*, or *Violations of Sovereignty* all require a varying degree of conclusive evidence, ultimately it falls to Judges' discrete assessment.[938] Various States have expressed their recognition of this dynamic. For instance, the Netherlands stated: "In the government's view, the burden of proof will indeed vary in accordance with the situation, depending on the seriousness of the act considered to be in breach of international law and the intended countermeasures."[939]

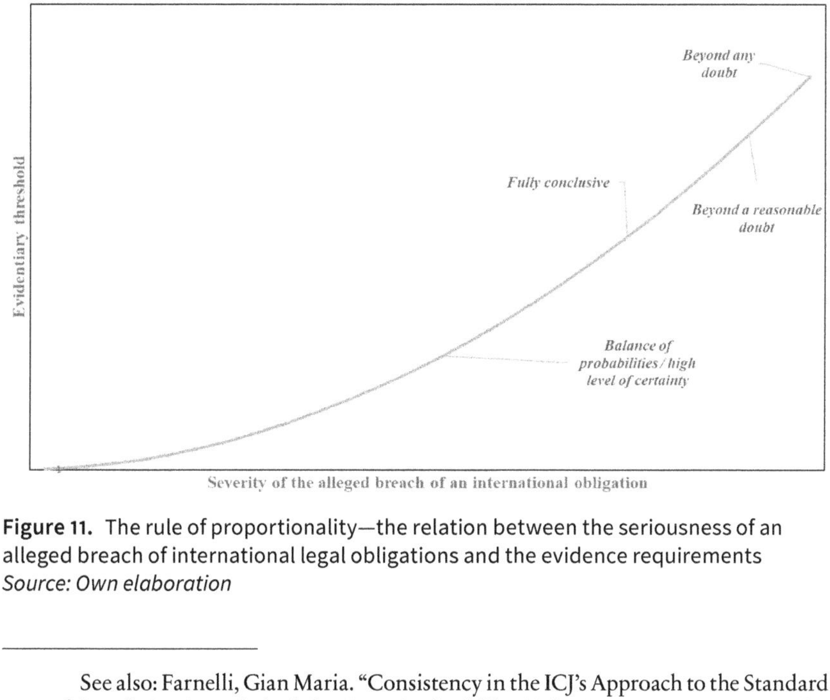

Figure 11. The rule of proportionality—the relation between the seriousness of an alleged breach of international legal obligations and the evidence requirements
Source: Own elaboration

See also: Farnelli, Gian Maria. "Consistency in the ICJ's Approach to the Standard of Proof: An Appraisal of the Court's Flexibility." The Law & Practice of International Courts and Tribunals 21, no. 1 (2022): pages 98–121. <https://doi.org/10.1163/15718034-12341466>.

938 Tsagourias, Nicholas. (2012). Cyber attacks, self-defence and the problem of attribution. Journal of Conflict and Security Law, 17(2), pages 229–244. <https://doi.org/10.1093/jcsl/krs019>.

939 The government of Netherlands. Letter to the parliament on the international legal order in cyberspace, September 26, 2019. Page 7. <https://www.government.nl/documents/parliamentary-documents/2019/09/26/letter-to-the-parliament-on-the-international-legal-order-in-cyberspace>.

The ICJ recognized in the so-called Iran-Contras ruling that the main challenge in attributing events and resulting obligations to States in Public International Law is *the process of tracing material proof*, that precedes determination of an *Internationally Wrongful Act*.[940] This means that how much conclusive evidence is required for determination of an Internationally Wrongful Act is possibly the most impactful aspect of seeking redress via the ICJ and other international judiciary bodies.

Access to evidence in the context of international legal disputes is notoriously constrained due to its confidential character. Most relevant materials have the status of classified intelligence, publication of which could hurt the victim State, on top of the damage caused by the disputed event. In the ruling on the *Corfu Channel* case from 949 between the United Kingdom and Albania, the ICJ acknowledged the problem of collecting evidence from third States, which are not directly involved in the dispute and have no incentive in sharing confidential materials. In such a situation, the ICJ stated that in a case, in which the ability to render a decision is constrained by lack of access, *a more liberal recourse to inferences of fact and circumstantial evidence* is possible.[941] The approach confirmed that the ICJ enjoys much latitude in assessing the evidence in a case-by-case manner.

5.3.1.3 Admissibility of evidence obtained without consent

Would evidence obtained without necessary consent of another State or in an otherwise wrongful way be admissible in front of the ICJ or another public international judiciary body? The ICJ handbook leaves this question conspicuously out of its Statute and other Rules. However, the established precedent implies that the answer would be positive, although within limits.

In the *Corfu Channel* judgment, the ICJ accepted evidence procured by the United Kingdom, despite the fact that it was obtained unlawfully from another State. In the justification of its conduct, the United Kingdom stated: "According to that Government, the *corpora delicti* must be secured as quickly as possible, for fear they should be taken away, without leaving traces, by

---

940 Case Concerning Military and Paramilitary Activities in and Against Nicaragua, Nicaragua v. United States. I.C.J Reports 14, ICGJ 112 (ICJ 1986). (1986). Paragraph 57. Retrieved February 15, 2022, from <https://www.icj-cij.org/en/case/70/judgments>.

941 Case Concerning Corfu Channel I.C.J. Reports 1949, 24, Page 18. Retrieved February 2022. <https://www.icj-cij.org/case/1>.

the authors of the minelaying or by the Albanian authorities."[942] The Court rejected this logic, labeling the U.K.'s conduct as unlawful. At the same time, the collected evidence was accepted for consideration by the Court. It did, however, refrain from formally analyzing the validity of that evidence, leaving open the possibility of such unlawful methods potentially deeming evidence inadmissible.

5.3.2 Application of the general framework on evidence in the cyber context

5.3.2.1 Transposition of the rules on burden of proof in the cyber context

The 11 *Voluntary Non-Binding Norms For Responsible State Behaviour in the Use of ICT*, issued by the UN GGE in 2015, set the general outline of the international legal framework applying to hostile cyber operations. While the norms are not part of binding Public International Law yet, the UN GGE has expressed their desire for such a transition to take place in the future. In fact, the process of *opinio juris* forming in that direction has already started, with no objection to the contents of the 11 norms registered from any State and with two regional organizations (ASEAN, the EU) and a number of States formally accepting them "in principle."[943] In this context, it is worth fleshing out the structure of the attribution model proposed by the 11 norms as well as its legal and casuistic underpinnings while being cognizant of their non-binding character.

The UN GGE stated in its final 2013 report (whose conclusions were incorporated into the 2015 one) that *States must meet their international obligations regarding internationally wrongful acts attributable to them* (in regard to ICT-related activities).[944] In doing so, the UN GGE drew directly on the

---

942 Case Concerning Corfu Channel I.C.J. Reports 1949, 24, Page 34. Retrieved February 2022. <https://www.icj-cij.org/case/1>.

943 "The UN Norms of Responsible State Behaviour in Cyberspace." Australian Strategic Policy Institute. Retrieved November 30, 2023. <https://www.aspi.org.au/report/un-norms-responsible-state-behaviour-cyberspace>.

944 United Nations General Assembly Resolution. (2013, June 24). Group of Governmental Experts on Developments in the Field of Information and Telecommunications in the Context of International Security—Note by the Secretary-General. Retrieved February 15, 2022, from <https://undocs.org/A/68/98>.

Draft Articles, extending their application to cyberspace. This stance was echoed by other organizations, most prominently the NATO Cooperative Cyber Defence Centre of Excellence, which issued the Tallinn Manual, one of the most seminal scholarly publications on Public International Law in cyberspace. The organization worked to collect the most highly qualified experts and legal publicists with focus on application of international law in cyberspace from various countries for the sake of process, aiming to put forward the publication as *subsidiary means for the determination of rules of law* as per Article 38 of the Statute of the International Court of Justice.[945] This seems to have been a largely successful bid, as the document has been quoted by the UN GGE, which elevates its status.[946] While the publication does not have the status of international law, it can be construed as informal espousal of the UN GGE *Voluntary Non-Binding Norms* by NATO. The Group of International Experts gathered by NATO Cooperative Cyber Defence Centre of Excellence stated in Rule 6 of the Tallinn Manual:

> A state bears international legal responsibility for a cyber operation attributable to it and which constitutes a breach of an international obligation.[947]

There exist, however, certain divergences between the general rules on proving wrongfulness and their application in cyberspace, specifically when it comes to attribution and the burden of proof. While the general notion of proving claims and facts in front of judiciary bodies applies in the cyber context, States are highly reluctant to reveal the technical details and insights that are the basis of their attribution of cyber operations. This might be due to the fact that such details are a result of a sophisticated process involving

---

945 International Court of Justice. (1945, June 26). Statute of the Court. Retrieved February 15, 2022, from <https://www.icj-cij.org/en/statute. Article 38>.

946 United Nations General Assembly Resolution. (2013, June 24). Group of Governmental Experts on Developments in the Field of Information and Telecommunications in the Context of International Security— Note by the Secretary-General. Retrieved February 15, 2022, from <https://undocs.org/A/68/98>.

947 Tallinn Manual Initiative. (n.d.). NATO Cooperative Cyber Defence Center of Excellence. Retrieved February 13, 2022, from <https://ccdcoe.org/research/tallinn-manual/>

a number of IT experts and confidential protocols. Much of that work is done by the IT branches of intelligence and counterintelligence services. This is not usually the case with conventional operations where evidence of attribution can be procured without revealing confidential capabilities of a State. For these reasons, France,[948] Netherlands,[949] the United Kingdom,[950] and the United States[951] have publicly stated that an attribution of a hostile cyber operation to another State and a subsequent response to it do not require providing technical evidence.

It remains to be seen whether the norms regulating the burden of proof in cyberspace will develop to constitute *lex specialis* relative to the general rules that allows for more secrecy on behalf of injured States. While the States that appear to support this stance are some of the most influential ones, they constitute a small minority of the international community. The dynamic also appears to match the imbalance of global power. Western States that enjoy high cyber capacity gravitate toward looser regulations in cyberspace while the rest of States have so far not supported such a notion. This split might prevent consistent *opinio juris* from forming. Nevertheless, State practice effectively moves in the direction of less access to evidence validating attribution of a hostile cyber operation to a perpetrator State.

---

948 The government of France. (2019a). International Law Applied to Operations in Cyberspace. Page 11. Retrieved February 19, 2022, from <https://www.defense.gouv.fr/content/download/567648/9770527/file/international+law+applied+to+operations+in+cyberspace.pdf>.

949 The government of Netherlands. Letter to the parliament on the international legal order in cyberspace, September 26, 2019. Page 6.
<https://www.government.nl/documents/parliamentary-documents/2019/09/26/letter-to-the-parliament-on-the-international-legal-order-in-cyberspace>.

950 The government of the United Kingdom. "Cyber and International Law in the 21st Century." (2018). Speech by Attorney General Jeremy Wright QC MP on 23 May 2018 <https://www.gov.uk/government/speeches/cyber-and-international-law-in-the-21st-century>

951 Egan, Brian J. (2017). International Law and Stability in Cyberspace. Berkeley Journal of International Law, 35(1), 1–26.
<https://www.law.berkeley.edu/wp-content/uploads/2016/12/BJIL-article-International-Law-and-Stability-in-Cyberspace.pdf>.

5.3.2.2 Proposed modification to the standard for assessing the level of required evidence in the cyber context

As described in Chapters 1 and 2, States frequently avoid making a formal attribution, preferring instead to keep the fact of being targeted by another State's hostile cyber operation a secret or to limit their response to a political denouncement only. This can happen for a variety of reasons. As explained in Chapters 1 and 2, one of them is the difficulty of procuring sophisticated technical evidence tracing an international operation back to its source. The fact that perpetrator States can use services of non-State actors, such as hacker groups, to pursue their goals makes the process only more challenging. The resulting situation makes for an impression of a dysfunctional legal system that does not serve its function of delivering redress and preventing proliferation of *Internationally Wrongful Acts.* To alleviate this situation, the UN GGE has proclaimed in its 2015 report, endorsed by the UN General Assembly that attribution can draw on the broad context of a hostile cyber operation:

> In case of ICT incidents, States should consider all relevant information, including the larger context of the event, the challenges of attribution in the ICT environment and the nature and the extent of the consequences.[952]

In this context, a few States, notably Estonia and the United States, have advocated to modify the rules on the standard of proof in cyberspace to allow for "reasonable conviction" instead of certainty as the minimum threshold of required evidence. Kersti Kaljulaid, then-president of Estonia, stated in 2019 at a NATO Cyber Conflict conference in Tallinn: "At the end of the day what is required from the attributing state, is not absolute certainty but what is reasonable."[953] Similar stance came earlier in 2016 from the United States, which as a permanent member of the UN Security Council and a leading world power has much influence in shaping global *opinio juris.* The

---

952 United Nations General Assembly Resolution. (2015, July 22). Group of Governmental Experts on Developments in the Field of Information and Telecommunications in the Context of International Security—Note by the Secretary-General. UN Doc A/70/174. Retrieved February 15, 2022, from <https://documents-dds-ny.un.org/doc/UNDOC/GEN/N15/228/35/PDF/N1522835.pdf?OpenElement>;

953 International cyber law: interactive toolkit. "Attribution - President Kersti Kaljulaid." International cyber law: interactive toolkit, July 28, 2023. <https://cyberlaw.ccdcoe.org/wiki/Attribution>.

U.S. Department of State proclaimed at the time that Public International Law only requires attributing States to only: "act reasonably under the circumstances when they gather information and draw conclusions based on that information."[954]

Using the framework laid out in Figure 11, earlier in this chapter, we can position the standard of "reasonableness" around the lowest rung—the balance of probabilities and in fact "reasonableness" draws on the ICJ jurisprudence that developed this standard. Applying the standard of "reasonableness" to hostile cyber acts in a blanket fashion, which appears to be implied in statements by Estonia and the United States, would make it easier for a victim State to implicate the perpetrator one. So far there has been no public pushback against that stance from other States although a number of international scholars critiqued this trend of lowering standard of proof requirements in cyberspace. For example, Przemysław Roguski claimed that the standard of reasonableness is too easy to meet, creating a risk of an attribution that is wrong and yet extends preclusion of wrongfulness to response actions conducted by a victim State. He wrote:

> this standard of "reasonableness" is problematic and requires further clarification. (…) If "reasonableness" were a *duty of care*, [a victim State] might argue that—acting "reasonably under the circumstances"—it has discharged its *duty of care* [in attempting to attribute a hostile cyber operation] and would therefore not bear international responsibility for violating rights of [a State to which the operation was erroneously attributed].[955]

If the standard of reasonableness was applied in Public International Law concerning cyberspace, it would constitute a conflation of the intention and the objective result of a State action. This logic is to some extent present in domestic criminal codes, where a crime committed under a mistaken impression can oftentimes be excused. However, this concept is not

---

[954] Egan, Brian J. (2016). Remarks on International Law and Stability in Cyberspace. United States Department of State, pages 1–26. <https://2009-2017.state.gov/s/l/releases/remarks/264303.htm>.

[955] Roguski, Przemysław. "Application of International Law to Cyber Operations: A Comparative Analysis of States' Views." The Hague Program for Cyber Norms, 2020. Page 15. <https://ruj.uj.edu.pl/xmlui/bitstream/handle/item/153989/roguski_application_of_international_law_to_cyber_operations_2020.pdf?sequence=1>.

applicable in international law.[956] The *Draft Articles on Responsibility of States for Internationally Wrongful Acts* for instance state that *Countermeasures* can only be lawful when taken in response to an existing *Internationally Wrongful Act*, which injured the victim State.[957] The linguistic interpretive logic implies that a wrongful attribution strips *Countermeasures* of their legality. There is no room for tolerable error in that regard if reasonable care was applied by the victim State when collecting evidence.

The proposition to introduce the standard of "reasonableness" can then be perceived as an attempt to improve effectiveness of a dysfunctional system, which in its present form makes it very difficult for victim States to seek redress via formal means. However, this adaptation would create risks that could easily outweigh the benefits of a more efficient attribution process. For that reason, it has to be assessed negatively.

5.3.2.3 Types of evidence and evidence-gathering techniques in cyberspace

Access to evidence in the context of international legal disputes is notoriously challenging. This challenge is only compounded in the cyber context, as laid out in the two previous sections. The confidential and sophisticated character of both hostile cyber acts and operations aimed at preventing and attributing them compels most States to conceal their evidence. Important materials often have the status of classified intelligence, publication of which could hurt the victim State, on top of the damage caused by a hostile cyber intrusion. Additionally, unlike for conventional operations, most evidence in cyberspace has non-physical character, making it difficult to bring it forward for the sake of attribution. Three main aspects of the process of gathering

---

956 Cassese, Antonio, Paola Gaeta, and Jones John R W D. The Rome Statute of the International Criminal Court: A commentary: A commentary. Oxford University Press, 2002. Page 394.

957 United Nations International Law Commission. (2001). Draft articles on Responsibility of States for Internationally Wrongful Acts with commentaries. United Nations Office of Legal Affairs. Page 130, Commentary to the article 49. Retrieved February 15, 2022, from <https://legal.un.org/ilc/texts/instruments/english/commentaries/9_6_2001.pdf.page>

evidence for the sake of attribution in cyberspace require particular attention, as they shape the process of seeking redress in the system of Public International Law:

- Techniques for obtaining evidence in cyberspace;
- Computer records as documentary evidence in public international judiciary;
- The role of the private sector in enabling attribution of hostile cyber operations to perpetrator States.

Techniques for obtaining evidence in cyberspace

The scope of possible techniques for obtaining evidence in cyberspace can be understood twofold: as the available technical means that can validate an attribution and as the legal range that indicates which techniques remain lawful from the standpoint of Public International Law. The latter question is answered in the next section, which deals with the issue of admissibility of evidence obtained through prohibited means. In terms of available technical means, a few States have expressed their general understanding of what possible methods are. France claimed that evidence-gathering techniques can include:

> identification of the attack and transit infrastructure for the cyberoperation and its location, identification of the adversary methods of operation (AMO), the overall chronology of the perpetrator's activities, the scale and gravity of the incident and the compromised perimeter, or the effects sought by the attacker[958]

The following cyber evidence can be brought in front of the ICJ and other international judiciary bodies for the sake of attribution:

- **Computer code** such as the code of a computer virus or pieces thereof can be utilized by a victim State to validate attribution to a State. As

958 The government of France. (2019a). International Law Applied to Operations in Cyberspace. Page 10. Retrieved February 19, 2022, from <https://www.defense.gouv.fr/content/download/567648/9770527/file/international+law+applied+to+operations+in+cyberspace.pdf>.

shown in the following case study on the 2013 cyber assault on an Indian Bank, a cyber forensic analysis that dissects the code of malware can procure tangible evidence.

- **Server logs** that display activities conducted by perpetrators during a hostile cyber operation can help establish the sequence of events, map the route of a hostile operation, assess the scale of the operation, and identify its targets (regardless of whether the hostile cyber act succeeded or not).
- **IP addresses** of sources of a hostile cyber operation can be collected and presented in front of the Court. If they all point to the likely perpetrator State and come from within governmental institutions, they can facilitate an attributive claim.
- **Serial numbers** are unique identifiers attached to a computer or other IT device by its producer. They come in two forms: physical marking on the device and the embedded number within software of the machine. They can serve as supplemental material that can strengthen other pieces of evidence.
- **Media Access Control (MAC) codes** are unique identifiers of the devices called Network Interface Controllers that connect a computer to the internet. Each MAC code is assigned by the device producer and is permanent.
- **Dataflow tracking** is a method that consists of tracking all the data as it enters and exits a network via routers.[959]

Oftentimes all the earlier listed methods are combined to help identify a perpetrator State. When that is the case, the resulting multi-pronged approach is labeled as cyber forensic analysis, in reference to advanced methods utilized by

---

959 Wheeler, David, and Larsen, Gregory N. (2003). Techniques for Cyber Attack Attribution. ResearchGate, pages 1–85. Page 82. <https://www.researchgate.net/publication/235170094_Techniques_for_Cyber_Attack_Attribution>;

Lahmann Henning. Unilateral Remedies to Cyber Operation. Self-defence, Countermeasures, Necessity, and the Question of Attribution, Cambridge University Press 2020, page 125.

domestic police units dealing with criminal cases. For example, France went on record identifying a range of methods it reserves a right to pursue such as:

> identification of the attack and transit infrastructure for the cyberoperation and its location, identification of the adversary methods of operation (AMO), the overall chronology of the perpetrator's activities, the scale and gravity of the incident and the compromised perimeter, or the effects sought by the attacker.[960]

While trying to identify the best ways to attribute hostile cyber operations to foreign entities, the U.S. Department of Defense commissioned the Institute for Defense Analyses (IDA) with providing guidelines on technical source identification techniques. In its report, IDA has identified 17 different techniques that States can deploy in order to identify the perpetrator that represent combinations of the earlier listed core components.[961] The authors acknowledged that due to a large number of intermediary servers usually used during a hostile cyber operation, the ability to attribute by States is inherently limited. Many attribution techniques are still immature and will require additional funding in order to become operational.[962] The existing techniques mostly rely on tracing back the server links and nodes that a cyber assault came from.

A good example is the 2013 hack of an Indian bank ICICI that was traced back to North Korea by utilizing an array of techniques. After the 2013 attack on an Indian bank, attributed to North Korean government-affiliated hackers based on IP address and server log traces, it was revealed that the main author of the cyber operation left a signature *kut_rsc1994* in the code. The cyber experts realized this was most likely Ryu Song Chol, a hacker employed by the North Korean Government Reconnaissance General Bureau. Ryu Song Chol who was born in 1994 and graduated from Kim Chaek University (*KUT* is the school's established acronym). The experts realized this might be the

---

960 The government of France. (2019a). International Law Applied to Operations in Cyberspace. Page 10. Retrieved February 19, 2022, from <https://www.defense.gouv.fr/content/download/567648/9770527/file/international+law+applied+to+operations+in+cyberspace.pdf>.

961 Wheeler, David, and Larsen, Gregory N. (2003). Techniques for Cyber Attack Attribution. ResearchGate, pages 1–85. Page 82. <https://www.researchgate.net/publication/235170094_Techniques_for_Cyber_Attack_Attribution>.

962 Ibid.

meaning of the signature because some of them had actually met him in person two years prior during the 2011 International Math Olympiad in Amsterdam, Netherlands. Ryu Song Chol, still a student at the time, was representing North Korea at the competition.[963]

The earlier example shows analysis that rested on decoding social cues in the code. However, most of the forensic analysis is based on familiarity with various coding approaches deployed by government-backed hacking units and the statistical analysis recognizing patterns in coding approaches that are not visible to a human eye. Oftentimes, the most notorious hacker groups, many of them enjoying protection from the host State government, develop their unique styles of hacking that can be discerned by professional IT experts.[964] That is the case with Chinese, Korean, Russian, and Israeli hackers, all known for their unique styles. Forensic Analysis was the method used to attribute the 2010 *Stuxnet* attack on the Iranian nuclear facilities to the United States and Israel,[965] although in that case, the Israeli hackers also left a signature by way of embedding references to a biblical story involving ancient Persia and Israel in the malware code. Simon Choi, a South-Korean government cybersecurity expert, stated that world-class government hackers, instead of attempting to conceal their identity, frequently leave signatures of sort embedded into malicious code on purpose as a sign of defiance and impunity.

Techniques utilized by perpetrator States to conceal their identity and prevent an attribution

At the current stage of development of technology and Public International Law, States perpetrating hostile cyber operations have the upper hands. It is difficult to effectively attribute a hostile cyber act. It involves much IT expertise and for every attributive technique, there exists a way to defy it. Below are some of the most frequently utilized ones:

---

963 Caesar, Ed. (2021b, April 19). The Incredible Rise of North Korea's Hacking Army. The New Yorker. <https://www.newyorker.com/magazine/2021/04/26/the-incredible-rise-of-north-koreas-hacking-army>.

964 United Nations Institute for Disarmament Research. (2017, March). Report of the International Security Cyber Issues Workshop Series. <https://www.unidir.org/files/publications/pdfs/report-of-the-international-security-cyber-issues-workshop-series-en-656.pdf>.

965 Ibid.

- **Forging IP addresses, serial numbers, and MAC codes (spoofing)** The identifiers of a device are supposed to be permanent. In reality however, hackers found ways to manipulate them, obscuring the source of a hostile cyber operation and deflecting attention in the wrong direction. That is the case with IP,[966] serial numbers,[967] as well as MAC.[968] While there exist counter-spoofing techniques,[969] these can also be anticipated by hackers, resulting in a complex arms race between both sides. As a result, the identifiers are not a reliable way of attributing a hostile cyber operation.
- **Weaponizing innocent computers and networks** Perpetrators can utilize the "reflector hosts technique," which consists of providing wrong sender details to the victim's system when overflooding them data requests. When the victim's systems respond to the data requests, they connect to that reflector host, who is not the actual source. The resulting communication between servers overwhelms the bandwidth of IT systems, leading to disruption of their service.[970]
- **Erasing the track records of where a cyber assault came from** Attackers can hide their identity and location by using a "laundering" host. A laundering host is a system that transforms data in some manner. A laundering host that immediately passes that data without processing is termed a stepping stone. For example, if an attacker logs into system A and then uses system A to log into system B then system A is a stepping stone between the attacker and system B. Oftentimes, these computers are hijacked by hackers for the effort, becoming "zombie" nodes in the process of preventing attribution to the actual perpetrator (see Figure 12 for an example).[971]

---

966 Delerue, François. Cyber Operations and international law. Cambridge: Cambridge University Press, 2020. Pages 65–67.

967 Ibid. Page 58.

968 Ibid. Page 61.

969 Wheeler, D., & Larsen, G. N. (2003). Techniques for Cyber Attack Attribution. ResearchGate, 82, 1–85.

970 Grzegorz Pilarski: Cyberprzestrzeń—relacje w wojnie hybrydowej, Warszawa 2020. <https://ksiegarnia.akademia.mil.pl/produkt/cyberprzestrzen-relacje-w-wojnie-hybrydowej/?lang=en>, pages 69–73.

971 Ibid.

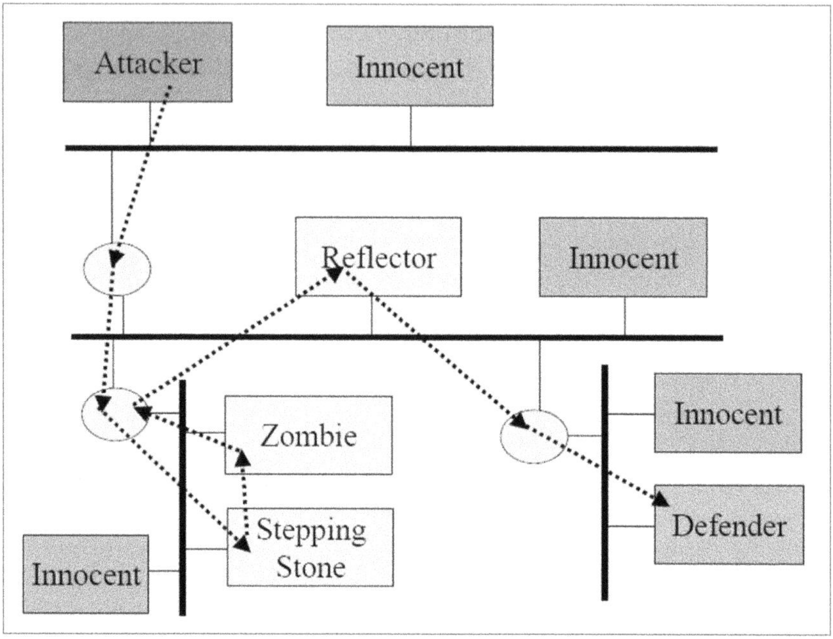

Figure 12. A scheme of the way a perpetrator State can use a number of intermediate computers to conceal its identity.
Source: Wheeler, D., & Larsen, G. N. (2003). Techniques for Cyber Attack Attribution

The role of the private sector in enabling attribution of hostile cyber operations to States

In light of insufficient attribution capacity on the part of many governments, a whole private industry has emerged that States rely on to buttress their defenses and intruder identification abilities. Private companies are increasingly the repositories of forensic knowledge on international hackers' patterns, which blurs the lines between the private and the international public sector in the area of cyber security. Just like the hostile cyber operations impact both the public and the private sector, the solutions to them are also being developed at the intersection of the two spheres. Most of the assaults mentioned in this book were technically attributed to a State by a private cyber security company. Governments rely on that expertise to make their own attribution choices that carry an actual international legal weight.

The ecosystem of companies providing cyber security services and evidence needed for attribution to governments (both at the central and local level) is expanding fast. The industry is a natural extension of the antivirus and antimalware software sector that has so far been catering to private clients and companies. Some of the main companies with the ability to technically attribute an hostile cyber operation to a foreign government have gone public at the New York Stock Exchange. A good example is Crowdstrike, the company that substantiated with its technical analysis the claim that the 2018 Olympics hack can be attributed to the Russian Federation (see Section 2.1). In 2020, the company experienced a year-on-year revenue increase of around 100%, revealing just how fast the sector of public cyber security is growing.[972] There are now thousands of such companies, readily providing attribution expertise to governments. BCG has compiled a visual map of 1,000 most prominent such companies and startups and grouped them into sub-sectors, showing that the private sector is playing a fundamental role in this area (see Figure 13). This private-public hybrid model has potential impact on how the evidence, necessary for facilitating an international legal claim of a cyber assault, is being collected. All this goes to show that trends in international cyber law are shaped not only by governments and international organizations but to a large extent also by private sector entities.

Computer records as documentary evidence in public international judiciary

Evidence in the documentary form is the most common type presented by States in ICJ proceedings.[973] Definitionally, "documentary evidence" is evidence that is available in the form of written documents.[974] The question then is whether electronic files or even creations such as computer code

---

972 The Software Report. (2020, December). The Top 25 Cybersecurity Companies of 2020. <https://www.thesoftwarereport.com/the-top-25-cybersecurity-companies-of-2020/>

973 Malintoppi, Loretta. "Fact Finding and Evidence before the International Court of Justice (Notably in Scientific-Related Disputes)Etablissement Des Faits et Question de La Preuve Devant La Cour Internationale de Justice (Notamment Dans Le Cadre de Différends Liés à Des Questions Scientifiques)." Journal of International Dispute Settlement 7, no. 2 (2016): 421–44. <https://doi.org/10.1093/jnlids/idw009>.

974 Delerue, François. Cyber Operations and international law. Cambridge: Cambridge University Press, 2020. Page 94.

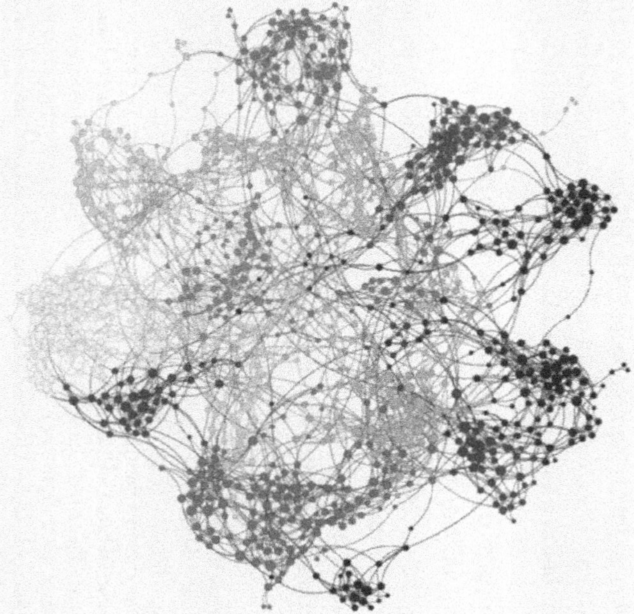

CYBERSECURITY CLUSTERS	Startups (%)	Funding (%)
Mobile device security	13	16
Penetration testing & incident response	13	6
Cloud security	10	10
Data security & solutions	9	13
Endpoint security	8	10
Disaster recovery & secure hosting	8	6
Email security	6	8
Identity & access management solutions	6	7
Network security	6	8
Identify theft & authentication	6	3
Web application security	5	2
Secure enterprise communication	4	4
Security analytics	4	5
Managed security services	2	2

Figure 13. Mapping of 1,000 existing companies offering cybersecurity services to States
Source: Boston Consulting Group Center for Innovation Analytics

count as a written document. As it turns out, the ICJ implies that this is the case, separating the notion of "writtenness" from the physical process of inscribing or printing words on paper. The provision IXbis of the Practice Directions of the Court states:

> a document that can be considered part of a publication readily available under Article 56 (4) of the Rules of Court may be in a any format (physical or electronic), form (physical or online, such as posted on the internet) or on any data medium (no paper, on digital or any other media).[975]

This broad framing can include all types of electronic outputs, including the code and server logs. In case of any doubt, these pieces of information could also be nested within a report or other document that would then pass the ICJ's muster. The system appears then to be well prepared to accept and process evidence. The expansion of the definition of written documents to include electronic records is a necessary step that prepares the system of Public International Law for situations where most State interactions and documentation thereof are of virtual nature.

The challenge is then not the lack of capacity to utilize digital records in front of the ICJ but the fact that States' interests do not align with the notion of sharing such attributive evidence publicly. To date, no hostile cyber operation has been brought in front of any international judiciary body. However, in those few instances where a State came forward publicly attributing hostile cyber acts to another State, oftentimes with help of a private sector IT company, they always presented digital records as conclusive evidence. That was the case in 2010 when the company Symantec published a report attributing the virus Stuxnet, which damaged Iranian nuclear facilities, to Israel and which utilized computer code as proof.[976] In 2013, a U.S.-based company called Mandiant delivered proof of the Chinese government being behind

---

975 International Court of Justice. (1945, June 26). Revisions to Practice Directions IX and XI of the Court. Practice Direction IXbis. Retrieved February 15, 2022, from <https://icj-cij.org/files/press-releases/0/000-20061213-PRE-01-00-EN.pdf>.

976 Stuxnet 0.5: The missing link. George Washington University. Retrieved November 30, 2023. <https://nsarchive2.gwu.edu/NSAEBB/NSAEBB424/docs/Cyber-088.pdf>.

the hacking activity of a group called APT 1.[977] The U.S. government then utilized that attribution to formulate critique of China.

5.3.2.4 Admissibility of evidence obtained without consent in cyberspace

The ambiguity on the status of evidence obtained using prohibited means traces back to the ICJ's 1949 Corfu Channel judgment, discussed already in the Subsection 5.3.1.3. At the time, the Court refrained from analyzing the admissibility of the evidence although it did consider it in its deliberations. On the other hand, it also issued a critique of the prohibited methods utilized by the United Kingdom to obtain, which violated the territorial sovereignty of Albania.

This state of flux creates uncertainty in the system of Public International Law. In the cyber context however, States have pushed especially strongly to accept evidence procured by utilizing methods that are not always lawful. To a large extent this is related to the unique features of cyberspace. It takes sophisticated IT capabilities to attribute a cyber act. Additionally, the de-territorialized nature of cyberspace means that servers located in other States are oftentimes affected by efforts to trace back hacks, risking violations of territorial sovereignty. As a result, the most frequent State organs that conduct such evidence-gathering activities are intelligence and counterintelligence units, oftentimes nested within armed forces. Netherlands stated that gathered evidence in cyberspace can encompass "both information obtained through regular channels and intelligence."[978] Estonia proclaimed that attributive evidence in the cyber context can include "technical information, political context, established behavioural patterns and other relevant indicators."[979] The Australian government went on record writing that it "relies on the

---

977 Mandiant Intelligence Center Report, "APT1: Exposing One of China's Cyber Espionage Units." Retrieved November 30, 2023. <https://www.mandiant.com/resources/reports/apt1-exposing-one-chinas-cyber-espionage-units>.

978 The government of Netherlands. Letter to the parliament on the international legal order in cyberspace, September 26, 2019. Page 6. <https://www.government.nl/documents/parliamentary-documents/2019/09/26/letter-to-the-parliament-on-the-international-legal-order-in-cyberspace>.

979 The government of Estonia. (2019, May 29). Remarks from President of the Republic of Estonia at the opening of CyCon 2019. Retrieved February 19, 2022, from <https://ceipfiles.s3.amazonaws.com/pdf/CyberNorms/LawStatements/

assessments of its law enforcement and intelligence agencies, and consultations with its international partners" in assessing cyber evidence.[980]

As discussed in Chapter 3, there exists no general prohibition of spying in Public International Law, although its methods might be deemed prohibited if they violate Sovereignty of spied-on States. Based on this general foundation, a new norm is potentially emerging to treat cyber spying that utilizes penetrative methods as prohibited.[981] This same logic can be applied to the question of admissibility of cyber evidence. The cyber evidence obtained using non-penetrative methods, such as analysis of a virus code or server logs is unquestionably lawful. The evidence obtained by breaking into systems within jurisdiction of another State, without its consent, has penetrative character and is potentially unlawful. However, since many States are openly admitting that they are using potentially penetrative methods and see those as acceptable, a special norm might be under development, whereas penetrative methods of obtaining evidence for the sake of attribution of a hostile cyber act are lawful, despite the matter being not settled in the broader framework of Public International Law. The Corfu Channel judgment might provide some guidelines for limitations of admissibility of evidence obtained in such a way. In that case, the United Kingdom invoked the principle of *Necessity*, as the reason why it had to act fast to secure evidence.[982] A State pursuing penetrative cyber methods to obtain attributive evidence might have then to act only within the limits if what is necessary and reasonable for the materials to be admissible. Certain international legal scholars, such as François Delerue, appear to support this formulation.[983]

Remarks+by+the+President+of+the+Republic+of+Estonia+at+the+Opening+of+CyCon+2019.pdf>

980 The government of Australia. "Australia's International Cyber Engagement Strategy," November 2020. <https://www.internationalcybertech.gov.au/sites/default/files/2020-11/The%20Strategy.pdf>.

981 See section I.3.2—"Status of espionage in the context of hostile cyber operations" for in-depth analysis of this subject.

982 Case Concerning Corfu Channel I.C.J. Reports 1949, 24, Page 36. Retrieved February 2022. <https://www.icj-cij.org/case/1>.

983 Delerue, François. Cyber Operations and international law. Cambridge: Cambridge University Press, 2020. Page 70.

5.4 Categories of entities, whose hostile cyber operations can be legally attributed to a State

5.4.1 Overview of entities to whom hostile cyber operations can be attributed in Public International Law

Attribution of an *Unfriendly Act* must be done against an entity that has formal standing in Public International Law in order to be effective. This adds to the complexity of the process of attribution as States oftentimes enjoy plausible deniability, rejecting accusations that they are responsible for hostile acts launched from within their jurisdiction. This problem is present in the context of conventional hostilities and only gets more intense in cyberspace due to its transnational and anonymity-inducing nature.

The 2001 *Draft Articles on State Responsibility for Internationally Wrongful Acts* published by the UN ILC proposed a general framework that classifies types of entities, whose actions can be attributed to a State.[984] Twenty-one years after its publication, this framework enjoys wide consensus in the international community and belongs to the part of the *Draft Articles* that is perceived as a reflection of the existing customary law.[985] Therefore, it can be utilized as the basis for considerations, with caveats required to account for the unique character of cyberspace.

There are three key rules included in the *Draft Articles* that bear relevance in terms of identifying the types of entities whose actions are attributable to a State. These are:

- Article 4—Organs of a State;
- Article 8—Entities directed or controlled by a State;
- Article 11—Entities whose conduct was acknowledged and adopted by a State as its own.[986]

---

984 United Nations International Law Commission. (2001). Draft articles on Responsibility of States for Internationally Wrongful Acts with commentaries. United Nations Office of Legal Affairs. Retrieved February 15, 2022, from <https://legal.un.org/ilc/texts/instruments/english/commentaries/9_6_2001.pdf>.

985 Crawford, James. (2002). The ILC's Articles on Responsibility of States for Internationally Wrongful Acts: A Retrospect. American Journal of International Law, 96(4), pages 874–890. <https://doi.org/10.2307/3070683>.

986 United Nations International Law Commission. (2001). Draft articles on Responsibility of States for Internationally Wrongful Acts with commentaries. United Nations Office

Additionally, in 2011, the UN ILC also adopted its final version of the *Draft Articles on the Responsibility of International Organizations.*[987] The status of the norms included in them is still hotly debated in the international community. However, a consensus is now slowly emerging that such entities can commit *Internationally Wrongful Acts,* similarly to States. While not formally attributable to member States, the liability for *Internationally Wrongful Acts* of an international organization eventually burdens them in a collective way (see Figure 14 for details).

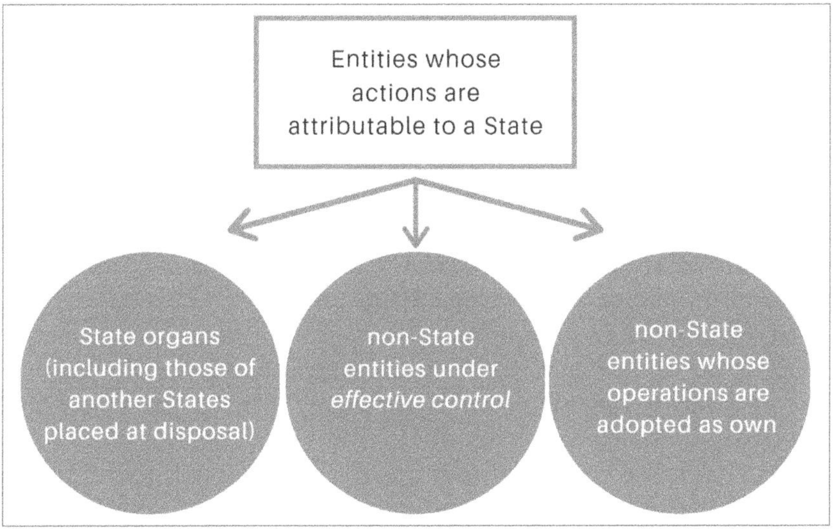

Figure 14. Entities whose cyber operations can be attributed to a State in international law
Source: Own elaboration

of Legal Affairs. Retrieved February 15, 2022, from <https://legal.un.org/ilc/texts/instruments/english/commentaries/9_6_2001.pdf>.

987 United Nations International Law Commission. (2011). Draft articles on Responsibility of International Organizations. United Nations Office of Legal Affairs. Retrieved February 15, 2022, from <https://legal.un.org/ilc/texts/instruments/english/draft_articles/9_11_2011.pdf>.

5.4.2 Attribution of actions conducted by State organs

5.4.2.1 Existing rules on attributing actions of State organs in Public International Law

Article 4 of the Draft Articles on State Responsibility states:

> 1. The conduct of any State organ shall be considered an act of that State under international law, whether the organ exercises legislative, executive, judicial or any other functions, whatever position it holds in the organization of the State, and whatever its character as an organ of the central Government or of a territorial unit of the State. (...)

Article 4 lays out an existing norm of international law, confirmed by the ICJ in a number of rulings—States are held accountable for the actions conducted by their own organs. Being an organ is defined in this context as an entity vested with exercising elements of government authority according to internal law or regulation.[988] For the purpose of attribution, formal organs of a State (e.g., national intelligence agencies), organizational actors that are not formally State organs but have *complete dependence on* the State, organs of other States placed at disposal of a State, and organizations or even just groups of persons, which have been vested with *exercising elements of government authority* by a State qualify as State organs.[989] The ICJ found in its 2007 ruling on the *Bosnia Genocide Case* that the atrocities committed in Srebrnica were not attributable to the State of Serbia because the perpetrators could not be qualified as its organ, showing that an internal legal empowerment to exercise elements of government authority (or alternatively complete dependence on State government) is a necessary requirement for qualification as an organ.[990] Similar conclusion was reached regarding the *Contras* militia in

---

988 Ibid. Article 6.

989 Ibid. Article 5. Paragraph 7.

990 Case Concerning the Application of the Convention on the Prevention and Punishment of the Crime of Genocide (Bosnia and Herzegovina v. Serbia). ICJ Reports 43. (2007). Paragraphs 385 -395. <Https://Www.Icj-Cij.Org/En/Case/91/Judgments>. Retrieved February 16, 2022, from <https://www.icj-cij.org/en/case/91/judgments>.

the Nicaragua v. United States case, where the *Contrast* were deemed not to be effective organs of the United States.[991]

The so-called *ultra vires* acts, that is, acts by State organs that are in excess of their authority or instructions are still attributable to the host State.[992] Per commentary provided by the UN International Law Commission, this type of responsibility likely covers not only offensive actions but also the defensive and retributive ones (although the customary legal status of this provision is uncertain at present).[993]

Actions of both *de jure* and *de facto* organs of a State are attributable to it. According to the *Draft Articles*, a State cannot avoid accountability for its organ's actions "merely by denying it that status under its own law."[994] Importantly, the category of *de facto* organs must be distinguished from non-State entities, whose actions are attributable to a State. Organs are always vested with exercising of government authority while non-State entities are only liable to effective control, as shown in the following subsection. This notion of accountability for actions of *de facto* organs was invoked by the ICJ in its Bosnia and Herzegovina v. Serbia and Montenegro (*Bosnia Genocide*) judgment,[995] as well as the Nicaragua judgment,[996] and the Armed Activities

---

991 Case Concerning Military and Paramilitary Activities in and Against Nicaragua, (Nicaragua v. United States). I.C.J. Reports 14, ICGJ 112 (ICJ 1986). (1986). Paragraph 221. <https://Www.Icj-Cij.Org/En/Case/70/Judgments. Retrieved February 15, 2022, from https://www.icj-cij.org/en/case/70/judgments>.

992 United Nations International Law Commission. (2001). Draft articles on Responsibility of States for Internationally Wrongful Acts with commentaries. United Nations Office of Legal Affairs. Article 7, paragraph 9 of the Commentary. Retrieved February 15, 2022, from <https://legal.un.org/ilc/texts/instruments/english/commentaries/9_6_2001.pdf>.

993 Ibid.

994 United Nations International Law Commission. (2011). Draft articles on Responsibility of International Organizations. United Nations Office of Legal Affairs. Commentary to Article 4, paragraph 11. Retrieved February 15, 2022, from <https://legal.un.org/ilc/texts/instruments/english/draft_articles/9_11_2011.pdf>.

995 Case Concerning the Application of the Convention on the Prevention and Punishment of the Crime of Genocide (Bosnia and Herzegovina v Serbia). ICJ Reports 43. (2007). Paragraph 391. <Https://Www.Icj-Cij.Org/En/Case/91/Judgments>. Retrieved February 16, 2022, from <https://www.icj-cij.org/en/case/91/judgments>.

996 Case Concerning Military and Paramilitary Activities in and Against Nicaragua, (Nicaragua v. United States). I.C.J. Reports 14, ICGJ 112 (ICJ 1986). (1986). Paragraphs

on the Territory of Congo judgment.[997] The Nicaragua judgment is especially prominent since it stated that a group operates as an organ of a State if it is under "strict control" of its government. This provided a tangible test that actions of non-State entities can be compared to. However, in neither of those cases did the ICJ recognize groups responsible for conducting *Internationally Wrongful Acts* as *de facto* organs, opting instead to label them as non-State entities under effective control. This goes to show how rare it is for the *de facto* organ label to be utilized in practice.

5.4.2.2 Transposition of rules on attributing actions of State organs in the cyber context

The threshold established for determining whether the perpetrator of a hostile cyber operation is a State organ is problematic in the cyber context. Establishing a relation between a State and a hacker group operating on its behalf is notoriously challenging. For these reasons, anything other than overt conduct by a State organ, is likely to be captured in the category of non-State entities under effective control (analyzed in the next subsection). François Delerue stated: "it is generally difficult to distinguish state-sponsored cyber operations from cybercrime. Even if the perpetrating group is controlled or sponsored by a State, the difficulty of attribution makes it almost impossible to clearly establish their relationship. (…) Cyber operations might present a new challenge for the agency test, and the rigidity of the strict control test might be called into question."[998] Other scholars, such as Scott Shackelford,[999] expressed a similar stance.

109–110. <https://Www.Icj-Cij.Org/En/Case/70/Judgments>. Retrieved February 15, 2022, from <https://www.icj-cij.org/en/case/70/judgments>.

997 Armed Activities on the Territory of the Congo (Democratic Republic of the Congo v. Uganda)—Judgment. International Court of Justice. ICJ Reports 2005. (2005, December 19). Paragraph 160. Retrieved February 17, 2022, from <https://www.icj-cij.org/en/case/116>.

998 Delerue, François. Cyber Operations and international law. Cambridge: Cambridge University Press, 2020. Page 122.

999 Shackelford, Scott J., From Nuclear War to Net War: Analogizing Cyber Attacks in International Law (April 28, 2009). Berkley Journal of International Law (BJIL), Vol. 25, No. 3, 2009. Page 192. <https://ssrn.com/abstract=1396375>.

The landmark UN GGE Report from 2015 introduced the notion of responsibility of States for hostile cyber operations conducted by their organs.[1000] The direct transposition of norms reflected in the *Draft Articles* was also espoused by the authors of the Tallinn Manual 2.0, a key NATO-sponsored publication composed by a selected group of international experts and scholars.[1001] This includes *ultra vires* cases of abuse as well as actions done by organs of another State put at disposal of a government. For example, if a State puts an ICT experts unit (usually labeled as a *CERT*—Computer Emergency Readiness Team) at another State's disposal to help it defend itself from a cyber assault, and then that team goes on to launch a retributive action against the intruding State, going beyond its original remit, the receiving State bears international legal responsibility for all of the unit's actions since it was acting as its own organ. This will be the case even if the receiving State has never authorized that team to strike back at the intruding State.[1002]

There exist important divergences between the conventional and cyber context in terms of applicability of the earlier stated rule. In the non-cyber context, usage of State resources such as government infrastructure or sophisticated army-owned weapons is perceived as a near-irrefutable proof of an organ activity being attributable to a State.[1003] That is not the case

---

1000 United Nations General Assembly Resolution. (2015, July 22). Group of Governmental Experts on Developments in the Field of Information and Telecommunications in the Context of International Security—Note by the Secretary-General. Paragraph 28(b). Retrieved February 15, 2022, from <https://documents-dds-ny.un.org/doc/UNDOC/GEN/N15/228/35/PDF/N1522835.pdf?OpenElement>;

Kostadinov, Dimitar. (2021, November 28). The attribution problem in cyber attacks. Infosec Resources. <https://resources.infosecinstitute.com/topics/hacking/attribution-problem-in-cyber-attacks/>; Tsagourias, Nicholas. (2012). Cyber attacks, self-defence and the problem of attribution. Journal of Conflict and Security Law, 17(2), pages 229–244. <https://doi.org/10.1093/jcsl/krs019>.

1001 Schmitt, Michael. N. & NATO Cooperative Cyber Defence Centre of Excellence. (2017). Tallinn Manual 2.0 on the International Law Applicable to Cyber Operations. Cambridge University Press. Rule 14, Commentary.

1002 United Nations International Law Commission. (2001). Draft articles on Responsibility of States for Internationally Wrongful Acts with commentaries. United Nations Office of Legal Affairs. Rule 15, Commentary. Retrieved February 15, 2022, from <https://legal.un.org/ilc/texts/instruments/english/commentaries/9_6_2001.pdf>.

1003 Jensen, Eric. T. (2017). The Tallinn Manual 2.0: highlights and insights. Georgetown Journal of International Law, 48(735), 735–778. Page 751. <https://papers.ssrn.com/sol3/papers.cfm?abstract_id=2932110>

in the cyber context. Due to the evidentiary problems described earlier in this chapter, especially the ability to route hostile cyber operations through third-State infrastructure, the same standard is difficult to be applied. The internet infrastructure is dual-purpose and allows for concealment of the source of operation. Even some of the clearest cases, such as the assault of Iranian hackers on an American bank in wake of the Stuxnet operation who appeared to possess confidential intelligence provided by the government, were never publicly attributed to the host State. Legal attribution of cyber assaults directly to a State organ is frequently impossible. This shifts the balance of importance away from Article 4 of the *Draft Articles* and toward Article 8, concerning non-State entities under effective control rather than organs. This shift means that the route of attribution conceived of as the fundamental one becomes near-irrelevant in the cyber context. Instead, an alternative attribution route has become the dominant as it is the most effective tool at the disposal of injured States.

François Delerue proposed a three-step test for proving that hackers behind a hostile operation were acting as a State-organ.[1004] The test applies the general rules on such attribution in the cyber context and is modeled on how activities of private military and mercenary companies can be attributed to a State in the conventional context.[1005] Thus, a hacker group, oftentimes in the form of a cybersecurity company that resembles mercenaries for hire, acts as a State organ if the order to exercise hacking activity:

- has been conferred directly by a State;
- the conferral was made explicitly through a formal act;
- the hacking activity constitutes an exercise of sovereign functions of the State or is connected to them.

The model of transposing rules of attribution developed in the context of military mercenaries for hire by States is compelling although it contains weaknesses that greatly limit its applicability. Specifically, the requirement of

1004 Delerue, François. Cyber Operations and international law. Cambridge: Cambridge University Press, 2020. Page 124.

1005 Lehnardt, Chia. "Private Military Companies and State Responsibility." From Mercenaries to Market, 2007, pages 139–57. <https://doi.org/10.1093/acprof:oso/9780199228485.003.0009>.

a formal conferral of power to exercise cyber hostilities goes against observed practice. Governments can easily and effectively conceal the nature of their relationship with hacking groups within their jurisdiction. While also possible in the conventional context, it is much less likely, which allowed for development of this requirement in the first place. This challenge only strengthens the conclusion that attribution of cyber hostile operations by means of proving hackers were acting as a State organ is not a feasible legal path for injured States.

5.4.3 Attribution of actions conducted by non-State entities under State control

5.4.3.1 Existing rules on attributing actions of non-State entities under State control in Public International Law

Article 8 of the *Draft Articles on State Responsibility for Internationally Wrongful Acts*, which reflects a customary legal norm states:

> The conduct of a person or group of persons shall be considered an act of a State under international law if the person or group of persons is in fact acting on the instructions of, or under the direction or control of that State in carrying out the conduct.[1006]

The most sensitive and ambiguous part of the article is the *instruction, direction or control*. What does it mean for a State to have a non-State entity under its instruction, direction, or control? The commentaries provided by the UN ILC to the *Draft Articles* claim that the most frequent example of *acting* on the *instructions of, the direction, or control of* a State are the so-called *auxiliaries*, which are private persons or groups, who serve a State organ but remain outside of the State's organizational structure.[1007]

Importantly, unlike in the case of State organs, *ultra vires* acts by non-State actors that are under *effective control* of a State are not attributable to the said

1006 United Nations International Law Commission. (2001). Draft articles on Responsibility of States for Internationally Wrongful Acts with commentaries. United Nations Office of Legal Affairs. Rule 8, Commentary. Retrieved February 15, 2022, from <https://legal.un.org/ilc/texts/instruments/english/commentaries/9_6_2001.pdf>.

1007 Ibid. Paragraph 7 of the Commentary.

State.[1008] This means in case of formal State organs, the State is responsible for all actions while in case of non-State entities, such entities only incur responsibility to a State, to a point to which the latter had effective control over their actions.

The term was introduced by the ICJ's ruling on the Case Concerning the Military and Paramilitary Activities in and Against Nicaragua in 1986. In it, the ICJ stated that: *Financing, organising, training, supplying, and equipping ..., the selection of its military or paramilitary targets, and the planning of the whole of its operation' has been found insufficient to reach the 'effective control' threshold.*[1009] While in that case, the threshold of effective control was not reached, the ICJ embraced the notion that such a situation could potentially take place and lead to legal attribution of acts to a State. In the case adjudicated by the Court, the United States was supporting anti-government guerrilla militias in Nicaragua, the so-called Contras, in a variety of profound ways. Nevertheless, the relationship between the U.S. government and Contras did not reach a level that would allow for attribution of the group's actions to the United States. The key element that was missing was a measure of control over actual execution.[1010]

Identification of the evidentiary threshold for *effective control* is complicated by the fact that the definition of the term is still crystallizing. In the case pertaining to Nicaragua, ruled on in 1986, the ICJ distinguished between *effective control* and *general control*, the former being a stricter term that was also selected as the threshold for attributing actions to a State. In the 2007 case pertaining to Bosnia Genocide, where the level of control by the Serbian government over Bosnia-based militias was also deemed insufficient, the ICJ spoke of *strict control* or alternatively *a great degree of control* as the necessary

---

1008 United Nations International Law Commission. (2001). Draft articles on Responsibility of States for Internationally Wrongful Acts with commentaries. United Nations Office of Legal Affairs. Article 8, paragraphs 6-8 of the Commentary. Retrieved February 15, 2022, from <https://legal.un.org/ilc/texts/instruments/english/commentaries/9_6_2001.pdf>.

1009 Case Concerning Military and Paramilitary Activities in and Against Nicaragua, (Nicaragua v. United States). I.C.J. Reports 14, ICGJ 112 (ICJ 1986). Paragraph 115. Retrieved February 15, 2022, from <https://www.icj-cij.org/en/case/70/judgments>.

1010 University of Oslo. (2016, April). When do cyber operations amount to use of force and armed attack, and what response will they justify? Page 41. <https://www.duo.uio.no/bitstream/handle/10852/50840/723.pdf?sequence=1>

threshold.[1011] These terms are similar in meaning but some differences can still be identified. Specifically, the ICJ's 2007 interpretation appears to be narrower and more restrictive. This way, the ICJ framing from the *Bosnia Genocide Case* seems to aim to limit the scope of potential attributable actions. The ICJ wrote in its ruling:

> At any rate, a high degree of control is required because 'to equate persons or entities with State organs when they do not have that status under internal law must be exceptional. (...) If, however, 'some qualified, but real, margin of independence' exists, the entity does not become a de facto organ and its conduct will not be attributed to a State.[1012]

In a sign of a less restrictive approach, The International Criminal Tribunal for the former Yugoslavia (ICTY), a UN court tasked with dealing with war crimes that took place during the Balkan War, offered a different formula than the one suggested by the ICJ. In the case concerning Duško Tadić ruled on in 1997 (related to crimes against humanity committed during the war in former Yugoslavia), the ICTY differentiated between unorganized and organized groups in terms of the threshold necessary for attribution of activities to a State. According to the ICTY, in the former case, the stricter *effective control* requirement must be met because of a less formalized nature of such groups. In the case of well-structured organizations, meeting the softer *overall control* requirement would suffice to hold a State accountable.

Some scholars, such as François Delerue, call out ICTY for allegedly misunderstanding the ICJ's definitions.[1013] The ICJ developed the strict control test to gauge whether a non-State entity can qualify as an organ of a State and the effective control test to gauge whether a non-State entity can qualify as being under instructions of a State. By introducing the overall control test, the ICTY widened the scope of potential attributability. The specific nature of the Duško Tadić Case (individual responsibility for crimes against humanity)

1011 Case Concerning the Application of the Convention on the Prevention and Punishment of the Crime of Genocide (Bosnia and Herzegovina v. Serbia). ICJ Reports 43. (2007). Paragraph 393. Retrieved February 16, 2022, from <https://www.icj-cij.org/en/case/91/judgments>.

1012 Ibid. Paragraphs 393, 394.

1013 Delerue, François. Cyber Operations and international law. Cambridge: Cambridge University Press, 2020. Page 138.

and the fact that the ICJ later strongly rebutted the *overall control* threshold opining that it *stretches too far, almost to a breaking point, the connection which must exist between the conduct of a State's organs and its international responsibility*[1014] imply that this more expansionary approach was a one-off exception rather than a new legal standard.

The European Court of Human Rights also engaged with the question of attribution of acts of non-State actors to a State. In the judgment on the Loizidou v. Turkey case, it was dealing with the question of attributability of actions by Turkish occupational forces in the northern part of Cyprus (self-proclaimed Turkish Republic of Northern Cyprus) to the Republic of Turkey.[1015] The ECHR developed its own threshold—effective overall control, which appears to blend together the notions of effective and overall control developed by the ICJ. This test is effectively more inclusive than the strict "effective control" one. This case is relevant since in the judgment, the court actually did attribute actions of TRNC to Turkey, providing a precedent in that respect. However, the weaker rank of the ECHR as compared to the ICJ means that the impact of its jurisprudence is lesser than that of the ICJ in terms of setting up new norms.[1016] In neither of the two ICJ-ruled cases (Nicaragua and Bosnia genocide) did the Court recognize effective or strict control by the State that would qualify the adjudicated activities as attributable to them. The fact that a wide range of influence that the United States and Serbian governments had over the non-State entities involved in the adjudicated activities was still insufficient to declare *effective control* implies that this requirement is a high threshold for attribution and that it is difficult to meet.

Historic difficulties with clearing the *effective control* threshold, as shown by jurisprudence, make its applicability limited. The ICJ never recognized any action by a non-State entity to be attributable to a State, leaving the question

---

1014 Case Concerning the Application of the Convention on the Prevention and Punishment of the Crime of Genocide (Bosnia and Herzegovina v. Serbia). ICJ Reports 43. (2007). Paragraph 406. Retrieved February 16, 2022, from <https://www.icj-cij.org/en/case/91/judgments>.

1015 Loizidou v. Turkey, Judgment. ECtHR Application no. 15318/89, Reports 1996-VI, paragraphs 49–57. Retrieved February 16, 2022, from <https://hudoc.echr.coe.int/fre#%7B%22itemid%22:[%22001-57920%22]%7D>.

1016 Ibid. Tadic's Appeal (n 34), Paragraphs 131–137.

of what would be enough to allow for an attribution to a State. The UN ILC appears to seek middle ground in its framing of the notion of control, sitting in between the strict ICJ definition and the laxer one proposed by ICTY. Specifically, it refrains from endorsing *overall control* as sufficient proof that an unorganized group of individuals acted under State control, opting instead to require specific instructions or directions that would prove it. In that it is aligned with the ICJ's approach of *effective control* although it does offer a somewhat broader scope of alternative pathways of achieving attribution (instructions/directions/control) than the Court. Figure 15 summarizes various definitional positions assumed by international judiciary bodies as well as the UN ILC.

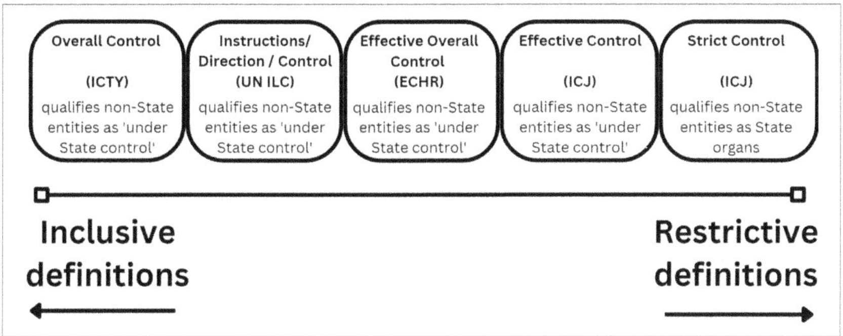

Figure 15. Various interpretations by international judiciary bodies and the UN ILC on what degree of control over non-State entities allows for attribution of their conduct to a State
Source: Own elaboration

5.4.3.2 Transposition of rules on attributing actions of non-State entities under State control in the cyber context

The *effective control* test established by the ICJ in the 1986 Nicaragua judgment, with its many interpretations proposed since by other judiciary bodies and the UN ILC, is the main tool for attributing hostile cyber operations to a State. This creates a subtle difference between the cyber and conventional context. Labeling hacker groups as organs of a State was conceived of as the main mode of attribution in the conventional context (although practice showed this to be a very difficult evidentiary threshold to clear even there).

The most common line of defense that perpetrator States assume when hacking activity is traced back to them is to claim that the hackers were private citizens, unaffiliated with any of its organs. This tactic of plausible deniability creates an aura of impunity, which gives hostile governments much latitude in pursuing targets abroad.[1017] The doctrine of *effective control* can introduce more accountability due its open-ended formulation. For instance, cyber operations of companies (State-owned or otherwise controlled) which depend on their own financial resources for organizational sustenance and are not officially exercising any measure of government authority that characterizes State organs can only be attributed to the host State based on the *effective control* doctrine.[1018] Internet Research Agency, located in Sankt Petersburg, Russia is a good example of a company that has been notoriously found to be involved in international cyber hostilities aligned with the policies of its host State.[1019] The norm is especially relevant in light of modern challenges related to hybrid operation and hostile cyber activity by State-affiliated hackers. Karol Karski and Paweł Mielniczek pointed out the challenge of blurring the distinction between the civilian and military spheres: "Hybrid warfare reflects a wide range of activities that state and non-state actors undertake in order to gain military and political advantages. (…) One common denominator for hybrid warfare, as opposed to the traditional, is a blurring of the

---

1017 Denning, Dorothy. (2015). The Rise of Hacktivism. Georgetown Journal of International Affairs, pages 1–3. <https://www.georgetownjournalofinternationalaffairs.org/online-edition/the-rise-of-hacktivism/>; Geary, S. (2017, February 24). Cyber Proxies: A Central Tenet of Russia's Hybrid Warfare. The Cipher Brief. <https://www.thecipherbrief.com/cyber-proxies-a-central-tenet-of-russias-hybrid-warfare-2>.

1018 Jensen, Eric. T. (2017). The Tallinn Manual 2.0: highlights and insights. Georgetown Journal of International Law, 48(735), pages 735–778. Page 752. <https://papers.ssrn.com/sol3/papers.cfm?abstract_id=2932110>

1019 Barret, Devlin, Horwitz, Sari, and Helderman, Rosalind S. (2018, February 16). Russian Troll farm, 13 suspects indicted in 2016 Election Interference. The Washington Post. <https://www.washingtonpost.com/world/national-security/russian-troll-farm-13-suspects-indicted-for-interference-in-us-election/2018/02/16/2504de5e-1342-11e8-9570-29c9830535e5_story.html>;

Agencja Bezpieczeństwa Wewnętrznego. Zespół Reagowania na Incydenty Bezpieczeństwa Komputerowego. (2014). Raport o stanie bezpieczeństwa cyberprzestrzeni RP w 2014 roku. <https://csirt.gov.pl/cer/publikacje/raporty-o-stanie-bezpi/738,Raport-o-stanie-bezpieczenstwa-cyberprzestrzeni-RP-w-2014-roku.html>.

distinction between military and civilian."[1020] This blurring is even more compounded in the cyber context. International hostile cyber operations by non-State actors under *effective control* of a government can be construed as a form of *hybrid warfare*, undermining a sovereign State while avoiding an open confrontation.

In the cyber context, the level of control necessary to meet the threshold of *effective control* would probably have to be manifested by a government's clear ability to unleash and stop cyber activities of hackers at its will. Other aspects of *effective control* such as giving instructions and directions are much more difficult to register in the cyber context as they leave no physical footprint. In the conventional context such activity might be visible in the form of moving heavy arms or training activities, captured on photos taken by geo-spatial satellites. None of the preparatory work for a hostile cyber operation is physically visible.

For those reasons, scholars such as Scott Shackelford and Johann-Christoph Woltag argued that the threshold set by the ICJ for *effective control* is too high in the cyber context and should be adjusted down in cyberspace as a form of *lex specialis*.[1021] Such a development would make it easier for injured States to seek redress within the framework of Public International Law although it must be critiqued for the hazards it would also create. Specifically, the risk of false flag operations and false accusations would grow exponentially if the threshold of *effective control* is lowered too much. Mistaken attribution followed by a misconceived retribution would also become more likely. Despite challenges, scholars, including François Delerue, expressed three additional reasons, on top of easier concealment of preparatory work mentioned in the previous paragraph, for why application of the threshold in cyberspace could be modified as opposed to the general rules:

1020 Karski, Karol, and Mielniczek, Paweł (2019). The notion of hybrid warfare in international law and its importance for NATO. NATO Legal Gazette, 39, 67–80. <https://www.act.nato.int/application/files/7616/0999/3871/legal_gazette_39.pdf>.

1021 Shackelford, Scott J., From Nuclear War to Net War: Analogizing Cyber Attacks in International Law (April 28, 2009). Berkley Journal of International Law (BJIL), Vol. 25, No. 3, 2009. Page 203. <https://ssrn.com/abstract=1396375>; Woltag, Johann-Christoph, Computer Network Operations Below the Level of Armed Force (May 26, 2011). ESIL 2011 4th Research Forum. Page 91. Retrieved on November 29, 2023. <https://ssrn.com/abstract=1967593>.

- Lower level of organizational cohesiveness needed in cyberspace Both the ICJ and ICTY distinguished non-State entities based on their level or organizational cohesiveness. However, cyberspace allows for delivery of sophisticated hostile acts at a much lower level of organization than it is the case in the conventional realm. For instance, a loosely connected group of hackers conducted hostile cyber operations in support of the Zapatista Army of National Liberation (ZANL), a separatist movement in south Mexico. They assaulted governmental websites of Mexico in 2013 despite never having met in person.[1022] Other hacks, such as the ones conducted by the FloodNet group against the United States, show a similar trait of low level of organization and coordination coupled with a highly effective impact.[1023] This weakens the notion of a high level of organization as an element facilitating attribution to a State in cyberspace.
- Easier way of incentivizing non-State entities to conduct hostile operations supporting State policies in cyberspace As shown by the example of Iran providing data and means for private hackers to assault IT systems of the United States as a response to the Stuxnet virus,[1024] the element of "arming and training," developed by the ICJ in the Nicaragua judgment, takes on a different meaning in cyberspace. Replication of digital means is practically costless. Additionally, a State disseminating cyber tools enabling digital assaults another State can do so with relative impunity. All it takes is an anonymous leak on the internet. Przemysław Roguski postulated that the existing multilateral regime designed for controlling international weapons transfers could potentially accommodate cyber

1022 "Hackers Disrupt Mexico Defense Ministry Website." Phys.org, January 17, 2013. <https://phys.org/news/2013-01-activists-hack-mexican-army-website.html>.

1023 Buck, Stephanie. "One of the First Cyberattacks Was an 'art Project' That Targeted the Pentagon." Medium, March 1, 2017. <https://timeline.com/electronic-disturbance-theater-bace73446dda>.

1024 Hanna, Andrew. "The Invisible u.s.-Iran Cyber War." The Iran Primer, November 1, 2021. <https://iranprimer.usip.org/blog/2019/oct/25/invisible-us-iran-cyber-war>.

tools.[1025] The Wassenaar Arrangement is an international treaty that limits exports of weapons, including "dual-use intrusion software," which it defines as "software designed to avoid being detected by monitoring tools" or to break through "protective countermeasures of a computer" and conducting "extraction of data or modification of the standard execution path of a program or process in order to allow the execution of externally provided instructions."[1026] If code utilized to execute hostile cyber operations could be included in the operational definitions of the Wassenaar Arrangement, it would make their legal attribution easier. The definition of "arming and training," as developed by the ICJ jurisprudence, could then be made broader to capture non-physical cyber means as arms and their one-sided dissemination on the internet as training. This wish, however, has not been expressed by any subject of Public International Law so far and remains an academic postulate. It would also create a risk of misattribution and false flag operations.

- Geographically fragmented evidence requires a higher degree of coordination of the international community in cyberspace While cyberspace is a realm that is ubiquitous and de-territorialized, its physical foundation, in the form of servers and connectors, is not. In fact, when a State is working to trace back hostile cyber operations, pieces of evidence can be disseminated on servers around the world spanning various State jurisdictions. It is then the question of goodwill of each of the host States to allow access to data facilitating attribution. Additionally, there is the challenge of logistics of this process. As a result, injured States have to rely on coordination of the international community more when proving *effective control* in cyberspace, as compared to the conventional realm.

1025 Roguski, Przemysław. "An Inspection Regime for Cyber Weapons: A Challenge Too Far?" AJIL Unbound 115 (2021): pages 111–15. <https://doi.org/10.1017/aju.2021.6>.

1026 Wassenaar Arrangement, List of Dual-Use Goods and Technologies and Munitions List, Cat 4 5P2, WA-LIST (19) 1, page 223. Retrieved on February 26, 2022. <https://www.wassenaar.org/>

Despite these suggestions, modification of the threshold of *effective control* in cyberspace is not realistically possible in the current context. States hesitate to support such changes to the framework of Public International Law for a variety of reasons, one of them being that cyberspace grows and evolves so fast that solutions implemented now could soon become obsolete, only contributing to a sense of flux and dysfunction. In this context, it is important to continue to observe State practice and their *opinio juris* in search of potential trends that can set the ground for future evolution of Public International Law in the cyber context.

5.4.4 Attribution of actions conducted by non-State entities adopted as own by a State

Article 11 of the *Draft Articles on State Responsibility for Internationally Wrongful Acts* which reflects customary a customary legal norm states:

> Conduct which is not attributable to a State under the preceding articles shall nevertheless be considered an act of that State under international law if and to the extent that the State acknowledges and adopts the conduct in question as its own.[1027]

The definition contains two requirements: acknowledgment and adoption, the latter being perceived by scholars, including the ones who wrote the official commentary to the *Draft Articles,* in a cumulative fashion, meaning that it also includes in itself the former one.[1028]

The only historic legal case where the ICJ recognized actions of non-State actors to be attributable to a State based on adoption was in its 1979 ruling on the *Case Concerning United States Diplomatic and Consular Staff in Tehran*. Specifically, in that case the pro-Islamist protesters who stormed the U.S. embassy in Tehran were deemed to act on behalf of the government, their

---

1027 United Nations International Law Commission. (2001). Draft articles on Responsibility of States for Internationally Wrongful Acts with commentaries. United Nations Office of Legal Affairs. Rule 11, Commentary. Retrieved February 15, 2022, from <https://legal.un.org/ilc/texts/instruments/english/commentaries/9_6_2001.pdf>.

1028 United Nations International Law Commission. (2001). Draft articles on Responsibility of States for Internationally Wrongful Acts with commentaries. United Nations Office of Legal Affairs. Article 8, paragraphs 6–8 of the Commentary. Article 11. Retrieved February 15, 2022, from <https://legal.un.org/ilc/texts/instruments/english/commentaries/9_6_2001.pdf>.;

actions attributable to the State under Public International Law. This conclusion was made possible by the government of the new Islamic Republic of Iran, which approved and perpetuated the escalation after the building had been stormed by protesters.[1029]

A situation where a newly established State acknowledges and adopts conduct of its non-State precursors, such as pro-independence militias or autonomous self-government is the only type adoption so far experienced in international law.[1030] That was the case in 1913 when Greece adopted prior conduct of the Greek self-government of Crete from the time when the island was still controlled by the Ottoman Empire.[1031] It was also the case during the "Year of Africa" in 1960, when several new States on the continent adopted international legal responsibility for behavior of pro-independence movements that had taken place prior to declaring independence. One exception from that pattern is one of the cases adjudicated by The International Criminal Tribunal for the Former Yugoslavia, which considered whether the Serbian government adopted abusive conduct of soldiers at the Sušica detention camp, ruling against that conclusion.[1032]

Potentially, State could claim conduct of non-State entities in other situations too, including hostile cyber operations. This, however, remains a hypothetical scenario. States have no incentive to adopt *Internationally Wrongful Acts* as their own. In fact, the known practice of States goes in the exact opposite direction—creating a context of plausible deniability that allows governments to deny any wrongdoing. For these reasons, adoption of wrongful conduct by a State might be an even rarest occurrence in the cyber context than it is in the conventional one.

1029 United States Diplomatic and Consular Staff in Tehran (United States of America v. Iran). International Court of Justice. ICJ Reports 1980. (1980, May 24). Page 3. Retrieved February 17, 2022, from <https://www.icj-cij.org/en/case/64>.

1030 Delerue, François. Cyber Operations and international law. Cambridge: Cambridge University Press, 2020. Page 152.

1031 Affaire relative à la concession des phares de l'Empire ottoman (Grèce, France). Reports Of International Arbitral Awards vol.XII. Page 155. Retrieved February 15, 2022, from <https://legal.un.org/riaa/cases/vol_XII/155-269_Concession.pdf>.

1032 Prosecutor v. Dragan Nikolic (Decision on Defence Motion Challenging the Exercise of Jurisdiction by the Tribunal), 2002. Case no. IT-94-2-PT. ICTY, Trial Chamber II. Paragraphs 60–64. <https://www.icty.org/x/file/Legal%20Library/jud_supplement/supp37-e/nikolic.htm>

The closest case that resembles State adoption of wrongful conduct in cyberspace that otherwise was not formally attributed to it is the reaction of the Israeli military establishment to the success of the Stuxnet virus in damaging Iranian nuclear facilities. In 2011, an Israeli Armed Forces general Gabi Ashkenazi threw a party to celebrate his transition into retirement. Israel Defense Forces' staff displayed a presentation during the event that showcased the main successes during the general's tenure, which included deployment of Stuxnet. The photos from the event, including the snapshots of the presentation were then leaked to the media.[1033] This however was not a formal adoption by a State and remains an isolated case.

5.4.5 Attribution of hostile cyber operations to international organizations

International organizations and various types of international collaboration initiatives are some of the most active entities in the cyber realm (for instance, NATO, The Five Eyes Alliance, the European Union). The role of the UN ITU and multilateral initiatives at various stages of formalization in the effort of formalization of attribution processes and more broadly Public International Law on cyberspace was highlighted in Chapters 1 and 2. Some of them have developed expertise and IT capabilities that far outweigh those of most States. This begs the question of legal responsibility in cyberspace of subjects of international law other than States. The precondition for an international organization's formal responsibility is having legal personhood that is different from that of the member States. This narrows down the scope of potential subjects to treaty-based organizations that have legal capacity to make formal decisions on its own behalf.[1034] the ICJ confirmed the notion of

---

1033 Williams, Christopher. "Israel Video Shows Stuxnet as One of Its Successes." The Telegraph, February 15, 2011. <https://www.telegraph.co.uk/news/worldnews/middleeast/israel/8326387/Israel-video-shows-Stuxnet-as-one-of-its-successes.html>.

1034 Fitzmaurice, Gerald G. Definition of the term "international organization." First report on the law of treaties. Yearbook of the International Law Commission 1956, vol. II, document A/CN.4/101, p. 108. <https://legal.un.org/ilc/publications/yearbooks/english/ilc_1956_v2.pdf>; Institute of International Law (Institut De Droit International). Lisbon resolution on the legal consequences for member states of

international legal responsibility of international organizations in its advisory opinion on the Interpretation of the Agreement of 25 March 1951 between Egypt and the World Health Organization:

International organizations are bound by any obligations incumbent upon them under general rules of international law, under their constitutions or under international agreements to which they are parties.[1035]

The *Draft Articles on the Responsibility of International Organizations*, published by the UN ILC in 2011, replicate the model for States' responsibility for *Internationally Wrongful Acts*, and apply it to international organizations. Article 4 of the 2011 *Draft Articles* states:

> There is an internationally wrongful act of an international organization when conduct consisting of an action or omission:

(a) is attributable to that organization under international law; and
(b) constitutes a breach of an international obligation of that organization.[1036]

The two requirements: existence of a breach and attributability of it to an international organization mirror the ones set for responsibility of States. The same is the case with organs of international organizations placed at disposal of another international organizations and *ultra vires* acts, that is, *Internationally Wrongful Acts* committed by organs of an international organization that go against or beyond the instructions provided by the international organization, yet were committed in the official capacity and within their overall function.[1037]

---

the non-fulfillment by international organizations of their obligations toward third parties. (Institute of International Law, Yearbook, vol. 66, Part II, Session of Lisbon (1995), page 445. <https://www.idi-iil.org/app/uploads/2017/06/1995_lis_02_en.pdf>.

1035 Interpretation of the Agreement of 25 March 1951 between the WHO and Egypt, Advisory Opinion, I.C.J. Reports 1980, page 73, paragraph 37.

1036 United Nations International Law Commission. (2011). Draft articles on Responsibility of International Organizations. United Nations Office of Legal Affairs. Commentary. Retrieved February 15, 2022, from <https://legal.un.org/ilc/texts/instruments/english/commentaries/9_11_2011.pdf>.

1037 Ibid. Commentary on Articles 6–8.

This is not a purely hypothetical challenge. International legal responsibility of the United Nations for wrongful conduct of peacekeeping forces in Kosovo (UNMIK and KFOR) was considered by the European Court of Human Rights in 2007 in a number of cases: *Behrami and Behrami v. France, Saramati v. France, Germany and Norway, Kasumaj v. Greece, Gajić v. Germany*, and *Berić and others v. Bosnia and Herzegovina*.[1038] In 2008, The District Court of The Hague considered attribution of actions taken by the Dutch contingent in the UNPROFOR peacekeeping mission to the United Nations during the massacre in Srebrenica, Yugoslavia.[1039]

Similar considerations took place in front of the Court of First Instance of Brussels in 2010, which considered the case of abandoning of the Kigali refugee camp in Rwanda by personnel of the UNAMIR peacekeeping mission, which enabled violations of human rights, international humanitarian law, and international refugee law to take place there.[1040] Mishandling of the MONUC mission in the Democratic Republic of Congo by the United Nations led to a settlement and monetary compensation, the basis for which was Public International Law violations.[1041]

As of 2025, no attribution of any hostile cyber operations has been made that would implicate an international organization. However, it remains a distinctive possibility that could actualize in the future.

[1038] Grand Chamber decision of 2 May 2007 (Admissibility), Application nos. 71412/01 and 78166/01, European Court of Human Rights. <http://hudoc.echr.coe.int>.

[1039] H. N. v. the Netherlands, Case No. 265615/HA ZA 06-1671, Judgment of 10 September 2008, District Court of The Hague, para. 4.8. <http://deeplink.rechtspraak.nl/uitspraak?id=ECLI:NL:RBSGR:2008:BF0181>.

[1040] Mukeshimana-Ngulinzira and Others v. Belgium and Others, RG Nos. 04/4807/A and 07/15547/A, Judgment of 8 December 2010, Court of First Instance of Brussels, Oxford Reports on International Law in Domestic Courts, vol. 1604 (BE 2010), paragraph 38; <https://www.cambridge.org/core/services/aop-cambridge-core/content/view/EE37C3B257746BD5D4E4B5AAC3B7D355/S000293002000007Xa.pdf/mukeshimana-ngulinzira-and-others-v-belgium-and-others.pdf>.

[1041] United Nations, Treaty Series, vol. 535, No. 7779 (1966), page 191. <https://treaties.un.org/doc/Publication/UNTS/Volume%20535/v535.pdf>

5.5 State Jurisdiction

5.5.1 The established norms on State jurisdiction in international law

5.5.1.1 Definitional scope of State jurisdiction

Analogously to other key elements of the system of Public International Law, there is no one source of law containing a comprehensive legal definition of jurisdiction. The concept reaches back thousands of years and has undergone a complex evolution and expansion throughout history that results in its current shape. Having said that, there exists consensus on the key components of its definition, grounded in treaties, State practice, and judgments of the ICJ and other international judiciary bodies.

The term jurisdiction stems from the Latin *jurisdictio* and is a combination of two words: *juris* (law) and *dictio* (stating or telling). In that, this Roman legal term denotes the power to define what is the applicable law in any given situation. Since in the ancient empire non-Roman citizens were subject to a different set of rules (called *jus gentium*) than the citizens, the concept of jurisdiction originally helped distinguish those separate legal cases. In the modern context, the term rose to prominence in the post-1648 Westphalian Western world order, alongside the notions of sovereignty and sovereign equality.[1042] Since then, the ability to wield the sole authority on what is the binding law has been perceived as an attribute of sovereignty and a core competence of an independent State. In that, jurisdiction took on a near-absolute character, becoming an important demonstration of a fully self-governing nation. Emergence of the post-World-War-2 system of international law, centered around the UN Charter and protection of basic human rights, led in turn to more emphasis on the role of *jus cogens* and binding decisions made by the UN Security Council as guardrails limiting abusive excesses perpetrated by States within their jurisdiction. While the notion of jurisdiction is a term nested within the framework of Public International Law, it has tangible impacts on domestic legal orders and accountability of individuals. In that it serves as a connective tissue between international

1042 Ryngaert, Cedric (2014). The Concept of Jurisdiction in International Law, Utrecht University Papers, page 3. <https://unijuris.sites.uu.nl/wp-content/uploads/sites/9/2014/12/The-Concept-of-Jurisdiction-in-International-Law.pdf>

and national legal orders. The doctrine has identified three main elements of jurisdiction in international law:

- Prescriptive element;
- Enforcement element;
- Adjudicative element.[1043]

The prescriptive element refers to a State's competence to legislate or otherwise define what the binding legal rules are. The 1927 *Lotus* judgment, adjudicated by the PCIJ, asserted that States are in principle free to exercise prescriptive jurisdiction over any situation on their sovereign territory, unless there exists a *jus cogens* rule in international law prohibiting it.[1044] While the core of the prescriptive element is defining law over sovereign territory, there exist a number or rules that extend the scope beyond that basic scope, most relevantly in the context of international criminal law, where nationals of a given State are usually subject to their domestic criminal jurisdiction regardless of their physical location.

Jurisdiction's enforcement element is the logical consequence of the prescriptive element. Jurisdiction is only meaningful if the prescribed norms are being enforced and actions are held accountable accordingly. This element and its aspects were also confirmed by the PCIJ's *Lotus* judgment[1045] and additionally discussed in the Tadić judgment by the ICJ.[1046] Enforcement might take on the form, for example, of making the prohibited conduct cease.

Finally, the adjudicative element denotes the ability to subject physical and legal entities to court or arbitrage proceedings that follow the State's law.

Control of territory is at the core of the notion of State sovereignty. By that logic, jurisdiction, which is a core part of State sovereignty, is intrinsically

---

1043 Ibid. Page 4.

1044 The Case of the S.S. Lotus (France v. Turkey). Permanent Court of International Justice, Award. September 7, 1927. Permanent Court of International Justice (series A). Pages 18–19. Retrieved February 17, 2022. <https://www.icj-cij.org/public/files/permanent-court-of-international-justice/serie_A/A_10/30_Lotus_Arret.pdf>.

1045 Ibid.

1046 Prosecutor vs. Tadić, signature IT-94-1-A (July 15, 1999). International Criminal Tribunal for the former Yugoslavia. United Nations. Retrieved February 17, 2022. <https://www.icty.org/en/case/tadic>

connected to the notion of territory. In fact, historically, the first sphere of jurisdiction was that over territory. Every other realm of where State jurisdiction extends, including water, air, outer space, or even cyberspace followed later and those are still perceived as derivative ones compared to the foundational realm that is territory.

The notion of territory has evolved over centuries. At present, territory in Public International Law is defined to encompass land within a State's borders, its territorial waters, that is, waters within three nautical miles of the permanently exposed land,[1047] archipelago waters, and airspace up until the border with outer space, customarily understood to be at the altitude of around 80–120 km above the sea level (the lowest level at which satellites can hover without falling back on Earth).[1048] The underground part of the land is also part of the territory and spans all the way to the Earth's core in a cone-like fashion until the point of singularity at the planet's center.[1049] As the technological frontiers are evolving and additional spheres are included in States' jurisdiction, such as satellites in outer space or cyberspace, we are observing a slow process of de-territorialization of jurisdiction.[1050] According to the current state of Public International Law, a State can exercise its jurisdiction in the following types of space:

1047 United Nations. (1982, December 10). United Nations Convention on the Law of the Sea. Section II—Territorial Sea And Contiguous Zone. Retrieved February 17, 2022, from <https://www.un.org/Depts/los/convention_agreements/texts/unclos/part2.htm> Encyclopedia Britannica. (n.d.). Terrritorial Waters in international law. Retrieved February 17, 2022, from <https://www.britannica.com/topic/territorial-waters>.

1048 International law does not formally define the upper-elevation boundary of sovereign airspace. The two proposals in circulation are the so-called *Kármán Line* set by the Fédération Aéronautique Internationale (FAI) at 100 kilometers and the alternative proposal of the US Air Force at ~ 80 kilometers (50 miles). See: von der Dunk, Frans. G. (2005). The Sky Is the Limit–But Where Does It End? Space, Cyber, and Telecommunications Law Program Faculty Publications, 34, pages 84–94.

1049 Worona, Joanna, "Cyberprzestrzeń a Prawo Międzynarodowe - Status Quo i Perspektywy." Ph.D. dissertation, University of Bialystok, 2017. Page 490.

1050 Rivkin, David W. "The Importance of Extraterritorial Jurisdiction - Report of the Task Force on Extraterritorial Jurisdiction." International Bar Association. Retrieved November 30, 2023. Page 33. <https://www.ibanet.org/MediaHandler?id=ECF39839-A217-4B3D-8106-DAB716B34F1E>.

- within its territorial borders;
- within the airspace over its territory;
- within its territorial waters and the exclusive economic zone;
- within its diplomatic and consular missions;
- on vessels and aircraft under its national ensign;
- on the satellites, which it has launched into outer space.

This is a universal scope of State jurisdiction that is applicable beyond just cyberspace. It stems from application of the *Principle of Sovereignty* as well as a number of international treaties and related customary norms that together define the scope of State jurisdiction.[1051]

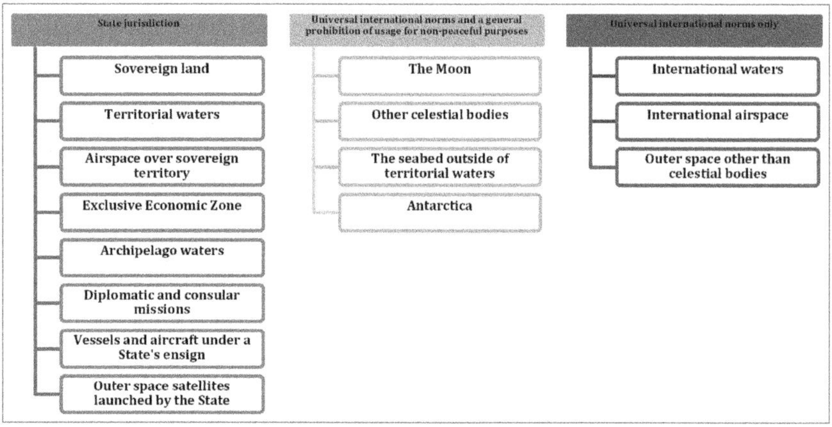

Figure 16. Jurisdiction spheres in Public International Law
Source: Own elaboration

Figure 16 presents types of jurisdiction applicable in different areas. Frequently jurisdictions of various States overlap, for example, when a ship under a national ensign is moored in a port in a foreign country.

From the perspective of Public International Law, any space can be categorized as either claimed by jurisdiction of a State or unclaimable

1051 Moynihan, Harriet. (2019, December). The Application of International Law to State Cyberattacks. Chatham House. Page 13. <https://www.chathamhouse.org/2019/12/application-international-law-state-cyberattacks>.

by any State. The latter category can be further split. There exist spaces where universal international law applies alongside a general prohibition of non-peaceful activities (the Moon, other celestial bodies, the seabed outside of territorial waters, and Antarctica). There are also spaces where universal international law applies without any specific prohibition of non-peaceful activities. These include international waters, international airspace, and outer space (except for celestial bodies).[1052] Authors such as Janusz Gilas offer an alternative way to categorize spaces unclaimable by State jurisdiction, splitting them into *res usum publicum* (common usage space), *res communis* (collective ownership space), and no-man's land.[1053]The first category includes open seas and outer space and is based on the notion of free passage and exploration that applies there. The second category includes the seabed outside of territorial waters and is based on the fact that the international community arranged for extraction of natural resources from seabed outside of any State's jurisdiction. The basis for this is the framework developed in the 1982 United Nations Convention on the Law of the Sea.[1054] The third category relates to territory unclaimed by any State, which at present is nearly non-existent except for special cases such as the Bir Tawil area between Egypt and Sudan.

Cyberspace defies these existing divisions as various layers of it are covered by either a State jurisdiction or the *res communis/res usus publicum* regulations. The exact contours of that distinction are debated within the community of scholars and are scrutinized closely in Section 5.5.2. In order to set up the context for that analysis, Subsection 5.5.1.2 analyzes the historical development of the notions of international waters, open seas and the outer space's status as common heritage of mankind, as these debates directly influence the emerging consensus on the status of cyberspace.

1052 Worona, Joanna, "Cyberprzestrzeń a Prawo Międzynarodowe - Status Quo i Perspektywy." Ph.D. dissertation, University of Bialystok, 2017. Pages 486–487.

1053 Ibid. Page 1240

1054 United Nations. (1982, December 10). United Nations Convention on the Law of the Sea. Section II—Territorial Sea And Contiguous Zone. Retrieved February 17, 2022. <https://www.un.org/Depts/los/convention_agreements/texts/unclos/part2.htm>

5.5.1.2 Development of the notion of open seas, seabed, and the outer space as *res communis* in international law

Open seas

The concept of permissibility of open-sea warfare and more broadly the rule of freedom of open sea has been a *de facto* part of the system of international law since time immemorial, stretching as far back as antiquity. During the early era of transatlantic exploration, the Spanish and Portuguese empires confirmed the freedom of navigation in open sea in several bilateral treaties that were then utilized as the legal basis when other European powers, such as France, Netherlands, and England, joined the race to conquer overseas lands.[1055] In 1609, Hugo Grotius argued in his treatise *Mare Liberum* that the principle of freedom of navigation in open seas is a natural right that supersedes man-made legal orders.[1056] This approach reflects the status of the norm at the time. It is also the first instance of framing open sea as *res communis* (a term utilized by Hugo Grotius in the treatise). It implied that much like a shared pasture in a shepherd community, the open sea could not be claimed by any specific entity as its own. Instead, everyone was allowed to use it. The 1958 Geneva Conventions on the Law of the Sea embraced the notion of *res communis* in application to open seas. It defined open sea as any sea or ocean that is not part of any State's territorial waters and declared it "open to all the nations."[1057]

The international legal framing of the seabed below the open sea and outer space follows an analogous but slightly different formulation, namely that of "common heritage of mankind" that stays under collective oversight of the international community. This represents a shift compared to the *res communis* framing developed to regulate the open sea. In 1967, Arvida Pardo and Aldo Cocca presented this formulation to the UN General Assembly,[1058] which was soon espoused by the majority of developing countries and was endorsed by the UN General Assembly in its 1971 resolution on the status of

1055 Worona, Joanna, "Cyberprzestrzeń a Prawo Międzynarodowe - Status Quo i Perspektywy." Ph.D. dissertation, University of Bialystok, 2017. Page 493.

1056 Ibid. Page 494.

1057 United Nations. (1956, April 29). Geneva Conventions on the Law of the Sea. Retrieved February 17, 2022. <https://legal.un.org/avl/ha/gclos/gclos.html>.

1058 United Nations General Assembly. (1967, November 1) Twenty-second session. First Committee 1515th Meeting. Official Records. <https://www.un.org/depts/los/convention_agreements/texts/pardo_ga1967.pdf>

seabed.[1059] The common heritage framing was also integrated into the 1982 United Nations Convention on the Law of the Sea in reference to seabed, even establishing the Sea-Bed Authority to oversee this space.[1060] The important distinction between framing these spaces as common heritage rather than *res communis* is that the latter implies free access to exploration and utilization of natural resources, while the former implies limited ability to extract resources that is regulated collectively by the international community.[1061]

Expansion of their jurisdiction over the 200-nautical-mile-long exclusive economic zones by coastal States in the world in the second half of the twentieth century has limited the scope of open seas.[1062] However, it did not directly infringe on the principle of innocent passage, which is an important component of the notion of open seas. The principle of innocent passage is also applicable outside of open seas and allows foreign ships to pass through a State's territorial waters, exclusive economic zones, and archipelago waters unobstructed within 3,200 nautical miles from the permanently exposed land of a coastal State as long as its passage is not prejudicial to the peace, good order or security of the said State. This customary norm was confirmed by the 1982 United Nations Convention on the Law of the Sea.[1063] It was however part of the system of international law long before. The ICJ's *Corfu Channel* judgment from 1949 confirmed the principle and importantly asserted that

1059 United Nations General Assembly Resolution. Declaration of Principles Governing the Sea-Bed and the Ocean Floor, and the Subsoil Thereof, beyond the Limits of National Jurisdiction. 25th session (1970). Retrieved February 17, 2022. <https://digitallibrary.un.org/record/201718?ln=en>.

1060 United Nations. (1982, December 10). United Nations Convention on the Law of the Sea. Section II—Territorial Sea And Contiguous Zone. Retrieved February 17, 2022. <https://www.un.org/Depts/los/convention_agreements/texts/unclos/part2.htm>; Encyclopedia Britannica. (n.d.). Terrritorial Waters in international law. Retrieved February 17, 2022. <https://www.britannica.com/topic/territorial-waters>.

1061 Worona, Joanna, "Cyberprzestrzeń a Prawo Międzynarodowe - Status Quo i Perspektywy." Ph.D. dissertation, University of Bialystok, 2017. Page 493.

1062 The government of the United States. "What Is the 'EEZ'?" What is the "EEZ"?: Exploration Facts: NOAA Office of Ocean Exploration and Research. Accessed December 1, 2023. <https://oceanexplorer.noaa.gov/facts/useez.html>.

1063 United Nations. (1982, December 10). United Nations Convention on the Law of the Sea. Section II - Territorial Sea And Contiguous Zone. Articles 18, 19. Retrieved February 17, 2022. <https://www.un.org/Depts/los/convention_agreements/texts/unclos/part2.htm>

a coastal State is not obliged to be aware of all the movements by foreign vessels taking place within waters covered by its jurisdiction.[1064] This assertion can potentially have a substantial impact on international legal norms regulating cyberspace, as laid out in Sections 5.6 and 5.7.

Outer space

Soon after the launch of the first satellite into outer space in 1958, the United Nations General Assembly formed the Committee on the Peaceful Uses of Outer Space (COPUOS), which exists until today.[1065] The two States which launched the first satellites: the Soviet Union and the United States, did it under open assumption that such conduct was legal from the Public International Legal perspective. Lack of resistance of the international community to it cemented this understanding as a new legal norm. The COPUOS's work alongside several international treaties regulating outer space, most importantly the Outer Space Treaty of 1967, have defined the shape of regulations covering this new domain of State activity. The selected model is that of common heritage of mankind, analogous to the one applied to seabed, rather than the *res communis* model applied to open seas. This can be deduced from Article I or the Outer Space Treaty, which states:

> Article I
> The exploration and use of outer space, including the moon and other celestial bodies, shall be carried out for the benefit and in the interests of all countries, irrespective of their degree of economic or scientific development, and shall be the province of all mankind.
>
> Outer space, including the moon and other celestial bodies, shall be free for exploration and use by all States without discrimination of any kind, on a basis of equality and in accordance with international law, and there shall be free access to all areas of celestial bodies. (...)[1066]

1064 Case Concerning Corfu Channel I.C.J. Reports 1949, 24, Page 28. Retrieved February 2022. <https://www.icj-cij.org/case/1>.

1065 Wickramatunga, Robert. "United Nations - Office for Outer Space Affairs." COPUOS History. Accessed December 1, 2023. <https://www.unoosa.org/oosa/en/ourwork/copuos/history.html#:~:text=In%201958%2C%20shortly%20after%20the,the%20specialized%20agencies%20and%20other>.

1066 United Nations. (1966, December 19). Treaty on Principles Governing the Activities of States in the Exploration and Use of Outer Space, including the Moon and Other

The practical implications of this choice are that exploration and exploitation of resources in outer space can only proceed in the interest of the whole international community, rather than a singular State. However, the practice of exploration of outer space appears to be in-between the frameworks of *res communis* and common heritage. Lukasz Kaluga has pointed out that technologically advanced States and private companies draw commercial benefits from outer space activity that oftentimes fits best the *res communis* approach of free access, despite a notional commitment to the common heritage of mankind model.[1067]

The analogy between open sea, seabed, and outer space created a pattern, according to which, new types of spaces available for States' exploration could be regulated based on adaptation of the existing model of either *res communis* or common heritage of mankind. This has practical implications for the legal framework regulating States' cyber-activity as laid out in the next subsection.

5.5.2 Application of the norms concerning State jurisdiction in cyberspace

5.5.2.1 The proposed framework on structuring State jurisdiction in cyberspace

Application of the notion of jurisdiction in cyberspace is the source of an ongoing debate. There exists no consensus among States nor international jurisprudence on the subject. However, by way of analogy, historical judgments and opinions of international judiciary bodies as well as emerging patterns of State practice can serve as guidelines for what it might be. The internet infrastructure is a mesh that envelops the planet and parts of its orbit, blurring State boundaries. There are no fixed physical boundaries that easily define jurisdiction areas of each country. This presents a challenge to the process of legal attribution of cyber operations. An attack that is routed through undersea cables and outer space satellites can pass through several jurisdictions. It creates a question regarding not only where the attack came from, but also which State is eligible to perceive its jurisdiction as being

---

Celestial Bodies. Retrieved February 17, 2022. <https://www.unoosa.org/oosa/en/ourwork/spacelaw/treaties/outerspacetreaty.html>.

1067 Worona, Joanna, "Cyberprzestrzeń a Prawo Międzynarodowe - Status Quo i Perspektywy." Ph.D. dissertation, University of Bialystok, 2017. Page 503.

affected and enact self-help measures such as countermeasures against the perpetrator State. There is an ongoing legal debate on the extent to which pass-through States are entitled to raise such legal claims.[1068]

While States have jurisdiction over ICT infrastructure that sits within their sovereign territory, there is an open debate on the so-called pass-through States in the cyber context. Since the internet network is a system that effectively covers all the countries in the world, many of them might end up involuntarily lending their ICT infrastructure to a hostile cyber operation as it passes through it. This situation is not directly comparable with any conventional context. Many scholars are of the opinion that a pass-through State does not enjoy jurisdiction over such activities and their impact elsewhere because of its *de minimis* connection with sit.[1069] However, there is no established State practice or jurisprudence in that regard. So far though, on the few occasions that a government would publicly attribute a hostile cyber operation to another State, they never mentioned pass-through countries, implying that they are not to be held accountable for cyber operations that pass through their territory.

Several scholars, including the International Group of Experts who authored the Tallinn Manual[1070] as well as Tomasz Welanyk,[1071] have proposed their frameworks. Doing so requires resolving several legal points of tension as described. The general consensus emerging from the work of the UN OEWG, including its reports endorsed by the UN General Assembly, is that the ICT infrastructure that sustains the internet and cyberspace physically located within territory of a State is always covered by its jurisdiction.[1072] This however creates a challenge that stems from the nature of cyberspace.

1068 Tsagourias, Nicholas., & Buchan, Russell. (2021). Research Handbook on International Law and Cyberspace (Research Handbooks in International Law series) (2nd ed.). Edward Elgar Publishing. Section "The legal status of cyberspace," Summary Point 13.

1069 Schmitt, Michael. N. & NATO Cooperative Cyber Defence Centre of Excellence. (2017). Tallinn Manual 2.0 on the International Law Applicable to Cyber Operations. Cambridge University Press. Page 56.

1070 Ibid. Commentary.

1071 Welanyk, Tomasz, "Istnienie i granice suwerenności w cyberprzestrzeni. Analiza prawna." Ph.D. dissertation, University of Warsaw, 2019. Page 33.

1072 United Nations General Assembly Resolution. Open-ended working group on developments in the field of information and telecommunications in the context of international security - Final Substantive Report. A/AC.290/2021/CRP.2.

At any given moment, a stream of data flows through the ICT infrastructure of States, en route from one part of the globe to another. If placing the ICT infrastructure within jurisdiction were to include all activity that takes place on it, effectively all States would hold jurisdiction over just about everything that takes place over the internet at all times. This would lead to problematic conclusions and destabilization of the system of Public International Law. A number of States with no meaningful connection to a hostile cyber operation could enact *Countermeasures* or be targeted by them based on the fact that related data passed through servers located within their territory for a fraction of a second.

Authors of the Tallinn Manual argued that the solution to that tension is to perceive the international internet data flows like ships passing through the territorial waters (ICT infrastructure) of a State.[1073] This analogy would allow for extension of the principle of innocent passage to cyberspace. It would also apply the requirement of the cyber activities flowing through the servers located in a State not being prejudicial to its peace, good order or security. Transposition of this requirement would create a convenient threshold that would explain why most internet data flows taking place via national ICT infrastructure are not a responsibility of the host State. It would also allow for application of existing international jurisprudence on the matter of territorial waters. Most importantly, the Corfu Channel judgment, which absolved a coastal State from a hypothetical requirement of knowing of all the movements in all its territorial waters at all times would apply.[1074] However, this proposed model is simplistic and does not solve all the conceptual problems posed by cyberspace. As pointed out by Tomasz Welanyk, there exists no State practice or *opinio juris* that would point to the data flows on national ICT infrastructure being always subject to the host State's jurisdiction.[1075]

Retrieved February 17, 2022. <https://front.un-arm.org/wp-content/uploads/2021/03/Final-report-A-AC.290-2021-CRP.2.pdf>.

1073 Welanyk, Tomasz, "Istnienie i granice suwerenności w cyberprzestrzeni. Analiza prawna." Ph.D. dissertation, University of Warsaw, 2019. Page 29.

1074 Case concerning Corfu Channel (United Kingdom of Great Britain and Northern Ireland v. Albania). I.C.J. Reports 1949, 244, Gen L No. 1. (1949). Judgment. Retrieved February 15, 2022. <https://www.icj-cij.org/en/case/1>.

1075 Welanyk, Tomasz, "Istnienie i granice suwerenności w cyberprzestrzeni. Analiza prawna." Ph.D. dissertation, University of Warsaw, 2019. Page 30.

If anything, the evidence points to the opposite, States do not exercise jurisdiction over any random data flows that appear on its servers for a fraction of a second. Meanwhile, ships in a State's territorial waters are always subject to the host State's jurisdiction. The analogy also does not explain how to treat certain types of hostile malware that lingers on the ICT infrastructure. For instance, would spying software nested on a State's ICT infrastructure that collects intelligence data on a third State be prejudicial to the host State's peace, good order or security? The Tallinn Manual's authors engaged with this question and were not able to answer it.[1076]

The framework structuring State jurisdiction in cyberspace should start with a distinction between its material/physical and non-material/cyber components. Following is a proposition on its possible shape. On the one end of the spectrum, we have the physical infrastructure upholding the system. It is physically located within a State jurisdiction and is covered by it. The ICJ's *Rainbow Warrior* judgment pointed out that any non-consensual hostile physical impact within a State's territory violates its sovereignty and therefore constitutes an *Internationally Wrongful Act*.[1077] This conclusion applies to the ICT infrastructure too. Any harm, tampering, or otherwise hostile conduct toward the physical infrastructure is subject to the host State's jurisdiction. States also have full jurisdiction over data stored on servers located in their territory. On the other end of the spectrum there are the accidental internet data flows that create the non-material part of cyberspace. The emerging State practice points in the direction of no jurisdiction over them of the States, whose infrastructure was used as an accidental pass-through for hostile cyber operation, constituting a space similar in nature to open seas res communis. Data flows here are similar

---

1076 Schmitt, Michael. N. & NATO Cooperative Cyber Defence Centre of Excellence. (2017). Tallinn Manual 2.0 on the International Law Applicable to Cyber Operations. Cambridge University Press. Paragraph 6.

1077 Case concerning the difference between New Zealand and France concerning the interpretation or application of two agreements, concluded on 9 July 1986 between the two States and which related to the problems arising from the Rainbow Warrior Affair. International Court of Justice. ICJ Reports 1990. (1990, April 30). Page 254. Retrieved February 18, 2022, from <https://legal.un.org/riaa/cases/vol_XX/215-284.pdf>.

to a vessel temporarily passing through non-territorial open international waters, en route to its destination. For instance, no pass-through State has claimed jurisdiction over the Sony hack operation attributed to North Korea. If the usage of ICT infrastructure is more than accidental and fleeting, some States are arguing *for Due Diligence* responsibility of the pass-through State (*Due Diligence* in cyberspace is the subject of the next section).[1078] While this postulate has not yet solidified into a binding legal norm, if and when it does, it would define a part of the data space that most closely resembles territorial waters where a certain threshold of severity of an act has to be met in order to trigger State responsibility over it.

Finally, there are parts of non-material cyberspace that constitute the extension of territory of a State, akin to the status of diplomatic missions. These are websites in the.gov domain (alongside other governmental domains) that represent the sovereign authority of a State and deliver essential services to citizens that qualify as part of the State's *domaine réservé*. Any digital assault on such websites by another State likely amounts to an *Internationally Wrongful Act* regardless of the threshold of severity, analogously to how there is no minimal threshold for open hostilities against diplomatic missions and sovereign functions of a State, as confirmed is, by the ICJ's *United States Diplomatic and Consular Staff in Tehran* judgment from 1980[1079] and the Vienna Convention on the Law of Treaties from 1969.[1080] Of course, this framework focuses on jurisdiction of States solely from the public international legal perspective. Jurisdiction over individuals and personal criminal accountability are regulated separately and their application to cyber acts is well established and uncontroversial. Figure 17 summarizes the proposed framework:

1078 See the next section—V.5.2.2. for more further analysis of this subject.

1079 United States Diplomatic and Consular Staff in Tehran (United States of America v. Iran). International Court of Justice. ICJ Reports 1980. (1980, May 24). Page 3. Retrieved February 17, 2022, <from https://www.icj-cij.org/en/case/64>.

1080 Vienna Convention on the Law of Treaties (May 23, 1969). UN Doc A/Conf39/27. Article 31(1) Retrieved February 15, 2022, from <https://legal.un.org/ilc/texts/instruments/english/conventions/1_1_1969.pdf>.

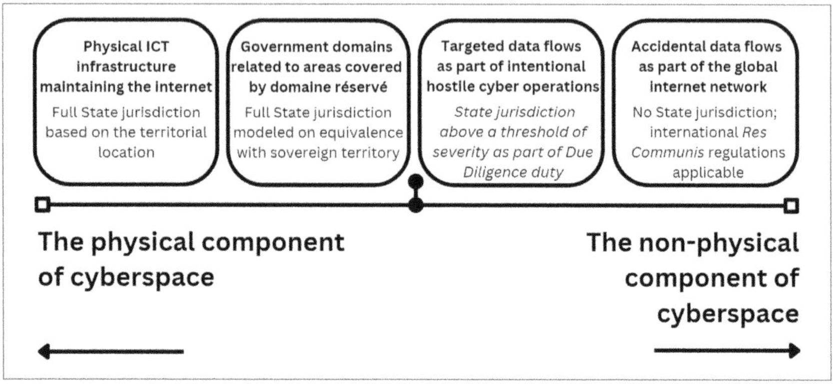

Figure 17. The extent of State jurisdiction in cyberspace, a proposed framework
Source: Own elaboration

5.5.2.2 The process of deterritorialization of jurisdiction in cyberspace

As highlighted earlier, the *Principle of Territoriality* is at the core of the notion of State jurisdiction. Control over land, which is the foundational component of territory, was at the center of Treaty of Westphalia of 1648.[1081] However, over centuries that have passed since, State jurisdiction has been slowly expanding onto non-territorial spaces, such as ships, airplanes, and orbit satellites. Cyberspace represents a new stage in this process. This requires analysis of how jurisdiction might cover hostile cyber operations conducted in spaces other than sovereign land.

Cyber operations launched from airplanes and other flying objects can be regulated according to the 1944 Convention on International Civil Aviation (ICAO, also known as the *Chicago Convention*). Article 1 of the Convention states:

> Article 1: Every state has complete and exclusive sovereignty over airspace above its territory.[1082]

1081 Ryngaert, Cedric (2014). The Concept of Jurisdiction in International Law, Utrecht University Papers, page 5. <https://unijuris.sites.uu.nl/wp-content/uploads/sites/9/2014/12/The-Concept-of-Jurisdiction-in-International-Law.pdf>

1082 United Nations—International Civil Aviation Organization. (1947, December 7). Convention on International Civil Aviation. Retrieved February 17, 2022, from

By confirming expansion of sovereignty over airspace, the Convention allowed for application of the principle of inviolability of sovereignty and the possibility of *Countermeasures* as well as other legal action aimed at remedying any violations. There is no reason to believe that these provisions do not apply to cyber operations. A possible example in this area could include disrupting communication between airplanes and control towers by means of a hacker assault. Jurisdiction over airborne airplanes should also apply in principle to unmanned flying vessels such as drones.[1083] This implies that hostile cyber operations taking place onboard are technically within the jurisdiction of the State owning the aircraft regardless of its geographic location at the moment of a cyber assault.

As mentioned in the previous subsection, the basis for classifying State conduct within an exclusive economic zone (EEZ) is the United Nations Convention on the Law of the Sea from 1982.[1084] The Convention includes the so-called right of innocent passage within the area of 3,200 nautical miles from permanently exposed land of a State, itself a formalization of earlier customary norms. Innocent passage by definition precludes non-innocent behavior such as perpetrating hostile cyber operations. This means that a State can perceive a cyber operation launched toward it from a vessel located inside its EEZ as an *Internationally Wrongful Act.* That logic also applies to operations conducted on or targeting underwater cables and pipelines located within an EEZ. In case of identifying an *Internationally Wrongful act* of this kind, a State is allowed to deploy *Countermeasures* and other forms of lawful self-help and raise legal claims against the perpetrator

---

<https://www.icao.int/publications/pages/doc7300.aspx#:~:text=%E2%80%8BConvention%20on%20International%20Civil,Organization%20(PICAO)%20was%20established>.

1083 Karski, Karol. (2015). Wojskowe bezzałogowe statki powietrzne a prawo międzynarodowe, [in:] Perkowski, Maciej (ed.), Szymański, Janusz (ed.), and Zdanowicz, Mieczysława (ed). Księga dedykowana Profesorowi Bogdanowi Wierzbickiemu. Człowiek i prawo międzynarodowe. Temida 2.

1084 United Nations. (1982, December 10). United Nations Convention on the Law of the Sea. Retrieved February 17, 2022, from <https://www.un.org/Depts/los/convention_agreements/texts/unclos/part2.htm>.

State.[1085] This also applies to a coastal State's contiguous zone, and archipelagic waters.[1086]

The basis for understanding of the status of the ICT infrastructure at diplomatic and consular missions is the Vienna Convention on Consular Relations from 1963.[1087] The key premise of that treaty—inviolability of the premises—sets the context for application of the rules to cyber operations affecting equipment located inside premises. Such equipment enjoys diplomatic status protections granted to ICT infrastructure within the jurisdiction of the State, to which the premises belong.[1088] There is however one important limitation to that status. Such ICT infrastructure located at diplomatic posts should not be utilized for purposes different than specifically defined in the diplomatic mandate (most importantly, it cannot be used for conducting hostile cyber operations).[1089] If that provision is breached, the host State can intervene to put an end to hostile cyber operations.

The international waters are under no jurisdiction of any State, which raises the issue of State responsibility for cyber operations aimed at ships as well as cables and pipes laid in such waters. There exists a need for codifying responsibility for willful or negligent damage to ships and submarine infrastructure in international waters. Their status as *Res Communis* implies not only collective ownership by the international community but also collective responsibility. This issue has been already raised by a number of international scholars.[1090] For now however, this subject remains unregulated. As a progressively larger

---

1085 Schmitt, Michael. N. & NATO Cooperative Cyber Defence Centre of Excellence. (2017). Tallinn Manual 2.0 on the International Law Applicable to Cyber Operations. Cambridge University Press. Paragraphs 240–245.

1086 Ibid. Rules 52, 53.

1087 United Nations. (1963, April 24). Vienna Convention on Consular Relations. Retrieved February 17, 2022, from <https://legal.un.org/ilc/texts/instruments/english/conventions/9_2_1963.pdf>.

1088 United Nations. (1961, April 18). Vienna Convention on Diplomatic Relations. Article 22(3). Retrieved February 17, 2022, from <https://legal.un.org/ilc/texts/instruments/english/conventions/9_1_1961.pdf>.

1089 United Nations. (1963, April 24). Vienna Convention on Consular Relations. Article 31. Retrieved February 17, 2022, from <https://legal.un.org/ilc/texts/instruments/english/conventions/9_2_1963.pdf>;

1090 Schmitt, Michael. N. & NATO Cooperative Cyber Defence Centre of Excellence. (2017). Tallinn Manual 2.0 on the International Law Applicable to Cyber Operations. Cambridge University Press. Rule 39, paragraphs 213–214, 258.

part of the world's cyber infrastructure relies on underwater cables in the international waters (see Figure 18), this will progressively become more urgent to be addressed. Just in 2023, members of the Russian Security Cabinet have threatened several times to destroy this infrastructure.[1091]

Unlike the national airspace, international airspace generally allows for cyber operations. There are no national sovereignty concerns that would give rise to an *internationally wrongful act* in that regard. If for example a hacking team located on one aircraft in the international airspace attacked another aircraft in the international airspace, there would be no specific norm forbidding that. The only limitation in such a context would be universal international law prescriptions such as the human rights law, *Prohibition of Use of Force*, and prohibition of jeopardizing the safety of international aviation. However, as long as a hostile cyber operation does not reach the level of intensity required for it to qualify as such a delict, the activity remains legal.[1092]

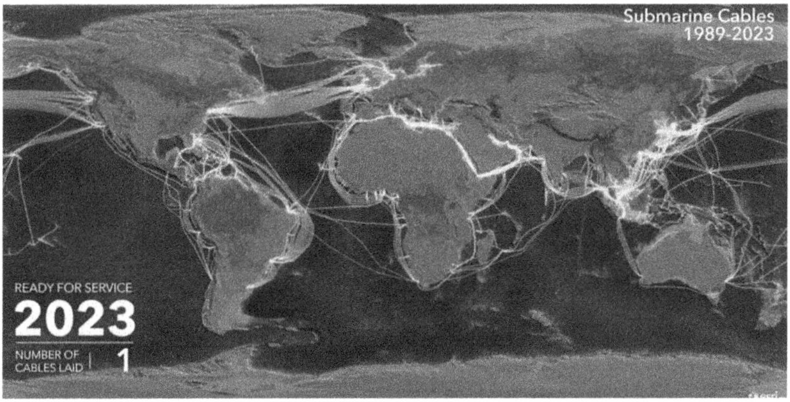

Figure 18. Map of ICT infrastructure located in international waters
Source: ESRI animated maps

1091 Faulconbridge, Guy. "Russia Now Has Free Hand to Destroy Undersea Communications Cables, Putin Ally Says." Reuters, June 14, 2023. <https://www.reuters.com/world/europe/russias-medvedev-says-moscow-now-has-free-hand-destroy-enemies-undersea-2023-06-14/>.

1092 Schmitt, Michael. N. & NATO Cooperative Cyber Defence Centre of Excellence. (2017). Tallinn Manual 2.0 on the International Law Applicable to Cyber Operations. Cambridge University Press. Rule 39, paragraphs 265–268.

As mentioned earlier, the distinction between the national airspace and outer space is not precisely defined in international law. However, State and multilateral practice suggests it is located somewhere at the altitude of 80–120 kilometers. There exists no *State Sovereignty* beyond that point, a norm strongly established by the United Nations in the 1967 Outer Space Treaty.[1093] This means that no State can claim sovereignty over any celestial body or other part of outer space. At the same time, it is possible to conceive of a State conducting cyber operations from an outer space aimed at another State. Importantly, the Outer Space Treaty makes a distinction between the Moon and other celestial bodies on one side and the rest of the space on the other. It set up an additional legal norm applicable to the former category. The Treaty states:

> The Moon and other celestial bodies shall be used exclusively for peaceful purposes.[1094]

Since breaching another State's sovereignty is a non-peaceful purpose, it can be derived from this Treaty that a customary norm exists preventing States from using celestial bodies (including the Moon) to conduct international hostile cyber operations. The International Group of Experts behind the NATO-sponsored Tallinn Manual 2.0 published a similar viewpoint.[1095] Unfortunately no specific prohibition of that kind exists in terms of other parts of outer space. This means that bilateral offensive cyber operations within outer space are lawful. This would happen if for instance one spacecraft launched a cyber assault against another. Similarly, the rules governing open seas and airspace not covered by national sovereignty, potential perpetrators are still limited in their scope of activity by universal international norms such as the human rights law, *Prohibition of Use of Force*, and prohibition of jeopardizing the safety of international aviation.

1093 United Nations Office for Outer Space Affairs. (1966). The Outer Space Treaty. Retrieved February 17, 2022, from <https://www.unoosa.org/oosa/en/ourwork/spacelaw/treaties/introouterspacetreaty.html>.

1094 Ibid.

1095 Schmitt, Michael. N. & NATO Cooperative Cyber Defence Centre of Excellence. (2017). Tallinn Manual 2.0 on the International Law Applicable to Cyber Operations. Cambridge University Press. Rule 58.

According to the Outer Space Treaty, satellites in outer space are covered by jurisdiction of the nation that launched them.[1096] This means that cyber operations targeting or utilizing such satellites can result in a breach of sovereignty of the State the satellite belongs to. This regulation becomes progressively more relevant as a higher and higher share of internet traffic is routed through communication satellites. A hostile cyber operation channeled through a satellite can be seen as a violation of sovereignty taking place within a State's jurisdiction, even if it is not the final target. The rules about above-the-minimis impact of such a violation would apply but otherwise, such activity can constitute an *Internationally Wrongful Act*.

5.6 Obligation of *Due Diligence* in cyberspace

5.6.1 Historical development of the notion of *Due Diligence* responsibility of States

Duty of *Due Diligence* by States is an established principle of international law. However, the limits of its definition and application scope are unclear and intensely debated. Joanna Kulesza proposed that the principle denotes an obligation of States not to knowingly allow use of their territory for conducting acts that go against the international legal rights of other States (more on the definition in the next subsection).[1097] The phrasing *Due Diligence* has been embraced in the cyber context, including most prominently in the UN GGE 2015 report endorsed by a UN General Assembly resolution, where it is presented as a voluntary non-binding norm. Historically, the notion of *Due Diligence* assumed various labels in international law. Most frequently it has been stated as the *no-harm principle*.[1098] The norm was invoked for example in the 1872 *Alabama* arbitration case pertaining to the duties of

---

1096 United Nations Office for Outer Space Affairs. (1966). The Outer Space Treaty. Retrieved February 17, 2022, from <https://www.unoosa.org/oosa/en/ourwork/spacelaw/treaties/introouterspacetreaty.html>;
Moynihan, Harriet. (2019, December). The Application of International Law to State Cyberattacks. Chatham House. Page 14. <https://www.chathamhouse.org/2019/12/application-international-law-state-cyberattacks>.

1097 Kulesza, Joanna. Due diligence in international law. Leiden: Brill Nijhoff, 2016. Page 57.

1098 Ibid.

the United Kingdom (then effectively extending over the now-sovereign State of Canada) to stay neutral during the American Civil War.[1099] It was also invoked by the Permanent Court of Arbitration in the 1928 *Island of Palmas* arbitration case, being presented as a collateral consequence of territorial sovereignty: *Territorial sovereignty (…) involves the exclusive right to display activities of a State. This right has a corollary duty: the obligation to protect within the territory the rights of other States, in particular, their right to integrity and inviolability in peace and in war*[1100]

The logic of the Permanent Court of Arbitration tied together the notion of sovereignty, control over territory, and a duty that can be captured with the term *Due Diligence*. Importantly, the *Alabama* case pertained to the context of war-related activities. The *Island of Palmas* case pertained to competing claims of sovereignty over an island by two States, in a peaceful context (the case was the result of Netherlands and the United States agreeing to pass their disagreement to the Permanent Court of Arbitration for a binding ruling). The two cases confirmed application of the norm in the context of war and peace respectively. The 1938 *Trail Smelter* arbitration case, pertaining to economic activities by a private entity also invoked the *Due Diligence* obligation: *State owes at all times a duty to protect other States against injurious acts by individuals from within its jurisdiction.*[1101]

The *Trail Smelter* case has had profound legal impact. It confirmed a State's international legal responsibility for actions of private entities taking place on its sovereign territory. It has become the core of international environmental law and its key conclusions, including the duty of prevention of harmful effects emanating onto other States, have formed the so-called *environmental no-harm principle*. At present, they are perceived as

---

1099 Tribunal of arbitration established by Article I of the Treaty of Washington of 8 May 1871. (1871, May 8). Alabama claims of the United States of America against Great Britain. United Nations. Pages 125–134. Retrieved February 17, 2022, from <https://legal.un.org/riaa/cases/vol_XXIX/125-134.pdf>.;

1100 Island of Palmas Case (or Miangas), United States v Netherlands, Award, (1928). April 4, 1928, Permanent Court of Arbitration, II RIAA 829, ICGJ 392. Page 839.

1101 Trail smelter case (United States, Canada). Permanent Court of Arbitration. (1941, March 11). Page 1963. Retrieved February 17, 2022, from <https://legal.un.org/riaa/cases/vol_III/1905-1982.pdf>.

part of customary law. The UN ILC has included the no-*harm principle* in its 2001 *Draft Articles on Prevention of Transboundary Harm from Hazardous Activities*, seen by States and international scholars as a reflection of existing customary norms.[1102]

The *Due Diligence* principle was also affirmed in the 1949 *Corfu Channel* judgment by the ICJ:

> It is every State's obligation not to allow knowingly its territory to be used for acts contrary to the rights of other States.[1103]

In that case, the Court confirmed the obligation of a State to notify ships of deathly mines floating in its territorial waters.[1104] The 1980 ICJ judgment concerning *United States Diplomatic and Consular Staff in Tehran* confirmed every State's obligation to protect diplomatic and consular staff as well as premises on its sovereign territory from harm.[1105] The 1986 ICJ judgment on *Military and Paramilitary Activities in and against Nicaragua* invoked the norm to lay out States' obligation to curb flows of unregistered arms onto territory of neighboring States.[1106] A similar logic was applied by the ICJ in its 2005

1102 United Nations International Law Commission. Draft articles on Prevention of Transboundary Harm from Hazardous Activities, with commentaries. United Nations Office of Legal Affairs (2001). Retrieved February 15, 2022. <https://legal.un.org/ilc/texts/instruments/english/commentaries/9_7_2001.pdf>;

Ellis, Jaye (2010). Bratspies, Rebecca M.; Miller, Russell A. (eds.). "Has International Law Outgrown Trail Smelter?". Transboundary Harm in International Law: Lessons from the Trail Smelter Arbitration. Cambridge: Cambridge University Press.

1103 Case concerning Corfu Channel (United Kingdom of Great Britain and Northern Ireland v. Albania).. I.C.J. Reports 1949, 244, Gen L No. 1. (1949). Page 22. Retrieved February 15, 2022, from <https://www.icj-cij.org/en/case/1>.

1104 Ibid. point 22 (Merits).

1105 United States Diplomatic and Consular Staff in Tehran (United States of America v. Iran). International Court of Justice. ICJ Reports 1980. (1980, May 24). Paragraph 68. Retrieved February 17, 2022, from <https://www.icj-cij.org/en/case/64>.

1106 Case Concerning Military and Paramilitary Activities in and Against Nicaragua, Nicaragua v. United States. International Court of Justice. I.C.J. Reports 14, ICGJ 112 (ICJ 1986). (1986). Paragraphs 157–168. Retrieved February 15, 2022, from <https://www.icj-cij.org/en/case/70/judgments>.

Armed Activities on the Territory of Congo judgment to mark as wrongful a State's toleration of rebel groups using its territory to cross into neighboring States and challenge their governments.[1107]

The notion took on a new expanded meaning following the 9/11 terrorist attacks. Tolerating the presence of organizations such as Al-Qaeda by some States on their territory while they were preparing terrorist assaults inside other States became an international issue. In this context, lack of *Due Diligence* could be equated to toleration and unwillingness to curb malign non-State actors on the part of host States. The United States used the argument of toleration to launch its invasion of Afghanistan in 2001. In their communication, the U.S. government framed the invasion as a self-defense measure following inaction and toleration of the Afghan authorities in face of terrorist activities perpetrated by Al-Qaeda. This argument had been used earlier to condemn the government of Afghanistan by the UN Security Council in a resolution, providing a basis for the U.S.' rationale for the invasion.[1108]

Despite its appeal and continuous relevance, it is uncertain whether the principle of *Due Diligence* spans onto every branch of Public International Law, including the one covering cyberspace. Some international scholars, such as Joanna Kulesza, stated that they believe this is the case[1109] while others remain more skeptical.[1110] There are also other aspects of the term that require further clarification, all of which are laid out in the subsequent subsection.

1107 Armed Activities on the Territory of the Congo (Democratic Republic of the Congo v. Uganda). International Court of Justice. ICJ Reports 2005. (2005, December 19). Paragraph 301. Retrieved February 17, 2022, from <https://www.icj-cij.org/en/case/116>.

1108 United Nations Security Council. (1999, October 15). RESOLUTION 1267 (1999) Adopted by the Security Council at its 4051st meeting on 15 October 1999. Retrieved February 17, 2022, from <https://www.undocs.org/S/RES/1267%20(1999)>.

1109 Kulesza, Joanna. Due diligence in international law. Leiden: Brill Nijhoff, 2016. Page 58.

1110 McDonald, Neil. (2019). The Role Of Due Diligence In International Law. International & Comparative Law Quarterly, 68(4), pages 1041–1054. <https://doi:10.1017/S0020589319000344>

5.6.2 Identification of the definitional scope of the term *Due Diligence* obligation in the conventional realm

5.6.2.1 Core aspects of the definition of *Due Diligence* in international law

Just as it is the case with many other norms in Public International Law, there exists no source that would provide one cohesive definition of the duty of *Due Diligence*. However, an attempt can be made to reconstruct this definition, to the extent that is possible, by utilizing existing treaties, proofs of customary conduct, and additionally research by international scholars as a subsidiary means. Fundamentally, *Due Diligence* is a duty of conduct rather than actual effect.[1111] This introduces the element of probability into the definition. As the International Law Association has stated: "At its heart, due diligence is (...) a standard of reasonableness, of reasonable care, that seeks to take account of the consequences of wrongful conduct and the extent to which such consequences could feasibly have been avoided."[1112] The core source for this phrasing is the 1949 *Corfu Channel* judgment discussed in the previous subsection. A State should make best efforts to prevent *Internationally Wrongful Acts* from taking place on its sovereign territory. However, if those efforts are unsuccessful and an *Internationally Wrongful Act* is committed, the State can prove it is not liable by demonstrating its proper conduct. On the other hand, State practice suggests that this logic does not operate in the opposite direction—lack of proper conduct coupled with no instances of *Internationally Wrongful Acts* does not result in a breach of *Due Diligence* by a careless State. Thus, for the obligation of *Due Diligence* to be breached, two conditions must be met:

- An *Internationally Wrongful Act* occurred against a State's rights, emanating from sovereign territory of another State;

1111 Pellet, Alain et al. Droit International Public (8th edition). LGDJ 2009. Pages 859–862. Paragraph 473; Delerue, François. Cyber Operations and international law. Cambridge: Cambridge University Press, 2020. Page 354.

1112 ILA Study Group on Due Diligence in International Law Second Repor July 2016 Tim Stephens (Rapporteur) and Duncan French (Chair). International Law Association. Page 2. <https://www.ila-hq.org/en_GB/documents/draft-study-group-report-johannesburg-2016>

- The State, whose territory was used for perpetrating the *Internationally Wrongful Act*, has not made its best efforts to prevent such acts from taking place.

This formula was used for example by the ICJ in 2007 to assess the conduct of the State of Serbia and Montenegro during the Yugoslavian war in relation to militias operating on its territory.[1113] International judiciary bodies listed in the previous section are in consensus that who has committed the wrongful act does not matter. This includes responsibility for wrongfulness of accidents that infringe upon rights of other States. The *Trail Smelter* case also confirmed that State responsibility spans onto non-State actors such as private companies acting on its sovereign territory. Sovereign control over territory implies an all-enveloping responsibility that can only be suspended by precluding circumstances, such as *Force Majeure* or *Necessity* discussed Chapter 4 earlier.

Due Diligence is frequently involved in international arrangements and disputes, although the four areas of Public International Law where it takes place most consistently are: environmental, diplomatic, and consular affairs.[1114] The contents of the *Due Diligence* obligation are also not fixed. Many areas of international law enjoy more lenient standards of *Due Diligence* while others experience more matured and stricter ones. In general, the international community is moving toward higher standards of care as States gain additional capacities. A good example are environmental reviews, which were first considered as a voluntary aspect by the ICJ but are now perceived as a mandatory element of projects that give rise to disputes considered by the Court.[1115] For this reason, the definitional extent of the *Due Diligence* duty is

---

1113 Case Concerning the Application of the Convention on the Prevention and Punishment of the Crime of Genocide (Bosnia and Herzegovina v. Serbia)—Judgment. International Court of Justice Reports 43, February 26, 2007. Paragraph 430. <https://www.icj-cij.org/en/case/91/judgments>.

1114 Delerue, François. Cyber Operations and international law. Cambridge: Cambridge University Press, 2020. Page 354.

1115 Case Concerning (Argentina v Uruguay) (Merits) (2010) ICJ Rep 14 (Pulp Mills Case); Certain Activities Carried out by Nicaragua in the Border Area (Costa Rica v. Nicaragua) <https://www.icj-cij.org/case/150>; Construction of a Road in Costa Rica along the San Juan River (Nicaragua v Costa Rica), Judgment. ICJ Reports, December 16, 2015. <https://www.icj-cij.org/case/152>. (Separate Opinion of Judge

a moving target that is also at various stages of crystallization and stringency in various branches of international law.

Most of the jurisprudence gravitates toward expansionary scope of the definition of *Due Diligence*, ensuring State accountability in international law. However, *Due Diligence* can also have the opposite effect. A State can demonstrate that it has made its best efforts to prevent an act from taking place, thus bearing no responsibility for the fact that it took place anyway. The degree of best efforts will also vary by State, with developed ones having generally far stronger capacity to make such efforts while developing ones having weak capacity. This problematic two-tier system of *Due Diligence* responsibility means a dilution of accountability on part of many States and is especially obvious in cyberspace, which will be discussed later in this section.

5.6.2.2 Duty of States to act to stop wrongful acts against other States taking place on their sovereign territory

A logical conclusion of the *Due Diligence* duty is that a State should take action to stop *Internationally Wrongful Acts* against other States which take place on its sovereign territory. Michael Schmitt, Liis Vihul, François Delerue, and Karine Bannelier-Christakis all suggested this duty is part of the *Due Diligence* obligation.[1116] However, this view has to be critiqued on the structural and definitional ground. It is a separate type of legal obligation as it addresses real effects of hostilities that have demonstrably actualized, while *Due Diligence* requires preventive conduct by States that lowers the hypothetical probability of occurrence of *Internationally Wrongful Acts.* Stopping ongoing abuse that carries the burden of wrongfulness stems from the general provisions of the UN Charter pertaining to sovereign equality and pursuit of peaceful relations between States in its Chapter 1. Such duty was reinforced by the ICJ's *Corfu Channel* judgment and subsequent rulings listed in the previous two subsections. For these reasons, it is much more established within the framework of Public International Law and universal, whereas the *Due Diligence* duty is applied to varying degrees in different branches of that system.

Donoghue's Where she observed that due diligence and environmental impact assessment should not be fixed and prescribed, and that there should be "scope for variation in the way that States of origin conduct the assessment').

1116 Delerue, François. Cyber Operations and international law. Cambridge: Cambridge University Press, 2020. Page 366.

Michael Schmitt and Liis Vihul suggested that a State confronted with its sovereign territory being used to breach rights of another State is only obliged to take measures to stop such a wrongful act from the moment it gains knowledge of it.[1117] The International Law Association added that such post-factum action is still subject to the overarching standard of reasonableness and feasibility. This means that a State is only obliged to act to an extent that is defined by what is reasonable given circumstances.[1118] For example, a State under strain of a natural disaster has less capacity to act than that same State when facing no emergency.

Knowledge of the existence of Internationally *Wrongful Acts* can come from two sources. Either a State finds it out by itself, or it is notified of it. Since, as laid out earlier in the chapter, the burden of proof falls on the injured State, the notification might offer a way of ensuring there is no room for interpretational ambiguity. Additionally, the ICJ has provided interpretative guidance on what a reasonable and feasible response means in the context of *Due Diligence.* In the 2007 Bosnia Genocide judgment, it equated such a response to making best efforts.[1119] Such "best efforts" must be assessed on a case-by-case basis due to varying degrees of State capacity and unique sets of context. In terms of the rapidness of the response, the *Corfu Channel* case provides guidance that an instantaneous reaction is not required. Instead, the State whose territory is used for breaching rights of another State must have sufficient amount of time to be made aware and react.[1120]

1117 Schmitt, Michael N., and Vihul, Liis. "Respect for Sovereignty in Cyberspace." Texas Law Review, 95(7), 2017, pages 1639–1670. <https://texaslawreview.org/respect-sovereignty-cyberspace/>.

1118 ILA Study Group on Due Diligence in International Law Second Repor July 2016 Tim Stephens (Rapporteur) and Duncan French (Chair). International Law Association. Page 7. <https://www.ila-hq.org/en_GB/documents/draft-study-group-report-johannesburg-2016>

1119 Case Concerning the Application of the Convention on the Prevention and Punishment of the Crime of Genocide (Bosnia and Herzegovina v. Serbia). ICJ Reports 43. (2007). Paragraph 430. Retrieved February 16, 2022, from <https://www.icj-cij.org/en/case/91/judgments>.

1120 Case concerning Corfu Channel (United Kingdom of Great Britain and Northern Ireland v. Albania).. I.C.J. Reports 1949, 244, Gen L No. 1. (1949). Page 22–23. Retrieved February 15, 2022, from <https://www.icj-cij.org/en/case/1>.

5.6.2.3 Contested aspects of the definition of *Due Diligence* in Public International Law

Two definitional aspects of *Due Diligence* are especially a source of contention among international scholars:

- Responsibility of transit States, through whose territory unlawful conduct passed to reach another State;
- Threshold of harm required to invoke a breach of *Due Diligence.*

Due Diligence duty implies a general obligation of a State to monitor activities taking place on its sovereign territory to the extent that it is reasonably feasible. However, international law is clear that ability to do so has its limit and no State can have absolute knowledge in that regard. The ICJ stated in the *Corfu Channel* judgment:

> it cannot be concluded from the mere fact of the control exercised by a State over its territory and waters that that State necessarily knew, or ought to have known, of any unlawful act perpetrated therein, nor yet that it necessarily know, or should have known, the authors.[1121]

The responsibility of a State for acts transiting through its territory on their way toward the target State boils down to what is reasonably feasible. This in turn depends on the individual context of each State and includes the geographic features, the degree of a State's technical capabilities, and the amount of time it takes for transit to take place. Some scholars state that transit States always bear responsibility on par with those from which a hostile act originated while others suggest that *Due Diligence* responsibility only arises when a transit State has a reasonable amount of time to identify and prevent such an act.[1122]

Some international scholars, including François Delerue,[1123] claimed there exists no particular threshold of harm that would trigger a breach of the *Due*

1121 Ibid. Merits, page 18.

1122 Bannelier, Karine and Christakis, Theodore, Cyber-Attacks—Prevention-Reactions: The Role of States and Private Actors (February 25, 2017). Les Cahiers de la Revue Défense Nationale, Paris, 2017. Page 28. <https://ssrn.com/abstract=2941988>.

1123 Delerue, François. Cyber Operations and international law. Cambridge: Cambridge University Press, 2020. Pages 364–365.

Diligence duty, seeing this logic as the consequence of the norm being based on the standard of State conduct rather than the actual effect. However, this view can be critiqued for being absolutist and inconsistent with the state of international law. Firstly, The Trail Smelter Arbitral Award defined two requirements in terms of assessing the harm:

- Serious consequence;
- Injury is established by clear and convincing evidence.[1124]

While this is not a precise threshold but rather guidelines for identifying it in a case-by-case manner, it does imply the existence of it. The Arbitral Award considered one specific dispute but it has since been elevated to the status of a source of generally applicable customary law. Secondly, more broadly, as laid out in Chapter 3, any *Unfriendly Act* must reach the severity level of at least a *Violation of Sovereignty*, which contains a threshold of harm, in order to be considered an *Internationally Wrongful Act.* This applies to all types of State obligations, including the duty to deliver *Due Diligence* care over its sovereign territory. Thirdly, State practice demonstrates that no State has invoked the *no-harm principle* or *Due Diligence* without certain actual damage present. François Delerue suggested that the *Due Diligence* duty should depend on theoretical "potential damage" rather than actual one.[1125] This hypothetical-based interpretation would reduce the element of stability in Public International Law and open space for less unverifiable accusations. Thus, from the perspective of the systemic interpretative logic, it would be a sub-par solution.

5.6.3 Application of the notion of *Due Diligence* in cyberspace

5.6.3.1 Is *Due Diligence* in cyberspace a binding norm of Public International Law?

The way the duty of *Due Diligence* should be applied in cyberspace is subject to an ongoing debate within the international community. The obligation would imply that a certain high degree of negligence in overseeing the

---

1124 Trail smelter Case (United States v. Canada). Permanent Court of Arbitration, March 11, 1941. N 8. <https://legal.un.org/riaa/cases/vol_III/1905-1982.pdf>.

1125 Delerue, François. Cyber Operations and international law. Cambridge: Cambridge University Press, 2020. Pages 365.

ICT infrastructure by a State on its sovereign territory that resulted in an *Internationally Wrongful Act* being perpetrated against another State constitutes an *Internationally Wrongful Act* in its own right.

In fact, the UN General Assembly already in the year 2000 recognized in a resolution titled "Combating the criminal misuse of information technologies" the validity of a norm expecting that States ensure their jurisdiction spaces do not become safe havens for illicit activity.[1126] However, the resolution did not reflect any existing norm of international law. The 2015 Report by UN GA, formally approved by the United Nations General Assembly in a resolution,[1127] says that States *should* rather than *must* exercise *Due Diligence* in cyberspace:

> (g) States should take appropriate measures to protect their critical infrastructure from ICT threats, taking into account General Assembly resolution 58/199 on the creation of a global culture of cybersecurity and the protection of critical information infrastructures, and other relevant resolutions;[1128]

This provision is identified as one of *voluntary, non-binding norms of responsible State behavior*. Its interpretation, provided by the UN GGE itself and facilitated by experts, is that *Internationally Wrongful Acts* committed using ICTs by anyone on a State's sovereign territory are attributable to said State if it can be ascertained that its negligence allowed for that to happen.[1129] The stated intention of the UN GGE was for these norms to become binding in

---

1126 United Nations General Assembly Resolution. (2001, January 22). 55/63. Combating the criminal misuse of information technologies. Point 1(a). Retrieved February 17, 2022, from <https://documents-dds-ny.un.org/doc/UNDOC/GEN/N00/563/17/PDF/N0056317.pdf?OpenElement>.

1127 United Nations General Assembly Resolution. (2015, July 22). Group of Governmental Experts on Developments in the Field of Information and Telecommunications in the Context of International Security—Note by the Secretary-General. Retrieved February 15, 2022. <https://documents-dds-ny.un.org/doc/UNDOC/GEN/N15/228/35/PDF/N1522835.pdf?OpenElement>.

1128 Ibid.

1129 United Nations Office for Disarmament Affairs. (2017). Voluntary, Non-Binding Norms for Responsible State Behaviour in the Use of Information and Communications Technology: A Commentary. Civil Society and Disarmament—United Nations Publications, E.18(IX.3), pages 1–296. <https://digitallibrary.un.org/record/3934467?ln=en>.

the future, should State practice and the prevailing *opinio juris* align in that direction. This explicitly contradicts the claim of cyber *Due Diligence* being mandatory at present, a claim that has been supported by various international scholars, including Michael Schmitt,[1130] Henning Lahmann,[1131] and François Delerue.[1132] Tallinn Manual 2.0 suggested that *Due Diligence* is a binding norm in the international cyberspace:

> Rule 6—Due diligence (general principle)
> A State must exercise due diligence in not allowing its territory, or territory or cyber infrastructure under its governmental control, to be used for cyber operations that affect the rights of, and produce serious adverse consequences for, other States.[1133]

Despite the strong language of Rule 6 in Tallinn Manual 2.0, it is far from obvious whether States *must* respect *Due Diligence* obligations in the cyber context. The International Group of Experts' work is not a source of international law and even they hedged the interpretation of the Rule in their commentaries, stating that *Due Diligence* obligation is only applicable if a State has knowledge of a malicious cyber operation being launched using its ICT infrastructure at the time of the operation.[1134] This interpretation would limit the scope of *Due Diligence* to reactive behavior, that is, stopping an ongoing malicious operation. Such an interpretation does not oblige governments to, for example, take preventive measures or run systemic stress tests.

The non-binding character of the cyber *Due Diligence* norm was further strengthened by the EU Council's Decision Concerning Restrictive Measures Against Cyber-Attacks Threatening The Union Or Its Member States in

---

1130 Schmitt, Michael. N. & NATO Cooperative Cyber Defence Centre of Excellence. (2017). Tallinn Manual 2.0 on the International Law Applicable to Cyber Operations. Cambridge University Press. Rule 6, Commentary.

1131 Lahmann, Henning. Unilateral Remedies to Cyber Operation. Self-defence, Countermeasures, Necessity, and the Question of Attribution, Cambridge University Press 2020. Chapter IX—Possible elements of the cyber emergency regime, page 228. <https://doi.org/10.1017/9781108807050>

1132 Delerue, François. Cyber Operations and international law. Cambridge: Cambridge University Press, 2020. Pages 359.

1133 Schmitt, Michael. N. & NATO Cooperative Cyber Defence Centre of Excellence. (2017). Tallinn Manual 2.0 on the International Law Applicable to Cyber Operations. Cambridge University Press. Rule 6.

1134 Ibid. Commentary, paragraphs 39, 41.

2019. In it, the EU used the phrase *should seek to* rather than *must,* implying an expectation that States provide their best effort to limit the risk of ICT infrastructure abuse by international hostile cyber operations but are not actually obliged to do so: *[States] should seek to ensure that their territory is not used by non-State actors to commit such acts.*[1135]

Nevertheless, some governments are now expressing their conviction that *Due Diligence* is undergoing a transition toward becoming a binding norm of international law. These include France[1136] and the Netherlands.[1137] If that would be the case, a breach of international law could be attributed to a State that does not ensure that minimum *Due Diligence* requirements are met in case of an international cyber assault against another State exploiting that weakness. This notion however is still being debated and has not enjoyed a broad consensus within the international community.[1138] The latest UN GGE Report, published in 2021, left the issue open to further debate.[1139] Given this impasse and lack of consistent *opinio juris* suggesting otherwise, it must be concluded that unlike in some other domains of Public International Law, duty of *Due Diligence* is currently not a binding rule in cyberspace. This

1135 Council of the European Union. (2019, May 14). COUNCIL DECISION concerning restrictive measures against cyber-attacks threatening the Union or its Member States. Retrieved February 17, 2022, from <https://data.consilium.europa.eu/doc/document/ST-7299-2019-INIT/en/pdf>.

1136 Schmitt, Michael. (2019, September 16). France's Major Statement on International Law and Cyber: An Assessment. Just Security. <https://www.justsecurity.org/66194/frances-major-statement-on-international-law-and-cyber-an-assessment/>.

1137 Jensen, Eric. T., & Watts, Sean. (2016). The Duty of Due Diligence and Cyber Incitements to Violence. Texas Law Review. Pages 1555–1577. <https://doi.org/10.2139/ssrn.2894070>.

1138 Breau, Susan C., & Samuel, Katja L. H. (2016). Research Handbook on Disasters and International Law (Research Handbooks in International Law series). Edward Elgar Publishing. Pages 406–427; Sklerov, Matthew J. (2009). Solving the Dilemma of State Responses to Cyberattacks: A Justification for the Use of Active Defenses against States Who Neglect Their Duty to Prevent. Military Law Review, 201, pages 1–85. Page 43.

1139 UN Group of Governmental Experts on Advancing responsible State behaviour in cyberspace in the context of international security. (2021, May 28). Final Report of the Group of Governmental Experts on Advancing responsible State behaviour in cyberspace in the context of international security. Retrieved February 17, 2022, from <https://front.un-arm.org/wp-content/uploads/2021/06/final-report-2019-2021-gge-1-advance-copy.pdf>.

deems immaterial the questions of what the threshold of cyber harm would be that triggers the norm or what thew reasonable level of cyber oversight by States is. Those questions however remain potentially relevant if and when the international community overcomes the obstacle of the currently non-binding character of the *Due Diligence* duty in the cyber realm.

5.6.3.2 Duty of States to act to stop hostile cyber operations against other States taking place via ICT infrastructure within their jurisdiction

Stopping an ongoing hostile cyber operation against a third State by the State, whose ICT infrastructure is used to perpetrate it goes beyond just the duty of *Due Diligence*, although it is closely associated with it. As laid out in the Subsection 5.6.2.2, unlike *Due Diligence*, it is a universal norm of Public International Law. A State that is aware that ICT infrastructure located on its territory is used for perpetrating hostile cyber operations against another State that reaches the threshold of an *Internationally Wrongful Act* has to make best efforts to stop it.[1140]

However, unique characteristics of cyber operations influence applicability of this norm in the new context. The ICJ's *Corfu Channel* judgment underscored the relevance of the time dimension. An immediate response is actually not required.[1141] This however means that most hostile cyber operations could proceed uninterrupted as it takes a fraction of time needed to execute conventional hostilities and the preparation stage is much more easily concealable. This challenge, that can potentially render the whole norm inapplicable in the cyber context, has not been addressed yet.

A separate challenge is related to the distinction of States, whose territory is only utilized as a transit node in a hacking act and those whose territory is the source of a hostile cyber operations. Transit States are covered by the obligation to make their best efforts to stop the wrongful conduct. However, the balance of what is reasonable and feasible will play out differently in both

---

1140 Schmitt, Michael N., and Vihul, Liis. "Respect for Sovereignty in Cyberspace." Texas Law Review, 95(7), 2017. Rule 7.

1141 Case concerning Corfu Channel (United Kingdom of Great Britain and Northern Ireland v. Albania)—Judgment (Merits). International Court of Justice Reports, April 9, 1949. Gen L No. 1. Pages 22–23. <https://www.icj-cij.org/en/case/1>.

cases. The source States are more easily held accountable as that is where hackers are usually physically located or where the hostile cyber operation has its host server that can be turned off. However, transit through a third State in the cyber context can take only a few seconds and does not involve the physical presence of persons perpetrating an act, making it extremely challenging to stop hostile cyber acts. Only those transit acts that involve hackers' physical presence in another State for the purpose of physical manipulation of the ICT infrastructure or use of the "territorial" part of the virtual side of cyberspace by a hostile cyber operation would give rise to the responsibility of a State to stop the transit. As laid out in Section 4.5, a State's jurisdiction does not extend over the part of virtual cyberspace data traffic, that only happens to flow through its ICT infrastructure. Hence, the "non-territorial" part of the virtual side of cyberspace remains part of the *Global Commons* and the flow of information there is too much of a rapid element to give rise to a transit State's responsibility. Additionally, while it would be theoretically possible to stop the transit of a hostile cyber operation by shutting down all of internet connectivity in a State or a region of it, it would not meet the test of reasonableness and feasibility. Too many vital services and people's livelihoods depend on it in most parts of the globe.

A few States weighed in on what they see as a mandatory response of a government upon learning that its sovereign territory is being used to perpetrate a hostile cyber operation. Australian stated that a State confronted with such a situation "should take reasonable steps consistent with international law."[1142] This vague statement implies that some action must be taken but it refrains from committing Australia to any particular interpretation of how such action should look. Estonia released a statement, in which it claimed that a State whose territory is used to conduct cyber *Internationally Wrongful Acts* must "make reasonable efforts to ensure that their territory is not used to adversely affect the rights of other states." It specified that reasonable efforts include cooperating with the victim State on the matters of identification, attribution, and investigation. The scale of the reasonable efforts depends

---

1142 The government of Australia. "Australia's International Cyber Engagement Strategy," November 2020. Page 91. <https://www.internationalcybertech.gov.au/sites/default/files/2020-11/The%20Strategy.pdf>.

on the capacities of each State, including its cyber expertise.[1143] Netherlands joined in on endorsing the reasonable efforts threshold, stating: "a state must take measures which, in the given circumstances, may be expected of a state acting in a reasonable manner [when countering hostile cyber operations]." It also claimed that the obligation to provide support to an injured State is not dependent on whether a hostile cyber act caused physical damage (a requirement suggested by some international scholars).[1144] France issued a policy statement, agreeing with the standard of "reasonable efforts" in countering hostile cyber acts against a third State that utilize a State's territory. It also included a caveat stating that "wrongful acts against other States perpetrated from its territory by non-state actors (…) cannot constitute an exception to the prohibition of the use of force."[1145]

This last point deserves special attention. After the 9/11 terrorist attacks, the U.S. government has spearheaded the theory of the "unwilling or unable test," that purported that a State injured by actions of non-State actors utilizing territory of another State might resort to *Use of Force* and even an outright invasion to put an end to hostile conduct.[1146] Most of the international community turned against this proposal, even though it had been invoked during the U.S. invasions of Afghanistan in 2001 and Iraq in 2003.[1147] No consistent State practice or *opinio juris* means that the "unwilling or unable test" is not currently a norm of Public International Law. Should it however

---

1143 International cyber law: interactive toolkit. "Attribution - President Kersti Kaljulaid." International cyber law: interactive toolkit, July 28, 2023. <https://cyberlaw.ccdcoe.org/wiki/Attribution>.

1144 The government of Netherlands. Letter to the parliament on the international legal order in cyberspace, September 26, 2019. Page 4. <https://www.government.nl/documents/parliamentary-documents/2019/09/26/letter-to-the-parliament-on-the-international-legal-order-in-cyberspace>.

1145 The government of France. (2019a). International Law Applied to Operations in Cyberspace. Page 10. Retrieved February 19, 2022, from <https://www.defense.gouv.fr/content/download/567648/9770527/file/international+law+applied+to+operations+in+cyberspace.pdf.>

1146 Corten, Olivier. (2016). The "Unwilling or Unable' Test: Has it Been, and Could it be, Accepted? Leiden Journal of International Law, 29(3), pages 777–799. <https://doi:10.1017/S0922156516000315>

1147 Simma, Bruno et al. (2013). The Charter of The United Nations 3E, Vol 1. Oxford Commentaries on International Law, 1. Page 802. <https://doi.org/10.1093/law/9780199639762.001.0001>.

be seen as such within the realm of international law covering cyberspace? In other words, can a State targeted with a hostile cyber operation hack back at the assailants? This tool would provide additional measure of deterrence, although it would go against the core systemic logic of the UN Charter system, which is to restore compliance with international legal obligations and restore peaceful relations rather than to exact a revenge.[1148] It would also create the risk of a vicious cycle of escalation. The right way to respond by a State whose territory is used to assault a third State is to make best efforts to stop the hostile operation, assist the injured State in attribution, and in extreme cases, resort to *Countermeasures* and other regulated self-help measures.

5.6.3.3 Tension between developed and developing States on the subject of the duty of *Due Diligence* in cyberspace

The main reason for why *Due Diligence* in cyberspace is not currently a binding norm of Public International Law is the lack of consistent State practice and *opinio juris* on the matter. In fact, as mentioned in the Subsection 5.6.2.1, there exists a split between States with a high degree of cyber capabilities and those with a low one. Implementing the *Due Diligence* obligation in cyberspace would be asymmetrically difficult for States lacking cyber capabilities. While States such as Brazil, Estonia, Finland, France, the Republic of Korea, the Netherlands, and Germany publicly expressed their support for *Due Diligence* becoming a binding international norm, Israel and Argentina voiced their opposition.[1149] For that reason, the most recent UN GGE Report from 2021 avoided the subject, leaving it for future deliberations.[1150] The position of Israel is interesting in that regard as the State appears to defy the political division and oppose cyber *Due Diligence* when other high-capability States mostly support it. This stance, however, only deepens the disagreement that prevents the norm from becoming binding law.

1148 Schmitt, Michael N. & NATO Cooperative Cyber Defence Centre of Excellence. (2017). Tallinn Manual 2.0 on the International Law Applicable to Cyber Operations. Cambridge University Press. Pages 90–94.

1149 Schmitt, Michael (2021, October 8). The Sixth United Nations GGE and International Law in Cyberspace. Just Security. <https://www.justsecurity.org/76864/the-sixth-united-nations-gge-and-international-law-in-cyberspace/>.

1150 Ibid.

Another axis of tension is that between the developed and developing States. While there exist developing States with high cyber capabilities, such as Russia and China, for the most part, richer States have much stronger cyber expertise at their disposal. A risk would emerge that States at low levels of economic development, oftentimes collectively called "The Global South," lacking State capacity to provide basic services, much less disciplined army or IT expert units, would be the most vulnerable to being accused of breaching *Due Diligence* duties. This dynamic undermines the political legitimacy of cyber *Due Diligence.*

Debate over what the threshold of "reasonable efforts" dictated by the duty of *Due Diligence* should reflect these tensions. On one hand, malicious low-capability States might abuse the flexible nature of the "reasonable efforts" standard that *Due Diligence* rests upon to willfully allow malicious actors to use their territory and infrastructure for conducting hostile acts abroad. On the other hand, low-capacity States might find themselves subject to a new challenging duty that is hardly feasible given their level of economic and technological development. It is worth recalling that only a handful of States currently possess highly operational cyber capabilities. This debate has not been concluded yet and its outcome will be of seminal impact on the shape of the international legal framework regulating cyber operations.

5.6.4 *Due Diligence* duty as an alternative solution to limitations of other ways to attribute hostile cyber operations to States

The norm of *Due Diligence* could potentially create a second-order impact on the shape of Public International Law regulating cyberspace that goes beyond establishing minimum standards of infrastructure oversight by States. It would pertain to attribution of hostile cyber operations perpetrated by non-State actors to their host States. This is because States' *Due Diligence* obligation in cyberspace would cover all types of hostile operations infringing upon rights of other States, including those launched by non-State actors. This could create a situation where it would be easier to attribute a breach of *Due Diligence* duties to a State than to prove it had *effective control* over the hackers residing on its territory.

In cases where *effective control* requirement is too difficult to prove, *Due Diligence* could potentially provide a more universal and easier standard that would allow victim States to seek a remedy. This position has been expressed by some experts in the field of international law.[1151] In this context, lack of *Due Diligence* would amount to toleration and unwillingness to curb malign non-State actors on the part of the host State, a standard proposed already by the United States to call out Afghanistan's toleration of Al-Qaeda's presence in the run-up to the 9/11 terrorist attacks.[1152] To an extent, this logic is reflected in the Singapore Norm Package released by the Global Commission on the Stability of Cyberspace, mentioned already in Chapter 2.[1153] This multilateral initiative proposed the so-called Norm 7 fuses together the requirements of *Due Diligence* ("should prevent") and response to ongoing cyber hostilities ("and respond") by non-State actors:

> Non-state actors should not engage in offensive cyber operations and state actors should prevent and respond to such activities if they occur.[1154]

The general norm of duty to respond to an ongoing breach of rights of a third State that utilizes the sovereign territory of a State is applicable in cyberspace. However, the approach that perceives this route as a way to hold the host State accountable without going through the *effective control* test has to be critiqued. Utilizing *Due Diligence* duty and the related norm of duty to respond in order to circumvent the requirement of proving *effective control* over non-State actors, established by the ICJ and other international judicial bodies, would erode the latter and only provide a surface-level solution to the existing challenges of attribution in cyberspace. It would risk destabilizing the framework of Public International Law and reducing its long-term effectiveness. The difficulties with providing technical and legal attribution should be addressed in a systemic fashion rather than by way of developing a secondary unintended function for legal norms, straying from their stated

---

1151 Schmitt, Michael. (2015). In Defense of Due Diligence in Cyberspace. Yale Law Journal Forum, 68, 1–14. <https://papers.ssrn.com/sol3/papers.cfm?abstract_id=2622077>.

1152 United Nations Security Council. (1999, October 15). RESOLUTION 1267 (1999) Adopted by the Security Council at its 4051st meeting on 15 October 1999. Retrieved February 17, 2022, from <https://www.undocs.org/S/RES/1267%20(1999)>.

1153 See Section II.4.2—"Efforts to establish norms regulating conduct of States in cyberspace"

1154 Global Commission on the stability of Cyberspace. (2018, November). Norm Package Singapore. Retrieved February 15, 2022, from <https://cyberstability.org/wp-content/uploads/2018/11/GCSC-Singapore-Norm-Package-3MB.pdf>.

goals. The potential systemic solutions to the challenge of attribution in cyberspace are the subject of the next section.

5.7 Potential future legal frameworks facilitating attribution of *Internationally Wrongful Acts* in cyberspace

In the current context, public attribution is mostly the domain of States possessing high cyber capabilities. The United States, United Kingdom, and Canada are among the most vocal members of the international community in that regard. Their Five Eyes intelligence alliance (also including Australia and New Zealand) is a source of some of the best technical expertise (supported by the United States' control over the core internet infrastructure) allowing them to confidently attribute cyber assaults to a State. A number of States, including China, Russia, France, and Brazil have voiced their discontent with an asymmetrical international dynamic in regard to attributive power. More broadly, the wide gap in technical capabilities between States gave rise to a debate on developing a multilateral body that would facilitate identification and attribution of malicious cyber activity between States.

Three key initiatives have been proposed by non-State organizations on potential changes to the international legal attribution process that would make the process more accessible to States with low cyber capability. Such a body would also be the standard bearer in terms of technical expertise and protocols utilized for attribution in cyberspace. Each of these proposals draws on a different existing model within the framework of Public International Law and presents a unique set of strengths and weaknesses. Those proposed models are:

- Multilateral Cyber Attribution and Adjudication Council modeled on the International Atomic Energy Agency (IAEA);
- Digital Geneva Convention modeled on the Second Geneva Convention;
- Global Cyber Attribution Consortium modeled on the UN 1267 Terrorist Sanctions Committee.

The Atlantic Council called for establishment of a Multilateral Cyber Attribution and Adjudication Council (MCAAC). The body would have a status of a multilateral organization and would provide an international mechanism for attributing cyber assaults.[1155] This proposal was published in 2014 in the context of cyber assaults associated with the beginning of the occupation of Ukrainian Crimea by the Russian Federation. In its formulation, MCAAC would draw on existing models such as the Biological Weapons Convention and even more importantly the International Atomic Energy Agency (IAEA).[1156] The latter organization is responsible for monitoring nuclear activity conducted by States and attribute illicit acts in that regard to perpetrating States. This technical act is then used by the international community to prevent the perpetrating States, which are not authorized to develop nuclear weapons, from doing so. MCAAC would also identify the character of a cyber assault, delineating between generic breaches of territorial sovereignty, *Armed Attacks*, *Prohibited Use of Force*, *Prohibited Interventions*, and other. The project also anticipates arbitration capacity on the part MCAAC.[1157]

The call for a Digital Geneva Convention is an initiative launched by Microsoft in 2017.[1158] The initiative aims to *commit governments to protecting civilians from nation-state attacks in times of peace*. It also calls for establishment of *Digital Switzerland*, an intergovernmental body with a strong presence of private technological companies, which would have the capacity to attribute cyber assaults by mustering strong technical competences with political and legal access to overlook the internet network.[1159] Later, Microsoft modified

1155 Atlantic Council. (2014, November). Confidence-Building Measures In Cyberspace—A Multistakeholder Approach For Stability And Security. The NATO Science for Peace and Security Programme. <https://www.atlanticcouncil.org/wp-content/uploads/2014/11/Confidence-Building_Measures_in_Cyberspace.pdf>.

1156 Chesterman, Simon. Shared secrets: Intelligence and collective security. Double Bay, N.S.W.: Lowy Institute for International Policy, 2006. Page 29;

1157 Ibid.

1158 Smith, Brad. (2018, May 15). The need for a Digital Geneva Convention. Microsoft. Retrieved February 13, 2022, from <https://blogs.microsoft.com/on-the-issues/2017/02/14/need-digital-geneva-convention/>;

Microsoft Policy Papers. (n.d.). An attribution organization to strengthen trust online. Microsoft. Retrieved February 17, 2022, from <https://query.prod.cms.rt.microsoft.com/cms/api/am/binary/RW67QI>.

1159 Ibid.

its approach, suggesting the new attributive body should have a non-governmental character, akin to a UN body. The initiative remained an open-ended proposal but it nevertheless encouraged a debate on the subject.

Internet Governance Project (IGP), a non-governmental body set up to provide expertise on global internet governance, proposed in 2017 establishing a Global Cyber Attribution Consortium (GCAC).[1160] Its structure and competences would be modeled on the UN 1267 Terrorist Sanctions Committee, the SWIFT Global Payment Framework, ICANN, and to some extent IAEA. It would be a non-governmental body of a semi-international character. IGP claims that States would be incentivized to provide the GCAC with sensitive intelligence materials in order to shape its verdicts on technical attribution, in a fashion that is similar to how the UN 1267 Terrorist Sanctions Committee operates.

To add complexity, the debate on establishing a multilateral attribute organization is tied to a broader conversation about the need for an all-encompassing treaty regulating the cyber realm, akin to the United Nations Convention on the Law of the Sea signed in 1982 (and which entered into force in 1994). Interestingly, the most vocal supporters of such a treaty so far have been Russia and China, accompanied by a number of developing States. Meanwhile, Western powers remain resistant to the idea, perceiving the status quo as more beneficial to their interests. This impasse prevents a global consensus from emerging.

A few years have passed since the aforementioned initiatives for an attributive body have been proposed. However, as of 2023, none of them have come to fruition. The main obstacle appears to be lack of an incentive to support such a project on the part of the biggest world powers, which are also the States with the strongest cyber capabilities. Being among the few States capable of effectively attributing a cyber operation to a foreign entity, they would have to accept giving up on this privilege for a body like MCAAC, a Digital Switzerland, or GCAC to be formed. As more States gain cyber operational abilities, this balance of power might shift to enable an independent body

---

1160 Mueller, Milton(2017, November 20). A Global Cyber-Attribution Organization—Thinking it through. Internet Governance Project. Retrieved February 17, 2022, from <https://www.internetgovernance.org/2017/06/04/a-global-cyber-attribution-org/>.

to emerge. In the meantime, the ability to legally attribute State-sponsored cyber assaults remains a competence that is held by a select few States.

5.8 Conclusion

Legal attribution of *Internationally Wrongful Acts* is the key element in the process of holding States accountable for breaches of their legal obligations. It is therefore crucial in ensuring that the emerging international law framework covering cyberspace is effective in providing the twin purpose of stability and fairness. At present however, the well-established rules on attribution, with the existing track record of legal rulings and multilateral treaties in force, cannot be easily transposed into cyberspace. This is because cyberspace is notorious for its ability to conceal the source of hostile operations, which can be originated by a seemingly private hacker group and channeled through a string of pass-through States and private servers.

This context sets it apart from conventional acts, where gathering evidence is significantly easier. Since, however, conclusive technical attribution is a prerequisite of legal attribution, only States that have developed the most sophisticated technological capacity enabling such a process can effectively utilize existing international norms to attribute internationally wrongful acts to other States and holding them accountable. State practice has developed the notion of three distinctive tiers of attribution for hostile cyber acts:

- acknowledgment of existence of a hostile cyber act without any other action,
- political attribution to another State without technical evidence or legal consequence,
- legally binding attribution that includes necessary technical evidence.

However, as evidence shows, even the most technologically capable governments, like the one of the United States, are not always able to conclusively attribute foreign hacking incursions, revealing the limits of modern-day available methods in that regard. In this context, most States shy away from utilizing international legal remedies when being targeted by foreign hostile cyber operations, reverting instead to name-and-shame tactics, political backlash, or simply pretending that nothing has happened. Data suggests that the latest option might be the most widespread type of State response at present. This situation lends itself to the hypothesis that the current dynamics impair development of the international legal rules on cyberspace as States prefer to adopt other, non-legal solutions, limiting the volume of judiciary cases that would facilitate emergence of new customary norms.

One of the challenges faced by international cyberspace law is also the evidentiary threshold established through judiciary practice of the ICJ and other courts and arbitrage bodies. The more severe the alleged breach of an international obligation, the higher the evidence threshold that must be met in order for the legal case to be ruled in favor of the plaintiff State, following the principle of proportionality. The combination of potentially very intrusive nature of hostile cyber operations (e.g., shutting down of the power grid in Western Ukraine in 2015) and difficulties with tracing them back to a sovereign State, makes collecting a sufficient amount of evidence an uphill battle. There are signs however that this situation might shift as attribution capacity grows among States and legal rules evolve to accommodate the unique context of cyberspace. One of such postulates is to lower the evidentiary threshold for proving *Internationally Wrongful Acts* committed by States in cyberspace. This could be achieved by relying on the notion of *reasonableness* to guide the process of attribution where the evidence file is thinner than what would be required in the conventional context. Such proposals, however, have not yet been tested in front of an international judiciary body, making them highly hypothetical, despite being endorsed by a number of States. In the meantime, to fill the evidence gap, a whole branch of the private sector has emerged that helps governments around the world identify offending States behind hostile cyber acts. This outsized role of private companies in the evidentiary process is a unique feature of the Public International Law concerning cyberspace and contributes to the blurring of distinction between civilian and State capabilities that is already advanced given the dual status of the internet infrastructure.

At the time of writing this book, a number of States are expressing their conviction that activities of hacker groups, which are not per se State organs, might be attributed to their host government for as long the latter retains *Effective Control* over said activities. In fact, there exist some scholars that even argue for lowering the threshold of *Effective Control* in the cyber context due to its unique evidentiary challenges. While the definition of *Effective Control* in cyberspace is still uncertain (much like it is the case in the conventional realm), State practice validates the impression that the process of adaptation and forming of *opinio juris* on the matter has arguably commenced. In fact, the *Effective Control* model has emerged as the main path for attribution to a State in the context of cyberspace. Proving that a hacker group acted as an organ creates practically insurmountable evidentiary obstacles. As a result, a legal path (*Effective Control* test) that has been originally envisioned as an alternative route to the organ test became the main one in cyberspace.

The 2015 UN GGE Report proposed a voluntary non-binding norm of *Due Diligence* in cyberspace. The norm implies a duty of a State hosting physical ICT infrastructure that is part of the global internet system to monitor its network and prevent the most abusive excesses against public international legal rights of third States utilizing said network that could take place. The norm is present within other branches of Public International Law, such as humanitarian law, where it has the binding status. The introduction of such a norm would imply a threshold of severity beyond which the State hosting infrastructure utilized by an offending State to infringe upon the rights of a third State is obliged to take action to stop the hostile cyber operation from continuing. While the norm has acquired a binding status in some areas of Public International Law, applying it to cyberspace would be problematic as it would put a heavy burden on the shoulders of underdeveloped States with limited IT capabilities. It could however offer an alternative path to curbing hostile cyber activity and even hold accountable States that utilize proxy hacker groups to seek impunity while targeting other States with hostile cyber acts. This however would represent a maladaptation of the system of Public International Law, whose main focus should remain making the baseline paths for attribution functional and effective.

The structure of State jurisdiction in cyberspace is still being debated although early State practice points to a hybrid model emerging. The model appears to rest on the distinction between the physical and non-physical components of cyberspace. While State jurisdiction over the physical infrastructure of the host State is unquestionable, confirmed by the UN GGE reports and the UN GA resolutions fully endorsing it, the situation of the non-physical part of cyberspace, that is, the domains, and data flows is more complex. Governmental domains such as.gov constitute an extension of

State institutions discharging duties within *domaine réservé*, which puts them firmly within State jurisdiction as an extension of sovereign territory of sorts. Data flows that are part of hostile cyber operations could be subject to State jurisdiction if they reach a certain level of severity (this however would only apply if the norm of cyber *Due Diligence* ever becomes legally binding). Finally, data flows that are accidental, below the threshold of severity and constitute part of global cyberspace are not subject to jurisdiction of the State in whose territory physical infrastructure maintaining the flows is located. Otherwise, effectively every State on earth could claim jurisdiction over any activity on the internet, which usually involves complex global data flows, each taking a minuscule fraction of a second.

Ambitious initiatives are also being raised at the United Nations and other forums regarding creating a new multilateral body that would facilitate or even render attribution decisions with regard to hostile cyber operations perpetrated by States. The existing models of the International Atomic Energy Agency (IAEA), the UN 1267 Terrorist Sanctions Committee, and the Second Geneva Convention are the ones most frequently quoted as the best blueprints for such a new body. The formation of such an entity would mark a milestone in the development of Public International Law concerning cyberspace. Theoretically, the UN ITU would be the natural place to host the body. Unfortunately, persistent lack of consensus within the international community on the subject will likely prevent such a decision from taking place anytime soon. Political dynamics around international technical oversight over the internet are bound to prevent any shifts from the current status quo favoring the developed States with formidable ICT capabilities, most prominently the United States of America, for the foreseeable future.

CHAPTER 6

Cyberspace norms as a special regime of Public International Law

6.1 Introduction

Public International Law is evolving to adapt to the novel challenges posed by the emergence of cyberspace. Over the course of this book, a number of key developments in that area have been highlighted and analyzed. They spanned various dimensions of the cyberspace phenomenon, including its semantic framing, its history, its capacity to shape lawful and unlawful interactions between States, as well as the jurisdictional and attributive aspects. The aim of this chapter is to take a step back and offer a panoramic view of all these processes. To structure the analysis, the chapter draws on the theory of law, theory of legal systems, and most importantly the notion of special regimes of Public International Law. Using these methodological tools, one can determine the level of maturity of unique cyberspace regulations within the broader international legal framework.

The focus of this work is to answer the question whether cyberspace law is a special regime of Public International Law or at least in the process of becoming one. The consequences of such a development would be momentous. Special regimes have the capacity to diverge from the general system by developing their own internal rules and principles that shape behavior of States and resolution of disputes between them. This is the case with some of the most prominent special regimes, such as the international trade law centered around the World Trade Organization or the international environmental law.

Since cyberspace's importance in human life and functioning of States only grows, early signs and patterns we can observe at present can have an exponential impact on the future of the international community. That is why it is important to consolidate and translate a broader analysis done in this book into a tangible insight on the future direction of the evolution of the public international legal framework covering cyberspace.

6.2 Conceptual context of the notion of special regimes of Public International Law

The notion of self-contained legal regimes or special legal regimes, as they are primarily referred to in this book, must be situated within a broader theory of legal systems. At its core, a special regime represents the idea of a subset of specialized rules within a bigger normative system like a branch sprouting from the main trunk of a tree, separate but also integrated into and part of a bigger whole. Zygmunt Ziembiński developed a world-renowned theory of law, which encompasses six normative requirements for a coherent legal system:

- Indication of the legal system's justification (its ideological rationale);
- Indication of the law-making competence of the designated legislative entities;
- Determination of the status of applicable customs and precedents;
- Compilation of a catalog of agreed-upon interpretative rules;
- Compilation of a catalog of agreed-upon rules of logical inference;
- Compilation of a catalog of agreed-up collision rules.[1161]

From a logical perspective, every legal framework, either an overarching or a specialized one, has to meet these requirements, that is to clarify its core rules, their axiological source, and a legitimate way they can be modified. Additionally, Zygmunt Ziembiński postulated that every legal system should maintain internal rationality in three dimensions: the linguistic one (which pertains to consistency of terms used across the system, the axiological one (which pertains to consistency motives and core beliefs that determine the

---

1161 Kordela, Marzena. "Teoria Prawa Zygmunta Ziembińskiego." Filozofia Publiczna i Edukacja Demokratyczna 4, no. 1 (2018): pages 230–49. Page 233. <https://doi.org/10.14746/fped.2015.4.1.12>.

system's purpose), and the praxeological one (which pertains to the system's efficacy in achieving its purpose, that is effectively influencing human behavior).[1162] In a similar fashion, Jerzy Apanowicz, analyzing the broader notion of intellectual systems, determined that the internal methodological rationality of any such system is facilitated by four main intellectual mechanisms: inference, deduction, induction, and classification.[1163] Jerzy Wróblewski, developing a model of rational law-making, proposed that any use of binding norms to achieve a desired effect must cover three fundamental components: a) rational law-making according to an accepted policy; (b) rational application of law according to the policy (by way of, e.g., decisions and judgments); (c) rational enforcement of law.[1164]

This framework enables us to understand key tenets of a functioning legal system, such as rationality and a cohesive set of rules, but it must be complemented by answering at least two other questions: what is a legal system and why would one ever need special legal systems nested within a bigger legal system, especially in the context of Public International Law? The academic doctrine offers a few ways to define the phenomenon of legal systems. Hans Kelsen postulated that a legal system attaches a sanction to certain behaviors and thus qualifies the behavior conditioning the sanction as a delict. Its existence is thus predicated on its efficacy in attaching said sanctions if said behavior occurs.[1165] Stephen Krasner, one of the leading scholars on the U.S.-led rules-based world order, proposed an explanation for special international regimes that is steeped in the game theoretical concepts and the logic of the post-World War II international system. He wrote:

> A basic analytic distinction must be made between regimes and agreements. Agreements are ad hoc, often "one-shot," arrangements. The purpose of regimes is more than the following of short-run self-interest. (...) In a world of sovereign states the basic function of regimes is to coordinate state behavior to achieve desired

---

1162 Ibid. Page 234.

1163 Apanowicz, Jerzy. Metodologia Ogólna. Gdynia: Wyższa Szkoła Administracjii i Biznesu, 2002. Page 9.

1164 WRÓBLEWSKI, JERZY. "A Model of Rational Law-Making." ARSP: Archiv Für Rechts- Und Sozialphilosophie/Archives for Philosophy of Law and Social Philosophy 65, no. 2 (1979): pages 187–201. Page 189. <http://www.jstor.org/stable/23679192>.

1165 Raz, Joseph. The concept of a legal system: An introduction to the theory of legal system. Oxford: Clarendon, 1980. Page 93.

> outcomes in particular issue-areas. Such coordination is attractive under several circumstances. Stein and Keohane posit that regimes can have an impact when Pareto-optimal outcomes could not be achieved through uncoordinated individual calculations of self-interest. The prisoners' dilemma is the classic game-theoretic example. (...) Stein also argues that purely autonomous behavior could lead to disastrous results for both parties. Haas and others suggest that regimes may have significant impact in a highly complex world in which ad hoc, individualistic calculations of interest could not possibly provide the necessary level of coordination.[1166]

More contemporarily, Cornell Law School offered a definition that describes a legal system as a framework of rules, procedures, and institutions that human collectives use to interpret and enforce their laws.[1167] A more specific definition from the same source of an international legal system describes it as a set of rules and principles governing the relations and conduct of sovereign states with each other, as well as with international organizations and individuals.[1168] The United Nations defines international law as a system setting legal responsibilities of States in their conduct with each other, and their treatment of individuals within State boundaries.[1169] All these definitions focus on legal systems' purpose of impacting human behavior (including collective human behavior as is the case with State conduct) in a desired direction.

With this focus on effective impact on human behavior in mind, we can engage with the question of why special legal regimes might develop in international law. The UN ILC defined self-contained regimes as "geographically or functionally limited international legal systems" in its historic 2006 report on the matter, endorsed by the UN General Assembly.[1170] Every new special regime emerges not by accident but in response to new needs that are not

1166 Krasner, Stephen D. "Structural Causes and Regime Consequences: Regimes as Intervening Variables." International Organization 36, no. 2 (1982): pages 185–205. Page 191. <https://doi.org/10.1017/s0020818300018920>.

1167 "Legal Systems." Legal Information Institute - Cornell University. Retrieved December 1, 2023. <https://www.law.cornell.edu/wex/legal_systems#:~:text=A%20legal%20system%20is%20the,legal%20system%20across%20the%20globe>.

1168 "International Law." Legal Information Institute—Cornell University. Retrieved December 1, 2023. <https://www.law.cornell.edu/wex/international_law>.

1169 "Uphold International Law." United Nations. Retrieved December 1, 2023. <https://www.un.org/en/our-work/uphold-international-law>.

1170 United Nations International Law Commission. (2006). Fragmentation Of International Law: Difficulties Arising From The Diversification And Expansion

met well enough by the general international legal system. Legal systems strive to impact human behavior effectively in order to achieve prescribed goals. Each special regime has its own foundational rationale and a purpose that can be framed in those terms. They aim to impact human behavior more effectively than the general system. As the UN ILC has put it, each such special regime comes with its unique modifications to legal rules and sometimes even completely new rules, its unique expertise, and its unique "ethos" as compared with the general system of international law or other special regimes.[1171] The UN ILC has argued that special regimes can either improve effectiveness of general rules by providing a narrower, more contextual interpretation or fill in gaps in case no relevant rules exist.[1172] It stated:

> That Special law has priority over general law is justified by the fact that such special law, being more concrete, often takes better account of the particular features of the context. (…) Its application may also often create a more equitable result and it may often better reflect the intent of the legal subjects.[1173]

Wilfred Jenks wrote in 1953 that special regimes tend to develop according to functional, geographic, and historic groupings of States,[1174] highlighting multidimensionality of evolution of special regimes that responds to a variety of existing factors in its drive for achieving the most effective rules. Additionally, he pointed out the lack of a designated legislative body in the international law system that would be vested with law-making power, the way national parliaments are in domestic orders, which accelerates the phenomenon of divergence of rules into special regimes.[1175] This is consistent with the second requirement proposed by Zygmunt Ziembiński that postulates a link between having such a body and coherence of a legal system.

The intrinsic problem of allowing for a legal system to develop special regimes within it is that the unity and coherence of the overall framework

---

Of International Law. United Nations Office of Legal Affairs. Page 31. Retrieved February 15, 2022, from <https://digitallibrary.un.org/record/574810?ln=en>.

1171 Ibid.

1172 Ibid. Page 19.

1173 Ibid. Page 105.

1174 Jenks, Wilfred. "The conflict of law-making treaties," British Year Book of International Law 1953, vol.30, pages 401–403.

1175 Fragmentation of International Law: difficulties arising

as a whole suffer. After all, deviations from what was offered by the general system before is exactly why special regimes emerge. This risk was pointed out by the UN ILC in its 2006 report on the matter, which encapsulated various aspects of this risk with one overarching term—fragmentation of a legal system.[1176] It is fundamentally important to the system of international law that any special regime is not seen as a closed circuit but rather an outgrowth of the system. In fact, the very name *special regime* reflects that adherence to a bigger whole, which is one of the reasons why it fits the purpose better than the term "self-contained regime" that functions in parallel to describe the same phenomenon. There are certain core rules in international law that cannot be muted by way of developing a special regime, such as the preemptory norms *jus cogens* or the principle of *pacta sunt servanda*. It is now customarily understood that all norms of international law are subject to the general and supplementary rules of interpretation, verbalized in articles 31 and 32 of the Vienna Convention on the Law of Treaties.[1177] Additionally, the very mechanisms of emergence of special regimes are part of the system of international law. From the perspective of systemic coherence then, the notion of a special regime can be seen at its core as an interpretative tool, helping better apply the existing system to a new context, rather than the system's competition.

An alternative view, insisting on detachment of special regimes from the body of general international law, would somewhat resemble the nineteenth century notion of dualism of international and domestic legal orders. In actuality, special regimes, while enjoying a varying degree of autonomy, are a part of the general system and cannot be seen as separate organisms. At this point, this notion was confirmed by several international judiciary bodies. For example, in the 2003 *Oil Platforms* judgment (Iran v. United States of

1176 United Nations International Law Commission. (2006). Fragmentation Of International Law: Difficulties Arising From The Diversification And Expansion Of International Law. United Nations Office of Legal Affairs. Page 12. Retrieved February 15, 2022, from <https://digitallibrary.un.org/record/574810?ln=en>.

1177 United Nations International Law Commission. (2013). Report of the International Law Commission—Subsequent Agreements And Subsequent Practice In Relation To The Interpretation Of Treaties, Sixty-fifth session. Page 17. <https://legal.un.org/ilc/reports/2013/english/chp4.pdf>.

America), the Court invoked the article 31 of the Vienna Convention on the Law of Treaties as universally applying and stated:

> Under general rules of treaty interpretation, as reflected in the 1969 Vienna Convention on the Law of Treaties, interpretation must take into account 'any relevant rules of international law applicable in the relations between the parties.' (…) The application of the relevant rules of international rules of international law relating to this question thus forms an integral part of the task of interpretation.[1178]

Practically speaking, special regimes' rules consist of a series of lex specialis and lex posterior norms as compared to the general system of international law. The aforementioned 2006 UN ILC report on special self-contained regimes utilizes the Vienna Convention on the Law of Treaties and its regulations on lex specialis and lex posterior as the main framework.[1179] Lex specialis rules retain primacy over general rules in principle although there are limits to that relationship that will be fleshed out in Section 6.3.3 where the shape of the special regime framework is presented. Lex specialis rules can have a range of impact on general rules, which is consequential for special regimes. They can cancel, modify, or expand application of the general norms. In general, however, they do not erase those general norms, which still loom in the background. As long as special regimes expand the application of norms or clarify it in a new context, they remain non-controversial. It is the cancellation and modification of general norms that arouses most resistance as it provides the biggest risk of incoherence to the system. These considerations guided the international community as it oversaw development of special regimes of international law. The subsequent sections analyze this process and then consider how it applies in the context of cyberspace.

1178 Oil Platforms (Islamic Republic of Iran v. United States of America)—Judgment. International Court of Justice. (ICJ 2003). Page 182. Retrieved February 15, 2022, from <https://www.icj-cij.org/case/90>.

1179 United Nations International Law Commission. (2006). Fragmentation Of International Law: Difficulties Arising From The Diversification And Expansion Of International Law. United Nations Office of Legal Affairs. Page 10. Retrieved February 15, 2022, from <https://digitallibrary.un.org/record/574810?ln=en>.

6.3 Historical development of special regimes of Public International Law

6.3.1 International jurisprudence supporting the notion of special regimes

The foundational judgments and legal opinions that shaped the framing of special regimes in international law are the following:

- 1923 United Kingdom and Others v. Germany (S. S. Wimbledon) judgment by the PCIJ;
- 1980 United States v. Iran (U.S. Diplomatic and Consular Staff in Tehran) judgment by the ICJ;
- 1986 Nicaragua v. United States of America (Nicaragua) judgment by the ICJ;
- 2000 ruling of the Arbitration Tribunal set up as part of the UN Convention on the Law of the Sea on the Japan Fisheries case;
- 2006 Opinion by the ICJ Judge Bruno Simma;
- 2006 UN ILC Report approved by a UN GA resolution titled "Fragmentation of the international law: difficulties arising from the diversification and expansion of international law."

6.3.1.1 1923 United Kingdom v. Germany (S. S. Wimbledon) judgment by the PCIJ

The *Wimbledon* case was one of the first large legal disputes brought before the Permanent Court of International Justice, set up as part of the League of Nations system established after World War I. The case pertained to navigation through the Kiel Canal in north Germany, which bypasses the Skagerrak strait. Prior to the war, the man-made canal was part of Imperial Germany's internal waterways. However, following the defeat in the war, France insisted on setting up a separate legal regime for it in the Treaty of Versailles of 1919 that would grant unconstrained access to foreign vessels. This was perceived as a national humiliation among the leadership circles of the Weimar Republic, and they refused to fully implement the provisions. This stand-off eventually led to a legal case in front of the PCIJ when the British ship *Wimbledon* was not allowed to pass through. This put the PCIJ in a position to consider the nature of the special international regime set up to regulate the unique status of the Kiel Canal. In its judgment, where it ruled against Germany, it stated:

> Although the Kiel Canal, having been constructed by Germany in German territory, was, until 1919, an internal waterway of the State holding both banks, the Treaty [of Versailles] has taken care not to assimilate it to the other internal navigable waterways of the German Empire. A special section has been created at the end of Part XII (…) and in this special section rules exclusively designed for the Kiel Canal have been inserted; these rules differ on more than one point from those to which other internal navigable waterways of the Empire are subjected (…) This difference appears more especially from the fact that the Kiel Canal is open to the war vessels and transit traffic of all nations at peace with Germany, whereas free access to the other German navigable waterways … is limited to the Allied and Associated Powers alone (…) The provisions relating to the Kiel Canal … are therefore self-contained (…) The idea which underlies [them] is not to be sought by drawing an analogy from [provisions on other waterways] but rather by arguing a contrario, a method of argument which excludes them.[1180]

There are long-lasting consequences of this ruling. First, it is the first time when the phrase *Self-contained regime* was used by a subject of international law in its legal decision. While it is not the most accurate way to capture the nature of special regimes (as described in the previous subsection), it expresses well the notion of legality of some areas of the system of international law system developing in their own directions. Second, the PCIJ described the special regime regulating the Kiel Canal as not just a way of context-specific interpretation of existing rules but as a modification and cancellation of some general rules due to Germany's unique obligations accepted in the Treaty of Versailles. Such framing of special regimes allows for a much deeper differentiation. The PCIJ has confirmed primacy of rules in a *Self-contained regime* over the general ones, even if the former materially modify or cancel the latter, in its 1925 Advisory Opinion on the Exchange of Greek and Turkish Populations that drew directly on the *Wimbledon* judgment.[1181]

1180 The Case of S.S. "Wimbledon" Judgment (Series A, No. 1). Permanent Court of International Justice. (1923, August 17).Pages 23–24. Retrieved February 18, 2022, from <https://legal.un.org/PCIJsummaries/documents/english/5_e.pdf>.

1181 Exchange of Greek and Turkish Populations, Advisory Opinion of 21 February 1925, Permanent Court of International Justice, Series B, No. 10, page 20. <https://www.icj-cij.org/pcij-series-b>.

6.3.1.2 1980 United States v. Iran (U.S. Diplomatic and Consular Staff in Tehran) judgment by the ICJ

In the 1980 case in front of the ICJ, the newly formed Islamic Republic of Iran was aiming to excuse its own breaches of international law, namely the storming of the U.S. embassy in Tehran and killing of its staffers, as a justified reaction to the United States' conduct. The ICJ rejected this logic, stating that the diplomatic and consular law is a *Self-contained regime* that includes several types of response and self-help by an injured State that provide a "fully efficacious" solution. In this case, no resort to general rules or other branches of international law is warranted. Specifically, Iran could have invoked the rule *persona non grata* and expel unwanted diplomats if it had seen it fit, instead of killing them.[1182] Thus, the notion of countermeasures, invoked by Iran was not an available legal route. Diplomatic and consular law replaces the norms of countermeasures and retorsions with an alternative framework that fits the specialized context better.

6.3.1.3 1986 Nicaragua v. United States of America (Nicaragua) judgment by the ICJ

The ICJ judgment concerning funding of the *Contras* insurgents in Nicaragua by the CIA with funds unlawfully obtained by selling arms to the Islamic Republic of Iran is one of the most consequential decisions of the Court in its history so far. The focus of the case was not special regimes but since the Court had to consider the relationship between specialized treaties and general customary norms, the verdict had a collateral impact on that subject. Specifically, the Court ruled that:

> In general, treaty rules being lex specialis, it would not be appropriate that a State should being a claim based on a customary-law rule if it has by treaty already provided means for settlement of such a claim.[1183]

[1182] United States Diplomatic and Consular Staff in Tehran (United States of America v. Iran). International Court of Justice. ICJ Reports 1980. (1980, May 24). Paragraph 83–86. Retrieved February 17, 2022, from <https://www.icj-cij.org/en/case/64>.

[1183] Case Concerning Military and Paramilitary Activities in and Against Nicaragua, Nicaragua v. United States. International Court of Justice. I.C.J. Reports 14, ICGJ 112 (ICJ 1986). (1986). Page 137. Retrieved February 15, 2022, from <https://www.icj-cij.org/en/case/70/judgments>.

This ruling supported the notion already developed in the *Tehran* judgment that to the extent that specialized regulations can bring full relief to a case, it should be resolved using those regulations instead of reverting back to the general framework of international law.

6.3.1.4 2000 ruling of the UN Arbitration Tribunal on the Japan Fisheries case

The issue of the relation between general rules of international law and those within a special regime came into sharp relief in the 1993 legal case on fishing activity of Japanese vessels. Japanese fishers are notorious for breaching international regulations on preserving endangered marine species such as whales. In the 1993 arbitration case, brought before the Tribunal set up as part of the UN Convention on the Law of the Sea, the Japanese government argued that the 1993 Convention for the Conservation of Southern Bluefin Tuna is a special regime that absolves Japanese vessels from adhering to general rules stemming from the 1982 United Nations Convention on the Law of the Sea that had no equivalent in the special regime. The Arbitration Tribunal confirmed that the 1993 convention created a special regime but otherwise rejected Japan's logic, stating that to the extent that it is possible, treaties and customs defining general and special regimes should be interpreted in parallel, ensuring that objectives of both are met efficaciously. Lack of specific constraints in the special regime does not mean the general ones are replaced with a vacuum.[1184]

The two rulings: the 1980 Tehran one by the ICJ and the 2000 one by the UN Arbitration Tribunal, set respectively the lower and upper bound in terms of the legal impact of special regimes on the general system. The special regimes have the power to modify and replace the legal rules but their interpretation will always gravitate toward reconciling both frameworks, preserving the maximum possible application of both.

1184 Southern Bluefin Tuna Case between Australia and Japan and between New Zealand and Japan, decision of 4 August 2000 (jurisdiction and admissibility), UNRIAA, vol. XXIII, p. 23, para. 38 (c). <https://legal.un.org/riaa/cases/vol_XXIII/1-57.pdf>.

6.3.1.5 2006 Opinion by the ICJ Judge Bruno Simma

Bruno Simma has been one of the most influential judges of the ICJ. A native of German Saarland, he served on the bench for ten years, between 2003 and 2012. During that time he published a widely cited article in the European Journal of International Law on the matter of *Self-contained regimes.* While his research is not legally binding, his formal capacity and status as one of leading international experts have resulted in the article's elevated impact. For example, it was cited in the subsequent UN ILC Report on the matter that was approved by the UN GA. In fact, Bruno Simma has been exploring the subject of *Self-contained regimes* since the 1980s.[1185] In the article, Judge Simma aimed to reconcile the tension between the general framework of international law and special regimes. He argued against their fully isolated character as well as their complete integration into general law as mere interpretative guidelines. Instead, he argued that general rules still apply, although they can be partially muted or modified in the specialized context. Whenever a specialized regime fails to efficaciously solve a case, the general rules activate, filling in the gap. This organic relationship between special regimes and the underlying general system is symbiotic rather than adversarial, even if divergence between the two is material.[1186]

6.3.1.6 2006 UN ILC Report approved by a UN GA resolution titled "Fragmentation of the international law: difficulties arising from the diversification and expansion of international law."

The 2006 UN ILC Report was the result of years of scholarly work, led by Martti Koskenniemi. The report offered a framework of special regimes in international law that is presented and analyzed in the next subsection. Additionally, it formulated the principle of synergistic interpretation between specialized and general rules that ensures harmonization of the overall system of international law.[1187] The report presents the cumulative achievements of

---

1185 Simma, Bruno. (1985). Self-contained regimes. Netherlands Yearbook of International Law, 16, pages 111–136. <https://doi:10.1017/S0167676800003482>

1186 Simma, Bruno, and Pulkowski, Dirk. Of Planets and the Universe: Self-contained Regimes in International Law, European Journal of International Law, Volume 17, Issue 3, 1 June 2006, pages 483–529, <https://doi.org/10.1093/ejil/chl015>.

1187 United Nations International Law Commission. (2006). Fragmentation Of International Law: Difficulties Arising From The Diversification And Expansion

international jurisprudence on the matter and structures them into a cohesive framework. In that, it is a reflection of the existing state of law rather than a novel postulate. The fact that the report was approved by a UN General Assembly resolution points to the international community's *opinio juris* that lends the framework enough credence to serve as the basis for the analysis of the status of emerging cyberspace law.

6.3.2 Framework of types of special regimes of international law

6.3.2.1 Structure of the framework of special regimes of international law

Weak and strong special regimes

Distinction between different types of special regimes boils down to the difference between principles, primary rules, and secondary rules. The distinction has been endorsed by the UN ILC in its report:[1188]

- **Principles** are general underlying rules that permeate a whole regime, influencing interpretation of each norm. They are at their core a value judgment that indicates priority and emphasis put on certain objectives within a regime. For example, the international trade law regime, centered around the World Trade Organization (WTO), emphasizes balancing competitive advantage in the market as the guiding principle. The international environmental law strives for reduction of damage to the environment as the overarching principle. Meanwhile, the general system of international law retains focus on respecting State sovereignty and sovereign equality between States as the main principle. As Neil MacCormick put it: "The commonplace distinction between rules and principles captures a relationship between norms of a lower and higher degree of abstraction."[1189]

Of International Law. United Nations Office of Legal Affairs. Page 15. Retrieved February 15, 2022, from <https://digitallibrary.un.org/record/574810?ln=en>.

1188 Ibid. Page 31.

1189 MacCormick, Neil. Legal Reasoning and Legal Theory, Oxford, Clarendon Press, 1978, page 156.

- **Primary rules** define States' and other international law subjects' rights and obligations.[1190]
- **Secondary rules** determine application of primary rules, their interpretation and meaning in a specific context, and consequences of breaching obligations and preventing rights from being realized by subjects of international law.[1191]

Based on this distinction, three types of special regimes of international law can be identified: one that only contains secondary rules—a weak special regime, one that contains both primary and secondary rules—a strong special regime, and one that contains unique principles, primary rules, and secondary rules—a very strong special regime. Figure 19 presents this distinction.

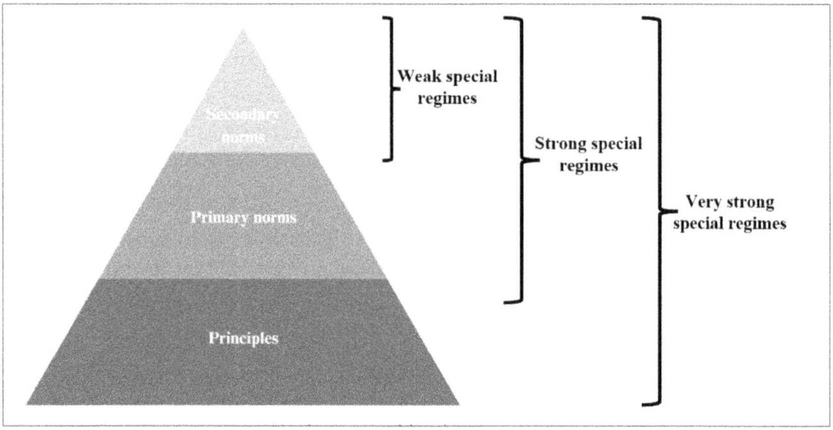

Figure 19. Three types of special regimes of international law
Source: own elaboration

Let us take a moment to consider the legal magnitude of each of the three types of special regimes. Weak special regimes function as interpretative tools, helping apply the general framework of international law in a specific context without formally affecting any of the rights and obligations of

1190 Shaw, Malcolm N. International Law (Cambridge University Press, Cambridge, 2003) page 117.

1191 Ibid.

subjects of international law. This soft version of a special regime creates no stress on the system. In fact, by facilitating effective application of existing rules, it makes it more efficacious without any negative trade-off. The UN ILC did not extend the label "Self-contained regime" to this type of special regime, reserving it for the two stronger categories only.[1192] The existing specialized dispute settlement mechanism, set up by States or groups of States to strengthen accountability and safeguarding of their contractual rights are a good example. Another example can be a treaty system regulating border disputes between States in a region. Strong special regimes create unique rights and obligations for States and offer specialized mechanisms of their interpretation and safeguarding. This kind of regime still provides an obvious benefit to the overall system. Specialized norms can ensure efficacious functioning of arrangements between States, while adhering to all general principles of international law. It must be noted that States across the world never have a uniform set of rights and obligations so enshrining that fact by way of a special regime does not breach the notion of sovereign equality.[1193] It is the third category, very strong special regimes, that is the most controversial. Establishing a set of unique underlying principles, different from the ones defining the general system of international law, leads to a different systemic logic and diverging jurisprudence.

Definition of lex specialis

Proper delineation of the term "lex specialis" is required in order to make a clear distinction between the general rules and the ones contained within a specialized regime, be it in terms of principles, primary norms, or secondary norms. As a matter of fact, there exists no formalized distinction between lex specialis and lex generalis in international law. UN ILC offered a simple guideline: *whenever two or more norms deal with the same subject matter, priority*

1192 United Nations International Law Commission. (2006). Fragmentation Of International Law: Difficulties Arising From The Diversification And Expansion Of International Law. United Nations Office of Legal Affairs. Page 36. Retrieved February 15, 2022, from <https://digitallibrary.un.org/record/574810?ln=en>.

1193 United States Diplomatic and Consular Staff in Tehran (United States of America v. Iran). International Court of Justice. ICJ Reports 1980. (1980, May 24). Paragraph 86. Retrieved February 17, 2022, from <https://www.icj-cij.org/en/case/64>.

should be given to the norm that is more specific.[1194] Lex specialis can cover a certain thematic area, such as human rights, diplomatic relations, or indeed cyberspace. However, it can also take on geographic dimensions, allowing States to develop legal specificities of regional nature or pertain to commercial arrangements. For instance, many international lex specialis rules concern subjecting treaty commitments and interests to scrutiny of arbitrage bodies in London or New York City. The division between lex generalis and specialis has to be ascertained in a case-by-case manner, based on the context and by applying the most reasonable interpretative logic. The UN ILC has dealt with the subject of lex specialis in its *Draft Articles on Responsibility of States for Internationally Wrongful Acts*, endorsed by the UN GA. Article 55 of the document states:

Article 55. Lex specialis

> These articles do not apply where and to the extent that the conditions for the existence of an internationally wrongful act or the content or implementation of the international responsibility of a State are governed by special rules of international law.[1195]

The derogation of the *Draft Articles* in case of existence of special rules is just one example of lex specialis that only pertains specifically to responsibility for *Internationally Wrongful Acts*. Nevertheless, it gave the UN ILC an opportunity to delve into the subject in general. In the commentary, it stated:

> For the lex specialis principle to apply it is not enough that the same subject matter is dealt with by two provisions; there must be some actual inconsistency between them, or else a discernible intention that one provision is to exclude the other.[1196]

1194 United Nations International Law Commission. (2006). Fragmentation Of International Law: Difficulties Arising From The Diversification And Expansion Of International Law. United Nations Office of Legal Affairs. Page 8. Retrieved February 15, 2022, from <https://digitallibrary.un.org/record/574810?ln=en>.

1195 United Nations International Law Commission. Draft articles on Responsibility of States for Internationally Wrongful Acts with commentaries. United Nations Office of Legal Affairs (2001). Article 55. Retrieved February 15, 2022. <https://legal.un.org/ilc/texts/instruments/english/commentaries/9_6_2001.pdf>.

1196 Ibid. Paragraph (4) of the Commentary to Article 55.

Based on this interpretation, there has to be some measure of inconsistency between the two provisions for one of them to be seen as lex specialis replacing or modifying the other in a more specific context. If there exists no distinguishable difference, one is just the repetition of the other. A borderline case of lex specialis are provisions that specify application of general rules in a new context without modifying their core substance. This approach explains why the UN ILC claimed that special regimes of international law that only contain secondary norms are "weak" and do not actually reach the threshold of a *Self-contained regime.* Secondary norms do not modify rights and obligations of States but only clarify application of general rules in a specific context and mechanisms for ensuring responsibility in case of a breach. A good example of a set of secondary norms that clarify application of the general ones without changing their core substance are the provisions of the 1987 Montreal Protocol on Substances that Deplete the Ozone Layer.[1197] Article 2 of the Protocol contains the schedule of emission reduction per State that creates specific commitments. The Protocol is one of the follow-up treaties to the 1985 Vienna Convention for the Protection of the Ozone Layer. The Convention is general in nature and does not contain specific reduction commitments.[1198]

Principle of harmonization and systemic integration

James Crawford has observed in his capacity as a member of the UN ILC, there is no assumption in the system of international law that it must be "one size fits all."[1199] At the same time, the UN ILC aimed to set limitations to how far apart various special regimes can evolve. One of them is the principle

---

1197 United Nations. Montreal Protocol on Substances that Deplete the Ozone Layer. United Nations, Treaty Series, vol. 1522. 16 September 1987. Retrieved November 30, 2023. <https://treaties.un.org/Pages/ViewDetails.aspx?src=IND&mtdsg_no=XXVII-2-a&chapter=27&clang=_en>.

1198 United Nations. Vienna Convention for the Protection of the Ozone Layer. United Nations, Treaty Series. 22 March 1985. Retrieved November 30, 2023. <https://legal.un.org/avl/ha/vcpol/vcpol.html#:~:text=The%20Vienna%20Convention%2C%20concluded%20in,that%20harm%20the%20ozone%20layer>.

1199 Crawford, James. (2002). The ILC's Articles on Responsibility of States for Internationally Wrongful Acts: A Retrospect. American Journal of International Law, 96(4), pages 874–890. Page 880. <http://doi:10.2307/3070683>.

of harmonization.[1200] It states that interpretation of rights and obligations across various areas of international law has to be rendered in a way that maximizes compatibility and consistency across them. This effort serves the purpose of systemic integration of the whole framework. This objective is understandable although sometimes difficult to secure, as demonstrated by accusations leveled at the WTO's Court interpretation of sovereign equality of States in the context of trade disputes.[1201]

The principle of harmonization has a long track record that predates the debate on special regimes of international law. Article 31 of the Vienna Convention on the Law of Treaties contains general rules of interpretation that include invocation of relevant rules of international law, which facilitates harmonization across diverse treaty regimes.[1202]

Jus cogens, obligations erga omnes, and other limitations of special regime provisions

As noted earlier, all special regimes are part of the overall system of international law and not truly self-contained. They are subject to its foundational paradigms and the principle of harmonization. What follows is that States cannot derogate or modify any existing rights and obligations. Special regimes are not a blanket permission to avoid accountability. Following are six limitations applicable to special regimes. The first five stem from their confirmed status in the system of international law, including via ICJ jurisprudence and enshrinement in the UN Charter, superbly researched by Zdzisław Galicki during his tenure at the UN ILC.[1203] The last one was additionally argued for by the UN ILC in its 2006 report.

1200 United Nations International Law Commission. (2006). Fragmentation Of International Law: Difficulties Arising From The Diversification And Expansion Of International Law. United Nations Office of Legal Affairs. Page 15. Retrieved February 15, 2022, from <https://digitallibrary.un.org/record/574810?ln=en>.

1201 World Trade Organization. "Top 10 Reasons to Oppose the World Trade Organization? Criticism, yes … misinformation, no!." Retrieved December 1, 2023. <https://www.wto.org/english/thewto_e/minist_e/min99_e/english/misinf_e/09sov_e.htm>.

1202 Vienna Convention on the Law of Treaties (May 23, 1969). UN Doc A/Conf39/27. Article 31(1) Retrieved February 15, 2022, from https://legal.un.org/ilc/texts/instruments/english/conventions/1_1_1969.pdf.

1203 Galicki, Zdzisław. "4. Hierarchy in International Law within the Context of Its Fragmentation." International Law between Universalism and Fragmentation, n.d., pages 41–60. <https://doi.org/10.1163/ej.9789004167278.v-1086.21>.

- **Preemptory norms of international law**—jus cogens *Jus cogens* is explicitly non-derogable by any subject of international law, in any context.[1204] The catalog of *jus cogens* provision has some core positions although the exact list is most determined and is subject to evolution. At present, the most agreed-upon list includes: launching aggressive war, committing crimes against humanity, war crimes, maritime piracy, genocide, apartheid, slavery, torture, and executing juvenile offenders.[1205]
- **International legal obligations erga omnes** Both *jus cogens* and obligations *erga omnes* denote certain obligations of all individual States toward the international community as a whole. The key difference is that *jus cogens* pertains to the most severe imaginable breaches in that respect while obligations *erga omnes* are a broader category of obligations that is constructed in an affirmative way.[1206] For example, in its 2004 Advisory Opinion, the ICJ identified "the right of peoples to self-determination" to be an obligation *erga omnes*,

---

1204 United Nations International Law Commission. (2019). Report on the work of the seventy-first session. United Nations Office of Legal Affairs. Chapter V—Peremptory norms of general international law (jus cogens). Retrieved November 15, 2023. <https://legal.un.org/ilc/reports/2019/english/chp5.pdf>;

See also: Dispute Concerning Access to Information under Article 9 of the OSPAR Convention, (Ireland v. United Kingdom) (Final Award, 2 July 2003) ILR vol. 126 (2005) page 364, paragraph 84. Retrieved November 15, 2023. <https://pca-cpa.org/en/cases/34/>

1205 United Nations General Assembly. Official Records of the General Assembly, Fifty-sixth Session, Supplement 10 (A/56/10). Commentary to article 40 of the draft articles on State Responsibility, paragraphs (4)-(6) & Commentary to article 26, paragraph (5). <https://legal.un.org/ilc/documentation/english/reports/a_56_10.pdf>; See also: Case concerning armed activities on the territory of the Congo (Democratic Republic of the Congo v.Rwanda) I.C.J. Reports 2006, para. 64. <https://www.icj-cij.org/case/116>; Prosecutor v. Furundžija, International Criminal Tribunal for the Former Yugoslavia, 2002, 121 International Law Reports 213 (2002). <https://www.icty.org/x/cases/furundzija/tjug/en/>;

Bossuyt, Marc and Wouters, Jan (2005). Grondlijnen van internationaal recht, Intersentia, Antwerp, etc., page 92.

1206 Memeti, Ardit, and Nuhija, Bekim. "The Concept of Erga Omnes Obligations in International Law," New Balkan Politics, Issue 14, 2013. <https://papers.ssrn.com/sol3/papers.cfm?abstract_id=3502662#:~:text=law%2C%20in%20general-,legal%20theory%20the%20concept%20%E2%80%9Cerga%20omnes%E2%80%9D%20(Latin%3A%20%E2%80%9E,obligations%20or%20rights%20towards%20all>.

to be recognized and respected by all subjects of international law.[1207] While *erga omnes* is a softer category than *jus cogens*, due to its more gradual character, neither can be derogated by a special regime. This prohibition reflects a hierarchy of norms in international law. Special regimes must defer to the foundational norms of the general framework they are part of.

- **Articles 25 and 103 of UN Charter as the ultimate collision resolution rules** By the same token, all special regimes are unconditionally subject to universally applicable norms of the UN Charter. The two most seminal ones in that regard are expressed in articles 25 and 103. Article 25 states: *The Members of the United Nations agree to accept and carry out the decisions of the Security Council in accordance with the present Charter.*[1208] The UN Security Council can weigh on any international legal matter at any time, even if it concerns customary law or agreement between States that are not members of the United Nations. For a UN Security Council resolution to be binding, it must be unanimously approved by the required majority of its members, with no dissent from any of the permanent members. Article 103 states: *In the event of a conflict between the obligations of the Members of the United Nations under the present Charter and their obligations under any other international agreement, their obligations under the present Charter shall prevail.*[1209] It lays out a collision resolution norm that applies to special regimes. It clearly expresses the hierarchy of legal order. In case of any conflict, obligations stemming from the UN Charter, which is at the center of the general framework of international law, take precedence over the rules of any special regime.
- **Article 31 and 32 of the Vienna Convention on the Law of Treaties** Articles 31 and 32 provide rules of interpretation of treaty-derived

---

[1207] Legal Consequences of the Construction of a Wall in the Occupied Palestinian Territory. International Court of Justice. ICJ Report 136, 2004. (2004, July 9). Paragraph 88. Retrieved February 18, 2022, from <https://www.icj-cij.org/en/case/131>.

[1208] United Nations. Charter of the United Nations, June 26, 1945. 1 UNTS XVI. Article 25. <https://www.un.org/en/about-us/un-charter>.

[1209] Ibid. Article 103.

obligations and rights of States. They are currently recognized as representing customary international law that applies beyond just the signatories of the Convention. It is also presumed that they cannot be revoked by special regime provisions.[1210] The elevated status of these two articles is predicated on the principle of harmonization and systemic integration across all branches of international law.

- Pacta sunt servanda—**special regimes cannot infringe upon rights of third parties** *Pacta sunt servanda* is a timeless legal principle that has been already recognized by ancient Romans and transcends the division between domestic and international law. It also applies in the context of special regimes. Its practical ramification is that States or entities engaged in development of a special regime are not allowed to infringe this way upon rights of third parties. In case a special regime emerges by itself, without any specific entity consciously driving the process, the principle still applies and shapes the regime's evolution.[1211]
- **Public law-nature treaties—special regimes cannot undermine their public law commitments via special regime development** The last limitation applicable to provisions of special regimes pertains to a category of treaties that can be described as *Public Law-Nature Treaties*. This category was proposed by the UN ILC in its considerations of the subject of special regimes of international law. Since the report was endorsed by the UN GA in a resolution, the category now enjoys demonstrated *opinio juris*, although its binding status has not been yet fully tested in practice. What the UN ILC meant by the category are treaties that set up a set of rules that serve the international community as a whole, not quite obligations *erga omnes*, but close enough to be considered immune to modifications

---

1210 United Nations International Law Commission. (2006). Fragmentation Of International Law: Difficulties Arising From The Diversification And Expansion Of International Law. United Nations Office of Legal Affairs. Page 8. Retrieved February 15, 2022, from <https://digitallibrary.un.org/record/574810?ln=en>.

1211 Sadat-Akhavi, Seyed-Ali. Methods of Resolving Conflicts between Treaties, Leiden, Martinus Nijhoff, 2003, pages 5–7.

via special regimes.[1212] A great example of such a Public-law nature treaty is the 1982 United Nations Convention on the Law of the Sea, which serves the purpose of preservation of the common heritage of mankind that is the global sea network, including all its marine life. The failed attempt of Japan attempting to derogate commitments stemming from the Convention set up to protect Bluefin tuna based on the special provisions of the 1993 Convention for the Conservation of Southern Bluefin Tuna, mentioned earlier in this section, can be an example of a State attempting to breach this limitation. UN ILC also put in the category of public law-nature treaty commitments, not to be undermined by special regimes, the constituent instruments of international organizations.[1213]

6.3.2.2 Limitations of special regimes of international law

The special regime framework has been developed to provide a useful function within the realm of international law. However, there exist risks of this tool becoming dysfunctional. Four issues that might arise while deploying a special regime are presented as follows:

- *Non liquet*—a situation where there are no applicable norm within a special regime that was developed to cover a certain area or the norms are inadequate If a special regime fails to regulate or adjudicate a case that is nominally within its scope, the general rules of international law fill in the gap. This is at once an expression of systemic integration of special regimes into the overall system and of the hierarchy of regimes, with the general one always looming in the background. This notion was confirmed in the George Pinson case of 1928, where the Arbitral Award, considering special regulations on dual citizenship depending

[1212] United Nations International Law Commission. (2006). Fragmentation Of International Law: Difficulties Arising From The Diversification And Expansion Of International Law. United Nations Office of Legal Affairs. Page 29. Retrieved February 15, 2022, from <https://digitallibrary.un.org/record/574810?ln=en>.

[1213] Ibid.

on the State, decided as much.[1214] The expression *non liquet* comes from Latin "it is not clear" and was introduced into the vocabulary of international law via British lawyers who developed the term within the Commonwealth legal framework.[1215] The UN GA resolution endorsing the UN ILC report on the matter supported the notion, offering a very wide definition of the fall-back rule. Not only can lack of relevant norms trigger the fall-back but also persistent non-compliance by the special regime's parties, withdrawal by parties instrumental for the regime, or even general non-fulfillment of its stated purpose by the regime.[1216]

- **Lack of clarity pertaining to the scope of** jus cogens **norms and** erga omnes **obligations** UN ILC has refrained from specifying the definition or scope of *jus cogens* norms and *erga omnes* obligations in any of its documents. In fact, it acknowledged as much, stating that *jus cogens* is a "thin doctrine" that is too abstract and unspecific to effectively curtail negative developments within the system.[1217]
- **Competing jurisprudence regimes centered around specialized international courts** One of the questions unanswered by the UN ILC report on the subject of special regimes mentioned earlier pertained to courts, frequently set up to adjudicate legal disputes within special regimes. In terms of the evolution of international law, such courts can play a twofold function. First, they can accelerate the accretion of differences between the regime and the general system, including in terms of primary norms and even the principles. Second, their jurisprudence might emerge as competition to the ruling by the general international legal courts, especially the ICJ. Lack of engagement on

---

1214 Georges Pinson case (France v. United Mexican States) Award of 13 April 1928, UNRIAA, vol. V, page 422. Retrieved November 15, 2023, from <https://legal.un.org/riaa/cases/vol_V/327-466.pdf>

1215 Cross, Rupert, and J. W. Harris. Precedent in English law (4th Edition). Oxford: Clarendon, 2004. Page 121.

1216 United Nations International Law Commission. (2006). Fragmentation Of International Law: Difficulties Arising From The Diversification And Expansion Of International Law. United Nations Office of Legal Affairs. Page 13. Retrieved February 15, 2022, from <https://digitallibrary.un.org/record/574810?ln=en>.

1217 Ibid. Page 84.

that issue by the UN ILC was called out by a number of legal scholars, including Christian Leathley,[1218] Sean Murphy,[1219] Ole Kristian Fauchald and André Nollkaemper,[1220] and Suzannah Linton and Firew Kebede Tiba.[1221] There is no easy solution to this challenge and the most feasible one would be for the ICJ to become a more activist court, decisively weighing in on growing discrepancies between regimes as they arise, which carries its own risks and limitations.

- **The challenge of diluting legal standards by way of establishing a special regime** The challenge of dilution of legal standards by way of developing special regimes was framed by Prosper Weil in 1983, although the problem has been considered even earlier, albeit in a more focused way.[1222] Initially the concern was specifically about the preemptory norms *jus cogens* that could be diluted by way of setting up a regional special regime. For that reason, the Vienna Convention on the Law of Treaties, included article 66 (a), which designates the ICJ as the ultimate decisive power on interpretation of *jus cogens*-related treaty provisions.[1223] However, over time the focus shifted to lower-rank international legal norms that could fall prey

1218 Leathley, Christian. "An Institutional Hierarchy to Combat the Fragmentation of International Law: Has the ILC Missed an Opportunity?" 40 N.Y.U. INT'L L. & POL. 259 (2007). <https://nyujilp.org/wp-content/uploads/2013/02/40.1-Leathley.pdf>.

1219 Sean D. Murphy, Deconstructing Fragmentation: Koskenniemi's 2006 ILC Project, Temple International & Comparative Law Journal. George Washington University. Page 5. <https://scholarship.law.gwu.edu/cgi/viewcontent.cgi?article=2207&context=faculty_publications#:~:text=The%20Report%20began%20by%20explaining,possibly%2C%20the%20loss%20of%20an>

1220 Fauchald, Ole Kristian, and Andre Nollkaemper. The practice of international and National Courts and the (de-) fragmentation of international law. Oxford: Hart Publishing, 2012.

1221 Linton, Suzannah and Tiba, Firew Kebede, The International Judge in an Age of Multiple International Courts and Tribunals (2009). Chicago Journal of International Law, Vol. 9, No. 2, 2009. Page 297. <http://dx.doi.org/10.2139/ssrn.2635379>

1222 Weil, Prosper. (1983). Towards Relative Normativity in International Law? American Journal of International Law, 77(3), 413–442. <https://doi:10.2307/2201073>.

1223 Vienna Convention on the Law of Treaties. United Nations. (1969, May 23). Article 66 (a). Retrieved February 18, 2022, from <https://legal.un.org/ilc/texts/instruments/english/conventions/1_1_1969.pdf>.

to dilution more easily. The Japan fisheries case mentioned earlier is a great case in point as it concerns a State attempting to utilize special regime provisions of Bluefin tuna preservation to dilute the standards contained within a more generic UN Convention on the Law of Sea.[1224]

All these challenges present in applying special regimes are not a reason for the concept to be abandoned. Special regimes provide utility to the global community. It is important however to stay aware of the fact that they are not a silver bullet solution, fit for purpose in every area of international law. It is especially important to be cognizant of both the benefits and the challenges when considering applying the framework to a completely new sphere, such as cyberspace, which is the subject of the final section of this book—VI.5.

6.3.2.3 Ways for special regimes of international law to emerge

There are two processes that can contribute to development of a special regime of international law:

- Treaty or a series of treaties;
- Custom.

Of course, these two processes can also blend together to facilitate emergence of a new special regime. However, the UN ILC has been skeptical regarding the possibility of a special regime to emerge purely by way of custom—State practice coupled by their consistent *opinio juris.* They called this prospect "exceptional."[1225] Historically, customary development has been the case with some of the oldest special regimes, such as the diplomatic and

---

1224 Southern Bluefin Tuna Case between Australia and Japan and between New Zealand and Japan, decision of 4 August 2000 (jurisdiction and admissibility), UNRIAA, vol. XXIII, p. 23, para. 38 (c). <https://legal.un.org/riaa/cases/vol_XXIII/1-57.pdf>.

1225 United Nations International Law Commission. (2006). Fragmentation Of International Law: Difficulties Arising From The Diversification And Expansion Of International Law. United Nations Office of Legal Affairs. Page 38. Retrieved February 15, 2022, from <https://digitallibrary.un.org/record/574810?ln=en>.

consular law. They emerged organically, via centuries and millennia of State practice. Nevertheless, in the modern context of the post-World War II, UN Charter-centric system of international law, special regimes are much more intentional creations that involve extensive cooperation, for which signing a treaty is the most obvious way.

Roman Kwiecień aptly pointed out that it is customary law that is the actual foundation of the system of international law, not treaties. The latter tend to are largely based on existing customs. He wrote: "It is custom and general principles of law that constitute the normative underpinnings of international law. Without these sources, the process of codification of international law would be pointless. The codification treaties, in turn, can be seen as the primary evidence of the normative validity of the unwritten general law."[1226] Nevertheless, it is that codification effort that makes a big difference when it comes to special regimes. Treaties that create new rights and obligations in a niche field, unlike those already existing in the general system, create a strong precedent, based on which customary norms might develop in a unique way that creates a measure of separateness from the broader framework.

Special regimes can accrue their separateness gradually or all at once. It is conceivable to think of a set of secondary rules on application emerging first, and then, as the new field matures, primary rules on area-specific rights and obligations are recognized, followed by emergence of unique principles.

In practice, the most effective way of deepening and strengthening of an existing special regime is by having a separate court system. A separate court can expand the range of application of norms, identify novel context-specific rights and obligations, and in some cases even start the process of shifting toward new underlying principles. This has been the case with the European Economic Community and the World Trade Organization, both of which advanced their respective unique special regimes by way of court activism. For

---

1226 Kwiecień, Roman, The Formal Sources of International Law, the Relationship between Treaties and Custom, and the International Law-Making Process (September 24, 2022). Page 65. <https://ssrn.com/abstract=4310365>.

example, many of the foundational rules concerning the European Internal Market are a creation of the Court of the European Union.[1227]

6.4 Currently established special regimes of Public International Law

Determining the list of existing special regimes is not a straightforward task. A few unresolved issues make for various interpretative approaches that can result in different answers. For example, certain international scholars insist that a special regime can only be established by a treaty, while the UN ILC, alongside many other scholars, allow for a possibility of emergence by way of customary practice.[1228] Additionally, the list of the "weak" regimes, as defined in the previous section, remains an open-ended question as many potential special regimes include secondary norms that are optional in nature, undermining their impact. Math Noorton offered the list of the core special regimes of international law, whose status enjoys a broad consensus among States and academics:

- Human rights law,
- Law of war,
- European Union law,
- World Trade Organization law,
- International environmental law,
- Diplomatic and consular law,
- Nuclear non-proliferation law,
- Various existing case-specific dispute settlement mechanisms,

---

1227 "The European Single Market - Historical Events in the European Integration Process (1945–2009) - CVCE Website." Luxembourg Center for Contemporary and Digital History. Retrieved December 1, 2023. <https://www.cvce.eu/en/education/unit-content/-/unit/02bb76df-d066-4c08-a58a-d4686a3e68ff/fc955c85-4a39-4187-9ae7-935d67d1656b>.

1228 Runersten, Michael. "Defining 'Self-contained Regime' -A Case Study of the International Covenant on Civil and Political Rights," Faculty Of Law - University of Lund. Page 43. <https://lup.lub.lu.se/luur/download?func=downloadFile&recordOId=1561624&fileOId=1565696>

- Various existing constituent instruments of international organizations providing for suspension and termination of memberships[1229]

Utilizing the framework developed in the previous section, we can categorize these eight special regimes. Case-specific dispute settlement mechanisms as well as instruments regulating suspension and termination of membership in international organizations are some of the weakest special regimes. They do not contain any specific primary rights or obligations and have a purely secondary character. The Nuclear Non-Proliferation law framework has a stronger character as it contains primary rights and obligations of States that are inherent to it. The 1970 Treaty on the Non-Proliferation of Nuclear Weapons is at the center of the system, with its framework that acknowledges nuclear powers and forbids any other States from developing nuclear weapons.[1230] The system is complemented by a series of UN GA resolutions[1231] and the International Atomic Energy Agency, which actually predates the 1970 treaty by some 13 years.[1232] At the same time, the legal framework did not develop a competing set of foundational principles that would replace the universal ones underlying the UN-based system. Nuclear non-proliferation regime espouses peaceful coexistence, accountability, and sovereign equality between States that acknowledges the special status and role of the UN Security Council permanent members.[1233] Similarly, diplomatic and consular law is a source of primary rights and obligations, putting it in the strong

1229 Noortmann, Math. Enforcing international law: From self-help to self-contained regimes. Ashgate Publishing Limited, Hampshire, 2005. Page 141. The system of Public International Law embraced the model of identifying special regimes based on their subject, which reflects the way in which unique binding norms are emerging in it. For alternative ways of making semantic distinctions between fields see: Kotarbiński, Tadeusz. Elementy teorii Poznania, logiki formalnej I Metodologii Nauk. Warszawa: Akademicka Spółdzielnia Wydawnicza, 1947. Page 189.

1230 United Nations. Treaty on the Non-Proliferation of Nuclear Weapons. United Nations, Treaty Series. 1 July 1968. Retrieved November 30, 2023. <https://disarmament.unoda.org/wmd/nuclear/npt/#:~:text=The%20NPT%20is%20a%20landmark,and%20general%20and%20complete%20disarmament>.

1231 Ibid.

1232 "History of the UN IAEA." International Atomic Energy Agency, June 8, 2016. <https://www.iaea.org/about/overview/history>.

1233 "Statute of the UN IAEA." International Atomic Energy Agency, December 28, 1989. <https://www.iaea.org/sites/default/files/statute.pdf>.

regime category, while adhering to the overall underlying principles of the international legal system.

Finally, the international environmental law, the WTO system, the EU system, and the Human Rights system, all belong in the category of very strong special regimes of international law. Not only do they contain primary and secondary legal norms, but they have also developed their own set of abstract principles that guide the process of systemic interpretation. The international environmental legal framework is an expansive system comprising more than 3,000 legal arrangements between States spanning a variety of issues.[1234] There have also been a number of legal cases brought in front of international judiciary bodies. The caseload of the International Tribunal for the Law of the Sea is largely of environmental character.[1235] The United States of America, Canada, and Mexico created the Commission for Environmental Compliance that can hear dispute submissions from the three parties or citizens under the USCMA free trade agreement.[1236] The ICJ, UN Permanent Court of Arbitration, and the European Court of Justice have also issued a number of landmark rulings.[1237] As a result, the system has developed its own set of overarching principles such as: The Precautionary Principle, Environmental Impact Assessment, and Common but Differentiated Responsibilities, among several others.[1238] In case these principles clash with the ones espoused broadly in the general system of international law, the interpretation might oftentimes

---

1234 Mitchell, Ronald B. "International Environmental Agreements (IEA) Database Project." University of Oregon. Accessed December 1, 2023. <https://iea.uoregon.edu/>;

Hunter, David. International Environmental Law—Insights on law and Society. American Bar Association, January 5, 2021. <https://www.americanbar.org/groups/public_education/publications/insights-on-law-and-society/volume-19/insights-vol-19-issue-1/international-environmental-law/>.

1235 "Annual Reports." International Tribunal for the Law of the Sea: Annual Reports. Retrieved December 1, 2023. <https://www.itlos.org/en/main/the-tribunal/annual-reports/>.

1236 "United States - Mexico - Canada Agreement (USMCA)." United States Trade Representative. Retrieved December 1, 2023. <https://ustr.gov/usmca>.

1237 United Nations Environment Programme (2022). Environmental Courts and Tribunals—2021: A Guide for Policy Makers. Page 3. <https://wedocs.unep.org/20.500.11822/40309>.

1238 Hunter, David. International Environmental Law—Insights on law and Society. American Bar Association, January 5, 2021. <https://www.americanbar.org/

lean toward the former. This conflict came into sharp relief in the Gabčíkovo-Nagymaros Project judgment, where the ICJ had to balance sovereign rights of a State over its territory and an array of environmental principles, including the precautionary one.[1239]

A combination of primary norms and a series of judiciary rulings appears to be the fastest way for a special regime to develop from a strong one to a very strong one, meaning one that has established its own set of unique overarching principles. Having a specialized judiciary body at the center of the system is the best way of achieving such an outcome, as it can serve as the main driving force of the process of developing a cohesive framework of interpretative principles. In this context, it makes sense that an alliance called The ICE Coalition pushes for creation of the International Court of Environment.[1240] The objective of having a dedicated judiciary body at the center of a special regime system has been achieved by the other frameworks: the EU, the WTO, the Law of War, and the Human Rights Law. In case of the last two, the judiciary system is more fragmented, as it consists of a patchwork of regional courts. The Human Rights Law specialized courts are: the European Court of Human Rights, the African Court on Human and Peoples' Rights, and the Inter-American Court of Human Rights. The Law of war system has so far seen the following dedicated judiciary bodies: Nuremberg Tribunal, International Military Tribunal for the Far East, International Criminal Tribunal for the former Yugoslavia, International Criminal Tribunal for Rwanda, and the International Criminal Court (in a narrow area of personal responsibility regulated by international law). The EU has its Court of Justice of The European Union[1241] and the WTO is centered around the famous Dispute

---

groups/public_education/publications/insights-on-law-and-society/volume-19/insights-vol-19-issue-1/international-environmental-law/>.

1239 Case Concerning Gabčíkovo-Nagymaros Project (Hungary/Slovakia)—Judgment. International Court of Justice. Reports 7, 54, para 79. I.C.J Reports 14, ICGJ 112 (ICJ 1986). Retrieved February 15, 2022, from <https://www.icj-cij.org/case/92>.

1240 "International Court for Environment Coallition." ICE Coalition. Retrieved December 1, 2023. <http://www.icecoalition.org/>.

1241 "Court of Justice of the European Union (CJEU)." European Union. Retrieved December 1, 2023. <https://european-union.europa.eu/institutions-law-budget/institutions-and-bodies/search-all-eu-institutions-and-bodies/court-justice-european-union-cjeu_en>.

Settlement Body.[1242] These systems have managed to develop their own set of unique principles that create an interpretative path dependence for any future legal cases. Because of that, they can be considered to be very strong special regimes of international law.

6.5 Application of the framework of special regimes of Public International Law in the context of cyberspace

6.5.1 Existing proposals of framing the emerging norms regulating cyberspace

6.5.1.1 Proposed rationale for a special regime of Public International Law for cyberspace

As mentioned earlier in this chapter, every new special regime emerges not by accident but in response to new needs that are not met well enough by the general international legal system. The universal aim is to regulate human behavior more effectively than the general system. The analysis of the performance of the general international legal framework in application to cyberspace reveals dysfunctionalities that make the case for a special regime robust. At the root of the need for a special regime are special characteristics of cyberspace, already discussed in-depth in previous chapters: partial de-territorialization of cyberspace (it is a hybrid phenomenon that combines both a physical and non-physical component to a create a unique, novel type of space), blending of public and private actors (e.g., hacker groups acting on the instructions of a State), and conflation of domestic and international rules (e.g., ICANN regulations and exclusion of the UN ITU and other multilateral bodies from oversight to the benefit of U.S.-based nonprofit organizations). There are also several additional unique factors setting cyberspace apart and making established international laws ineffective. The impossibilities of technical and legal attribution, and a stark mismatch of IT capabilities across States are just some of examples brought up in this book. The policy of "ambiguity and silence" in cyberspace, which is a stance assumed by most

---

1242 "WTO Dispute Settlement Body." World Trade Organization. Retrieved December 1, 2023. <https://www.wto.org/english/tratop_e/dispu_e/dispu_e.htm>.

States when affected by international cyber hostilities, is a result of a system that cannot offer effective problem resolution.

This sentiment is now enjoying a broad consensus both among States[1243] and within the academic community. For example, Joel Reidenberg identified three aspects of cyberspace that require urgent international regulation: sensitive information ownership and protection, intellectual property rights, and the status of data passing through infrastructure of various States.[1244] Joanna Kulesza, in her research article titled "International Internet Law," argued for an International Framework Convention as a desirable way to further consolidate a slowly emerging new special regime of international law. She also stated: "Autonomous cyberspace law would be desirable most of all due to elimination of jurisdictional uncertainty (…) and development of unique legal notions that apply solely in the cyber context."[1245]

However, the same reasons that create a strong rationale for a special regime of international law on cyberspace, limit its development. The existing structure of States' vested interests pitches developed States, led by the United States, against the developing ones. The United States benefits from preserving the current setup, which contains a tremendous set of privileges connected to the fact that the international technical governance of cyberspace takes place on its sovereign soil and on its terms. Conflicting interests have led to inertia that stalls development of customary laws and reduces likelihood of a multilateral treaty on the subject in the predictable future down to near-zero. The uniquely active cyber private sector has filled the void by providing standards and practical regulations that shape up the legal space without enjoying formal status in Public International Law. The end result of this inertial evolution is yet to be determined although so far it validates the impression that solutions meant to be temporary often tend to be some of the most enduring ones.

1243 See Chapter II for an in-depth analysis of these dynamics.

1244 Reidenberg, Joel R. (1998)."Lex Informatica: The Formulation of Information Policy Rules through Technology," Texas Law Review 1998, vol. 76, no. 3, page 554. <https://ir.lawnet.fordham.edu/faculty_scholarship/42>.

1245 Kulesza, Joanna. International Internet law, Global Change, Peace & Security (2012), 24:3, pages 351–364. <https://10.1080/14781158.2012.716417>, page 291.

6.5.1.2 History of proposals of special regime of Public International Law for cyberspace

The first academic propositions of defining cyberspace law at the international public level emerged in the middle of the 1990s. David Johnson and David Post postulated in 1996 that cyberspace is so unique in its functioning that it will inevitably give rise to an autonomous international legal order.[1246] Among the main arguments that they brought up was the de-territorialized nature of cyberspace and the unique ways in which subjects of international law can interact in it. At the time, the debate on the subject was at a very early stage and one of the main objectives they set out for themselves was to convince international scholars, lawyers, and politicians to take the idea seriously, before any intricacies of the proposed solutions could be even analyzed. There existed strong pushback to the notion of cyberspace requiring unique international legal norms.[1247] For example, Frank Easterbrook ridiculed the idea by comparing the need for a special legal regime on cyberspace to the need for a special legal regime on horses.[1248] To make their point about the need for an international legal regime regulating cyberspace, David Johnson and David Post wrote: "(Internet) radically subverts a system of rule-making based on borders between physical spaces, at least with respect to the claim that cyberspace should naturally be governed by territorially defined rules."[1249] Their proposals were ambitious, including derogating territorial jurisdiction of States on the matters taking place within cyberspace, to be replaced by an relatively vaguely defined international democratic framework ensuring accountability.[1250]

1246 Johnson, David R., and David Post. "Law and Borders: The Rise of Law in Cyberspace." Stanford Law Review 48, no. 5 (1996): pages 1367–1402. <https://doi.org/10.2307/1229390>.

1247 Easterbrook, Frank H. "Cyberspace and the Law of the Horse," 1996 University of Chicago Legal Forum 207 (1996). <https://chicagounbound.uchicago.edu/cgi/viewcontent.cgi?referer=&httpsredir=1&article=2147&context=journal_articles>

1248 Ibid.

1249 Johnson, David R., and David Post. "Law and Borders: The Rise of Law in Cyberspace." Stanford Law Review 48, no. 5 (1996): pages 1367–1402. Page 1370. <https://doi.org/10.2307/1229390>.

1250 Johnson David R., and Post, David G. The New "Civic Virtue" of the Internet; A Complex Systems Model for the Governance of Cyberspace, in The Emerging

The distinction between the public international and private international legal dimensions of cyberspace was even less delineated back then than it is now. Cyberspace was and is a phenomenon that easily escapes this separation. For that reason, David Johnson's and David Post's ideas received much criticism. Jack Goldsmith implied that removing cyberspace from within States' territorial jurisdiction is a straight path to "cyberanarchy."[1251] Andrew Shapiro offered an alternative approach in 1998 that would acknowledge the deeply embedded role of private actors and infrastructure in the functioning of the internet, recognizing that a clean split between Public International Law and Private International Law is practically impossible in the cyber context. He also criticized David Johnson's and David Post's approach for ignoring that reality when they pushed for a full internationalization of accountability. Rather than making an effort to develop cyberspace law, he suggested focusing on a more flexible category of cyberspace code instead, that would refrain from the traditional distinctions and blend together public and private as well as international and domestic regulations.[1252] Lawrence Lessig, the creator of the widely popular Creative Commons copyrights license that was designed to fit the nature of cyberspace, expressed his support for the idea of a new legal order tailored to such unique aspects.[1253] Janusz Bart and Ryszard Markiewicz, experts in the area of intellectual property, were also among the first public supporters of the idea.[1254] In 2003, the subject was brought up by Shabtai Rosenne, who claimed that the international legal vacuum concerning activity in cyberspace can be filled by way of an agreement

---

Internet (C. Firestone ed., 1998), available at <http://www.temple.edu/lawschool/dpost/Newcivicvirtue.html>

1251 Goldsmith, Jack L. (1998). "Against Cyberanarchy," University of Chicago Law Review: Vol. 65: Iss. 4. Pages 1199–1200. <https://chicagounbound.uchicago.edu/uclrev/vol65/iss4/2>.

1252 Shapiro, Andrew (1998). "The Disappearance of Cyberspace and the Rise of Code," Berkman Klein Center. <https://cyber.harvard.edu/works/shapiro/Disappearance.pdf>.

1253 Kulesza, Joanna. (2008). Internet Governance and the Jurisdiction of States: Justification of the Need for an International Regulation of Cyberspace. SSRN Electronic Journal. <https://dx.doi.org/10.2139/ssrn.1445452>.

1254 Barta, Janusz, and Markiewicz, Ryszard (1997). "Prawo cyberprzestrzeni i stare konwencje," Rzeczpospolita November 15, 1997. <https://archiwum.rp.pl/>.

between subjects of Public International Law.[1255] On the other hand, Karol Dobrzeniecki presented in 2004 an alternative approach, in which conduct in cyberspace should be effectively regulated within domestic jurisdictions of States, with no part of it left to any de-territorialized international oversight mechanisms.[1256]

In 2008, Joanna Kulesza argued in favor of "international regulation of cyberspace." She critiqued the outsize role of U.S.-based NGOs and the American government in defining the legal contours of the internet and proposed that evolution toward a multilateral framework that would benefit further development of cyberspace.[1257] In 2010, Joanna Kulesza further championed the debate by advocating for development of *Jus Internet*. While acknowledging the challenge of de-territorialization of cyberspace, well defined by David Johnson and David Post, she critiqued their proposed solution of complete internationalization of cyberspace governance.[1258] While focusing mostly on the private international legal side of the internet's functioning, she suggested that a comprehensive regulatory framework of *Jus Internet*, including the domestic regulatory aspects, would require a multilateral agreement on a public international legal foundation, a postulate she further developed in a book dedicated to the subject in 2012.[1259] Similar sentiment was expressed by Marcin Rojszczak, who argued for international harmonization of rules pertaining to human rights in cyberspace.[1260]

1255 Rosenne, Shabtai. The perplexities of modern international law, General Course on Public International Law, RCADI, 2003, vol. III. Page 349.

1256 Dobrzeniecki, Karol. Prawo a etos cyberprzestrzeni, Wydawnictwo Adam Marszałek, 2004.

1257 Kulesza, Joanna. (2008). Internet Governance and the Jurisdiction of States: Justification of the Need for an International Regulation of Cyberspace. SSRN Electronic Journal. <https://dx.doi.org/10.2139/ssrn.1445452>.

1258 Kulesza, Joanna. (2010). Ius Internet. Publio. <https://www.publio.pl/files/samples/bd/c9/94/48179/Ius_internet_demo.pdf.>

1259 Kulesza, Joanna, Magdalena Arent, and Wojciech Wołoszyk. International internet law. London: Routledge, 2013.

1260 Rojszczak, Marcin. "Does global scope guarantee effectiveness? Searching for a new legal standard for privacy protection in cyberspace." Information & communications technology law 29, no. 1 (2020): page 26. <https://doi.org/10.1080/13600834.2020.1705033>.

The 2010s and 2020s brought gradual legal concretization of the once-undefined field of international cyberspace. At one end of the spectrum, the UN Group of Government Experts started issuing its reports, subsequently endorsed by the UN General Assembly, slowly setting up the legal framework in a top-down fashion. On the other end of the spectrum, dynamic development of private entities with deep cyber expertise, coupled with functioning of the technical governance framework centered around ICANN led to emergence of bottom-up rules of conduct that slowly started shaping up actions of not only individuals and domestic entities but also States and other subjects of international law. Thus, the uncertainty gap started slowly closing, albeit in a very idiosyncratic manner, compared to other areas of Public International Law. With the outsize role of private entities, a partially de-territorialized character, and a conflation of domestic and international regulations, it took on a unique path of evolution. In response, some scholars advocate for embracing of this unique model, frequently captured with the term *Lex Informatica*, which is the focus of the following subsection.

6.5.1.3 *Lex Informatica* as a proposal of a legal framework regulating cyberspace

Lex Informatica is a term first proposed in 1996 by Willem Van Broom and Sjef Van Erp to describe the unique evolution path of the international regulatory framework covering cyberspace.[1261] The inspiration was the Medieval *Lex Mercatoria* (Law of Merchants), a set of rules and judiciary procedures that organically developed to regulate trade relations between European merchants. The system had a bottom-up character and depended on customary laws, spontaneously emerging based on precedent cases and prevailing practice.[1262] Some scholars trace its lineage back to the ancient times, when Mediterranean merchants were crisscrossing the sea to reap benefits servicing clients in economic powerhouses at the time: Rome, Constantinople, Alexandria, and others. The merchants sought stable rules that would allow

[1261] Scott, Colin. Regulation in the Age of Governance: The Rise of the Post Regulatory State, [in:] Jordana, Jacint And Levi-Faur, DAvid (red.), The Politics of Regulation: Institutions and Regulatory Reforms for the Age of Governance. Cheltenham 2004, s. 162–164.

[1262] Baker, JH. "The Law Merchant and the Common Law," Cambridge Law Journal 38, no. 295 (1979). Pages 295–322. <https://doi.org/10.1017/S0008197300094204>.

for smooth functioning of commerce across borders. The basis of authority of the law was not State sovereignty, as we would put it nowadays, but the traders' community, including the customs, track record of personal reputation, and the notions of fairness and common sense.[1263] However, the custom, as understood in *Lex Mercatoria*, differs substantially from the custom of Public International Law, in that it did not require States' *opinio juris*, or even their consistent practice.[1264] In essence, the system was voluntary and non-binding although merchants felt effectively forced to participate in it as a requirement for being a member of the international trade network and enjoying its benefits. By the thirteenth century, a variant *Lex Mercatoria* was utilized by the Hansa League, and specialized *Lex Mercatoria* courts were established to resolve trade disputes near main marketplaces in France, Italy, and England.[1265] The system blended the private and international legal components as a self-governing fluid organism.

The idea of *Lex Informatica* as a symbolic heir of the *Lex Mercatoria* captures much of the essence of how cyberspace operates. In the absence of a comprehensive top-down legal framework, private actors spontaneously developed a set of standards and norms that fill the void. Just like *Lex Mercatoria* was not attached to jurisdiction of one sovereign State so does cyberspace, which defies physical territorial borderlines. The norms are guided by practice and efficiency and do not make a proper distinction between the domestic and international legal orders. For example, infrastructure-related standards set by private companies determine the ability to trace back hacker activity or exert control over international data flows taking place. Cybersecurity companies frequently possess stronger offensive and defensive cyber capabilities than governments and are hired by the latter to execute sovereign functions or actions that have an international legal impact. The original authors of the term *Lex Informatica* only meant

---

1263 Ibid.; de Ruysscher, Dave. (2020). Conceptualizing Lex Mercatoria: Malynes, Schmitthoff and Goldman compared. Maastricht Journal of European and Comparative Law, 27(4), pages 465–483. <https://doi.org/10.1177/1023263X20938247>

1264 Lindquist, Stefanie A. and Frank C. Cross. (2010). "Stability, Predictability And The Rule Of Law: Stare Decisis As Reciprocity Norm." University of Texas School of Law. <https://law.utexas.edu/conferences/measuring/The%20Papers/Rule%20of%20Law%20Conference.crosslindquist.pdf>

1265 Ibid.

it as a way to frame potential collision norms that cyberspace might generate between various legal orders.[1266] In time however, the idea took on as a broader description of the evolution of cyberspace law. *Lex Informatica* captures both the organic bottom-up, customary nature of the regulatory framework but also the uneasy relationship between it and the sovereign States that are formally vested with regulating cyberspace but are largely passive recipients of norms at the moment.

Karol Dobrzeniecki stated that *Lex Informatica* derives its ability to set effective norms by way of technical architecture of cyberspace, specifically the software code that dictates its functioning. Those that control the contents of the code possess power that extends sometimes all the way to how subjects of international law operate.[1267] At present, these are largely private IT infrastructure companies, internet providers, and the technical oversight bodies located in the United States, especially ICANN and IAB. The idea of such a setup leading to emergence of a bottom-up customary legal order regulating cyberspace on the international level has been supported by other scholars too, for instance Aron Mefford,[1268] Trotter Hardy,[1269] and Przemysław Polanski,[1270] Joanna Worona,[1271] and Tomasz Welanyk.[1272] Other authors pro-

1266 Mefford, Aron. (1997)"Lex informatica: Foundations of Law on the Internet." Indiana Journal of Global Legal Studies. vol. 5, no 1, page 211. <https://www.repository.law.indiana.edu/cgi/viewcontent.cgi?referer=&httpsredir=1&article=1116&context=ijgls>

1267 Dobrzeniecki, Karol. Autonomiczne prawo cyberprzestrzeni: mit czy rzeczywistość?, [in:] O. Bogucki, S. Czepita (ed.), System prawny a porządek prawny, Szczecin 2008, page 320.

1268 Mefford, Aron. (1997)"Lex informatica: Foundations of Law on the Internet." Indiana Journal of Global Legal Studies. vol. 5, no 1, page 211. <https://www.repository.law.indiana.edu/cgi/viewcontent.cgi?referer=&httpsredir=1&article=1116&context=ijgls>

1269 Hardy, Trotter I. (1994). "The Proper Legal Regime for Cyberspace," University of Pittsburgh Law Review. Vol. 55, page 1010.

1270 Polański, Przemysław. (2006). „Zarys autonomicznego prawa Internetu," Studia Iuridica 2006, vol. 45, page 179. <https://bibliografia.icm.edu.pl/g2/main.pl?mod=p&id=56052&a=1&s=35115&imie=Przemys%B3aw&nazwisko=Pola%F1ski&lim=25&ord=1>.

1271 Worona, Joanna, "Cyberprzestrzeń a Prawo Międzynarodowe - Status Quo i Perspektywy." Ph.D. dissertation, University of Bialystok, 2017. Page 540.

1272 Welanyk, Tomasz, "Istnienie i granice suwerenności w cyberprzestrzeni. Analiza prawna." Ph.D. dissertation, University of Warsaw, 2019. Page 136.

posed similar framings such as Lex Digitalis, Lex Electronica, and Internet *Lex Mercatoria*.[1273]

Joanna Worona hypothesized that given the unique dynamic in the area of international cyberspace law, the most feasible way forward could be by way of soft law, which would enable subjects of international law to set rules that would draw on *Lex Informatica* and circumnavigate the challenge of the lack of consistent *opinio juris*.[1274] This would reconcile the tension between the established framework of international law and Lex Informatic, which is currently a form of a wild outgrowth that defies the existing system. She also argues that it is a distinctively unique feature of cyberspace that it is open, decentralized and a-territorial, whereas the system of international law strives to establish norms that are of hierarchical nature and bound to territoriality of State sovereignty. Hence, *Lex Informatica*, while going against the grain of that system, is the logical consequence of the nature of cyberspace.[1275]

Tomasz Welanyk highlighted lack of required wide *opinio juris* as one of the main advantages of *Lex Informatica*, allowing it to develop unimpeded by the impasse we currently experience among States on the subject.[1276] He suggested that applying the model of *Lex Mercatoria* to the existing dynamics concerning cyberspace, would be close in nature to voluntary mediation and arbitrage based on established customs alongside the principle of *ex aequo et bono* between willing parties in a case-by-case manner.[1277]

However, closer inspection of the *Lex Informatica* proposal leads to the conclusion that the model displays a series of limitations that make it unfit as a replacement for a traditional international legal framework. The main three challenges are the following:

1273 Człapka, Filip. Internet jako wyzwanie dla współczesnych systemów prawa, [in:] Galewska, E., and Kotecka, S. (ed.), X-lecie. Księga pamiątkowa z okazji dziesięciolecia Centrum Badań Problemów Prawnych i Ekonomicznych Komunikacji Elektronicznej i Studenckiego Koła Naukowego—Blok Prawa Komputerowego, Wrocław 2012, page 478.

1274 Worona, Joanna, "Cyberprzestrzeń a Prawo Międzynarodowe - Status Quo i Perspektywy." Ph.D. dissertation, University of Bialystok, 2017. Page 568.

1275 Ibid. Page 551.

1276 Welanyk, Tomasz, "Istnienie i granice suwerenności w cyberprzestrzeni. Analiza prawna." Ph.D. dissertation, University of Warsaw, 2019. Page 12.

1277 Ibid. Page 137.

- Lack of certainty on the contents of the norms;
- No mechanism for the rules becoming binding;
- Conflation of legal spheres further entrenches uncertainty and lack of accountability.

Standards and norms developed by entities that have no legal standing in the international legal system are a multicentric patchwork that is subject to constant change and is highly dependent on domestic context. *Lex Informatica* conflates technical and legal aspects of the functioning of cyberspace into one unstructured blend. There is no clarity on what the contents of the purported *Lex Informatica* norms are and there exists no judiciary body that would establish it with any measure of formal authority. For example, what is applicable in a low-capability developing State will not be the case in Sweden, the United Kingdom, or other highly developed State that enjoys more hands-on control over its digital space. The scope of entities shaping *Lex Informatica* is uncertain too. Which organization exactly would have a standing to shape the norms? Introducing both those types of uncertainty might create more harm to the system of international law than benefit. A special regime must offer more stability and predictability than the general one. Otherwise, there is no case for developing it.

Lex Informatica has the practical benefit of circumventing the requirement for consistent and stable *opinio juris* by States, coupled by their practice. However, long-term this might be more of a problem than an advantage. While short-term, this allows for recognition of existing practice as some form of law, it offers no pathway to elevate such "law" to the status of a binding norm within the existing system. The established rules of Public International Law are demanding in that respect but they compensate for that by extending a binding status to those norms that pass the muster. A system without binding norms is not exactly law, which implies an obligation to comply, but rather a set of guidelines. As such, it is a less robust foundation to build a system on and a sub-par replacement for the established methods of setting up a special regime of international law. A counter-argument could be that *Lex Informatica* could serve as soft law that slowly turns into customary law in the traditional sense, as States start observing it. However, by reducing the States' role in shaping the norms, they disincentivize them from ever doing so, opening a possibility instead of freezing in place the current practice of non-committal conduct by States captured with the term "ambiguity and silence" that does not imply *opinio juris*.

Finally, one of the main challenges of cyberspace right now is avoidance of accountability by States by way of utilizing private entities (such as hacker groups) and by routing cyber operations via IT infrastructure in various domestic jurisdictions in order to make attribution difficult. Much effort is made to clarify the application of the rules of attribution and accountability in this novel context. *Lex Informatica* developed as a result of this confluence of various legal spheres but it does not offer solutions to those core challenges. In fact, by entrenching the conflation of public and private, as well as domestic, and international legal spheres, it indirectly entrenches that challenge.

For the aforementioned reasons, the *Lex Informatica* model, understood as recognition of the mesh of practical rules created by private entities as a sort of exceptional customary international soft law framework, should be seen as a sub-par proposition. It does not offer enough benefits to validate a serious carve-out to the established international legal order. It would offer a short-term reconciliation of the tension created by the unique developmental path of cyberspace but would not solve any of the core challenges and would even create a risk of their further entrenchment.

6.5.2 Situating emerging cyberspace norms in the framework of special regimes of Public International Law

6.5.2.1 Academic debate on emerging patterns of State conduct in the cyber context

Besides creative proposals for regulating cyberspace at the public international legal level, such as *Lex Informatica*, a more conventional evolution is taking place. State practice emerges organically and with each passing year, the international community has a better sense of the range of possible conduct in cyberspace available to subjects of international law. While a framework treaty remains politically infeasible, soft law proposals, championed by the United Nations, alongside some multilateral initiatives such as the Internet Governance Forum, the Global Commission on the Stability of Cyberspace and The Global Commission on Internet Governance, define the debate that can usher in a binding customary system in the future. It is a slow process, but it does display progress and it sets up the stage for the emergence of consistent *opinio juris*, at least on the most agreed upon norms. The eventual emergence of a special regime of international law on cyberspace, in the UN ILC's framing of the term, now appears to be an inevitability, albeit one that is happening in an extremely slow motion.

As we analyze this glacial process, Joanna Kulesza suggested that the guiding principle should be subsidiarity, which means that new or modified solutions should be embraced and advocated for only if and to the extent that they complement and improve the functioning of the general systemic rules.[1278] This is in line with the general norms of special regimes of international law, although it helps focus minds in order to avoid treating every idiosyncrasy of State conduct in cyberspace as a pretext for claiming emergence of a new legal norm. Joel Reidenberg highlighted in his research that the universal requirement of any State practice and *opinio juris* being consistent and enduring applies in cyberspace.[1279] This is especially difficult in a field that is novel and evolving in a dramatically dynamic fashion. The way the internet functioned in the year 2003 is different from 2023. Its current context will be in turn inapplicable in the year 2043. The established rules for identifying new norms of Public International Law minimize the risk that some temporary phenomena get unnecessarily elevated to the status of legal rules.

In the absence of a specialized international court, a feature that accelerated the emergence of many other special regimes, some scholars argued that the World Intellectual Property Organization Center for Arbitration and Mediation can be considered as the closest equivalent for cyberspace. This idea was championed by scholars such as Maud Piers and Chrisitan Aschauer.[1280] While it is true that the Center adjudicates the majority of domain-related disputes, including those where States are a side of the dispute, it is an imperfect analogy. States participate in the proceedings of the Center

---

1278 Kulesza, Joanna, Magdalena Arent, and Wojciech Wołoszyk. International internet law. London: Routledge, 2013. Chapter 4. From Internet Governance to International Internet Law.

1279 Reidenberg, Joel R. (1998)."Lex Informatica: The Formulation of Information Policy Rules through Technology," Texas Law Review 1998, vol. 76, no. 3, page 554. <https://ir.lawnet.fordham.edu/faculty_scholarship/42>

1280 Piers, Maud, and Christian Aschauer. Arbitration in the digital age: The brave new world of arbitration. Cambridge i pozostałe: Cambridge University Press, 2018. Page 283

for Arbitration and Mediation, so to say, in their *jure gestionis* rather than *jure imperii*, which means that they protect their commercial interests rather than rights deriving from their sovereign standing as subjects of international law. Secondly, the disputes considered by the Center have a very narrow scope and consider only intellectual property-related disputes, which are not directly covered by Public International Law and mostly belong in the realm of Private International Law (with some limited exceptions).

Hence, of the three "engines" that a special regime could potentially utilize to propel its emergence: treaties, a specialized judiciary body, and State practice-based custom, cyberspace only relies on the last one, with some limited support from non-binding soft law proposed by the UN and multilateral initiatives. Even those limited "engines" are put in question by some scholars. Tomasz Welanyk claimed that achieving consistent and enduring *opinio juris* and State practice in the cyber context appears simply impossible.[1281] These concerns are valid. As described in this book, there is no consensus in the international community on how governance over cyberspace should be structured and application of even fundamental notions such as *State Sovereignty* and *Illegal Intervention* are disputed. At the same time, the nucleus of agreement is slowly emerging and some notions are gaining widespread approval. Therefore, skepticism as to whether any *opinio juris* would ever emerge might be too harsh.

Finally, some scholars began offering hypotheses as to what the unique principles of the potential future special regime on cyberspace might be. This is definitely premature since, as explained earlier in this chapter, a separate set of principles is characteristic of the strongest special regimes in existence. They also always feature a set of primary and secondary norms and usually also include a dedicated international judiciary body that can champion and develop the separate systemic logic of the regime. Cyberspace is nowhere near that status. However, hypothesizing about future principles is already taking place. One such principle could be placing fundamental emphasis on free and unconstrained flow of pass-through data that moves between servers within territory of various States without being subject to their jurisdiction as a systemic value. Some scholars, such as John Vogler, argue that this part

---

1281 Welanyk, Tomasz, "Istnienie i granice suwerenności w cyberprzestrzeni. Analiza prawna." Ph.D. dissertation, University of Warsaw, 2019. Page 158.

of cyberspace could be perceived as equivalent to *res communis*, open sea, or outer space and be immune to any claims by States.[1282] However, to the extent that the evolution path of other special regimes can be a guideline here, cyberspace should first develop secondary and then primary legal rights and obligations, passing initially as a weak special regime that then becomes stronger over time, eventually laying claim to its own systemic logic expressed by unique principles. Therefore, the next subsection takes stock of all the State practice that could indicate emergence of any such norms, shedding light on what stage the process is at currently.

6.5.2.2 The current stage of development of the special regime of Public International Law covering cyberspace

Over the course of this book, several types of emergent unique State practice in the realm of cyberspace were presented and discussed. A distinction must be made here between expanding application of general norms of international law to cyberspace and genuinely new State practice, which might consist of either modified, original way of said application or completely new norms without an earlier precedent that respond to the unique features of cyberspace. The first category (which includes developments such as recognizing that cyber acts can constitute an *Internationally Wrongful* Act or that *State Sovereignty* applies in cyberspace) does not contribute to establishment of a special regime and rather indicates maturing of the field, as it is brought into the fold of the general system. The second category is a potential resource for identifying a trend toward a special regime. Table 6 summarizes eight most relevant cases of unique State practice in cyberspace that might indicate potential development of new legal norms of Public International Law, all of which are discussed in this book.

1282 Vogler, John. The Global Commons: A regime analysis. Chichester: Wiley, 1995. Page 2; Vogler, John. (2012). "Global Commons Revisited," Global Policy 2012, vol. 3, no. 1, page 63.

Table 6. Summary of unique State practice in the realm of cyberspace

Unique State Practice	***Opinio Juris***	**Primary or Secondary Character**
1. A lower threshold of tolerance toward cyber espionage; perceiving all cyber espionage as internationally wrongful as opposed to conventional espionage, which is lawful in principle	Very limited; *opinio juris* only declared by France and supported by some doctrine, opposing State practice and *opinio juris* from the United States and the United Kingdom	Secondary
2. Avoidance of legal attribution to the perpetrator States by States subject to a hostile cyber operation; prevalence of the policy of "ambiguity and silence"; a lower threshold for required evidence to prove attribution of *Internationally Wrongful Acts* in cyberspace based on the Doctrine of R*easonableness*	Limited; the United States and Estonia supported the notion publicly with no pushback from other States so far	Secondary
3. Modified doctrine of *Effects and Scale* that places special importance on IT critical infrastructure being targeted when assessing severity of *Prohibited Use of Force*	Limited; Australia, Estonia, Romania, and partially the United States supported the notion. Several other States endorsed the opposing approach of equivalence with conventional *Effects and Scale*	Secondary
4. Classifying an accumulation of cyber *Unfriendly Acts* below the severity threshold as one cumulative *Internationally Wrongful Act*	Very limited; only United States, United Kingdom, Israel, and France have supported the norm in general and only France has supported it so far in the cyber context	Secondary
5. Classification of cyberspace as a separate "fifth domain" (after land, sea, air, and outer space) with its own way of applying general norms	NATO States endorsed the notion at the behest of the United States in the context of warfare and defensive matters	Quasi-secondary

(Continued)

Table 6. *(Continued)*

Unique State Practice	*Opinio Juris*	Primary or Secondary Character
6. Derogation of the role of UN ITU and more broadly of the UN and multilateral system from technical oversight over the internet, as compared to all other communication technologies, and vesting outsize agency with the United States government instead	Strong; while opposition to the current governance norms remains vocal, essentially all States recognize and accept the existence of a unique set of rights and obligations that put the United States in a privileged position as a binding fact	Primary
7. Collective *Countermeasures* in cyberspace	Very limited; Only supported formally by Estonia and Poland, repudiated by France	Primary
8. Duty of *Due Diligence* by States in cyberspace	Very limited, France and Netherlands support the claim that the norm is in the process of *becoming* binding; other States, the UN, and the EU claim that it is still a voluntary norm although that it could become binding in the future	Primary

Source: own elaboration

Each of these eight sets of unique State practice in the cyber context is described in more detail in the following paragraph. Additionally, four more proposals for new norms in cyberspace that have not yet left the academic debate are highlighted afterwards.

1. A lower threshold of tolerance toward cyber espionage; perceiving all cyber espionage as internationally wrongful as opposed to conventional espionage, which is lawful in principle

Cyber espionage is the most widespread form of hostile cyber operations between States, constituting more than 80% of the total volume. While there exists no general prohibition of espionage in Public International Law, it can still constitute an *Internationally Wrongful Act*, if the methods it employs reach the threshold of severity qualifying it as a *Violation of Sovereignty*. State practice and statements start shaping in the direction of seeing cyber espionage as different from conventional one. The key difference between conventional and cyber espionage might be that the latter is much more likely to breach sovereignty of the target State. This is mostly due to the penetrative character of cyber espionage. A breach into a protected IT system is almost by default a *Violation of Sovereignty* and can have much more compounded impacts than a conventional act of intercepting information, for example, by way of reading confidential print-outs. Importantly, even if the wedge between treatment of conventional and cyber espionage were to become an established norm, it would not define any new rights or obligations but rather focus on adjusted implementation and interpretation of existing ones in a new context. For this reason, this cyberspace-related State practice can amount to a secondary norm at most.

So far, only France expressed its explicit *opinio juris* that any intrusive cyber activity by another State would constitute an *Internationally Wrongful Act.*[1283] At the same time, denouncement of cyber espionage by foreign governments as unlawful by several States affected by it offers State practice supporting the notion.[1284] However, none of those affected States expressed their conviction that unlawfulness of cyberspace is a binding norm, focusing rather on the penetrative nature of their specific case. Additionally, the United Kingdom expressed a much more permissive stance than France, rejecting the notion that any penetrative cyber act by a State is automatically unlawful, leaning instead toward lawfulness of cyber espionage in principle.[1285] Other States, such as the United States and China, expressed an in-between stance, recognizing that some types of cyber espionage can

1283 The government of France. (2019, October 4). Communiqué—La France s'engage à promouvoir un cyberespace stable, fondé sur la confiance et le respect du droit international. French Ministry of Defense. <https://www.defense.gouv.fr/fre/salle-de-presse/communiques/communique_la-france-s-engage-a-promouvoir-un-cyberespace-stable-fonde-sur-la-confiance-et-le-respect-du-droit-international>.

1284 See section I.3.2—"Status of espionage in the context of hostile cyber operations" for in-depth analysis on this subject.

1285 The government of the United Kingdom. "Cyber and International Law in the 21st Century." (2018). Speech by Attorney General Jeremy Wright QC MP on 23 May 2018 <https://www.gov.uk/government/speeches/cyber-and-international-law-in-the-21st-century>.

be unlawful by default but not all.[1286] In the absence of consensus and limited *opinio juris*, special treatment of cyber espionage as unlawful by default, professed by some States, might not gain formal recognition as a customary norm in the foreseeable future.

2. Avoidance of legal attribution to the perpetrator States by States subject to a hostile cyber operation; prevalence of the policy of "ambiguity and silence"

Most States maintain a policy of ambiguity and silence in terms of their stance on how international law applies in cyberspace. This non-committal approach has led to four types of response to State-on-State hostilities in cyberspace: acknowledgment without attribution, political attribution, technical attribution, and finally legal attribution. A legal attribution is the most consequential one and at the same time the one least frequently invoked by States. This is because invoking specific norms of international law allegedly breached by another State requires presenting at least an outline of evidence facilitating such an accusation. Political, technical, and legal attribution types are oftentimes conflated in the public discourse on hostile cyber operations. Only the legal attribution has formal consequences in Public International Law, with the political one being in the gray zone, potentially providing rationale for lawful *Unfriendly Acts* in response. However, legal attribution is usually shunned by States subject to cyber hostilities mounted by another State. Instead, they revert to name-and-shame tactics, political backlash, or simply pretending that nothing has happened. Data suggests that the latest option might be the most widespread type of State response at present. There were however a few cases when a State made an attribution. For example, in 2018 the United Kingdom accused the Russian Federation of "a reckless campaign of cyber assaults leading to flagrant violations of international law."[1287] The announcement was made in coordination with Canada and Ukraine, two countries also targeted by Russian hostile cyber operations,

---

[1286] The government of the United States of America. (2015, September 25). Fact Sheet: President Xi Jinping's State Visit to the United States. <https://obamawhitehouse.archives.gov/the-press-office/2015/09/25/fact-sheet-president-xi-jinpings-state-visit-united-states>.

[1287] The government of United Kingdom. (n.d.). Reckless campaign of cyber attacks by Russian military intelligence service exposed. United Kingdom National

which purportedly aimed to disrupt work done by the World Anti-Doping Agency in Montreal, and the transport oversight systems in Kyiv respectively. Attribution was facilitated by technical analysis delivered by the U.K. National Cyber Security Centre. This, however, remains an exception to the norm. Usually, States stop short of formally attributing a hostile cyber operation, option instead for a softer response.

To a large extent, this State practice reflects the limitations of the current international legal framework when faced with the unique aspects of a novel field that is cyberspace. States do not see value in pursuing redress via formal channels, resulting in a dearth of cases of legal attribution. It also reflects the fact that gathering evidence in cyberspace is much harder than it is the case in the conventional context. Since, however, conclusive technical attribution is a prerequisite of legal attribution, only States that have developed the most sophisticated technological capacity enabling such a process can effectively utilize existing international norms to attribute internationally wrongful acts to other States and holding them accountable. However, as evidence shows, even the most technologically capable governments, like the one of the United States, are not always able to conclusively attribute foreign hacking incursions, revealing the limits of modern-day available methods in that regard. This situation lends itself to the hypothesis that the current dynamics impair development of the international legal rules on cyberspace as States prefer to adopt other, non-legal solutions, limiting the volume of judiciary cases that would facilitate emergence of new customary norms.

This State practice, if enduring and consistent enough, could lead to the development of *sui generis* secondary rules. One practical result of this process is that several States have called for a lower threshold for required evidence to prove attribution of *Internationally Wrongful Acts* in cyberspace, grounding this postulate in the doctrine of *Reasonableness.* Specifically, Estonia and the United States have advocated to modify the rules on the standard of proof in cyberspace to allow for "reasonable conviction" instead of certainty as the minimum threshold of required evidence. Kersti Kaljulaid, then-president of Estonia, stated in 2019 at a NATO Cyber Conflict conference in Tallinn:

Cyber Security Center. <https://www.ncsc.gov.uk/news/reckless-campaign-cyber-attacks-russian-military-intelligence-service-exposed>.

"At the end of the day what is required from the attributing state, is not absolute certainty but what is reasonable."[1288] Similar stance came earlier in 2016 from the United States, which as a permanent member of the UN Security Council and a leading world power has much influence in shaping global *opinio juris*. The U.S. Department of State proclaimed at the time that Public International Law only requires attributing States only to: "act reasonably under the circumstances when they gather information and draw conclusions based on that information."[1289]

Using the framework laid out in Figure 15 in Chapter 5, we can place the standard of "reasonableness" around the lowest rung—"the balance of probabilities," which is the easiest standard of proof ever utilized by the ICJ. Applying the standard of "reasonableness" to hostile cyber acts in a blanket fashion, which appears to be implied in statements by Estonia and the United States, would make it easier for a victim State to implicate the perpetrator one. So far there has been no public pushback against that stance from other States although several international scholars critiqued this trend of lowering standard of proof requirements in cyberspace. For example, Przemysław Roguski claimed that the standard of reasonableness is too easy to meet, creating a risk of an attribution that is wrong and yet extends preclusion of wrongfulness to response actions conducted by a victim State. He wrote: "this standard of "reasonableness" is problematic and requires further clarification. (…) If "reasonableness" were a duty of care, [a victim State] might argue that—acting "reasonably under the circumstances"—it has discharged its duty of care [in attempting to attribute a hostile cyber operation] and would therefore not bear international responsibility for violating rights of [a State to which the operation was erroneously attributed]." [1290]

1288 International cyber law: interactive toolkit. (2019) "Attribution - President Kersti Kaljulaid." International cyber law: interactive toolkit, July 28, 2023. <https://cyberlaw.ccdcoe.org/wiki/Attribution>.

1289 Egan, Brian J. (2016). Remarks on International Law and Stability in Cyberspace. United States Department of State, pages 1–26. <https://2009-2017.state.gov/s/l/releases/remarks/264303.htm>.

1290 Roguski, Przemysław. "Application of International Law to Cyber Operations: A Comparative Analysis of States' Views." The Hague Program for Cyber Norms, 2020. Page 15. <https://ruj.uj.edu.pl/xmlui/bitstream/handle/item/153989/roguski_application_of_international_law_to_cyber_operations_2020.pdf?sequence=1>.

3. **Modified doctrine of** Effects and Scale **that determines severity of** Prohibited Use of Force **placing special importance on IT critical infrastructure**

The main doctrine for assessing whether the threshold of severity of *Prohibited Use of Force* has been met in case of State-on-State hostilities is called *Effects and Scale*. Some State practice has emerged that operates utilizing a modified version of it. The modifications mostly pertain to the status of IT critical infrastructure. Critical infrastructure plays an outsized role in the context of International Public Law regulating cyberspace. Whether a hostile cyber operation targeted critical infrastructure can influence the legal classification of an act. This introduces the notion of the Doctrine of *Target* and is due to the penetrative and potentially extremely harmful impacts of breaching into such systems. The established Doctrine of Scale and Effects only focuses on actual damage that was made or was attempted to be made. Critical IT infrastructure is a nervous system of a State that permeates all its regions and is enmeshed in all its vital functions. It does not matter that a hostile cyber operation did not fully utilize the destructive potential that was extended by breaching in. The mere potential is enough to convince some States to treat cyber breaches more severely. Such a stance was supported by Australia, Estonia, Romania, and partially by the United States in a report commissioned and endorsed by the UN General Assembly.[1291] However, in the same report, two States endorsed an opposing approach that calls for a more straightforward approach of equivalence with conventional *Effects and Scale* when gauging *Use of Force* in cyberspace. These were Brazil and Germany. A number of other States, whose statements were also collected for the report maintained a more ambiguous approach that overall accepted the application of the Doctrine of *Effects and Scale* in cyberspace, without specifying their stance on the question of targeting IT critical infrastructure.

1291 United Nations General Assembly Resolution. (2021, July 13). 73/266. Official compendium of voluntary national contributions on the subject of how international law applies to the use of information and communications technologies by States submitted by participating governmental experts in the Group of Governmental Experts on Advancing Responsible State Behaviour in Cyberspace in the Context of International Security established pursuant to General Assembly resolution. <https://front.un-arm.org/wp-content/uploads/2021/08/A-76-136-EN.pdf>.

4. Classifying an accumulation of cyber Unfriendly Acts **below the severity threshold as one cumulative** Internationally Wrongful Act

Classifying an accumulation of events as one *Internationally Wrongful Act*, a legal theory that has been on the cusp of becoming a norm of Public International Law for decades but never achieved that status, is getting a new lease of life in the cyber context. States such as France are now officially espousing the notion specifically in the cyber context, where it is more applicable than in the conventional one.[1292]

The notion of "accumulation of events" did not get endorsement of the UN Security Council when it was discussed there. At the same time, several States such as the United States, the United Kingdom, and Israel, have utilized the terms, both in front of the ICJ and outside of it.[1293] Additionally, the UN International Law Commission proposed in its Draft Articles on State Responsibility introduction of a composite Internationally Wrongful Act as a formal category. The article 15(1) of the Draft Articles states:

> The breach of an international obligation by a State through a series of actions or omissions defined in aggregate as wrongful occurs when the action or omission occurs which, taken with the other actions or omissions, is sufficient to constitute the wrongful act.[1294]

The Draft Articles are a combination of formalization of existing customary rules and proposed rules that the UN ILC hopes might become binding in the future. Article 15 belongs to the latter category. However, the support by such a respected body as the ILC might solidify State practice in that direction. Some State practice already suggests that. For example, France has formally espoused the Public International Norm of accumulation of events in the context of hostile cyber operations.

1292 See section III.6.2.5—"Accumulation of hostile cyber operations that collectively amount to Use of Force" for in-depth analysis of this subject.

1293 See III.6.2.5 Accumulation of hostile cyber operations that collectively amount to Use of Force for in-depth analysis of the subject.

1294 United Nations International Law Commission. Draft articles on Responsibility of States for Internationally Wrongful Acts with commentaries. United Nations Office of Legal Affairs (2001). Article 15(1). <https://legal.un.org/ilc/texts/instruments/english/commentaries/9_6_2001.pdf>.

Whether the rule is a binding norm yet is not clear and additional State practice coupled by *opinio juris* is needed to provide more clarification. So far, only a handful of States endorsed the norm in general and only France did it in the cyber context in particular. If the rule emerged as part of customary law, it would create a unique feature of the international legal framework covering cyberspace.

5. Classification of cyberspace as a separate "fifth domain" (after land, sea, air, and outer space) with its own way of applying general norms
Treating cyberspace as the "fifth domain" does not automatically create any rights or obligations for subjects of international law. It is also not a secondary norm per se, as no specific modification to existing rights and obligations can be derived just yet if the "fifth domain claim" is endorsed by the international community. However, if established, it creates interpretative space for adjusting application of existing rights and obligations to account for the unique cyber context. A similar process took place for the other "new" domain—outer space (that was added to the existing three: land, water, and air), where acceptance of their separateness led to organic development of unique secondary norms that would account for it. For this reason, the notion can be perceived as a quasi-secondary norm, setting up ground for development of subsequent secondary norms in the future.

The notion of cyberspace has been championed by the U.S. military and traveled the path from the American war doctrine, via endorsement of the U.S. government, until endorsement by all NATO members during the Warsaw summit in 2016.[1295] Although the NATO designation applies in the context of warfare and defensive activities, it also sets a precedent for perceiving cyberspace as a fifth domain in the context of peaceful activities, in a fashion similar to which airspace law has developed. However, such expansion has not been made yet stated or proposed by any State in a way that could be construed as *opinio juris*. Additionally, the doctrine is split on the matter with some scholars questioning whether cyberspace

---

[1295] North Atlantic Treaty Organization. "NATO Recognises Cyberspace as a 'domain of Operations' at Warsaw Summit." NATO CCDCOE, July 9, 2016. <https://ccdcoe.org/incyder-articles/nato-recognises-cyberspace-as-a-domain-of-operations-at-warsaw-summit/>.

is meaningful enough to be regarded on par with physical tangible spaces that are the other four domains.[1296] Overall however, the notion of cyberspace as the fifth domain of warfare appears to be sufficiently established with potential of being expanded onto Public International Law pertaining to peacetime activities.

6. Derogation of the role of UN ITU and more broadly of the UN and multilateral system from technical oversight over the internet, as compared to all other communication technologies, and vesting outsize agency with the United States government instead

By the time the internet became a global phenomenon in the mid-1990s, the international community was faced with a status quo of a unique governance system over the system that defied established norms. It vested an outsize role with nonprofit domestic organizations located in the United States and to a large extent directly with the U.S. government. The details of the historical development of this framework and the subsequent pushback have been described in Chapter 2 of this book.[1297] Despite attempts to upend the system, it won staying rights and was accepted as part of the larger system of Public International Law. As a result, a unique balance of rights and obligations has emerged that gives the United States much formal and practical power in the area of cyberspace. For instance, its control over the root DNS servers means it can limit or turn off internet access in any country it decides to. This happened once in 2014 in North Korea as a penalty for hacking Sony. The norms that developed in that regard are of primary character as they identify unique rights and obligations, essentially splitting them between the United States and the rest of the world. While opposition to this situation remains vocal, led by the Russian Federation, China, and South Africa, they do not declare the system unlawful or not binding but rather call for its modification and rebalancing, thus recognizing its established character.

1296 Delerue, François. Cyber Operations and international law. Cambridge: Cambridge University Press, 2020. Page 298; Hoisington, Matthew. "Cyberwarfare and the Use of Force Giving Rise to the Right of Self-Defense." SSRN Electronic Journal, 2009. Page 447. <https://doi.org/10.2139/ssrn.1542223>.

1297 See section II.3.2—"Establishment of the unique international system regulating the internet" for in-depth analysis on the subject.

7. Collective Countermeasures in cyberspace

In 2019, during the opening remarks at the International Conference on Cyber Conflict, then-president of Estonia Kersti Kaljulaid put forward a bold proposal of collective Countermeasures in cyberspace:

> Estonia is furthering the position that States which are not directly injured may apply Countermeasures to support the State directly affected by the malicious cyber operation. The Countermeasures applied should follow the principle of proportionality and other principles established within the international customary law. It is therefore important that States may respond collectively to unlawful cyber operations where diplomatic action is insufficient, but no lawful recourse to use of force exists. Allies matter also in cyberspace.[1298]

Estonia has been the target of hostile cyber operations for years. The most publicized case, the Bronze Soldier incident of 2007, led to a denouncement by NATO and creation of the NATO Cyber Defence Centre of Excellence in Tallinn. This context explains the State's support for collective Countermeasures. The idea is analogous to the Self-defense provision included in Article 5 of the North Atlantic Treaty that obligates NATO member States to support any of them experiencing an Armed Attack.[1299]

The notion of third States weighing in with *Countermeasures* in support of their allies as a response to hostile cyber operations was supported by Poland. However, France has repudiated it in a stark statement soon after Estonia's initial proposal in 2019.

8. Duty of Due Diligence by States in cyberspace

The 2015 UN GGE Report proposed a voluntary non-binding norm of *Due Diligence* in cyberspace. The norm implies a duty of a State hosting physical ICT infrastructure that is part of the global internet system to monitor its network and prevent the most abusive excesses against public international legal rights of third States utilizing said network that could take place. The non-binding character of the cyber Due Diligence norm was further

---

1298 International cyber law: interactive toolkit. (2019) "Attribution - President Kersti Kaljulaid." International cyber law: interactive toolkit, July 28, 2023. <https://cyberlaw.ccdcoe.org/wiki/Attribution>.

1299 See section IV.4.3—"Collective Countermeasures" for in-depth analysis on the subject.

strengthened by the EU Council's Decision Concerning Restrictive Measures Against Cyber-Attacks Threatening The Union Or Its Member States in 2019.[1300] The norm is present within other branches of Public International Law, such as humanitarian law, where it has the binding status. The introduction of such a norm would imply a threshold of severity beyond which the State hosting infrastructure utilized by an offending State to infringe upon the rights of a third State is obliged to take action to stop the hostile cyber operation from continuing. While analogous norms have acquired a binding status in some areas of Public International Law, applying it in cyberspace would be problematic as it would put a heavy burden on the shoulders of underdeveloped States with limited IT capabilities. It could however offer an alternative path to curbing hostile cyber activity and even hold accountable States that utilize proxy hacker groups to seek impunity while targeting other States with hostile cyber acts. This, however, would represent a maladaptation of the system of Public International Law, whose focus should remain making the baseline paths for attribution functional and effective. Nevertheless, some governments are now expressing their conviction that Due Diligence is undergoing a transition toward becoming a binding norm of international law. These include France[1301] and the Netherlands.[1302] The odds are however stacked against the norms becoming binding anytime soon, as no other State has supported the notion and the non-binding voluntary status still formally figures in the official UN and EU documents, anchoring its status as such for now.

Besides emergent State practice with potential of turning into customary norms listed earlier, international scholars proposed other rules that could be considered as part of the hypothetical special regime on cyberspace. The most prominent and widely supported ones are:

1300 Council of the European Union. (2019, May 14). COUNCIL DECISION concerning restrictive measures against cyber-attacks threatening the Union or its Member States. Retrieved February 17, 2022, from <https://data.consilium.europa.eu/doc/document/ST-7299-2019-INIT/en/pdf>.

1301 Schmitt, Michael. (2019, September 16). France's Major Statement on International Law and Cyber: An Assessment. Just Security. <https://www.justsecurity.org/66194/frances-major-statement-on-international-law-and-cyber-an-assessment/>.

1302 Jensen, Eric. T., & Watts, S. (2016). The Duty of Due Diligence and Cyber Incitements to Violence. Texas Law Review. Pages 1555–1577. <https://doi.org/10.2139/ssrn.2894070>.

- Lower threshold for invoking *Urgent Countermeasures* in cyberspace, which entails no requirement of prior notification of their target State;
- A lower threshold of demonstrated *effective control* for attributing actions of hacker groups to their host State;
- Hybrid model of jurisdiction in cyberspace.

Lower threshold for invoking Urgent Countermeasures in cyberspace, which entails no requirement of prior notification of their target State

One of the requirements for a State conducting *Countermeasures* is the obligation of prior notification of the offending State. This is problematic in cyberspace where the element of surprise is more important for the success of an operation than it is the case with conventional operations. In fact, usually the success of a cyber operation rests entirely on the element of surprise. Hostile cyber operations can cut deeper and in a radically quicker fashion than conventional acts, but they can also be prevented more much more easily if information about the preparations is available. Notifying the target State could easily neutralize the whole operation and defy the purpose of *Countermeasures*. There are two notification requirements listed in the ICJ jurisprudence: the first one demanding cessation of the offending conduct and the second one signaling the *Countermeasure* that is about to be taken. Of the two, the second one specifically is the most problematic.

The existing framework of Public International Law allows for an exception that could accommodate this specific nature of cyber operation—*Urgent Countermeasures*. This is not a fully formed norm of international law—cases of State practice and *opinio juris* are too scarce and not consistent enough yet. However, there exist legal precedents that point to a potential process of forming of the norm. For example, Protocol Additional to the Geneva Conventions from August 12, 1949, when relating to the Protection of Victims of International Armed Conflicts states that:

> In the case of bombardment by long-distance projectiles or bombs dropped from aircraft, giving warning may be inconvenient when the element of surprise in the

> attack is a condition of its success. For this reason the rule allows for derogation: "unless circumstances do not permit."[1303]

The passage comes from the International Committee of the Red Cross and applies to *jus in bello*, that is, it pertains to States in the midst of an armed conflict. This is an obstacle to a direct transposition of the logic into the context of cyber *Countermeasures*, which pertain to the peacetime context. Emergence of urgent cyber *Countermeasures* that do not require prior notification would mean taking a partially formed exception rule from another realm of Public International Law and applying it in the cyber context as a standard one. However, such expansionary transposition in the context of cyber *Countermeasures* would help adapt the existing legal framework to the new context. In fact, some scholars, including Michael Schmitt, have called for this solution.[1304] Others, including François Delerue[1305] and Mary O'Connell[1306] have critiqued the idea. Since no State has come forward supporting such an expansion as of yet, the notion of urgent cyber *Countermeasures* remains only a proposition.

A lower threshold of demonstrated *effective control* for attributing actions of hacker groups to their host State

Effective control over a non-State entity, such as giving instructions and directions, is much more difficult to register in the cyber context than in the conventional one. In the conventional context such activity is likely to leave a physical footprint such as moving heavy arms or training activities, captured

---

1303 International Committee of the Red Cross. (1977b, June 8). Commentary to Protocol Additional to the Geneva Conventions of 12 August 1949, and relating to the Protection of Victims of International Armed Conflicts (Protocol I). Retrieved February 18, 2022, from <https://ihl-databases.icrc.org/applic/ihl/ihl.nsf/1a13044f3bbb5b8ec12563fb0066f226/d80d14d84bf36b92c12563cd00434fbd>.

1304 Schmitt, Michael N. & NATO Cooperative Cyber Defence Centre of Excellence. (2017). Tallinn Manual 2.0 on the International Law Applicable to Cyber Operations. Cambridge University Press. Supra note 14, paragraph 120.

1305 Delerue, François. Cyber Operations and international law. Cambridge: Cambridge University Press, 2020. Page 445.

1306 O'Connell, Mary E. "Attribution and Other Conditions of Lawful Countermeasures to Cyber Misconduct," 10 Notre Dame J. Int'l Comp. L. 1 (2020). Page 251. <https://scholarship.law.nd.edu/law_faculty_scholarship/1437>

on photos taken by geo-spatial satellites. None of the preparatory work for a hostile cyber operation is physically visible.

For those reasons, scholars such as Scott Shackelford and Johann-Christoph Woltag argued that the threshold set by the ICJ for *effective control* is too high in the cyber context and should be adjusted down in cyberspace as a form of *lex specialis.*[1307] Such a development would make it easier for injured States to seek redress within the framework of Public International Law although it must be critiqued for the hazards it would also create. Specifically, the risk of false flag operations and false accusations would grow exponentially if the threshold of *effective control* is lowered too much. Mistaken attribution followed by a misconceived retribution would also become more likely. Despite challenges, scholars, including François Delerue, expressed three additional reasons, on top of easier concealment of preparatory work mentioned in the previous paragraph, for why application of the threshold in cyberspace could be modified as opposed to the general rules:

- Lower level of organizational cohesiveness needed in cyberspace Both the ICJ and ICTY distinguished non-State entities based on their level or organizational cohesiveness. However, cyberspace allows for delivery of sophisticated hostile acts at a much lower level of organization than it is the case in the conventional realm. For instance, a loosely connected group of hackers conducted hostile cyber operations in support of the Zapatista Army of National Liberation (ZANL), a separatist movement in south Mexico. They assaulted governmental websites of Mexico in 2013 despite never having met in person.[1308] Other hacks, such as the ones conducted by the FloodNet group against

---

1307 Shackelford, Scott J., From Nuclear War to Net War: Analogizing Cyber Attacks in International Law (April 28, 2009). Berkley Journal of International Law (BJIL), Vol. 25, No. 3, 2009. Page 203. <https://ssrn.com/abstract=1396375>; Woltag, Johann-Christoph, Computer Network Operations Below the Level of Armed Force (May 26, 2011). ESIL 2011 4th Research Forum. Page 91. Retrieved on November 29, 2023. <https://ssrn.com/abstract=1967593>.

1308 "Hackers Disrupt Mexico Defense Ministry Website." Phys.org, January 17, 2013. <https://phys.org/news/2013-01-activists-hack-mexican-army-website.html>.

the United States, show a similar trait of low level of organization and coordination coupled with a highly effective impact.[1309]

- Easier way of incentivizing non-State entities to conduct hostile operations supporting State policies in cyberspace As shown by the example of Iran providing data and means for private hackers to assault IT systems of the United States as a response to the Stuxnet virus,[1310] the element of "arming and training," developed by the ICJ in the Nicaragua judgment, takes on a different meaning in cyberspace. Replication of digital means is practically costless. Additionally, a State disseminating cyber tools enabling digital assaults another State can do so with relative impunity. All it takes is an anonymous leak on the internet.
- Geographically fragmented evidence requires a higher degree of coordination of the international community in cyberspace While cyberspace is a realm that is ubiquitous and de-territorialized, its physical foundation, in the form of servers and connectors, is not. In fact, when a State is working to trace back a hostile cyber operation, pieces of evidence can be disseminated on servers around the world spanning various State jurisdictions. It is then the question of goodwill of each of the host States to allow access to data facilitating attribution. Additionally, there is the challenge of logistics of this process.

Despite these suggestions, modification of the threshold of *effective control* in cyberspace is not realistically possible in the current context. The proposal for this novel secondary norm remains a hypothetical possibility for the future.

Hybrid model of jurisdiction in cyberspace

While States have jurisdiction over ICT infrastructure that sits within their sovereign territory, there is an open debate as to the so-called pass-through States in the cyber context. Since the internet network is a system that

1309 Buck, Stephanie. "One of the First Cyberattacks Was an 'art Project' That Targeted the Pentagon." Medium, March 1, 2017. <https://timeline.com/electronic-disturbance-theater-bace73446dda>.

1310 Hanna, Andrew. "The Invisible u.s.-Iran Cyber War." The Iran Primer, November 1, 2021. <https://iranprimer.usip.org/blog/2019/oct/25/invisible-us-iran-cyber-war>.

effectively covers all the countries in the world, many of them might end up involuntarily lending their ICT infrastructure to a hostile cyber operation as it passes through it. This situation is not directly comparable with any conventional context. Many scholars are of the opinion that a pass-through State does not enjoy jurisdiction over such activities and their impact elsewhere because of its *de minimis* connection with it.[1311] However, there is no established State practice or jurisprudence in that regard. So far though, on the few occasions that a government would publicly attribute a hostile cyber operation to another State, they never mentioned pass-through countries, implying that they are not to be held accountable for cyber operations that pass through their territory.

Several scholars, including the International Group of Experts who authored the Tallinn Manual[1312] as well as Tomasz Welanyk,[1313] have proposed their frameworks to resolve this novel situation. The general consensus emerging from the work of the UN OEWG, including its reports endorsed by the UN General Assembly, is that the ICT infrastructure that sustains the internet and cyberspace physically located within territory of a State is covered by its jurisdiction.[1314] This however creates a challenge that stems from the nature of cyberspace. At any given moment, a stream of data flows through the ICT infrastructure of States, en route from one part of the globe to another. If placing the ICT infrastructure within jurisdiction were to include all activity that takes place on it, effectively all States would hold jurisdiction over just about everything that takes place over the internet at all times. This would lead to problematic conclusions and destabilization of the system of Public International Law. A number of States with no meaningful connection to a hostile cyber operation could enact *Countermeasures* or be

1311 Schmitt, Michael N. & NATO Cooperative Cyber Defence Centre of Excellence. (2017). Tallinn Manual 2.0 on the International Law Applicable to Cyber Operations. Cambridge University Press. Page 56.

1312 Ibid.

1313 Welanyk, Tomasz, "Istnienie i granice suwerenności w cyberprzestrzeni. Analiza prawna." Ph.D. dissertation, University of Warsaw, 2019. Page 33.

1314 United Nations General Assembly Resolution. Open-ended working group on developments in the field of information and telecommunications in the context of international security—Final Substantive Report. A/AC.290/2021/CRP.2. <https://front.un-arm.org/wp-content/uploads/2021/03/Final-report-A-AC.290-2021-CRP.2.pdf>.

targeted by them based on the fact that related data passed through servers located within their territory for a fraction of a second.

Authors of the Tallinn Manual argued that the solution to that tension is to perceive the international internet data flows like ships passing through the territorial waters (ICT infrastructure) of a State.[1315] This analogy would allow for extension of the principle of innocent passage to cyberspace. It would also apply the requirement of the cyber activities flowing through the servers located in a State not being prejudicial to its peace, good order or security. Transposition of this requirement would create a convenient threshold that would explain why most internet data flows taking place via national ICT infrastructure are not a responsibility of the host State. It would also allow for the application of existing international jurisprudence on the matter of territorial waters by analogy, most importantly, the Corfu Channel judgment, which absolved a coastal State from a hypothetical requirement of knowing of all the movements in all its territorial waters at all times would apply.[1316] However, this proposed model is simplistic and does not solve all the conceptual problems posed by cyberspace. As pointed out by Tomasz Welanyk, there exists no State practice or *opinio juris* that would point to the data flows on national ICT infrastructure being always subject to the host State's jurisdiction.[1317] If anything, the evidence points to the opposite—States do not exercise jurisdiction over any random data flows that appear on its servers for a fraction of a second. Meanwhile, ships in a State's territorial waters are always subject to the host State's jurisdiction. The analogy also does not explain how to treat certain types of hostile malware that lingers on the ICT infrastructure. For instance, would spying software nested on a State's ICT infrastructure that collects intelligence data on a third State be prejudicial to the host State's peace, good order

---

1315 Welanyk, Tomasz, "Istnienie i granice suwerenności w cyberprzestrzeni. Analiza prawna." Ph.D. dissertation, University of Warsaw, 2019. Page 29.

1316 Case concerning Corfu Channel (United Kingdom of Great Britain and Northern Ireland v. Albania)—Judgment (Merits). International Court of Justice Reports, April 9, 1949. Gen L No. 1. Paragraphs 69–70. <https://www.icj-cij.org/en/case/1>.

1317 Welanyk, Tomasz, "Istnienie i granice suwerenności w cyberprzestrzeni. Analiza prawna." Ph.D. dissertation, University of Warsaw, 2019. Page 30.

or security? The Tallinn Manual's authors engaged with this question and were not able to answer it.[1318]

The framework structuring State jurisdiction in cyberspace should start with a distinction between its material/physical and non-material/cyber components. A proposition on its possible shape is discussed next. At one end of the spectrum, we have the physical infrastructure upholding the system. It is physically located within a State jurisdiction and is covered by it. The ICJ's *Rainbow Warrior* judgment pointed out that any non-consensual hostile physical impact within a State's territory violates its sovereignty and therefore constitutes an *Internationally Wrongful Act.*[1319] This conclusion applies to the ICT infrastructure too. Any harm, tampering, or otherwise hostile conduct toward the physical infrastructure is subject to the host State's jurisdiction. On the other end of the spectrum there are the accidental internet data flows that create the non-material part of cyberspace. The emerging State practice points in the direction of no jurisdiction over them of the States, whose infrastructure was used as an accidental pass-through for hostile cyber operation, constituting a space similar in nature to open seas res communis. For instance, no pass-through State has claimed jurisdiction over the Sony hack operation attributed to North Korea. If the usage of ICT infrastructure is more than accidental and fleeting, some States are arguing *for Due Diligence* responsibility of the pass-through State (*Due Diligence* in cyberspace is the subject of the next section).[1320] While this postulate has not yet solidified into a binding legal norm, if and when it does, it would define a part of the data space that most closely resembles territorial waters where a certain threshold of severity of an act has to be met in order to trigger State responsibility over it. Finally, there are parts of non-material cyberspace that constitute the extension

---

1318 Schmitt, Michael. N. & NATO Cooperative Cyber Defence Centre of Excellence. (2017). Tallinn Manual 2.0 on the International Law Applicable to Cyber Operations. Cambridge University Press. Paragraph 6.

1319 Case concerning the difference between New Zealand and France concerning the interpretation or application of two agreements, concluded on 9 July 1986 between the two States and which related to the problems arising from the Rainbow Warrior Affair. International Court of Justice. ICJ Reports 1990. (1990, April 30). Page 254. Retrieved February 18, 2022, from <https://legal.un.org/riaa/cases/vol_XX/215-284.pdf>.

1320 See the section—V.5.2.2 "The process of deterritorialization of jurisdiction in cyberspace" for further analysis on the subject.

of territory of a State, akin to the status of diplomatic missions. These are websites in the.gov domain (alongside other governmental domains) that represent the sovereign authority of a State and deliver essential services to citizens that qualify as part of the State's *domaine réservé*. Any digital assault on such websites by another State likely amounts to an *Internationally Wrongful Act* regardless of the threshold of severity, analogously to open hostilities on diplomatic missions and sovereign functions of a State, as confirmed is, by the ICJ's *United States Diplomatic and Consular Staff in Tehran* judgment from 1980[1321] and the Vienna Convention on the Law of Treaties from 1969.[1322]

These discussions are so far confined mostly to the scholarly sphere. There is a lack of clarity in terms of State practice or *opinio juris* on the subject of the limits of State jurisdiction in cyberspace. For this reason, the notion of a layered model, despite potentially providing clarity on many outstanding jurisdictional issues, remains an academic proposal.

6.6 Conclusion

Special regimes of Public International Law were devised as a tool making the overall system more effective. However, this possibility contains an inherent trade-off. As regimes get more specialized in order to address the specific features and needs of the niche they cover, a risk emerges of reduced coherence of the overall legal system they are a part of. Zygmunt Ziembiński laid out the requirement of internal rationality for any legal system to be able to function: the linguistic one (which pertains to consistency of terms used across the system, the axiological one (which pertains to consistency motives and core beliefs that determine the system's purpose). Special regimes are walking a fine line between improving applicability of Public International Law in a specific context and maintaining cohesiveness across the system's different branches.

The main framework for understanding special regimes was formulated by the UN ILC in 2006 and endorsed by the UN General Assembly that same

1321 United States Diplomatic and Consular Staff in Tehran (United States of America v. Iran). International Court of Justice. ICJ Reports 1980. (1980, May 24). Page 3. <https://www.icj-cij.org/en/case/64>.

1322 Vienna Convention on the Law of Treaties (May 23, 1969). UN Doc A/Conf39/27. Article 31(1). <https://legal.un.org/ilc/texts/instruments/english/conventions/1_1_1969.pdf>.

year. It draws on more than a century of international jurisprudence and reflects customary developments that have since become part of established international law. A key feature of the framework is a distinction of three main types of special regimes: the weak, the strong, and the very strong ones. The main difference between them is that the weak ones only contain secondary norms that clarify application and interpretation of existing rights and obligations in a specific context, the strong ones contain norms that generate new rights and obligations of States and other subjects of international law, while the very strong ones contain their own principles that define the systemic interpretation across the whole special regime.

Several special regimes are well established although the exact number and their contours are subject to a hot academic debate. The main ones include: Human rights law, Law of war, European Union law, World Trade Organization law, International environmental law, and Diplomatic and consular law. Analysis of the historical development of these special regimes allows for identification of the three main "engines" that can propel their differentiation and evolution away from the general system. These are: treaties, customary law, and a dedicated international judiciary body. The last component is especially important for those regimes that managed to develop their own systemic principles that can modify or even in certain instances replace those of the general system of Public International Law. Such judiciary bodies can serve as champions of a special regime, articulating its rationale and weaving together a systemic logic by means of their judgments, advisory opinions, and arbitration rulings.

The case for a special regime on cyberspace is robust. The field displays an array of unique features that create uncertainty as to how general rules should be applied there. Certain novel characteristics of cyberspace present legal challenges that have not been experienced before by humanity and have no equivalent in the conventional realm. However, lack of consensus in the international community and States' proclivity to avoid seeking formal redress when they are targeted by cyber hostilities creates a dearth of legal material for a special regime to be built with. Of the three "engines," only one is available, customary developments in State practice, and even that one is limited. In this challenging context, creative solutions were proposed by some scholars to disregard established sources of international law lean instead toward alternative ones. One such solution that gained the most prominence is the notion of *Lex Informatica*, a system of rules inspired by the medieval framework maintained by the community of itinerant European merchants called *Lex Mercatoria*. In this proposed approach, a system of rules would develop bottom-up by all users of cyberspace, regardless of their status in international law, and its enforcement would rely on the communal mechanisms of reputation and collegial marketplace courts rather than sovereign power. Transposing this idea into the cyber realm would entail removing the distinction between domestic and international law and between private and public entities, embracing organic patterns of conduct that emerge at the intersection of these spheres. While an interesting proposition, *Lex Informatica* is not a viable path for development for cyberspace law. Indeed, the lack of semantic and hierarchical structure of *Lex Informatica* might reflect the nature of cyberspace a little better than the traditional legal frameworks. However, long-term lack of clarity and accountability, coupled with no clear ways for binding norms to emerge and to be enforced effectively would stunt development of international cyberspace law rather than foster it.

It is worth then shifting gears back to the established mechanisms of Public International Law. Situating unique State practice that has thus far developed in the cyber context reveals eight potential norms that have received a measure of consistent practice and *opinio juris* from **some** States. These nascent State practice patterns are:

1. A lower threshold of tolerance toward cyber espionage; perceiving all cyber espionage as internationally wrongful as opposed to conventional espionage, which is internationally lawful in principle;
2. Avoidance of legal attribution to the perpetrator States by States subject to a hostile cyber operation; prevalence of the policy of "ambiguity and silence"; a lower threshold for required evidence to prove attribution of *Internationally Wrongful Acts* in cyberspace based on the Doctrine of Reasonableness;
3. Modified doctrine of Effects and Scale that places special importance on IT critical infrastructure being targeted when assessing severity of Prohibited Use of Force;
4. Classifying an accumulation of cyber *Unfriendly Acts* below the severity threshold as one cumulative *Internationally Wrongful Act*;

5. Classification of cyberspace as a separate "fifth domain" (after land, sea, air, and outer space) with its own way of applying general norms;
6. Derogation of the role of UN ITU and more broadly of the UN and the multilateral system from the technical oversight over the internet, as compared to all other communication technologies, and vesting outsized control over it with the government of the United States of America instead;
7. Existence of collective *Countermeasures* in cyberspace;
8. Duty of *Due Diligence* by States in cyberspace.

Unfortunately, except for one, none of these proposed norms enjoy the scale and consistency of State practice and *opinio juris* that would place them even close to becoming binding customary law. That one exception pertains to the arrangements on the governance over the cyberspace infrastructure and international data flows (point 6. on the list), currently putting the United States of America, the birthplace of cyberspace, at a disproportionately privileged and advantageous position compared to any other State. While recognized as existing and binding by other States, even these norms are subject to tremendous pressure by the international community, which is collectively seeking a more balanced arrangement.

Given these dynamics, it can be determined that cyberspace law is **not yet** a special regime of Public International Law. In fact, there is not much binding law there in the first place. This conclusion follows the guiding principle established by Jan Woleński for identifying binding legal norms, which is to focus on the actual existing state of law and State practice, rather than aspirations for their future evolution.[1323]

Nevertheless, State practice appears to be evolving toward establishing a weak special regime eventually and even potentially a strong one further into the future. Of the eight identified norms, five are of secondary character and three are of primary character. Additional four secondary norms are at various stages of development on the academic plane and were supported by the group of experts who authored the widely recognized Tallinn Manual. State practice displays continuous readiness to explore

---

[1323] Woleński, Jan. Z zagadnień analitycznej filozofii prawa, 1st Edition. Nakład Uniwersytetu Jagiellońskiego Kraków-Warszawa 1981. Page 26.

such opportunities for specialized norms in cyberspace. The *sui generis* international governance regime and emergent framing of cyberspace as the "fifth domain," while in themselves not nearly enough to constitute a special regime, set up ground for future evolution of the field. This gives the process a forward momentum, a sense of direction, and a clear end-goal—eventual establishment of a special regime of Public International Law covering cyberspace.

Summary

Cyberspace contains within itself an inherent duality: tremendous potential and tremendous risks. This duality is well captured by two contradicting quotes by Henry Kissinger and Zbigniew Brzeziński, each expressing a different sentiment. Henry Kissinger wrote optimistically in 2014: "Principles of networked communication, if applied correctly to the realm of international affairs, could help solve age-old problems of violent conflict. Traditional ethnic and sectarian rivalries may be muted in the Internet age." Just a few months prior, Zbigniew Brzeziński struck a radically different tone stating: "If someone used nuclear weapons 20 years ago against us, or we used them against someone else, the party affected would know where these weapons came from. One of my concerns here is that this kind of indirect [cyber] warfare becomes more pervasive and simultaneously more destructive and more anonymous in origin. And that, I think, is just a paralyzing, frightening prospect for humanity, and could undermine the stability of the international system." While disparate, both those statements ring true, which speaks to how impactful yet fraught the effort to regulate cyberspace is.

Cyberspace constitutes a completely new area of human interactions, qualitatively different from physical locations such as land, water, air, or outer space. For this reason, it is now considered as the 5th domain by key members of the international community, which sets ground for its autonomous legal evolution. Given the rapidness of technological progress and adoption of cyber means in all dimensions of State functioning, structuring rules of conduct in cyberspace might be one of the main objectives for the system of Public International Law in the twenty-first century. Adoption of cyber means only accelerated during the COVID pandemic, when the United Nations and most States moved the bulk of their activity online. The potential of cyberspace now represents a bold new frontier, as promising and unchartered as outer space.

There is no binding definition of cyberspace in international law although several propositions exist in circulations, put forward by States, multilateral initiatives, and academic scholars. While there is consensus on inclusion of the Internet as the underlying platform and the related IT infrastructure as core components of cyberspace, other aspects remain disputed. The two main questions are whether cyberspace must include human interactions and whether networks only occasionally connected to the internet (such as electricity plant systems) should be included in the definition. The definition currently most broadly used was provided by the *Tallinn Manual*, a publication put forward by the NATO Cooperative Cyber Defence Centre of Excellence. It states: "Cyberspace is the environment formed by physical and non-physical components characterized by the use of computers and the electro-magnetic spectrum to store, modify and exchange data using computer networks." This definition allows for inclusion of non-permanently networked systems and disregards the social component, thus creating the broadest possible definitional scope of cyberspace. This not a moot consideration, since it allows for qualification as cyber hostilities such incidents as the 2010 Stuxnet virus, which damaged Iranian nuclear facilities (which are not directly connected to the Internet). It also accounts for the fact that most interactions and information transfers in cyberspace do not involve any humans. Instead, they are a mesh of sometimes very complex automated communication between servers, a phenomenon only bound to strengthen with the rise of AI.

These considerations demonstrate how challenging it is to apply existing norms of Public International Law in cyberspace, a *sui generis* environment that defies conventional norms and limitations. An information transfer in cyberspace might pass through a number of States on its way to the end target in a fraction of a second, all while not involving any humans at all. Cyberspace is decentralized and web-like, lacking any center and physically permeating all States, disregarding traditionally set borders. It also allows for a high measure of anonymity and plausible deniability on behalf of States that utilize cyberspace to conduct international hostilities. It blends together the physical and non-physical elements, thus creating a dimension for human activity of no past precedent. It is everywhere and nowhere in particular at the same time. The most tangible part of it, the internet infrastructure, conforms to conventionally established rules of sovereignty and jurisdiction zones. However, the same cannot be said about the cyber part of it that is sustained by the infrastructure and cannot be easily located in geographic terms.

It is then no surprise that the existing legal rules in the system of Public International Law most under strain when applied to cyberspace are those pertaining to jurisdiction spheres and attribution. The traditional notion of territory as the core of State jurisdiction, already slowly diminishing, is being openly challenged by the ways cyberspace is structured and utilized.

The purpose of this book is to verify the hypothesis whether the emerging unique State practice and statements concerning cyberspace constitute a special regime of Public International Law. To that end, it takes stock of all relevant customary State practice, available *opinio juris*, historical international legal context and precedents, multilateral treaties and initiatives, *soft law* documents, jurisprudence, as well as work by renowned international legal scholars. It proposed a framework to structure and evaluate the emerging patterns in order to provide an answer to the hypothesis question given the current context and suggest how likely future developments might impact it. Special regimes of Public International Law are a formally defined category that allows for certain branches of international law to develop autonomously, establishing their own binding norms. The UN International Legal Commission proposed, based on existing practice, that depending on whether those rules only pertain to interpretation of existing rights and obligations, set up novel rights and obligations, or go beyond that and formulate unique systemic principles, a special regime can be either described as weak, strong, or very strong. This structure allows for comparison between emerging practice concerning cyberspace and the existing special regimes of various strength.

The analysis leads to the conclusion that emerging cyberspace law is not yet a special regime of Public International Law, not even a weak one. In fact, there is not much unique binding law concerning cyberspace to begin with. Constrained by lack of international consensus and States' propensity to hide their cyber operations and international policies, cyberspace law suffers from lack of material from, that an emerging special regime could draw on. However, State practice appears to be evolving toward establishing a weak special regime and even potentially a strong one further down the road. This conclusion can made based on most States' formal recognition of cyberspace as a separate domain (similarly to land, sea, airspace, and outer space), cyberspace's separate *sui generis* international governance regime, and States' continuous readiness to propose new international legal norms concerning cyberspace. At present, eight such norms are enjoying a measure of consistent State practice and expressed *opinio juris*, five of which would re-interpret existing conventional rights and obligations for the sake of application in cyberspace and three would establish completely new rights and obligations of States.

The reasons for why there is hardly any international consensus on what rules for cyberspace should be are rooted in the historical development of the field. The existing international legal framework for overseeing communication technologies hails back to the original arrangements set up for telegraph. The UN ITU is the multilateral body in charge of that framework and should presumably exert governance control over development of internet. However, the internet defied the established international norms, being governed instead by an ecosystem of NGOs based in the United States, the birth country of the technology. The situation gives one State a tremendous advantage over all others, that translates to effective power over direction of technical evolution of cyberspace as well as insight into and control over international data flows in cyberspace. The United States as the only existing global superpower resists all and any attempts to rebalance this situation, leading to a stalemate in the field.

This is, however, not the only brake put on the development of Public International Law concerning cyberspace. Most States embrace the approach of *ambiguity and silence* in cyberspace, which limits development of consistent *opinio juris* or demonstrated State practice. Those States that have strong offensive cyber capabilities, which also tend to be the most powerful States in general, are reluctant to advocate for more regulation that could curtail their space for maneuver. Those States that become a target of hostile cyber operations have no incentive to popularize their vulnerability given no effective redress can be provided via the system of Public International Law. This situation lays bare how inadequate the existing international legal tools are in the cyber context but in paradoxical twist also hamper their development. To circumvent this impasse, the United Nations has resorted to *soft law* propositions, hoping that they can usher in development of binding customary norms. Similar approach was assumed by some prominent multilateral initiatives such as NATO's *Tallinn Manual* or Global Commission on the Stability of Cyberspace's *Singapore Package*. These efforts, however, are still to bear any fruit.

One of the few aspects of cyberspace that the international community was able to agree on was the general applicability of the existing framework of Public International Law in cyberspace. This historic achievement was the result of the work of the UN Group of Government Experts, which successfully submitted such a conclusion for the UN GA's consideration in 2013. What follows is that the structuring of the main categories of *Internationally Wrongful Acts* should be utilized when identifying hostile State behavior in cyberspace. The main categories in that regard: *Violation of Sovereignty*, *Prohibited Intervention*, *Act of Aggression*, and *Armed Attack*, alongside other auxiliary types. Despite being stablished categories in Public International Law, for each of these main types, cyberspace poses an interpretative challenge. States proposed several adjustments and modifications that can lay a foundation for the special regime that might develop in the future. One of them pertains to the sensitivity of critical infrastructure to cyber hostilities. Just like hitting a nervous system of an organism, a well-tailored hostile cyber operation against critical infrastructure can generate tremendous damage that sends shockwaves throughout every region of a victim State. For that reason, a number of States proposed gauging severity of such hostile operation following the *Doctrine of Target*, which would a deviation from the commonly applied *Doctrine of Effects and Scale*, that has been the default one since at least the landmark *Nicaragua* judgment by the ICJ in 1986. Another example of a proposed adjustment is classification of several small-scale cyber hostilities as one collective *Internationally Wrongful Act*. Such proposals, each broached by a State or a small number of States have not been yet tested in practice, limiting their effective relevance.

Following the logic of general application of the existing Public International Law to cyberspace also creates the possibility of lawful cyber hostilities between States. Actions such as *Self-defense*, *Countermeasures*, or *Retorsions* are just some examples. Here too, caveats and interpretative modifications must be applied to account for cyberspace's unique features. This is reflected in some States' push for collective *Countermeasures* or a proposal that *Countermeasures* in cyberspace need not be preceded by a notification to the targeted State, lest the action is completely futile. The dual nature of internet infrastructure, inevitably encompassing both private and public activity, led some scholars to insist that the requirements that have to be met by a potential *Countermeasure* in terms of collateral damage are stricter than it is the case in the conventional space.

Establishing a category of an *Internationally Wrongful Act* in cyberspace is one thing. Attributing it to a State is another. As it turns out, attribution is radically harder in cyberspace than in the conventional realm. It is already a notoriously difficult aspect of public international legal proceedings in general. In cyberspace, limited track record of formal attributions limits legal development of the whole field. This is due to lack of sufficient State practice and associated *opinio juris* that could emerge from such activity. Evidence shows, that even the most technologically capable governments, like the one of the United States, are not always able to conclusively attribute foreign hacking incursions, revealing the limits of modern-day available methods in that regard. In this context, most States shy away from utilizing international legal remedies when being targeted by foreign hostile cyber operations, reverting instead to name-and-shame tactics, political backlash, or simply pretending that nothing has happened. Data suggests that the latest option might be the most widespread type of State response at present. One idea on how address this challenge is to lower the evidentiary threshold for proving *Internationally Wrongful Acts* committed by States in cyberspace, as proposed by some States, most vocally Estonia and the United States. This could be achieved by relying on the notion of *reasonableness* to guide the process of attribution where the evidence file is thinner than what would be required in the conventional context. Similar proposals were brought up with regard to proving *effective control* of hacker groups by their host States. Such proposals, however, have not yet been tested in front of an international judiciary body, making them highly hypothetical. In the meantime, to fill the evidence gap, a whole branch of the private sector has emerged that helps governments around the world identify offending States behind hostile cyber acts by utilizing advanced IT expertise. This outsized role of private companies in the evidentiary process is a unique feature of the Public International Law concerning cyberspace and contributes to the blurring of distinction between civilian and State capabilities that is already advanced given the dual status of the internet infrastructure.

Some of the *soft law* proposed by the United Nations and multilateral initiatives such as the Global Commission on the Stability of Cyberspace pertains to attribution, recognizing it as one of the key frontiers of development of the field. The norm to avoid tampering and the norm against offensive cyber operations by non-State actors are examples of rules that are geared toward reinforcing accountability in cyberspace. Arguably the biggest effort in that regard however is around the proposal to establish *Due Diligence* duty of States. The norm would create a new obligation forcing States to take responsibility for any hostile cyber operations taking place from within their jurisdiction against another State. This would simplify the attributive process for actions done by hacker groups and other non-State actors. However, the norm, while endorsed by the UN and some States, is explicitly labeled as non-binding and voluntary. It is possible that it gestates into a more binding commitment over time, but the lack of international consensus is currently blocking that process from taking place.

Ambitious initiatives are also being raised at the United Nations and other forums regarding creating a new multilateral body that would facilitate or even formally attribute hostile cyber operations perpetrated by States, serving the function of a global prosecutor of sorts. The existing models of the International Atomic Energy Agency (IAEA), the UN 1267 Terrorist Sanctions Committee, and the Second Geneva Convention are the ones most frequently quoted as the best blueprints for such a new body. The formation of such an entity would mark a milestone in the development of Public International Law concerning cyberspace. Theoretically, the UN ITU would be the natural place to host the body. Unfortunately, persistent lack of consensus within the international community on the subject will likely prevent such a decision from taking place anytime soon.

In this challenging context, creative solutions were proposed by some scholars to disregard established sources of international law lean instead toward alternative ones. One such creative solution is the proposal to remove cyberspace from the purview of Public International Law altogether, relying instead fully on domestic legal orders to deal with all and any cyber incidents. However, ever since the UN GGE 2013 Report that recognized applicability of Public International Law in cyberspace, such arguments are moot. There is now consensus among States that cyberspace will not be framed as an element of *domaine réservé*, instead being subject to the international community's oversight. Additionally, extensive research by scholars such as Joanna Kulesza or François Delerue has demonstrated that Public International Law is uniquely positioned to address the most perplexing conundrums posed by cyberspace, such as deterritorialization of global cyber activity or hostile operations conducted by non-State actors against foreign States. Another proposal that gained prominence is the notion of *Lex Informatica*, a system of rules inspired by the medieval framework maintained by the community of itinerant European merchants called *Lex Mercatoria*. The system would develop bottom-up and its enforcement would rely on the communal mechanisms of reputation and collegial marketplace courts rather than sovereign power. Transposing this idea into the cyber realm would entail removing the distinction between domestic and international law and between private and public entities, embracing organic patterns of conduct that emerge at the intersection of these spheres. While an interesting proposition, *Lex Informatica* is not a viable path for development for cyberspace law. The lack of semantic and hierarchical structure might reflect the nature of cyberspace a little better than the traditional legal frameworks. However, long-term lack of clarity and accountability, coupled with no clear ways for binding norms to clearly emerge and be enforced effectively would stunt development of international cyberspace law rather than foster it. From that perspective, it would represent a short-term maladaptation rather than an enduring solution.

The development of the special regime of Public International Law on cyberspace might then be the most feasible and robust solution, despite all the existing challenges. However, it is shaping up to be a slow and grueling process, punctuated by the international community's response to especially egregious acts, such as was the case with the Stuxnet incident at the nuclear facilities in Iran or the WannaCry virus paralyzing hospitals in the United Kingdom. Ultimately however, adoption of cyber capabilities among States is an unstoppable and inevitable process that could lead to a future where most State interactions, friendly or otherwise, are taking place in cyberspace. The most logical way out of the deadlock could be a treaty that would establish rules concerning legal definitions, attribution, and accountability that are tailored to the unique cyber context. Nevertheless, in the absence of readiness among world powers to commit to a large codification effort, a slow process of building consensus on specific aspects of the framework and developing customary norms based on it appears to be the most feasible way forward. In that new context, most Public International Law would be effectively cyber space related. Until we reach that point, the transitional stage we are currently in might be marked by occasional volatility and uncertainty as relevant State practice organically develops in a case-based fashion.

Some hope for a more formalized process can be provided by the examples of the on the Non-Proliferation of Nuclear Weapons and the International Atomic Energy Agency (IAEA). The treaty was not embraced by the totality of the international community at first, instead being joined a continuous trickle of States over decades since its inception in 1968. A similar evolution took place in the case of the IAEA since its opening in 1957. Had both required full unanimous support of the international community to enter into force, neither the agency nor the treaty would be presently part of the system of Public International Law. These success stories can provide a roadmap for States determined to improve public international regulation of cyberspace. Establishing an international agency that is open to universal membership and slowly accrues participating States over years while it provides monitoring services and attributive legal and technical expertise could be a practical solution to the problem of accountability in cyberspace and a catalyst for development of a special regime of Public International Law that would help humanity navigate the new digital era of civilization.

Bibliography

A. Normative acts

A.1 Normative & executive acts of States

The Government of Australia. Australia's International Cyber Engagement Strategy with an International Law Supplement on how international law applies to State conduct in cyberspace. 2019. <https://www.internationalcybertech.gov.au/sites/default/files/2020-11/2019%20Legal%20Supplment_0.PDF>.

The Government of Australia. Critical Infrastructure Resilience Strategy: Policy statement. <https://www.tisn.gov.au/Site%20Documents/CriticalInfrastructureResilienceStrategyPolicyStatement.PDF>.

The Government of Austria. Bundesgesetz über Aufgaben und Befugnisse im Rahmen der militärischen Landesverteidigung, April 27, 1999. Section 20(a). <https://www.ris.bka.gv.at/GeltendeFassung.wxe?Abfrage=Bundesnormen&Gesetzesnummer=20000864>.

The Government of China. China's International Strategy of Cooperation on Cyberspace. Xinhua Press Agency. March 1, 2017. <http://www.xinhuanet.com//english/china/2017-03/01/c_136094371_5.htm>.

The Government of Estonia. Statement: Use of Force in International Law. November 16, 2021. <https://cyberlaw.ccdcoe.org/wiki/Use_of_force#Estonia>.

The Government of France—Ministry of Armed Forces. Communiqué -La France s'engage à promouvoir un cyberespace stable, fondé sur la confiance et le respect du droit international. October 4, 2019. <https://www.defense.gouv.fr/fre/salle-de-presse/communiques/communique_la-france-s-engage-a-promouvoir-un-cyberespace-stable-fonde-sur-la-confiance-et-le-respect-du-droit-international>.

The Government of France - Ministry of Armed Forces. Droit International Applique Aux Operations Dans Le Cyberspace. 2019. <https://www.defense.gouv.fr/salle-de-presse/>

The Government of France - Ministry of the Armed Forces. International Law Applied to Operations in Cyberspace. 2019.<https://www.defense.gouv.fr/content/download/567648/9770527/file/international+law+applied+to+operations+in+cyberspace.pdf>.

The Government of Germany—Federal Foreign Office. Cyber Security as a Dimension of Security Policy - Ambassador Norbert Riedel, Commissioner for International Cyber Policy. May 18, 2015. <https://www.auswaertiges-amt.de/en/newsroom/news/150518-ca-b-chatham-house/271832.>

The government of Germany. Die Souveränität Deutschland. March 25, 2009. <https://www.bundestag.de/resource/blob/579364/034b11190e6f59ada9686600ee020f37/WD-3-119-09-pdf-data.pdfmenschenrechte-data.pdf.>

The Government of Germany. Gesetz über den Bundesnachrichtendienst (BND-Gesetz – BNDG). 1990. <https://www.gesetze-im-internet.de/bndg/BJNR029790990.html>

The Government of Netherlands. Letter of 5. July 2019 from the Minister of Foreign Affairs to the President of the House of Representatives on the international legal order in cyberspace. July 5, 2019. <https://www.government.nl/ministries/ministry-of-foreign-affairs/documents/parliamentary-documents/2019/09/26/letter-to-the-parliament-on-the-international-legal-order-in-cyberspace>

The government of Netherlands. Wet op de inlichtingen- en veiligheidsdiensten 2017. Sections 1–2. <https://wetten.overheid.nl/BWBR0039896/2022-01-01#:~:text=2%20De%20Algemene%20Inlichtingen%2D%20en,zijn%20verstrekt%20dat%20noodzakelijk%20maken>

The Government of Poland – Internal Security Agency. Bezpieczeństwo w cyberprzestrzeni ze stanowiska prawa międzynarodowego. 2016. <https://www.abw.gov.pl/download/1/2170/TomaszRAleksandrowicz.pdf.>

The Government of Poland – Internal Security Agency. Raport o stanie bezpieczeństwa cyberprzestrzeni RP w 2014 roku. 2014. <https://csirt.gov.pl/cer/publikacje/raporty-o-stanie-bezpi/738,Raport-o-stanie-bezpieczenstwa-cyberprzestrzeni-RP-w-2014-roku.html.>

The Government of Poland - Ministry of Foreign Affairs Republic of Poland. The Republic of Poland's Position on the Application of International Law in Cyberspace. December 29, 2022. <https://www.gov.pl/web/diplomacy/the-republic-of-polands-position-on-the-application-of-international-law-in-cyberspace.>

The Government of Switzerland. Bundesgesetz vom 3. Oktober 2008 über die Zuständigkeiten im Bereich des zivilen Nachrichtendienstes (ZNDG). October 3, 2008. Articla 1(a). <https://www.fedlex.admin.ch/eli/cc/2009/809/de.>

The Government of the United Kingdom. Cyber and International Law in the 21st Century—position of the United Kingdom on applying international law to cyberspace. May 23, 2018. <https://www.gov.uk/government/speeches/cyber-and-international-law-in-the-21st-century.>

The Government of the United States—Cybersecurity and Infrastructure Security Agency CISA. Cyber-Attack against Ukrainian Critical Infrastructure. March 4, 2021. <https://www.cisa.gov/news-events/ics-alerts/ir-alert-h-16-056-01.>

The Government of the United States - Department of Defense. An Assessment of International Legal Issues In Information Operations. May, 1999. <https://irp.fas.org/eprint/io-legal.pdf;>

The Government of the United States - Department of State. International Law in Cyberspace, Response #9. September 18, 2012. <https://2009-2017.state.gov/s/l/releases/remarks/197924.htm.>

The Government of the United States. Letter dated 2001/10/07 from the Permanent Representative of the United States of America to the United Nations addressed to the President of the Security Council. United Nations Digital Library System. October 7, 2001. <https://digitallibrary.un.org/record/449476?ln=en;>

The Government of the United States. Presidential Executive Order - Blocking the Property of Persons Engaging in Significant Malicious Cyber-Enabled Activities. April 1, 2015. <https://www.federalregister.gov/documents/2015/04/02/2015-07788/blocking-the-property-of-certain-persons-engaging-in-significant-malicious-cyber-enabled-activities.>

The Government of the United States. The Designation of Election Systems as Critical Infrastructure. September 18, 2019. <https://sgp.fas.org/crs/misc/IF10677.pdf.>

The Government of the United States. USA PATRIOT Act - Promulgation. October 26, 2001. <https://www.fincen.gov/resources/statutes-regulations/usa-patriot-act.>

The Government of United Kingdom. Letter from the Charge d'affaires ai of the Permanent Mission of the United Kingdom of Great Britain and Northern Ireland to the United Nations addressed to the President of the Security Council. United Nations Digital Library. October 7, 2001. <https://digitallibrary.un.org/.>

The Government of United Kingdom. Regulation of Investigatory Powers Act. July 20, 2000. Section 8(4). <https://www.legislation.gov.uk/ukpga/2000/23/contents;>

The Parliament of Germany. Antwort - Deutscher Bundestag - Krieg im "Cyber-Raum" – offensive und defensive Cyberstrategie des Bundesministeriums der Verteidigung. December 10, 2015. <https://dserver.bundestag.de/btd/18/069/1806989.pdf.>

United States Code. 42 U.S. Code § 5195C(e) - Critical Infrastructures Protection. Legal Information Institute. <https://www.law.cornell.edu/uscode/text/42/5195c.>

United States Code. 47 U.S. Code § 230. Protection for Private Blocking and Screening of Offensive Material." Legal Information Institute. <https://www.law.cornell.edu/uscode/text/47/230#f_1.>

United States Code. Supplement 3 Title 50. Section 1708 - War And National Defense. <http://www.govinfo.gov/app/details/USCODE-2021-title50/USCODE-2021-title50-chap35-sec1708.>

United States government. ICANN - Affirmation of Commitments Information. Internet Corporation for Assigned Names and Numbers. September 30, 2009. <https://www.icann.org/resources/pages/governance/aoc-en.>

A.2 Normative & executive acts of the European Union

Council of Europe. Convention on Cybercrime. ETS No. 185. November 23, 2001. <https://www.coe.int/en/web/conventions/full-list?module=treaty-detail&treatynum=185.>

Council of Europe. European Convention for the Peaceful Settlement of Disputes. April 29, 1957. <https://rm.coe.int/1680064586.>

Council of Europe. European Convention on Human Rights. November 4, 1950. <https://www.echr.coe.int/documents/convention_eng.pdf.>

Council of the European Union. (2019, May 14). COUNCIL DECISION concerning restrictive measures against cyber-attacks threatening the Union or its Member States <https://data.consilium.europa.eu/doc/document/ST-7299-2019-INIT/en/pdf.>

Council of the European Union. Council Conclusions on the Joint Communication to the European Parliament and the Council: Resilience, Deterrence and Defence: Building strong cybersecurity for the EU. November 20, 2017. <https://www.consilium.europa.eu/media/31666/st14435en17.pdf.>

Council of the European Union. Council Decision concerning restrictive measures against cyber-attacks threatening the Union or its Member States. May 14, 2019. <https://data.consilium.europa.eu/doc/document/ST-7299-2019-INIT/en/pdf.>

Council of the European Union. Directive 2008/114/EC on the identification and designation of European critical infrastructures and the assessment of the need to improve their protection. Official Journal of the European Union. December 8, 2008. <https://eur-lex.europa.eu/LexUriServ/LexUriServ.do?uri=OJ:L:2008:345:0075:0082:EN:PDF.>

Council of the European Union. Statement on Cyber attacks: EU ready to respond with a range of measures, including sanctions. June 19, 2017. <https://www.consilium.europa.eu/en/press/press-releases/2017/06/19/cyber-diplomacy-toolbox/.>

European Parliament. The internal market: General principles. June 19, 2017. <https://www.europarl.europa.eu/factsheets/en/sheet/33/the-internal-market-general-principles.>

European Parliament. Resolution on the forthcoming World Conference on International Telecommunications (WCIT-12) of the International Telecommunication Union, and the possible expansion of the scope of international telecommunication regulations. November 19, 2012. <https://www.europarl.europa.eu/doceo/document/B-7-2012-0499_EN.html?redirect.>

A.3 International normative & executive acts

African Union. African Union Convention on Cyber Security and Personal Data Protection. June 27, 2014. <https://au.int/en/treaties/african-union-convention-cyber-security-and-personal-data-protection.>

African Union. Constitutive Act Of The African Union. July 11, 2000. <https://au.int/sites/default/files/pages/34873-file-constitutiveact_en.pdf.>

Association of Southeast Asian Nations. The ASEAN Charter. January, 2008. <https://asean.org/wp-content/uploads/images/archive/publications/ASEAN-Charter.pdf.>

Commonwealth Heads of Government Meeting. Commonwealth Cyber Declaration. April 20, 2018. <https://production-new-commonwealth-files.s3.eu-west-2.amazonaws.com/migrated/inline/Commonwealth-Cyber-Declaration.pdf.>

Governments of India, Brazil, and South Africa. Statement: IBSA Multistakeholder Meeting on Global Internet Governance. September 2, 2011. <https://web.archive.org/web/20111005063245/http://www.culturalivre.org.br/artigos/IBSA_recommendations_Internet_Governance.pdf.>

Hague Convention II on the Laws and Customs of War on Land. 1899. <https://ihl-databases.icrc.org/en/ihl-treaties/hague-conv-ii-1899.> <https://documents-ddsny.un.org/doc/UNDOC/GEN/N04/602/31/PDF/N0460231.pdf?OpenElement.>

Institute for International Law and Justice. Convention for the Definition of Aggression. July 3, 1933. <https://www.iilj.org/wp-content/uploads/2016/08/Convention-for-the-Definition-of-Aggression-1933.pdf.>

Institute of International Law (Institut De Droit International). Lisbon resolution on the legal consequences for member states of the non-fulfillment by international organizations of their obligations toward third parties. 1995. <https://www.idi-iil.org/app/uploads/2017/06/1995_lis_02_en.pdf.>

International Committee of the Red Cross. Customary International Humanitarian Law - Rule 65: Perfidy. <https://ihl-databases.icrc.org/customary-ihl/eng/docindex/v1_rul_rule65.>

International Committee of the Red Cross. Additional Protocol I to the Geneva Conventions. June 8, 1977. <https://www.icrc.org/en/doc/assets/files/other/icrc_002_0321.pdf.>

International Committee of the Red Cross. Customary International Humanitarian Law - Rule 54: Attacks against Objects Indispensable to the Survival of the Civilian Population. <https://ihl-databases.icrc.org/en/customary-ihl/v1/rule54.>

International Committee of the Red Cross. Customary International Humanitarian Law - Rule 147: Reprisals against Protected Objects. <https://ihl-databases.icrc.org/customary-ihl/eng/docs/v1_rul_rule147.>

International Committee of the Red Cross. Customary International Humanitarian Law - Rule 148: Reprisals in Non-International Armed Conflicts. <https://ihl-databases.icrc.org/customary-ihl/eng/docs/v1_rul_rule148;>

International Committee of the Red Cross. Treaties, States parties, and Commentaries - Geneva Convention (I) on Wounded and Sick in Armed Forces in the Field. 2016. <https://ihl-databases.icrc.org/ihl/full/GCI-commentaryArt3.>

International Court of Justice. Revisions to Practice Directions IX and XI of the Court. June, 1945. <https://icj-cij.org/files/press-releases/0/000-20061213-PRE-01-00-EN.pdf.>

International Court of Justice. Statute of the Court. June, 1945 <https://www.icj-cij.org/en/statute.>

International Criminal Court. Rome Statute of the International Criminal Court, with later modifications. July 17, 1998. <https://www.icc-cpi.int/resource-library/documents/rs-eng.pdf.>

Internet Corporation for Assigned Names and Numbers. Montevideo Statement on the Future of Internet Cooperation. October 7, 2013. <https://www.icann.org/en/announcements/details/montevideo-statement-on-the-future-of-internet-cooperation-7-10-2013-en.>

League of Nations. The Covenant of the League of Nations. December, 1924. <https://avalon.law.yale.edu/20th_century/leagcov.asp.>

North Atlantic Treaty Alliance (NATO). NATO's official Outer Space Policy. June 20, 2019. <https://www.nato.int/cps/en/natohq/topics_175419.htm.>

North Atlantic Treaty Organization (NATO). Statement: Invocation of Article 5 confirmed. October 2, 2001. <https://www.nato.int/docu/update/2001/1001/e1002a.htm.>

North Atlantic Treaty Organization (NATO). The North Atlantic Treaty. April 4, 1949. <https://www.nato.int/cps/en/natolive/official_texts_17120.htm.>

Organisation for Economic Co-operation and Development. Critical Information Infrastructures Protection. 2008 <https://www.oecd.org/sti/ieconomy/ciip.htm.>

Organization for Security and Co-operation in Europe. Decision no. 1202 of the OSCE Permanent Council: Confidence-building Measures to Reduce the Risks of Conflict Stemming from the Use of Information and Communication Technologies. March 10, 2016. <https://www.osce.org/files/f/documents/d/a/227281.pdf.>

Organization for Security and Co-operation in Europe. Helsinki Final Act. August 1, 1975. <https://www.osce.org/helsinki-final-act.>

Organization for Security and Co-operation in Europe. СОВЕЩАНИЕ ПО БЕЗОПАСНОСТИ И СОТРУДНИЧЕСТВУ В ЕВРОПЕ - ЗАКЛЮЧИТЕЛЬНЫЙ АКТ. August 1, 1975. <https://www.osce.org/files/f/documents/0/c/39505_1.pdf.>

Organization Of American States. Charter of the Organization of American States. 1948. <https://www.oas.org/en/sla/dil/inter_american_treaties_A-41_charter_OAS.asp.>

Organization of American States. Montevideo Convention on the Rights and Duties of States - Additional Protocol Relative to Non-intervention. December 23, 1936. <https://history.state.gov/historicaldocuments/frus1947v08/d566.>

Organization of American States. Montevideo Convention on the Rights and Duties of States. December 26, 1933. <https://www.jus.uio.no/english/services/library/treaties/01/1-02/rights-duties-states.xml.>

Shanghai Cooperation Organization. Agreement of the Member States of the Shanghai Cooperation Organization on Cooperation in the Field of International Information Security. June 16, 2009. <https://ccdcoe.org/uploads/2018/10/SCO-090616-IISAgreement.pdf.>

Shanghai Cooperation Organization. The Tashkent Declaration of the Fifteenth Anniversary of the Shanghai Cooperation Organization, July 18, 2018. <https://uzbekistan.lv/en/the-tashkent-declaration-of-the-fifteenth-anniversary-of-the-shanghai-cooperation-organization/.>

UN General Assembly. Resolution - 2005 World Summit Outcome document. September 20, 2005. <https://documents-dds-ny.un.org/doc/UNDOC/GEN/N05/487/60/PDF/N0548760.pdf.>

UN General Assembly. Resolution - Open-ended working group on developments in the field of information and telecommunications in the context of international security: Final Substantive Report. March 10, 2021. <https://front.un-arm.org/wp-content/uploads/2021/03/Final-report-A-AC.290-2021-CRP.2.pdf.>

UN Human Rights Council. Resolution: On the Promotion and Protection and Enjoyment of Human Rights on the Internet. June 26, 2012. <https://ap.ohchr.org/documents/alldocs.aspx?doc_id=20280.>

UN International Telecommunication Union. Resolution 73 of the ITU Plenipotentiary Conference. 1998. <https://www.itu.int/net/wsis/docs/background/resolutions/73.html.>

United Nations - International Civil Aviation Organization. Convention on International Civil Aviation. December 7, 1944. <https://www.icao.int/publications/pages/doc7300.aspx.>

United Nations - International Law Commission. Commentary to the Draft Articles on Responsibility of States for Internationally Wrongful Acts. September 6, 2001. <https://legal.un.org/ilc/texts/instruments/english/commentaries/9_6_2001.pdf.>

United Nations - International Law Commission. Definition of the term "international organization." November, 1956. <https://legal.un.org/ilc/publications/yearbooks/english/ilc_1956_v2.pdf.>

United Nations - International Law Commission. Draft articles on State Responsibility Provisionally Adopted by the Drafting Committee on Second Reading. January, 2000. <https://legal.un.org/ilc/texts/instruments/english/commentaries/9_6_1996.pdf>

United Nations - International Law Commission. Draft articles on Responsibility of International Organizations. September 11, 2011. <https://legal.un.org/ilc/texts/instruments/english/draft_articles/9_11_2011.pdf>

United Nations - International Law Commission. Draft articles on Prevention of Transboundary Harm from Hazardous Activities, with commentaries. September 7, 2001. <https://legal.un.org/ilc/texts/instruments/english/commentaries/9_7_2001.pdf.>

United Nations - International Law Commission. Draft conclusions on identification and legal consequences of peremptory norms of general international law (jus cogens). September, 2022. <https://legal.un.org/ilc/texts/instruments/english/draft_articles/1_14_2022.pdf>

United Nations - International Law Commission. Draft Declaration on Rights and Duties of States with commentaries. December 6, 1949. <https://legal.un.org/ilc/texts/instruments/english/commentaries/2_1_1949.pdf.>

United Nations - International Law Commission. Formal Report - Peremptory norms of general international law (jus cogens). December 20, 2019. <https://legal.un.org/ilc/reports/2019/english/chp5.pdf;>

United Nations - International Law Commission. Official Records of the General Assembly, Fifty-sixth Session, Supplement 10 (A/56/10). Commentary to the draft articles on State Responsibility. August 10, 2001.<https://legal.un.org/ilc/documentation/english/reports/a_56_10.pdf.>

United Nations - International Law Commission. Report - Subsequent Agreements And Subsequent Practice In Relation To The Interpretation Of Treaties, Sixty-fifth session. May 31, 2013. <https://legal.un.org/ilc/reports/2013/english/chp4.pdf.>

United Nations - International Law Commission. Yearbook Of The International Law Commission 1958. March 6, 1958. <https://legal.un.org/ilc/publications/yearbooks/english/ilc_1958_v2.pdf.>

United Nations - International Telecommunication Union. Final Acts of World Administrative Telegraph and Telephone Conference. 1989. <https://www.itu.int/dms_pub/itu-t/oth/3F/01/T3F010000010001PDFE.pdf.

United Nations - International Telecommunication Union. World Conference on International Telecommunications - WCIT-12 Final Acts Signatories. December 14, 2012. <https://www.itu.int/osg/wcit-12/highlights/signatories.html.>

United Nations - Internet Governance Forum. Organization Mandate. December 16, 2015. <http://www.intgovforum.org/en/about.>

United Nations - Office for Disarmament Affairs. Voluntary, Non-Binding Norms for Responsible State Behaviour in the Use of Information and Communications Technology. September, 2017. <https://digitallibrary.un.org/record/3934467?ln=en.>

United Nations - Working Group on Internet Governance. Report of the Working Group on Internet Governance. June, 2005. <http://www.wgig.org/WGIG-Report.html.>

United Nations General Assembly Resolution 174 (II). Establishment of an International Law Commission, A/RES/174(II) (1947, November 21). <https://daccess-ods.un.org/access.nsf/Get?OpenAgent&DS=A/RES/174(II)&Lang=E.>

United Nations General Assembly Resolution: Creation of a global culture of cybersecurity and the protection of critical information infrastructures. December 23, 2003. <https://digitallibrary.un.org/record/509571?ln=en>

United Nations General Assembly Resolution: World Summit on the Information Society. January 31, 2002. <https://undocs.org/en/A/RES/56/183.>

United Nations General Assembly. Letter dated 9 January 2015 from the Permanent Representatives of China, Kazakhstan, Kyrgyzstan, the Russian Federation, Tajikistan and Uzbekistan addressed to the Secretary-General. January 13, 2015. <https://documents-dds-ny.un.org/doc/UNDOC/GEN/N15/014/02/PDF/N1501402.pdf?OpenElement;>

United Nations General Assembly. Official Records - Twenty-second session, First Committee 1515th Meeting. November 1, 1967. >https://www.un.org/depts/los/convention_agreements/texts/pardo_ga1967.pdf>

United Nations General Assembly. Resolution - A More Secure World: Our Shared Responsibility – Report of the High-level Panel on Threats Challenges and Change. 2004. <https://www.un.org/peacebuilding/sites/www.un.org.peacebuilding/files/documents/hlp_more_secure_world.pdf>

United Nations General Assembly. Resolution. Combating the criminal misuse of information technologies. January 22, 2001. <https://documents-dds-ny.un.org/doc/UNDOC/GEN/N00/563/17/PDF/N0056317.pdf?OpenElement.>

United Nations General Assembly. Resolution: 2005 World Summit Outcome. October 24, 2005. <https://peacemaker.un.org/node/95#:~:text=A%2FRES%2F60%2F1,World%20Summit%20Outcome%20%7C%20UN%20Peacemaker&text=The%202005%20World%20Summit%20Outcome,strengthening%20of%20the%20United%20Nations.>

United Nations General Assembly. Resolution: Creation of a global culture of cybersecurity and taking stock of national efforts to protect critical information infrastructures. March 17, 2010. <https://undocs.org/pdf?symbol=en/A/RES/64/211.>

United Nations General Assembly. Resolution: Declaration of Principles Governing the Sea-Bed and the Ocean Floor, and the Subsoil Thereof, beyond the Limits of National Jurisdiction. December 17, 1970. <https://digitallibrary.un.org/record/201718?ln=en.>

United Nations General Assembly. Resolution: Declaration on Principles of International Law concerning Friendly Relations and Cooperation among States in Accordance with the Charter of the United Nations. October 24, 1970. <https://legal.un.org/avl/ha/dpilfrcscun/dpilfrcscun.html.>

United Nations General Assembly. Resolution: Declaration on Principles of International Law concerning Friendly Relations and Cooperation among States in Accordance with the Charter of the United Nations. October 24, 1970. <https://legal.un.org/avl/ha/dpilfrcscun/dpilfrcscun.html.>

United Nations General Assembly. Resolution: Declaration on the Enhancement of the Effectiveness of the Principle of Refraining from the Threat or Use of Force in International Relations. November 18, 1987. <https://legal.un.org/avl/ha/ga_42-22/ga_42-22.html.>

United Nations General Assembly. Resolution: Declaration on the Inadmissibility of Intervention in the Domestic Affairs of States and the Protection of Their Independence and Sovereignty. December 21, 1965. <https://legal.un.org/avl/ha/ga_2131-xx/ga_2131-xx.html.>

United Nations General Assembly. Resolution: Definition of Aggression General Assembly resolution. December 14, 1974. <https://legal.un.org/avl/ha/da/da.html.>

United Nations General Assembly. Resolution: Developments in the field of information and telecommunications in the context of international security. December 18, 2003. <https://undocs.org/A/RES/58/32>

United Nations General Assembly. Resolution: Developments in the field of information and telecommunications in the context of international security. December 11, 2018. <https://undocs.org/en/A/RES/73/27.>

United Nations General Assembly. Resolution: Developments in the field of information and telecommunications in the context of international security - Report of the Secretary-General. July 15, 2011. <https://www.un.org/ga/search/viewm_doc.asp?symbol=A/66/152.>

United Nations General Assembly. Resolution: Establishment of an International Law Commission. November 21, 1947. <https://www.un.org/ga/search/view_doc.asp?symbol=A/RES/174(II)>

United Nations General Assembly. Resolution: Follow-up to the outcome of the Millennium Summit - Note by the Secretary-General. December 2, 2003. <https://www.un.org/en/ga/62/plenary/millennium/bkg.shtml.>

United Nations General Assembly. Resolution: General and complete disarmament - A Prohibition of the dumping of radioactive wastes. January 9, 1995. <https://digitallibrary.un.org/record/193267?ln=en.>

United Nations General Assembly. Resolution: Group of Governmental Experts on Developments in the Field of Information and Telecommunications in the Context of International Security - Note by the Secretary-General. July 22, 2015. <https://documents-dds-ny.un.org/doc/UNDOC/GEN/N15/228/35/PDF/N1522835.pdf?OpenElement.>

United Nations General Assembly. Resolution: Group of Governmental Experts on Developments in the Field of Information and Telecommunications in the Context of International Security - Note by the Secretary-General. July 14, 2021. <https://front.un-arm.org/wp-content/uploads/2021/08/A_76_135-2104030E-1.pdf.>

United Nations General Assembly. Resolution: Group of Governmental Experts on Developments in the Field of Information and Telecommunications in the Context of International Security - Note by the Secretary-General. July 30, 2010. <https://undocs.org/A/65/201.>

United Nations General Assembly. Resolution: Group of Governmental Experts on Developments in the Field of Information and Telecommunications in the Context of International Security - Note by the Secretary-General. June 24, 2013. <https://undocs.org/A/68/98.>

United Nations General Assembly. Resolution: International Convention for the Suppression of Terrorist Bombings. United Nations Treaty Collection. December 15, 1997. <https://treaties.un.org/pages/ViewDetails.aspx?src=IND&mtdsg_no=XVIII-9&chapter=18&clang=_en.>

United Nations General Assembly. Resolution: Official compendium of voluntary national contributions on the subject of how international law applies to the use of information and communications technologies by States submitted by participating governmental experts in the Group of Governmental Experts on Advancing Responsible State Behaviour in Cyberspace in the Context of International Security established pursuant to General Assembly resolution. July 13, 2021. <https://front.un-arm.org/wp-content/uploads/2021/08/A-76-136-EN.pdf.>

United Nations General Assembly. Resolution: Open-ended working group on developments in the field of information and telecommunications in the context of international security - Final Substantive Report. March 10, 2021. <https://front.un-arm.org/wp-content/uploads/2021/03/Final-report-A-AC.290-2021-CRP.2.pdf>

United Nations General Assembly. Resolution: Programme of action to advance responsible State behaviour in the use of information and communications technologies in the context of international security. October 13, 2022. <https://digitallibrary.un.org/record/3991743?ln=en.>

United Nations General Assembly. Resolution: Protection of the environment in times of armed conflict. United Nations Digital Library System. February 9, 1993. <https://digitallibrary.un.org/record/158808?ln=en.>

United Nations General Assembly. Resolution: Report of the Special Committee on the Problem of Defining Aggression. November, 1968. <https://digitallibrary.un.org/record/774843/files/A_7185_Rev-1-EN.pdf#page=11.>

United Nations General Assembly. Resolution: Responsibility of States for internationally wrongful act. January 28, 2002. <https://documents-dds-ny.un.org/doc/UNDOC/GEN/N01/477/97/PDF/N0147797.pdf?OpenElement.>

United Nations Office for Outer Space Affairs. The Outer Space Treaty. December 19, 1966. <https://www.unoosa.org/oosa/en/ourwork/spacelaw/treaties/introouterspacetreaty.html.>

United Nations Office of Disarmament Affairs. Submission by the Islamic Republic of Iran to the Open Ended Working Group on Developments in the Field of Information and Telecommunications in the context of

International Security. September 2019. <https://ceipfiles.s3.amazonaws.com/pdf/CyberNorms/UNGGE/Submission+by+the+Islamic+Republic+of+Iran+to+the+Open-Ended+Working+Group+on+Developments+in+the+Field+of+Information+and+Telecommunications+in+the+Context+of+International+Security.pdf.>

United Nations Security Council. Resolution: Call For Suppressing Financing of Terrorism and Improving of International Cooperation. September 28, 2001. <https://www.un.org/press/en/2001/sc7158.doc.htm>

United Nations Security Council. Resolution: Condemnation of the terrorist acts of 11 September 2001. September 12, 2001. <https://digitallibrary.un.org/record/448051?ln=en.>

United Nations Security Council. Resolution: Limited air embargo and assets freeze on the Taliban. October 15, 1999. <https://documents-dds-ny.un.org/doc/UNDOC/GEN/N99/300/44/PDF/N9930044.pdf?OpenElement>

United Nations. Communique from the UN Under-Secretary-General For Economic and Social Affairs issued on the adoption of WSIS+10 outcome document. December 16, 2015. <http://www.intgovforum.org/cms/Message%20from%20Mr%20Wu_adoption%20outcome%20doc%20WSIS_16%20Dec%202015.pdf.>

United Nations. Convention on the Territorial Sea and the Contiguous Zone. April 29, 1958. <https://treaties.un.org/pages/ViewDetails.aspx?src=TREATY&mtdsg_no=XXI-1&chapter=21.>

United Nations. Declaration on Environment and Development at the Rio Conference on Environment and Development. June 14, 1992. <https://www.jus.uio.no/lm/environmental.development.rio.declaration.1992/24.html.>

United Nations. International Covenant on Civil and Political Rights. December 16, 1966. <https://www.ohchr.org/en/professionalinterest/pages/ccpr.aspx.>

United Nations. Montreal Protocol on Substances that Deplete the Ozone Layer. September 16, 1987. <https://treaties.un.org/Pages/ViewDetails.aspx?src=IND&mtdsg_no=XXVII-2-a&chapter=27&clang=_en.>

United Nations. Treaty on Principles Governing the Activities of States in the Exploration and Use of Outer Space, including the Moon and Other Celestial Bodies. December 19, 1966. <https://www.unoosa.org/oosa/en/ourwork/spacelaw/treaties/introouterspacetreaty.html.>

United Nations. Treaty on the Non-Proliferation of Nuclear Weapons. July 1, 1968. <https://disarmament.unoda.org/wmd/nuclear/npt/#:~:text=The%20NPT%20is%20a%20landmark,and%20general%20and%20complete%20disarmament.>

United Nations. Treaty Series vol. 535 - Treaties and international agreements registered or filed and recorded with the Secretariat of the United Nations. 1966. <https://treaties.un.org/doc/Publication/UNTS/Volume%20535/v535.pdf>

United Nations. United Nations Convention on the Law of the Sea. December 10, 1982. <https://www.un.org/Depts/los/convention_agreements/texts/unclos/part2.htm>

United Nations. Vienna Convention for the Protection of the Ozone Layer. March 22, 1985. <https://legal.un.org/avl/ha/vcpol/vcpol.html#:~:text=The%20Vienna%20Convention%2C%20concluded%20in,that%20harm%20the%20ozone%20layer.>

United Nations. Vienna Convention on Consular Relations. 1963, April 24, 1963. <https://legal.un.org/ilc/texts/instruments/english/conventions/9_2_1963.pdf.>

United Nations. Vienna Convention on Diplomatic Relations. April 18, 1961. <https://legal.un.org/ilc/texts/instruments/english/conventions/9_1_1961.pdf.>

United Nations. Vienna Convention on the Law of Treaties. May 23, 1969. <https://legal.un.org/ilc/texts/instruments/english/conventions/1_1_1969.pdf.>

United States Trade Representative. United States - Mexico - Canada Agreement (USMCA). July 1, 2020. <https://ustr.gov/usmca.>

Wassenaar Arrangement, List of Dual-Use Goods and Technologies and Munitions List. July 12, 1996. <https://www.wassenaar.org/>

World Trade Organization. Marrakesh Agreement Establishing the World Trade Organization. April 15, 1994. <https://www.wto.org/english/docs_e/legal_e/04-wto_e.htm.>

B. Judicature

Advisory Opinion on Exchange of Greek and Turkish Populations. Permanent Court of International Justice. Series B. February 21, 1925. <https://www.icj-cij.org/pcij-series-b.>

Advisory Opinion on Interpretation of the Agreement of March 25, 1951 between the WHO and Egypt. International Court of Justice. ICJ Reports. December 20, 1980. <https://www.icj-cij.org/case/65>

Advisory Opinion on Legality of the Threat or Use of Nuclear Weapons. International Court of Justice. ICJ Reports. July 8, 1996. <https://www.icj-cij.org/en/case/95.>

Advisory Opinion on Nationality Decrees Issued in Tunis and Morocco. Permanent Court Of International Justice. February 7, 1923. <https://www.icj-cij.org/en/pcij-series-b.>

Advisory Opinion on the Legal Consequences of the Construction of a Wall in the Occupied Palestinian Territory. International Court of Justice. ICJ Reports. July 9, 2004. <https://www.icj-cij.org/en/case/131.>

Affaire relative à la concession des phares de l'Empire ottoman (Grèce, France). Reports Of International Arbitral Awards. Permanent Court of Arbitration. July 27, 1956. <https://legal.un.org/riaa/cases/vol_XII/155-269_Concession.pdf.>

Air Service Agreement (United States of America, France). Reports of International Arbitral Awards. Permanent Court of Arbitration. December 9, 1978. <https://legal.un.org/riaa/cases/vol_XVIII/417-493.pdf.>

Alabama claims of the United States of America against Great Britain. Tribunal of arbitration established by the Treaty of Washington. May 8, 1871. https://legal.un.org/riaa/cases/vol_XXIX/125-134.pdf.

Anaconda Iran Ltd. v. Iran, 13. Iran-US Claims Tribunal. December 10, 1986. <http://translex.uni-koeln.de/231800/_/iran-us-claims-tribunal-anaconda-iran-ltd-v-iran-13-iran-us-ctr-1986-at-199-et-seq/.>

Annual Reports. International Tribunal for the Law of the Sea. <https://www.itlos.org/en/main/the-tribunal/annual-reports/.>

Armed Activities on the Territory of the Congo (Democratic Republic of the Congo v. Uganda). International Court of Justice. ICJ Reports. December 19, 2005. <https://www.icj-cij.org/en/case/116.>

Arrest and Return of Savarkar (France v. Great Britain). Permanent Court of Arbitration. United Nations - Report of International Arbitral Awards. February 24, 1911. <https://opil.ouplaw.com/view/10.1093/law:icgj/401pca11.case.1/law-icgj-401pca11.>

Canada: Claim Against The Union Of Soviet Socialist Republics For Damage Caused By Soviet Cosmos 954. International Legal Materials. 1978.

Case between CMS Gas Transmission Company and The Argentine Republic. The World Bank - International Centre For Settlement Of Investment Disputes. May 12, 2005. <http://icsidfiles.worldbank.org/icsid/ICSIDBLOBS/OnlineAwards/C4/DC504_En.pdf.>

Case Concerning Construction of a Road in Costa Rica along the San Juan River (Nicaragua v. Costa Rica), International Court of Justice. ICJ Reports. December 16, 2015. <https://www.icj-cij.org/case/152.>

Case concerning Corfu Channel (United Kingdom of Great Britain and Northern Ireland v. Albania) International Court of Justice. ICJ Reports. April 9, 1949. <https://www.icj-cij.org/en/case/1.>

Case Concerning Military and Paramilitary Activities in and Against Nicaragua (Nicaragua v. United States). International Court of Justice. ICJ Reports. November 26, 1986. <https://www.icj-cij.org/en/case/70/judgments.>

Case Concerning Oil Platforms (Iran v. United States). International Court of Justice. ICJ Reports. November 6, 2003. <https://www.icj-cij.org/en/case/90.>

Case Concerning the Application of the Convention on the Prevention and Punishment of the Crime of Genocide (Bosnia and Herzegovina v Serbia). International Court of Justice. ICJ Reports. February 26, 2007. <https://www.icj-cij.org/en/case/91/judgments.>

Case concerning the difference between New Zealand and France concerning the interpretation or application of two agreements, concluded on July 9, 1986 between the two States and which related to the problems arising from the Rainbow Warrior Affair. International Court of Justice. ICJ Reports. April 30, 1990. <https://legal.un.org/riaa/cases/vol_XX/215-284.pdf.<

Case concerning the Gabčikovo-Nagymaros Project. International Court of Justice. ICJ Reports. September 27, 1997. <https://www.icj-cij.org/case/92>

Case Concerning The Payment In Gold Of Brazilian Federal Loans Contracted In France (France v. Brazil). Permanent Court Of International Justice. Series A. July 12, 1929 <https://www.icj-cij.org/public/files/permanent-court-of-international-justice/serie_A/A_20/64_Emprunts_Bresiliens_Arret.pdf.>

Case Concerning the Payment of Various Serbian Loans Issued in France (France v. Kingdom of the Serbs, Croats and Slovenes). Permanent Court Of International Justice. Series A. July 12, 1929 <https://www.icj-cij.org/public/files/permanent-court-of-international-justice/serie_A/A_20/62_Emprunts_Serbes_Arret.pdf.>

Certain Activities Carried Out by Nicaragua in the Border Area (Costa Rica v. Nicaragua). International Court of Justice. ICJ Reports. December 16, 2015. <https://www.icj-cij.org/case/150;>

Counter-Memorandum and Counter-Claim submitted by the United States of America in the Oil Platforms case (Islamic Republic of Iran v. United States of America). International Court of Justice. ICJ Reports. November 6, 2003. <https://www.icj-cij.org/case/90.>

Dispute Concerning Access to Information under Article 9 of the OSPAR Convention, (Ireland v. United Kingdom). Permanent Court of Arbitration. ILR. July 2, 2003. <https://pca-cpa.org/en/cases/34/.>

Enron Corporation and Ponderosa Assets, L.P. v The Argentine Republic. Argentina-US Bilateral Investment Treaties Arbitration Body. May 22, 2007. <https://www.biicl.org/files/3909_2007_enron_v_argentina.pdf.>

Fisheries Jurisdiction (Spain v. Canada). International Court of Justice. ICJ Reports. December 4, 1998. <https://www.icj-cij.org/en/case/96/judgments.>

Georges Pinson case (France v. United Mexican States). Arbitral Tribunal. United Nations - Report of International Arbitral Awards. April 13, 1928. <https://legal.un.org/riaa/cases/vol_V/327-466.pdf.>

German-Portugese Arbitral Award (The Naulilaa Case). Arbitral Commission. June 30, 1930. United Nations - Report of International Arbitral Awards. <https://legal.un.org/riaa/cases/vol_III/1371-1386.pdf;>

Gould Marketing, Inc. v. Ministry of National Defence. Iran-U.S. Claims Tribunal. July 27, 1983. <http://translex.uni-koeln.de/230700/_/iran-us-claims-tribunal-gould-marketing-inc-v-ministry-of-national-defence-3-iran-us-ctr-at-147-et-seq/.>

Grand Chamber decision on Admissibility of Application nos. 71412/01 and 78166/01. European Court of Human Rights. May 2, 2007. <http://hudoc.echr.coe.int.>

H. N. v. the Netherlands, Case No. 265615/HA ZA 06-1671. District Court of The Hague. September 10, 2008 <http://deeplink.rechtspraak.nl/uitspraak?id=ECLI:NL:RBSGR:2008:BF0181.>

Island of Palmas Case (or Miangas) (United States v. Netherlands). Permanent Court of Arbitration. United Nations - Report of International Arbitral Awards. April 4, 1928. <https://pca-cpa.org/en/cases/94/.>

Land and Maritime Boundary between Cameroon and Nigeria (Cameroon v. Nigeria: Equatorial Guinea intervening). International Court of Justice. ICJ Reports. October 10, 2002. <https://www.icj-cij.org/case/94.>

Legal case United States v. Morris. Case Brief for Law School. LexisNexis. March 7, 1991. <https://www.lexisnexis.com/community/casebrief/p/casebrief-united-states-v-morris.>

LG&E International Inc. v. The Argentine Republic. Argentina-US Bilateral Investment Treaties Arbitration Body. July 25, 2007. <https://www.biicl.org/files/3908_2007_lg&e_v_argentina.pdf.>

Libyan Arab Foreign Investment Company (Lafico) v. the Republic of Burundi. International Law Review. World Trade Organization Arbitration Body. March 4, 1991. <https://www.cambridge.org/core/journals/international-law-reports/article/abs/libyan-arab-foreign-investment-company-lafico-and-the-republic-of-burundi/62B205440734B90983D02B51A712780D.>

Loizidou v. Turkey (Application no. 15318/89). European Court of Human Rights. ECHR Reports. March 23, 1995. <https://hudoc.echr.coe.int/fre#%7B%22itemid%22:[%22001-57920%22]%7D.>

Minqueirs and Ecrehos (France v. United Kingdom). International Court of Justice. ICJ Reports. November 17, 1953. <https://www.icj-cij.org/case/17.>

Mukeshimana-Ngulinzira and Others v. Belgium and Others., Court of First Instance of Brussels. Oxford Reports on International Law in Domestic Courts. June 8, 2018. <https://www.cambridge.org/core/services/aop-cambridge-core/content/view/EE37C3B257746BD5D4E4B5AAC3B7D355/S000293002000007Xa.pdf/mukeshimana-ngulinzira-and-others-v-belgium-and-others.pdf.>

Portugal v. Germany. (The Cysne Case). Hamburg Prize Court. Cambridge University - Annual Digest of Public International Law Cases. June 30, 1930. <https://www.cambridge.org/core/journals/annual-digest-of-public-international-law-cases/article/abs/portugal-v-germany-the-cysne/AC04379DA13F524F709EF6789D825D4A.>

Prosecutor v. Dragan Nikolic (Decision on Defence Motion Challenging the Exercise of Jurisdiction by the Tribunal). International Criminal Tribunal for the former Yugoslavia. United Nations. October 9, 2002. <https://www.icty.org/x/file/Legal%20Library/jud_supplement/supp37-e/nikolic.htm>

Prosecutor v. Furundžija. International Criminal Tribunal for the Former Yugoslavia. United Nations. December 10, 1998. <https://www.icty.org/x/cases/furundzija/tjug/en/.>

Prosecutor vs. Tadić, International Criminal Tribunal for the former Yugoslavia. United Nations. January 26, 2000. <https://www.icty.org/en/case/tadic.>

Sempra Energy International v. Argentine Republic. Argentina-US Bilateral Investment Treaties Arbitration Body. September 28, 2007. <https://www.biicl.org/files/3906_2007_sempra_energy_v_argentina.pdf.>

The Case of S.S. "Wimbledon" Judgment. Permanent Court of International Justice. Series A. August 17, 1923. <https://legal.un.org/PCIJsummaries/documents/english/5_e.pdf.>

The Case of the SS Lotus (France v. Turkey). Permanent Court of International Justice. Series A. September 7, 1927. <https://www.icj-cij.org/public/files/permanent-court-of-international-justice/serie_A/A_10/30_Lotus_Arret.pdf.>

The Opinions of the Badinter Arbitration Committee for Yugoslavia - A Second Breath for the Self-Determination of Peoples. Arbitration Commission of the Peace Conference on Yugoslavia. November 29, 1991. <http://www.ejil.org/pdfs/3/1/1175.pdf.>

Trail smelter Case (United States v. Canada). Permanent Court of Arbitration. March 11, 1941. <https://legal.un.org/riaa/cases/vol_III/1905-1982.pdf.>

United States Diplomatic and Consular Staff in Tehran (United States of America v. Iran). International Court of Justice. ICJ Reports. May 24, 1980. <https://www.icj-cij.org/en/case/64.>

C. Monographs, books, & dissertations

Apanowicz, Jerzy. (2002) Metodologia Ogólna. Gdynia, Wyższa Szkoła Administracjii i Biznesu.

Black, Henry., & Garner, Bryan. (2009). Black's Law Dictionary. St. Paul, MN: West.

Bossuyt, Marc and Wouters, Jan (2005). Grondlijnen van internationaal recht, Intersentia, Antwerp.

Breau, Susan C., & Samuel, Katja L. H. (2016). Research Handbook on Disasters and International Law (Research Handbooks in International Law series). Edward Elgar Publishing.

Brenner, Joel. (2011). America the Vulnerable: Inside the New Threat Matrix of Digital Espionage, Crime, and Warfare. Penguin Press.

Buchan, Russell J. (2019) The International Legal Regulation of Cyber Espionage - The International Legal Regulation of State-Sponsored Cyber Espionage. [in:] Osula, A.-M. and Rõigas, H., (eds.) International Cyber Norms: Legal, Policy & Industry Perspectives. NATO CCD COE Publications.

Buchan, Russell J. (2019) Cyber espionage and international law (1st Edition). Oxford: Hart.

Cassese, Antonio, Paola Gaeta, and Jones John (2002). The Rome Statute of the International Criminal Court: A commentary: A commentary. Oxford University Press.

Chesterman, Simon. (2006). Shared secrets: Intelligence and collective security. Double Bay, N.S.W.: Lowy Institute for International Policy.

Cłapka, Filip. Internet jako wyzwanie dla współczesnych systemów prawa. (2012). [in:] Galewska, E., and Kotecka, S. (ed.), X-lecie. Wrocław,

Księga pamiątkowa z okazji dziesięciolecia Centrum Badań Problemów Prawnych i Ekonomicznych Komunikacji Elektronicznej i Studenckiego Koła Naukowego - Blok Prawa Komputerowego.

Corten, Olivier. (2020). Le droit contre la guerre: L'interdiction du recours à la force en droit international contemporain. Paris: Éditions Pédone.

Crawford, James, and Ian Brownlie. (2019). Brownlie's principles of Public International Law. Oxford: Oxford University Press.

Crawford, James, and Kate Parlett. (2013). The law of international responsibility. Oxford: Oxford University Press.

Crawford, James. (2013). State responsibility the general part. Cambridge: Cambridge University Press.

Cross, Rupert, and J. W. Harris. (2004). Precedent in English law (4th Edition). Oxford: Clarendon.

Czapliński, Władysław, and Anna Wyrozumska. (2014). Prawo Międzynarodowe publiczne: Zagadnienia Systemowe. Warszawa: Beck.

D'Aspremont, Jean. (2012). Participants in the International Legal System: Multiple Perspectives on Non-State Actors in International Law (Routledge Research in International Law) (1st ed.). Routledge.

Delerue, François. (2020). Cyber Operations and international law. Cambridge: Cambridge University Press.

Dobrzeniecki, Karol. (2008). Autonomiczne prawo cyberprzestrzeni: mit czy rzeczywistość?, [in:] O. Bogucki, S. Czepita (ed.), System prawny a porządek prawny. Szczecin, Wydawnictwo Naukowe Uniwersytetu Szczecińskiego.

Dobrzeniecki, Karol. (2004) Prawo a Etos cyberprzestrzeni. Toruń, Wydawnictwo Adam Marszałek.

Dörr, Oliver, and Randelzhofer Albrecht. (2012). "Ch.I Purposes and Principles, Article 2 (4)." [in:] Simma, Bruno, and Nikolai Wessendorf. The charter of the United Nations: A commentary. Oxford: Oxford University Press.

Dubuisson, François, and Agatha Verdebout. (2018). Espionage in International Law. Oxford Bibliographies.

Ellis, Jaye, Bratspies, Rebecca M, andMiller, Russell A. (eds.). (2010). Has International Law Outgrown Trail Smelter?. Transboundary Harm in International Law: Lessons from the Trail Smelter Arbitration. Cambridge: Cambridge University Press.

Fauchald, Ole Kristian, and Andre Nollkaemper. (2012). The practice of international and National Courts and the (de-) fragmentation of international law. Oxford: Hart Publishing.

Fisher, Smith Norman Alfred. (1985). History of technology. London: Mansell Publishing.

Gazzini, Tarcisio. (2005). The changing rules on the use of force in international law. Huntington, NY: Juris Publ.

Gibson, William. (1984). Neuromancer. New York, Penguin Group.

Grey, Christine. (2018). International Law and the Use of Force Oxford University Press.

Pilarski, Grzegorz. (2020). Cyberprzestrzeń - relacje w wojnie hybrydowej. Warszawa, Wydawnictwo Akademii Sztuki Wojennej.

Harris, David, and Sivakumaran, Sandesh. (2020). Cases and Materials on International Law (9th edition). Sweet & Maxwell.

Huurdeman, Anton A. (2003). The worldwide history of Telecommunications. Hoboken, NJ: J. Wiley.

Jenks, Wilfred. (1953). The conflict of law-making treaties. British Year Book of International Law.

Karski, Karol. (2015). Wojskowe bezzałogowe statki powietrzne a prawo międzynarodowe, [in:] Perkowski, Maciej (ed.), Szymański, Janusz (ed.), and Zdanowicz, Mieczysława (ed). Księga dedykowana Profesorowi Bogdanowi Wierzbickiemu. Człowiek i prawo międzynarodowe. Temida 2.

Klein, Robert E. (1990). Oral history interview with Robert E. Kahn. Charles Babbage Institute.

Kolb, Robert. (2014). La Court Internationale de Justice.

Kotarbiński, Tadeusz. (1947). Elementy teorii Poznania, logiki formalnej I Metodologii Nauk. Warszawa, Akademicka Spółdzielnia Wydawnicza.

Kramer, Franklin D., Stuart H. Starr, and Larry K. Wentz. (2009). Cyberpower and national security. Washington, D.C.: Center for Technology and National Security Policy.

Kranz, Jerzy, and Barcz, Jan. (2015). Pojęcie Suwerenności we Współczesnym Prawie Międzynarodowym. Warszawa, Dom Wydawniczy Elipsa.

Kulesza, Joanna, Magdalena Arent, and Wojciech Wołoszyk. (2013). International internet law. London: Routledge.

Kulesza, Joanna. (2016). Due diligence in international law. Leiden: Brill Nijhoff.

Lahmann, Henning. (2020). Unilateral Remedies to Cyber Operations: Self-Defence, Countermeasures, Necessity, and the Question of Attribution 1st edition. Cambridge, Cambridge University Press.

Lane, Thomas, Pabriks, Artis, Purs, Aldis, & Smith, David J. (2002). The Baltic States: Estonia, Latvia and Lithuania (Postcommunist States and Nations) 1st edition. Routledge.

Lawrence, Thomas. J. (1910). The Principles of International Law. Forgotten Books.

Lin, Herbert. (2011). Responding to Sub-Threshold Cyber Intrusions: A Fertile Topic for Research and Discussion. Georgetown University Press.

Loshin, Peter. (2011). Practical anonymity hiding in plain sight online. Syngress.

Lubell, Noam. (2011). Extraterritorial use of force against non-state actors. Oxford: Oxford University Press.

MacCormick, Neil. (1978). Legal Reasoning and Legal Theory, Oxford, Clarendon Press.

MacKinnon, Rebecca. (2013). Consent of the Networked - The Worldwide Struggle For Internet Freedom. Basic Books.

Malamud, Carl. (1993). Exploring the internet: A technical travelogue. Englewood Cliffs, N.J: Prentice Hall, 1993.

Marland, E. A. (1964). Early Electrical Communication. London: Abelard-Schuman.

Math Noortman and Cedric Ryngaert. (2010). Non-State Actor Dynamics in International Law: From Law-Takers to Law-Makers. Routledge.

Menon, R. V. G. (2012). Technology and Society. Pearson India.

Michaelis, Anthony R. (1965). From semaphore to satellite. UN International Telecommunication Union.

Nagel, Ernest et al. (1969). Philosophy, Science, and Method: Essays in Honor of Ernest Nagel. St. Martin's Press.

Nichols, Tom M. (2008). Eve of Destruction: The Coming Age of Preventive War. University of Pennsylvania Press.

Noortmann, Math. (2005). Enforcing international law: From self-help to self-contained regimes. Ashgate Publishing Limited, Hampshire.

Ohlin, Jens David, Kevin Govern, and Claire Oakes Finkelstein. (2015). Cyberwar: Law and ethics for virtual conflicts. Oxford, Oxford University Press.

Oppenheim, Lassa, Robert Y. Jennings, and Arthur Watts. (2008). Oppenheim's international law. Oxford, Oxford University Press.

Oppenheim, Lassa. F. (1996). International Law A Treatise Vol. 1. Peace (9th ed.). Longman.

Oppenheim, Lassa. (1903). International Law: a Treatise, vol. II, War and Neutrality. Longmans.

Orji, Uchenna Jerome. International Telecommunications Law and policy. (2018). Newcastle upon Tyne, Cambridge Scholars Publishing.

Pellet, Alain et al. (2009). Droit International Public 8th edition. LGDJ.

Piers, Maud, and Christian Aschauer. (2018). Arbitration in the digital age: The brave new world of arbitration. Cambridge i pozostałe: Cambridge University Press.

Quintana, Juan Jose. (2015). Litigation at the International Court of Justice. Brill Nijhoff.

Radziwill, Yaroslav. (2015). Cyber-attacks and the exploitable imperfections of International Law. BRILL.

Raz, Joseph. (1980). The concept of a legal system: An introduction to the theory of legal system. Oxford, Clarendon.

Riddell, Anna, and Plant, Brendan. (2009). Evidence before the International Court of Justice. British Institute of International and Comparative Law.

Rivier, Alphonse. (1896). Principes du droit des gens, vol II. A Rousseau.

Rojszczak, Marcin. (2019). Ochrona prywatności W cyberprzestrzeni Z uwzględnieniem Zagrożeń Wynikających Z nowych Technik Przetwarzania Informacji. Warszawa, Wolters Kluwer.

Roscini, Marco. (2016). Cyber Operations and the use of force in international law. New York, Oxford University Press.

Rosenne, Shabtai. (2003). The perplexities of modern international law, General Course on Public International Law. RCADI.

Sadat-Akhavi, Seyed-Ali. (2003). Methods of Resolving Conflicts between Treaties. Leiden, Martinus Nijhoff.

Salmon, Jean (ed.). (2001). Dictionnaire de droit international public. Bruxelles, Bruyant/AUF.

Schmitt, Michael N. et al. (2017). Tallinn Manual 2.0 on the International Law Applicable to Cyber Operations. Cambridge, Cambridge University Press.

Schmitt, Michael N. (2013). Tallinn Manual on the international law applicable to cyber warfare. Cambridge, Cambridge University Press.

Scott, Colin. (2004). Regulation in the Age of Governance: The Rise of the Post Regulatory State. [in:] Jordana, Jacint And Levi-Faur, DAvid (red.). The Politics of Regulation: Institutions and Regulatory Reforms for the Age of Governance. Cheltenham.

Shaw, Malcolm N. (2003). International Law. Cambridge, Cambridge University Press.

Simpson, Gerry J. (2004). Great powers and outlaw states: Unequal sovereigns in the International Legal Order. Cambridge, Cambridge University Press.

Szurek, Sandra. (2010). Circumstances precluding Wrongfulness in the ILC Articles on State Responsibility: Force Majeure. [in:] James Crawford, Alain Pellet, and Simon Olleson. The Law of International Responsibility.

Tadeusiewicz, Ryszard. (2007). Wychowywanie dla cyberprzestrzeni jednym z warunków zapobiegania cyberuzależnieniom. [in:] Mastalerz, Elżbieta, Krzysztof Pytel, and Henryk Noga. Cyberuzależnieni: Przeciwdziałanie uzależnieniom od Komputera I Internetu: Publikacja Pokonferencyjna. Kraków, Niezależne Zrzeszenie Studentów Akademii Pedagogicznej.

Tsagourias, Nicholas, and Buchan, Russell. (2021). Research Handbook on International Law and Cyberspace (Research Handbooks in International Law series) 2nd edition. Edward Elgar Publishing.

Tyranowski, Jerzy. (1990). Integralność Terytorialna, nienaruszalność granic i Samostanowienie w Prawie Międzynarodowym. Warszawa, Państwowe Wydawnictwo Naukowe.

Vattel, Emer D., Chitty, Joseph, and Ingraham, Edward D. (1758). The Law of Nations: Or, Principles of the Law of Nature, Applied to the Conduct and Affairs of Nations and Sovereigns.

Ventre, Daniel. (2011). Cyberespace et acteurs du cyberconflit. Paris: Hermès Science publications.

Vogler, John. (1995). The Global Commons: A regime analysis. Chichester, Wiley.

Wade, Wyn Craig. (1992). The Titanic: End of a dream. New York, USA. Penguin Books.

Welanyk, Tomasz. (2019). Istnienie i granice suwerenności w cyberprzestrzeni. Analiza prawna. Doctoral Dissertation, University of Warsaw.

Wingfield, Thomas C. (2000). The law of information conflict: National security law in Cyberspace. Falls Church, Aegis Research Corp.

Woleński, Jan. (1981). Z zagadnień analitycznej filozofii prawa, 1st Edition. Nakład Uniwersytetu Jagiellońskiego Kraków-Warszawa 1981.

Worona, Joanna. (2017) "Cyberprzestrzeń a Prawo Międzynarodowe - Status Quo i Perspektywy." Doctoral Dissertation, University of Bialystok.

Zetter, Kim. (2015). Countdown to zero day: Stuxnet and the launch of the world's first digital weapon. New York: Broadway Books

Ziolkowski, Katharina. (2013). Peacetime regime for state activities in cyberspace: international law, international relations and diplomacy. NATO Cooperative Cyber Defence Centre of Excellence Publications

D. Peer-reviewed scientific papers & reports

Easterbrook, Frank H. (1996). "Cyberspace and the Law of the Horse," University of Chicago Legal Forum 207. <https://chicagounbound.uchicago.edu/cgi/viewcontent.cgi?referer=&httpsredir=1&article=2147&context=journal_articles>

Allison, A. L. (1993). "Meeting the Challenges of Change: The Reform of the International Telecommunication Union," Federal Communications Law Journal, 45, pages 491–498.

Aloupi, Niki. (2015). "The Right to Non-Intervention and Non-Interference." Cambridge Journal of International and Comparative Law 4, no. 3, pages 566–587. <https://doi.org/10.7574/cjicl.04.03.566.>

Ansley, Rachel. (2017). Tallinn Manual 2.0: Defending Cyberspace. Atlantic Council. <https://www.atlanticcouncil.org/blogs/new-atlanticist/tallinn-manual-2-0-defending-cyberspace/.>

Ansley, Rachel. (2017). "Tallinn Manual 2.0: Defending Cyberspace." Atlantic Council. <https://www.atlanticcouncil.org/blogs/new-atlanticist/tallinn-manual-2-0-defending-cyberspace/.>

AT&T. (2022). "2022 AT&T Cybersecurity Insights Report." <https://www.business.att.com/categories/cybersecurity-insights-report.html.>

Aufricht, Hans (1950). "Extrinsic Evidence in International Law." Cornell Law Review, vol. 35. <https://scholarship.law.cornell.edu/cgi/viewcontent.cgi?article=1574&context=clr.>

Baker, JH. (1979). "The Law Merchant and the Common Law," Cambridge Law Journal 38, no. 295. Pages 295–322. <https://doi.org/10.1017/S0008197300094204.>

Bannelier, Karine and Christakis, Theodore. (2017). Cyber-Attacks—Prevention-Reactions: The Role of States and Private Actors. Les Cahiers de la Revue Défense Nationale, Paris, 2017. <https://ssrn.com/abstract=2941988.>

Bannelier, Karine and Christakis, Theodore, Cyber-Attacks—Prevention-Reactions: The Role of States and Private Actors (February 25, 2017). Les Cahiers de la Revue Défense Nationale, Paris, 2017. <https://ssrn.com/abstract=2941988.>

Barela, Steven. J. (2016). Jens David Ohlin, Kevin Govern and Claire Finkelstein (eds),Cyber War: Law and Ethics for Virtual Conflicts. Journal of International Criminal Justice, 14(1), pages 225–226. <https://doi.org/10.1093/jicj/mqw003.>

Beim, Jared (2018) "Enforcing a Prohibition on International Espionage," Chicago Journal of International Law: Vol. 18: No. 2, Article 6.

Besson, Samantha. (2011). Sovereignty. Max Planck Encyclopedias of International Law. <https://opil.ouplaw.com/view/10.1093/law:epil/9780199231690/law-9780199231690-e1472?prd=MPIL.>

Buchan, Russell. (2014). Cyber Operations and the Use of Force in International Law. By MARCO ROSCINI. British Yearbook of International Law, 84(1), pages 385–389. <https://doi.org/10.1093/bybil/bru014.>

University of Oslo. (2016, April). When do cyber operations amount to use of force and armed attack, and what response will they justify? <https://www.duo.uio.no/bitstream/handle/10852/50840/723.pdf?sequence=1>

Centre for European Policy Studies. The impact of the German NetzdG law, November 30, 2018. <https://www.ceps.eu/ceps-projects/the-impact-of-the-german-netzdg-law/.>

Choucri, Nazli. (2014). "Co-Evolution of Cyberspace and International Relations: New Challenges for the Social Sciences." SSRN Electronic Journal, October 13, 2014, pages 3–23. <https://doi.org/10.2139/ssrn.2514532.>

Codding, George. A. Jr. (1995). "The International Telecommunications Union: 130 Years of Telecommunications Regulation." Denver Journal of International Law and Policy, 23, pages 501–513

Corn, Gary P., and Taylor, Robert. (2017). "Sovereignty in the Age of Cyber." AJIL Unbound, 111, August 22, 2017. <https://doi.org/10.1017/aju.2017.57.>

Corten, Olivier. (2016). The 'Unwilling or Unable' Test: Has it Been, and Could it be, Accepted? Leiden Journal of International Law, 29(3), pages 777–799. <https://doi:10.1017/S0922156516000315.>

Crawford, James. (2002). The ILC's Articles on Responsibility of States for Internationally Wrongful Acts: A Retrospect. American Journal of International Law, 96(4), pages 874–890. <http://doi:10.2307/3070683.>

Crawford, James. (2012). Sovereignty as a legal value. The Cambridge Companion to International Law. <https://doi.org/10.1017/cco9781139035651.009.>

Crowdstrike. (2018). "2018 Global Threat Report: Blurring The Lines Between Statecraft And Tradecraft." <https://go.crowdstrike.com/2018ThreatReport.html.>

Crowdstrike. (2019). "2019 Global Threat Report: Adversary Tradecraft and the Importance of Speed." <https://www.crowdstrike.com/blog/2019-global-threat-report-shows-it-takes-innovation-and-speed-to-win-against-adversaries/.>

Crowford, James. "State Responsibility: Fourth Report on State Responsibility." United Nations International Law Commission, April 3, 2001. <https://legal.un.org/ilc/documentation/english/a_cn4_517.pdf.>

Crawaford, James. (2000, August 15). Third report on State responsibility. United Nations Digital Library System. Paragraph 386. <https://digitallibrary.un.org/record/420754?ln=en.>

Czapliński, Władyslaw. (2003). UN Codification of Law of State Responsibility. Archiv Des Völkerrechts, 41(1), pages 62–82. <https://doi.org/10.1628/0003892034410754.>

Damrosch, Lori. F. (1989). Politics Across Borders: Nonintervention and Nonforcible Influence Over Domestic Affairs. American Journal of International Law, 83(1), pages 1–50. <https://doi.org/10.2307/2202789.>

Darrel C. Menthe. (1998)Jurisdiction in Cyberspace: A Theory of International Spaces. 4 Mich. Telecomm. & Tech. L. Rev. 69.

de Ruysscher, Dave. (2020). Conceptualizing Lex Mercatoria: Malynes, Schmitthoff and Goldman compared. Maastricht Journal of European and Comparative Law, 27(4), pages 465–483. <https://doi.org/10.1177/1023263X20938247>

Deeks, Ashley (2015). An International Legal Framework for Surveillance. Virginia Journal of International Law, 55(291), 300–319. <https://www.ilsa.org/Jessup/Jessup16/Batch%202/DeeksLegalFramework.pdf.>

Pun, Darien. (2017). Rethinking Espionage in the Modern Era. Chicago Journal of International Law, pages 353, 359–368. <https://chicagounbound.uchicago.edu/cjil/vol18/iss1/10/.>

Deeks, Ashley. (2014). "An International Legal Framework for Surveillance." Virginia Journal of International Law, 55(291), pages 300–319. <https://www.ilsa.org/Jessup/Jessup16/Batch%202/DeeksLegalFramework.pdf;>

Denning, Dorothy. (2015). The Rise of Hacktivism. Georgetown Journal of International Affairs, pages 1–3. <https://www.georgetownjournalofinternationalaffairs.org/online-edition/the-rise-of-hacktivism/.>

Geary, Sean. (2017). Cyber Proxies: A Central Tenet of Russia's Hybrid Warfare. The Cipher Brief. <https://www.thecipherbrief.com/cyber-proxies-a-central-tenet-of-russias-hybrid-warfare-2.>

Dinniss, Heather H. (2012). Cyber Warfare and the Laws of War (Cambridge Studies in International and Comparative Law). Cambridge University Press. <https://doi.org/10.1017/CBO9780511894527.>

Dinstein, Yoram. (2002). Computer Network Attacks and Self-Defense. International Law Studies, 76, pages 99–114. <https://digital-commons.usnwc.edu/cgi/viewcontent.cgi?article=1397&context=ils.>

Dinstein, Yoram. (2013). Cyber War and International Law: Concluding Remarks at the 2012 Naval War College International Law Conference. International Law Studies of the U.S. Naval War College, 89, pages 275–287. <https://digital-commons.usnwc.edu/ils/vol89/iss1/2/.>

Dinstein, Yoram. (2013). Cyber War and International Law: Concluding Remarks at the 2012 Naval War College International Law Conference. International Law Studies of the U.S. Naval War College. Page 88.

Dubuisson, François, and Agatha Verdebout. (2018). "Espionage in International Law." Oxford Bibliographies Online Datasets. <https://doi.org/10.1093/obo/9780199796953-0173.>

Jupillat, Nicolas. (2017). "From the Cuckoo's Egg to Global Surveillance: Cyber Espionage that Becomes Prohibited Intervention.." North Carolina Journal of International Law and Commercial Regulation, Vol. 42, No. 4, 2017. <https://ssrn.com/abstract=3050619.>

Efrony, Dan, and Shany, Yuval. (2018). A Rule Book on the Shelf? Tallinn Manual 2.0 on Cyberoperations and Subsequent State Practice. American Journal of International Law, 112(4), pages 583–657. <https://doi.org/10.1017/ajil.2018.86.>

Egan, Brian J. (2017). International Law and Stability in Cyberspace. Berkeley Journal of International Law, 35(1), pages 1–26. <https://www.law.berkeley.edu/wp-content/uploads/2016/12/BJIL-article-International-Law-and-Stability-in-Cyberspace.pdf.>

Enzo Cannizzaro. (2001)."The Role of Proportionality in the Law of International Countermeasures." European Journal of International Law 889, pages 899–900.

Farnelli, Gian Maria. (2022). "Consistency in the ICJ's Approach to the Standard of Proof: An Appraisal of the Court's Flexibility." The Law & Practice of International Courts and Tribunals 21, no. 1 (2022): pages 98–121. <https://doi.org/10.1163/15718034-12341466.>

Feldstein, Steven. (2017). "Why Internet Access Is a Human Right. Carnegie Endowment for International Peace." <https://carnegieendowment.org/2017/06/01/why-internet-access-is-human-right-pub-70151.>

Fidler, David P. (2015). Whither the Web?: International Law, Cybersecurity, and Critical Infrastructure Protection. Georgetown Journal of International Affairs - Articles by Maurer Faculty, 2452, pages 8–20. <https://www.repository.law.indiana.edu/cgi/viewcontent.cgi?article=3452&context=facpub.>

Finnemore, Martha, and Hollis, Duncan B. (2020). Beyond Naming and Shaming: Accusations and International Law in Cybersecurity. European Journal of International Law, 31(3), pages 969–1003. <https://doi.org/10.1093/ejil/chaa056.>

French, D. (2019). Russell Buchan, Cyber Espionage and International Law, Hart Publishing, 2018, 248pp. Leiden Journal of International Law, 32(4), pages 883–885. <https://doi:10.1017/S0922156519000359.>

Galicki, Zdzisław. (2008). "4. Hierarchy in International Law within the Context of Its Fragmentation." International Law between Universalism and Fragmentation, n.d., pages 41–60. <https://doi.org/10.1163/ej.9789004167278.v-1086.21.>

Ghafur Saira et al., (2019). "A retrospective impact analysis of the WannaCry cyberattack on the NHS." Nature, 2019, pages 1–6. <https://doi.org/10.1038/s41746-019-0161-6.>

Goldsmith, Jack L. (1998). "Against Cyberanarchy," University of Chicago Law Review: Vol. 65: Iss. 4. Pages 1199–1200. <https://chicagounbound.uchicago.edu/uclrev/vol65/iss4/2/.>

Gorodnichenko, Yuriy, Tho Pham, and Oleksandr Talavera. (2018). Social media, sentiment and public opinions: Evidence from #Brexit and #uselection, May 2018, pages 1–40. <https://doi.org/10.3386/w24631.>

Grafton Wilson, G. (1925). "A Treatise on International Law." By William Edward Hall, M.A. 8th Edition. Edited by A. Pearce Higgins Professor. New York: Oxford University Press, 1924. pp. xlvii, 952. American Journal of International Law, 19(3), pages 656–657. <https://doi:10.2307/2188905.>

Guarnieri, Massimo. (2014). "The Conquest of the Atlantic [Historical]." IEEE Industrial Electronics Magazine 8, no. 1 2014, pages 53–67. <https://doi.org/10.1109/mie.2014.2299492>

Haataja, Samuli. (2022). "Cyber Operations against Critical Infrastructure under Norms of Responsible State Behaviour and International Law." International Journal of Law and Information Technology 30, no. 4 (2022): pages 423–443. <https://doi.org/10.1093/ijlit/eaad006.>

Hardy, Trotter I. (1994). "The Proper Legal Regime for Cyberspace," University of Pittsburgh Law Review. Vol. 55, page 1010. <https://scholarship.law.wm.edu/cgi/viewcontent.cgi?referer=&httpsredir=1&article=1536&context=facpubs.>

Henkin, Louis. (1971). "The Reports of the Death of Article 2(4) Are Greaty Exaggerated." American Journal of International Law, 65(3), pages 544–548. <https://doi.org/10.2307/2198975.>

Henry, Joseph. "Inventor of the Telegraph?." 2007. <https://siarchives.si.edu/oldsite/siarchives-old/history/jhp/joseph20.htm.>

Hoisington, Matthew. "Cyberwarfare and the Use of Force Giving Rise to the Right of Self-Defense." SSRN Electronic Journal, 2009. Page 447. <https://doi.org/10.2139/ssrn.1542223.>

Hoisington, Matthew. (2009) "Cyberwarfare and the Use of Force Giving Rise to the Right of Self-Defense." SSRN Electronic Journal, 2009. Page 447. <https://doi.org/10.2139/ssrn.1542223.>

Holzgrefe, Jeff L. (2009). Humanitarian Intervention: Ethical, Legal and Political Dilemmas. Cambridge University Press. Page 18. <https://doi.org/10.1017/CBO9780511494000.>

Hoover Institution. (2018). Strengths Become Vulnerabilities - How a Digital World Disadvantages the United States in Its International Relations (Aegis Series Paper No. 1806). <https://www.hoover.org/sites/default/files/research/docs/381100534-strengths-become-vulnerabilities.pdf.>

Howard, Philip N., and Bence Kollanyi. (20016). "Bots, #strongerin, and #Brexit: Computational Propaganda during the U.K.-EU Referendum."

SSRN Journal, June 21, 2016, pages 1–6. <https://doi.org/10.2139/ssrn.2798311;>

Woltag, Johann-Christoph. (2011). Computer Network Operations Below the Level of Armed Force (May 26, 2011). ESIL 2011 4th Research Forum. Page 91. <https://ssrn.com/abstract=1967593.>

Hunter, David. (2021). International Environmental Law - Insights on law and Society. American Bar Association, January 5, 2021. <https://www.americanbar.org/groups/public_education/publications/insights-on-law-and-society/volume-19/insights-vol-19-issue-1/international-environmental-law/.>

Stephens, Tim, and French, Duncan. (2016). ILA Study Group on Due Diligence in International Law Second Report. International Law Association. Page 2. <https://www.ila-hq.org/en_GB/documents/draft-study-group-report-johannesburg-2016>

International Civil Aviation Organization. (2012). Working Paper on Cyber Security for Civil Aviation, Twelfth Air Navigation Conference. <https://www.icao.int/meetings/anconf12/workingpapers/anconfwp122.1.1.enonly.pdf.>

International Committee on the Red Cross. (2020). "ICRC Position Paper - International Humanitarian Law and Cyber Operations during Armed Conflicts." <https://unoda-web.s3.amazonaws.com/wp-content/uploads/2020/01/icrc_ihl-and-cyber-operations-during-armed-conflicts.pdf.>

International Institute for Strategic Studies. (2021). "Cyber Capabilities and National Power: A Net Assessment," June 28, 2021. <https://www.iiss.org/blogs/research-paper/2021/06/cyber-capabilities-national-power.>

Jamnejad, Maziar., & Wood, Michael. (2009). "The Principle of Non-intervention," Leiden Journal of International Law, 22(2), pages 345–381. Page 381. <https://doi.org/10.1017/s0922156509005858.>

Jensen, Eric T. (2002). Computer Attacks on Critical National Infrastructure: A Use of Force Invoking the Right of Self-Defense. Stanford Journal of International Law, 38(207), 207–240. Page 231. <https://digitalcommons.law.byu.edu/faculty_scholarship/212/.>

Jensen, Eric T. (2017). "The Tallinn Manual 2.0: highlights and insights," March 15, 2017. Georgetown Journal of International

Law, 48(735), pages 735–778. <https://papers.ssrn.com/sol3/papers.cfm?abstract_id=2932110.>

Jensen, Eric. T., & Watts, Sean. (2016). The Duty of Due Diligence and Cyber Incitements to Violence. Texas Law Review. Pages 1555–1577. <https://doi.org/10.2139/ssrn.2894070.>

Johnson David R., and Post, David G. (1998). The New "Civic Virtue" of the Internet; A Complex Systems Model for the Governance of Cyberspace, in The Emerging Internet. C. Firestone ed. <http://www.temple.edu/lawschool/dpost/Newcivicvirtue.html>

Johnson, David R., and David Post. (1996). "Law and Borders: The Rise of Law in Cyberspace." Stanford Law Review 48, no. 5 (1996): pages 1367–1402. <https://doi.org/10.2307/1229390.>

Juurvee, Ivo, and Anna-Mariita Mattiisen. (2007). "The Bronze Soldier Crisis of 2007: Revisiting an Early Case of Hybrid Conflict." International Centre for Defence and Security. <https://icds.ee/en/the-bronze-soldier-crisis-of-2007/.>

Karlin, Mara E., Suzanne Maloney, Tea Ivanovic Sasha Toperich, Maya Nir Marsin Alshamary, Ranj Alaaldin, Kevin Huggard Jeffrey Feltman, Adrianna Pita Patricia M. Kim, and Yingyi Ma. (2022). "Imperfect Allies and Non-State Actors: Lessons from the 1991 No-Fly Zone in Iraq." Brookings, March 9, 2022. <https://www.brookings.edu/articles/imperfect-allies-and-non-state-actors-lessons-from-the-1991-no-fly-zone-in-iraq/.>

Karska, Elżbieta, & Karski, Karol. (2015). Introduction: Extraterritorial Scope of Human Rights. International Community Law Review, 17(4–5), pages395–401. <https://doi.org/10.1163/18719732-12341311.>

Karska, Elżbieta. (2010). „Dorobek Konferencji Rewizyjnej Statutu MTK ze szczególnym uwzględnieniem poprawki definiującej zbrodnię agresji. Kwartalnik Prawa Publicznego," 2010(3), pages 9–39. <https://bazhum.muzhp.pl/media/files/Kwartalnik_Prawa_Publicznego/Kwartalnik_Prawa_Publicznego-r2010-t10-n3/Kwartalnik_Prawa_Publicznego-r2010-t10-n3-s9-39/Kwartalnik_Prawa_Publicznego-r2010-t10-n3-s9-39.pdf.>

Karski, Karol, and Mielniczek, Paweł (2019). The notion of hybrid warfare in international law and its importance for NATO. NATO Legal Gazette, 39, pages 67–80. <https://www.act.nato.int/application/files/7616/0999/3871/legal_gazette_39.pdf.>

Kelly, Thomas. (1982). “Thucydides and Spartan Strategy in the Archidamian War.” The American Historical Review 87, no. 1 (1982). Page 25. <https://doi.org/10.2307/1863307;>

Kilovaty, Ido. (2017). World Wide Web of Exploitations—The Case of Peacetime Cyber Espionage Operations Under International Law: Towards a Contextual Approach. Columbia University Science and Technology Law Review, 18(1), 42–78. Page 53. <https://doi.org/10.7916/stlr.v18i1.4012.>

Kirstein, Peter T. “Early Experiences with the ARPANET and INTERNET in the U.K.,” City University of London. <http://www0.cs.ucl.ac.uk/research/darpa/internet-history.html.>

Koh, Harold. H. (2012). International Law in Cyberspace. Harvard International Law Journal, 54, pages 1–12. <https://harvardilj.org/wp-content/uploads/sites/15/2012/12/Koh-Speech-to-Publish1.pdf;> U.S. Department of Defense. (2020, March 2).

Kordela, Marzena. “Teoria Prawa Zygmunta Ziembińskiego.” Filozofia Publiczna i Edukacja Demokratyczna 4, no. 1 (2018): pages 230–49. Page 233. <https://doi.org/10.14746/fped.2015.4.1.12.>

Kostadinov, Dimitar. (2021, November 28). The attribution problem in cyber attacks. Infosec Resources. <https://resources.infosecinstitute.com/topics/hacking/attribution-problem-in-cyber-attacks/;>

Kowalski, Michał. (2005). Ius ad bellum a systemowy charakter prawa międzynarodowego. Wydawnictwo UMCS. Page 190.

Kozłowski, Andrzej. (2014). Comparative Analysis of Cyberattacks on Estonia, Georgia and Kyrgyzstan. European Scientific Journal ESJ, 10(7). <http://dx.doi.org/10.19044/esj.2014.v10n7p%25p.>

Kranz, Jerzy. (2005). “Suwerenność państwa. Rekonstrukcja i znaczenie idei w prawie międzynarodowym,” Roman Kwiecień, Kraków 2004: [recenzja]. Kwartalnik Prawa Publicznego, 5(1/2), pages 329–334. <https://bazhum.muzhp.pl/media/files/Kwartalnik_Prawa_Publicznego/Kwartalnik_Prawa_Publicznego-r2005-t5-n1_2/Kwartalnik_Prawa_Publicznego-r2005-t5-n1_2-s329-334/Kwartalnik_Prawa_Publicznego-r2005-t5-n1_2-s329-334.pdf.>

Krasner, Stephen D. “Structural Causes and Regime Consequences: Regimes as Intervening Variables.” International Organization

36, no. 2 (1982): pages185–205. Page 191. <https://doi.org/10.1017/s0020818300018920.>

Krasner, Stephen D. "Transforming International Regimes: What the Third World Wants and Why." International Studies Quarterly 25, no. 1 (1981): pages 119–28. <https://doi.org/10.2307/2600213.>

Kretzmer, David. (2013). "The Inherent Right to Self-Defence and Proportionality in Jus Ad Bellum." European Journal of International Law, 24(1), pages 235–282. <https://doi.org/10.1093/ejil/chs087.>

Kretzmer, David. "The Inherent Right to Self-Defence and Proportionality in Jus Ad Bellum." European Journal of International Law 24, no. 1 (April 1, 2013): pages 235–282. Page 244. <https://doi.org/10.1093/ejil/chs087.>

Kreuzer, Michael P. "Cyberspace Is an Analogy, Not a Domain: Rethinking Domains and Layers of Warfare for the Information Age." The Strategy Bridge, July 8, 2021. <https://thestrategybridge.org/the-bridge/2021/7/8/cyberspace-is-an-analogy-not-a-domain-rethinking-domains-and-layers-of-warfare-for-the-information-age.>

Krippendorff, Klaus. "The Growth of Cyberspace and the Rise of a Design Culture, workshop on Social Theory and Social Computing." University of Hawaii. May 22, 2010. <https://www.iosrjournals.org/iosr-jce/papers/Vol17-issue3/Version-6/C017361724.pdf.>

Kuehl, Daniel T. "From Cyberspace to Cyberpower:" Cyberpower and National Security, June 16, 2009, page 25. <https://doi.org/10.2307/j.ctt1djmhj1.7.>

Kulesza, Joanna. (2008). Internet Governance and the Jurisdiction of States: Justification of the Need for an International Regulation of Cyberspace. SSRN Electronic Journal. <https://dx.doi.org/10.2139/ssrn.1445452.>

Kulesza, Joanna. (2008). Internet Governance and the Jurisdiction of States: Justification of the Need for an International Regulation of Cyberspace. SSRN Electronic Journal.

Kulesza, Joanna. (2010). Ius Internet. Publio.

Kulesza, Joanna. International Internet law, Global Change, Peace & Security (2012), 24:3, pages 351–364. <https://10.1080/14781158.2012.716417, page 291.>

Kwiecień, Roman (2022), "Aggression and Responsibility Under International Law—A Case of the Aggression of the Russian Federation Against Ukraine." Page 201. <https://www.nomos-elibrary.de/10.5771/0030-6444-2022-2-201.pdf.>

Kwiecień, Roman, The Formal Sources of International Law, the Relationship between Treaties and Custom, and the International Law-Making Process (September 24, 2022). Page 65. <https://ssrn.com/abstract=4310365.>

Leathley, Christian. "An Institutional Hierarchy to Combat the Fragmentation of International Law: Has the ILC Missed an Opportunity?" 40 N.Y.U. INT'L L. & POL. 259 (2007). <https://nyujilp.org/wp-content/uploads/2013/02/40.1-Leathley.pdf.>

Lefkow, Leslie. "Darfur Destroyed - Ethnic Cleansing by Government and Militia Forces in Western Sudan." Human Rights Watch, March 28, 2023. <https://www.hrw.org/report/2004/05/06/darfur-destroyed/ethnic-cleansing-government-and-militia-forces-western-sudan.>

Lehnardt, Chia. "Private Military Companies and State Responsibility." From Mercenaries to Market, 2007, pages 139–57. <https://doi.org/10.1093/acprof:oso/9780199228485.003.0009.>

Leonhard Kreuzer, 'Disentangling the Cyber Security Debate', Völkerrechtsblog, 20 June 2018. <https://doi.org/10.17176/20180620-183041-1.>

Libicki, Martin C. "Cyberspace is Not a Warfighting Domain." I/S A Journal of Law and Policy for the Information Society 8, no. 2 (2012). Pages 325–340. <https://kb.osu.edu/server/api/core/bitstreams/0f5c21be-28f3-5951-926c-6bdcab243319/content>

Lin, Herbert. "Responding to Sub-Threshold Cyber Intrusions: A Fertile Topic for Research and Discussion," 2011. Georgetown Journal of International Affairs, 2011, Pages 127–135.

Lindquist, Stefanie A. and Frank C. Cross. (2010). "Stability, Predictability And The Rule Of Law: Stare Decisis As Reciprocity Norm." University of Texas School of Law. <https://law.utexas.edu/conferences/measuring/The%20Papers/Rule%20of%20Law%20Conference.crosslindquist.pdf>

Linton, Suzannah and Tiba, Firew Kebede. (2009). "The International Judge in an Age of Multiple International Courts and Tribunals,"

Chicago Journal of International Law, Vol. 9, No. 2, 2009. Page 297. <http://dx.doi.org/10.2139/ssrn.2635379>

Lubin, Asaf M. (2018). "Cyber Law and Espionage Law as Communicating Vessels," 2018. SSRN Electronic Journal, Pages 203–225. <https://doi.org/10.2139/ssrn.3099769.>

Lubin, Asaf. M (2020). The Liberty to Spy. Harvard International Law Journal, 61(185), Pages 1–61. <https://www.repository.law.indiana.edu/facpub/2905/.>

Mačák, Kubo. (2019). "On the Shelf, But Close at Hand: The Contribution of Non-State Initiatives to International Cyber Law," AJIL Unbound, 113, pages 81–86. <https://www.cambridge.org/core/journals/american-journal-of-international-law/article/on-the-shelf-but-close-at-hand-the-contribution-of-nonstate-initiatives-to-international-cyber-law/B2B45B05750572E78FBD835D104E7EAD.>

Malintoppi, Loretta. (2016). "Fact Finding and Evidence before the International Court of Justice (Notably in Scientific-Related Disputes) Etablissement Des Faits et Question de La Preuve Devant La Cour Internationale de Justice (Notamment Dans Le Cadre de Différends Liés à Des Questions Scientifiques)," Journal of International Dispute Settlement 7, no. 2 (2016), pages 421–44. <https://doi.org/10.1093/jnlids/idw009.>

Mandiant Intelligence Center Report (2023). "APT1: Exposing One of China's Cyber Espionage Units." <https://www.mandiant.com/resources/reports/apt1-exposing-one-chinas-cyber-espionage-units.>

Mary E. O'Connell. (2020). "Attribution and Other Conditions of Lawful Countermeasures to Cyber Misconduct," 10 Notre Dame J. Int'l Comp. L. 1 (2020). Page 251. <https://scholarship.law.nd.edu/law_faculty_scholarship/1437.>

McDonald, Neil. (2019). The Role Of Due Diligence In International Law. International & Comparative Law Quarterly, 68(4), pages 1041–1054. <https://doi:10.1017/S0020589319000344.>

McGuffin, Chris, and Paul Mitchell. (2014). "On Domains: Cyber and the Practice of Warfare," International Journal: Canada's Journal of Global Policy Analysis 69, no. 3 (2014): Page 411. <https://doi.org/10.1177/0020702014540618.>

McKinsey Global Institute. (2011). "Internet Matters: The Net's Sweeping Impact on Growth, Jobs, and Prosperity,

May, 2011. Page 3. <https://www.mckinsey.com/industries/technology-media-and-telecommunications/our-insights/internet-matters.>

Mefford, Aron. (1997). "Lex informatica: Foundations of Law on the Internet," Indiana Journal of Global Legal Studies. vol. 5, no 1, page 211. <https://www.repository.law.indiana.edu/cgi/viewcontent.cgi?referer=&httpsredir=1&article=1116&context=ijgls>

Melzer, Nils. (2009). "Targeted Killing in International Law (Oxford Monographs in International Law) 1st edition," Oxford University Press. Page 16.<https://doi.org/10.1093/law/9780199577903.001.0001.>

Memeti, Ardit, and Nuhija, Bekim. (2013). "The Concept of Erga Omnes Obligations in International Law," New Balkan Politics, Issue 14, 2013. <https://papers.ssrn.com/sol3/papers.cfm?abstract_id=3502662#:~:text=law%2C%20in%20general-,legal%20theory%20the%20concept%20%E2%80%9Cerga%20omnes%E2%80%9D%20(Latin%3A%20%E2%80%9E,obligations%20or%20rights%20towards%20all.>

Meyer, Timothy. (2014). "Collective Decision-Making in International Governance." AJIL Unbound 108 (2014), pages 30–36. <https://doi.org/10.1017/s239877230000180x.>

Microsoft Policy Papers. (n.d.). An attribution organization to strengthen trust online. Microsoft. <https://query.prod.cms.rt.microsoft.com/cms/api/am/binary/RW67QI.>

Morgan, Steven. (2021). "Cybercrime To Cost The World $10.5 Trillion Annually By 2025," Cybercrime Magazine. <https://cybersecurityventures.com/hackerpocalypse-original-cybercrime-report-2016/.>

Moynihan, Harriet. (2019). The Application of International Law to State Cyberattacks. Chatham House (December 2019). Page 50. <https://www.chathamhouse.org/2019/12/application-international-law-state-cyberattacks.>

Murphy, Sean. (2002). "Terrorism and the Concept of Armed Attack in Article 51 of the U.N. Charter." 43 Harvard International Law Journal. 41 (2002). Page 50

North Atlantic Treaty Organization (NATO). (2022). "Kosovo Air Campaign (March-June 1999)." NATO, May 17, 2022. Https://www.nato.int/cps/en/natohq/topics_49602.htm.

Navarrete Inaki Mr., & Buchan, Russell. (2019). Out of the Legal Wilderness: Peacetime Espionage, International Law and the Existence of Customary Exceptions. Cornell International Law Journal, 51(4), pages 897–953. <https://scholarship.law.cornell.edu/cilj/vol51/iss4/4/.>

Nguyen, Reese. (2013). "Navigating Jus ad Bellum in the Age of Cyber Warfare." California Law Review, 101(4), 1079–1130. Page 1117. <https://www.jstor.org/stable/23784325.>

Ning, Huansheng, Xiaozhen Ye, Mohammed Amine Bouras, Dawei Wei, and Mahmoud Daneshmand. (2018). "General Cyberspace: Cyberspace and Cyber-Enabled Spaces." IEEE Internet of Things Journal 5, no. 3 (2018): 1843–56. <https://doi.org/10.1109/jiot.2018.2815535.>

North Atlantic Treaty Organization (NATO). (2016). "NATO Recognises Cyberspace as a 'domain of Operations' at Warsaw Summit." NATO CCDCOE, July 9, 2016. <https://ccdcoe.org/incyder-articles/nato-recognises-cyberspace-as-a-domain-of-operations-at-warsaw-summit/.>

O'Connell, Mary E. (2020). "Attribution and Other Conditions of Lawful Countermeasures to Cyber Misconduct," 10 Notre Dame J. Int'l Comp. L. 1 (2020). Page 251. <https://scholarship.law.nd.edu/law_faculty_scholarship/1437.>

Ohlin, Jens D. (2018). Did Russian Cyber-Interference In The 2016 Election Violate International Law? Cornell University Law School - Cornell Law School Research Paper, 17(15), pages 1–24. <https://archive.law.upenn.edu/live/files/6477-ohlin-jens-david-did-russina-cyber-interference-in.>

Ossoff, William. (2021). Hacking the Domaine Reserve: The Rule of Non-Intervention and Political Interference in Cyberspace. Harvard International Law Journal, 62(1), pages 1–40. <https://journals.law.harvard.edu/ilj/2021/04/hacking-the-domaine-reserve-the-rule-of-non-intervention-and-political-interference-in-cyberspace/.>

Perl, Raphael. F. (2007). "National Strategy for Combating Terrorism: Background and Issues for Congress," November, 2007. Congressional Research Service. <https://sgp.fas.org/crs/terror/RL34230.pdf.>

Muchlinski, Peter. (2010). "Multinational Enterprises as Actors in International Law: Creating "Soft Law" Obligations and "Hard Law" rights," University of London. Page 14. <https://www.researchgate.net/publication/287448877_Multinational_enterprises_as_actors_in_international_law_Creating_'soft_law'_obligations_and_'hard_law'_rights.>

Polański, Przemysław. (2006). „Zarys autonomicznego prawa Internetu," Studia Iuridica 2006, vol. 45, page 179. <https://bibliografia.icm.edu.pl/g2/main.pl?mod=p&id=56052&a=1&s=35115&imie=Przemys%B3aw&nazwisko=Pola%F1ski&lim=25&ord=1.>

Pun, Darien. (2017). "Rethinking Espionage in the Modern Era," Chicago Journal of International Law," 353, Pages 359–368. <https://chicagounbound.uchicago.edu/cjil/vol18/iss1/10/;>

Ramcharan, Bertrand. (2015). "A new international Law of Security and Protection," UN Chronicle 2015 No. 4, page 42.

Reidenberg, Joel R. (1998)."Lex Informatica: The Formulation of Information Policy Rules through Technology," Texas Law Review 1998, vol. 76, no. 3, page 554. <https://ir.lawnet.fordham.edu/faculty_scholarship/42.>

Reinold, Theresa. (2011). "State Weakness, Irregular Warfare, and the Right to Self-Defense Post 9/11," 105 AJIL (2011), page 244.

Rid, Thomas. (2012). "Cyber War Will Not Take Place." Journal of Strategic Studies 35, no. 1 (2012): Pages 5–32. <https://doi.org/10.1080/01402390.2011.608939.>

Rivkin, David W. (2010). "The Importance of Extraterritorial Jurisdiction - Report of the Task Force on Extraterritorial Jurisdiction." International Bar Association. Page 33. <https://www.ibanet.org/MediaHandler?id=ECF39839-A217-4B3D-8106-DAB716B34F1E.>

Roberson, Walter G, and Leavenworth. Fort Ks. (2007). "British Military Intervention into Sierra Leone: A Case Study." DTIC, December 14, 2007. <https://apps.dtic.mil/sti/citations/ADA475595.>

Roguski, Przemysław. (2021). "An Inspection Regime for Cyber Weapons: A Challenge Too Far?" AJIL Unbound 115 (2021): pages 111–15. <https://doi.org/10.1017/aju.2021.6.>

Roguski, Przemysław. (2020). "Application of International Law to Cyber Operations: A Comparative Analysis of States' Views." The Hague

Program for Cyber Norms, 2020. Page 7. <https://ruj.uj.edu.pl/xmlui/bitstream/handle/item/153989/roguski_application_of_international_law_to_cyber_operations_2020.pdf?sequence=1.>

Rojszczak, Marcin. (2020). "Does global scope guarantee effectiveness? Searching for a new legal standard for privacy protection in cyberspace." Information & communications technology law 29, no. 1 (2020): page 26. <https://doi.org/10.1080/13600834.2020.1705033.>

Roscini, Marco. (2010). World Wide Warfare - "Jus Ad Bellum" and the Use of Cyber Force. Max Planck Yearbook of United Nations Law, 14, 85–130. Page 106. <https://papers.ssrn.com/sol3/papers.cfm?abstract_id=1683370.>

Roscini, Marco. (2014). Cyber Operations and the Use of Force in International Law. British Yearbook of International Law, 84(1), pages 385–389. <https://doi.org/10.1093/bybil/bru014.>

Rothkopf, David. (1997). "In Praise of Cultural Imperialism?," Foreign Policy, No. 107 July 1997, pages 38–53. <https://doi.org/10.2307/1149331.>

Runersten, Michael. (2008). "Defining 'Self-contained Regime' -A Case Study of the International Covenant on Civil and Political Rights," Faculty Of Law - University of Lund. Page 43. <https://lup.lub.lu.se/luur/download?func=downloadFile&recordOId=1561624&fileOId=1565696.>

Ryngaert, Cedric (2014). "The Concept of Jurisdiction in International Law," Utrecht University Papers, page 3. <https://unijuris.sites.uu.nl/wp-content/uploads/sites/9/2014/12/The-Concept-of-Jurisdiction-in-International-Law.pdf.>

Sander, Barrie. (2019). "The Sound of Silence: International Law and the Governance of Peacetime Cyber Operations." 2019 11th International Conference on Cyber Conflict (CyCon), 2019, pages 1–21. <https://doi.org/10.23919/cycon.2019.8756882.>

Schachter, Oscar. (1994). "Dispute Settlement and Countermeasures in the International Law Commission." American Journal of International Law 88, no. 3 (1994): pages 471–77. <https://doi.org/10.2307/2203714.>

Schaller, Chrisitan. (2016). "Beyond Self-Defense and Countermeasures: A Critical Assessment of the Tallinn Manual's Conception of Necessity" 2016, 95 Texas Law Review, page 1619.

Schmitt, Michael N. (2014). "Below the threshold" cyber operations: the countermeasures response option and international law. Virginia Journal of International Law, 54(3), 697–732. pages 718–719. <https://centaur.reading.ac.uk/89821/1/SSRN-id2353898.pdf.>

Schmitt, Michael N., & Watts, Sean. (2021). Collective Cyber Countermeasures? Harvard National Security Journal, 12, 373–411. <https://harvardnsj.org/wp-content/uploads/sites/13/2021/07/HNSJ-Vol-12-Schmitt-and-Watts-Collective-Cyber-Countermeasures.pdf.>

Schmitt, Michael N., and Christopher M. Pitts. (2020). "Cyber Countermeasures and Effects on Third Parties: The International Legal Regime." International Law from a Baltic Perspective, 2020, pages 258–80. <https://doi.org/10.1163/9789004433151_011.>

Schmitt, Michael N., and Vihul, Liis. (2017). "Respect for Sovereignty in Cyberspace." Texas Law Review, 95(7), 2017, pages 1639–1670. <https://texaslawreview.org/respect-sovereignty-cyberspace/;>

Schmitt, Michael. (2015). "In Defense of Due Diligence in Cyberspace," Yale Law Journal Forum, 68, 1–14. <https://papers.ssrn.com/sol3/papers.cfm?abstract_id=2622077.>

Sean D. Murphy. (2006). "Deconstructing Fragmentation: Koskenniemi's 2006 ILC Project," Temple International & Comparative Law Journal. George Washington University. Page 5. <https://scholarship.law.gwu.edu/cgi/viewcontent.cgi?article=2207&context=faculty_publications#:~:text=The%20Report%20began%20by%20explaining,possibly%2C%20the%20loss%20of%20an.>

Seebeck, Lesley. "Why the Fifth Domain Is Different." Australian Strategic Policy Institute, September 4, 2019. <https://www.aspistrategist.org.au/why-the-fifth-domain-is-different/.>

Shackelford, Scott J., From Nuclear War to Net War: Analogizing Cyber Attacks in International Law (April 28, 2009). Berkley Journal of International Law (BJIL), Vol. 25, No. 3, 2009. Page 192. <https://ssrn.com/abstract=1396375.>

Shapiro, Andrew (1998). "The Disappearance of Cyberspace and the Rise of Code," Berkman Klein Center. <https://cyber.harvard.edu/works/shapiro/Disappearance.pdf.>

Shimbun, Yomiuri. (2012). "Japanese Govt Working on Defensive Cyberweapon." Communications of the ACM, January 4, 2012. <https://cacm.acm.org/news/144941-japanese-govt-working-on-defensive-cyberweapon/fulltext?mobile=false.>

Silver, Daniel B. (2002). "Computer Network Attack as a Use of Force under Article 2(4) of the United Nations Charter." Page 85.https://core.ac.uk/download/pdf/236321477.pdf. Schmitt, Michael N. (2017). "Computer Network Attack and the Use of Force in International Law: Thoughts on a Normative Framework." The Use of Force in International Law, 2017, pages 379–431. <https://doi.org/10.4324/9781315084992-17.>

Simma Bruno et al. (2013). "The Charter of The United Nations," Vol 1. Oxford Commentaries on International Law, 1. Pages 1419–1420. <https://doi.org/10.1093/law/9780199639762.001.0001.>

Simma, Bruno, and Pulkowski, Dirk. (2006). "Of Planets and the Universe: Self-contained Regimes in International Law," European Journal of International Law, Volume 17, Issue 3, 1 June 2006, pages 483–529, <https://doi.org/10.1093/ejil/chl015.>

Simma, Bruno. (1985). "Self-contained regimes," Netherlands Yearbook of International Law, 16, pages 111–136. <https://doi:10.1017/S0167676800003482>

Simma, Bruno. (1999). "NATO, the UN and the use of force: legal aspects," European Journal of International Law, 10(1), 1–22, page 3. <https://doi.org/10.1093/ejil/10.1.1.>

Sklerov, Matthew J. (2009). "Solving the Dilemma of State Responses to Cyberattacks: A Justification for the Use of Active Defenses against States Who Neglect Their Duty to Prevent," Military Law Review, 201, pages 1–85. page 43.

Spaulding Ryan, P. (2012). "The ITU and the Internet's Titanic Momen," 2012. Stanford Technology Law Review, 2012(8), pages 8–36. <https://papers.ssrn.com/sol3/papers.cfm?abstract_id=2110509#.>

Stahn, Carsten. (2006). "Jus ad bellum," "jus in bello" … "jus post bellum"? -Rethinking the Conception of the Law of Armed Force. European Journal of International Law, 17(5), 921–943. <https://doi.org/10.1093/ejil/chl037.>

McDonald, Geoff et al. "Stuxnet 0.5: The missing link," George Washington University. <https://nsarchive2.gwu.edu/NSAEBB/NSAEBB424/docs/Cyber-088.pdf.>

Tams, Christian. (2009). "The Use of Force against Terrorists," 20 EJIL (2009), supra note 49, page 388.

Thibault, Edward A. (1973). "Thucydides on the influence of sea power." Naval War College Review 25, no. 4 (1973), pages 31–35. <http://www.jstor.org/stable/44639794.>

Thimm, J., & Schaller, C. (2014). "Internet Governance and the ITU: Maintaining the Multistakeholder Approach - The German Perspective. Council on Foreign Relations." Council for Foreign Relations. <https://www.cfr.org/report/internet-governance-and-itu-maintaining-multistakeholder-approach.>

Ticehurst, Rupert. (1997). "The Martens Clause and the Laws of Armed Conflict." ICRC, April 30, 1997. Paragraphs 3–5. <https://www.icrc.org/en/doc/resources/documents/article/other/57jnhy.htm.>

Tsagourias, Nicholas. (2012). "Cyber attacks, self-defence and the problem of attribution." Journal of Conflict and Security Law, 17(2), pages 229–244. <https://doi.org/10.1093/jcsl/krs019.>

Tsagourias, Nicholas. (2018). "Law, Borders and the Territorialisation of Cyberspace." SSRN Electronic Journal, 2018, page 19. <https://doi.org/10.2139/ssrn.3213511.>

Tsagourias, Nicholas. (2019). "The Slow Process of Normativizing Cyberspace." AJIL Unbound 113 (2019): pages 71–75. <https://doi.org/10.1017/aju.2019.9;>

U.S. Army Center of Military History. (2015). "After Action Report – Intervention in Somalia." <https://history.army.mil/html/documents/somalia/SomaliaAAR.pdf.>

U.S. Naval War College. (2014). "Anticipatory Self-Defense in the Cyber Context." Digital Commons: U.S. Naval War College Research. <https://digital-commons.usnwc.edu/.>

Ronen, Yaël. (2007). "Israel, Hizbollah, and the Second Lebanon War." Yearbook of International Humanitarian Law 2007, pages 362–393. <https://doi.org/10.1007/978-90-6704-755-5_10.>

United Nations Institute for Disarmament Research. (2017). “Report of the International Security Cyber Issues Workshop Series.” <https://www.unidir.org/files/publications/pdfs/report-of-the-international-security-cyber-issues-workshop-series-en-656.pdf.>

University of Oslo Faculty of Law. (2016). “When do cyber operations amount to use of force and armed attack, and what response will they justify?.” Page 24. <https://www.duo.uio.no/bitstream/handle/10852/50840/723.pdf?sequence=1.>

Verdebout, Agatha. (2021). Rewriting Histories of the Use of Force: The Narrative of “Indifference.” Cambridge University Press. <https://doi.org/10.1017/9781108937375.>

Vogler, John. (2012). “Global Commons Revisited,” Global Policy 2012, vol. 3, no. 1, page 63.

von der Dunk, Frans. G. (2005). The Sky Is the Limit–But Where Does It End? Space, Cyber, and Telecommunications Law Program Faculty Publications, 34, pages 84–94.

Wasilewski, Janusz. (2013). “Zarys Definicyjny Cyberprzestrzeni.” Przegląd Bezpieczeństwa Wewnętrznego 5, no. 9 (2013): pages 225–34. <http://cejsh.icm.edu.pl/cejsh/element/bwmeta1.element.desklight-fad9287e-d6f2-4713-ad9e-472717378ab4.>

Watts, Sean, and Richard, Theodore. T. (2018). “Baseline Territorial Sovereignty and Cyberspace,” 2018. Lewis & Clark Law Review, pages 866–867. <https://papers.ssrn.com/sol3/papers.cfm?abstract_id=3142272.>

Watts, Sean. (2015). Low-Intensity Cyber Operations and the Principle of Non-Intervention. Baltic Yearbook of International Law Online, 14(1), pages 137–161. <https://doi.org/10.1163/22115897-90000111.>

Weil, Prosper. (1983). Towards Relative Normativity in International Law? American Journal of International Law, 77(3), pages 413–442. <https://doi:10.2307/2201073.>

Wheeler, David, and Larsen, Gregory N. (2003). Techniques for Cyber Attack Attribution. ResearchGate, pages 1–85. Page 82.<https://www.researchgate.net/publication/235170094_Techniques_for_Cyber_Attack_Attribution;>

Wiltse, Charles M. (1973). Daniel Webster and the British Experience. Proceedings of the Massachusetts Historical Society, 85, pages 58–77. <https://www.jstor.org/stable/25080745.>

Wróblewski, Jerzy. (1979). "A Model of Rational Law-Making," ARSP: Archiv Für Rechts- Und Sozialphilosophie/Archives for Philosophy of Law and Social Philosophy 65, no. 2 (1979): pages 187–201. Page 189. <http://www.jstor.org/stable/23679192.>

Yehuda Z. Blum. (1976). "State Response to Acts of Terrorism," 19 German Yearbook Of International Law 223 (1976).

Zemanek, Karl. (2013, October). Definition of an Armed Attack in International Law. Max Planck Encyclopedias of International Law - Oxford Public International Law. Paragraph 21. <https://opil.ouplaw.com/view/10.1093/law:epil/9780199231690/law-9780199231690-e241.>

E. Articles

"Obama On Russian Hacking: 'We Need To Take Action. And We Will'". Detrow, Scott (December 15, 2016). National Public Radio.

"Prawo cyberprzestrzeni i stare konwencje," Barta, Janusz, and Markiewicz, Ryszard (1997). Rzeczpospolita November 15, 1997. <https://archiwum.rp.pl/.>

"7 Days Before Obama Gives Away Internet & National Security." Westby, J. (2016, September 24). Forbes. <https://www.forbes.com/sites/jodywestby/2016/09/24/7-days-before-obama-gives-away-internet-national-security/.>

"A Cybersecurity Firm's Sharp Rise and Stunning Collapse," Khatchadourian, R. (2019, October 28). The New Yorker. <https://www.newyorker.com/magazine/2019/11/04/a-cybersecurity-firms-sharp-rise-and-stunning-collapse.>

"A Declaration of the Independence of Cyberspace." Barlow, John P. Electronic Frontier Foundation, April 8, 2018. <https://www.eff.org/cyberspace-independence.>

"A Global Cyber-Attribution Organization - Thinking it through." Mueller, Milton(2017, November 20). Internet Governance Project. <https://www.internetgovernance.org/2017/06/04/a-global-cyber-attribution-org/.>

"A product demo may have revealed what could be the biggest ever government data breach." Hackett, Robert. (2015, June 13). Fortune. <https://www.govinfo.gov/content/pkg/CHRG-114hhrg99659/html/CHRG-114hhrg99659.htm.>

"A significant demonstration of Morse Code," The Telegraph. May 4, 2017. The Telegraph. <https://www.telegraph.co.uk/technology/connecting-britain/significant-demonstration-morse-code.>

"A tour of the worm," Seeley, Donn. February 1989. University of Utah Computer Science Technical Report, 89(009). Pages 1–16. <https://collections.lib.utah.edu/details?id=702918.>

"Africa in OEWG and Ad Hoc Cybercrime Committee - Diplo Resource." Diplo, January 25, 2023. <https://www.diplomacy.edu/resource/report-stronger-digital-voices-from-africa/africa-participation-international-processes-cybersecurity-cybercrime/#Cybersecurity_UN_GGE_and_OEWG.>

"An Updated Draft of the Code of Conduct Distributed in the United Nations – What's New?" Rõigas, H. (n.d.). NATO Cooperative Cyber Defence Center of Excellence. <https://ccdcoe.org/incyder-articles/an-updated-draft-of-the-code-of-conduct-distributed-in-the-united-nations-whats-new/;>

"Assault on key Yemeni port would endanger 300,000 children and 'choke off' aid for millions more: UNICEF chief." United Nations. (2018, June 15). <https://news.un.org/en/story/2018/06/1012032.>

"Back to Square One? The Fifth UN GGE Fails to Submit a Conclusive Report at the United Nations General Assembly." CCDCOE. <https://ccdcoe.org/incyder-articles/back-to-square-one-the-fifth-un-gge-fails-to-submit-a-conclusive-report-at-the-un-general-assembly/.>

"Bernie Sanders has a $150 billion plan to turn the internet into a public utility with low prices and fast speeds — here's how his plan works," Gilbert, Ben. January 22, 2020. Business Insider Nederland. <https://www.businessinsider.nl/bernie-sanders-internet-as-utility-plan-explainer-2019-12?international=true&r=US;>

"Brazil's Rousseff ousted by Senate, Temer sworn in." Marcello, M. A., & Boadle, A. (2016, September 1). Reuters. <https://www.reuters.com/article/us-brazil-impeachment/brazils-rousseff-ousted-by-senate-temer-sworn-in-idUSKCN114071.>

"British security minister says North Korea was behind WannaCry hack on NHS." Withnall, Adam. (2017, October 27). The Independent. <https://www.independent.co.uk/news/uk/home-news/wannacry-malware-hack-nhs-report-cybercrime-north-korea-uk-ben-wallace-a8022491.html.>

"Browser wars of the wireless telegraphy age," Dawson, Keith. March 1, 1999. Technology Front. <https://tbtf.com/resource/telegraph-browser-wars.html.>

"Bush administration annexes internet." McCarthy, K. (2005, July 1). The Register. <https://www.theregister.com/2005/07/01/bush_net_policy/.>

"Carry Forward the Five Principles of Peaceful Coexistence To Build a Better World Through Win-Win Cooperation." The government of China. (2014, June 28). <https://www.fmprc.gov.cn/mfa_eng/wjdt_665385/zyjh_665391/201407/t20140701_678184.html.>

"China Is "Leading Suspect" in OPM Hacks, Says Intelligence Chief James Clapper." Pepitone, Julianne (2015, June 25). NBC News. <https://www.nbcnews.com/tech/security/clapper-china-leading-suspect-opm-hack-n381881.>

"China's Hacking Spree Will Have a Decades-Long Fallout." Graff, Garrett. M. (2020, February 11). Wired. <https://www.wired.com/story/china-equifax-anthem-marriott-opm-hacks-data/.>

"Citing Internet Standoff, U.S. Rejects International Telecommunications Treaty." Pfanner, E. (2012, December 14). The New York Times. <https://www.nytimes.com/2012/12/14/technology/14iht-treaty14.html;>

"Computer virus in Iran actually targeted larger nuclear facility." Melman, Yossef. <https://www.haaretz.com/1.5118389.>

"Confidence-Building Measures In Cyberspace - A Multistakeholder Approach For Stability And Security." The NATO Science for Peace and Security Programme. Atlantic Council. (2014, November). <https://www.atlanticcouncil.org/wp-content/uploads/2014/11/Confidence-Building_Measures_in_Cyberspace.pdf.>

"Connect the Dots on State-Sponsored Cyber Incidents - Compromise of a Power Grid in Eastern Ukraine." Council on Foreign Relations, December 2015. <https://www.cfr.org/cyber-operations/compromise-power-grid-eastern-ukraine.>

"Court Backs Rules Treating Internet as Utility, Not Luxury," Kang, Cecilia. June 14, 2016. The New York Times. <https://www.nytimes.com/2016/06/15/technology/net-neutrality-fcc-appeals-court-ruling.html;>

"Cyber Operations during the Russo-Ukrainian War." Mueller, Grace B., Benjamin Jensen, Brandon Valeriano, Ryan C. Maness, and Jose M. Macias. CSIS, July 13, 2023. <https://www.csis.org/analysis/cyber-operations-during-russo-ukrainian-war.>

"Cyber-attack: US and UK blame North Korea for WannaCry." British Broadcasting Corporation. (2017, December 19). <https://www.bbc.com/news/world-us-canada-42407488.>

"Cyber-Attack: US and UK Blame North Korea for WannaCry." British Broadcasting Corporation. December 19, 2017. <https://www.bbc.com/news/world-us-canada-42407488.>

"Cyberattacks trigger talk of hacking back." Timberg, Craig, Nakashima, Ellen, & Douglas-Gabriel, Danielle. (2014, October 9). The Washington Post. <https://www.washingtonpost.com/business/technology/cyberattacks-trigger-talk-of-hacking-back/2014/10/09/6f0b7a24-4f02-11e4-8c24-487e92bc997b_story.html.>

"Cybersecurity Statistics and Trends for 2021," Sobers, Robert. March 13, 2021. Varonis. <https://www.varonis.com/blog/cybersecurity-statistics.>

"Defending a New Domain: The Pentagon's Cyberstrategy." Lynn III, W. J. (2020, October 16). Foreign Affairs. <https://www.foreignaffairs.com/articles/united-states/2010-09-01/defending-new-domain.>

"Details of the First-Ever Control System Malware (FAQ)." Mills, Elinor. CNET, July 21, 2010. <https://www.cnet.com/news/privacy/details-of-the-first-ever-control-system-malware-faq/.>

"Disentangling the cyber security debate." Kreuzer, Leonhard. (2020, December 9). Völkerrechtsblog. <https://voelkerrechtsblog.org/disentangling-the-cyber-security-debate/.>

"Estonia Fines Man for 'Cyber War.'" British Broadcasting Corporation. January 25, 2008. <http://news.bbc.co.uk/2/hi/technology/7208511.stm.>

"EU Confronts U.S. over Reports It Spies on European Allies." Deighton, Ben, and Annika Breidthardt. Reuters, July 1, 2013.<https://www.reuters.com/article/usa-eu-spying-reports/

eu-confronts-u-s-over-reports-it-spies-on-european-allies-idINDEE95T06G20130701/.>

"Exclusive: DOJ probes allegations that Tiversa lied to FTC about data breaches." Schectman, J. (2016, March 18). Reuters.<https://www.reuters.com/article/us-tiversa-doj-probe-exclusive-idUSKCN0WK027.>

"Exclusive: Inside Washington's Quest to Bring Down Edward Snowden." Leopold, J. (2015, June 4). Vice. <https://news.vice.com/en/article/qv54gd/exclusive-inside-washingtons-quest-to-bring-down-edward-snowden;>

"Facts About W3C." World Wide Web Consortium. <https://www.w3.org/Consortium/facts>

"France and Partners Propose a Programme of Action for Advancing Responsible State Behaviour in Cyberspace." Digital Watch Observatory, February 26, 2022. <https://dig.watch/updates/france-and-partners-propose-programme-action-advancing-responsible-state-behaviour.>

"France's Major Statement on International Law and Cyber: An Assessment." Schmitt, Michael. (2019, September 16). Just Security. <https://www.justsecurity.org/66194/frances-major-statement-on-international-law-and-cyber-an-assessment/.>

"From the first email to the first YouTube video: a definitive internet history," Meltzer, Tom, and Phillips, Sarah. October 23, 2009. The Guardian. <https://www.theguardian.com/technology/2009/oct/23/internet-history.>

"Georgia Takes a Beating in the Cyberwar with Russia." Markoff, John. The New York Times, August 11, 2008. <https://archive.nytimes.com/bits.blogs.nytimes.com/2008/08/11/georgia-takes-a-beating-in-the-cyberwar-with-russia/.>

"Germany Detects New Cyber Attack by Russian Hacker Group - Spiegel." Reuters, November 30, 2018.<https://www.reuters.com/article/germany-cyber-russia/germany-detects-new-cyber-attack-by-russian-hacker-group-spiegel-idUSL8N1Y47J5/.>

"Google attacks UN's internet treaty conference." BBC News. (2012, November 21). <https://www.bbc.co.uk/news/technology-20429625.>

"Hackers Disrupt Mexico Defense Ministry Website." Phys.org, January 17, 2013. <https://phys.org/news/2013-01-activists-hack-mexican-army-website.html.>

"Hackers Disrupt Mexico Defense Ministry Website." Phys.org, January 17, 2013. <https://phys.org/news/2013-01-activists-hack-mexican-army-website.html.>

"History of the UN IAEA." International Atomic Energy Agency, June 8, 2016. <https://www.iaea.org/about/overview/history.>

"House approves resolution to keep Internet control out of UN hands." Kasperowicz, P. (2016, February 3). TheHill. <https://thehill.com/blogs/floor-action/house/271153-house-approves-resolution-to-keep-internet-control-out-of-un-hands.>

"How the Dutch foiled Russian "cyber-attack" on OPCW." British Broadcasting Corporation. (2018, October 4). <https://www.bbc.com/news/world-europe-45747472.>

"How the Notpetya Attack Is Reshaping Cyber Insurance." Villasenor, John, and Nicol Turner Lee Norman Eisen. Brookings, December 1, 2021. <https://www.brookings.edu/articles/how-the-notpetya-attack-is-reshaping-cyber-insurance/.>

"How the NSA is still harvesting your online data." Greenwald, G., & Ackerman, S. (2017, July 15). The Guardian. <https://www.theguardian.com/world/2013/jun/27/nsa-online-metadata-collection.>

"IETF and the Internet Society. Internet Society." Cerf, Vint. September 28, 2021. <https://www.internetsociety.org/internet/history-of-the-internet/ietf-internet-society/.>

"In China, the 'Great Firewall' Is Changing a Generation," Wang, Yaqiu. September 1, 2020. Politico. <https://www.politico.com/news/magazine/2020/09/01/china-great-firewall-generation-405385>

"In NSA-intercepted data, those not targeted far outnumber the foreigners who are." Gellman, B., Tate, J., & Soltani, A. (2014, July 6). The Washington Post. <https://www.washingtonpost.com/world/national-security/in-nsa-intercepted-data-those-not-targeted-far-outnumber-the-foreigners-who-are/2014/07/05/8139adf8-045a-11e4-8572-4b1b969b6322_story.html.>

"India changes its internet governance position — backs away from UN proposal." Kaul, M. (2012, October 29). Uncut. <https://web.archive.org/web/20121103094900/http://uncut.indexoncensorship.org/2012/10/india-internet-governance/.>

"Inside Olympic Destroyer, the Most Deceptive Hack in History." Greenberg, Andrew. (2019b, October 17). Wired. <https://www.wired.com/story/untold-story-2018-olympics-destroyer-cyberattack/.>

"International Cyber Law Politicized: The UN GGE's Failure to Advance Cyber Norms." Schmitt, Michael, and Vihul, Liis. (2017, June 30). Just Security. <https://www.justsecurity.org/42768/international-cyber-law-politicized-gges-failure-advance-cyber-norms/.>

"International Telegraph Conference (Madrid, 1932)," UN International Telecommunication Union. October 7, 2007. <https://www.itu.int/en/history/Pages/PlenipotentiaryConferences.aspx?conf=4.5;>

"International Telegraph Convention, May 17, 1865." UN International Telecommunication Union. ITU. <https://search.itu.int/history/HistoryDigitalCollectionDocLibrary/4.1.43.fr.201.pdf.>

"International Telegraph Convention, UN International Telecommunication Union. May 17, 1865." ITU. <https://search.itu.int/history/HistoryDigitalCollectionDocLibrary/4.1.43.fr.201.pdf.>

"Internet Research Task Force," Internet Research Task Force. January 11, 2022. <https://irtf.org/.>

"Is Yemen's Man-Made Famine the Future of War?" Ferguson, Jane. (2018, July 11). The New Yorker. <https://www.newyorker.com/news/news-desk/is-yemen-intentional-starvation-the-future-of-war.>

"Israel video shows Stuxnet as one of its successes." Williams, Christopher. The Telegraph, February 15, 2011. <https://www.telegraph.co.uk/news/worldnews/middleeast/israel/8326387/Israel-video-shows-Stuxnet-as-one-of-its-successes.html.>

"It's Time For An Internet-For-All Public Utility (Before Corona Crashes It)," March 31, 2020. Andriole, Steve. Forbes. <https://www.forbes.com/sites/steveandriole/2020/03/30/its-time-for-an-internet-for-all-public-utility-before-corona-crashes-it/#2638b7f2af95.>

"Japan, West snub rules for Net curbs," The Japan Times Online. (2012, December 16). Japan Times. <https://web.archive.org/web/20121221143609/http://www.japantimes.co.jp/text/nn20121216a7.html>

"Massive ransomware cyber-attack hits nearly 100 countries around the world." Wong, Julia C., and Solon, Olivia. (2017, November 28). The Guardian. <https://www.theguardian.com/technology/2017/may/12/global-cyber-attack-ransomware-nsa-uk-nhs.>

"Merkel Says U.S. Spying an Unacceptable Breach of Trust." Baker, Luke, and Andreas Rinke. Reuters, October 24, 2013. <https://www.reuters.com/article/uk-eu-summit-idUKBRE99N0ED20131024/.>

"Monroe Doctrine - December 2, 1823." Yale University Law School. (n.d.). Avalon Project.. <https://avalon.law.yale.edu/19th_century/monroe.asp.>

"Morse Code & the Telegraph," November 9, 2009. History.com Editors. <http://www.history.com/topics/inventions/telegraph.>

"New BND Spy Scandal – German Intelligence Admits to Spying in Afghanistan." Deutsche Welle, December 7, 2008. <https://www.dw.com/en/german-intelligence-admits-to-spying-on-charities-in-afghanistan/a-3855839;>

"New global telecoms treaty agreed in Dubai." United Nations International Telecommunication Union. (2012, December 14). <https://www.itu.int/net/pressoffice/press_releases/2012/92.aspx>

"NHS cyber-attack: GPs and hospitals hit by ransomware." British Broadcasting Corporation. (2017a, May 13). <https://www.bbc.com/news/health-39899646;>

"NHS Cyber-Attack: GPS and Hospitals Hit by Ransomware." British Broadcasting Corporation. May 12, 2017.

"North Korea Blames U.S. for Internet Outages, Calls Obama 'Monkey.'" Kim, Jack. Reuters, December 27, 2014. <https://www.reuters.com/article/us-northkorea-cybersecurity/north-korea-blames-u-s-for-internet-outages-calls-obama-monkey-idUSKBN0K502920141228.>

"North Korean government behind NHS cyber attack, says Microsoft boss." Hills, Joel. (2017, October 13). iTV. <https://www.itv.com/news/2017-10-13/hacking-threat-is-as-serious-as-terrorism-says-microsoft-boss;>

"Obama Order Sped Up Wave of Cyberattacks Against Iran." Sanger, David E. The New York Times, June 1, 2012. <https://www.nytimes.com/2012/06/01/world/middleeast/obama-ordered-wave-of-cyberattacks-against-iran.html.>

"Obama says Sony hack not an act of war. Reuters." Holland, Steve., & Chiacu, Doina. (2014, December 22). <https://www.reuters.com/article/us-sony-cybersecurity-usa/obama-says-sony-hack-not-an-act-of-war-idUSKBN0JX1MH20141222.>

“One of the First Cyberattacks Was an ‘art Project’ That Targeted the Pentagon.” Buck, Stephanie. Medium, March 1, 2017. <https://timeline.com/electronic-disturbance-theater-bace73446dda.>

“On-Line Pizza Idea Is Clever but Only Half-Baked,” Schrage, Michael. March 6, 2019. Los Angeles Times. <https://www.latimes.com/archives/la-xpm-1994-08-25-fi-31168-story.html.>

“Opinio Juris (international law).” Cornell University - Legal Information Institute. (n.d.). <https://www.law.cornell.edu/wex/opinio_juris_(international_law).>

“Opinio Juris.” Oxford University References. (n.d.). <https://www.oxfordreference.com/view/10.1093/oi/authority.20110803100251755.>

“Overview of ITU’s History.” UN International Telecommunication Union. <https://itu.int/en/history/documents/itu-history-overview.pdf.>

“Plenipotentiary Conferences.” ITU. UN International Telecommunication Union. <https://www.itu.int/en/history/Pages/PlenipotentiaryConferences.aspx?conf=4.1.>

“Pluralistic, Not Imperialistic,” Negroponte, Nicholas. March 1, 1996. Wired. <https://www.wired.com/1996/03/negroponte-51/.>

“Poland’s Position on International Law and Cyber Operations: Sovereignty and Third-Party Countermeasures.” Roguski, Przemysław. Just Security, January 18, 2023. <https://www.justsecurity.org/84799/polands-position-on-international-law-and-cyber-operations-sovereignty-and-third-party-countermeasures/.>

“Press Briefing on the Attribution of the WannaCry Malware Attack to North Korea.” (2017, December 21). U.S. Embassy & Consulate in the Republic of Korea. <https://kr.usembassy.gov/121917-press-briefing-attribution-wannacry-malware-attack-north-korea/.>

“Putin Likens Western Sanctions to War as Russian Assault Traps Ukrainian Civilians.” Polityuk, Pavel, and Aleksandar Vasovic. Reuters, March 5, 2022. <https://www.reuters.com/markets/europe/top-wrap-1-europes-largest-nuclear-power-plant-fire-after-russian-attack-mayor-2022-03-04/.>

“Quietly, symbolically, US control of the internet was just ended.” Farrell, M. (2017, February 21). The Guardian. <https://www.theguardian.com/technology/2016/mar/14/icann-internet-control-domain-names-iana.>

"Radio Regulations Board (RRB): It's place, role and functioning in the ITU (by Wladyslaw Moron, Member RRB)," UN International Telecommunication Union. March 22, 2010. <https://www.itu.int/net/ITU-R/information/promotion/e-flash/4/article7.html>

"Reagan Approved Plan to Sabotage Soviets." Hoffman, David E. The Washington Post, February 27, 2004. <https://www.washingtonpost.com/archive/politics/2004/02/27/reagan-approved-plan-to-sabotage-soviets/a9184eff-47fd-402e-beb2-63970851e130/.>

"Researchers say Stuxnet was deployed against Iran in 2007." Finkle, Jim. (2013, February 26). Reuters. <https://www.reuters.com/article/us-cyberwar-stuxnet-idUSBRE91P0PP20130226.>

"Resolution on the Programme of Action (POA) on Cybersecurity Adopted." Digital Watch Observatory. <https://dig.watch/updates/resolution-on-the-programme-of-action-poa-on-cybersecurity-adopted>

"Russia Accused of Unleashing Cyberwar to Disable Estonia." Traynor, Ian. The Guardian, May 17, 2007. <https://www.theguardian.com/world/2007/may/17/topstories3.russia;>

"Russia internet: Law introducing new controls comes into force," British Broadcasting Corporation. November 1, 2019. <https://www.bbc.com/news/world-europe-50259597.>

"Russia Now Has Free Hand to Destroy Undersea Communications Cables, Putin Ally Says." Faulconbridge, Guy. Reuters, June 14, 2023. <https://www.reuters.com/world/europe/russias-medvedev-says-moscow-now-has-free-hand-destroy-enemies-undersea-2023-06-14/.>

"Russia Says 'unfriendly' EU Sanctions Will Hinder Ties." Reuters, July 10, 2014. <https://www.reuters.com/article/us-ukraine-crisis-sanctions-russia/russia-says-unfriendly-eu-sanctions-will-hinder-ties-idUSKBN0FF1A820140710.>

"Russian spies hacked the Olympics and tried to make it look like North Korea did it, U.S. officials say." Nakashima, Ellen. (2018, February 25). Washington Post. <https://www.washingtonpost.com/world/national-security/russian-spies-hacked-the-olympics-and-tried-to-make-it-look-like-north-korea-did-it-us-officials-say/2018/02/24/44b5468e-18f2-11e8-92c9-376b4fe57ff7_story.html.>

"Russian Troll farm, 13 suspects indicted in 2016 Election Interference." Barret, Devlin, Horwitz, Sari, and Helderman, Rosalind S. (2018, February 16). The Washington Post. <https://www.washingtonpost.com/world/national-security/russian-troll-farm-13-suspects-indicted-for-interference-in-us-election/2018/02/16/2504de5e-1342-11e8-9570-29c9830535e5_story.html;>

"Russian Twitter Accounts Promoted Brexit Ahead of Eu Referendum - Times Newspaper," Reuters. November 15, 2017. <https://www.reuters.com/article/us-britain-eu-russia/russian-twitter-accounts-promoted-brexit-ahead-of-eu-referendum-times-newspaper-idUSKBN1DF0ZR;>

"Russians hacked key Ukrainian company in Trump impeachment inquiry, researchers say." Haaretz. (2020, January 14). <https://www.haaretz.com/world-news/europe/russians-hacked-key-ukrainian-company-in-trump-impeachment-inquiry-researchers-say-1.8399586.>

"Shamoon virus targets energy sector infrastructure." British Broadcasting Corporation. (2012a, August 17).

"Situation in Ukraine: ICC Judges Issue Arrest Warrants against Vladimir Vladimirovich Putin and Maria Alekseyevna Lvova-Belova." International Criminal Court, March 17, 2023.

"Stuxnet may have destroyed 1,000 centrifuges at Natanz." Katz, Yaakov B. The Jerusalem Post, December 24, 2010. <https://www.jpost.com/defense/stuxnet-may-have-destroyed-1000-centrifuges-at-natanz.>

"Stuxnet Worm 'Targeted High-Value Iranian Assets.'" Fildes, Jonathan B. BBC, September 23, 2010. <https://www.bbc.com/news/technology-11388018.>

"Tallinn Manual 2.0 – Advancing the Conversation. Just Security." Corn, Gary C. (2021, October 8). <https://www.justsecurity.org/37812/tallinn-manual-2-0-advancing-conversation/#more-37812.>

"Tallinn Manual 2.0 – Advancing the Conversation." Corn, Gary. Just Security, October 8, 2021. <https://www.justsecurity.org/37812/tallinn-manual-2-0-advancing-conversation/#more-37812.>

"TechCrunch is part of the Yahoo family of brands." Whittaker, Zack. (2019, May 12). TechCrunch. <https://techcrunch.com/2019/05/12/wannacry-two-years-on/.>

"The 1865 International Telegraph Conference." UN International Telecommunication Union. <https://www.itu.int/en/history/Pages/ITUBorn1865.aspx.>

"The Bronze Soldier Crisis of 2007: Revisiting an Early Case of Hybrid Conflict." Juurvee, Ivo, and Anna-Mariita Mattiisen. International Centre for Defence and Security, February 14, 2022.

"The Case for Internet Access as a Human Right," Bode, Karl. Vice. November 13, 2019. <https://www.vice.com/en/article/3kxmm5/the-case-for-internet-access-as-a-human-right;>

"The European Single Market - Historical Events in the European Integration Process (1945–2009) - CVCE Website." Luxembourg Center for Contemporary and Digital History. <https://www.cvce.eu/en/education/unit-content/-/unit/02bb76df-d066-4c08-a58a-d4686a3e68ff/fc955c85-4a39-4187-9ae7-935d67d1656b.>

"The History of IANA An Extended Timeline with Citations and Commentary," Internet Society. November, 2016. <https://www.yumpu.com/en/document/view/56851186/the-history-of-iana-an-extended-timeline-with-citations-and-commentary.>

"The Incredible Rise of North Korea's Hacking Army." Caesar, Ed. (2021, April 19). The New Yorker. <https://www.newyorker.com/magazine/2021/04/26/the-incredible-rise-of-north-koreas-hacking-army.>

"The internet as a human right. Brookings Institution," Howell, Catherine, and West, Darrell. M. 2016, November 4, 2016. <https://www.brookings.edu/blog/techtank/2016/11/07/the-internet-as-a-human-right/;>

"The Invisible u.s.-Iran Cyber War." Hanna, Andrew. The Iran Primer, November 1, 2021. <https://iranprimer.usip.org/blog/2019/oct/25/invisible-us-iran-cyber-war.>

"The need for a Digital Geneva Convention." Smith, Brad. (2018, May 15). Microsoft. <https://blogs.microsoft.com/on-the-issues/2017/02/14/need-digital-geneva-convention/.>

"The need for urgent collective action to keep people safe online: Lessons from last week's cyberattack." Smith, Brad. (2017, May 14). Microsoft. <https://blogs.microsoft.com/on-the-issues/2017/05/14/need-urgent-collective-action-keep-people-safe-online-lessons-last-weeks-cyberattack/#Idi5LfUGG87joatu.99.>

"The OPM hack explained: Bad security practices meet China's Captain America." Fruhlinger, Josh. (2020, February 12). CSO Online. <https://www.csoonline.com/article/3318238/the-opm-hack-explained-bad-security-practices-meet-chinas-captain-america.html;>

"The pandemic proves internet should be a public utility," Livni, Ephrat. March 26, 2020. Quartz. <https://qz.com/1826043/the-coronavirus-crisis-proves-internet-should-be-a-public-utility/;>

"The Ship That Became a Bomb." Caesar, Ed. (October 4, 2021). The New Yorker. <https://www.newyorker.com/magazine/2021/10/11/the-ship-that-became-a-bomb.>

"The Sixth United Nations GGE and International Law in Cyberspace." Schmitt, Michael (2021, October 8). Just Security. <https://www.justsecurity.org/76864/the-sixth-united-nations-gge-and-international-law-in-cyberspace/.>

"The Strange and Violent History of Kites." Manheim, Noa. Haaretz, June 28, 2018. <https://www.haaretz.com/israel-news/2018-06-28/ty-article-magazine/.premium/the-strange-and-violent-history-of-kites/0000017f-db94-d856-a37f-ffd483610000.>

"The Stuxnet Attack On Iran's Nuclear Plant Was 'Far More Dangerous' Than Previously Thought," Kelley, Michael B. Business Insider, November 20, 2013.

"The telegraphic age dawns," BT Group Connected Earth Online Museum. 2010. Page 129

"The Top 25 Cybersecurity Companies of 2020." "The Software Report. (2020, December). <https://www.thesoftwarereport.com/the-top-25-cybersecurity-companies-of-2020/>

"The U.N. Threat to Internet Freedom." McDowell, Robert. M. (2012, February 21). The Wall Street Jorunal. <https://www.wsj.com/articles/SB10001424052970204792404577229074023195322.>

"The U.N.'s Internet Power Grab." Crovitz, G. L. (2012, June 18). Crovitz: The Wall Street Journal. <https://www.wsj.com/articles/SB10001424052702303822204577470532859210296.>

"The UN Norms of Responsible State Behaviour in Cyberspace." Australian Strategic Policy Institute. <https://www.aspi.org.au/report/un-norms-responsible-state-behaviour-cyberspace.>

"The Updated Commentary on the First Geneva Convention – a New Tool for Generating Respect for International Humanitarian Law." International Review of the Red Cross, November 1, 2016. Pages 1209 – 1226. <https://international-review.icrc.org/articles/updated-commentary-first-geneva-convention-new-tool-generating-respect-international.>

"Top 10 Reasons to Oppose the World Trade Organization? Criticism, yes … misinformation, no!." World Trade Organization. <https://www.wto.org/english/thewto_e/minist_e/min99_e/english/misinf_e/09sov_e.htm.>

"Twitter Bots Helped Trump and Brexit Win, Economic Study Says." Smialek, Jeanna. Bloomberg, May 21, 2018. <https://www.bloomberg.com/politics/articles/2018-05-21/twitter-bots-helped-trump-and-brexit-win-economic-study-says.>

"Ukraine Computers Hit by Data-Wiping Software as Russia Launched Invasion." Reuters, February 24, 2022. <https://www.reuters.com/world/europe/ukrainian-government-foreign-ministry-parliament-websites-down-2022-02-23/.>

"UN at odds over internet's future." BBC News - Technology. (2005, July 18). <http://news.bbc.co.uk/2/hi/technology/4692743.stm.>

"United Nations - Office for Outer Space Affairs." Wickramatunga, Robert. COPUOS History. <https://www.unoosa.org/oosa/en/ourwork/copuos/history.html#:~:text=In%201958%2C%20shortly%20after%20the,the%20specialized%20agencies%20and%20other.>

"United Nations Environment Programme (2022)." Environmental Courts and Tribunals: A Guide for Policy Makers. Page 3. <https://wedocs.unep.org/20.500.11822/40309.>

"United Nations Office on Genocide Prevention and the Responsibility to Protect." United Nations. <https://www.un.org/en/genocideprevention/about-responsibility-to-protect.shtml.>

"Uphold International Law." United Nations. <https://www.un.org/en/our-work/uphold-international-law.>

"US Department of State's Transparency Regarding International Law in Cyberspace," Egan, Brian. 2019. Just Security. <https://www.justsecurity.org/34465/transparency-international-law-cyberspace/.>

"US Transparency Regarding International Law in Cyberspace." Brian Egan (2019a, March 21). Just Security. <https://www.justsecurity.org/34465/transparency-international-law-cyberspace/.>

"Vladimir Putin: cyber espionage is direct violation of state's sovereignty," Interfax. July 11, 2014. <https://interfax.com/newsroom/top-stories/41982/.>

"WAM - Emirates News Agency." Hamdan bin Mohammed launches Dubai Metaverse Strategy - الإمارات أنباء وكالة, July 18, 2022. <https://wam.ae/en/details/1395303067141.>

"WannaCry ransomware has links to North Korea, cybersecurity experts say." Solon, Olivia. (2017, September 5). The Guardian. <https://www.theguardian.com/technology/2017/may/15/wannacry-ransomware-north-korea-lazarus-group.>

"War in the fifth domain," The Economist. July 6, 2010. <https://www.economist.com/briefing/2010/07/01/war-in-the-fifth-domain.>

"War in the Fifth Domain." The Economist, July 6, 2010. <https://www.economist.com/briefing/2010/07/01/war-in-the-fifth-domain.>

"What Are Jus Ad Bellum and Jus in Bello?" International Committee of the Red Cross, November 12, 2015. <https://www.icrc.org/en/document/what-are-jus-ad-bellum-and-jus-bello-0.>

"What does ITU do?." UN International Telecommunication. <https://www.itu.int/en/about/Pages/whatwedo.aspx.>

"What Is the Slammer Worm/SQL Worm/Sapphire Worm?" North Carolina State University. <https://ethics.csc.ncsu.edu/abuse/wvt/Slammer/study.php.>

"Where Does the Word Cyber Come From?" Oxford University Press Editorial. July 10, 2015. <https://blog.oup.com/2015/03/cyber-word-origins/.>

"Whistleblower accuses cybersecurity company of extorting clients." Pagliery, J. (2015, May 7). CNNMoney. <https://money.cnn.com/2015/05/07/technology/tiversa-labmd-ftc/index.html.>

"World Summit on Information Society: Tunis Agenda for the Information Society." United Nations International Telecommunication Union. (2005, November 18). <https://www.itu.int/net/wsis/docs2/tunis/off/6rev1.html>

"WSIS: Declaration of Principles - Building the Information Society: a global challenge in the new Millennium," UN International Telecommunication Union. December 3, 2003. <https://www.itu.int/net/wsis/docs/geneva/official/dop.html.>

"Your Internet is working. Thank these Cold War-era pioneers who designed it to handle almost anything," Timberg, Craig. April 6, 2020. The Washington Post. <https://www.washingtonpost.com/technology/2020/04/06/your-internet-is-working-thank-these-cold-war-era-pioneers-who-designed-it-handle-almost-anything/.>

Department of Defense General Counsel Remarks at U.S. Cyber Command Legal Conference. The Government of the United States. <https://www.defense.gov/News/Speeches/Speech/Article/2099378/dod-general-counsel-remarks-at-us-cyber-command-legal-conference/;>

NSA hacked Al-Jazeera and Russia's Aeroflot – report. Russia Today International. (2013, September 1). Russia Today International. <https://www.rt.com/news/nsa-jazeera-aeroflot-spy-272/.>

Singapore International Cyber Week 2018 - Highlights and Testimonials. Cyber Security Agency of Singapore. (2018, September 20). <https://www.csa.gov.sg/news/press-releases/sicw-2018-highlights-and-testimonials>

F. Websites

"Court of Justice of the European Union (CJEU)." European Union. <https://european-union.europa.eu/institutions-law-budget/institutions-and-bodies/search-all-eu-institutions-and-bodies/court-justice-european-union-cjeu_en.>

"English Standard Version Online - Literal Word." English Standard Version Bible. <https://esv.literalword.com/.>

"International Court for Environment Coallition." ICE Coalition. <http://www.icecoalition.org/.>

"International Law." Legal Information Institute - Cornell University. <https://www.law.cornell.edu/wex/international_law.>

"Legal Systems." Legal Information Institute - Cornell University. <https://www.law.cornell.edu/wex/legal_systems#:~:text=A%20legal%20system%20is%20the,legal%20system%20across%20the%20globe.>

"Unfriendly Act - Definition in the Public International Law." Oxford University Public International Law. <https://opil.ouplaw.com/display/10.1093/law:epil/9780199231690/law-9780199231690-e423.>

"WTO Dispute Settlement Body." World Trade Organization. <https://www.wto.org/english/tratop_e/dispu_e/dispu_e.htm.>

Area 1 Security, Inc. (n.d.). Area 1 Security, Inc. <https://www.area1security.com/.>

Center for Strategic & International Studies. "Significant International Cyber Incidents - a list." <https://www.csis.org/programs/strategic-technologies-program/significant-cyber-incidents>

Centre National de Ressources Textuelles et Lexicales. "TLFI." Cybernétique : Définition de Cybernétique. <https://www.cnrtl.fr/definition/cybern%C3%A9tique.>

Cerf, Vint. "The Internet Activities Board Memo. Internet Engineering Task Force, May 1, 1990. <https://www.ietf.org/rfc/rfc1160.txt.>

Charter of Trust. (2020). Charter of Trust. <https://www.charteroftrust.com/.>

Congressional Records – GovInfo. "48 Congressional Records S7282 - Statement of Sen. Smith," May 28, 1912. <https://www.govinfo.gov/app/collection/crecb/_crecb/Volume%20048%20(1912).>

Council on Foreign Relations. "Cyber Operations Tracker." <https://www.cfr.org/cyber-operations/.>

Cybersecurity Tech Accord. (2019, October 12). Cybersecurity Tech Accord. <https://cybertechaccord.org/about/.>

Demand Digital Peace Now. (2020, June 24). Demand Digital Peace Now. <https://digitalpeacenow.org/.>

Encyclopedia Britannica. "Entebbe raid." Encyclopedia Britannica. https://www.britannica.com/event/Entebbe-raid; Swift, John. "U.S. invasion of Grenada." Encyclopedia Britannica. <https://www.britannica.com/event/U-S-invasion-of-Grenada.>

Encyclopedia Britannica. (n.d.). Terrritorial Waters in international law. <https://www.britannica.com/topic/territorial-waters.>

Geneva Dialogue. <https://genevadialogue.ch/.>

Geneva Internet Platform. (2022, January 28). UN GGE and OEWG. Digital Watch Observatory. <https://dig.watch/processes/un-gge.>

Geneva Internet Platform. “UN OEWG in 2023.” Digital Watch Observatory, October 18, 2023. <https://dig.watch/processes/un-gge/.>

Georgetown University Law School. “Guides: International and Foreign Cyberspace Law Research Guide: Tallinn Manual & Primary Law Applicable to Cyber Conflicts.” Guides at Georgetown Law Library. <https://guides.ll.georgetown.edu/cyberspace/cyber-conflicts.>

Global Commission on the stability of Cyberspace. (2018, November). Norm Package Singapore. <https://cyberstability.org/wp-content/uploads/2018/11/GCSC-Singapore-Norm-Package-3MB.pdf.>

Global Commission on the stability of Cyberspace. (2018, November). Norm Package Singapore. <https://cyberstability.org/wp-content/uploads/2018/11/GCSC-Singapore-Norm-Package-3MB.pdf.>

Government of France. Against information manipulation, November 20, 2018. <https://www.gouvernement.fr/en/against-information-manipulation.>

Hunter, David. International Environmental Law - Insights on law and Society. American Bar Association, January 5, 2021. <https://www.americanbar.org/groups/public_education/publications/insights-on-law-and-society/volume-19/insights-vol-19-issue-1/international-environmental-law/.>

Internet Corporation for Assigned Names and Numbers. “ICANN’s Major Agreements and Related Reports.” <https://www.icann.org/resources/pages/agreements-en.>

Internet World Stats. “World Internet Users Statistics and 2021 World Population Stats,” March 31, 2021. <https://www.internetworldstats.com/stats.htm.>

Max Planck Encyclopedia of Public International Law. (n.d.). State Practice. Oxford Public International Law. <https://opil.ouplaw.com/view/10.1093/law:epil/9780199231690/law-9780199231690-e1107?prd=MPIL#:%7E:text=State%20practice%20is%20creative%2C%20or,law%2C%20or%20opinio%20iuris).>

Mitchell, Ronald B. “International Environmental Agreements (IEA) Database Project.” University of Oregon. <https://iea.uoregon.edu/;>

NATO Cooperative Cyber Defence Center of Excellence. “The Tallinn manual Initiative.” <https://ccdcoe.org/research/tallinn-manual/.>

Online Etymology Dictionary. “Cybernetics (n.).” Etymology. <https://www.etymonline.com/word/cybernetics?ref=etymonline_crossreference.>

Oxford Public International Law. Domaine Réservé - definition. <https://opil.ouplaw.com/view/10.1093/law:epil/9780199231690/law-9780199231690-e1398;>

Oxford Public International Law. Unfriendly Act - definition. <https://opil.ouplaw.com/view/10.1093/law:epil/9780199231690/law-9780199231690-e423.>

Permanent Mission of Switzerland to the United Nations. (2017). The GA Handbook A practical guide to the United Nations General Assembly. <https://www.eda.admin.ch/dam/mission-new-york/en/documents/UN_GA__Final.pdf.>

Postel, Jon. “RFC 349 - Proposed Standard Socket Numbers. Internet Engineering Task Force,”May 30, 1972. <https://datatracker.ietf.org/doc/html/rfc349.>

Root Server Technical Operations Association. (n.d.). Root Server Technical Operations Association. <https://root-servers.org/.>

Schaller, Christian. Spies. In: Rüdiger Wolfrum (ed.), The Max Planck Encyclopedia of Public International Law (2008), online edition. <https://www.mpepil.com.>

State of California - Business Portal. California Secretary of State - California Business Search. <https://web.archive.org/web/20070321194344/http://kepler.ss.ca.gov/corpdata/ShowAllList?QueryCorpNumber=C2121683.>

The government of the United States of America. Fact Sheet: President Xi Jinping’s State Visit to the United States. September 25, 2015. <https://obamawhitehouse.archives.gov/the-press-office/2015/09/25/fact-sheet-president-xi-jinpings-state-visit-united-states.>

U.S. House of Representatives, Committee on Science. “Public Hearing on Internet Domain Names, Part I,” September 25, 1997. U.S. House of Representatives Committee Hearings. <http://commdocs.house.gov/committees/science/hsy268140.000/hsy268140_0.HTM.>

UN International Telecommunication Union. (“Agenda of the 2001 Session of Council,” June 19, 2001. <https://www.itu.int/itudoc/gs/council/c01/pdagn/001rev1.html.>

United Nation Internet Governance Forum. (2014, April). The Global Multistakeholder Forum for Dialogue on Internet Governance Issues. <http://intgovforum.org/cms/2014/IGFBrochure.pdf.>

United Nations - Department for General Assembly and Conference Management. (n.d.). United Nations Regional Groups. <https://www.un.org/dgacm/.>

United Nations - Office for Outer Space Affairs. Space Law Treaties and Principles. <https://www.unoosa.org/oosa/en/ourwork/spacelaw/treaties.html#:~:text=These%20five%20treaties%20deal%20with,with%20space%20activities%20and%20the.>

United Nations - Office on Drugs and Crime. Countering Chemical, Biological, Radiological and Nuclear Terrorism. <https://www.unodc.org/unodc/en/terrorism/expertise/countering-chemical-biological-radiological-and-nuclear-terrorism.html.>

United Nations Office for Disarmament Affairs. (n.d.). Developments in the field of information and telecommunications in the context of international security – UNODA. <https://www.un.org/disarmament/ict-security/.>

United Nations Office for Disarmament Affairs. (n.d.-b). Fact Sheet Developments In The Field Of Information And Telecommunications In The Context Of International Security. <https://unoda-web.s3.amazonaws.com/wp-content/uploads/2019/07/Information-Security-Fact-Sheet-July-2019.pdf.>

United Nations Office for Disarmament Affairs. (n.d.-c). Open-ended Working Group – UNODA. <https://www.un.org/disarmament/open-ended-working-group/.>

United Nations. "List of the member states." <https://www.un.org/en/about-us/member-states.>

World Economic Forum. (2014, January 20). Global Commission on Internet Governance (2014–2016). Centre for International Governance Innovation. <https://www.cigionline.org/activities/global-commission-internet-governance-2014-2016/.>

Ziegler, Katja. S. (n.d.). Domaine Réservé. Max Planck Encyclopedias of International Law. https://opil.ouplaw.com/view/10.1093/law:epil/9780199231690/law-9780199231690-e1398.

Index

Ius, Lex et Res Publica
Studies in Law, Philosophy and Political Cultures

Edited by
Barbara Janusz-Pohl

Vol. 1 Anna Jaron: Socio-Economic Constitutional Rights in Democratisation Processes. An Account of the Constitutional Dialogue Theory. 2012.

Vol. 2 Stanisław Filipowicz: Democracy – The Power of Illusion. 2013.

Vol. 3 Teresa Dukiet-Nagórska (ed.): The Postulates of Restorative Justice and the Continental Model of Criminal Law. As Illustrated by Polish Criminal Law 2014.

Vol. 4 Agnieszka Kupzok: Enforcement of Patents on Geographically Divisible Inventions. An Inquiry into the Standard of Substantive Patent Law Infringement in Cross-Border Constellations. 2015.

Vol. 5 Alicja Jagielska-Burduk / Wojciech Szafrański: Legal Issues in Cultural Heritage Management. A Polish Perspective. 2016.

Vol. 6 Maciej Mataczyński (ed.): The Takeover of Public Companies as a Mode of Exercising EU Treaty Freedoms. 2017.

Vol. 7 Maciej Barczewski (ed.): Value of Information. Intellectual Property, Privacy and Big Data. 2018.

Vol. 8 Pawel Smoleń, Marcin Burzec: Introduction to Polish Tax Law. 2018.

Vol. 9 Łukasz Pohl, Konrad Burdziak: Judicial Interpretation of the 1997 Criminal Code Provisions on Self-Defence. 2019.

Vol. 10 Adam Szot: Judicial Review of Administrative Discretion. The Influence of Court Decisions on Administrative Actions. 2019.

Vol. 11 Michał Peno / Konrad Burdziak (eds.): The Concept of Modern Law. Polish and Central European Tradition. 2019.

Vol. 12 Leszek Leszczyński / Bartosz Lińewski / Adam Szot (eds.): Potential of Precedent in the Statutory Legal Order. 2019.

Vol. 13 Łukasz Bolesta: In Search of a Model for the Legal Protection of a Whistleblower in the Workplace in Poland. A legal and comparative study. 2020.

Vol. 14 Paweł Chmielnicki / Adam Sulikowski (eds.): New Perspectives on Legislation. A Comparative Approach. 2020.

Vol. 15 Marcin Burzec / Beata Kucia-Guściora / Paweł Smoleś: Agricultural Activity in Poland: A Fiscal and Legal Study. 2020.

Vol. 16 Magdalena Półtorak / Ilona Topa (eds.): Women, Children and (Other) Vulnerable Groups. Standards of Protection and Challenges for International Law. 2021.

Vol. 17 Josef Albert Fox: Die polnische Verfassung vom 3. Mai 1791. Hintergründe der Entstehung und der Außerkraftsetzung. Stellung Polens im Zeitalter der Aufklärung. 2021.

Vol. 18 Barbara Janusz-Pohl (ed.): Juvenile Justice Systems: Poland-Brazil-Portugal. 2021.

Vol. 19 Leszek Leszczyński: General Reference Clauses in the Judicial Process. Context of Legislative Intentions Interpretative Discretion. 2021.

Vol. 20 Francisco J. Campos Zamora: Das Problem der Begründung richterlicher Entscheidungen. Eine Analyse auf der Grundlage der Theorie der juristischen Argumentation. 2021.

Vol. 21 Aneta Skorupa-Wulczyńska: Language Rights of the Citizen of the European Union. 2022.

Vol. 22 Mateusz Osiecki: International Legal Aspects of Aerial Terrorism. Methods of Law Enforcement in Aviation. 2022.

Vol. 23 Vladimír Sharp / Gabriela Blahoudková / Jakub Handrlica (eds.): Law, Pandemics and Ownership Restrictions. 2022.

Vol. 24 Piotr Kasprzyk / Anna Konert: Drones – Future of Aviation Law? Interference of Public Law in Private Law. 2023.

Vol. 25 Szymon Pawelec (ed.): Consensual Mechanisms in Criminal Proceedings – Integrative and Comparative Perspective. 2023.

Vol. 26 Dorota Pudzianowska: Statelessness in Public Law. 2023.

Vol. 27 Boguslaw Przywora / Aleksander Wróbel: Formalised Access to Pre-jurisdictional Free Legal Aid. 2023.

Vol. 28 Ewa Dawidziuk / Patricia Panero / Anny Tarwacka (eds.): Family, Law, and Society: from Roman Law to the Present Day. 2024.

Vol. 29 Marian Grzybowsk / Boguslaw Przywora / Aleksandra Syryt (eds.): Free Legal Aid, Theory, Legal Basis and Practice. European Standards. 2024.

Vol. 30 Karolina Gmerek: Trial as a Social Communication Occurrence. 2024.

Vol. 31 Pawel Wiliński (ed.): Effective Legal Remedies in Criminal Justice System. European Perspective. 2024.

Vol. 32 Jakub Hanc / Olga Sitarz / Anna Jaworska-Wieloch: On the (non)existence of the right to religious freedom of persons deprived of liberty. 2024.

Vol. 33 Marian Grzybowsk / Boguslaw Przywora / Aleksandra Syryt (eds.): Free Legal Aid – A Comparative Approach. 2024.

Vol. 34 Dominik Gajewski (ed.): Functioning of Administrative Judiciary in the Context of Economic Changes. 2024.

Vol. 35 Mikołajczyk, Barbara: Older Migrants – Vulnerable and Excluded. 2024.

Vol. 36 Świder, Maciej: The Exercise of the Right to a Fair Trial in the Era of the COVID-19 Pandemic. 2024.

Vol. 37 Tomasz Barankiewicz / Boguslaw Przywora (eds.): Public and Civil Service in Poland. 2024.

Vol. 38 Daniele Vicoli (ed.): Effective Justice 1. Effective Justice. International and Comparative Approaches. 2025.

Vol. 39 Barbara Janusz-Pohl (ed.): Effective Justice 2. Effective Justice. International and Comparative Approaches. 2025.

Vol. 40 Kinga Anna Gajda / Marta Pietras-Eichberger / Małgorzata Skawińska (eds.): Mediation as an Inclusive and Sustainable Method of Resolving Conflicts. 2025.

Vol. 41 Ewa Dawidziuk / Anna Tarwacka / Sławomir Kursa (eds.): Historical and Contemporary Issues of Democracy, Person and Human Rights. 2025.

Vol. 42 Jakub Kępiński: The impact of Directive 2005/29/EC on Polish law on combating unfair competition. 2025.

Vol. 43 Paul von Chamier Cieminski: Hostile Cyber Operations between States in International Law. 2026.

www.peterlang.com

www.ingramcontent.com/pod-product-compliance
Ingram Content Group UK Ltd.
Pitfield, Milton Keynes, MK11 3LW, UK
UKHW020833290926
15470UKWH00004B/1321

9 783631 930458